W9-COA-443

Research Methods in Psychology

Third Edition

Research Methods in Psychology

John J. Shaughnessy
Hope College

Eugene B. Zechmeister
Loyola University of Chicago

McGraw-Hill, Inc.
New York St. Louis San Francisco Auckland Bogotá Caracas
Lisbon London Madrid Mexico City Milan Montreal
New Delhi San Juan Singapore Sydney Tokyo Toronto

RESEARCH METHODS IN PSYCHOLOGY

This book is printed on acid-free paper.

4 5 6 7 8 9 0 AGM AGM 9 0 9 8 7 6 5

ISBN 0-07-056691-7

This book was set in Palatino by Ruttle, Shaw, & Wetherill, Inc.
The editors were Jane Vaicunas and David Dunham;
the production supervisor was Annette Mayeski.
The cover was designed by Robin Hessel Hoffmann.
Arcata Graphics/Martinsburg was printer and binder.

Library of Congress Cataloging-in-Publication Data

Shaughnessy, John J., (date).
Research methods in psychology / John J. Shaughnessy, Eugene B. Zechmeister. — 3rd ed.
p. cm.
Includes bibliographical references and indexes.
ISBN 0-07-056691-7 (alk. paper)
1. Psychology—Research—Methodology. 2. Psychology, Experimental. I. Zechmeister, Eugene B., (date). II. Title.
BF76.5.S46 1994
150'.72—dc20 93-18859

This book is printed on acid free recycled paper containing a minimum of 50% total recycled fiber with 10% post consumer de-inked fiber.

About the Authors

JOHN J. SHAUGHNESSY is Professor of Psychology at Hope College, a relatively small, select, undergraduate liberal arts college in Holland, Michigan. After completing the B.S. degree at Loyola University of Chicago in 1969, he received the Ph.D. in 1972 from Northwestern University. He is a Fellow of the American Psychological Society, and he has been a frequent contributor of research on human memory, a reviewer for several journals, and coauthor, with Benton J. Underwood, of *Experimentation in Psychology* (Wiley, 1975). He was selected by students in 1992 as the Hope Outstanding Professor Educator, and his teaching expertise has been recognized by his colleagues' selection of him as a campus teaching consultant.

EUGENE B. ZECHMEISTER is Professor of Psychology at Loyola University of Chicago, a large metropolitan university where he has taught both undergraduate and graduate courses since 1970. Professor Zechmeister completed his B.A. in 1966 at the University of New Mexico. He later received both the M.S. (1968) and Ph.D (1970) from Northwestern University. A specialist in the field of human cognition, Professor Zechmeister authored, with S. E. Nyberg, *Human Memory: An Introduction to Research and Theory* (Brooks/Cole, 1982), and with J. E. Johnson, *Critical Thinking: A Functional Approach* (Brooks/Cole, 1992). He is a Fellow of both of the American Psychological Association (Divisions 1 and 3) and the American Psychological Society. Professor Zechmeister currently is the Undergraduate Program Director for the Loyola University of Chicago Psychology Department.

About the Authors

To Kathy and Martha
and to the Memory of Granny (J.J.S.)

To Ruth O'Keane and to the Memory of James O'Keane,
and to the Memory of My Mother (E.B.Z.)

Contents

Preface

We have written a broad-based introduction to research methods in psychology. Various methodological approaches in psychology (naturalistic observation, survey research, and experimentation, for example) are viewed as complementary. In short, we have emphasized a multimethod approach to hypothesis testing.

Most students who take research methodology will be research consumers rather than research producers. For many students, the psychology research methods course will be their only opportunity to study the processes by which conclusions emerge from research. This book attempts to teach students to be discerning research consumers. At the same time, it provides the necessary background for students who will do research as part of their undergraduate or professional careers. Rather than emphasize specific content areas, we have illustrated concepts and methods with research from many areas of psychology. Students who use this book will find it an introduction to many contemporary and historical problems in psychology, ranging from cognitive interpretations of depression, to social attribution theory, to clinical treatment of maladaptive behavior, to program evaluation of crime deterrence programs using helicopter patrols. As students progress, they will find that they have learned much about psychology in general while coming to understand psychological research methods. Of course, by using a variety of examples from the psychology literature, we also hope to make this introduction to research methods inherently interesting.

We also have emphasized the problem-solving nature of research. We believe that, by taking this problem-solving approach, a research methods course can develop students' critical thinking abilities. We believe that these critical thinking skills generalize well to actual problem-solving situations.

The success of the second edition prompted many instructors and students to suggest how to make the book even better. We are indebted to the many individuals who contributed ideas for improving this third edition, and we have tried to incorporate as many of these suggestions as possible.

CHANGES IN THE THIRD EDITION

We tried in this third edition to go by the maxim: If it isn't broken, don't fix it. Nevertheless, while perhaps not broken, through the helpful guidance of faithful users and reviewers we identified some cracks, a few missing pieces, and a segment or two out of order. Thus, some minor repairs were in order for this edition.

Many users of the first two editions requested that the ethics material be integrated with the main text. Coincidentally, the American Psychological Association (APA) published a new ethics code since the previous edition appeared. This required a new introduction and commentary. Thus, while incorporating the new ethics material from APA, we moved our discussion of ethical issues in psychological research into a more prominent position in the text, as Chapter 2. Our original intent in placing this material in an appendix had been to allow for different approaches to presenting ethical issues. Specifically, some instructors introduce this material only after information about specific research methods has been presented. We are now convinced that there are a substantial number of others who wish to introduce ethical issues early in the course. These instructors should find the new position in the text to their liking. Those who wish to present ethics material later in the term will find it easy to skip Chapter 2 and return to it when it seems most appropriate for their course. The case studies from the earlier editions have been replaced with brief research proposals to permit students to better appreciate the process of ethical decision making required before research is initiated.

Other material that has been moved in this edition includes the discussion of case-study methodology, information about questionnaire construction, and material dealing with statistical issues in psychological research. The case-study material, previously in Chapter 4, has been moved to a newly revised Chapter 10: Single-Case Research. This change required reducing the material on operant and classical conditioning which served as background for $N = 1$ experimental designs. We are convinced that it is better pedagogy to put a discussion of case-study methology and $N = 1$ designs in the same place. Previous users will recognize that the old Chapter 3: Surveys and Questionnaires, has been renamed Correlational Research: Surveys and Tests (Chapter 4). Two major changes are found under this name change. First, we made the material on questionnaire construction an appendix to the book. Many students in their first research methods course do not actually engage in questionnaire construction. When instructors wish to include this material, or class projects require its use, the guidelines for constructing questionnaires can be accessed easily in

Appendix B. This change has made it possible to discuss the use of tests in psychological research. Because so much correlational research is based on test outcomes, we thought that this was a needed addition to the new edition.

We remain convinced that an introduction to research methods is incomplete without a thorough discussion of the role of inferential statistics in research. In this edition we have retained a brief discussion of conceptual issues pertaining to statistical inference in Chapter 6 (Independent Groups Designs) and Chapter 8 (Complex Designs). However, we have also included a new chapter (Chapter 9: Analysis of Experiments) at the end of the section on experimental methods that provides an introduction to the use of analysis of variance in independent groups, within-subjects, and complex designs. In the previous edition a discussion of analysis of variance had been included in the chapter covering a particular experimental design. The change in this edition was made as part of the never-ending quest to integrate design and analysis in a way that makes sense to both instructor and student. For many students, grasping the logic of experimental methodology and statistical analysis represents their most difficult assignment in the research methods course. The approach in this edition should make the task a bit easier by presenting the major discussion of statistical issues in experimental psychology after our coverage of experimental designs, a sort of divide and conquer approach. The new organization should also aid instructors in planning when and how much of this material to introduce to students. Finally, this change has allowed us to introduce the important topics of effect size, power, and meta-analysis in Chapter 9, which is new material for this edition. Some computational procedures for statistical tests are presented in Appendix A, as they were in the previous edition; however, users will note that the step-by-step computational guide to analysis of variance has been replaced with a discussion and illustration of computer-based analyses. Our emphasis in this section of Appendix A is on interpreting the computer output.

Additional new material is found in Chapter 1, wherein we have increased substantially the discussion of the role of theories in psychological research. Minor changes have also been made throughout the text when we thought that a new example was timely or an update of previous work was needed. Previous users will notice a significant reduction in the number of boxes that contained material intended to elaborate on concepts presented in the text. We have incorporated much of this material in the text so that students will not need to shift from reading the main text in order to learn a little history or gain additional information about an important concept. A major deletion from the previous edition is the material on psychophysics and scaling, which had been found in Appendix D. We have retained some of this material in Chapters 5 and 7. The three appendixes in the third edition represent something of a how-to section: how to do statistical analyses, how to construct questionnaires, how to write an APA paper. We believe that this practical information will be helpful to students as they approach research projects.

This edition retains a structure that permits instructors to have maximum flexibility in planning their courses. The following chapters, in our view, represent a "basic course" in research methodology: Chapters 1, 3, 6, 7, 8, and 11.

The remaining chapters and appendixes can be used to expand on this core material according to each instructor's preferences.

We hope that in making changes for this edition we have helped students to understand better the process of psychological research while continuing to convey to them the excitement of psychological research.

WORDS OF THANKS

We would like to thank the following reviewers for their many helpful comments and suggestions: Robert C. Beck, Wake Forest University; Terry L. Davidson, Purdue University; Rosemary T. Hornak, Meredith College; Rosanne Lorden, Eastern Kentucky University; Emil J. Posavac, Loyola University of Chicago; Richard Smith, University of Kentucky; and Paul J. Wellman, Texas A & M University.

A number of people made important contributions to this new edition. We want to thank Kathy Adamski, Departmental Assistant in the Psychology Department of Hope College, for her excellent work on the Instructor's Manual, and for her encouragement throughout the project. We also want to thank Michelle Nainys and Paula Nadeau Shaughnessy for their dedicated help with many important, but often tedious tasks, and for their unwavering confidence that things would get done. Elizabeth Zechmeister did a wonderful job completing the indexes under substantial time pressure. Katie Zechmeister also pitched in to help with correspondence regarding permissions.

Finally, as we move into this third edition, the list of colleagues with whom we have discussed aspects of the book grows longer. Space does not permit (neither, unfortunately, does our memory) a complete listing of all those who have commented about what they liked or didn't like about the previous editions, and which influenced us when writing this new edition. We especially want to thank, however, our colleagues in the Psychology Departments at Hope College and at Loyola University of Chicago for their contributions and support. Also, as anyone in the textbook writing business knows, there are many people behind the scenes in the publishers' offices, as well as some on stage, including both major players and those with small but important roles, who make a book possible. Some people who played major roles in the production of our book were Jane Vaicunas, Beth Kaufman, and David Dunham at McGraw-Hill, Inc. Thanks to all.

John J. Shaughnessy
Eugene B. Zechmeister

Permissions/Acknowledgments

CHAPTER 1

Page 5. Photos courtesy of The Bettman Archive and Culver Pictures. Figure 1.1. Photos courtesy of the Research Center for Language and Semiotic Studies, Indiana University, Bloomington. Figure 1.2. Photo by Emil Posavac. Figure 1.3. From R. V. Levine, "The pace of life." *American Scientist* (1990), *78,* 450–459. Figure 3, page 453. Copyright 1990 by Sigma Xi, The Scientific Research Society, Inc. Used with permission of the publisher and author.

CHAPTER 2

Figure 2.1. Photos taken by Eugene B. Zechmeister and John L. Zechmeister. Special thanks go to Erica, Linda, and Hilary Bryant, Eaaron Henderson, and members of his social psychology class, Candy Baguilat, Lynda Cafasso, and Peter Bergquist for being willing subjects for these photos; we thank Dick Fay and Bill Shofner for helping us obtain pictures of the animal subjects. We also wish to acknowledge the cooperation of the Parmly Institute of Loyola University of Chicago as well as Rich Bowen for providing experimental settings for some of these photos. Ethical principles 6.06–6.26 of the American Psychological Association, "Ethical principles of psychologists and code of conduct," *American Psychologist, 47,* 1597–1611. Copyright 1992 by the American Psychological Association. Reprinted by permission of the publisher. Neither the original nor this reproduction can be republished, photocopied, reprinted, or distributed in any form, without the prior written permission of the APA.

CHAPTER 3

Figure 3.1 from D. A. Jenni and M. A. Jenni, "Carrying behavior in humans: Analysis of sex differences." *Science* (1976), *194*, 859–860. Figure 1, page 859. Copyright 1976 by the American Association for the Advancement of Science. Reprinted by permission of publisher and author. Table 3.2 From J. R. Dickie, and S. C. Gerber, "Training in social competence: The effect on mothers, fathers, and infants." *Child Development* (1980), *51*, 1248–1251. Materials from Jane Dickie, Psychology Department, Hope College, Holland, MI. 49423. Table 3.4. From M. LaFrance and C. Mayo, "Racial differences in gaze behavior during conversations: Two systematic observational studies." *Journal of Personality and Social Psychology* (1976), *33*, 547–552. Table 2, page 550. Copyright 1976 by the American Psychological Association. Reprinted by permission of the publisher and author.

CHAPTER 4

Tables 4.1, and 4.2. From A Campbell, *The sense of well-being in America* (1981). New York: McGraw-Hill. Appendix Table 2 and Appendix Table 8, respectively. Copyright 1981 by McGraw-Hill, Inc. Reprinted by permission of publisher.

CHAPTER 5

Table 5.1. Based on material from E. J. Webb, D. T. Campbell, R. D. Schwartz, L. Sechrest, and J. B. Grove, *Nonreactive measures in the social sciences*, 2nd ed. (1981). Boston: Houghton Mifflin. Copyright 1981 by Harper & Row, Publishers, Inc. Used with permission of Harper Collins Publishers. Figure 5.1. From D. P. Phillips, "Motor vehicle fatalities increase just after publicized suicide stories." *Science* (1977), *196*, 1464–1465. Figure 1, page 1465. Copyright 1977 by the American Association for the Advancement of Science. Reprinted by permission of publisher and author. Table 5.2. Adapted from material in R. M. Brandt, *Studying behavior in natural settings* (1972). New York: Holt, Rinehart & Winston. (Republished 1981 by University Press of America, Washington, D.C.). Pages 203–206. Used by permission of author.

CHAPTER 6

Figure 6.1. Photo by Jonathan Hoffman, from D. G. Myers, *Social psychology* (1990). New York: McGraw-Hill. Used with permission of the publisher and photographer.

CHAPTER 7

Figure 7.1. From H. A. Sackheim, R. C. Gur, and M. C. Saucy, *Science* (1978), *202*, 434–436. Figure 1, page 434. Copyright 1978 by the American Association for the Advancement of Science. Reprinted by permission of publisher and author.

CHAPTER 8

Table 8.1. From R. G. Hass, I. Katz, N. Rizzo, J. Bailey, and D. Eisenstadt. "Cross-racial appraisal as related to attitude abivalence and cognitive complexity." *Personality and Social Psychology Bulletin* (1991), *17,* 83–92. Based on Table 1, page 86. Copyright 1991 by Sage Publications, Inc. Adapted by permission of the publisher and author. Data for 2 × 2 illustration from J. E. Johnson, T. P. Petzel, L. M. Hartney, and R. A. Morgan, "Recall and importance ratings of completed and uncompleted tasks as a function of depression." *Cognitive Therapy and Research* (1983), *7,* 51–56. Copyright 1983 by Plenum Publishing Corporation. Adapted by permission of publisher and author. Figure 8.5. From J. V. Hinrichs and L. R. Novick, "Memory for numbers: Nominal versus magnitude information." *Memory & Cognition* (1982), *10,* 479–486. Figure 1, page 484. Copyright 1982 by the Psychonomic Society. Reprinted by permission of publisher and author. Figure 8.6. From W. P. Wallace and B. J. Underwood, "Implicit responses and the role of intralist similarity in verbal learning by normal and retarded subjects." *Journal of Educational Psychology* (1964) *55,* 362–370. Figures 1 and 2, page 361. Copyright 1964 by the American Psychological Association. Adapted by permission of publisher and author. Table 8.3 and Figure 8.9. From M. L. Dittmar, D. B. Berch, and J. S. Warm, "Sustained visual attention in deaf and hearing adults." *Bulletin of the Psychonomic Society* (1982), *19,* 339–342. Figure 1, page 341. Copyright 1982 by the Psychonomic Society. Adapted by permission of publisher and author. Table 8.4. From J. L. Rodman and J. M. Burger, "The influence of depression on the attribution of responsibility for an accident." *Cognitive Therapy and Research* (1985) *9,* 651–657. Copyright 1985 by Plenum Publishing Corporation. Used with permission of publisher and author.

CHAPTER 9

Figure 9.1. Photo courtesy of Sonya Jacobs/The Stock Market.

CHAPTER 10

Case study illustration from I. Kirsch, "Teaching clients to be their own therapists: A case study illustration." *Psychotherapy: Theory, Research and Practice* (1978), *15,* 302–05. Reprinted by permission of Donald K. Freedheim, Editor. Figure 10.1. From S. V. Horton, "Reduction of disruptive mealtime behavior by facial screenings." *Behavior Modification* (1987), *11,* 53–64. Figure 1, page 60. Copyright 1987 by Sage Publications, Inc. Adapted by permission of Sage Publications, Inc., and author. Reprinted by permission of publisher and author. Figure 10.2. From M. G. Allison and T. Ayllon, "Behavioral coaching in the development of skills in football, gymnastics, and tennis." *Journal of Applied Behavioral Analysis* (1980), *13*, 297–304. Figure 1, page 301. Copyright 1980 by the Experimental Analysis of Behavior, Inc. Reprinted by permission of publisher and author.

CHAPTER 11

Figure 11.2. From D. T. Campbell, "Reforms as experiments." *American Psychologist* (1969), *24*, 409–429. Figure 5 and Figure 6, page 416. Copyright 1969 by the American Psychological Association. Reprinted by permission of publisher and author. Figure 11.3. From A. S. Ross and S. White, "Shoplifting, impaired driving, and refusing the breathalyzer." *Evaluation Review* (1987), *11*, 254–260. Figure 1, page 257. Copyright 1987 by Sage Publications, Inc. Reprinted by permission of Sage Publications, Inc. and author. Figure 11.4. From A. J. McSweeney, "Effects of response cost on the behavior of a million persons: Charging for directory assistance in Cincinnati." *Journal of Applied Behavior Analysis* (1978), *11*, 47–51. Copyright 1978 by the Society for the Experimental Analysis of Behavior, Inc. Reprinted by permission of publisher and author. Figure 11.5. From J. F. Schnelle, R. E. Kirchner, J. W. Macrae, M. P. McNees, R. H. Eck, S. Snodgrass, J. D. Casey, and P. H. Uselton, Jr., "Police evaluation research: An experimental and cost benefit analysis of a helicopter patrol in a high-crime area." *Journal of Applied Behavior Analysis* (1979), *11*, 11–21. Copyright 1978 by the Society for the Experimental Analysis of Behavior, Inc. Reprinted by permission of publisher and author. Page 356. Figure from G. Salomon, "Basic and applied research in psychology: Reciprocity between two worlds." *International Journal of Psychology* (1987), *22*, 441–446. Figure 2, page 444. Reprinted by permission of Elsevier Science Publishers, Academic Publishing Division, and author.

APPENDIX A

Computer-generated analyses and output shown on computer Screens A.1 through A.7 used with permission of SYSTAT, Inc., 1800 Sherman Avenue, Evanston, IL 60201. Permission to use statistical tables in Appendix A is acknowledged with tables in Appendix A.

APPENDIX B

Table B.3. Questionnaire used in a survey conducted by researchers at the Institute for Social Research (ISR), University of Michigan. Reprinted by permission of Willard Rodgers, ISR, Ann Arbor, MI 48106, and Sage Publications, Inc. Table B.4. Questionnaire given to authors, who were passengers on Amtrak's Chicago–St. Louis train, by representatives of the Illinois Department of Transportation.

APPENDIX C

Table C.3. "Guidelines for Nonsexist Language" and extensive quotations from *Publication Manual of the American Psychological Association*, 3rd ed. (1983). Washington, D.C. Copyright 1983 by the American Psychological Association. Reprinted by permission of publisher. Neither the original nor this reproduction can be republished, photocopied, reprinted, or distributed in any form, without the prior written permission of the APA. Table C.4. From M. Anisfeld, "A course to develop competence in critical reading of empirical research in psychology." *Teaching of Psychology* (1987), *14*, 224–227. Table 1, page 225. Copyright 1987 by Lawrence Erlbaum Publishers. Adapted by permission of the publisher and author. Figure C.4. Courtesy of Eastman Kodak Company.

Part I

General Issues

Chapter 1

Introduction

Outline

PSYCHOLOGY AS A SCIENCE

There is no record of who first observed behavior carefully and systematically, who conducted the first public opinion survey, or even of who performed the first psychology experiment. We don't really know exactly when psychology first became an independent discipline. It emerged gradually, with its roots in the thinking of Aristotle (the "father" of all psychology; Keller, 1937), in the writings of later philosophers such as Descartes and Locke, and, more recently, in the work of early 19th-century physiologists and physicists.

The date usually taken to mark psychology's official beginning is 1879. In that year Wilhelm Wundt established a formal psychology laboratory in Leipzig, Germany. Wundt, like many scientists of his time, had a doctoral degree in medicine. He even published for awhile in the fields of anatomy and physiology. These experiences gave Wundt a basis for his ideas about a "physiological psychology" that led to his scientific approach to psychology. Dozens of researchers from around the world came to his psychology laboratory to learn about the "new" discipline. As a consequence, from Wundt's laboratory a scientific psychology spread quickly to the intellectual centers of the world. According to Boring (1950), Wilhelm Wundt was the "first man who without reservation is properly called a psychologist" (p. 316).

Whatever exact date one accepts for the beginning of a scientific psychology, we can see that the enterprise is little more than a hundred years old. Near the end of the 19th century, in 1892, the American Psychological Association (APA) was formed, with G. Stanley Hall as its first president. Hall had been a student at Harvard of the well-known American philosopher and psychologist William James. In 1878, James bestowed upon Hall the first Ph.D. in psychology given

Wilhelm Wundt
(1832-1920)

William James
(1842-1910)

in the United States. After receiving his degree, Hall left the United States to study with Wundt in Germany (Boring, 1950). Still later, in 1887, Hall founded the first psychology journal in the United States, the *American Journal of Psychology.* The APA had only a few dozen members in its first year; 100 years later, in 1992, when the APA celebrated its 100th birthday, there were approximately 70,000 members (see American Psychological Association, 1991).

Psychology has changed significantly since its beginnings. Wundt and his colleagues were primarily interested in questions dealing with sensation and perception—for instance, visual illusions and imagery. Experiments on reaction time also were conducted with the goal of measuring the time necessary for various cognitive processes, such as those involved in making a choice (Boring, 1950). Psychologists continue to be interested in sensation and perception, and Wundt's procedures form the basis of some of the experimental methods in use today. However, research on sensation and perception represents but a fraction of the research undertaken in contemporary psychology. Today psychologists are interested in a myriad of topics, including those in such general areas as clinical, social, industrial, counseling, physiological, cognitive, educational, and developmental psychology.

Psychology has also not developed strictly as a laboratory science. Although laboratory investigation remains at the heart of psychological inquiry, psychologists and other behavioral scientists do research in schools, clinics, businesses, hospitals, and other nonlaboratory settings. Many research psychologists, for instance, are engaged in *program evaluation,* a type of research in which the impact of large-scale interventions on groups or institutions is evaluated. Program evaluators confront questions such as whether a new management-labor relations program will lead to increased employee morale and company productivity, or whether the nationwide Head Start program has significantly raised the IQ of hundreds of thousands of preschoolers (see Chapter 11).

Promotion of psychological research is a concern of APA as well as the recently founded American Psychological Society (APS). Formed in 1988 to emphasize mainly scientific issues in psychology, APS grew at a phenomenal rate. In just its first two years, membership increased to over 10,000 (McGaugh, 1990). While many psychologists choose to join either APA or APS, many join both. APA and APS both sponsor annual conventions which psychologists attend to learn about the most recent developments in their fields; each organization also publishes scientific journals in order to communicate the latest research findings to its members and to society in general; and both organizations encourage student affiliation, which provides educational and research opportunities for both undergraduate and graduate psychology students. By affiliating with APA and APS, students can subscribe to major psychology journals at a relatively low cost as well as become involved at an early stage in a career in psychology.

THE SCIENTIFIC METHOD

There is one way in which psychology has not changed in the one hundred years or so of its existence: the **scientific method** is still emphasized as the basis for investigation. The founding of Wundt's laboratory marked the beginning of the formal application of the scientific method to problems in psychology. This method is not identified with particular kinds of equipment, nor is it associated exclusively with specific research procedures. The scientific method is something abstract. It is an approach to knowledge that is best described by distinguishing it from what might be called *nonscientific* or "everyday" approaches to knowledge.

SCIENTIFIC AND NONSCIENTIFIC APPROACHES TO KNOWLEDGE

Several major differences between a scientific and a nonscientific approach to knowledge are outlined in Table 1.1. Collectively, the characteristics listed under "Scientific" define what is called the **scientific method.** The distinctions made in Table 1.1 between a scientific and a nonscientific approach are intended to highlight differences that frequently exist between "everyday," or informal, kinds of thinking and thinking that is characteristic of the scientist's approach to knowledge. These distinctions are briefly summarized as follows.

General Approach Many everyday judgments are made intuitively. This usually means that we act on the basis of what "feels right" or what "seems reasonable." Intuition is not based on a formal decision process, such as that of deductive logic, nor is it based on information that was taught to us or that we acquired through direct experience. The many everyday inferences and conclusions reached intuitively are the product of insight and of what we quickly perceive as true.

Intuition is a valuable cognitive process. We frequently have little to go on other than what intuition suggests is the right answer or the proper course to

TABLE 1.1 CHARACTERISTICS OF SCIENTIFIC AND NONSCIENTIFIC (EVERYDAY) APPROACHES TO KNOWLEDGE*

	Nonscientific (everyday)	Scientific
General Approach:	Intuitive	Empirical
Observation:	Casual, uncontrolled	Systematic, controlled
Reporting:	Biased, subjective	Unbiased, objective
Concepts:	Ambiguous, with surplus meanings	Clear definitions, operational specificity
Instruments:	Inaccurate, imprecise	Accurate, precise
Measurement:	Not valid or reliable	Valid and reliable
Hypotheses:	Untestable	Testable
Attitude:	Uncritical, accepting	Critical, skeptical

*Based in part on distinctions suggested by Marx (1963).

follow. Intuition can also help us make decisions in situations that we have not encountered before. Consider, for example, what intuition might suggest as the answer to a question based on the following situation:

> Assume that on two different occasions you are the victim of a street crime. Let us say that you are walking down the street and someone tries to grab your wallet or purse. The thief begins to wrestle with you in order to get it. You find yourself in need of assistance. On one occasion there is a crowd of bystanders who witness the attempted robbery. On the other occasion there is only one person who sees the event.
>
> The question is: In which situation would you be more likely to receive help, when many people are present or when only one person is present?

Intuition would suggest that the more people present, the greater the chances that you will receive help. Surprisingly, social psychologists have determined that just the opposite is true. A bystander is more likely to act in an emergency when alone than when a group of people is present (Latané & Darley, 1970; see also Chapter 3 in this book).

Our intuition about what is true does not always agree with what is actually true because we fail to recognize that our perceptions may be distorted by what are called cognitive biases or because we neglect to weigh available evidence appropriately (Kahneman & Tversky, 1973; Tversky & Kahneman, 1974). One such cognitive bias, called *illusory correlation,* is our tendency to perceive a relationship between events when none exists. Ward and Jenkins (1965) showed their subjects the results of a hypothetical 50-day cloud-seeding experiment. For each of the 50 days, subjects were told whether cloud seeding had been done and whether it had rained on that day. Ward and Jenkins constructed the results such that there was actually no relationship between cloud seeding and the likelihood of rain—rain was equally likely on days when seeding had and had not been done. Nonetheless, subjects were convinced that the evidence supported their intuitive supposition that cloud seeding and rain varied together. One possible basis for the illusory-correlation bias is that we are more likely to notice events that are consistent with our beliefs than events that violate them. Thus, subjects in the cloud-seeding experiment may have been more likely to notice and remember the days on which cloud seeding was followed by rain than the days on which clouds were seeded in vain.

The scientific approach to knowledge is empirical rather than intuitive. An **empirical approach** emphasizes direct observation and experimentation as a way of answering questions. This does not mean that intuition plays no role in science. Any scientist can probably recount tales of getting empirical outcomes or experimental results that intuition had suggested would emerge. On the other hand, the same scientist is also likely to have come up with just as many findings that were counterintuitive. Research at first may be guided by what the scientist's intuition suggests is the proper direction to take. Eventually, however, the scientist strives to be guided by what direct observation and experimentation reveal to be true.

Observation We can learn a great deal about behavior by simply observing the actions of others. However, everyday observations are not always made carefully or systematically. Most people do not attempt to control or eliminate factors that might influence the events that they are observing. As a consequence, erroneous conclusions are often drawn. Consider, for instance, the classic case of Clever Hans. Hans was a horse who was said by his owner, a German mathematics teacher, to have amazing talents. Hans could count, do simple addition and subtraction (even involving fractions), read German, answer simple questions ("What is the lady holding in her hands?"), and give the date, and tell time (Watson, 1914/1967). Hans answered questions by tapping with his forefoot or by pointing with his nose at different alternatives shown to him. His owner considered Hans to be truly intelligent and denied using any tricks to guide his horse's behavior. And, in fact, Clever Hans was clever even when the questioner was someone other than his owner.

Newspapers carried accounts of Hans's performances, and hundreds of people came to view this amazing horse (see Figure 1.1). In 1904 a scientific commission was established with the goal of discovering the basis for Hans's abilities. The scientists found that Hans was no longer clever if either of two circumstances existed. First, Hans did not know the answers to questions if the questioner also did not know the answers. Second, Hans was not very clever if he could not see his questioner. It was discovered that Hans was responding to very slight movements of the questioner. A slight bending forward by the questioner would start Hans tapping, and any movement upward or backward would cause Hans to stop tapping. The commission demonstrated that questioners were unintentionally cueing Hans in this way.

This famous account of Clever Hans illustrates the fact that scientific observation (unlike casual observation) is systematic and controlled. Indeed, it has been suggested that **control** is the essential ingredient of science, distinguishing it from nonscientific procedures (Boring, 1954; Marx, 1963). In the case of Clever

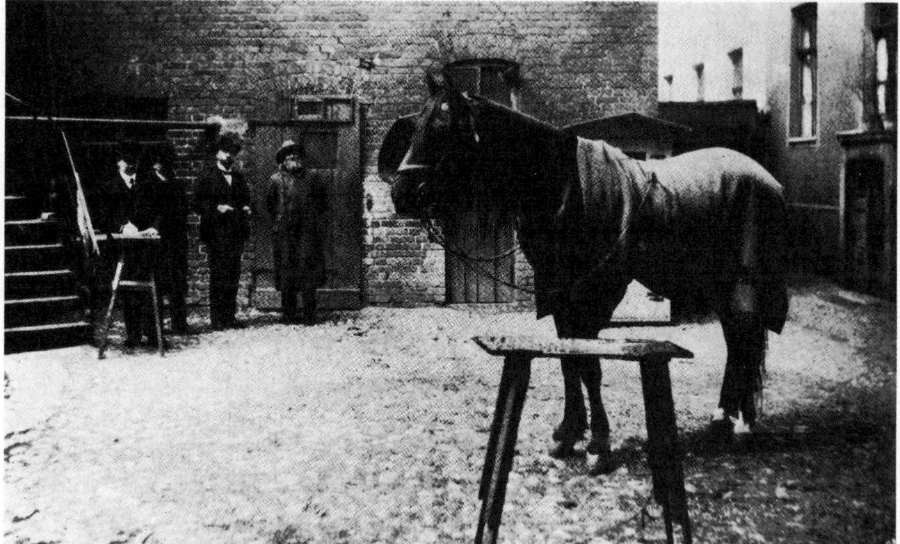

FIGURE 1.1 Top: Clever Hans performing before onlookers. Bottom: Hans being tested under more controlled conditions when Hans could not see the questioner.

Hans, investigators exercised control by manipulating, *one at a time,* conditions such as whether the questioner knew the answer to the questions asked and whether Hans could see the questioner (see Figure 1.1). By exercising control, taking care to investigate the effect of various factors one by one, the scientist seeks to gain a clearer picture of the factors that actually produce a phenomenon.

The factors that the researcher controls or manipulates in order to determine their effect on behavior are called the **independent variables.** In the simplest of studies, the independent variable has two levels. These two levels often represent the presence and the absence of some treatment, respectively. The condition in which the treatment is present is commonly called the *experimental condition;* the condition in which the treatment is absent is called the *control condition.* If we wanted to study the effect of drinking alcohol on the ability to process complex information quickly and accurately, for example, the independent variable would be the presence or absence of alcohol in a drink that subjects were given. Subjects in the experimental condition would receive alcohol, while subjects in the control condition would receive the same drink without alcohol.

The levels of the independent variable do not always represent the presence and the absence of some treatment; moreover, an independent variable may have more than two levels. What is critical is that the levels differ with respect to the variable of interest. For example, Heath and Davidson (1988) recruited female college students to participate in a study designed to aid in the development of a rape-prevention pamphlet. When volunteers appeared in the laboratory, they were asked to review one of three packages of materials that they were told was being considered for possible inclusion in the pamphlet. The three packages of materials varied in the manner in which rape was described. Specifically, the materials to be reviewed presented rape as being very controllable, somewhat controllable, or not at all controllable. After reviewing the materials, the women were asked a series of questions regarding their own perceptions of the risk of rape. The independent variable in this study was the degree of control emphasized in the pamphlet materials; it had three levels (high, medium, low).

Sometimes the levels of the independent variable are selected by a researcher rather than manipulated. This is typically the case when a **subject variable** serves as the independent variable. A subject variable is a characteristic or trait that varies consistently across subjects. For example, a researcher may be interested in the effect of age on the ability to process complex information. Do older adults, for instance, process verbatim and inferential information differently from younger adults? (See Till, 1985.) Age would be the independent variable in this study. Age is a subject variable and necessarily would not be manipulated by a researcher; rather, the researcher controls this independent variable by systematically selecting individuals of particular ages or within specific age groups. Intelligence, aggressiveness, gender, and fraternity or sorority membership are other examples of subject variables.

The term *independent variable* is used both for subject variables when levels of the variable are selected and for nonsubject variables when levels can be manipulated. There are important differences, however, between these kinds of independent variables. As we will see later in this chapter and in Chapter 6, manipulating the levels of an independent variable has considerable advantages over selecting the levels of a subject variable. Studying the effects of subject variables poses additional challenges of control. Nonetheless, subject variables are of significant interest in many areas of research in psychology.

The measures of behavior that are used to assess the effect (if any) of the independent variables are called **dependent variables.** In our example of a study which investigates the effects of alcohol on processing complex information, the researcher might measure the number of errors made by control and experimental subjects when playing a difficult video game. Errors, then, would be the dependent variable. When Till (1985) investigated the ability of young and elderly adults to process verbatim and inferential messages appearing in a list of unrelated sentences, he recorded the subjects' answers to twenty-four questions based on information in the sentences. The number of questions answered correctly was the dependent variable. Most studies in psychology are done in order to discover the nature of the relationship between particular independent and dependent variables.

In the Heath and Davidson (1988) rape study, there were several dependent variables, which represented the women's responses to questions on the rape-perception questionnaire. The results showed that women who read materials emphasizing rape as an uncontrollable event reported higher anxiety when outside on the street or inside their homes, and a greater intention to take precautionary steps, than did women who reviewed the materials describing rape as more controllable. Interestingly, results of additional experiments carried out by Heath and Davidson (1988) indicated that although uncontrollable rape is definitely viewed as anxiety producing, the "intent" to be more cautious reported by their subjects may not always be followed by actual changes in behaviors. Unfortunately, when rape is perceived as an uncontrollable event some women may view attempts to reduce their vulnerability to attacks as futile.

If changes in the dependent variable are to be interpreted as a result of the effects of the independent variable, control techniques must be used properly. The control techniques available to scientists can be divided into three types: manipulation, holding conditions constant, and balancing. We have already seen how *manipulation* of the levels of an independent variable can be used as a control technique. The second type of control, holding conditions constant, is probably the one that is most commonly associated with the word *control.* If we were studying the effect of drinking alcohol on errors made while playing a video game, we would *not* want to test the experimental subjects using a large color screen and the control subjects using a small black-and-white screen. Instead, we would want to make sure that the same screen was used for all subjects, thereby *holding constant* the potentially significant variable of type of display screen.

When an independent variable is manipulated, at least one set of factors typically cannot be held constant—the characteristics of the subjects tested. Just as the researcher would not want experimental and control subjects in the alcohol study to use different screens, the researcher also would not want control and experimental subjects to differ systematically in terms of some subject characteristic that affects video-game performance. People are likely to differ in the amount of experience they have had playing video games. It would be important that control and experimental subjects have similar amounts of experience playing video games. Researchers control factors that are not manipulated and that cannot be held constant by *balancing* the influence of these factors across the conditions. The most common technique used to avoid imbalance is to assign subjects randomly to the different groups being tested. Without random assignment, we might find that one group had more young people, more women, more overweight people, and so on—all differences that might distort the results of the study. Of course, even groups whose members are randomly assigned are not all perfectly equivalent in all characteristics, but any imbalance is likely to be minor and unlikely to affect research results. Throughout this text, we will be describing specific procedures for the use of each of the three types of control (see especially Chapters 6 and 7).

When the independent variable is a subject variable, such as age, and levels of the independent variable must be selected rather than manipulated, it should be apparent that balancing subject characteristics through random assignment is not feasible. Young and elderly adults, for example, are selected from natural groups to represent levels of an age variable; thus, it is not possible to assign subjects randomly to different levels of the independent variable. The process of selecting subjects to represent different levels of a subject variable serves to define the levels of the independent variable. However, subject characteristics other than the one which is explicitly defined also may differentiate the groups. A researcher who sets out to investigate the effect of age on the ability to play video games must acknowledge that the subjects are likely to differ in ways other than age. In other words, elderly adults are not only "older" (by definition) than younger adults but also likely to have had less experience playing video games than are younger adults. Video games simply were not around when today's elderly were adolescents. Elderly adults also may differ from younger adults in their motivation to play video games, or in terms of many other relevant characteristics. Because it is not possible to balance these factors between young and elderly groups through randomization, the researcher must deal with the fact that differences in performance associated with age need not be (nor are they even likely to be) due to differences in "age" per se. Suggestions for dealing with the interpretation of differences across levels of a subject variable are presented in Chapter 8.

Reporting If we ask someone to *report* to us about events that occurred in our absence, we probably want the report to be unbiased and objective. Otherwise we will be unable to determine exactly what happened. As you might imagine, personal biases and subjective impressions often enter into everyday reports that we receive. Ask anyone to describe an event to you and you are likely to receive not merely details of the event but also personal impressions. You may also find that the details reported to you are not the ones that *you* would have reported. We often report events in terms of our own interests and attitudes. Obviously, these interests and attitudes do not always coincide with those of others. The next time you take a class examination, poll several classmates on their impressions of the test. Their reports are likely to vary dramatically, depending on such factors as how well prepared they were, what they concentrated on when they studied, and their expectations about what the instructor was going to emphasize on the test.

When scientists report their findings, they seek to separate what they have observed from what they conclude or infer on the basis of these observations. For example, consider the photograph in Figure 1.2. How would you describe to someone what you see there? One way to describe this scene is to say that two people are running along a path with one person in front of the other. You might also describe this scene as one person *chasing* the other. If you use this second description, you are reporting an inference drawn from what you have seen and not just reporting what you have observed. The description of two people running would be preferred in a scientific report.

This distinction between description and inference in reporting can be carried to extremes. For example, describing what is shown in Figure 1.2 as running could be considered an inference, the actual observation being that two people are moving their legs up and down and forward in rapid, long strides. Such a literal description also would not be appropriate. The point is that, in scientific reporting, observers must guard against a tendency to draw inferences

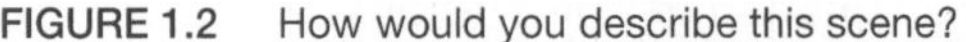

FIGURE 1.2 How would you describe this scene?

too quickly. Further, events should be described in sufficient detail without including trivial and unnecessary minutiae. We will discuss proper methods for making observations and reporting them in Chapter 3.

Scientific reporting also seeks to be unbiased and objective. One accepted check on whether a report is unbiased is whether it can be verified by more than one independent observer. A measure of interobserver agreement, for example, is usually found in observational studies (see Chapter 3). Unfortunately, many biases are subtle and not always detected even in scientific reporting. Consider the fact that there is a species of fish in which the eggs are incubated in the mouth of the male parent until they hatch. The first scientist to observe the eggs disappear into their father's mouth could certainly be forgiven for assuming, momentarily, that he was eating them. That's simply what we expect organisms to do with their mouths! But the careful observer waits, watches for unexpected results, and takes *nothing* for granted.

Concepts We use the term *concepts* to refer to things (both living and inanimate), to events (things in action), and to relationships among things or events, as well as to their characteristics (Marx, 1963). "Dog" is a concept, as is "barking," and so is "obedience." Concepts are the symbols by which we ordinarily communicate. Clear, unambiguous communication of ideas requires that we use concepts that are clearly defined. This means that the concepts we use should be free of unwarranted or surplus meaning. That is, a concept should not convey more meaning than was intended.

In everyday conversation we can often get by without having to worry too much about how we define a concept. Many words, for instance, are commonly used and apparently understood even though neither party to the communication knows *exactly* what the words mean. We are suggesting that people frequently communicate with one another without being fully aware of what they are talking about. This may sound ridiculous but, to prove our point, try the following.

Ask a few people whether they believe that intelligence is mostly inherited or mostly acquired. You might try arguing a point of view opposite to theirs just for the fun of it. After having engaged them in a discussion about the roots of intelligence, ask them what they mean by "intelligence." You will probably find that most people have a difficult time defining this concept. Yet people are frequently willing to debate an important point regarding intelligence, and even take a definite stand on the issue, without being able to say exactly what "intelligence" is. When someone does provide a definition, it is unlikely to be exactly the same as that given by another person. That is, "intelligence" means one thing to one person and something else to another. Clearly, in order to attempt to answer the question of whether intelligence is mainly inherited or mainly acquired, we must provide an exact definition that all parties involved can accept. On the other hand, we can talk about it, even argue about it, on an everyday basis without knowing exactly what it is we are talking about!

One way in which a scientist gives meaning to a concept is by defining it operationally. An **operational definition** explains a concept solely in terms of the operations used to produce and measure it. Intelligence, for instance, can be defined operationally by specifying a paper-and-pencil test emphasizing understanding of logical relationships, short-term memory, and acquaintance with the meaning of words. Some may not like this operational definition of intelligence, but once a particular test has been identified, there can at least be no argument about what intelligence means *according to this definition.* Operational definitions facilitate communication, at least among those who know how and why they are used.

Although exact meaning is conveyed via operational definitions, this approach to communication has not escaped criticism. One problem has been alluded to already. That is, if we don't like one operational definition of intelligence, there is nothing to prevent us from giving intelligence another operational definition. Does this mean that there are as many kinds of intelligence as there are operational definitions? Each time a new set of questions is added to a paper-and-pencil test of intelligence do we have a new definition of intelligence? The answer, unfortunately, is that we don't really know. To determine whether a different procedure yields a new definition of intelligence, we would have to seek additional evidence. For example, do people who score high on one test also score high on the second test? If they do, the new test may be measuring the same thing as the old one.

Another criticism of using operational definitions is that the definitions are not always meaningful. For example, defining intelligence in terms of how long one can balance a ball on one's nose is an operational definition that most people would not find very meaningful. How do we decide whether a concept has been meaningfully defined? Once again, the solution is to appeal to other forms of evidence. How does performance on a balancing task compare to performance on other tasks that *are* commonly accepted as measures of intelligence? We must also be willing to apply common sense to the situation. Do people usually consider balancing a ball evidence of intelligence? Scientists are generally aware of the limitations of operational definitions; however, the clarity of communication that derives from this approach is assumed to outweigh the problems it raises.

Instruments You depend on instruments to measure events more than you probably realize. The speedometer in the car, the clock in the bedroom, and the thermometer used to measure body temperature are all instruments that we would find it difficult to do without. And you can appreciate the problems that arise if one of these instruments is inaccurate. *Accuracy* refers to the difference between what an instrument says is true and what is known to be true. A clock that is consistently 5 minutes slow is not very accurate. Inaccurate clocks can make us late, inaccurate speedometers can earn us traffic tickets, and inaccurate thermometers can lead us to believe that we are ill when we are not. The accuracy of an instrument is determined by *calibrating* it, or checking it with another instrument known to be true. Thus, we periodically call the telephone company to check the accuracy of our clocks based on the recorded messages telling us "the time at the tone," which we assume represent the true time. The accuracy of speedometers can be checked using a combination of observations of roadside distance markers and the seconds ticking off on an accurate watch.

Measurements can be made at varying levels of *precision.* A measure of time in tenths of a second is not as precise as one that is in hundredths of a second. One instrument that yields imprecise measures is the gas gauge in most cars. Although reasonably accurate, gas gauges do not give very precise readings. Most of us have wished at one time or another that the gas gauge would permit us to determine whether we had that extra half gallon of gas that would get us to the next service station.

We also need instruments to measure behavior. Wundt used reaction-time apparatus to measure the time required for cognitive processing. You can be assured that the precision, and even the accuracy, of instruments of this kind have improved significantly in the last hundred years. Today electronic counters provide precise measures of reaction time in milliseconds (thousandths of a second). Many other instruments are employed in contemporary psychology. To perform a biofeedback experiment requires instruments that give accurate feedback to a participant regarding such internal states as heart rate and blood pressure. Tests of anxiety sometimes employ instruments to measure galvanic skin response (GSR). Other behavioral instruments are of the paper-and-pencil variety. Questionnaires and tests are popular instruments used by psychologists to measure behavior (see especially Chapter 4). So, too, are the rating scales used by human observers (see Chapter 3). For instance, rating aggression in children on a 7-point scale ranging from not at all aggressive (1) to very aggressive (7) can yield relatively accurate (although perhaps not too precise) measures of aggression. It is the responsibility of the behavioral scientist to use instruments that are as precise and as accurate as possible.

Measurement Psychologists must deal with two types of measurement. The first type, physical measurement, involves dimensions for which there is an agreed-upon standard and an instrument for doing the measuring. Length is a dimension that can be scaled with physical measurement, and there are agreed-upon standards for units of length. For instance, 1 meter was at one time defined as 1/10,000,000 of the distance between the North Pole and the equator. This proved impossible to measure precisely, so the definition of 1 meter was changed to the distance between two points on a platinum-iridium bar kept under controlled conditions near Paris, France. Although this provided accuracy to one part in a million, greater precision was sought. In 1960 the meter was defined as 1,650,763.73 wavelengths of the red-orange radiation of the inert gas krypton-86. But even this proved not precise enough for scientists. (When using the krypton measure to determine the distance from the earth to the moon, scientists found themselves in error by more than 1.5 meters.) Recently, the definition of the meter was changed to the length of the path traveled by light in a vacuum in 1/299,792,458 of a second.

In most research in psychology, however, the dimensions to be measured do not involve physical measurement. Rulers do not exist for measuring beauty, aggression, or intelligence. For these dimensions we must use a second type of measurement: *psychological measurement.* Agreement among a certain number of observers provides the basis for psychological measurement. If several independent observers agree that a certain action warrants a rating of 3 on a 7-point rating scale of aggression, we can say that we have a psychological measurement of the aggressiveness of the action. Of course, many dimensions that can be scaled physically can also be measured using psychological measurement. Observers can be asked to judge which of two lines is longer, and, if they consistently select the longer one, we know the observers can "measure" length. This type of measurement is called psychophysical measurement and it represents one of the earliest areas of experimental investigation in psychology.

It is important that measurement be both valid and reliable. In general, **validity** refers to the "truthfulness" of a measure. A valid measure of a concept is one that measures what it claims to measure. We discussed this aspect of measurement when we mentioned possible operational definitions of intelligence. Intelligence, it was suggested, could be defined in terms of performance on a task requiring one to balance a ball on one's nose. According to the principle of operationalism, this is a perfectly permissible definition. However, we would be led to ask whether this is really a measure of intelligence; in other words, we would want to question the validity of the measure. Can intelligence actually be measured by how long we can keep a ball twirling on our nose? As we indicated earlier, evidence bearing on the validity of this definition would have to come from other sources. The validity of a measure is supported to the extent that subjects do as well on *it* as they do on independent measures that are presumed to measure the same concept. For example, if time spent balancing a ball is a valid measure of intelligence, then a person who does well on the balancing task should also do well on such measures as size of vocabulary, reasoning ability, and other accepted measures of intelligence. Note that an instrument, such as a stopwatch, may be very accurate and precise yet not provide a valid measure of the concept of intelligence.

The **reliability** of a measurement is indicated by its consistency. Several different kinds of reliability can be distinguished. When we speak of instrument reliability, we are discussing whether an instrument works consistently. The car that sometimes starts and sometimes doesn't when we engage the ignition is not very reliable. Observations made by two or more independent observers are said to be reliable if they show agreement—that is, if the observations are consistent from one observer to another. In the context of psychological testing, researchers need to be concerned with test reliability. Are the results obtained on a test consistent from one administration of the test to another? In subsequent chapters of this book we will discuss various kinds of validity and reliability and introduce you to various methods for measuring them.

Hypotheses A **hypothesis** is a tentative explanation for something. It frequently attempts to answer the questions "How?" and "Why?" At one level, a hypothesis may simply suggest how particular variables are related. For example, a researcher may hypothesize that elderly adults will remember less of inferential information than will young adults. At a more theoretical level, a hypothesis may offer a reason (the "why") for the way that particular variables are related. For example, Till (1985) hypothesized that older adults remember less inferential information because they are less able to encode (register) and retrieve (recall) such information than are younger adults.

Nearly everyone has proposed hypotheses to explain some human behavior at one time or another. Why do people commit apparently senseless acts of violence? What causes people to smoke cigarettes? Why are some students academically more successful than others? One characteristic often distinguishes the hypotheses proposed by the nonscientist from those offered by the scientist: testability. As attractive as it might be, if a hypothesis cannot be tested, it is of no immediate use to science (Marx, 1963).

Hypotheses are not testable if *the concepts to which they refer are not adequately defined*. To say that a would-be assassin shot a U.S. president or other prominent figure because he was mentally disturbed is not a testable hypothesis unless a definition of mentally disturbed can be agreed upon. Unfortunately, psychologists and psychiatrists cannot always agree on what terms such as "mentally disturbed" and "insane" mean. Often this occurs because an accepted operational definition is not available for these concepts. As one prominent researcher has commented, "a criterion of whether or not a so-called empirical concept is a scientific concept is whether or not it has been operationally defined" (Underwood, 1957, p. 52). Therefore, in addition to facilitating clarity in communication, operational definitions offer a means of evaluating whether our hypotheses contain scientifically acceptable concepts.

Hypotheses are also untestable if they are *circular*, in which case the event itself becomes an explanation for the event. It has been pointed out that using a definition of an event as an explanation for the event, that is, a *circular hypothesis*, is something you can "catch the late-night talk show hosts doing" all the time (Kimble, 1989). Kimble gives these examples (p. 495):

> "Your eight-year-old son is distractable in school and having trouble reading because he has an attention deficiency disorder."
>
> "The stock market crash of October 19, 1987, was caused by widespread economic panic."

This scientist goes on to say that "If [he] could make just one change in what the general public (and some psychologists) understand about psychology, it would be to give them an immunity to such misuses of definitions."

Finally, a hypothesis may be untestable if it *appeals to ideas or forces that are not recognized by science*. As we have shown, science deals with the observable, the demonstrable, the empirical. To suggest that people who commit horrendous acts of violence are under orders from the Devil is not testable because it invokes a principle (the Devil) that is not in the province of science. Such hypotheses might be of value to philosophers or theologians but not to the scientist.

Hypotheses in scientific research are often derived from a **theory.** The nature of scientific theories, their function, and how they are constructed and tested will be discussed later in this chapter.

Attitude More than anything else, scientists are skeptical. Not only do they want to "see it before believing it," but they are likely to want to see it again, and again, perhaps under conditions of their own choosing. Behavioral scientists come to this skepticism by recognizing two important facts. First, behavior is complex, and often many factors interact to give rise to a psychological phenomenon. Discovering these factors is often a difficult task. The explanations proposed are sometimes premature, not enough factors having been considered or the existence of one or more factors having gone unnoticed. Second, the behavioral scientist recognizes that science is a human endeavor. People make mistakes. Human inference, as we have suggested, is not always to be trusted. Therefore scientists are often skeptical about "new discoveries" and extraordinary claims.

The skepticism of scientists produces a cautiousness that is often lacking in those without scientific training. Too many people are apparently all too ready to accept explanations that are based on insufficient or inadequate evidence. This is illustrated by the widespread belief in the occult. Rather than approach cautiously the claims of those who promote belief in the paranormal, many people are uncritical in their acceptance. According to public opinion surveys, a large majority of Americans believe in ESP (*e*xtra*s*ensory *p*erception), and many people apparently are convinced that beings from outer space have visited earth. About 2 in 5 Americans give some credibility to astrology reports, and as many as 12 million adults report changing their behavior after reading astrology reports (Miller, 1986). Such beliefs are held despite minimal and often contradictory evidence of their validity. This human tendency to ignore certain kinds of evidence is not new. When scientists successfully demonstrated the means by which Clever Hans was so clever, many people continued to believe in his superior reasoning ability (Watson, 1914/1967).

What is responsible for this tendency to propose explanations based on the occult and to resist obvious evidence to the contrary? Singer and Benassi (1981) suggest that an uncritical attitude toward such events has several sources. First, there are many distortions in the media. The public is constantly exposed to television shows, newspaper accounts, and other reports of events presumably caused by supernatural forces. These reports are often presented with little critical evaluation, and scientific evidence for alternative explanations is frequently ignored. The sheer pervasiveness of such reports may lend credibility to them.

Another reason for the widespread acceptance of the occult may be deficiencies in human reasoning. As we emphasized earlier in this chapter, everyday inferences are susceptible to many biases, including the tendency to seek only confirmatory evidence, to jump to conclusions, and to perceive causality in events when none is actually present (see, for example, Zechmeister & Johnson, 1992). Finally, Singer and Benassi find fault with science education. Too often, they suggest, science is taught as a set of facts rather than as a way of approaching knowledge critically and systematically. Thus, people are often impatient with the scientific process and even confused when scientists appear to change their minds or when they attempt to clarify earlier findings. Singer and Benassi also find that the general public exhibits woefully little general scientific knowledge. Many people believe that islands float on the ocean surface, for instance, and that the moon is fixed in the sky but only visible at night. Belief in astrology reports and "lucky numbers," for example, is stronger among people with little formal education than it is among college-educated individuals (Miller, 1986).

Scientists do not, of course, automatically assume that unconventional interpretations of unexplained phenomena could not possibly be true. They simply insist on being allowed to test all claims and to reject those that are inherently untestable. Scientific skepticism is a gullible public's defense against charlatans and others who would sell them ineffective medicines and cures, impossible schemes to get rich, and supernatural explanations for natural phenomena.

GOALS OF THE SCIENTIFIC METHOD

The scientific method is intended to meet three goals: description, prediction, and understanding.

Description *Description* refers to the procedures by which events and their relationships are defined, classified, cataloged, or categorized. Clinical research, for instance, has provided practioners with many different sets of criteria for classifying mental disorders. Many of these are found in the American Psychiatric Association's *Diagnostic and statistical manual of mental disorders* (3rd ed., rev., 1987), also known as *DSM-III-R.* Consider, as one example, the criteria used to define the disorder labeled *psychogenic fugue.*

> **A.** The predominant disturbance is sudden, unexpected travel away from home or one's customary place of work, with inability to recall one's past.
> **B.** Assumption of a new identity (partial or complete).
> **C.** The disturbance is not due to Multiple Personality Disorder or to an Organic Mental Disorder (e.g., partial complex seizures in temporal lobe epilepsy). (*DSM-III-R*, 1987, p. 273)

Research also seeks to provide clinicians with descriptions of the prevalence of a mental disorder and their relationship to variables including, but not restricted to, gender and age. According to the *DSM-III-R* (1987), for instance, psychogenic fugue is relatively rare but more frequent in wartime or following a natural disaster. (Information about the relationship of this disorder to gender or family condition is lacking at present.) Clinical research frequently makes use of case studies, a procedure that will be discussed in Chapter 10.

Levine (1990) described the "pace of life" in various cultures and countries of the world. Measures of a country's tempo were made by noting the accuracy of outdoor bank clocks in a country's cities, by timing the walking speed of pedestrians over a distance of 100 feet, and by measuring the speed with which postal clerks processed a standard request for stamps. The investigator frequently enlisted the help of students to make observations while they traveled during summer vacations or semester breaks. The results of this study are shown in Figure 1.3. The citizens of Japan exhibited, overall, the fastest pace of life; the citizens of Indonesia were the slowest. United States citizens were second overall.

Psychology (like science in general) develops descriptions of phenomena using the *nomothetic approach.* The objective of the nomothetic approach is to establish broad generalizations and universal "laws" that apply to a wide population of organisms. As a consequence, psychological research frequently consists of studies involving large numbers of participants with the purpose of determining the "average," or typical, performance of a group. This average may or may not represent the performance of any one individual in the group. Not all citizens of Japan or the United States, for example, are on the fast track. In fact, Levine (1990) and his colleagues found wide differences in the pace of life among various cities within a country. Inhabitants of large cities walked faster than did those of medium-sized cities in the various countries that were visited. In the United States, differences in a city's tempo were found depending on the region of the country. Cities in the Northeast (e.g., Boston, New York)

FIGURE 1.3 Measures of accuracy of a country's bank clocks, pedestrian walking speed, and the speed of postal clerks performing a routine task served to describe the pace of life in a country. In the graph a longer bar represents greater accuracy of clocks or greater speed of walking and performing a task (from Levine, 1990).

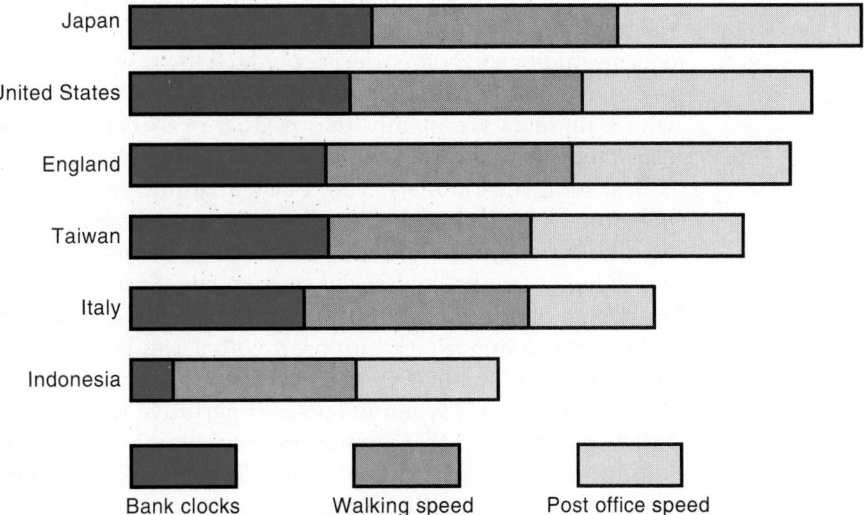

had a faster tempo than did cities on the West Coast (e.g., Sacramento, Los Angeles). Of course, there will be individual variations within cities as well. Not all citizens of Los Angeles are going to be slow-paced, nor are all New Yorkers going to be fast-paced. Nevertheless, the Japanese move *in general* at a faster pace than do Indonesians, and Americans on the West Coast exhibit, *on the average,* a slower pace of life than do residents of the Northeast.

The nomothetic approach does not deny that there are important differences among individuals; it simply seeks to identify the similarities that exist *among* these differences. For example, a person's individuality is not threatened by our knowledge that that person's heart, like the hearts of other human beings, is located in the upper left chest cavity. Similarly, we do not deny a person's individuality when we state that that person's behavior is influenced by patterns of reinforcement. Researchers merely seek to describe what organisms are like in general on the basis of the average performance of a group of different organisms.

Although the nomothetic approach predominates in psychological research, there is an alternative. Some psychologists, notably Allport (1961), argue that the nomothetic approach is inadequate—that the individual cannot be represented by an average value. Allport argues that the individual both is unique and exhibits behavior that conforms to general laws, or principles. He maintains that study built on the individual, called *idiographic research,* is important. A major form of idiographic research is the case study method, which we will describe in detail in Chapter 10.

Whether a researcher seeks to make generalizations about groups of individuals or is looking for the lawfulness found in one individual's behavior is based on a choice made by the researcher that is largely dictated by the nature of the question being asked. And while many researchers do mainly one or the other kind of research, others may do both. A clinical psychologist, for instance, may decide to pursue mainly idiographic investigations of a few clients in therapy but consider nomothetic issues when doing research with groups of college students. Another decision which the researcher must make is whether to do quantitative or qualitative research. *Quantitative research* refers to studies whose findings are mainly the product of statistical summary and analysis. *Qualitative research* produces research findings that are not arrived at by statistical summary or analysis and lack quantification altogether (see, for example, Strauss & Corbin, 1990). The data of qualitative research are most commonly obtained from interviews and observations and can be used to describe individuals, groups, and social movements (Strauss & Corbin, 1990). Reports describing and interpreting the way in which individuals faced death or describing how a minority group dealt with assimilation into the majority culture are examples of qualitative research. Some examples of qualitative research are found in Chapter 3 when we discuss narrative records of observed behavior. Just as psychological research is more frequently nomothetic than idiographic, it is also more typically quantitative than qualitative. And while both kinds of research can be usefully employed to describe behavior, our emphasis in this book is mainly on quantitative research.

Prediction A description of events and their relationships often provides a basis for *prediction,* the second goal of the scientific method. There are important questions in psychology that call for predictions. For example: Does the early loss of a parent make a child especially vulnerable to depression? Are children who are overly aggressive likely to have emotional problems as adults? Do stressful life events lead to increased physical illness? Research findings suggest an affirmative answer to all these questions. This information not only adds valuable knowledge to the discipline of psychology but is also helpful in both the treatment and the prevention of emotional disorders.

An important occupation of many psychologists is the prediction of later performance (for example, on the job, in school, or in specific vocations) on the basis of earlier performance on various standardized tests. For instance, a student's scores on the Graduate Record Examination (GRE), as well as undergraduate grade-point average (GPA), can be used to predict how well the student will do in graduate school. Interestingly, research has shown that faculty recommendations, which are usually required for graduate school admittance, are a rather poor predictor of whether a student will successfully complete a doctorate degree (Willingham, 1974). On the other hand, there is research showing that the amount of undergraduate research activity and ratings by peers of a student's commitment to psychology are better predictors of later success in psychology (as measured, for example, by number of scientific publications) than are the more traditional measures, such as GRE scores and GPA (Hirschberg & Itkin, 1978).

When scores on one variable can be used to predict scores on a second variable, we say that the two variables are correlated. A **correlation** exists when two different measures of the same people, events, or things vary together; that is, when particular scores on one variable tend to be associated with particular scores on another variable. For example, typically there is a correlation between first and last test scores in a large introductory psychology class. Test performance is correlated in that students who have high scores on the first test tend to have high scores on the last test, while students who score low on the first test tend to score low on the last test. Thus, if we know students' scores on the first test we are able to predict to some degree students' scores on the final test.

It is possible to determine quantitatively how well two measures vary together by computing a **correlation coefficient.** (See Appendix A for details on computing a correlation coefficient.) We can, therefore, obtain a quantitative index of how well we are able to predict one set of scores (for example, final test scores) based on another set of scores (for example, first test scores). A correlation coefficient expresses the degree of relationship between two variables in terms of both the direction and the magnitude of that relationship.

The *direction* of a correlation coefficient can be either positive or negative. A *positive correlation* indicates that, as the value of one measure increases, the value of the other measure also increases. Scores on the first and final tests in a large psychology class should be positively correlated. Similarly, Scholastic Aptitude Test (SAT) scores and the first-semester GPAs of college students are positively correlated. In a *negative correlation,* as the value of one measure increases, the value of the other measure decreases. We would expect time spent studying to correlate negatively with the number of errors made on a classroom examination. Thus, it is perhaps not surprising to learn that data from a national survey of high school seniors showed that the amount of time spent watching TV and the number of correct answers on an academic achievement test were negatively correlated (Keith, Reimers, Fehrmann, Pottebaum, & Aubrey, 1986).

The *magnitude* of a correlation coefficient can range from 0.0 to 1.00. A value of 0 indicates that we have no ability to predict one measure on the basis of knowing a value on another measure. The relationship between intelligence and mental illness exhibits a zero correlation; we cannot predict the likelihood that a person will become mentally ill by knowing the person's IQ. A value of +1.00 indicates a perfect positive correlation, and a value of −1.00 indicates a perfect negative correlation. Values between 0 and 1.00 indicate predictive relationships of intermediate strength. Remember, the sign of the correlation signifies only its direction; a correlation coefficient of −.46 indicates a stronger relationship than one of +.20. Degree of correlation can be assessed when data are presented in the form of a *scatterplot.* A scatterplot shows the intersecting points for each pair of scores in the data set. Hypothetical examples of scatterplots showing strong positive, practically zero, and strong negative correlations are shown in Figure 1.4.

Levine (1990) found a positive correlation of .50 between a city's pace of life and its deaths from heart disease. This indicates that the faster the pace in a city, the more likely its inhabitants are to die from heart disease. Death rates from heart disease, in other words, can be predicted by simply measuring how fast its inhabitants typically walk 100 feet or even by checking the accuracy of the city's clocks!

We will be concerned with issues of correlation at various points in this text and will discuss the more general topic of correlational research in Chapter 4. Correlational research, which seeks to describe predictive relationships among variables, such as scores on a paper-and-pencil personality test and frequency of hospitalization for depression, is a major area of psychological research.

FIGURE 1.4 Three scatterplots illustrating a strong positive (a), a zero (b), and a strong negative (c), correlation between scores on two variables: X and Y.

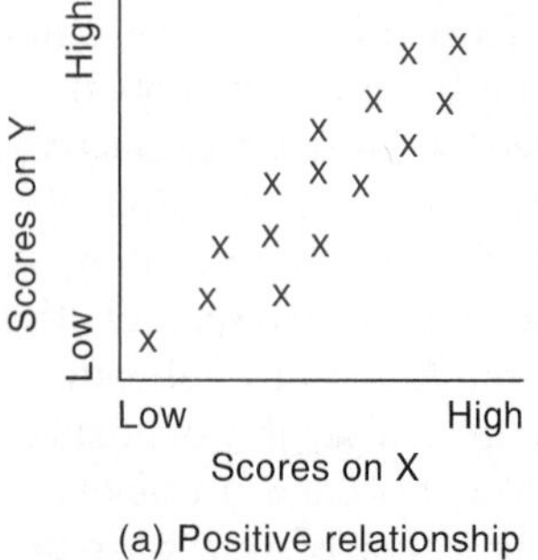

(a) Positive relationship

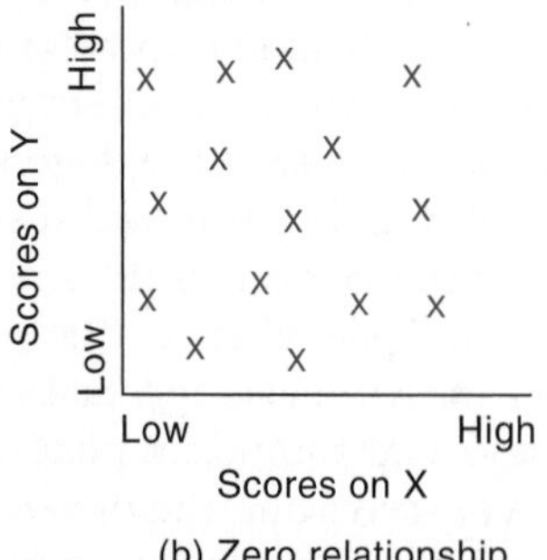

(b) Zero relationship

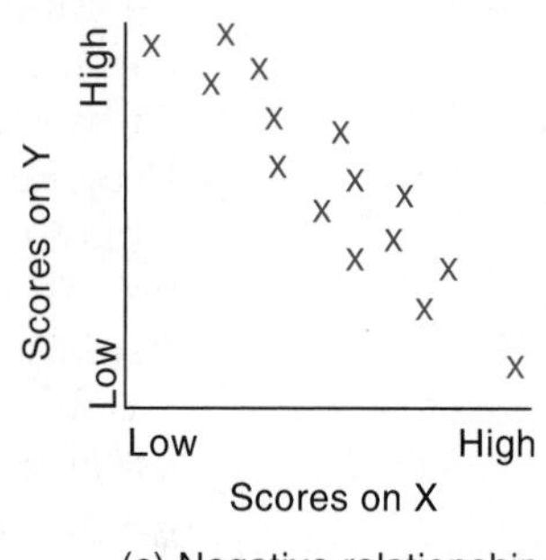

(c) Negative relationship

It is important to point out that successful prediction doesn't always depend on knowing *why* a relationship exists between two variables. Consider the report that the Chinese rely on observing animal behavior to help them predict earthquakes. Certain animals apparently behave in an unusual manner just before an earthquake. The dog that barks and runs in circles and the snake seen fleeing its hole, therefore, may be reliable predictors of earthquakes. If so, they could be used to warn people of forthcoming disasters. We might even imagine that in areas where earthquakes are likely, residents would be asked to keep certain animals under observation (as miners once kept canaries) to warn them of conditions of which they are as yet unaware. This would not require that we understand *why* certain animals behave strangely before an earthquake, or even why earthquakes occur.

You may remember that Levine (1990) showed that measures of the pace of a city can be used to predict death rates from heart disease. However, we can only speculate about why these measures are related. One possible explanation for this correlation suggested by the researchers is that people living in time-urgent environments engage in unhealthy behaviors, for example, cigarette smoking and poor eating habits, which increase their risk of heart disease (Levine, 1990).

Understanding Although they are important goals in themselves, description and prediction are only the first steps in understanding a phenomenon. *Understanding* is the third and most important goal of the scientific method. It is achieved when the cause or causes of a phenomenon are identified. The scientist sets three important conditions for making a **causal inference** and, hence, of understanding: *covariation of events; a time-order relationship;* and the *elimination of plausible alternative causes.* If one event is the cause of another, the two events must vary together; that is, when one changes, the other must also change. This is the principle of covariation. Further, the presumed cause must occur before the presumed effect. This is the second condition, a time-order relationship. Finally, causal explanations are accepted only when other possible causes of the effect have been ruled out—when plausible alternative causes have been eliminated.

Unfortunately, people have a tendency to conclude that all three conditions for a causal inference have been met when really only the first condition is satisfied. For example, research has shown that parents who are stern disciplinarians and who use physical punishment are more likely to have aggressive children than are parents who are less stern and use other forms of discipline. Parental discipline and children's aggressiveness obviously covary. Moreover, the fact that parents are typically assumed to influence how their children behave might lead us to think that the time-order condition has been met—parents use physical discipline and children's aggressiveness results. More recent research has shown, however, that infants vary in how active and aggressive they are and that the infant's behavior has a strong influence on the *parents'* responses in trying to exercise control. In other words, some children may be naturally aggressive and require stern discipline rather than stern discipline's producing aggressive children. Therefore, the direction of the causal relationship may be opposite to what we thought at first.

It is important to recognize, however, that the causes of events cannot be identified unless covariation has been demonstrated. The first objective of the scientific method, description, can be met by describing events under a single set of circumstances. The goal of understanding, however, requires more than this. For example, a teacher who emphasized active learning strategies could accurately describe the performance of a group of students who received instruction in this particular way. But before the teacher could claim that this performance was *caused* by the particular method of instruction, she would have to compare this method with some other reasonable approach that did not employ active learning strategies. Without showing that teaching strategy and performance covary, it is not possible to demonstrate conclusively that the strategy is the cause of any subsequent performance that is measured. This is why manipulation is such an important method of control for scientists. By manipulating independent variables, the investigator can determine whether any subsequent covariation occurs in the dependent variable. If it does, a bonus results from using manipulation: the time-order condition has also been met, because the researcher changes the independent variable and *subsequently* measures the changes, if any, in subjects' behavior.

By far the most challenging condition to be met in making a causal inference is eliminating other plausible alternative causes. The methods of control we mentioned earlier—manipulation, holding conditions constant, and balancing—are intended primarily to allow the researcher to eliminate alternative causes of an observed effect. For example, consider a study in which the effect of two different teaching approaches (active and passive) is to be assessed. You can see that one way *not* to assign students to teaching conditions in this study would be to have all men in one group and all women in the other. If this were done, the independent variable of teaching method would be "confounded" with the independent variable of gender. **Confounding** occurs when two potentially effective variables are allowed to covary simultaneously. When research is confounded, it is impossible to determine what variable is responsible for any obtained difference in performance. When no confoundings are present, a research study is said to have **internal validity.** Much of the discussion in this book will focus on developing skills in performing internally valid research by learning to identify and eliminate confoundings.

The internal validity of a study, which relates to our ability to make causal inferences from it, must be distinguished from the study's **external validity.** External validity involves the extent to which the research results can be generalized to different populations, settings, and conditions. A research finding may be internally valid and have little external validity. Although free of confoundings, the study may not be able to be generalized. Questions of external validity in science often arise when results obtained with animal subjects are claimed to apply to human subjects as well. Researchers frequently depend on experiments with animals to obtain information about human psychopathology. In one series of experiments, uncontrollable electric shock was used in an attempt to investigate in animal subjects the kinds of stressful experiences that are thought to cause ulcers and depression in humans (Weiss, 1977). Animal models have also been used to study drug addiction, minimal brain dysfunction, and various forms of mild to severe psychopathology (Maser & Seligman, 1977).

A major standard by which these laboratory models are evaluated is the degree to which they apply to real-life phenomena. Is the reaction of rats to uncontrollable electric shock the same as that observed in humans who experience unavoidable traumatic events (such as the death of a spouse or the loss of a job)? Validation of a laboratory model of psychopathology must be made in terms of its similarity to the course, symptoms, prevention, and cure of naturally occurring disorders (Abramson & Seligman, 1977). This problem of external validity is an extremely complex one. For instance, as Abramson and Seligman pointed out, although specific symptoms can be produced in the laboratory, this does not mean that naturally occurring symptoms are necessarily caused in the same way.

Because laboratory research, in general, is often conducted under more controlled conditions than are found in natural settings, an important task of the scientist is to determine whether laboratory findings generalize to "the real world." This is often the goal of what is called *field research.* By performing "in the field" (outside the laboratory) an experiment that is similar to an experiment that has been carried out in the laboratory, a researcher can provide evidence bearing on the external validity of laboratory results. Research conducted outside the laboratory often requires methods and procedures that are specifically designed for this less well controlled environment. Later in this book we will introduce some of the methods used by psychologists to conduct field research (see especially Chapters 3 and 11).

SCIENTIFIC THEORY CONSTRUCTION AND TESTING

Theories are "ideas" about how nature works. Psychologists propose ideas about why behavior occurs the way it does (e.g., what causes schizophrenia), about the nature of cognition (e.g., how people solve problems), and so on. A psychological theory can be developed on different levels: for example, it can be developed on a physiological or on a symbolic level (see Anderson, 1990; Simon, 1992). A theory of schizophrenia may, in other words, propose biological causes (e.g., specific genetic carriers), psychological causes (e.g., patterns of emotional conflict, stress), or both. The propositions contained in theories may be expressed as verbal statements, as mathematical equations, or even as computer programs.

An important dimension on which theories differ is scope. The *scope* of a theory refers to the range of phenomena that it seeks to explain. A theory of "flashbulb memory," for instance, attempts to explain why the personal circumstances surrounding particularly surprising and emotional events, such as the explosion of the space shuttle *Challenger,* are remembered better than are details associated with everyday events (see, for example, Brown & Kulik, 1977; McCloskey, Wible, & Cohen, 1988). Many older adults, for instance, can apparently remember precisely what they were doing when they heard about the assassination of President Kennedy. The scope of a theory of flashbulb memory is relatively restricted, proposing as it does an explanation of the nature and cause of an interesting but very specific memory phenomenon. A theory of human love, such as that proposed by Sternberg (1986), is an example of a psychological theory of much greater scope. Sternberg shows how the amount and kind of love one experiences is a function of three critical behavioral components: intimacy, passion, and decision/commitment. Anderson's (1990; Anderson & Milson, 1989) theory of human cognition offers an account of how cognition works in general, including ideas about learning, memory, problem solving, and so on. Clearly, the scope of a theory can be quite large. In general, the greater the scope of a theory the more complex it is likely to be. Complexity sometimes may be a necessary characteristic of psychological theories given the nature and range of phenomena psychologists try to understand. Complexity also can be a serious obstacle, however, to testing a theory. Most theories in contemporary psychology tend to be relatively modest in scope, attempting to account only for a limited range of phenomena.

The source of a scientific theory is a mixture of intuition, personal observation, and discovered knowledge (known facts and ideas). The famous philosopher of science Karl Popper (1976, p. 268–269) suggested that truly creative theories spring from a combination of "intense interest in a problem (and thus a readiness to try again and again)" and "critical imagination." *Critical imagination* is the ability to think critically, but there is more. It includes a readiness to challenge accepted ideas and an "imaginative freedom that allows us to see so far unsuspected sources of error" in previous thinking about a problem. Critical imagination, in other words, means traveling beyond what others have said are the boundaries (limits) of thinking about a problem. Assuming we have that important burning interest in a problem, one way we might approach constructing a scientific theory is by critically examining what is known, looking for flaws or unseen sources of error in that knowledge.

Whatever the nature and scope of a theory, whether it be expressed mathematically or verbally or developed at a physiological level or at some higher-order level, the theory includes certain assumptions and concepts that must be explained in order for it to be understood and tested. A theory of flashbulb memory, for instance, needs to state exactly what a flashbulb memory *is,* showing, for example, how flashbulb memory differs from other, more typical memory. To be complete, therefore, a theory must include definitions of various events or concepts (e.g., emotional events, test, accuracy), information about relationships between these events (e.g., the relationship between degree of emotional involvement and amount remembered), and so forth. Thus, we can offer the following formal definition of a scientific **theory:** a logically organized set of propositions (claims, statements, assertions) which serves to define events (concepts), describe relationships among these events, and explain the occurrence of these events.

The major functions of a theory are to *guide* research and to *organize* empirical knowledge (Marx, 1963). In the early 1960s, Rotter (1966) developed a theory of internal versus external locus of control. In this theory Rotter differentiates individuals who perceive a contingency between their behavior and what happens to them (internal locus of control) and those who perceive that their behavior has little consequence for what happens to them (external locus of control). Rotter developed a questionnaire to define this concept on the basis of the idea that individuals differ in locus of control because of the way they have been rewarded developmentally. The theory suggests a relationship between perceived locus of control and anxiety, with greater anxiety associated with greater perceived external locus of control. The theory has guided researchers for many years and has served to organize a body of empirical literature regarding self-efficacy, or the feeling of being able to cope with the environment (see, for example, Tedeschi, Lindskold, & Rosenfeld, 1985). The success of a psychological theory such as the locus-of-control theory can be measured by the degree to which it achieves the two important goals of guiding research and organizing empirical findings.

A scientific theory guides research by suggesting testable hypotheses. You may remember that hypotheses, like theories, are explanations for behavior; however, a hypothesis typically is simpler and more tentative than is a scientific theory (Marx, 1963). We reviewed previously several factors affecting the testability of hypotheses, including the important criterion of operational specificity of concepts. It is important that hypotheses derived from a theory attempt to meet these criteria.

Theories frequently require that we postulate intervening processes to account for observed behavior (Underwood, 1975). An intervening process is one that "mediates" between certain antecedent conditions and behavior. We have been discussing one such intervening process, memory. We can safely say that we have never "seen" memory. It is something that we infer based on observations of our own behavior and that of others when asked about a previous experience. We assume that there is some record of experiences somewhere inside us which we refer to when queried about a previous experience. The concept "memory" is proposed as an intervening process to explain the behavior we have observed. Mediating processes such as memory are called *intervening variables*. To be useful to the scientist, it is important that these concepts have a clear relationship to behavior (see Kimble, 1989). That is, while we might infer many kinds of unseen processes to help explain behavior, unless we tie down intervening processes to observed relationships between specific antecedents (independent variables) and behavior (dependent variables), our theories are scientifically weak. For example, a theory that proposes a "free-floating" process to explain behavior cannot be shown to be wrong. Because free-floating processes (e.g., "the little person inside me") are not tied to specific empirical relationships, they can be called into play in any and every situation to "explain" behavior.

How scientific theories should be evaluated and tested is one of the most complex and difficult issues in psychology and philosophy (e.g., Meehl, 1978, 1990a, 1990b; Popper, 1959). At least one scientist, however, suggests a rather straightforward procedure. Kimble (1989, p. 498) says quite simply, "The best theory is the one that survives the fires of logical and empirical testing." While somewhat simplistic, this is a good starting point. A theory can be evaluated first on the basis of its organization, its logical consistency. Are its propositions arranged in a meaningful way? Is the theory free of contradictions? Can specific deductions about expected behavior be made from it easily? Theories are tested logically by exposing their internal structure to the critical eye of members of the scientific community. A particular theory's propositions, assumptions, and definitions are frequently the topic of debate in scientific journals. Ideas about the exact definition of flashbulb memories, for example, have been debated at length in the psychology literature (e.g., Cohen, McCloskey, & Wible, 1990; Pillemer, 1990).

Kimble (1989) suggests that a theory is strengthened or weakened according to the outcomes of empirical tests of hypotheses derived from it. Successful tests of a hypothesis serve to increase the acceptability of a theory; unsuccessful tests serve to decrease the theory's acceptability. The best theory, in this view, is the one that passes these tests successfully. But there are serious obstacles to testing hypotheses and, as a consequence, confirming or disconfirming scientific theories. For example, a theory, especially a complex one, may produce many specific testable hypotheses. Therefore, a theory is not likely to fall on the basis of a single test (e.g., Lakatos, 1978). Moreover, theories may include propositions and concepts that have not been adequately defined or suggest intervening processes that are related to behavior and to each other in complex and even mysterious ways. Such theories may have a long life, but their value to science is questionable (see, for example, Meehl, 1978).

When constructing and evaluating a theory, scientists place a premium on parsimony (Marx, 1963). The *rule of parsimony* is followed when the simplest of alternative explanations is accepted. When choosing among theoretical propositions, scientists tend to favor the simplest of them. *Precision of prediction* is another criterion by which a theory can be evaluated. Theories that make precise predictions about behavior are preferred to those that make only general predictions (Meehl, 1990a). For instance, a theory of flashbulb memory that predicts the precise nature and duration of a "forgetting function" for such a memory is clearly a better theory than one that simply states that these memories will be remembered "longer" than other memories. Stated another way, some tests are easier for theories to pass than are others. A good scientific theory is one that is able to pass the most rigorous tests. *Rigorous testing* includes more tests that seek to falsify a theory's propositions than ones that seek to confirm them (Cook & Campbell, 1979). While confirming a particular theory's propositions provides support for the specific theory that is being tested, confirmation logically does not rule out other, alternative theories of the same phenomenon.

Although theories can be difficult and frustrating to work with, the process of constructing and evaluating scientific theories is at the core of the scientific enterprise and is absolutely necessary for the continuation of a science of psychology.

SCIENTIFIC INTEGRITY

Science is a search for truth. Fraud, lies, and misrepresentations should play no part in a scientific investigation. But science is also a human endeavor, and frequently much more is at stake than truth. Both scientists and the institutions that hire them compete for rewards in a game with jobs, money, and reputations on the line. The number of scientific publications authored by a university faculty member, for instance, is usually a major factor influencing decisions regarding promotion and tenure. Under these circumstances, there are unfortunate, but seemingly inevitable, cases of scientific misconduct.

A variety of activities constitute violations of scientific integrity. They include data fabrication, plagiarism, selective reporting of research findings, failure to acknowledge individuals who made significant contributions to the research, misuse of research funds, and unethical treatment of human or animal subjects (see, for example, Adler, 1991). Some transgressions are easier to detect than others. Out-and-out fabrication of data, for instance, can be revealed when, in the normal course of science, results are not able to be reproduced by independent researchers, or when logical inconsistencies appear in published reports. However, more subtle transgressions, such as reporting only data that meet expectations or misleading reporting of results, are difficult to detect. The dividing line between intentional misconduct and simply bad science is also not always clear.

To educate researchers about the proper conduct of science, and to help guide them around the many ethical pitfalls that are present, most scientific organizations have adopted formal codes of ethics. In Chapter 2 we will introduce you to the APA ethical principles governing research with humans and animals. As you will see, ethical dilemmas often arise. Consider the research by Heath and Davidson (1988) mentioned earlier in this chapter. You may remember that they asked groups of university women to help prepare a new rape-prevention pamphlet. Their subjects reviewed materials that presented rape as very controllable, somewhat controllable, or not at all controllable. Women who read the uncontrollable version reported greater levels of anxiety about rape than did women who read the other versions. However, the researchers did not actually intend to produce a new rape-prevention pamphlet. Participants in this research were deceived regarding the true purpose of the study: to investigate how perceived controllability of rape influences women's perceptions of vulnerability to rape. Under what conditions should researchers be allowed to deceive research participants?

Deception is just one of many ethical issues that researchers must confront. As yet another illustration of ethical problems, we mentioned that animal subjects sometimes are used to help understand human psychopathology. This may mean exposing animal subjects to stressful and even painful conditions. Again, we must ask about the ethical issues involved with this type of research. Under what conditions should research with animal subjects be permitted? The list of ethical questions raised by psychological research is a lengthy one. Thus, it is of the utmost importance that you become familiar with the APA ethical principles and their application at an early stage in your research career, and that you participate (as subject, assistant, or principal investigator) only in research that meets the highest standards of scientific integrity.

THE GOALS OF THIS BOOK

This book provides an introduction to the way in which the scientific method is applied in psychology. As you are probably aware, the scope of psychology is quite large, encompassing many problem areas. Moreover, no single research methodology can be said to answer all the questions raised in a particular area. Thus the best approach to answering a question about behavior or mental processes is frequently a multimethod one, that is, searching for an answer using different methodologies. Therefore there is much ground to cover. In the second part of the book we introduce you to what are called *descriptive methods*. Naturalistic observation, for instance, is an important tool of psychologists who want to describe behavior in a natural context (see Chapter 3). Surveys and tests are among the most commonly used instruments in psychology. The nature of surveys and tests is discussed in Chapter 4. Several less commonly used measures of behavior—those based on the examination of archival records and those derived from the study of physical traces—are treated in Chapter 5.

In the third part of the book we deal with experimental approaches to the study of behavior. The emphasis is on experiments done with groups of subjects (see Chapters 6–9). Experimental approaches are aimed chiefly at discovering cause-and-effect relationships. However, experimental methods used in the laboratory are not necessarily the same as those used outside the laboratory.

In the fourth part of the book we introduce you to the methods employed in applied research. In Chapter 10 there is a discussion of experiments conducted with small numbers of subjects, in fact, with single subjects ($N = 1$). In that chapter we also discuss the important case study method. The last chapter deals with quasi-experimental designs and with the important topic of program evaluation, which, as we have seen, is concerned with assessing the effects of "treatments" applied in natural settings (see Chapter 11).

This book is not just about research methods in psychology. We have attempted to incorporate many of the interesting facts and ideas in psychology that have been associated with particular research methods. For instance, the problem of bystander intervention, which was mentioned briefly in this chapter, will be used to illustrate concepts introduced in Chapters 3 and 4. We have avoided hypothetical examples describing situations that no one is likely to encounter. Instead, we have drawn on the rich field of psychology for examples. Accordingly, reading this book will increase your general knowledge of psychology. In this chapter you have already learned something about the historical basis for a scientific psychology and about scientists' concern regarding the public's uncritical acceptance of the occult. It is now time to get on with the study of specific research methods so that you can learn more about what psychologists have discovered and how they have gone about making these discoveries.

SUMMARY

Psychology's official beginning is marked by the establishment, in 1879, of a formal psychology laboratory in Leipzig, Germany, under the direction of Wilhelm Wundt. With this beginning came the first applications of the scientific method to problems of psychology. As an approach to knowledge, the scientific method is characterized by a reliance on empirical procedures, rather than intuition, and by an attempt to control (through manipulation, holding conditions constant, and balancing) the investigation of those factors believed responsible for a phenomenon. Those factors that are systematically controlled in an attempt to determine their effect on behavior are called independent variables. The measures of behavior used to assess the effect (if any) of the independent variable are called dependent variables. It is important to recognize when levels of an independent variable have been manipulated and when, as is the case for a subject variable, the levels have been selected.

Scientists seek to report results in an unbiased and objective manner. This goal is enhanced by giving operational meaning to concepts. Scientists also seek to measure phenomena as accurately and precisely as possible. Measurement involves both physical and psychological measurement. Scientists seek both validity and reliability of these measures.

Hypotheses are tentative explanations of events. To be useful to the scientist, however, hypotheses must be testable. Hypotheses that lack adequate definition, that are circular, or that appeal to ideas or forces outside the province of science are not testable. Hypotheses are often derived from theories. More than anything else, scientists are skeptical. A skeptical attitude is not always found among nonscientists, who may rush to accept "new discoveries" and extraordinary claims.

The goals of the scientific method are description, prediction, and understanding. Both quantitative and qualitative research are used to describe behavior. Observation is the principal basis of scientific description. When two measures correlate, we can predict the value of one measure by knowing the value of the other. A quantitative measure of our predictive ability is the correlation coefficient, which has both a direction (positive or negative) and a magnitude (0 to 1.00). Understanding is achieved when the causes of a phenomenon are discovered. This requires that evidence be provided for covariation of events, that a time-order relationship exist, and that alternative causes be eliminated. When two potentially effective variables covary such that the independent effect of each on behavior cannot be determined, we say that our research is confounded. Confounding must be avoided if we wish to produce a study with internal validity. The external validity of a study involves the extent to which research results can be generalized to different populations, settings, and conditions.

Scientific theory construction and testing provide the bases for a scientific approach to psychology. Theories have the important function of guiding research and organizing empirical knowledge. Finally, many ethical questions are raised by psychological research; it is important that the science of psychology be carried out according to the highest standards of scientific integrity.

KEY CONCEPTS

scientific method
empirical approach
control
independent variable
subject variable
dependent variable
operational definition
validity
reliability
hypothesis
correlation
correlation coefficient
causal inference
confounding
internal validity
external validity
theory

REVIEW QUESTIONS

1 For each of the following characteristics, indicate how the scientific approach differs from nonscientific (everyday) approaches to knowledge: general approach, observation, reporting, concepts, instruments, measurement, hypotheses, and attitudes.
2 Under what two circumstances did scientists demonstrate that Clever Hans was not too clever? To what conclusion did this lead the scientists?
3 Why is it important to distinguish between nonsubject variables, with levels that are manipulated, and subject variables, with levels that are selected?
4 Name and give an example of each of the three types of control used by scientists.
5 What is the major advantage of using operational definitions in psychology? What disadvantages are there in using operational definitions?
6 Distinguish between the accuracy of a measuring instrument and its precision.
7 What distinguishes physical measurement from psychological measurement?
8 What three shortcomings often keep hypotheses from being testable?
9 Why do behavioral scientists always seek to maintain a skeptical attitude?
10 What are the three goals of the scientific method?
11 What do we mean when we say that the nomothetic approach is used in science? How is the nomothetic approach different from the idiographic approach?
12 Provide an example both of quantitative research and of qualitative research.
13 Name and briefly describe the two characteristics of a correlation coefficient.

14 What three conditions must be met if one event is to be considered the cause of another?

15 Distinguish between the internal validity and the external validity of a research study.

16 Describe how a scientific theory can be used to guide and organize empirical research.

17 Identify at least three characteristics used to evaluate a theory.

18 Explain the use of intervening variables in theory construction. What important quality should an intervening variable have?

CHALLENGE QUESTIONS

1 In each of the following descriptions of research studies, you are to identify the independent variable(s). You should also be able to identify at least one dependent variable in each study.

A A psychologist was interested in the effect of food deprivation on motor activity. She assigned each of sixty rats to one of four conditions differing in the length of time for which the animals were deprived of food: 0 hours, 8 hours, 16 hours, 24 hours. She then measured the amount of time the animals spent in the activity wheel in their cages.

B A physical education instructor was interested in specifying the changes in motor coordination with increasing age in young children. He selected six groups of children and gave each child a test of motor coordination. The groups of children differed in age; that is, one group was made up of all 5-year-olds, the next group was all 6-year-olds, and so on up to the sixth group, which was all 10-year-olds.

C A developmental psychologist was interested in the amount of verbal behavior very young children displayed depending on who else was present. The study he did involved selecting children who were either 2, 3, or 4 years old. These children were observed in a laboratory setting for a 30-minute period. Half of the children of each age were assigned to a condition in which an adult was present with the child during the session. The other half of the children were assigned to a condition in which another young child was present during the session with the child being observed. The psychologist measured the number, duration, and complexity of the verbal utterances of each observed child.

2 In the following description the independent variable of interest is confounded with a potentially relevant independent variable. Identify the confounding variable and explain clearly how the confounding occurred. Also state exactly what conclusion can be supported on the basis of the evidence presented. Finally, suggest ways in which the study could be done so that it would be internally valid.

A physiological psychologist developed a drug that she thought would revolutionize the world of horse racing. She named the drug Speedo, and it was her contention that this drug would lead horses to run much faster than they do now. (Forget, for the sake of this problem, that it is illegal to give drugs to race horses.) She selected two groups of horses and gave one of the groups injections of Speedo once a week for 4 weeks. Because Speedo was known to have some negative effects on the horses' digestive systems, those horses given the Speedo had to be placed on a special high-protein diet. Those horses not given the Speedo were maintained on their regular diet. After the 4-week period, all the horses were timed in a 2-mile race and the mean times for the horses given Speedo were significantly faster than the mean times for those not given Speedo. The psychologist concluded that her drug was effective.

3 Two physicians did a study to try to determine why people who are allergic to cats still keep them as pets. They asked sixty-seven patients (twenty-two male and forty-five female) with an average age of 40 years to complete a questionnaire concerning the nature of their attachment to their cat. Even though eleven people had a history of emergency room visits following exposure to cats, thirty-eight said they would definitely replace their cat if it died and an additional sixteen reported they would have difficulty avoiding a new acquisition. Having someone to love and companionship were the most commonly selected reasons for having cats. The physicians concluded that cat ownership meets strong psychological needs in allergic patients. What comparison information is needed before reaching the conclusion that the psychological reasons for owning a cat are peculiar to allergic patients?

4 When presented with only correlational evidence, the investigator can only hypothesize about possible causal factors underlying a relationship between variables. A stage wherein the investigator thinks about possible causal factors and "tries them out" as explanations, perhaps during discussions with other researchers, is often a preliminary step to doing research which may provide evidence for the factors responsible for the reported relationship. For each of the following reports of covariation, identify a possible causal factor; that is, speculate on "why" these events are correlated.

A A study of nearly 5,000 Swedish women (20 to 44 years old) revealed that couples who live together before marriage have an 80 percent higher probability of getting divorced than do married couples who do not live together before marriage (*Behavior Today*, December 21, 1987).

B Dual-income couples now outnumber those with single incomes and questions have been raised about how career demands affect relationships. One study reported that among dual-income couples the greater the amount of togetherness, the more satisfactory was the relationship (*Psychology Today*, January, 1988).

C Married women are found to suffer from depression more than men. However, the greater is marital compatibility the less the risk of depression among women (*Behavior Today Newsletter*, July 28, 1986).

D In the late 1980s the National Institutes of Health sponsored a conference to assess available data regarding the "healing power of pets." The idea is that having pets is good for you. One investigator reported that among ninety-two coronary patients, pet owners were more likely to be alive one year after discharge from a coronary heart unit than were people who do not own a pet (*Science*, September 25, 1987).

ANSWER TO CHALLENGE QUESTION 1

1 A IV: hours of food deprivation with four levels; DV: time (in minutes) animals spent in activity wheel

B IV: age of children with six levels (distinguish selection of levels from manipulation in part A); DV: scores on test of motor coordination

C IV: age at three levels and additional person present with two levels (again, distinguish selection and manipulation); DV: number, duration, and complexity of child's verbal utterances

Chapter 2

Ethical Issues in the Conduct of Psychological Research

Outline

INTRODUCTION

A scientist has the responsibility of seeking knowledge, carrying out research in a competent manner, reporting results accurately, managing available resources honestly, fairly acknowledging, in scientific communications, the individuals who have contributed their ideas or their time and effort, considering the consequences to society of any research endeavor, and speaking out publicly on societal concerns related to a scientist's knowledge and expertise (see especially Diener & Crandall, 1978). In order to meet these obligations, the scientist must consider the numerous ethical issues and questions of scientific misconduct which we introduced briefly in Chapter 1. These issues may arise at any point in the research process. The American Psychological Association (APA) has formulated an Ethics Code to guide the behavior of psychologists in the course of their research as well as in other contexts, for example, as teachers, therapists, or administrators (see American Psychological Association, 1992a). The Ethics Code consists of an Introduction, a Preamble, six General Principles (A–F), and specific Ethical Standards dealing with such diverse issues as sexual harassment, fees for psychological services, test construction, classroom teaching, and expert witnesses.

The Introduction to the Ethics Code explains the goals and purposes of the Ethics Code, while the Preamble and General Principles describe the ideals psychologists should seek in their research and practice. For example, the Preamble requires from psychologists "a personal commitment to a lifelong effort to act ethically; to encourage ethical behavior by students, supervisees, employees, and colleagues, as appropriate; and to consult with others, as needed, concerning ethical problems" (p. 39). It is important for students of psychology also to make this commitment. They should familiarize themselves with the Ethics Code and make every effort to live up to its stated ideals and standards of behavior. A copy of the complete APA's Ethics Code can be obtained from the APA Order Department, American Psychological Association, 750 First Street, N.E., Washington, DC 20002-4242.

Many of the ethical standards in the APA's Ethics Code deal directly with psychological research (see especially Sections 6.06–6.26 of the Code). These standards deal with the treatment of both human and animal subjects. As with most ethical codes, the standards tend to be general in nature and require specific definition in particular contexts. It's usually the case that more than one ethical standard applies to a research situation, and at times the standards may even appear to contradict one another. For instance, ethical research requires that human participants be protected from physical injury; however, some research, for instance that using drugs or other invasive treatments, may place participants at risk of physical harm. The welfare of animal subjects should be protected; however, as we saw in Chapter 1, certain kinds of research may involve inflicting pain or other suffering on an animal subject. Solving these ethical dilemmas is not always easy. Thus, it is important not only that you become familiar with the ethical standards but that you practice applying them to real research situations. Ethical decisions are best made after consultation with others, including one's peers but also those who are more experienced or knowledgeable in a particular area. (In fact, as you will see, review of a research plan by persons *not* involved in the research is legally required in some situations.) In the remaining sections of this chapter, we identify those standards from the Ethics Code that deal specifically with psychological research. We also offer a brief commentary on some aspects of these standards and present several hypothetical research plans that raise ethical questions. By putting yourself in the position of having to make judgments about the ethical issues raised in these proposals, you will begin to learn to grapple with the application of particular ethical standards and with the difficulties of ethical decision making in general. We urge you to discuss these research proposals with your peers, teachers, and others who have had prior experience doing psychological research.

THINGS YOU NEED TO KNOW BEFORE YOU BEGIN TO DO RESEARCH

Because research psychologists must consider a host of ethical issues, problems can be averted only by planning carefully and consulting with appropriate individuals and groups *prior to doing the research.* Not only does the failure to conduct research in an ethical manner undermine the entire scientific process, retard the advancement of knowledge, and erode the public's respect for the scientific and academic communities, but it can also bring significant legal and financial penalties down on individuals and institutions. The following ethical standards spell out some things researchers must keep in mind as they begin to do psychological research.

FIGURE 2.1
Many ethical questions are raised when research is performed with animal and human subjects.

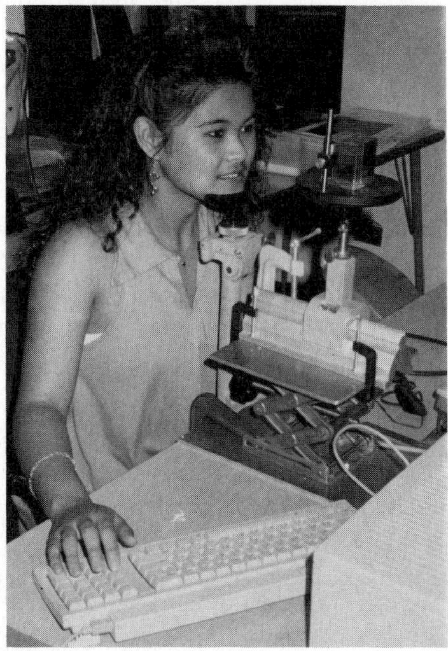

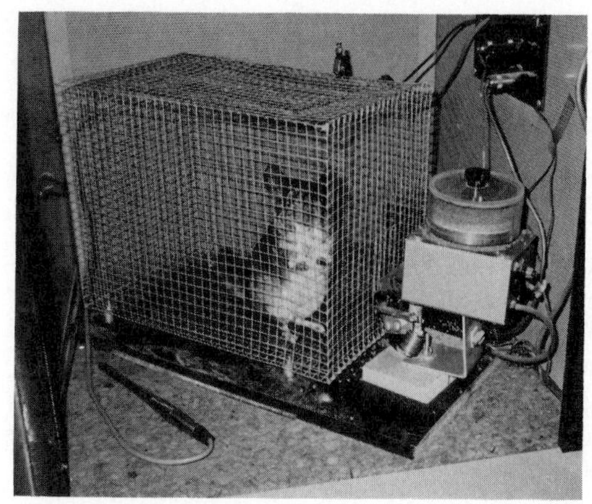

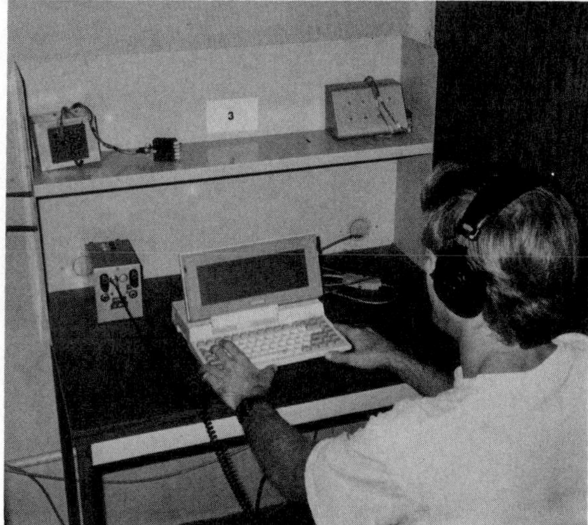
3

APA ETHICAL STANDARDS

6.06 Planning Research

1 (a) Psychologists design, conduct, and report research in accordance with recognized standards of scientific competence and ethical research.
(b) Psychologists plan their research so as to minimize the possibility that results will be misleading.
(c) In planning research, psychologists consider its ethical acceptability under the Ethics Code. If an ethical issue is unclear, psychologists seek to resolve the issue through consultation with institutional review boards, animal care and use committees, peer consultations, or other proper mechanisms.
(d) Psychologists take reasonable steps to implement appropriate protections for the rights and welfare of human participants, other persons affected by the research, and animal subjects.

6.07 Responsibility

1 (a) Psychologists conduct research competently and with due concern for the dignity and welfare of the participants.
(b) Psychologists are responsible for the ethical conduct of research conducted by them or by others under their supervision or control.
(c) Researchers and assistants are permitted to perform only those tasks for which they are appropriately trained and prepared.
(d) As part of the process of development and implementation of research projects, psychologists consult those with expertise concerning any special population under investigation or most likely to be affected.

6.08 Compliance With Law and Standards

Psychologists plan and conduct research in a manner consistent with federal and state law and regulations, as well as professional standards governing the conduct of research, and particularly those standards governing research with human participants and animal subjects.

6.09 Institutional Approval

Psychologists obtain from host institutions or organizations appropriate approval prior to conducting research, and they provide accurate information about their research proposals. They conduct the research in accordance with the approved research protocol.

COMMENTARY

As you can see, the importance of consulting with others about ethical issues prior to doing research cannot be overemphasized. It is particularly critical that a researcher obtain prior approval from the proper institutional committee before doing research.

The National Research Act, signed into law in 1974, resulted in the creation of the National Commission for the Protection of Human Subjects of Biomedical and Behavioral Research. This act requires that institutions, such as colleges and universities that seek research funds from specific federal agencies, establish committees to review research sponsored by the institution. These committees, referred to as Institutional Review Boards (IRBs), are frequently called on to review psychological research in order to safeguard the rights and welfare of human participants. Federal regulations impose very specific requirements on the make-up and duties of these committees (see *Federal Register,* June 18, 1991). For example, an IRB must be composed of at least five members with varying backgrounds and fields of expertise. Both scientists and nonscientists must be represented, and there must be at least one IRB member who is *not* affiliated with the institution. Responsibile members of the community, such as members of the clergy, lawyers, and nurses are asked to serve on these committees.

A psychology student seeking to do research with human participants is apt to be asked first to satisfy the regulations of a departmental committee charged with reviewing research conducted in the psychology department. Depending on the association of this departmental committee with an IRB, research falling into various well-defined categories is either reviewed at the departmental level or referred to the IRB, which has the authority to approve, disapprove, or require modifications prior to the approval of the research.

In a similar vein, in 1985, the Department of Agriculture, as well as the Public Health Service, formulated new guidelines for the care of laboratory animals (Holden, 1987). As a result, every institution doing research with animal subjects is now required to have an Institutional Animal Care and Use Committee (IACUC), whose members minimally must include a scientist, a veterinarian, and at least one person not affiliated with the institution. Review of animal research by IACUCs extends to more than simply overseeing the research procedures. Federal regulations governing the conduct of animal research extend to specifications of animal living quarters and the proper training of personnel who work directly with the animals (see Holden, 1987).

Given the complex nature of federal regulations, and the policies of most institutions requiring review of research with human and animal subjects, any individual who wants to do research should inquire of the proper authorities, prior to starting research, about the appropriate procedure for institutional review.

Nearly every college and university requires that all research conducted at the institution be reviewed at some stage by an independent committee. Violation of federal regulations regarding the review of research involving human or animal subjects can bring a halt to research at an institution, spell the loss of federal funds, and result in substantial fines (see Holden, 1987; Smith, 1977).

THE RISK/BENEFIT RATIO

In addition to checking if appropriate ethical principles are being followed, a major function of an IRB is to arrive at a consensus regarding what is sometimes called the *risk/benefit ratio.* Despite use of the term *ratio,* the risk/benefit ratio is nothing like a mathematical ratio with easily calculable components. The decision to do research must rest on a subjective evaluation of the costs both to the individual and to society. Failure to do research may cost society the benefits of the knowledge gained from the research and, ultimately, an opportunity to improve the human condition. To do research may at times exact a cost from individual participants—for example, research participants risk injury when exposed to potentially harmful circumstances. The principal investigator must, of course, be the first one to give consideration to these potential risks and benefits; however, determination of the ratio, and hence the decision to do research, is most appropriately made by knowledgeable individuals who do not have a personal interest in the research. As we have indicated, this is often the role played by an IRB.

In its simplest form, the **risk/benefit ratio** asks the question, Is it worth it? When the inconvenience and possible risks to subjects are considered, is there sufficient potential benefit to the individual and to society to carry out this research? Many factors affect a decision regarding the proper balance of risks and benefits of a particular research activity. The most basic are the nature of the risk and the magnitude of the probable benefit to the participant and to society. When the benefits to an individual or society are clear and immediate, a greater risk can be tolerated than when the benefits are less clear or their application is less immediate. For instance, in the context of research investigating the antecedents of psychotic behavior, the possible benefits to both the participants and society may be substantial if a proposed treatment has a good possibility of having a beneficial effect. Society will also benefit as psychologists come to understand more completely such behaviors as aggression, bystander intervention, deviance, and suicide. The benefits to be gained by investigating these behaviors, however, must be continually weighed against the risks to the participants.

In determining the risk/benefit ratio, a researcher must also take into account the probability that valid and interpretable results will be produced. An established scientist with a history of successful research in her field would reasonably be judged to have a greater chance of obtaining important results than would an undergraduate psychology major. When risk is present, a researcher must make sure that there are not alternative, low-risk procedures that might be substituted and that the research has been planned in a competent manner. Without a careful review of the psychological literature, for instance, a researcher might carry out research that has already been done, thus exposing subjects to needless risk.

DETERMINATION OF RISK

Determining whether subjects are "at risk" illustrates the difficulties involved in ethical decision making. Life itself is a risky affair. Commuting to work or school, crossing streets, and riding on elevators are all activities that have an element of risk. Simply showing up for an appointment to serve in a psychology experiment must be judged to entail some degree of risk. To say that human participants in psychological research can never risk injury would bring all research to a halt. Decisions about what constitutes risk must take into consideration those risks that are part of everyday life.

Any determination of risk must also consider the nature of the participants. Certain activities can reasonably be judged to pose a serious risk for some individuals but not for others. Running up a flight of stairs may substantially increase an elderly person's chance of suffering a heart attack; the same task would not be a serious risk for most young adults. Individuals who are exceptionally depressed or anxious might be expected to show more severe reactions to certain psychological treatments than would other people. Statements about what constitutes risk cannot be easily generalized to all individuals or populations.

Risk is often associated with the possibility of physical injury as when bodily harm is threatened. More often, however, participants in social science research risk social or psychological injury. The potential for social risk exists when information gained about an individual through her or his participation in psychological research is revealed to others. Simply knowing that someone completed a questionnaire inquiring about deviant sexual practices could cause social injury if those who knew reacted differently to that individual as a consequence of their knowledge. Information collected during the conduct of research may include important personal facts about intelligence, personality traits, and political, social, or religious beliefs. A research participant is not likely to want this information divulged to teachers, employers, or peers. Failure to protect the confidentiality of a subject's responses may significantly increase the possibility of social injury.

The potential for psychological injury exists whenever the procedures associated with a research activity are likely to induce serious mental or emotional stress in the participants. A subject who participates in a social psychology experiment involving a simulated emergency, as when smoke enters a room where she is waiting, may experience a substantial amount of emotional stress until the true, simulated character of the event is revealed. Merely participating in a psychology experiment is anxiety-provoking for some individuals. After learning a list of nonsense syllables, a subject once volunteered that he was sure the researcher now knew a great deal about him! The subject assumed that the psychologist was interested in his mental state as revealed by the associations he used when learning the list. In reality, this subject was participating in a simple memory experiment designed to measure forgetting. Even here, the researcher is responsible for putting the subject's mind at ease. A researcher is under an obligation to protect subjects from emotional or mental stress, including, when possible, that which might arise due to a participant's misconceptions about the nature of a psychological task.

MINIMAL RISK

A distinction is sometimes made between a subject "at risk" and a subject "at minimal risk." One definition of *minimal risk* is that followed by IRBs in their review of biomedical and behavioral research (*Federal Register*, January 26, 1981; amended *Federal Register*, June 18, 1991):

Minimal risk means that the probability and magnitude of harm or discomfort anticipated in the research are not greater in and of themselves than are those ordinarily encountered in daily life or during the performance of routine physical or psychological examinations or tests.

As an example of minimal risk, consider the fact that many psychology laboratory experiments involve lengthy paper-and-pencil tests intended to assess various mental abilities. Participants are frequently under time pressure to complete the tests and may receive specific feedback regarding their performance. No doubt some degree of mental or even emotional stress is associated with participation in these kinds of activities. Within limits, however, the risk of psychological injury in this situation would generally be assumed to be no greater than that of being a student. Therefore, subjects who are college students would be judged to incur only minimal risk in such experiments.

An IRB may waive certain requirements if it is judged that the risks that research participants are exposed to are minimal. However, when the possibility of injury is judged to be more than minimal, each subject is considered to be "at risk." More serious obligations fall on the researcher to protect the welfare of such participants.

DEALING WITH RISK

Even when only a slight potential for injury exists, the researcher should try to minimize the risk and provide safeguards for the participants. For instance, stating at the beginning of a memory experiment that the tasks are not intended to measure intelligence or personality reduces the level of stress that some participants experience. When substances are to be taken internally, subjects should be screened prior to participation in order to identify and excuse any individuals who might show unusual physical reactions. In situations where the possibility of harm is judged to be significantly greater than that occurring in daily life, the researcher's obligation to protect participants increases correspondingly. It is not unheard of for an IRB to require that a clinical psychologist be available to counsel subjects when, by participating in a psychology experiment, they are exposed to the possibility of serious emotional stress.

No research activity involving serious risk to subjects should be carried out unless alternative, low-risk methods of data collection have been explored. In some cases, descriptive approaches involving observation or questionnaires should be substituted for experimental treatments. It is also possible to take advantage of naturally occurring "treatments." For example, Anderson (1976) interviewed owner-managers of small businesses that had been damaged by hurricane floods. He found that the likelihood of problem-solving coping behaviors by the subjects showed an inverted U-shaped function when related on a graph to perceived stress, indicating that there is an optimal level of stress and that, when stress is higher or lower than this optimal level, performance decreases. A similar relationship has been demonstrated in a number of experimental laboratory tasks using experimenter-induced stress.

In order to protect subjects from social injury, the method of data collection used should preserve the anonymity of participants or, when this is not possible, ensure the confidentiality of responses. If at all possible, a researcher should obtain information about participants in a manner that does not require individuals to be identified. Simply not having subjects sign their names to the test instruments is obviously one way to keep participation anonymous. When the researcher must test subjects on more than one occasion or otherwise track specific individuals, numbers can be randomly assigned to participants at the beginning of a study. Only these numbers need appear on subjects' response sheets.

When anonymity cannot be preserved, confidentiality should be protected through some type of code system. If the information supplied by participants is particularly sensitive, such a scheme is necessary to minimize the risk of social injury. One procedure is to assign code numbers to participants. Names are linked with the code numbers on a master list. Access to this list is restricted by keeping it under lock and key. Even this system may not adequately protect participants if information about them is related to criminal activity. The master list could be legally subpoenaed. In at least one case, in order to safeguard the rights of his subjects, a researcher went so far as to place the master list with the information that linked coded data to specific individuals in the vault of a foreign bank (Diener & Crandall, 1978).

Assuring participants of their anonymity or the confidentiality of their responses can also benefit the researcher if such assurances lead the participant to be more honest and open when responding (Blanck, Bellack, Rosnow, Rotheram-Borus, & Schooler, 1992). It can be assumed that participants will be less likely to fabricate or withhold information if they do not have to worry about who will have access to their responses.

OBTAINING INFORMED CONSENT

The success of most human psychological research depends upon the willingness of students, patients, clients, and other members of the community to take part in a scientific investigation. At times, participants in psychological research are given money or other compensation for their time and effort. At other times, people simply respond to requests by researchers for volunteers to participate in a research endeavor and expect no compensation. Whichever is the case, researcher and subject enter into a social contract. This contract is sometimes an informal one; however, in other circumstances, the contract includes statements signed by both researcher and subject, as well as by witnesses. As part of this contract, the researcher has an ethical responsibility to make clear to the participant what the research entails, including any possible risk to the participant, and to respect the dignity and rights of the individual during the research experience.

Although it is not often discussed, the research subject also has an ethical responsibility to behave in an appropriate manner, for example, by paying attention to instructions and by performing tasks in the manner requested by the researcher. Lying, cheating, or otherwise fraudulent behavior on the part of someone who has agreed to participate in a scientific investigation is as much of a violation of the scientific integrity of the research situation as is the failure of a researcher to fully explain to the subject the risks inherent in the research task.

APA ETHICAL STANDARDS

6.10 Research Responsibilities

Prior to conducting research (except research involving only anonymous surveys, naturalistic observations, or similar research), psychologists enter into an agreement with participants that clarifies the nature of the research and the responsibilities of each party.

6.11 Informed Consent to Research

(a) Psychologists use language that is reasonably understandable to research participants in obtaining their appropriate informed consent (except as provided in Standard 6.12, Dispensing With Informed Consent). Such informed consent is appropriately documented.

(b) Psychologists inform participants of the nature of the research; they inform participants that they are free to participate or to decline to participate or to withdraw from the research; they explain the foreseeable consequences of declining or withdrawing; they inform participants of significant factors that may be expected to influence their willingness to participate (such as risks, discomfort, adverse effects, or limitations on confidentiality, except as provided in Standard 6.15, Deception in Research); and they explain other aspects about which the prospective participants inquire.

(c) When psychologists conduct research with individuals such as students or subordinates, psychologists take special care to protect the prospective participants from adverse consequences of declining or withdrawing from participation.

(d) When research participation is a course requirement or opportunity for extra credit, the prospective participant is given the choice of equitable alternative activities.

(e) For persons who are legally incapable of giving informed consent, psychologists nevertheless (1) provide an appropriate explanation, (2) obtain the participant's assent, and (3) obtain appropriate permission from a legally authorized person, if such substitute consent is permitted by law.

6.12 Dispensing With Informed Consent

Before determining that planned research (such as research involving only anonymous questionnaires, naturalistic observations, or certain kinds of archival research) does not require the informed consent of research participants, psychologists consider applicable regulations and institutional review board requirements, and they consult with colleagues as appropriate.

6.13 Informed Consent in Research Filming or Recording

Psychologists obtain informed consent from research participants prior to filming or recording them in any form, unless the research involves simply naturalistic observations in public places and it is not anticipated that the recording will be used in a manner that could cause personal identification or harm.

6.14 Offering Inducements for Research Participants

(a) In offering professional services as an inducement to obtain research participants, psychologists make clear the nature of the services, as well as the risks, obligations, and limitations. (See also Standard 1.18, Barter, [With Patients or Clients.])

(b) Psychologists do not offer excessive or inappropriate financial or other inducements to obtain research participants, particularly when it might tend to coerce participation.

COMMENTARY

Ethical research practice requires that subjects be informed of all features of the research that reasonably might be expected to influence their willingness to participate. The researcher is obligated to respond to any inquiries that subjects might make about the research and to inform subjects that they are free to withdraw their consent at any time without penalty or prejudice. Consent must be given freely, without undue inducement or pressure. **Informed consent** should always be obtained and is absolutely essential when subjects are exposed to the possibility of serious injury.

True informed consent cannot be obtained from certain individuals, such as the mentally impaired or emotionally disturbed, young children, and others who are recognized as having limited ability to understand the nature of research and the possible risks. In these cases, consent must be obtained from the subjects' parents or legal guardians. Developmental psychologists who want to test schoolchildren are often faced with the task of contacting dozens (if not hundreds) of parents in order to secure permission for the children to participate in psychological research. Ethical restrictions such as those involving informed consent also raise methodological issues (see Adair, Dushenko, & Lindsay, 1985). Results of one study revealed that children of parents who did not provide parental consent for a research project were academically less successful and were less popular with their peers than were children of parents who did provide consent (Frame & Strauss, 1987).

Consider, for example, the dilemma faced by one graduate student who was seeking to interview adolescents receiving services from a family planning clinic (Landers, 1988). Parental permission was not required for the teens to attend the clinic; thus, if the investigator asked the parents for permission for their children to participate in the study, she would be revealing to the parents the teens' use of the clinic's services. Yet, obtaining permission of parents before conducting research with minors is standard ethical practice and also is mandated by federal laws. To help make a decision regarding proper ethical procedures in this difficult case, the graduate student correctly sought advice from experts, specifically, from members of APA's Committee for the Protection of Human Participants in Research. In 1990, this committee was renamed Committee on Standards in Research, and the scope of its ethical concerns was enlarged (see Grisso et al., 1991). The student used the information obtained from the experts to formulate the procedures that she proposed to use as part of her dissertation research. Although advice should be sought from knowledgeable others whenever ethical dilemmas arise, final responsibility for conducting research in an ethical manner always rests with the investigator.

It is not always easy to decide what constitutes undue inducement or pressure to participate. Paying college students $5 an hour to take part in a psychology experiment would not generally be considered improper coercion. Recruiting very poor or disadvantaged persons from the streets with a $5 offer may be more coercive and less acceptable (see Kelman, 1972). Prisoners may believe that any refusal on their part to participate in a psychology experiment will be viewed by the authorities as evidence of uncooperativeness and will therefore make it more difficult for them to be paroled. Parents of schoolchildren may fear that their children will be less well treated by teachers if they refuse to give permission for their children to participate in research. When college students are asked to fulfill a class requirement by serving as subjects in psychology experiments (an experience that presumably has some educational value), an alternative method of earning class credit should be made available to those who do not wish to participate in psychological research. Such options should be equivalent, in terms of time and effort, with the requirements of research participation.

Serious ethical problems can arise when a researcher withholds certain information about a psychological treatment from a subject. The reason for withholding information may be a legitimate concern on the part of the researcher that informing subjects of all details of the experiment will negate the effect of a particular treatment. For example, research on conformity behavior often requires that subjects believe that responses of other persons in the situation represent those individuals' own opinions. Telling subjects before the experiment that responses made by other people will be purposely misleading would appear to make this type of research impossible.

Failure to obtain informed consent from subjects was at the center of the controversy surrounding a researcher who submitted copies of a fake article to a number of academic journals in the field of social work (Coughlin, 1988). It is standard practice for editors of journals to ask individuals with expertise in the area to critique articles submitted for possible publication. On the basis of these expert evaluations, the editor makes a decision regarding the suitability of the article for the journal. The researcher in question wanted to investigate the possibility that social-work journals exhibit a confirmational bias, namely, that editors tend to accept articles for publication that confirm the value of social-work interventions and reject articles that do not. Using fictitious names, he submitted two different versions of a bogus research study to various journals. One version showed a positive outcome from a social work-intervention;

the other version revealed no positive outcome. Only when the journal editors accepted or rejected his article did he notify them that they had been subjects in an experiment.

When the researcher submitted his findings as part of a legitimate article to a scholarly journal, the article was rejected by the editors and a complaint lodged against the researcher with the National Association of Social Workers. The complaint said that the researcher practiced deception and failed to obtain informed consent from the subjects (the journal editors and expert reviewers). Critics of the research pointed out that the evaluation and processing of the manuscript cost time and money, which, in the view of at least some editors, was not justified by the potential benefits of the findings. The researcher argued that the editorial policies of journals have a significant influence on the practice of science and thus warrant investigation. Many journal editors would undoubtedly agree. However, the question raised is whether the methods used by the researcher in this investigation were ethical.

In any event, IRBs require investigators to document that the proper informed-consent procedure has been followed for any research involving human participants. A sample informed-consent form for use with a normal adult population is shown in Box 2.1. This form may be submitted to an IRB for approval when deception is not present and *when no more than minimal risk is anticipated.* If the research involves more than minimal risk or if deception is used, the investigator has the responsibility to seek advice from those with experience in the particular problem area under investigation. Others should also be consulted, such as the chairperson of an IRB, in order to prepare a consent procedure that protects the rights of the participants. (General requirements of IRBs for informed consent, including a description of those conditions under which a consent procedure may be modified, have been published in the *Federal Register*, June 18, 1991.)

In some situations it may not be necessary to obtain informed consent. The most obvious example would be when researchers are observing individuals' behavior in public places without any intervention. An investigator, for instance, who wishes to gather evidence about race relations on a college campus by observing the frequency of mixed-race vs. unmixed-race groups sitting at tables in the college cafeteria or walking across campus would not ordinarily need to obtain students' permission before making the observations. (We will assume that the identity of specific individuals will not be recorded.) Such student behavior can be considered public, and the method that of naturalistic observation (see Chapter 3). However, deciding what is public vs. what is private behavior is not always easy.

Diener and Crandall (1978) identify three major dimensions to consider when deciding what information is private and what safeguards should be employed: sensitivity of the information, setting, and degree of dissemination of the information.

Clearly, some kinds of information are more sensitive than others. Subjects interviewed about their sexual practices, religious beliefs, or criminal activities

BOX 2.1

SAMPLE INFORMED-CONSENT FORM

[DATE]

I, [NAME OF PARTICIPANT], state that I am over 18 years of age and that I voluntarily agree to participate in a research project conducted by [NAME OF PRINCIPAL INVESTIGATOR, TITLE, INSTITUTIONAL AFFILIATION].

The research is being conducted in order to [BRIEF DESCRIPTION OF THE GOALS OF THE RESEARCH]. The specific task I will perform requires [DETAILS OF THE RESEARCH TASK, INCLUDING INFORMATION ABOUT THE DURATION OF PARTICIPANT'S INVOLVEMENT. ANY POSSIBLE DISCOMFORT TO PARTICIPATE ALSO MUST BE DESCRIBED.].

I acknowledge that [NAME OF PRINCIPAL INVESTIGATOR OR RESEARCH ASSISTANT] has explained the task to me fully; has informed me that I may withdraw from participation at any time without prejudice or penalty; has offered to answer any questions that I might have concerning the research procedure; has assured me that any information that I give will be used for research purposes only and will be kept confidential. [PROCEDURE FOR PROTECTING CONFIDENTIALITY OF RESPONSES SHOULD BE EXPLAINED.]

I also acknowledge that the benefits derived from, or rewards given for, my participation have been fully explained to me—as well as alternative methods, if available, for earning these rewards—and that I have been promised, upon completion of the research task, a brief description of the role my specific performance plays in this project. [THE EXACT NATURE OF ANY COMMITMENTS MADE BY THE RESEARCHER, SUCH AS THE AMOUNT OF MONEY TO BE PAID TO INDIVIDUALS FOR PARTICIPATION, SHOULD BE SPECIFIED HERE.]

____
[SIGNATURE OF RESEARCHER]

____
[SIGNATURE OF PARTICIPANT]

are likely to be more concerned about the dissemination of this information than subjects interviewed about who they believe will win the World Series. Similarly, organizations and businesses are likely to perceive some types of information about them as more sensitive than other types.

The setting in which behavior is observed is also a factor in defining what constitutes private activity. Individuals engaged in what reasonably might be considered public behaviors, such as attending a baseball game or other outdoor event, give up a certain degree of privacy. What is public behavior is not always easy to decide. Such behaviors as riding inside one's own car, using public bathrooms, or picnicking in a park are not easily classified. Decisions about ethical practice in these situations sometimes depend on the sensitivity of the data and the manner in which the information will be disseminated.

Dissemination of information in terms of group averages or proportions is unlikely to reflect on specific individuals. In other situations, code systems can be used to protect subjects' confidentiality. Dissemination of sensitive information about individuals or groups without their permission is a serious breach of ethics. When information about individuals has been collected unobtrusively (for example, by a concealed observer), one approach that has been suggested is to contact subjects after the observations have been made and ask whether this information can be used by the researcher.

As Diener and Crandall indicate, the most difficult decisions regarding privacy involve situations in which there is an obvious ethical problem on one dimension but not on others and situations in which there is a slight problem on all dimensions. For instance, the behavior of individuals in the darkened setting of a movie theatre would appear to have the potential of yielding sensitive information about the individual, but the setting could be reasonably classified as public. **Privacy** refers to the rights of individuals to decide how information about them is to be communicated to others. Whenever possible, the manner in which information about subjects will be kept confidential should be explained to participants in psychological research so that they may judge for themselves whether the safeguards taken to ensure confidentiality are reasonable. Implementing the principle of informed consent requires that the investigator seek to balance the need to investigate human behavior on the one hand with the rights of human participants on the other.

During the 1980s, the APA Committee for the Protection of Human Participants in Research became involved in a number of controversies over the ethical issues related to psychosocial research on acquired immune deficiency syndrome (AIDS) (Melton, Levine, Koocher, Rosenthal, & Thompson, 1988). Particularly salient among the ethical dilemmas posed by this research is that related to privacy. Control over knowledge about oneself and one's body is basic to respect for persons and is even constitutionally protected; on the other hand, the courts have supported the government's police power to curb threats to public health (see Melton & Gray, 1988). The transmission of AIDS is known to take place via the sharing of body fluids, such as sexual contact or sharing of needles for intravenous injections. Thus, to understand fully the spread of AIDS requires gathering data regarding individuals' sexual practices, drug use, medical history, travel, and acquaintances. Unfortunately, confidentiality cannot always be guaranteed to participants in AIDS research because of laws requiring the reporting of AIDS cases and the fact that records can sometimes be legally supoenaed (Gray & Melton, 1985). New federal and state laws may be needed to protect the privacy of participants in research involving diseases of this nature (Melton & Gray, 1988).

As in other areas when ethical dilemmas arise, the investigator is obligated to seek advice from knowledgeable others regarding the appropriateness of a research procedure. For example, consultation with members of IRBs, experienced researchers, members of ethics committees, and even representatives of the population at risk (see Melton et al., 1988) will help to ensure that the rights of participants are protected when the psychosocial aspects of communicable diseases are investigated.

DECEPTION IN PSYCHOLOGICAL RESEARCH

No ethical issue related to research is more controversial than that of deception. There are those who would argue that subjects should *never* be deceived in the context of psychological research. Deception runs counter to the principle of openness and honesty that ethical practice says should characterize the relationship between experimenter and subject. **Deception** can occur either through *omission,* the withholding of information, or *commission,* the presentation of misinformation to subjects about an aspect of the research. Either kind of deception contradicts the principle of informed consent. To some, deception is morally repugnant; it is no different from lying. Nevertheless, despite the increased attention given to deceptive methodological practices over the last couple of decades, the use of deception in psychological research has not declined (Adair, Dushenk, & Lindsay, 1985).

APA ETHICAL STANDARDS

6.15 Deception in Research

(a) Psychologists do not conduct a study involving deception unless they have determined that the use of deceptive techniques is justified by the study's prospective scientific, educational, or applied value and that equally effective alternative procedures that do not use deception are not feasible.

(b) Psychologists never deceive research participants about significant aspects that would affect their willingness to participate, such as physical risks, discomfort, or unpleasant emotional experiences.

(c) Any other deception that is an integral feature of the design and conduct of an experiment must be explained to participants as early as is feasible, preferably at the conclusion of their participation, but no later than at the conclusion of the research. (See also Standard 6.18, Providing Participants With Information About the Study.)

COMMENTARY

It is simply impossible to carry out certain kinds of research without withholding information from subjects about some aspects of the research. In other situations, it may be necessary to misinform subjects in order to have them adopt certain attitudes or behaviors. As you will see in Chapter 3, participant observers may find it necessary to give false information in order to gain access to a particular group or setting. Rosenthal's (1966) research investigating experimenter bias was based on the assumption that the subjects believed that they were experimenters working for a principal investigator. The "experimenters" were actually the subjects. The data collected by these subject-experimenters sometimes differed because of the expectations they had about the research outcome. Although deception is sometimes justified on methodological grounds, deceiving subjects for the purpose of getting them to participate in research in which they would not normally take part, or research that involves serious risk, is always unethical.

Milgram (1977) has questioned whether the term *deception* is a fair description of the procedures used by psychologists. He suggests that more neutral terms, such as *masking* or *technical illusions*, would be more appropriate. After all, illusions are sometimes created in real-life situations in order to make people believe something. When listening to a radio program, people are not generally bothered by the fact that the thunder they hear or the sound of a horse galloping are merely technical illusions created by a sound-effects specialist. Milgram argues that technical illusions should be permitted in the case of scientific inquiry. We deceive children into believing in Santa Claus. Why cannot scientists create illusions in order to help them understand human behavior?

Just as illusions are often created in real-life situations, in other situations, Milgram points out, there can be a suspension of a general moral principle. If we learn of a crime, we are ethically bound to report it to the authorities. On the other hand, a lawyer who is given information by a client must consider this information privileged even if it reveals that the client is guilty. Physicians perform very personal examinations of our bodies. Although it is morally permissible in a physician's office, the same type of behavior would not be condoned outside the office. Milgram argues that, in the interest of science, psychologists should occasionally be allowed to suspend the moral principle of truthfulness and honesty.

A basic assumption underlying the use of deception is that it is necessary to conceal the true nature of an experiment so that subjects will behave as they normally would or so that they will act in accordance with the stated instructions and cues provided by the experimenter. If people come to realize (and perhaps many already have) that psychologists often present misinformation and that serving in a psychology experiment means they are likely to be deceived, then the very assumption on which the use of deception is based will be lost. Subjects will no longer act in accordance with the instructions of the experimenter because they will no longer believe that the experimenter is telling the truth. Frequent and casual use of deception undermines the usefulness of deception as a methodological tool (Kelman, 1967).

The fact that psychologists are often identified with deceptive practices, and the fact that deception may be the basis for experimental manipulations in natural settings, also may affect the way people react to emergencies or other events that they witness. On one college campus a student was attacked and shot by another student. Witnesses did not try to help, and the assailant was not pursued. When bystanders were asked why they did not intervene, some said they thought it was just a psychology experiment (Diener & Crandall, 1978).

Kelman (1972) suggests that, before using deception, a researcher give very serious consideration to (a) the importance of the study to our scientific knowledge, (b) the availability of alternative, deception-free methods, and (c) the "noxiousness" of the deception. This last consideration refers to the degree of deception involved and to the possibility of injury to the participants. In Kelman's (p. 997) view: "Only if a study is very important and no alternative methods are available can anything more than the mildest form of deception be justified." When deception is used, the researcher must inform subjects after the experiment of the reasons for the deception, discuss any misconceptions that they may have, and remove any harmful effects of the deception. One goal of this "debriefing" is educating the subject about the need for deception. For example, after female participants were deceived about the true purpose of a study investigating women's perceptions of vulnerability to rape (see Chapter 1, Heath & Davidson, 1988), the researchers explained the reasons for the deception and corrected any misperceptions that had been created.

ADDITIONAL RESPONSIBILITIES TO RESEARCH PARTICIPANTS

Over the years, many researchers have fallen into the trap of viewing human participants in research chiefly as means to an end, as "objects" used to obtain data in order to meet the goals of a research study. While perhaps conscientiously giving participants the opportunity to give their informed consent and carefully safeguarding them from serious injury, researchers sometimes have considered their responsibility to participants to end when the last response was made or the final piece of data collected. A handshake or "thank you" was frequently all that marked the end of the research session. This meant that the research participant likely left with unanswered questions about specific aspects of the situation and with only the vaguest idea of what role was played in the scientific endeavor. It is important both in the planning and in the conduct of research to consider how the experience may affect the research participant and the participant's environment *after* the research is completed and to seek ways in which the subject will benefit from participation.

APA ETHICAL STANDARDS

6.16 Sharing and Utilizing Data

Psychologists inform research participants of their anticipated sharing or further use of personally identifiable research data and of the possibility of unanticipated future uses.

6.17 Minimizing Invasiveness

In conducting research, psychologists interfere with the participants or milieu from which data are collected only in a manner that is warranted by an appropriate research design and that is consistent with psychologists' roles as scientific investigators.

6.18 Providing Participants With Information About the Study

(a) Psychologists provide a prompt opportunity for participants to obtain appropriate information about the nature, results, and conclusions of the research, and psychologists attempt to correct any misconceptions that participants may have.

(b) If scientific or humane values justify delaying or withholding this information, psychologists take reasonable measures to reduce the risk of harm.

6.19 Honoring Commitments

Psychologists take reasonable measures to honor all commitments they have made to research participants.

COMMENTARY

Earlier we mentioned that protecting the confidentiality of a participant's responses brought benefits both to the participant (safeguarding from social injury) and to the researcher (increasing the probability of honest responding). **Debriefing** participants at the end of a research session also carries benefits both to participant and researcher (see Blanck et al., 1992). As we saw when discussing the use of deception, debriefing is necessary to remove any harmful effects or misconceptions about participation as well as to explain to participants the need for deception; however, debriefing also has the important goals of educating participants about the research (rationale, method, results) and of leaving them with positive feelings about their participation. Whenever possible, a researcher should take the time to explain the nature of the participant's specific performance and to show how it relates to group or normative data. If this is not feasible, participants should be given the opportunity at some future time to learn about the general outcome of the research. Some researchers take it upon themselves to mail a written report of a study's results to the participants; others, especially when testing captive populations such as college students, invite participants to come back later (for instance, at the end of a semester) to obtain a report summarizing the study's findings. In this way, participants can learn more about their particular contribution to the research study and, in doing so, feel more personally involved in the scientific process.

Debriefing is an opportunity for participants to learn more about research in general—by having the study's methodology explained to them, for instance, or by being introduced to various tests or instruments used in psychological research. Because the "educational value" of participation in psychological research is one reason given to justify the use of large numbers of volunteers from college introductory psychology classes, researchers using college subjects have an important obligation to attempt to educate their subjects about psychological research. In addition to being debriefed, student participants have sometimes been asked by classroom instructors to write brief reports about their research experience, including details about the study's purpose, the techniques used, and the significance of the research to understanding behavior. One evaluation of such a procedure revealed that students who wrote reports were more satisfied with the research experience and experienced a significantly greater overall educational benefit from it than did students who did not write reports (Richardson, Pegalis, & Britton, 1992).

Debriefing can help a researcher by providing an opportunity to find out how the participant viewed the situation and any treatments that were administered. For example, a researcher may wish to know whether a particular experimental procedure was perceived by the participant in the way that the investigator intended (Blanck et al., 1992). Studies of what is called incidental learning involve exposing participants to certain kinds of critical material (e.g., the contents of a room, another person, a list of words, and so on) and then later asking them what they can remember of this material. It is important that participants, when exposed to the critical material, be unaware that a memory test will later be given (otherwise, intentional, not incidental, learning will take place). Debriefing enables the investigator to find out how participants perceived the tasks given to them and whether they were aware that their retention would be tested.

Debriefing which seeks to discover how participants perceive a specific task or situation must be done in a manner that avoids pressing them to reveal information they believe they are not supposed to possess. Research participants generally want to help with the scientific process, and many realize that in any valid psychological study there may be information that is purposely withheld from them (see especially Orne, 1962). To tell the researcher that they really *did* know about these details may seem to participants to threaten the study's validity and hence "ruin" it. Thus if questioned directly, participants may withhold information about their perceptions in a misguided, albeit well-intentioned, attempt to protect the scientific integrity of the study. Debriefing should thus be carried out in an informal manner, with the participant carefully led by the investigator to respond honestly and openly. This is often best accomplished by using general questions in an open-ended format (e.g., What do you think this study was about?) and following up with more specific questions which, as much as possible, do not cue the participant in on what is expected (Orne, 1962).

Debriefing provides yet another benefit to researchers. It can provide them with "leads for future research and help identify problems in their current protocols" (Blanck et al., 1992, p. 962). Debriefing, in other words, can provide clues as to the reasons for a participant's performance, which may help when discussing the overall results or may set the stage for another study. Errors in experimental materials—for instance, missing information or ambiguous instructions—are sometimes detected through postexperimental interviews with participants. As we said, debriefing is good for both the participant and the scientist.

RESEARCH WITH ANIMALS

Each year millions of animals become subjects in laboratory investigations aimed at answering a wide range of important questions. New drugs are tested on animals before they are used with humans. Substances introduced into the environment must first be given to animals to test their effects. Animals are exposed to diseases in order that investigators may observe symptoms and test various cures. New surgical procedures—especially those involving the brain—are often first tried out on animals. Many animals are also used for behavioral research, for example by ethologists and experimental psychologists. These investigations yield much information that contributes to human welfare (see Miller, 1985). In the process, however, many animals are subjected to pain and discomfort, stress and sickness, and death. Although rodents, particularly rats and mice, are the largest group of laboratory animals, researchers use a wide variety of species in their investigations, including monkeys, fish, dogs, and cats. Specific animals are frequently chosen because they are good models of human responses. For example, psychologists interested in audition sometimes use chinchillas as subjects because their auditory processes are very similar to those of humans. Apparently, chimpanzees are the only nonhuman primates that can harbor the virus linked to AIDS (Landers, 1988). As a result, concern over the dwindling numbers of these animals has been expressed, not only by animal conservationists, who worry about the extinction of the species, but by biomedical researchers, who may have to depend upon these animals for laboratory research aimed at finding a vaccine for AIDS (Booth, 1988; Goodall, 1987).

APA ETHICAL STANDARDS

6.20 Care and Use of Animals in Research

(a) Psychologists who conduct research involving animals treat them humanely.

(b) Psychologists acquire, care for, use, and dispose of animals in compliance with current federal, state, and local laws and regulations, and with professional standards.

(c) Psychologists trained in research methods and experienced in the care of laboratory animals supervise all procedures involving animals and are responsible for ensuring appropriate consideration of their comfort, health, and humane treatment.

(d) Psychologists ensure that all individuals using animals under their supervision have received instruction in research methods and in the care, maintenance, and handling of the species being used, to the extent appropriate to their role.

(e) Responsibilities and activities of individuals assisting in a research project are consistent with their respective competencies.

(f) Psychologists make reasonable efforts to minimize the discomfort, infection, illness, and pain of animal subjects.

(g) A procedure subjecting animals to pain, stress, or privation is used only when an alternative procedure is unavailable and the goal is justified by its prospective scientific, educational, or applied value.

(h) Surgical procedures are performed under appropriate anesthesia; techniques to avoid infection and minimize pain are followed during and after surgery.

(i) When it is appropriate that the animal's life be terminated, it is done rapidly, with an effort to minimize pain, and in accordance with accepted procedures.

COMMENTARY

The use of animals as laboratory subjects has often been taken for granted. In fact, the biblical reference to man's "dominion" over all lesser creatures is sometimes invoked to justify the use of animals as laboratory subjects (see, for example, Johnson, 1990; Rollin, 1985). More often, however, research with animal subjects is justified by the need to gain knowledge *without putting humans in jeopardy* about aspects of nature that directly affect the human condition. Few cures, drugs, vaccines, or therapies have come about without experimentation on animals (see Rosenfeld, 1981). It would be difficult to contemplate the consequences of doing research on such diseases as cancer or muscular dystrophy without the opportunity first to examine the course of the disease or try out a new cure on animal subjects. Feeney (1987), for example, has called attention to the contributions that basic research with animal subjects has made to the treatment of patients recovering from brain and spinal-cord injury. He also points out that our understanding of the relationship between brain and behavior was advanced significantly by the now classic work in the 1960s of Roger Sperry, who won a Nobel Prize for his work on the "split brain" (the functioning of the brain after the corpus callosum has been cut). Early investigations by Sperry and others, using cats and monkeys as subjects, demonstrated that the two hemispheres of the brain can function independently in learning and memory.

Many questions have been raised about the role of animal subjects in laboratory studies, however (see, for example, Novak, 1991; Shapiro, 1991; Ulrich, 1991). These questions include the most basic one, whether animals should be used at all in scientific investigations, as well as equally important questions about the care and protection of animal subjects. Clearly, according to the APA principles, the researcher who uses animal subjects in an investigation has an ethical obligation to look out for their welfare and to treat them humanely. Only individuals qualified to do research and to manage and care for the particular species being used should be allowed to participate. When the research exposes the animals to pain or discomfort, it must be justified by the potential scientific, educational, or applied goals. As was noted earlier when institutional review was discussed, animal review boards (IACUCs) are now in place at research facilities receiving funds from the Public Health Service. These committees are charged with determining the adequacy of the procedures for controlling pain, carrying out euthanasia, housing animals, and training personnel, as well as determining whether the experimental design is sufficient to gain important new information and whether the animal model is appropriate or whether nonanimal models could be used (Holden, 1987).

Partly in response to calls from members of animal-rights groups during the 1980s, investigators must now meet a host of federal and state requirements, including inspection of animal facilities by veterinarians from the U.S. Department of Agriculture (see, for example, Landers, 1987a; 1987b). These regulations are often welcomed by members of the scientific community, and many animal researchers belong to groups such as the APA Committee on Animal Research and Experimentation (CARE) which seek to protect laboratory animals. (CARE has developed a list of specific guidelines to be followed when animal subjects are used in psychological research. A copy of these guidelines may be obtained by writing CARE, c/o Science Directorate, American Psychological Association, 750 First Street, N.E., Washington, DC 20002-4242.) As with any ethically sensitive issue, however, it is clear that compromises must be made. For example, until alternatives to animal research can be found, the need to conduct research using animal subjects in order to battle human disease and suffering must be balanced against the need for adequate control over the way animals are treated in laboratory research (see, for example, Goodall, 1987). Hovering above this discussion is the need for a balanced treatment of the issues (see, for example, Kelly, 1986). As APA's chief executive officer, Raymond Fowler, has pointed out, it is important that the use of animal subjects not be restricted because the application of the research is not readily apparent (Fowler, 1992). "The charges that animal research is of no value because it cannot always be linked to potential applications is a charge that can be made against all basic research." Such an indictment "threatens the intellectual and scientific foundation" of all psychology, including both "scientists and practitioners" (p. 2).

While few scientists would disagree that restrictions are necessary to prevent needless suffering in animals, most want to avoid a quagmire of bureaucratic restrictions and high costs that will undermine research. Feeney (1987) suggests that severe restrictions and high costs, as well as the negative publicity (and occasional terrorist acts) directed toward individuals and institutions by extremists within the animal-activists groups, may deter young scientists from entering the field of animal research. If such is the case, the result possibly could be to deprive the (presently) incurably ill or permanently paralyzed of the hope that comes through scientific research.

Clearly, the issues surrounding the debate over the relevance of animal research to the human situation are many and complex. As Ulrich (1992) has commented, discussion of these issues must be approached with "wisdom and balance" (p. 386).

REPORTING OF PSYCHOLOGICAL RESEARCH

Generally, once a psychological investigation is completed, the principal investigator prepares a manuscript for submission to one of the dozens of psychology-related scientific periodicals. Publication in a psychology journal not only achieves the scientific goal of communicating the results of a study to members of the scientific community and to society in general but, as we have seen, may also enhance the researcher's reputation and even the reputation of the institution that sponsored the research. But getting the results of a scientific investigation published is not always an easy process, especially if the researcher wishes to publish in one of the more prestigious scientific journals. Journals sponsored by APA, such as the *Journal of Abnormal Psychology, Journal of Educational Psychology, Journal of Experimental Psychology: Learning, Memory, and Cognition,* and *Psychological Review,* can have *rejection* rates as high as 90 percent (American Psychological Association, 1992b).

Manuscripts submitted for publication must be prepared according to strict stylistic guidelines (see Appendix C), meet rigorous methodological and substantive criteria, and be appropriate for the particular journal to which the manuscript is submitted. Problems in any of these three areas may be sufficient to deny publication; however, manuscripts are more commonly rejected because of problems in the methodology of the study, problems in the statistical treatment of the results, or because the results do not make a significant enough contribution to scientific progress in the field. Decisions about the acceptability of a scientific manuscript are made by the journal's editors, usually on the basis of comments made by the experts in the field who have been asked by the editors for their opinions about the manuscript's scientific worth. This process is known as *peer review,* and many scientists have had their hopes of being published dashed along this difficult scientific path. Despite the many pressures to publish in order to earn promotion or tenure at a university, it is imperative that all scientists adhere strictly to the code of ethics governing the reporting of results.

APA ETHICAL STANDARDS

6.21 Reporting of Results

(a) Psychologists do not fabricate data or falsify results in their publications.
(b) If psychologists discover significant errors in their published data, they take reasonable steps to correct such errors in a correction, retraction, erratum, or other appropriate publication means.

6.22 Plagiarism

Psychologists do not present substantial portions or elements of another's work or data as their own, even if the other work or data source is cited occasionally.

6.23 Publication Credit

(a) Psychologists take responsibility and credit, including authorship credit, only for work they have actually performed or to which they have contributed.
(b) Principal authorship and other publication credits accurately reflect the relative scientific or professional contributions of the individuals involved, regardless of their relative status. Mere possession of an institutional position, such as Department Chair, does not justify authorship credit. Minor contributions to the research or to the writing for publications are appropriately acknowledged, such as in footnotes or in an introductory statement.
(c) A student is usually listed as principal author on any multiple-authored article that is substantially based on the student's dissertation or thesis.

6.24 Duplicate Publication of Data

Psychologists do not publish, as original data, data that have been previously published. This does not preclude republishing data when accompanied by proper acknowledgment.

6.25 Sharing Data

After research results are published, psychologists do not withhold the data on which their conclusions are based from other competent professionals who seek to verify the substantive claims through reanalysis and who intend to use such data only for that purpose, provided that the confidentiality of the participants can be protected and unless legal rights concerning proprietary data preclude their release.

6.26 Professional Reviewers

Psychologists who review material submitted for publication, grant, or other research proposal review respect the confidentiality of and the proprietary rights in such information of those who submitted it.

COMMENTARY

The ethical standards governing the reporting of the results of a scientific investigation seem more straightforward than in other areas of ethical concern. There are areas of ethical decision making, however, in which the lines cannot always be drawn clearly. Consider, for example, ethical issues related to assigning *publication credit* to those who make contributions to a research project. Research is often a collaborative effort, involving, for instance, colleagues who offer suggestions about a study's design, graduate or undergraduate students who assist a principal investigator by testing subjects and organizing data, technicians who construct specialized equipment, and expert consultants who give advice about computer programs needed for statistical analyses. Because "authorship" of a published scientific study frequently is used to measure an individual's motivation and competence in a scientific field, it is important to acknowledge fairly those who have contributed to a project. However, deciding whether an individual should be credited by being an "author" of a scientific paper or whether that individual's contribution should be acknowledged in a less visible way, such as in a footnote, is not always easy. When research psychologists are surveyed about this issue, most report that a contribution should be evaluated mainly in terms of its scholarly importance (e.g., aiding the conceptual aspects of a study) and not by the time and energy invested in the study (see Bridgewater, Bornstein, & Walkenbach, 1981).

A rather troublesome area of concern, not only for some professionals but frequently for students, is that of **plagiarism.** Again, the ethical standard seems clear enough: Don't present substantial portions or elements of another's work as your own. But what constitutes "substantial portions or elements," and how does one avoid giving the impression that another's work is one's own? This can be like walking a tightrope. On one side is the goal of achieving recognition for contributing to the solution of a problem; on the other side is the goal of recognizing others who have previously contributed to its solution. The fact that both professionals and students are too often caught in the act of plagiarizing suggests that many veer from the tightrope by seeking their own recognition at the expense of giving due credit to the work of others. Sometimes acts of plagiarism result from sloppiness (failing to double-check a source to verify that an idea which is presented did not originate with someone else, for example). Errors of this kind are still plagiarism; ignorance is not a legitimate excuse. On other occasions, especially among students, plagiarism can result from failure to identify literal passages through the use of quotation marks or to acknowledge the use of secondary sources. A *secondary source* is one that discusses other (original) work. Most textbooks can be considered secondary sources. Again, ignorance concerning the proper form of citation is not an acceptable excuse, and on unfortunate occasions researchers—professors as well as students—have seen their careers ruined by accusations of plagiarism.

Mistakes can be made all too easily. For example, what constitutes a "substantial" element of another's thinking is not always determined by quantity, as is sometimes assumed. That is, researchers occasionally ask "how much" of a passage can be used without putting it in quotation marks or otherwise identifying its source. However, a substantial element can be a single word or short phrase if that element serves to identify a key idea or concept which is the result of another's thinking. Students and other novices in an academic discipline, who may not yet be cognizant of important concepts and ideas in an area of knowledge, must be particularly careful when referring to the work of others. *Whenever material is taken directly from a source* it should be placed in quotation marks and the source properly identified.

Because students and others new to a scientific field frequently rely on secondary sources, it is very important that they understand how to use and cite such sources, which include not only textbooks, but published reviews of research such as appear in scientific journals like the *Psychological Bulletin,* and any other sources whose authors refer to another's findings and ideas. It is always unethical to present an idea or result from an article or publication found in a secondary source *in a manner that suggests that you consulted the original work* when your only source of information about the critical material comes from the secondary source. For example, suppose that you wish to discuss the interesting work done by Levine (1990) on pace of life that was discussed in Chapter 1 of this text. Unless you are able to locate and peruse the original article, it is unethical for you simply to acknowledge Levine when citing his work; you must also cite the authors of the textbook that discussed his work. It is also bad scholarship because if your readers rely on your report, they will be relying on your interpretation of the textbook authors' interpretation of the original (Levine's) work. It isn't difficult to see how building a base of scientific knowledge on interpretations of interpretations (and so on, when others interpret *your* work) would quickly produce inconsistencies and contradictions.

Citing work mentioned in a secondary source should be avoided whenever possible (for example, by taking the time to locate and consult the original), but when it is necessary to do so, proper citation means informing your reader that you did *not* consult the original work (for example, by using the phrase "as cited in . . ." when referring to the original work). This gives your reader fair warning that the identification and interpretation of the criterial material did not originate with you. (Students of psychology are expected to be familiar with the stylistic rules and guidelines for manuscript preparation found in the *Publication Manual of the American Psychological Association,* 1983. See also Appendix C in this textbook.) As with other areas of ethical decision making, when in doubt *get advice* from others with experience in the area in which you have questions.

SUMMARY

Psychological research raises many ethical questions. Thus, before beginning a research project, it is important to consider the specific ethical issues, as well as the various federal and state laws, relevant to your project. In most cases formal institutional approval—for example, from an IRB or IACUC—must be obtained before beginning to do research. One function of an IRB is to reach a consensus regarding the risk/benefit ratio of the proposed research. Researchers must take special safeguards to protect human participants when more than minimal risk is present. Risk can involve physical, psychological, or social injury. Informed consent must be obtained from human participants in most psychological research. Serious ethical questions arise when researchers withhold information from participants; whenever deception is used, the researcher has the responsibility to debrief the participant. The debriefing should include providing information concerning the reasons for having used deception. Debriefing can also help human participants feel more fully involved in the research situation as well as help the researcher learn how the participants perceived the treatment or task. Psychologists testing animal subjects must obey a variety of federal and state guidelines and, in general, must treat the animals humanely. Animals may be subjected to pain or discomfort only when alternative procedures are not available and when the goals of the research are judged to justify such procedures. Reporting of psychological findings should be done in a manner that gives appropriate credit to the individuals who helped with the project. Appropriate acknowledgment must also be made of those individuals whose ideas or findings have previously been reported in the published literature and who therefore contributed to the investigator's planning or thinking about the study.

KEY CONCEPTS

risk/benefit ratio
minimal risk
informed consent
privacy
deception
debriefing
plagiarism

REVIEW QUESTIONS

1 Briefly summarize the role of Institutional Review Boards (IRBs) and Institutional Animal Care and Use Committees (IACUCs) in overseeing psychological research.
2 How is the "risk/benefit" ratio used in ethical decision making?
3 Differentiate among the following possible types of injury in psychological research: physical, psychological, social.
4 Give two or more examples of research tasks that in your judgment would involve no more than "minimal risk" to participants selected from a normal college student population.
5 How is the possibility of social risk typically safeguarded against?
6 Under what conditions do the APA ethical standards indicate that informed consent may not be necessary?
7 Identify four major features of an informed-consent form.
8 What do Diener and Crandall (1978) say are three important dimensions to consider when making decisions about what information is private?
9 When is it unethical to deceive human participants?
10 What are the major benefits of debriefing, both to the participant and to the researcher?
11 What kinds of special knowledge are required by the APA standards for those working with animal subjects?
12 According to the APA standards, what circumstances must be present before animals may be subjected to stress or pain?
13 What allows an individual to claim "authorship" of a published scientific report?
14 What specific ethical procedure should be followed when it is necessary to cite information from a secondary source?

CHALLENGE QUESTIONS

NOTE: Each of the challenge questions for Chapter 2 includes a hypothetical research proposal involving a rationale and method similar to that of actual published research. In order to answer these questions, you will need to be familiar with the APA ethical principles and other material on ethical decision making presented in this chapter. As you will see, your task is to decide whether specific ethical standards have been violated and to make recommendations regarding the proposed research, including the most basic recommendation of whether the investigator should be allowed to proceed. Unlike this section in other chapters, no answers to the questions are provided. In order to resolve the ethical dilemmas, you must be able not only to apply the appropriate ethical standards but to reach an agreement regarding the proposed research after discussion with others who have backgrounds and knowledge that differs from your own. You will therefore have to consider points of view different from your own. We urge you to approach these problems as part of a group discussion of these important issues.

I. Assume that you are a member of an Institutional Review Board (IRB). Besides yourself, the committee includes a clinical psychologist, a social psychologist, social worker, philosopher, a Protestant minister, a history professor, and a respected business executive in the community. The following are two summaries of research proposals that have been submitted to the IRB for review. For each proposal, you are asked to consider what questions you might want to ask the investigator and whether you would approve carrying out the study at your institution in its present form, whether modification should be made before approval, or whether the proposal should not be approved. (An actual research proposal submitted to an IRB would include more details than are presented here.)

PROPOSAL #1

Rationale

Psychological conformity occurs when people accept the opinions or judgments of others in the absence of significant reasons to do so or in the face of evidence to the contrary. Previous research has investigated the conditions under which conformity is likely to occur and has shown, for example, that conformity increases when people anticipate unpleasant events (e.g., shock) and when the pressure to conform comes from individuals with whom the individuals identify. The proposed research examines psychological conformity in the context of discussions about alcohol consumption among teenage students. The goal of the research is to identify factors that contribute to students' willingness to attend social events where alcohol is served to minors and to allow obviously intoxicated persons to drive an automobile. This research seeks to investigate conformity in a natural setting and in circumstances where unpleasant events (e.g., legal penalties, school suspension, injury, or even death) can be avoided by *not* conforming to peer pressure.

Method

The research will involve 36 high school students between the ages of 16 and 18 who have volunteered to participate in a research project investigating "beliefs and attitudes of today's high school students." Participants will be assigned to four-person discussion groups. Each person in the group will be given the same 20 questions to answer; however, they will be asked to discuss each question with members of the group before writing down their answers. Four of the 20 questions deal with alcohol consumption by teenagers and with possible actions that might be taken to reduce teenage drinking and driving. One member of the group will be appointed discussion leader by the principal investigator. Unknown to the participants, they will be assigned randomly to three different groups. In each group, there will be either 0, 1, or 2 students who are actually working for the principal investigator. Each of these "confederates" has received prior instructions from the investigator regarding what to say during the group discussion of the critical questions about teenage drinking. (The use of confederates in psychological research is discussed in Chapter 3.) Specifically, confederates have been asked to follow a script which presents the argument that the majority of people who reach the legal driving age (16), and all individuals who are old enough (18) to vote in national elections and serve in the armed forces, are old enough to make their own decisions about drinking alcohol; moreover, because it is up to each individual to make this decision, other individuals do not have the right to intervene if someone under the legal age chooses to drink alcohol. Each of the confederates "admits" to drinking alcohol on at least two previous occasions. Thus, the experimental manipulation involves either 0, 1, or 2 persons in the four-person groups suggesting that they do not believe students have a responsibility to avoid situations where alcohol is served to minors or to intervene when someone chooses to drink and drive. The effect of this argument on the written answers given by the actual subjects in this experiment will be evaluated. Moreover, audiotapes of the sessions will be made without participants' knowledge, and the contents of these audiotapes will be analyzed. Following the experiment, the nature of the deception and the reasons for making audiotapes of the discussions will be explained to the subjects.

PROPOSAL #2

Rationale

The proposed research seeks to determine the conditions which lead to unethical and illegal behavior in businesses and in society. Specifically, this study examines cheating behavior in a natural setting. Previous research has shown that cheating often is affected by situational variables such as the absence of witnesses and the ease with which the cheating can be accomplished. The present research seeks to investigate cheating behavior as a function of the gender of the cheater and the degree of opportunity to cheat. The situations chosen to investigate this behavior are those in which an automobile driver is asked to put money in a machine to gain access to a parking facility or to a highway. Two common situations of this type are unattended automated parking lots and tollways. The goal of the research is to shed light on the social conditions leading to unethical and illegal behavior.

Method

The research will be conducted with the cooperation of several parking-lot owners and with tollway authorities in the community. An opportunity to cheat will be manipulated by placing a sign next to a barrier (either to a tollway or a parking facility) which declares that the machine will take money but that the barrier (which is in the open position) is temporarily inoperable. In addition, in one condition the signs will further state that entering without paying the appropriate toll is punishable by a fine. No such warning will be present on the signs in the other condition. Observers will be positioned so that they can identify the gender of the driver and see whether the driver puts money in the machine. State regulations also require that a highway patrol officer be present when observations are made of drivers entering a tollway entrance. Of interest is whether the rate of cheating differs between males and females; whether the warning about legal penalties affects this behavior; and if the warning does have an effect, whether it influences one gender more than another.

II. Assume that you are a member of an Institutional Animal Care and Use Committee (IACUC). Besides yourself, the committee includes a veterinarian, a biologist, a philosopher, and a respected business executive in the community. The following is a summary of a research proposal that has been submitted to the IACUC for review. You are asked to consider what questions you might want to ask the investigator and whether you would approve carrying out this study at your institution in its present form, whether modification should be made before approval, or whether the proposal should not be approved. (An actual research proposal submitted to an IACUC would include more details than the one presented here.)

PROPOSAL #3

Rationale

The investigators seek to investigate the role of subcortical structures in the limbic system in moderating emotion and aggression. This proposal is based on previous research from this laboratory which has shown a significant relationship between damage in various subcortical brain areas of monkey subjects and changes in eating, aggressive, and other social behaviors (e.g., courtship). The areas under investigation are those that sometimes have been excised in psychosurgery with humans when attempting to control hyperaggressive and assaultive behaviors. Moreover, the particular subcortical area which is the focus of the present proposal has been hypothesized to be involved in controlling certain sexual activities that are sometimes the subject of psychological treatment (e.g., hypersexuality). Previous studies have been unable to pinpoint the exact areas thought to be involved in controlling certain behaviors; the proposed research seeks to improve on this knowledge.

Method

Two groups of rhesus monkeys will serve as subjects. One group ($N = 4$) will be a control group. These animals will undergo a sham operation, which involves anesthetizing the animals and drilling a hole in the skull. These animals then will be tested and evaluated in the same manner as the experimental animals. The experimental group will undergo an operation to lesion a small part of a subcortical structure known as the amygdala. Two of the animals will have lesions in one site; the remaining two will receive lesions in another site in this structure. After recovery, all animals will be tested on a variety of tasks measuring their food preferences, social behaviors with same and opposite-sex monkeys (normals), and emotional responsiveness (e.g., reactions to a novel fear stimulus: an experimenter in a clown face).

The animals will be housed in a modern animal laboratory; the operations will be performed and recovery monitored by a licensed veterinarian. After testing, the experimental animals will be sacrificed and the brains prepared for histological examination. (Histology is necessary to confirm the locus and extent of lesions.) The control animals will not be killed; they will be returned to the colony for use in future experiments.

Part

Descriptive Methods

Chapter 3

Observation

Outline

OVERVIEW

As was mentioned in Chapter 1, scientists and nonscientists alike rely on observation to learn about behavior. What distinguishes scientific observation from nonscientific observation is the manner in which observations are made. Nonscientists are likely to observe casually and are often unaware of personal and situational biases that may influence the observational process. Nonscientists rarely keep formal records of what they observe and consequently depend on memory for information about an event. Unfortunately, what one remembers about an event is not likely to be a literal record of what one experienced, and memory can be affected by information added after an event is observed (Bartlett, 1932; Loftus, 1979b). Scientific observation, on the other hand, is made under precisely defined conditions, in a systematic and objective manner, and with careful record keeping. When observations are made in this manner, valuable behavioral information and its antecedents can be obtained.

An important task of the psychologist is to describe behavior in its natural context and to identify relationships among variables that are present. Changes in behavior are frequently observed to result from the context in which behavior occurs. For example, Schaller (1963) observed that mountain gorillas regularly eat meat when in captivity, but he found no evidence of meat eating by gorillas in the wild. Moderately obese people eating in a cafeteria were observed to purchase less food and to consume fewer calories when eating with others than when eating alone (Krantz, 1979). By describing behavior in natural settings, the psychologist seeks to establish a basis for predicting future behavior.

Often, observation is also the first step in discovering the reasons why organisms behave the way they do. For example, both animals and humans are known to display distinctive reactions to novel or unfamiliar situations. Observing a group of 2- and 3-year-old children in the presence of an unfamiliar person or object, Kagan, Reznick, and Snidman (1988) identified those children who were consistently shy, quiet, and timid and those who were consistently sociable, talkative, and affectively spontaneous. When the same children were observed at 7 years of age, a majority of the children in each group exhibited similar behaviors. The researchers speculated that shyness in childhood as well as extreme social anxiety in adulthood are the result of temperamental differences present at birth.

Systematic observation is an important tool not only of psychologists but of anthropologists, sociologists, and ethologists. In this chapter we examine observational methods used to investigate behavior—especially, but not exclusively, in natural settings. As you will see, the scientist-observer is not always passive, present merely to record behavior. Researchers sometimes intervene in the situation in which they are observing behavior. Scientists' reasons for intervening in natural settings are discussed. Methods for recording data and techniques for analyzing data are also illustrated, and some limitations and problems associated with the observation of behavior are explained.

CLASSIFICATION OF OBSERVATIONAL METHODS

Observational methods can be classified according to the degree to which an observer intervenes in an observational setting as well as according to the way in which that behavior is recorded (see Willems, 1969). Hence we make an important distinction between observation with intervention and observation without intervention. Methods of recording behavior also generally differ in terms of whether all (or nearly all) of the behavior exhibited in a given setting is recorded or only particular units of behavior are recorded. In some situations an observer may seek a comprehensive description of behavior. This may be accomplished by the use of film, tapes, or lengthy verbal descriptions. More often, a researcher records specific units of behavior that are seen as related to the goals of a particular study. An investigator, for instance, who is interested in prosocial behavior likely will concentrate on specific behaviors which define this type of behavior. Chambers and Ascione (1987) observed that children who played an aggressive video game put less money in a donation box and volunteered to help sharpen pencils significantly less than did those who played a video game with prosocial content.

We will discuss observational methods first in terms of the extent of observer intervention and then in terms of methods of recording behavior.

OBSERVATION WITHOUT INTERVENTION

Observation of behavior in a more or less natural setting, without any attempt by the observer to intervene, is frequently called **naturalistic observation,** a *naturalistic field study*, or, more formally, *systematic observation in a natural setting*.

An observer using this method of observation acts as a passive recorder of what occurs. The events witnessed are those that occur naturally and have not been manipulated or in any way controlled by the observer. What exactly constitutes a natural setting is not easily identified (see Bickman, 1976; Willems & Raush, 1969). In general, we can consider a natural setting one in which behavior occurs ordinarily and one that has not been arranged specifically for the purpose of recording behavior. Observing people in a psychology laboratory would not, for instance, be considered naturalistic observation. The laboratory situation has been created specifically to study behavior and, in a manner of speaking, is an artificial rather than a natural setting. In fact, an important reason for doing naturalistic observation is to verify relationships between variables that have been identified in the psychology laboratory. Observation in natural settings serves, among other functions, as a way of establishing the external validity of laboratory findings.

The major goals of observation in natural settings are to describe behavior as it ordinarily occurs and to investigate the relationship among variables that are present. Hartup (1974) chose naturalistic observation to investigate the frequency and types of aggression exhibited by preschoolers in a St. Paul, Minnesota, children's center. He distinguished hostile aggression (person-oriented) from instrumental aggression (aimed at the retrieval of an object, territory, or privilege). Although he observed boys to be more aggressive overall than girls, his observations provided no evidence that the types of aggression differed between the sexes. Thus Hartup was able to conclude that, with respect to hostile aggression, there was no evidence that boys and girls were "wired" differently.

Hartup's study of children's aggression illustrates why a researcher may choose to use naturalistic observation rather than to manipulate conditions related to behavior. There are certain aspects of human behavior that moral or ethical considerations prevent us from controlling. Researchers may be interested in the relationship between early childhood isolation and later emotional and psychological development. However, we would object strenuously if they tried to take children from their parents in order to raise them in isolation. Alternative methods of data collection must be considered if this problem is to be investigated. For example, the effect of early isolation on later development has been studied through experimentation on animal subjects (Harlow & Harlow, 1966), case studies of children subjected to unusual conditions of isolation by their parents (Curtiss, 1977), and systematic observation of institutionalized children (Spitz, 1965). The nature of children's aggression is another aspect of behavior the investigation of which is subject to moral and ethical limitations. We would not want to see children intentionally harassed and picked on simply to record their reactions. However, as anyone knows who has observed children, there is plenty of naturally occurring aggression. Hartup's study shows how observation without intervention can be a useful alternative to methods of data collection that attempt to manipulate the behavior of interest.

Psychologists are not the only researchers who observe behavior in natural settings. Observation is a fundamental method of ethologists. Although related to psychology, **ethology** is generally considered a branch of biology (Eibl-Eibesfeldt, 1975). Ethologists study the behavior of organisms in relation to their natural environment. A major question they seek to answer is how natural selection has worked to produce particular behavior patterns in an animal species. The focus of an ethological investigation is often the development of an **ethogram.** This is nothing less than a complete catalog of all the behavior patterns of an organism, including information on frequency, duration, and context of occurrence.

Ethologists adopt a comparative approach to understanding behavior and often seek to explain behavior in one animal species on the basis of innate patterns of behavior observed in species lower on the evolutionary scale. Speculations about the role of innate mechanisms in determining human behavior are not uncommon among ethologists. For instance, Barash (1977) observed whether male and female human pedestrians visually scanned both directions before crossing a dangerous intersection in Seattle, Washington. When a male adult and a female adult were together, adult males scanned more than females. This was true regardless of whether children were also present. The ethologist-observer suggested an evolutionary explanation: Adult male monkeys and baboons in the wild generally function as lookouts to warn the rest of the group of approaching danger. An ethological perspective has proved important for the understanding of both normal and abnormal human behavior. An interesting example is the ethological analysis of psychiatric problems based on comprehensive descriptions of facial behavior of schizophrenic patients (see Pitman et al., 1987).

OBSERVATION WITH INTERVENTION

It is characteristic of the scientist to "tamper" with nature, to intervene, in order to make a point or to test a theory. Intervention rather than nonintervention characterizes most psychological research. Kinds of intervention vary widely in psychological studies, depending on such things as the purpose for investigating behavior, the nature of the behavior under observation, and the ingenuity of the researcher.

Although the types of intervention employed by psychologists are too numerous and diverse to classify, their reasons for intervening are generally one or more of the following:

1 To precipitate or cause an event that occurs infrequently in nature or that normally occurs under conditions that make it difficult to observe.

2 To investigate the limits of an organism's response by varying systematically the qualities of a stimulus event.

3 To gain access to a situation or event that is generally not open to scientific observation.

4 To arrange conditions so that important antecedent events are controlled and consequent behaviors can be readily observed.

5 To establish a comparison by manipulating one or more independent variables to determine their effect on behavior.

These reasons for intervening are illustrated in three methods of observation: participant observation, structured observation, and the field experiment. As we review these major observational techniques, the investigator's reasons for intervening will become clear.

PARTICIPANT OBSERVATION

Observation of behavior by someone who also plays an active and significant role in the situation or context in which behavior is recorded is called **participant observation.** In *undisguised* participant observation, the individuals who are being observed know that the observer is present for the purpose of collecting information about their behavior. This method is frequently used by anthropologists who seek to understand the culture and behavior of groups by living and working with members of the group.

When the observer's role is not known to those who are being observed, we speak of *disguised* participant observation. As you might imagine, people do not always behave in the way they ordinarily would when they know their behavior is being recorded. Politicians, for instance, often make different statements when speaking to the press, depending on whether their comments are "for" or "off" the record. Our own behavior is likely to be affected by knowing that we are being watched. This problem associated with observational methods will be discussed more fully later in the chapter. For now, let us simply say that researchers may decide to disguise their role as observers if they believe that subjects will not act as they ordinarily would if they know their activities are being recorded.

Disguised participant observation was used by Rosenhan (1973) to investigate the basis of psychiatric diagnosis in the context of a mental institution. Eight individuals (including psychologists, a pediatrician, and a housewife) misrepresented their names and occupations and sought admission to twelve different mental hospitals. Each complained of the same general symptom: that he or she was hearing voices. Rosenhan (p. 251) described these symptoms and the rationale for their selection by the observers as follows:

> Asked what the voices said, he replied that they were often unclear, but as far as he could tell they said "empty," "hollow," and "thud." The voices were unfamiliar and were of the same sex as the pseudopatient. The choice of these symptoms was occasioned by their apparent similarity to existential symptoms. Such symptoms are alleged to arise from painful concerns about the perceived meaninglessness of one's life. It is as if the hallucinating person were saying, "My life is empty and hollow." The choice of these symptoms was also determined by the *absence* of a single report of existential psychoses in the literature. Beyond alleging the symptoms and falsifying name, vocation, and employment, no further alterations of person, history, or circumstances were made.

Immediately after being put in the mental ward, the researchers stopped complaining of any symptoms and refrained from acting abnormally. In addition to observing patient-staff interactions, the observers were interested in how long it took for a "sane" person to be released from the hospital. Length of hospitalization ranged from 7 to 52 days. The researchers were never detected as sane and, when they were discharged, their schizophrenia was said only to be "in remission." Apparently, once the pseudopatients were labeled schizophrenic, they were stuck with that label no matter what the nature of their subsequent behavior.

Participant observation allows an observer to gain access to a situation that is not usually open to scientific observation. In addition, the participant observer is often in a position to have the same experiences as the subjects under study. This may provide important insights and understanding of individuals or groups. The pseudopatients in the Rosenhan study, for instance, felt what it was like to be labeled schizophrenic and not to know how long it would be before they could return to society. In the fall of 1959, John Howard Griffin set out to research "what it was like to be a Negro in a land where we keep the Negro down." Griffin, a white man, darkened his skin using medication and stain in order to pass himself off as black. For more than a month he traveled (walking, hitchhiking, riding buses) through Mississippi, Alabama, and Georgia. He described his experiences as a participant observer in his book *Black Like Me* (1960), which was an important precursor of the civil rights movement of the 1960s.

A participant observer's role in a situation can produce certain methodological problems. By identifying with the individuals under study, it is possible for an observer to lose the scientific objectivity that accurate and valid observation requires. Changes in a participant observer are sometimes dramatic and are not easily anticipated. Witness the experiences of a criminologist who used undisguised participant observation to study police officers at work. Kirkham (1975) went through police academy training like any recruit and became a uniformed patrol officer assigned to a high-crime area in a city of about half a million. His immersion in the daily activities of an officer on the beat led to marked changes in his attitudes and personality. As Kirkham (p. 19) himself noted:

> As the weeks and months of my new career as a slum policeman went by, I slowly but inexorably began to become indistinguishable in attitudes and behavior from the policemen with whom I worked. . . . According to the accounts of my family, colleagues and friends, I began to increasingly display attitudinal and behavioral elements that were entirely foreign to my previous personality—punitiveness, pervasive cynicism and mistrust of others, chronic irritability and free-floating hostility, racism, a diffuse personal anxiety over the menace of crime and criminals that seemed at times to border on the obsessive. A former opponent of capital punishment, I became its vociferous advocate in cases involving felony murder, kidnapping and the homicide of police officers—even though as a criminologist I continued to recognize its ineffectiveness as a deterrent to crime.

Participant observers must be aware of the threat to objective reporting that arises due to their involvement in the situation wherein they are recording behavior. This threat necessarily increases as degree of involvement increases.

Another problem with observer involvement is the effect the observer has on the behavior of those being studied. It is more than likely that the participant observer will have to interact with other people, make decisions, initiate activities, assume responsibilities, and otherwise act like everyone else in that situation. Whenever observers intervene in a natural setting, they must ask to what degree subjects and events are affected by the intervention. Is what is being observed the same as it would have been if the observer had never appeared? It is difficult to generalize results to other situations if intervention produces behavior that is specific to the conditions and events created by the observer.

In the case of participant observation, the extent of an observer's influence on the behavior under observation is not easily assessed. Several factors must be considered, such as whether participation is disguised or undisguised, the size of the group entered, and the role of the observer in the group. Griffin, for example, was not known to be a white man even by most of the blacks he associated with, and his entry into a subculture of literally thousands of disadvantaged blacks could not reasonably be expected to influence the nature of black-white interactions that he observed. Similarly, it does not appear that Rosenhan and his associates significantly affected the natural environment of the mental ward by assuming the role of mental patients. (However, some of the patients—though none of the staff—apparently detected the sanity of the pseudopatients, suggesting to the observers that they were there to check up on the hospital.)

When the group under observation is small or the activities of the participant are prominent, the observer is more likely to have a significant effect on subjects' behavior. This problem confronted several social psychologists who infiltrated a group of people who claimed to be in contact with beings from outer space (Festinger, Riecken, & Schachter, 1956). A leader of the group said he had received a message from the aliens predicting a cataclysmic flood on a specific date. The flood was to stretch from the Arctic Circle to the Gulf of Mexico. The prophecy was reported in the newspapers, and certain psychologists who read the account saw an opportunity to test a theory of group cohesion and reaction in the face of unfulfilled prophecy. (The psychologists assumed that the flood was not going to occur.) Because of the attitudes of members of the group toward "nonbelievers," the researchers were forced to make up bizarre stories in order to gain access to the group. This tactic worked too well. Not only were the disguised participant observers welcomed into the group, which never consisted of more than a dozen hard-core believers, but their stories were taken as signs from the extraterrestrial beings. One of the observers was even thought to be a spaceman bringing a message. The researchers had inadvertently reinforced the group's beliefs and influenced in an undetermined way the course of events that followed. By the way, the flood never occurred, but at least some of the group members came to use this disconfirmation as a means of strengthening their initial belief. They began to seek new members by arguing that their faith had prevented the prophesied flood.

STRUCTURED OBSERVATION

There are a variety of observational methods using intervention that are not easily categorized. Because researchers exert some control over the events, these procedures differ from naturalistic observation without intervention. However, the degree of control is often less than that seen in field experiments, which we will consider later. We have labeled these procedures **structured observation.** Often the observer intervenes in order to cause an event to occur or to "set up" a situation so that events can be more easily recorded than they would be without intervention. In other cases the observer may create quite elaborate procedures to investigate a particular behavior more fully.

Structured observations may occur in a natural setting or in a laboratory setting. Structured laboratory observations are often used by clinical psychologists when making behavioral assessments of parent-child interactions (see, for example, Hughes & Haynes, 1978). A parent and child who are seeking some sort of help come to a diagnostic clinic or laboratory and are asked to engage in specific tasks while being observed (often from behind a one-way window). Observations are made of various specific behaviors (for instance, tantrums or other emotional outbursts by the child) and of the general nature of the parent-child interactions. Partly on the basis of the results of this structured observation, the therapist plans a strategy to address the behavioral problems that exist. A group of educational psychologists observed elementary and junior high school students while they worked on class assignments in a private room containing various kinds of furniture, as well as a television set and radio (Patton, Routh, & Stinard, 1986). Results confirmed what had been reported previously for descriptions of study at home: A majority of the children preferred to study with the television set or radio turned on.

Structured observations are also frequently used by developmental psychologists. Perhaps most notable are the methods of the famous Swiss psychologist Jean Piaget. In many of Piaget's studies a child is first given a problem to solve and then given several variations on the problem to test the limits of the child's understanding. The observer acquaints the child with the nature of the problem and then usually asks questions to probe the child's reasoning processes. These structured observations have provided a wealth of information regarding children's cognition and are the basis for Piaget's "stage theory" of intellectual development. The methods have not escaped criticism, however. The fact that Piaget did not always follow exactly the same procedure from one observation to another, and the fact that his observations were frequently based on only a few (and sometimes very select) individuals, are viewed as problems with his observational techniques (see Brainerd, 1978).

In spite of these criticisms many researchers, including Piaget, see structured observation as a compromise between the passive nonintervention of naturalistic observation and the systematic manipulation of independent variables and precise control that characterize laboratory methods. Such a compromise permits observations to be made under conditions that are more natural than those imposed in a laboratory, but there may be a price to pay. The failure to follow similar procedures each time an observation is made may make it difficult for other observers to obtain the same results when investigating a problem. Uncontrolled, and perhaps unknown, variables may play an important part in producing the behavior under observation.

To reinforce this point regarding the possible influence of uncontrolled variables in structured observation, let us relate a historical anecdote about two well-known psychologists in the first half of the twentieth century (see Cohen, 1979).

In 1913, the same year he launched psychology on a new course with his remarks entitled, "Psychology as the Behaviorist Views It," John B. Watson set sail for the Tortugas islands off the coast of Florida. On a previous visit to the islands, he had begun observations of noddy and sooty terns in their natural habitat. This year Karl Lashley, who was a student of Watson's and who later did important physiological studies of brain function, went with Watson to help him make his observations and to help test the homing abilities of terns. At one point during the summer, Lashley removed thirty birds from their nests and took them with him on a boat trip to Mobile, Alabama, where he released fifteen of them. Traveling more than 100 miles farther to Galveston, Texas, Lashley set free the remaining fifteen birds. Watson waited on the island to record the arrival of the birds if, indeed, they were able to make it back as popular stories of the time suggested. Four days after Lashley released them, the birds began returning to the island. Watson and Lashley had demonstrated that terns could safely navigate across an open sea with no obvious landmarks from a distance of 1,000 miles. They were at a loss to explain how the birds managed their remarkable feat, and, as events transpired, Watson did not have the opportunity to carry out any more tests of the birds' homing abilities.

Suppose the procedure of taking the terns on board a ship caused some of the birds to become ill (something that had actually happened on a previous occasion, when the birds died in transit) and that their illness affected their homing behavior. When no birds returned to their nests after being released, the observers might have wrongly concluded that the animals had no homing instinct. This possibility does not seem that farfetched when you consider that more recent observations of bird navigation have revealed that homing pigeons make use of airborne odors to recognize the location of their lofts (see Wallraff & Sinsch, 1988). Birds who were allowed to smell only filtered air before being released did not show any tendency to return home. Although structured observations are often important for gathering information about behavior, and even for testing specific hypotheses, researchers must be aware of the limitations they impose when they allow some variables to remain uncontrolled and when procedures differ with the circumstances or the behavior of the subject under observation.

Ethologists frequently use structured observation to study the limits of an organism's response by varying systematically the characteristics of a stimulus event. For example, observations by Nobel Prize-winning ethologist Konrad Lorenz led to the discovery of imprinting (see Eibl-Eibesfeldt, 1975). Imprinting is a process by which certain animal species form an attachment to an object encountered during a critical or sensitive period in their lives. Immediately after hatching, for example, the young graylag gosling will imprint on almost any moving object in its environment and follow that object for some time afterward. Under ordinary conditions, the object of the bird's imprinting is its parent, and the innately triggered response is important for the young bird's survival. To understand the imprinting response better, ethologists have sometimes created models of both male and female parents and tested the young animal's response when the models were moving, when they made a noise, or when the imprinting response was punished (see Eibl-Eibesfeldt, 1975). Lorenz himself served as a model; many students of psychology have been introduced to ethology by scenes of the famous ethologist being energetically pursued over land and water by the young birds who attached themselves to him.

FIELD EXPERIMENTS

When an observer manipulates one or more independent variables in a natural setting in order to determine their effect on behavior, the procedure is called a **field experiment.** Although experimental methods will be discussed extensively in later chapters of this book, we mention the field experiment here because it represents one end of the nonintervention-intervention dimension that characterizes observational methods. In conducting a field experiment, the observer (now usually called the experimenter) seeks to control the antecedents of an event in order to measure systematically the effect of a variable on behavior. Control or comparison groups are used, and the experimenter usually dictates the assignment of subjects to conditions. The field experiment is probably the most frequently used field-observation technique in social psychology (Bickman, 1976). In most cases subjects are unaware that they are participating in an experiment. In a field experiment a researcher also typically makes use of **confederates.** A confederate is someone in the research situation who is instructed to behave in a certain way in order to produce an experimental situation. Confederates, for example, have been employed by social psychologists to pose as robbers when bystander reaction to a crime has been investigated (Latané & Darley, 1970) and to mimic the behavior of individuals cutting into a waiting line in order to study the reactions of those in line (Milgram, Liberty, Toledo, & Wackenhut, 1986).

Field experiments sometimes yield valuable practical knowledge. For example, research by Latané and Darley and others has helped us to understand the variables that affect a bystander's willingness to come to the aid of a victim.

Interestingly, many studies show that a bystander is more likely to aid a victim when the bystander is alone than when other bystanders are present. In a less serious, but also in a potentially practical vein, Crusco and Wetzel (1984) investigated the effect of touching on diners in a restaurant. Waitresses working as confederates touched restaurant customers on either the hand or the shoulder while returning change. The researchers speculated that a touch on the hand would produce positive affect toward the waitress whereas a touch on the shoulder, which may be seen as a sign of dominance, would not be viewed positively, especially by male diners. The subjects were 114 diners from two restaurants who were randomly assigned to three levels of the independent variable: Fleeting Touch, when the waitress twice touched the diner's palm for ½ second when returning change; Shoulder Touch, when she placed her hand for from 1 to 1½ seconds on the diner's shoulder as she gave back change; and No Touch, when no physical contact was made with the customers. The major dependent variable was the size of the gratuity. Results showed that males tipped overall more than females but that both male and female diners gave a significantly larger tip after being touched than when not touched. The results did not show, as the researchers had expected, that the nature of the touch made a difference; male and female diners were affected equally by both kinds of touches.

RECORDING BEHAVIOR

We have mentioned two important characteristics of observational methods. One is the degree of observer intervention, the other the method of recording behavior. Intervention is a dimension anchored at one end by the absence of any intervention (as is associated with passive observation in a natural setting) and at the other end by the active and systematic manipulation of antecedent events that characterizes field experiments. Observational methods also differ in the manner in which behavior is recorded, particularly the degree to which behavior is abstracted from the situation in which it is observed (see Willems, 1969, for a thorough discussion of this aspect of observational methods).

In general, methods of recording behavior can be classified as those that seek a comprehensive description of behavior and the situation in which it occurs and those that focus on only certain kinds of behavior or events. Whether *all* behavior in a given setting or only selected aspects are to be observed depends on the purposes or goals of an observational study. Decisions regarding the manner in which behavior is recorded also depend on whether the investigator is doing qualitative or quantitative research. As we saw in Chapter 1, the results of a qualitative study are presented chiefly in the form of verbal description and logical argument, whereas quantitative research emphasizes statistical description and analysis of data to support a study's conclusions. The important point for you to remember is that how the results of a study are eventually summarized, analyzed, and reported hinges on the way in which the behavior is initially recorded.

NARRATIVE RECORDS

Narrative records are intended to provide a more or less faithful reproduction of behavior as it originally occurred. Written descriptions of behavior made by an observer are one major type of narrative record. So are the spoken records produced by using a tape recorder and the visual records obtained with videotape or movie cameras. Ethologists are often interested in every detail of a behavioral event, so motion picture film turns out to be one of their most important means of recording behavior (Eibl-Eibesfeldt, 1975). To study the function of the "eyebrow flash" in social interactions, ethologists made use of 67 hours of film showing individuals in naturally occurring social situations (Grammer, Schiefenhovel, Schleidt, Lorenz, & Eibl-Eibesfeldt, 1988). Across three different cultures, the eyebrow flash, usually accompanied by a smile, was found to be a universal social signal, for example, as a sign of factual "yes."

Once narrative records are obtained, the observer can study, classify, and organize the records at leisure. Particular hypotheses or expectations about the behaviors under observation can be tested by examining the data. This constitutes an important difference between narrative records and other forms of behavior measurement wherein the classification or coding of behaviors is done at the time of observation. Thus, it is critical that narrative records capture the particular information that is critical for evaluating a study's goals or hypotheses. Henderson and Dias (1987) prepared narrative records of approximately 75 hours of infant problem-solving behavior. The goal of the study was to examine how children less than 1½ years of age adapted to situations that blocked ongoing behavior, the sort of thing that might occur, for example, when a baby swing becomes stuck or a door won't open. Observers were instructed to "make a running account of who and what the infant was attending to, the environmental conditions, and responses to stimuli" (p. 207) and to note apparent instances of blocks and responses to them. Observers were, however, told not to initiate interaction and to ignore initiation by the infant. Results showed that the infants encountered a problem on the average of once every 3 minutes and that about two-thirds of the problems were solved.

Illustrations One of the prominent psychologists who relied heavily on narrative records was Piaget. We have already mentioned how Piaget used structured observation to study the cognitive development of children. Having selected a problem to present to the child, Piaget then made a rather literal record of the child's attempts to solve the problem. The following narrative record was obtained by Piaget when investigating a 4-year-old child's understanding of quantity:

> The child is given two containers A and L of equal height, A being wide and L narrow. A is filled to a certain height (one-quarter or one-fifth) and the child is asked to pour the same quantity of liquid into L. The dimensions are such that the level will be four times as high in L as in A for the same amount of liquid. In spite of this striking difference in the proportions, the child at this stage proves incapable of grasping that the smaller diameter of L will require a higher level of liquid. Those

> children who are clearly still at this stage are satisfied that there is "the same amount to drink" in L when they have filled it to the same level as A.
>
> Blas (4.0): "Look, your mummy has poured out a glass of lemonade for herself (A) and she gives you this glass (L). We want you to pour into your glass as much lemonade as your mummy has in hers.—(She poured rather quickly and exceeded the level equal to that in A that she was trying to achieve.)—Will you both have the same like that?—*No.*—Who will have more?—*Me.*—Show me where you must pour to so that you both have the same.—(She poured up to the same level.)—Will you and mummy have the same amount to drink like that?—*Yes.*—Are you sure?—*Yes.*" (Piaget, J. [1965]. *The child's conception of number* [pp. 11–12]. New York: Norton. First published in French in 1941 under the title *Le Genèse du nombre chez l'enfant.*)

The narrative begins with the observer's comments to the child, Blas. The observer says, "Look, your mummy has poured out a glass of lemonade. . . ." After that follows an exact reproduction of what the observer said, what the child said, and what happened in this situation. The narrative contains little observer inference and the exact sequence of behaviors is recorded. His many observations of children's behavior led Piaget to a number of important conclusions about human cognitive development. As you can see, Piaget used the narrative record to illustrate that the 4-year-old has not yet mastered the principle of "conservation of volume." The two containers, which were of equal height but different width, were perceived by the child to hold the same amount of liquid when the level of the liquid was the same.

Hartup (1974) obtained narrative records as part of his naturalistic study of children's aggression. He investigated a number of different aspects of children's aggression, including the relationship between particular kinds of antecedent events and the nature of the aggressive episodes that followed. Here is a sample narrative record from Hartup's study (p. 339):

> Marian [a seven-year-old] . . . is complaining to all that David [who is also present] had squirted her on the pants she has to wear tonight. She says, "I'm gonna do it to him to see how he likes it." She fills a can with water and David runs to the teacher and tells of her threat. The teacher takes the can from Marian. Marian attacks David and pulls his hair very hard. He cries and swings at Marian as the teacher tries to restrain him; then she takes him upstairs. . . . Later, Marian and Elaine go upstairs and into the room where David is seated with a teacher. He throws a book at Marian. The teacher asks Marian to leave. Marian kicks David, then leaves. David cries and screams, "Get out of here, they're just gonna tease me."

Hartup (1974) instructed his observers to avoid making inferences about the intentions, motives, or feelings of the subjects and to use precise language in describing behavior. We are not told why David might want to throw a book at Marian or how Marian feels about being attacked. Hartup believed that certain antecedent behaviors were related to specific types of aggression. Because any inferences or impressions of the observers were strictly excluded, the content of the narrative records could be classified and coded in an objective manner. Individuals doing the coding would not be influenced by what the observer inferred was going on.

The narrative records obtained by Piaget and by Hartup are similar in that both are rather literal descriptions of behavior in a particular context. Observer inference is minimal, and nearly everything that occurs in a relatively brief period of time is recorded. As many details of the setting, context, and characteristics of the subjects are recorded as is necessary to give a meaningful description of what happened. The narratives focus on particular aspects of children's behavior. Piaget studied the problem-solving abilities of children, whereas Hartup focused on children's aggression.

An example of a narrative record that does not focus on particular behaviors, and one that does include inferences and impressions of the observer, is provided by a study of "a day in the life" of a midwestern schoolgirl (Barker, Wright, Schoggen, & Barker, 1978, pp. 56–58). Eight different observers took turns observing an 8-year-old girl from the time she awoke in the morning until she went to sleep at night. In reproducing her day, the researchers wanted to include information about the motives, feelings, and perceptions that were part of her daily activities. This required that the observers make a number of inferences. Generally, only the inferences that two or more of the observers agreed on were included. For example, people can often agree as to when someone is sad or happy or excited or calm. By recording their impressions of the girl's feelings and moods, the observers hoped to provide a record that was true to real life and might yield important information to those who seek to understand the more subjective aspects of human behavior. Personality and social psychologists might be able to learn from this record about the kinds of frustrations, anxieties, and other feelings an 8-year-old experiences in the course of her normal activities during one day in a small midwestern town. A comprehensive description of individuals in everyday contexts is an important goal of **ecological psychology.** The narrative record of this little girl's day was made on May 12, 1949. The complete record was about 100,000 words in length and was later determined to contain 969 different behavior episodes.

Although the narrative records we have discussed so far have differed in their focus as well as in the degree of observer inference allowed, each has been a rather complete description of behavior in a particular setting or context. Not all narrative records are as detailed as those we have examined. Often the narrative records of an observer are merely running descriptions of the participants, events, settings, and behaviors. These records are generally called **field notes.** Field notes are nothing more than the verbal records of a trained observer. Used by journalists, social workers, anthropologists, ethologists, and others, they do not always contain an exact record of everything that occurred. Events and behaviors that especially interest the observer are recorded and are likely to be interpreted in terms of the observer's specialized knowledge or field of expertise. In making notes about a particular patient, a psychiatrist might compare the client's symptoms with those of other patients or with a textbook definition. An ethologist might record how the behavior of one species appears to parallel that of another.

Field notes tend to be highly personalized (Brandt, 1972), but they are probably used more frequently than is any other kind of narrative record. Field notes have generated numerous revelations about behavior; they are the basis of Darwin's theory of evolution as well as Rosenhan's description of being sane in insane places. Their usefulness as scientific records depends on the accuracy and precision of their content. These in turn are related to the training of the observer and the extent to which the observations that are recorded can be verified by independent observers and through other means of investigation.

Considerations Practical, as well as methodological, considerations dictate the manner in which narrative records are made. As a general rule, records should be made as soon as possible after behavior is observed. The passage of time blurs details and makes it harder to reproduce the original sequence of actions. Adjang (1986) used a portable cassette recorder to make narrative records of his spoken observations of the teasing behavior of young chimpanzees; however, he then transcribed these spoken reports onto paper "as soon as possible" (p. 139). This rule is sometimes not easy to follow when observations are made in natural settings. An ethologist who is trying to record the behavior of animals in the wild is sometimes hampered by bad weather, animal migration, dwindling daylight, and so forth. Notes may have to be made quickly—even while the observer is quite literally on the run. At other times observers may have to wait until they return to camp to make written records of behavior. When Festinger et al. (1956) infiltrated the group of people waiting for spacemen to rescue them from a cataclysmic flood, the participant observers sometimes found it difficult to take notes without being seen by members of the group. Excuses had to be made to leave the group (to go to the bathroom, for example) in order to make written records of the group's activities.

Decisions regarding the content of a narrative record must be made prior to observing behavior. We have seen that verbal narratives may differ according to the degree of observer inference or how literal the record of behavior is. Table 3.1 contains suggestions for improving the quality of narrative records (see also Brandt, 1972). Once the content of narrative records is decided, observers must be trained to record behavior according to the criteria that have been set up. Practice observations may have to be conducted and records critiqued by more than one investigator before "real" data are collected.

OBTAINING QUANTITATIVE MEASURES OF BEHAVIOR

When only certain behaviors or specific aspects of individuals and settings are of interest, the behaviors typically are defined prior to beginning an observational study. Decisions are also made as to exactly how characteristics of their occurrence should be measured, that is, how the behavior can be *quantified*. For example, assume that you wish to observe reactions to individuals with obvious physical disabilities by those who do not have such disabilities. Unfortunately, research indicates that these reactions frequently can be classified as unfavorable (see, for example, Thompson, 1982). In order to conduct your study, it

TABLE 3.1 SUGGESTIONS FOR IMPROVING THE QUALITY OF NARRATIVE RECORDS*

1 Record what you observe as soon as possible after you observe it.
2 Decide whether observer inferences and interpretations of behavior are to be included. If they are, only those inferences should be included on which two independent observers could reasonably be expected to agree.
3 When a particular behavior or event is the focus of the observation, provide observers with a precise operational definition of what is to be observed.
4 Judge how literal and complete a record is needed. Exact reproductions of behavior sequences are difficult to record accurately, so you must decide what is and what is not to be recorded. Generally speaking, exact reproductions are possible only when the observation interval is relatively short. Always record enough details of the setting or context to indicate the "who, what, and where" of the behavior episode.
5 Decide on the key subjects or the major events and focus on them. The responses or reactions of minor subjects should be included only to the extent that they complement the activities of the main participants.
6 When observing particular sequences of behaviors or when focusing on specific behavior episodes (such as aggression or helping), decide what events mark the beginning of the episode and what events mark the end. Significant variations in observer reports can be expected unless all observers begin and end their observations at the same points.
7 Use language that is precise and unambiguous.
8 When conversations are to be recorded, decide whether direct quotations are necessary or summaries of what is said are sufficient. Be sure to distinguish (for example, by quotation marks) what is a direct quote from what is an indirect quote.
9 When possible use a tape recorder to record initial descriptions of behavior. Recorded material can be transcribed to written form later, and additional details (such as information about the context or setting) can be added.
10 In planning the content of the narrative, keep in mind how it will be analyzed. For example, if narratives are to be coded according to whether certain expressions are used in conversation, then direct quotes of what was said should be recorded.

* Based to a large extent on recommendations made by Brandt (1972).

would be necessary to define what constitutes a "reaction" to a physically disabled individual. Are you interested, for example, in helping behaviors, approach/avoidance behaviors, eye contact, length of conversation, or in some other behavioral reaction? As you consider what behaviors you will use to define people's "reactions," you will also have to decide how you will measure these behaviors. Assume, for instance, that you are planning a study using naturalistic observation and that you have chosen to measure people's reactions by observing eye contact between individuals who do not have obvious physical disabilities and those who do. Exactly how should you measure eye contact? Should you simply measure whether a passerby does or does not make eye contact, or do you want to measure the *duration* of any eye contact? The decisions you make will depend on the particular hypotheses or goals of your study, but they will also be influenced by information gained by examining previous studies that have used the same or similar behavioral measures. Of course, you may wish to make multiple measures, a research strategy that is recommended whenever it is feasible.

Defining a behavioral measure involves deciding what scale of measurement to use. Thus, it is important for you to be familiar with the types of measurement scales used in behavioral research.

Measurement Scales There are four levels of measurement, or **measurement scales,** that apply to both physical and psychological measurement. The lowest level, or scale, is called a *nominal scale;* it involves simply categorizing the stimulus to be measured into one of a number of discrete categories. For instance, we could measure the color of people's eyes by categorizing them as "brown-eyed" or "blue-eyed." When studying people's reactions to individuals with obvious physical disabilities, a researcher might use a nominal scale by measuring whether persons make eye contact or do not make eye contact with someone who has an obvious physical disability. This type of category system is called a **checklist.** A checklist is used to record the presence or absence of something in the situation under observation (Brandt, 1972). A further distinction can be made between *static* and *action* checklists. A static checklist contains descriptions of relatively permanent aspects of subjects or settings. Age, race, and sex are examples of subject characteristics that are often noted. Features of the setting—such as time of day, location, and whether other people are present—also may be part of a static checklist. An action checklist is used to record the presence or absence of specific behaviors. A classroom observer may note whether children are talking or are quiet. An environmental psychologist may be interested in whether people use seat belts or do not use seat belts or in whether people dispose of litter or do not dispose of litter.

As you might expect, static and action checklists are often combined. Specific characteristics of subjects as well as their behavior are likely to be of interest. For example, it is often informative to observe behavior as a function of certain static characteristics. Do males use seat belts more than females? Are people who drive inexpensive automobiles more likely to share a ride than people who drive expensive automobiles? These questions can be answered by observing the presence or absence of certain behaviors (seat-belt use or car pooling) for different categories of subjects and events (male and female, expensive and inexpensive automobiles).

Jenni (1976; also Jenni & Jenni, 1976) used a checklist to study the book-carrying behavior of male and female college students. Three types of book-carrying behaviors were defined: two major types and an "other" category. Figure 3.1 illustrates the two major types of carrying behavior. Students using Type I wrap one or both arms around the books, with the short edges of the books resting on the hip or in front of the body. Students using Type II support the books by one arm and hand at the side of the body, with the long edges of the books approximately horizontal to the ground. The "other" category included a variety of book-carrying methods that did not fit either Type I or Type II. For example, students occasionally hold books by the edges with both hands in front of the body (for instance, when reading while walking).

Observations of 2,626 individuals were made on six college campuses (three

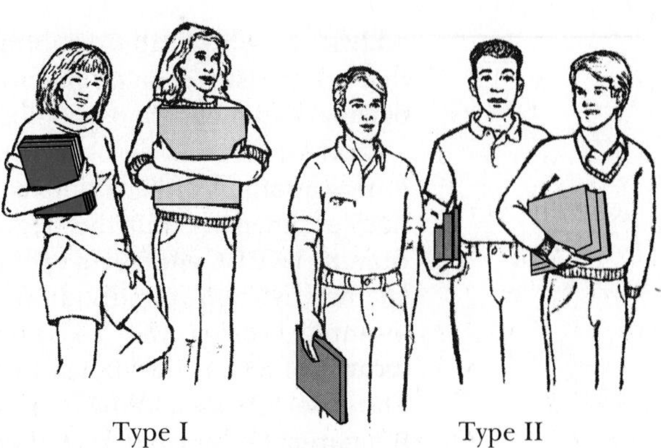

FIGURE 3.1 Two methods that students were observed to use to carry books. In the Type I method, the short edges of the book rest on the hip or in front of the body. In the Type II method, the books are either pinched from above or supported from below by the hand or by both the hand and the arm (from Jenni & Jenni, 1976).

in the United States, one in Canada, and two in Central America). Individuals were observed as they passed a certain point on campus. Type of carrying behavior and sex of the subject were noted. In terms of the arithmetic operations that we can perform on data recorded on a nominal scale, we can use only the relationships "equal" and "not equal." A common way of summarizing nominal data is to report the frequency or proportion of instances in each of the several categories. Across the six college campuses, 82 percent of the females were observed to use the Type I method, whereas only 3 percent of the males used this method. On the other hand, the observers found that 96 percent of the males used the Type II carrying method compared with 16 percent of the females. The "other" methods were used 2 percent of the time or less by both male and female students. It appears that book-carrying behavior among college students is almost totally sex-specific.

The second level, or scale, called an *ordinal scale,* involves ordering or ranking stimuli to be measured. Ordinal scales add the arithmetic relationships "greater than" and "less than" to the measurement process. One common example of an ordinal scale is class rank. We can order students in a class from highest to lowest, but if we know only their ranks we have no information about how far apart the students are in academic performance. When we know that an Olympic distance runner won a silver medal, we do not know whether she finished second in a photo finish or trailed 200 meters behind the gold-medal winner.

The third level, or scale, called an *interval scale,* involves specifying how far apart two stimuli are on a given dimension. On an ordinal scale, the difference between the stimulus ranked first and the stimulus ranked third does not necessarily equal the distance between the stimuli ranked third and fifth. On an interval scale, however, differences of the same numerical size in scale values *are* equal. For example, the difference between fifty and seventy correct answers on an aptitude test is equal to the difference between seventy and ninety correct answers, and thus the ratio of scale intervals is meaningful. What is missing from an interval scale is a meaningful zero point. For instance, if your score were zero on a verbal aptitude test, you would not necessarily have absolutely zero verbal ability. On the other hand, the standard arithmetic operations of addition, multiplication, subtraction, and division can be performed on data that are measured on an interval scale. Whenever possible, therefore, psychologists try to measure psychological dimensions using interval scales.

In the context of an observational study, observers are sometimes called on to make ratings of behaviors and events. This usually involves making subjective judgments about the degree or quantity of some trait or condition (see Brandt, 1972). Generally a rating system requires an observer to evaluate some characteristic of an individual or situation on a psychological dimension. For example, Dickie (1987) asked observers to rate parent-infant interactions in the context of a study designed to assess the effects of a parent training program. The observers visited the home and rated both the mother and the father while the parents interacted with their infant child. During most of the observation period, the observers sat in the room with the infant and asked the parents to "act as normal as possible—just as if we [the observers] weren't here." Structured observations involving assigned play with each parent were also used. Parent-infant interactions were rated on thirteen different dimensions, including degree of verbal, physical, and emotional interaction. For each dimension a continuum was defined that represented different degrees of this variable. A 7-point scale was used, whereon 1 represented the absence or very little of the characteristic and larger numbers represented increasingly more of the trait. Table 3.2 outlines one of the dimensions used by the observers in this study: warmth and affection directed toward the child. Note that precise verbal descriptions are given with the four odd-numbered scale values to help observers define different degrees of this trait. The even-numbered values are used by observers to rate events that they judge fall between the more clearly defined values. The investigators found that parents who had taken part in a program aimed at developing competency in dealing with an infant were rated higher than were untrained parents on many of the variables.

At first glance, a rating scale such as that used by Dickie would appear to represent an interval scale of measurement. There is no true zero, and the intervals seem to be equal. And, in fact, many researchers treat such rating systems *as if* they represented interval scales of measurement. Closer examination, however, reveals that most of the rating scales used by observers to evaluate people or events on a psychological dimension really yield only ordinal information. For a rating system to be truly an interval level of measurement, a rating of 2, for instance, would have to be the same distance from a rating of 3 as a rating of 4 is from 5 or a rating of 6 is from 7. It is highly unlikely that human observers can make subjective judgments of traits such as warmth, pleasure, aggressiveness, anxiety, and so forth in a manner that yields precise interval distances between ratings. Classification of measures according to level of measurement is not always easy, and advice should be sought from knowledgeable experts when in doubt. In this way you will be prepared to make the correct choices regarding the statistical description and analysis of your data.

TABLE 3.2 EXAMPLE OF RATING SCALE USED TO MEASURE A PARENT'S WARMTH AND AFFECTION TOWARD AN INFANT CHILD*

Scale value	Description
1	There is an absence of warmth, affection, and pleasure. Excessive hostility, coldness, distance, and isolation from the child are predominant. Relationship is on an attacking level.
2	
3	There is occasional warmth and pleasure in interaction. Parent shows little evidence of pride in the child, or pride is shown in relation to deviant or bizarre behavior by the child. Parent's manner of relating is contrived, intellectual, not genuine.
4	
5	There is moderate pleasure and warmth in the interaction. Parent shows pleasure in some areas but not in others.
6	
7	Warmth and pleasure are characteristic of the interaction with the child. There is evidence of pleasure and pride in the child. Pleasure response is appropriate to the child's behavior.

* From materials provided by Jane Dickie.

The fourth level of measurement is a *ratio scale.* A ratio scale has all the properties of an interval scale with the important additional quality of an absolute zero point. In terms of arithmetic operations, a zero point makes the ratio of scale values meaningful. For example, temperature as expressed on the Celsius scale represents an interval scale of measurement. A reading of 0 degrees Celsius does not really mean absolutely no temperature. Therefore it is not meaningful to say that 100 degrees Celsius is twice as hot as 50 degrees, or that 60 degrees is three times as warm as 20 degrees. On the other hand, the Kelvin scale of temperature does have an absolute zero, and the ratio of scale values can be meaningfully calculated. Physical scales measuring time, weight, and distance can usually be treated as ratio scales.

LaFrance and Mayo (1976) investigated racial differences in amount of eye contact between individuals of the same race engaged in conversation. Pairs of black individuals and pairs of white individuals were observed in natural settings. The amount of time each member of the pair spent looking into the face of the other member was recorded. *Duration* of eye contact represents a ratio level of measurement. The researchers found that blacks gazed less at another person while listening to conversation than did whites. LaFrance and Mayo suggest that subtle differences in eye contact may be a source of social misunderstandings. White speakers may feel that lack of eye contact by a black listener indicates untrustworthiness or lack of interest when it may merely be a manifestation of a cultural difference between the races.

Another important measure of behavior is *frequency* of occurrence. For example, in observing book-carrying behavior, Jenni (1976) made only one observation of each individual. As was noted, this represents a nominal level of measurement: Behaviors were recorded as falling in one of several mutually exclusive categories. Frequency of book-carrying behavior, therefore, was described in terms of the number (or percentage) of *different* individuals who used one method or another. Checklists also can be used to obtain information about the frequency of particular behaviors in the *same* individual or group of individuals. In this case, repeated observations of the same individual or group are made over a period of time. The presence or absence of specific behaviors is noted at the time of each observation. For instance, the Schedule for Classroom Activity Norms (SCAN) is a checklist that divides classroom behavior into twenty-seven discrete categories (McKinney, Mason, Perkerson, & Clifford, 1975). At repeated intervals of time, an observer records what each child in the classroom is doing. Many observations of the same child show which categories of behavior are most frequent for that child. In one study using the SCAN checklist, researchers looked for relationships between the frequency of certain classroom behaviors and performance on standard tests of academic achievement. Combining information obtained from observing the children's behavior with information obtained from IQ tests yielded a more accurate prediction of school achievement than could be obtained by using either observation or IQ information alone.

Frequency of responding usually can be assumed to represent a ratio level of measurement. If "units" of something (e.g., occasions when a child leaves classroom seat) are being counted, then zero represents an absence of units. Ratios of scale values would be meaningful as long as, for instance, an individual with 20 units had twice as many units as someone with 10.

Table 3.3 summarizes the characteristics of levels of measurement that we have discussed. You will need to keep these four types of scales in mind as you select statistical procedures for analyzing the results of the research you will be doing (see Appendix A).

Computer-Assisted Recording Recording behavior as part of an observational study has been aided by the development of hand-held microcomputers

TABLE 3.3 CHARACTERISTICS OF MEASUREMENT SCALES

Type of scale	Operations	Objective
Nominal	Equal/not equal	Sort stimuli into discrete categories
Ordinal	Greater than/less than	Rank-order stimuli on a single dimension
Interval	Addition/multiplication/subtraction/division	Specify the distance between stimuli in a given dimension
Ratio	Addition/multiplication/subtraction/division/formation of ratios of values	Specify the distance between stimuli in a given dimension and express ratios of scale values

which permit an observer to record complex information rapidly. In an observational study of family interactions of depressed women, the observers used microcomputers to record both static and active categories of relevant behavior (see Hops et al., 1987). Family members were given codes, as were various behaviors and characteristics of the family interaction, and these were recorded using hand-held high-technology devices. Kirmeyer and Biggers (1988) used a similar electronic recording device to record the duration and characteristics of activities of seventy-two police radio dispatchers as part of an observational study investigating Type A behavior (that is, "behavior characterized by ambitiousness, hostility, impatience, and competitiveness," p. 997). As in the previously mentioned study, codes were developed for both static and active aspects of behavior and observers were rehearsed prior to actual data collection in the use of the microcomputer recording system. Type A individuals were observed to place demands on themselves by initiating work tasks and by attending to multiple tasks.

SAMPLING TECHNIQUES

Before conducting an observational study, a researcher must make a number of important decisions abut the times when observations will be made and the conditions under which they will be made. In some cases, it might be possible to observe *all* the behavior of interest—for instance, the behavior patterns of certain short-lived organisms. In the vast majority of observational studies, however, the investigator must be satisfied with something considerably less than a complete record of behavior. Only certain behaviors occurring at particular times and in specific settings can generally be observed. In other words, behavior and settings must be sampled. The nature of these samples determines the extent to which generalizations are possible. Observations made of classroom behavior at the beginning of a school year, for instance, may not yield results that are typical of behavior seen at the end of the school year. Nor, for that matter, do observations made in the morning necessarily reveal the same pattern of classroom behavior as observations made in the afternoon. The frequency and type of aggression observed in children living in lower socioeconomic areas may not be representative of the aggression found in children from upper socioeconomic neighborhoods. As we saw in Chapter 1, our ability to generalize research findings depends upon the study's external validity. Results can reasonably be generalized only to subjects, conditions, and situations similar to those in the study in which the results were actually observed. Behavior sampling (including both time and event sampling) and situation sampling are techniques used to lend external validity to observational findings.

BEHAVIOR SAMPLING

Behavior sampling is generally accomplished by either time sampling or event sampling. Hartup (1974) used a combination of time and event sampling when studying children's aggression. In **time sampling,** the intervals at which observations are made are chosen either systematically or randomly with the goal of obtaining a representative sample of behavior. As examples, we might consider the application of these techniques in the context of observing a child's classroom behavior.

Suppose that observations are to be made for a total of 2 hours each day. As we indicated, restricting observations to certain times of the day (say, mornings only) would not necessarily permit us to generalize our findings to the rest of the school day. One approach to obtaining a representative sample is to schedule observation periods *systematically* throughout the school day. Observations might be made during four 30-minute periods beginning every 2 hours. The first observation period could begin at 9 A.M., the second at 11 A.M., and so forth. Another possibility would be to schedule 10-minute observation periods every half hour during the school day. A *random* time-sampling technique could be used in the same situation by distributing four 30-minute periods (or twelve 10-minute periods) randomly over the course of the day. A different random schedule would be determined each day on which observations are made. Times would vary from day to day but, over the long run, behavior would be sampled equally from all times of the school day.

Systematic and random time-sampling procedures are often combined, as when observation intervals are scheduled systematically but observations within an interval are made at random times. For example, having scheduled four 30-minute observation periods at the same time each day, an observer might then decide to observe only during 20-second intervals that are randomly distributed within each half-hour period. Or observation periods might be scheduled randomly during certain weeks of the school year but the weeks selected systematically from the early, middle, and late parts of the year. Whatever method is used, the observer must carefully scrutinize the schedule, noting both its limitations and its advantages in terms of yielding a representative record of behavior. Sampling plays a central role in conducting surveys. Many issues related to the topic of sampling will be discussed in Chapter 4 when survey methods are introduced.

Event sampling may be a more efficient method of sampling behavior than time sampling when the event of interest occurs infrequently. In this case researchers want to maximize their opportunities to observe an event in order to get enough information about its occurrence to make investigating it worthwhile. Not only may time sampling cause precious instances of an event to be missed, but if the event is of significant duration, time sampling may not permit an observer to be present at the beginning of an event or to witness an event in its entirety. In event sampling the observer records each event that meets a predetermined definition. Researchers interested in children's reactions to special events in school, such as a Christmas play, would want to use event sampling. The special event defines when the observations are to be made. Researchers would certainly *not* want to use time sampling in this situation in the hope that a special event might occur during one of their randomly selected observation periods.

In many situations in which event sampling is used, a formally scheduled event like a school play is not the event of interest. Instead, researchers are often interested in events that occur unpredictably. Researchers interested in victims' reactions to violent crimes are dependent on event sampling in selecting the occasions for making their observations. Whenever possible, observers try to be present in those situations and at those times when an event of interest has occurred or is likely to occur. Thus, in an ethological study of children's "rough-and-tumble" play, an observer positioned herself in the corner of a playground to observe members of a nursery school class (Smith & Lewis, 1985). Event sampling was the method of choice due to the relatively low frequency of this behavior. However, this manner of observing behavior can easily introduce biases into the behavioral record—as when, for instance, an observer samples at the times that are most "convenient" or only when an event is certain to occur. Characterization of events at these times may not be the same as at other times. In most situations, only through some form of time sampling is an observer likely to guarantee a representative sample of behavior.

SITUATION SAMPLING

The external validity of observational findings can be significantly increased through **situation sampling.** Whenever possible—and when it is in keeping with the goals of a study—behavior should be observed under many different circumstances, locations, and conditions. By sampling different situations researchers reduce the chance that their results will be peculiar to a certain set of circumstances or conditions. It is clear that behavior often changes as a function of the context in which it is observed. Animals do not behave the same way in zoos as they do in the wild. Children do not always behave the same way with one parent as they do with the other parent. By sampling different situations, a researcher can also increase the diversity of the subject sample and hence achieve greater generality than could be claimed if only particular types of individuals were observed. As part of a naturalistic observation of beer drinking among college students, investigators purposely sampled behavior in various settings where beer was served, including five town bars, a student center, and a fraternity party (see Geller, Russ, & Altomari, 1986). When LaFrance and Mayo (1976) investigated racial differences in eye contact, they sampled many different situations. Pairs of individuals were observed in college cafeterias, business-district fast-food outlets, hospital and airport waiting rooms, and restaurants. By using situation sampling the investigators were able to include in their sample subjects who differed in age, socioeconomic class, sex, and race. Their observations of an apparent cultural difference in eye-contact behavior have considerably greater external validity than if only certain types of subjects, or behavior in only a specific situation, had been studied.

ANALYSIS OF OBSERVATIONAL DATA

DATA REDUCTION

Analysis of Narrative Records Once they have been collected, narrative records can provide a wealth of information about behavior in natural settings. However, for meaningful information to emerge, data relevant to the goals of an observational study must be abstracted from the lengthy behavioral descriptions included in most narrative records. Results must be organized, and statements summarizing important findings must be prepared. This process of abstracting and summarizing in the analysis of behavioral data is called **data reduction.**

The first step in quantitative analysis of the content of narrative records often consists of identifying units of behavior, or particular events. This stage of data reduction involves **coding** behavioral records according to specific criteria. For instance, we previously noted that a narrative record describing a day in the life of a schoolgirl was found to contain 969 different behavior episodes (Barker et al., 1978, pp. 56–58). Hartup's (1974) 10-week observation of children's aggression yielded information about 758 units of aggression. As part of an ethological study of preschool children, McGrew (1972) identified 115 different behavior patterns. He classified patterns of behavior according to the body part involved, ranging from facial expressions such as bared teeth, grin face, and pucker face, to locomotion behaviors such as gallop, crawl, run, skip, and step. Coders classified these behavioral patterns while watching videotape records showing interactions of children attending nursery school.

Relevant units of behavior or events are often classified in terms of their apparent function or their particular antecedents. For instance, Hartup used nine categories to classify the nature of aggressive episodes. Antecedents of aggression were described using eighteen different categories. Relationships between antecedent events and types of aggression were then summarized, and comparisons were made between different age groups. When derogation ("put-down") elicited aggression, more younger children than older children retaliated via some form of physical aggression (such as hitting). McGrew (1972) found that children exhibit a "pout face" after losing a fight over a toy. This ethologist-observer noted that young chimpanzees show a similar expression when seeking reunion with their mother. A "pucker face" was observed in children particularly after being frustrated (and often just prior to weeping). Interestingly, there seems to be no record of a pucker face in nonhuman primates.

Descriptive Measures When events are classified into mutually exclusive categories, the most common descriptive measure is one of relative frequency. The proportion or percentage of times that various behaviors occur is expressed in terms of the total frequency of events observed. We have already seen several examples of this type of descriptive measure. Jenni (1976), for instance, reported the percentage of times that male and female students were observed to use three different book-carrying methods. Barash (1977) summarized his observations of pedestrian behavior in terms of the percentage of people in various social groupings who looked both ways.

When behavior is recorded on at least an interval scale of measurement, as when measures of time (duration, latency) are used and frequently when ratings are made, one or more measures of central tendency are generally reported. The most common measure is the *arithmetic mean,* or *average.* The mean describes the "typical" score in a group of scores and is an important summary measure of group performance. Measures of variability or dispersion of scores around the mean are necesary to describe group performance completely. The *standard deviation* approximates the average distance of a score from the mean. (Computational procedures for measures of central tendency and variability, as well as confidence intervals for the mean, are found in Appendix A.)

The mean and standard deviation as descriptive measures are illustrated in the results of the study by LaFrance and Mayo (1976). You may remember that these investigators observed other-directed looking behavior in pairs of black and white conversants. The number of seconds that each listener in a pair spent looking into the speaker's face was recorded. Table 3.4 gives the means and standard deviations that summarize the results of this study. As we noted previously, white listeners spent more time looking into the faces of white speakers than black listeners spent looking into the faces of black speakers. This was found for same-sex pairs as well as mixed-sex pairs.

OBSERVER RELIABILITY

In assessing the results of an observational study, we need to inquire about reliability of an observer. Would another observer viewing the same events obtain the same results?

TABLE 3.4 MEANS AND STANDARD DEVIATIONS DESCRIBING THE TIME (IN SECONDS) THAT LISTENERS SPENT LOOKING INTO THE FACE OF A SPEAKER PER 1-MINUTE OBSERVATION UNIT*

Group	Mean	Standard deviation
Black conversants		
Male pairs	19.3	6.9
Female pairs	28.4	10.2
Male-female pairs	24.9	11.6
White conversants		
Male pairs	35.8	8.6
Female pairs	39.9	10.7
Male-female pairs	29.9	11.2

* From LaFrance and Mayo (1976).

Interobserver Reliability The degree to which two independent observers are in agreement is referred to as **interobserver reliability.** Lack of agreement from one observer to another prevents us from generalizing research results. Low interobserver reliability can be due to characteristics of the observers or to the procedures and methods of observing. In the context of a behavioral study, differences between observers in terms of experience, attitude, fatigue, boredom, and outcome expectancies are possible reasons for low interobserver reliability. Observer reliability is generally increased by training observers and giving them specific feedback regarding any discrepancies between their observations and those of other observers (Judd, Smith, & Kidder, 1991).

Low interobserver reliability may also result when the event to be recorded is not clearly defined. Imagine Hartup (1974) asking his observers to record aggressive episodes among children without giving them an exact definition of *aggression.* What exactly is aggression? Some observers might decide to define aggression as one child's physical attack on another; other observers might include verbal assaults in their definition of aggression. What is a playful push and what is an angry shove? Without a clear definition of behavior or of the events to be recorded, observers do not always agree—and hence show low interobserver reliability. In addition to providing precise verbal definitions, giving concrete examples of a phenomenon generally helps increase reliability among observers. Showing observers the pictures of book-carrying methods in Figure 3.1, for example, could be assumed to improve their ability to classify behavior according to this characteristic.

High observer reliability is not necessarily sufficient evidence that observations are accurate. We can imagine two observers of behavior who are both "in error" to the same degree. For instance, both might be influenced in a similar way by what they expect the outcome of the observational study to be. It is conceivable that the two observers would agree about what they saw but neither observer would provide a valid record of behavior. Instances are occasionally reported in the media of several observers claiming to see the same thing (for instance, an unidentified flying object [UFO]), only to have the event or object turn out to be something other than what observers claimed it to be (for instance, a weather balloon). Nevertheless, when two independent observers agree, we are generally more inclined to believe that their observations are valid than we are when data are based on the observations of a single observer. The chance of both observers' being influenced to the same degree by outcome expectancies, fatigue, or boredom is generally so small that we can feel confident that what was reported actually occurred. Of course, the more independent observers who agree, the more confident we become.

Measures of Reliability How observer reliability is measured depends on the way in which behavior is measured. When events are classified according to mutually exclusive categories, such as when individuals are classified in terms of whether they show a certain behavior, observer reliability is generally assessed via a percentage agreement measure.

A formula for calculating percentage agreement between observers is:

$$\frac{\text{Number of times two observers agree}}{\text{Number of opportunities to agree}} \times 100$$

Barash (1977) reported that observers were 100 percent reliable when classifying pedestrians as to the type of social group that was present (adult male and female, female with children, and so on) and in agreement 97 percent of the time when deciding whether pedestrians scanned both directions before crossing the street. Hartup (1974) reported measures of reliability that ranged from 83 to 94 percent for judges who coded narrative records according to type of aggression and nature of antecedent events. Although there is no hard-and-fast percentage of agreement that defines low interobserver reliability, a perusal of the literature reveals that researchers generally report estimates of reliability that exceed 85 percent, suggesting that agreement much lower than that is unacceptable.

Because in many observational studies most of the data are collected by one observer, or by several observers who collect data at different times, measures of reliability are often based only on a sample of observations for any one observer. Two observers might be asked to record the same behavior according to some time-sampling procedure. Amount of agreement for these times can be used to indicate the degree of reliability for the study as a whole. For example, when studying beer drinking among college students, investigators reported the percent agreement for two independent observers who were present at slightly fewer than half of the 243 total observation periods; during the remaining periods only one observer was present (Geller et al., 1986). Observer reliability for home observations of family interactions involving depressed women was based on 86 (17 percent) of the 520 sessions (see Hops et al., 1987).

When observational data are of at least an interval nature, as is often assumed when ratings are made or when some variable such as time is measured, observer reliability can be measured using what is called the Pearson Product–Moment Correlation Coefficient *r*. (The formula for the Pearson *r* is found in Appendix A.) LaFrance and Mayo (1976) obtained measures of reliability when observers recorded how much of the time a listener gazed into the speaker's face during a conversation. The average correlation for observer reliability between pairs of observers was .92 in their study.

PROBLEMS IN THE CONDUCT OF OBSERVATIONAL RESEARCH

INFLUENCE OF THE OBSERVER

Reactivity The influence that an observer has on the behavior under observation is referred to as **reactivity.** Generally, we can think of reactive research situations as situations in which subjects "react" to the presence of an observer. Behavior in these situations may not be representative of behavior when an observer is not present. Underwood and Shaughnessy (1975) relate how a student, as part of a class assignment, set out to observe whether drivers came to a complete stop at an intersection with a stop sign. The student had hypothesized that drivers of high-priced cars would be less likely than drivers of low-priced cars to stop at the sign. The observer located himself on the street corner with clipbord in hand. However, he soon observed that *all* cars were stopping at the stop sign. He then realized that his presence was influencing the driver's behavior. When he concealed himself near the intersection, he found that drivers' behavior changed and he was able to gather data regarding his hypothesis.

Although human subjects may not exhibit innate reactions to an observer, as is the case with certain animals (for example, see Moore & Stuttard, 1979), they can respond in very subtle ways when they are aware that their behavior is being observed. For instance, subjects are sometimes apprehensive and more than a little anxious about participating in psychological research. Measures of arousal, such as heart rate and galvanic skin response (GSR), may show changes simply as a function of an observer's being present.

Social psychologists have long been aware that behavior is affected by the presence of another person. Research has shown that performance on simple tasks can be facilitated by the presence of another person, a so-called facilitation effect, whereas performance on more complex tasks is often inhibited, a so-called social-impairment effect (see, for example, Bond & Titus, 1983). As you might suspect, whether social-facilitation and impairment effects are found depends not only on the complexity of the task but on who is present. For example, if the other person present is someone whose job it is to evaluate performance, as would be the case if an experimenter or observer were present, then effects due to another's presence are rather robust (see Guerin, 1986). In this case, social facilitation is usually attributed to increased arousal brought about by anticipation of being evaluated or to an increased desire on the part of the subject to gain approval and do what is socially acceptable. Social impairment would be produced if increased arousal interfered with performance, as sometimes happens when an individual facing tough competition "chokes," or if the presence of an observer distracts a subject and brings about poorer performance than that found when the subject is alone. Although of interest as social psychological phenomena, these effects, of course, also help to define reactivity in a research situation and must be guarded against by the researcher.

Subjects may also attempt to behave in the way they think the researcher wants them to behave. Knowing that they are part of a scientific investigation, subjects usually want to cooperate and to be good subjects. "Being a good subject" may be seen by the participant in a psychological study as doing what is expected by the observer. Orne (1962) has referred to the cues and other information used by subjects to guide their behavior in a psychological study as the **demand characteristics** of the research situation. Orne suggests that subjects generally ask themselves the question "What am I supposed to be doing here?" By paying attention to cues present in the setting, including those that are part of the research procedure itself, or even by attending to implicit cues given by the researcher, the subjects can perhaps figure out what is "expected" of them and attempt to modify their behavior accordingly. Subject reactions to the demand characteristics of a research situation pose threats to both the external and the internal validity of psychological research. When subjects behave in a manner that is not representative of their behavior outside the psychological research setting, our ability to generalize the results is restricted. Also, by behaving in a manner that they think is expected of them, subjects may unintentionally make a research variable look more effective than it actually is or even nullify the effects of an otherwise significant variable.

Controlling Reactivity Problems of reactivity can be approached in several ways. Reactivity can be eliminated if observations are made in such a way that the presence of the observer is not detected by subjects. Measures of behavior in such circumstances are referred to as **unobtrusive (nonreactive) measures.** Obtaining nonreactive measures may involve concealing the observer or hiding mechanical recording devices such as tape recorders and videotape cameras. LaFrance and Mayo (1976) observed people in conversation without their knowledge. Observations were made in a variety of natural settings, such as restaurants and waiting rooms, so we can imagine that observers had to keep their stopwatches and data sheets hidden behind menus and potted plants in order to obtain unobtrusive measures of behavior. Yet another approach is for a researcher to adopt a role in the situation other than that of observer. Subjects do not know that an observer is present, so we assume that they act as they ordinarily would. To investigate honesty, Hays (1980) worked as a clerk in a college student union. When patrons asked for change for a dollar bill, he gave them a nickel extra. Only 45 percent of those patrons who were judged by the observer to be aware of the extra nickel returned the extra money.

Whenever individuals are observed without their knowledge, important ethical issues arise. In many circumstances, observing people without their consent can represent a serious invasion of privacy. And when subjects are involved in situations that are deliberately arranged by an investigator, as might happen in a field experiment, ethical problems associated with placing subjects at risk may arise. Ethical issues in psychological research were discussed at length in Chapter 2.

Another way of dealing with reactivity is to adapt subjects to the presence of an observer. It can be assumed that, as subjects get used to an observer's being present, they will come to behave normally in that person's presence. Adaptation can be accomplished through either habituation or desensitization.

In a *habituation* procedure observers simply introduce themselves into a situation on many different occasions until the subjects cease to react to their presence. In order to film a documentary entitled "An American Family," which was shown on public television in the early 1970s, observers (with their cameras) literally moved into a California home and recorded the activities of a family over a 7-month period. Although it is impossible to tell how much of their behavior was influenced by the observers' presence, the events that unfolded and remarks made by family members gave evidence of a habituation process having taken place. During filming the family broke up, the mother asking the father to move out of the house. When interviewed later about having the divorce announced to millions of television viewers, the father admitted that they could have asked the camera crew to get out but that, by this time, "we had gotten used to it" (*Newsweek*, 1973, p. 49). Habituation may also set in when undisguised participant observers spend a great deal of time with the subjects they are observing. Although they are still aware that an observer is present, subjects may begin to behave as though the observer were not present. As part of a study of aggressive behavior in preschool children, Addison (1986) reported that before actual data were collected a 5-day adaptation period was used to adapt the children to the presence of both the observer and the videotape equipment. Because the children often experienced classroom observers in the form of student teachers and other adults, there appeared to be no effect due to the presence of the researcher. Moreover, Addison (1986) stated that the children's interest in the videotape equipment diminished after a few days.

Desensitization as a means of dealing with reactivity is similar to the desensitization used in the behavioral treatment of phobias. In a therapy situation, an individual with a specific fear (say, an irrational fear of spiders) is first exposed to the fear stimulus at a very low intensity. The patient may be asked to think of things that are related to spiders, such as dusty rooms and cobwebs. At the same time the therapist helps the patient practice relaxing. Gradually the intensity of the stimulus is increased until the patient can tolerate the actual fear stimulus itself.

Desensitization is often used by ethologists to adapt animal subjects to the presence of an observer. Prior to a violent death in the land of her beloved subjects, Fossey (1981, 1983) conducted fascinating observational studies of the mountain gorilla in Africa. Over a period of time she moved closer and closer to the gorillas so that they would get used to her presence. She found that by imitating their movements—for instance, by munching the foliage they ate and by scratching herself—she could put the gorillas at ease. Eventually she was able to sit among the gorillas and observe them as they touched her and explored the research equipment she was using.

Finally, nonreactive measures of behavior can be obtained by observing behavior indirectly (see Webb, Campbell, Schwartz, Sechrest, & Grove, 1981). This may involve examining physical traces left behind or examining archival information, records kept by society about individuals and events. One researcher investigated the drinking behavior of people living in a town that was officially "dry" by counting empty liquor bottles in their trash cans. Another researcher used the records kept by a library to assess the effect on a community of the introduction of television. Withdrawals of fiction titles dropped, but the demand for nonfiction was not affected (see Webb et al., 1981). Physical traces and archival data are important unobtrusive measures that can be valuable sources of information about behavior. In Chapter 5 we will discuss more fully these indirect methods of observation.

OBSERVER BIAS

You may remember that, when Rosenhan (1973) and his colleagues observed the interaction between staff members and patients in mental hospitals, they found a serious bias on the part of the staff. Once patients were labeled schizophrenic, their behavior was interpreted solely in light of this label. Behaviors that might have been considered normal when performed by sane individuals were interpreted by the staff as evidence of the patients' insanity. For instance, note taking by the participant observers, which was done openly, was later discovered to have been cited by members of the staff as an example of the pseudopatients' pathological state. As a result of the staff's tendency to interpret patients' behavior in terms of the label that had been given them, the sanity of the pseudopatients was not detected. This example clearly illustrates the danger of **observer bias,** the systematic errors in observation that result from the observer's expectations.

Expectancy Effects Although we might hope that scientific observations are free from the kind of observer bias documented by Rosenhan, we know that this is not always the case. In many scientific studies the observer has some expectancy about what behavior should be like in a particular situation or should result from a specific psychological treatment. This expectancy may be created by knowledge of the results of past investigations or perhaps by the observer's own hypothesis about behavior in this situation. Expectancies can be a source of observer bias—*expectancy effects*—if they lead to systematic errors in observation (Rosenthal, 1966, 1976).

An example of a study designed to document observer bias will illustrate this problem (see Cordaro & Ison, 1963). The study required college student observers to record the number of head turns and body contractions made by two groups of flatworms. The observers were led to expect different rates of turning and contracting in the two groups. The worms in the groups were, however, essentially identical. What differed was the observers' expectations about what they would see. Results showed that the observers reported twice as many head turns and three times as many body contractions when a high rate of movement was expected than when a low rate was expected. Apparently, the students interpreted the actions of the worms differently depending on what they expected to observe.

Other Biases An observer's expectancies regarding the outcome of a study may not be the only source of observer bias. You might think that using automated equipment such as movie cameras would eliminate observer bias. Although automation reduces the opportunity for observer bias, it does not necessarily eliminate it. Consider the fact that, in order to record behavior on film, the observer must determine the angle, location, and time of filming. To the extent that they are influenced by personal biases of the observer, decisions about these aspects of the study can introduce systematic errors into the results. Altmann (1974) describes an observational study of animal behavior in which the observers biased the results by taking a midday break whenever the animals were inactive. Observations of the animals during this period of inactivity were conspicuously absent from the observational records. Furthermore, using automated equipment generally only postpones the process of classification and interpretation, and it is perfectly possible for the effects of observer bias to be introduced when narrative records are coded and analyzed.

Controlling Observer Bias Observer bias cannot be eliminated, but it can be controlled in several ways. As we mentioned, the use of automatic recording equipment can help, although the potential for bias is still present. Probably the most important control over observer bias is the awareness that it might be present.

Observer bias also can be reduced by limiting the information provided to observers. When Hartup (1974) analyzed the results of his observational study of children's aggression, the individuals who performed the analysis were not permitted to see all the narrative records. When the nature of the aggressive act was classified, the antecedent events were blacked out; and when antecedent events were coded, the nature of the aggressive act was blacked out. Therefore, in making their classifications, the coders could not be influenced by information related to the event that they were coding. In a manner of speaking the coders were "blind" to certain aspects of the study. Observers are *blind* when they do not know why the observations are being made or the goals of a study. When Burns, Haywood, and Delclos (1987) observed the problem-solving strategies of children from two different socioeconomic groups, they first videotaped the children while they worked on five tasks selected from standardized intelligence tests. When task strategies were observed and coded from the videotape records, however, the observer-coder was blind to which group the child was from. When LaFrance and Mayo (1976) investigated eye contact between individuals conversing in natural settings, their observers did not know that possible differences along racial lines were being probed. Using "blind" observers greatly reduces the possibility of introducing systematic errors due to observer expectancies.

SUMMARY

Observational methods can be characterized in terms of both the degree of observer intervention and the manner in which behavior is recorded. Observation in a natural setting without observer intervention is called naturalistic observation. On the other hand, both structured observation (frequently used by the developmental psychologist Piaget) and field experiments (often used by social psychologists) depend on some degree of observer intervention. The manner of record keeping in an observational study varies according to whether a comprehensive description of behavior is sought or the observer seeks only to describe certain predefined units of behavior. Whereas narrative records, including field notes, are used to provide comprehensive descriptions of behavior, checklists (action and static) are typically used when it is simply of interest whether a specific behavior has occurred. The frequency and duration of behaviors also may be recorded, and observers are sometimes called on to make subjective judgments, in the form of ratings, about the quality or degree of a characteristic of the subject or situation.

How quantitative data are described and analyzed depends on the scale of measurement used. The four levels of measurement used by psychologists are: nominal, ordinal, interval, and ratio.

Observations can rarely be made of all behavior that occurs. Consequently some form of behavior sampling (time and event) or situation sampling must be used. An important goal of sampling is to achieve a representative sample of behavior. When narrative records are made, some type of coding system is generally used as one step in the process of data reduction. Measures of frequency and duration, as well as ratings, are typically summarized, using descriptive statistics such as the mean and standard deviation.

It is essential to provide measures of observer reliability when reporting the results of an observational study. Depending on the level of measurement that has been used, either a percentage agreement measure or a correlation coefficient can be used to assess reliability. Finally, it is important to control for the possible influence of both reactivity and observer bias in any observational study.

KEY CONCEPTS

naturalistic observation
ethology
ethogram
participant observation
structured observation
field experiment
confederate
narrative records
ecological psychology
field notes
measurement scale
checklist
time sampling
event sampling
situation sampling
data reduction
coding
interobserver reliability
reactivity
demand characteristics
unobtrusive (nonreactive) measures
observer bias

REVIEW QUESTIONS

1 What three characteristics distinguish scientific observation from nonscientific observation?
2 What critical characteristics distinguish among naturalistic observation, participant observation, structured observation, and a field experiment?
3 What two dimensions can be used to classify observational methods?
4 What is meant by a comparative approach to understanding behavior?
5 There are five general reasons for intervening in conducting an observational study. Identify a study illustrating each reason—either from the studies cited in this chapter or from research you have read about in other psychology courses.
6 What two methodological problems arise in participant observation?
7 What factors in participant observation can be expected to influence the extent of the observer's influence on the behavior being observed?
8 What is the principal advantage of the structured-observation method?
9 Describe the role of a confederate in a field experiment.
10 In what ways does the narrative record from the study of a day in the life of a midwestern schoolgirl differ from that taken from Hartup's study of children's aggression?
11 What factors determine the usefulness of field notes as scientific records, and what determines the likelihood that these factors will be present?
12 How can the quality of narrative records be improved?
13 Define and give an example of a static checklist and an action checklist.
14 Name the four scales of measurement, and give an example of each.
15 What aspect of an observational study is the proper use of behavior sampling and situation sampling intended to ensure?
16 What are the most common descriptive measures (1) when events are classified into mutually exclusive categories and (2) when behavior is recorded on at least an interval scale?
17 What factors contribute to low interobserver reliability, and how can interobserver reliability be increased?
18 Does high interobserver reliability ensure the validity of observations? Why or why not?

19 Why are subjects' reactions to demand characteristics a threat to both the internal and the external validity of psychological research?
20 What ethical issues must one address when using unobtrusive measures?
21 Give an example of each of the two ways in which investigators attempt to mitigate reactivity by adapting subjects to the presence of the observer.
22 What is the best procedure to control observer bias?

CHALLENGE QUESTIONS

1 Students in a developmental psychology lab course conducted an observational study of parent-infant interactions in the home. When they first entered the home on each of the 4 days they did the observation of a given family, they greeted both the parents and the infant (and any other children at home). They instructed the family to follow its daily routine and they asked a series of questions about the activities of that day to determine whether it was a "normal" day or something unusual had happened. The students tried to make the family feel comfortable, but they also tried to minimize their interactions with the family and with each other. For any given 2-hour observation period there were always two student observers present in the home, and the two observers recorded their notes independently of each other. There were six pairs of students who were randomly assigned to carry out the 8 hours of observation on each of the twelve families who volunteered to serve in the study. The same pair of observers always observed a given family, and two families were assigned to each pair of observers. The observers used checklists to record behaviors on a number of different dimensions, such as mutual warmth and affection of the parent-infant interaction.

  A Cite *two* specific procedures used by the students to ensure the *reliability* of their findings.
  B Cite one possible threat to the external validity of the findings of this study; once again, cite a specific example from the description provided.
  C Cite one specific aspect of their procedure that indicated that the students were sensitive to the possibility that their measurements might be reactive. What other methods might they have used to deal with this problem of reactivity?

2 A naturalistic observation study was done to assess the effects of environmental influences on drinking by college students in a university-sponsored pub. Eighty-two subjects between the ages of 18 and 22 were observed. Observations were differentiated on the basis of whether the person being observed was with one other person or was in a group of two or more other people. The observations were made over a 3-month period; sessions were always from 3 P.M. to 1 A.M., and observations were made Monday through Saturday. Each subject was observed for up to 1 hour from the time the subject ordered the first beer. Two observers were always present during any observation session. The results showed that in terms of number of beers drunk per hour men drank more and faster than did women. Men drank faster when with other men, and women also drank faster with men present. Both men and women drank more in groups than when with one other person. These results do indicate that the environment within which drinking occurs plays an important role in the nature and extent of that drinking.

  A Identify the independent and dependent variables in this study.
  B What is the operational definition of a group in this study?

C Identify one specific aspect of this study that increases the external validity of the findings.

3 A friend of yours is absolutely convinced that he has a positive influence on the friendliness of conversations in which he is a participant. He has reached this conclusion on the basis of his everyday observations. You convince him that a systematic study is needed to confirm his hypothesis. Your friend (still smiling) carefully develops an operational definition of the friendliness of a conversation and records a rating for each of the next fifty conversations in which he is a participant. His results show that 75 percent of these conversations are rated "very friendly," 20 percent are rated "friendly" and 5 percent are rated neutral. Your friend returns to you—now convinced beyond a shadow of a doubt that he has a positive effect on the friendliness of a conversation. Although your friend won't be pleased with you, explain to him why the results of his study are essentially useless as a means of confirming his hypothesis. While you have this chance to lecture your friend on research methods, explain to him why it would be better for you or someone else to rate the friendliness of the conversations in a proper study testing your friend's hypothesis.

4 A recent carefully controlled observational study was undertaken to determine whether differences in student-teacher ratings correspond to genuine instructional differences among teachers. The subjects were forty-eight full-time social science faculty (thirty-nine males and nine females) at a major university. Ten were full professors, eighteen were associate professors, and twenty were assistant professors. A number of undergraduate students were carefully trained as observers. They used a checklist including 100 specific observable classroom behaviors, and their visits to the classrooms were unnoticed by the professors. Six to eight observers visited three separate 1-hour class periods taught by these instructors over a 3-month period. The results of the study showed that teachers who receive high ratings from students do in fact teach differently from instructors who receive average or poor ratings.

Use the above description to answer the following questions:

A Suggest what specific procedure was used in this study to avoid reactivity?
B What factor in this study is likely to have affected the reliability of the results?
C What factor in this study affected the external validity of the findings?
D Given the final conclusion, which goal of the scientific method (description, prediction, understanding) was the basis for this study?

ANSWER TO CHALLENGE QUESTION 1

1 A The students' procedures that enhanced reliability were as follows: observing each family for 8 hours, using two independent observers, and using checklists to provide operational definitions.

B One possible threat to the external validity of the findings was that the twelve families volunteered for the study and such families may differ from typical families.

C The students' efforts to minimize interactions with the family and with each other suggested that they were sensitive to the problem of reactivity. Two other methods they might have used are habituation and desensitization.

Chapter 4

Correlational Research: Surveys and Tests

Outline

OVERVIEW

During every presidential campaign we are inundated with the results of the "latest poll." The 1992 campaign may well have represented the peak of polling. The media seemed to be reporting results of polls daily. Analysts also appeared in the media interpreting the implications of the polls. There were even debates as to whether the polls were having an undue influence on the political process. The polls are intended to describe people's voting preferences at the time the poll is taken. Polls are also used, however, as a basis of predicting how people will vote at the time of the actual election. The results of polls can influence decisions made by candidates as to the places in which and the issues on which they will focus their campaigning. Political polls involve the use of survey-research methods. Surveys have a much broader application than their use in political polling; they are an important research tool in psychology.

As you will see in this chapter, survey research illustrates a more general approach to psychological research called *correlational research.* The goal of correlational research is to identify predictive relationships by assessing the covariation among naturally occurring variables. The results of correlational research have implications for making decisions such as identifying emotional disorders and selecting among job applicants.

Another research tool that is used extensively in correlational research is psychological testing. Tests and surveys share similar characteristics such as the use of sampling and the need to establish reliability and validity. Tests and surveys also have distinctive characteristics and uses that will be described in this chapter.

A major portion of this chapter includes a description of the basic logic and techniques of sampling—that is, the process of selecting a subset of a population to represent the population as a whole. The advantages and disadvantages of various survey-research methods and survey-research designs are then discussed. The correspondence between people's reported behavior and their actual behavior is also discussed briefly.

The remaining portion of the chapter introduces a few fundamental characteristics and uses of tests. We examine how key characteristics of tests such as reliability, validity, and fairness are established. We conclude the chapter with a discussion of the use of correlational research in meeting the scientific goal of developing predictive relationships and in decision making.

USES AND CHARACTERISTICS OF SURVEYS

In Chapter 3 we discussed how psychologists use observational methods in their study of human and animal behavior. You have seen how these methods can be used to describe behavior and its context. Results of these observations can be used to infer how people must have been thinking or feeling to have behaved in a certain way. We now turn our attention to a method designed to deal more directly with the nature of people's thoughts, opinions, and feelings. The method is called *survey research.* On the surface, survey research is deceptively simple. If you want to know what people are thinking, ask them! In a similar vein one could suggest that, if you want to know what people are doing, observe them! As we have seen, however, observation from which we hope to infer general principles of behavior requires considerably more sophistication. So, too, the proper use of the survey-research method requires more than simply asking people questions.

The deceptive ease of conducting a survey is illustrated in a report by a young girl named Bridgette that was published in a suburban grammar school's newsletter. The report read, "I surveyed fifty people on which candy bar they liked best. Here are my results in order of preference: Hershey bar—35, Snickers—10, Whachamacallit—5." These results may please the manufacturers of Hershey bars, but the operator of the school's vending machine should be wary of stocking it on the basis of these findings. Who were the "fifty people" surveyed and how were they selected? How was the survey conducted? Was each child interviewed separately? If other children were present during the interview, were they eating candy bars? If so, what brands? Do the children who claim to like Hershey bars best really eat them most often? These and many other questions must be answered before we can confidently interpret the results of this survey. You may be thinking at this point that we are taking Bridgette's survey more seriously than she intended, and you are probably right. Nonetheless, these questions are typical of those that should be asked when we read or hear a report of a nationwide survey indicating that, for example, a majority of Americans oppose gun control. After reading this chapter you should be better able to formulate such questions and to evaluate responses to them.

Surveys are used in research by social scientists such as political scientists, psychologists, and sociologists for a variety of reasons. For example, Jessor, Chase, and Donovan (1980) conducted a national survey to determine the extent of, and possible reasons for, drug and alcohol use by adolescents. Cherlin et al. (1991) conducted national surveys in Great Britain and the United States to investigate the effects of divorce on children. Campbell (1981) used surveys to study changes in people's sense of satisfaction in various domains of their lives during the 1970s. The specific survey-research techniques used in these studies and the major results of each study will be described later in this chapter.

Surveys are also used to meet the more pragmatic needs of political candidates, public health officials, and advertising and marketing directors. The scope and purpose of such surveys can be limited and specific, or they can be truly global. A very specific application occurred in connection with a personal injury suit in Chicago. The lawyer for the injured party hired a market-research team to conduct a survey of registered voters to determine what sort of person would identify with the victim and, therefore, be most likely to award a multimillion-dollar settlement. The lawyer used this information to screen prospective jurors. Gallup (1976), on the other hand, reported the results of surveys sampling two-thirds of the world's population to measure human needs and satisfactions. One objective was to establish an international data bank that would make it possible to measure and chart trends in global attitudes and behavior.

Though they differ in scope and purpose, most surveys have certain characteristics in common. Surveys generally involve sampling, a concept that was introduced in our discussion of observational methods (Chapter 3) and about which we will have more to say in the next section of this chapter. Surveys are also characterized by their use of a set of predetermined questions for all respondents. Oral or written responses to these questions constitute the principal data obtained in a survey. By using the same phrasing and ordering of questions, it is possible to summarize the views of all respondents succinctly. (The procedure for constructing questionnaires, the most commonly used instruments for administering surveys, are described in Appendix B.) A series of national surveys asked respondents the same questions about their attitudes toward premarital sex (Gallup, 1988). In 1969, 68 percent of the respondents condemned premarital sex as wrong. A decreasing percentage of respondents held this view in 1973 (48 percent) and in 1985 (39 percent). By 1987, however, 46 percent of the respondents said premarital sex was wrong, suggesting that negative attitudes toward premarital sex may be increasing. As this example illustrates, the study of trends over time is possible when the same survey question has been asked of comparable samples in successive surveys.

Properly conducted surveys are an excellent basis for describing people's attitudes and opinions. They are not, however, without their limitations. The consistent ordering and phrasing of questions is ill suited for in-depth examination of the thoughts or feelings of individual respondents. And, because questionnaires must be constructed prior to data collection and adhered to closely during data collection, surveys do not provide a good vehicle for exploratory studies. Less-structured "pilot" studies are the preferred method for exploratory studies, in which the research question and the method of attack take shape during the process of conducting the study.

SAMPLING TECHNIQUES

Assuming that you have determined the population of interest for your survey, the next step is to decide whom to interview. This involves selecting a sample of respondents to represent the population. The power and efficiency of sampling are aptly summarized by the noted survey researcher Angus Campbell (1981, p. 17):

> The method of choice for portraying all the variety of a large heterogeneous population is clearly that of the sample survey. Ever since statisticians and social scientists learned how to draw a sample from a large universe in such a way that every member of the universe has an equal chance of being chosen, it has been possible to describe the national population accurately by obtaining information from a few thousand carefully selected individuals.

Whether we are describing a national population or a much smaller one, such as the employees of a certain company, the procedures are the same. This section explains how to make that careful selection of individuals which Campbell describes.

BASIC TERMINOLOGY OF SAMPLING

In discussing sampling techniques, it is essential that we clearly understand the definitions of four terms: population, sampling frame, sample, and element. A **population** is the set of *all* the cases of interest. If you were interested in the attitudes of students on your campus toward the services provided by the library, your population would be all students on your campus. If we were conducting a census, we would attempt to obtain information from every member of the population; in a survey, for the sake of efficiency, we select a subset of the population to represent the population as a whole.

Most often a population is a hypothetical entity, and we need to develop a specific list of the members of the population. This specific list is called a **sampling frame** and is, in a sense, an operational definition of the population of interest. In a survey assessing the attitudes of students toward library services, the sampling frame might be a list obtained from the registrar's office of all currently enrolled students. It is easy to see that the extent to which the sampling frame reflects the population of interest determines the adequacy of the subset we ultimately select. The list provided by the registrar should provide a good sampling frame, but it is still possible that some students may be excluded, such as those who have just recently been processed for admission.

An inadequate sampling frame can pose a much more serious problem, as pollsters in the 1936 presidential election found out. In 1936 a *Literary Digest* poll involving a mail survey of almost 2 million voters predicted incorrectly that Alfred M. Landon would beat Franklin D. Roosevelt by a landslide. The sample of voters was drawn from telephone directories, magazine subscription lists, and automobile registration lists. Using this same technique, pollsters had correctly predicted the outcome of the previous four elections. Spurred by the Depression, however, increasing numbers of the poor voted in 1936 and they were not adequately represented on such lists. In the same election George Gallup used a different technique to predict Roosevelt's 1936 victory. Even so, in 1948 Gallup (and many other pollsters) confidently and incorrectly predicted that Dewey would defeat Truman.

The subset of the population actually drawn from the sampling frame is called the **sample.** We might select 100 students from the registrar's list to serve as the sample in our library survey. How closely the attitudes of this sample of students will correspond to those of all the students depends critically on how the sample is chosen. Each member of the population is called an **element,** and the identification and selection of those elements that will serve as a sample are the basis of all sampling techniques. The relationships among the four critical sampling terms are summarized in Figure 4.1.

Remember that samples are of little or no interest in themselves. Library policy would not be changed solely for the 100 students surveyed. Similarly,

FIGURE 4.1 Diagram illustrating relationships among basic sampling terms.

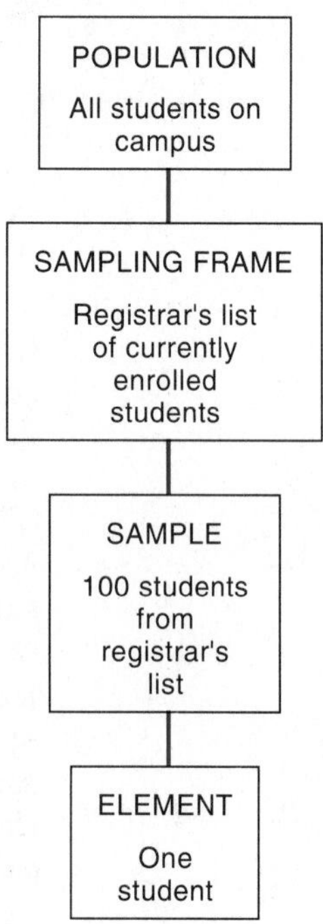

the social psychologist is not interested solely in the racial attitudes of the 50 people he surveyed, nor is the marketing director interested only in the preferences of the 200 consumers she surveyed. The "power" of descriptions derived from an analysis of the sample stems from the fact that they are assumed to be applicable to the population from which the sample was drawn. Populations, not samples, are of primary interest.

The ability to generalize from a sample to the population depends critically on the **representativeness** of the sample. Characteristics of individuals in the population are distributed in various ways. That is, the relative frequencies with which the characteristics appear in the population vary. For example, in one population there might be 40 percent males and 60 percent females, whereas in another the distribution might be 75 percent female and 25 percent male. A sample is representative to the extent that it exhibits the same distribution of characteristics as the population from which it was selected. If 30 percent of the students on your campus are sophomores, then your library survey sample of 100 students should include approximately 30 sophomores if it is to be representative.

The major threat to representativeness is bias. A **biased sample** is one in which the distribution of characteristics is *systematically* different from that of the target population. A sample that included 80 percent females and 20 percent males would be biased if the population that the sample was intended to represent was 40 percent female and 60 percent male. There are two sources of bias: *selection bias* and *response bias*. (We will discuss selection bias now and deal with response bias when we discuss response rates associated with various survey methods.) Selection bias occurs when the procedures used to select the sample result in the overrepresentation of some segment of the population or, conversely, in the exclusion or underrepresentation of a significant segment.

A particularly salient case of selection bias once led to some serious errors in estimating the public-health needs of the elderly. In the late 1950s a survey-research project was funded by the Foundation for Voluntary Welfare. This foundation was generally acknowledged to be opposed to public-welfare programs. The intended purpose of the study was to determine the needs and resources of the elderly by conducting a nationwide survey. The sample was selected in such a way that upper-class respondents were overrepresented. In addition, the sample excluded nonwhite persons over 65, individuals in nursing homes, and those receiving old-age assistance. The exclusion of these groups was particularly troublesome because the problems of aging are relatively severe in each of them. Not surprisingly, given this serious selection bias, the results showed that older people were more healthy and more satisfied with existing programs than earlier studies had indicated. As often happens, this survey had an impact beyond the confines of the research community. These findings were part of the basis of a national campaign mounted by the American Medical Association against federal programs for medical care for the elderly (Warwick & Lininger, 1975).

Survey researchers must be constantly alert to the threat of selection bias in sampling. Fortunately, as we will see, they have developed techniques that can minimize the risk.

APPROACHES TO SAMPLING

There are two basic approaches to sampling—nonprobability sampling and probability sampling. In **nonprobability sampling** there is no way to estimate the probability of each element's being included in the sample and no guarantee that each element has some chance of being included. If a researcher were to interview the first ten students she met after she walked out of her office, she would be using nonprobability sampling. Clearly, not all students on campus would be equally likely to be outside the researcher's office at that particular time, and some students would have essentially no chance of being included in the sample.

By contrast, if the researcher were to select ten students randomly from the registrar's list of enrolled students, she would be using **probablity sampling.** All students would have an equal chance of being included in such a sample. Only when probability sampling is used is it possible to estimate the likelihood that sample findings differ from the findings that would have emerged from studying the whole population. Hence probability sampling is far superior to nonprobability sampling in ensuring that selected samples will be representative samples. The principal advantages of nonprobability sampling are convenience and economy. In order to choose appropriately between nonprobability sampling and probability sampling, you will need to learn more about specific types of sampling plans.

Types of Nonprobability Samples Two types of nonprobability sampling are accidental samples and purposive samples. **Accidental samples** are those that result when availability and willingness to respond are the overriding factors used in selecting respondents. If an instructor who is interested in the attitudes of college students uses the students who happen to be enrolled in his classes that semester as his sample, he is using an accidental sample. On a Saturday afternoon at the beginning of the 1981 major league baseball strike, NBC surveyed its viewers about their attitudes toward the strike. Periodically during the program substituted for the scheduled telecast of a baseball game, an announcer asked those who favored the owners to call one telephone number and those who favored the players to call a different number. Clearly the respondents in this survey constituted an accidental sample: those who happened to be watching at that time.

Shere Hite's book *Women and Love: A Cultural Revolution in Progress* (1987) illustrates an extreme case of accidental sampling. She mailed 100,000 questionnaires to women who belonged to a variety of women's groups in forty-three states. These groups ranged from feminist organizations to church groups to garden clubs. Her questionnaires included 127 essay questions on topics ranging from hobbies to communication between spouses. Only 4.5 percent of the original sample responded to the survey. The problem is not the size of the sample; Shere Hite herself said, "It's 4,500 people. That's enough for me." The problem is whether these respondents can be considered representative of the intended population, women in the United States. Without additional information about the population it is impossible to confirm that an accidental sample is not representative. In this case, however, one can be quite certain that the survey respondents do not fairly represent the whole population. Even the initial 100,000 selected were not representative of women in general because they all belonged to some organization. It is also reasonable to expect that discontented women might be more likely to respond and therefore be overrepresented in the final sample. For example, Hite reported that 95 percent of women feel emotionally harassed by the men they love.

This finding contrasts sharply with other national surveys done about the same time using random samples in which half or more of women reported being completely satisfied with their marriage and only 3 percent said they were "not at all happy" (Peplau & Gordon, 1985). As a general rule, accidental samples should be considered biased unless there is strong evidence confirming their representativeness.

In the second type of nonprobability sampling, **purposive sampling,** the investigator handpicks the elements to be included in the sample on the basis of expert judgment. The individuals selected may be either those judged to have certain special characteristics or (more commonly) those who are likely to provide the most useful information for the purposes for which the study is being done. A small number of election districts are sometimes used as a purposive sample. These "key" districts are selected for polling because in previous years their election results have approximated overall state or national voting patterns. Goleman (1981) describes the use of purposive sampling in a survey for which respondents who were most likely to prove informative were selected. In developing new tests for use in personnel selection, psychologist David C. McClelland asked top management people to nominate "water walkers"—people who were so outstanding they could do no wrong. The managers were also asked to nominate employees who simply did their jobs well enough not to get fired. McClelland and his colleagues then conducted intensive interviews of the nominees from both groups and, from these interviews, developed a list of competencies that set the water walkers apart from the more typical employees. Job applicants were then screened on the basis of these competency-based tests to try to detect potential water walkers. In this situation the characteristics of workers in general were not McClelland's primary interest, so purposive sampling was ideally suited to the task at hand. When representative samples *are* essential, the method of choice is probability sampling.

Types of Probability Samples The distinguishing characteristic of probability sampling is that the researcher can specify, for each element of the population, the probability that it will be included in the sample. Three types of probability samples are used most often: simple random samples, stratified samples, and cluster samples. **Simple random sampling** is the basic technique of probability sampling, and it is incorporated in the other two types of probability sampling. In a simple random sample, each possible sample of a specified size in the population has an equal chance of being chosen. Because samples are usually drawn from large populations, it is not common practice to list all possible samples and then select one randomly. Instead, the most common definition of a random sample is that every element has an equal chance of being included in it. The procedures for selecting such a sample are outlined in Box 4.1.

The initial failures when polls were used to predict presidential elections were partly responsible for the development of probability sampling, the most respected survey research method in use today. The 1976 election provided what is perhaps the high point in the accuracy of presidential polling using probability sampling. The *Times*-CBS poll predicted 51.1 percent for Carter and 48.9 percent for Ford (ignoring undecideds)—the same as the actual vote totals! What makes this feat even more impressive is that samples of 2,000 voters were used to predict the voting of 80 million people. A word of caution about the accuracy of polls: Polls based on probability samples are accurate reflections of voting preferences *at the time the poll is taken*. The results of such polls, however, do not necessarily predict future voting preferences.

One critical decision that must be made in selecting a random sample is how large it should be. For now, we will simply note that the size of a random sample needed to ensure representativeness varies with the homogeneity of the population. College students in Ivy League schools represent a more homogeneous population than college students in all U.S. colleges. In the extreme case of homogeneity, where all members of the population are identical, a sample of one is representative regardless of the size of the population. At the other extreme, if the population were so heterogeneous that each member was completely different from all other members on all characteristics, then *no* sample, regardless of its size, could be representative. Every individual would have to be included to describe such a heterogeneous population. Fortunately, the populations with which survey researchers work fall somewhere between these two extremes. Thus the representativeness of samples, like the joy of eating a piece of chocolate cake, increases with increasing size—up to a point.

The size of the sample has an influence on another important aspect of survey results when probability sampling has been used. A given sample that has been randomly selected is just one of an infinite number of possible samples that could have been drawn from the population. Therefore, it is unlikely that the results for the given sample are exactly equal to the corresponding value for the population as a whole. It is possible to estimate, however, the **margin of error** between the sample results and the true population value (Judd et al., 1991). The margin of error is primarily determined by the size of the sample—the larger the sample size, the smaller the margin of error. The margin of error can be reduced by increasing the size of the sample, but increasing sample sizes can prohibitively increase the cost of doing the survey. The size of the margin of error is also influenced by the confidence we want to have in the accuracy of our estimate. (See further description of confidence intervals in

Appendix A.) Greater confidence will require a wider margin of error given a sample of a specific size. For example, a 99 percent confidence level would result in a larger margin of error than would a 90 percent confidence level (again, with the same sample size for the two different confidence levels). The margin of error for a given sample can be computed using the sample size and the specified confidence level. In practice, however, a desired margin of error (e.g., 3 percent) and confidence level (e.g., 95 percent) are selected and the sample size necessary to achieve these two objectives is then calculated.

Margins of error are routinely included when national surveys are reported in the media. For example, in late June of the 1992 presidential campaign an ABC News-*Washington Post* poll reported that 33 percent of respondents preferred Governor Clinton and 29 percent preferred President Bush. Ten days later an NBC News-*Wall Street Journal* poll reported that 31 percent favored President Bush and 28 percent favored Governor Clinton. The size of the two national samples for the surveys was 1,007 and 1,105 adults, respectively. With such large samples it would be tempting to conclude that Governor Clinton was the leading candidate in the first poll, but that President Bush was the leader in the later poll. In fact, the most reasonable conclusion is that the two candidates were in a virtual tie with each other in both polls. The margin of error for the first sample was 3.5 percent, and the margin of error in the second sample was 3 percent. Differences as large as the margin of error could occur due to sampling error (covered more extensively in Chapter 6) even when there were no real differences in voters' preferences for the two candidates. That is, there is no real difference in preferences for the two candidates that needs to be interpreted.

The use of the concept of margin of error in the interpretation of survey results illustrates a more general principle. Absolute differences in percentages are not directly interpretable; differences in percentages must be evaluated in terms of their size relative to the size of the differences expected due to sampling error (e.g., the margin of error). When it comes to interpreting survey results, a difference (unlike a rose) is not a difference.

The representativeness of the obtained sample can often be increased by using **stratified random sampling.** In this procedure, the population is divided into subpopulations called strata (singular, *stratum*) and random samples are drawn from each of these strata. Two general approaches are followed in determining how many elements should be drawn from each stratum. One approach (illustrated in the last example of Box 4.1) is to draw equal-sized samples from each stratum. The second approach is to draw elements for the sample on a proportional basis. For example, if there are three strata representing 40 percent, 40 percent, and 20 percent of the population, respectively, then a stratified sample of 200 would include 80 individuals from each of the first two strata and 40 from the third stratum.

Stratified random sampling is especially beneficial when the strata represent relatively homogeneous segments of the population. In addition to increasing the representativeness of samples, stratified random sampling is a useful tech-

BOX 4.1

SAMPLES OF RANDOM SAMPLES

The following names represent a scaled-down version of a sampling frame obtained from the registrar's office of a small college campus. Procedures for drawing both a simple random sample and a stratified random sample from this list are described below.

Adamski	F	Jr	Hedlund	F	So
Alderink	F	Sr	Johnson	F	Fr
Baxter	M	Sr	Knecht	F	Jr
Bowen	M	Fr	Mason	F	Sr
Broder	M	So	Nadeau	F	Sr
Brown	M	Jr	Nowaczyk	M	Jr
Bufford	M	So	O'Keane	F	Sr
Campbell	F	Fr	Osgood	M	So
Carnahan	F	So	Owens	F	So
Cowan	F	Fr	Penzien	M	Jr
Cushman	M	Sr	Powers	M	Sr
Dawes	M	Jr	Ryan	M	Fr
Dennis	M	Sr	Sawyer	M	Jr
Douglas	F	Fr	Shaw	M	Sr
Dunne	M	So	Sonders	F	Sr
Fahey	M	Fr	Suffolk	F	So
Fedder	M	Fr	Taylor	F	Fr
Foley	F	So	Thompson	M	Fr
Grossman	F	Jr	Watterson	F	Jr
Harris	F	Jr	Zimmerman	M	So

Drawing a simple random sample

Step 1. Number each element in the sampling frame: Adamski would be number 1, Harris number 20, and Zimmerman number 40.

Step 2. Decide on the sample size you want to use. This is just an illustration, so we will use a sample size of 5.

Step 3. Choose a starting point in the Table of Random Numbers in Appendix A (a finger stab with your eyes closed works just fine—our stab came down at column 8, row 22 at the entry 26384). Because our sampling frame ranges only from 1 to 40, we had decided *prior* to entering the table to use the left two numbers in each set of five and to go across the table from left to right. We could just as easily have decided to go up, down, or from right to left. We could also have used the middle two or the last two digits of each set of five, but one should make these decisions before entering the table.

Step 4. Identify the numbers to be included in your sample by moving across the table. We got the numbers 26, 06, 21, 15, and 32. Notice that numbers over 40 are ignored. The same would be true if we had come across a repetition of a number we had already selected.

Step 5. List the names corresponding to the selected numbers. In our case the sample will include Nowaczyk, Brown, Hedlund, Dunne, and Ryan.

An even easier system, called *systematic sam-*

pling, can be used to obtain a random sample. In this procedure you divide the sample size you want into the size of the sampling frame to obtain the value *k*. Then you select every *k*th element after choosing the first one randomly. In our example we want a sample size of 5 from a sampling frame of 40, so *k* would be 8. Thus we would choose one of the first eight people randomly and then take every eighth person thereafter. If Alderink were chosen from among the first 8, the remaining members of the sample would be Cowan, Foley, Nowaczyk, and Shaw. Note: This system should *not* be used if the sampling frame has a periodic organization—if, for example, you had a list of dormitory residents arranged by room and every tenth pair listed occupied a corner room. You can readily see that, in such a list, if your sampling interval was 10 you could end up with all people from corner rooms or no people from corner rooms.

Drawing a stratified random sample

Step 1. Arrange the sampling frame in strata. For our example we will stratify by class standing, so our sampling frame now looks like this:

Freshmen	Sophomores	Juniors	Seniors
1 Bowen	1 Broder	1 Adamski	1 Alderink
2 Campbell	2 Bufford	2 Brown	2 Baxter
3 Cowan	3 Carnahan	3 Dawes	3 Cushman
4 Douglas	4 Dunne	4 Grossman	4 Dennis
5 Fahey	5 Foley	5 Harris	5 Mason
6 Fedder	6 Hedlund	6 Knecht	6 Nadeau
7 Johnson	7 Osgood	7 Nowaczyk	7 O'Keane
8 Ryan	8 Owens	8 Penzien	8 Powers
9 Taylor	9 Suffolk	9 Sawyer	9 Shaw
10 Thompson	10 Zimmerman	10 Watterson	10 Sonders

In our example the strata are equal in size, but this need not be the case.

Step 2. Number each element within each stratum, as has been done in the foregoing list.

Step 3. Decide on the overall sample size you want to use. For our example we will draw a sample of 8.

Step 4. Draw an equal-sized sample from each stratum such that you obtain the desired overall sample size. For our example this would mean drawing 2 from each stratum.

Step 5. Follow the steps for drawing a random sample and repeat for each stratum. We used the previously determined starting point (column 8, line 22) in the Table of Random Numbers, but this time we used the last digit in each set of five. The numbers identified for each stratum were: Freshmen (4 and 1), Sophomores (6 and 4), Juniors (7 and 9), and Seniors (2 and 9).

Step 6. List the names corresponding to the selected numbers. Our stratified random sample would include Douglas, Bowen, Hedlund, Dunne, Nowaczyk, Sawyer, Baxter, and Shaw.

nique when you want to make general statements about portions of the population you have sampled. For example, a simple random sample of 100 students would be sufficient to survey students' attitudes on a campus of 2,000 students. It would be risky, however, to use views of the two chemistry students who happened to be included in this sample to represent those of the forty chemistry majors on campus. If the investigators knew in advance that they wanted to describe the views of students majoring in various departments, a simple random sample of the students on campus would not be the method of choice. Instead, a stratified random sample according to majors could be constructed without drastically increasing the overall sample size.

As the previous examples demonstrate, simple random sampling and stratified sampling involve the use of a sampling frame. Unfortunately, survey researchers are often faced with the task of sampling from populations for which sampling frames are not readily available.

Jessor et al. (1980) were confronted with the task of developing a national sample of adolescents. Needless to say, they did not have a sampling frame listing all adolescents presently living in the United States. They first drew a stratified random sample of fifty counties from a list of all the counties within the forty-eight contiguous states and the District of Columbia. They then used a sampling frame listing the homerooms of the junior and senior high schools in the fifty counties they had selected. Each homeroom represents a *cluster* of adolescents. The researchers randomly selected approximately 700 homerooms from the sampling frame; these 700 clusters provided an overall sample of approximately 16,000 adolescents.

In general, **cluster sampling** is a technique in which the sampling unit is not an individual element but some aggregate or cluster of elements in the population for which an appropriate sampling frame can be found. There was no available sampling frame for the individual adolescents (elements), but there was a sampling frame for homerooms (clusters) including several individual adolescents. As the Jessor et al. (1980) example illustrates, cluster sampling is somewhat more complex than either simple random sampling or stratified random sampling. But the objective of cluster sampling is still the same: to obtain a representative sample of the population of interest, in this case all adolescents residing in the continental United States.

SURVEY METHODS

In this section we describe the alternatives from which the survey researcher may choose in deciding *how* to conduct the interview. There are three general survey methods: mail surveys, personal interviews, and telephone interviews. As was true of sampling techniques, there is no one best method for all circumstances; each survey method has its own advantages and disadvantages. The challenge facing the survey researcher is to select the method that best fits the problem under study.

MAIL SURVEYS

Mail surveys represent the most common means of distributing self-administered questionnaires. A principal advantage of mail surveys is that they can be done relatively quickly. Because they are self-administered, mail surveys avoid the problems of interviewer bias (to be defined more completely in the next section). And among the three types of surveys, mail surveys are the best for dealing with highly personal or embarrassing topics, especially when anonymity of respondents is preserved.

Unfortunately, there are as many disadvantages to mail surveys as there are advantages. Some of these disadvantages are less serious than others. For instance, because the respondent will not be able to ask questions if a portion of the questionnaire is unclear, the questionnaire must be completely self-explanatory. A second minor disadvantage is that the researcher has little control over the order in which the respondent proceeds through the questionnaire. Different respondents may follow different sequences, and the order of questions may affect the way respondents answer certain of them. It is reasonable to expect that, when all respondents do not follow the same sequence, the variability among their responses to a given question is likely to increase.

A major problem with mail surveys, however, is one of bias—namely, *response bias.* Response bias is a threat to the representativeness of a sample because not all respondents complete the survey. Mail surveys exclude respondents with literacy problems and are generally intimidating to those of low educational background. Those with problems with their vision, such as many of the elderly, are also excluded. The major factor leading to response bias in mail surveys is the generally low response rate. Quite often people included in a sample are too busy or not interested enough in the study to return a completed questionnaire. Low response rates necessarily produce smaller samples. Generally, however, the size of the sample is not the most serious concern. The problem is that low response rates make it likely that response bias will affect the sample. For example, if 200 store managers are included in a survey about store security, but only 50 respond, the results may be affected by response bias because only those stores that are the least busy are represented. Unless the return rate is 100 percent, the potential for response bias exists regardless of how carefully the *initial* sample was selected. Nonetheless, the problem of response bias decreases with increasing response rate. A 50 percent response rate is considered adequate, 60 percent is good, and 70 percent is very good (Babbie, 1992). These are demanding standards in light of the fact that a typical return rate for a mail survey is around 30 percent. When it comes to ensuring the representativeness of the obtained sample, however, a demonstrated lack of response bias is much more crucial than the absolute level of the response rate.

Certain procedures should be followed in a mail survey to enhance response rate. For instance, the initial mailing should include a letter summarizing the purpose of the survey, explaining the basis on which the respondents were selected, and assuring the respondents of confidentiality. A postage-paid return envelope should also be included along with the questionnaire. As questionnaires are returned, the researcher should plot a cumulative response rate graph like that shown in Figure 4.2. Numbering the returned questionnaires in the order received allows researchers to make comparisons such as that between early and late respondents. Plateaus in the cumulative response rate graph indicate that a follow-up mailing should be sent. To obtain a 70 percent response rate, it is often necessary to send three mailings. These should be spaced about 2 to 3 weeks apart or when a plateau appears on the cumulative response rate graph. Because the original copy is likely to have been lost, a new copy of the questionnaire should be sent with each mailing.

Several factors contribute to higher than usual return rates. Return rates will be highest when the questionnaire has a "personal touch," when it requires a minimum of effort for the respondent, when the topic of the survey is of intrinsic interest to the respondent, and when the respondent identifies in some way with the organization or researcher sponsoring the survey. Warwick and Lininger (1975) describe a survey that met these requirements. About 100,000 members of women's religious congregations in the United States were surveyed. The study was sponsored by, and had the support of, the religious congregations. It was done by a visible and respected member of one of the religious orders, and the subject matter was of great interest to the respondents. The result was an almost perfect response rate. Warwick and Lininger note, however, that most mail surveys fall far short of this ideal. Fortunately, survey researchers have available other survey methods that generate much higher response rates than mail surveys.

PERSONAL INTERVIEWS

When personal interviews are used to collect survey data, respondents are usually contacted in their homes and trained interviewers administer the questionnaire. The personal interview allows much greater flexibility in asking questions than does the mail survey. In a personal interview the respondent can obtain clarification of unclear questions, and the trained interviewer can

FIGURE 4.2 Graph illustrating cumulative response rate for a mail survey. On Wednesday, September 16, 500 surveys were mailed.

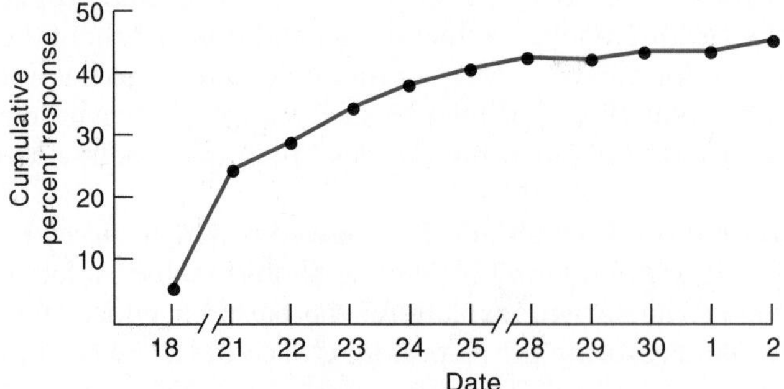

pursue incomplete or ambiguous answers to open-ended questions. Respondents are also much less likely to fail to respond to an item on the questionnaire, and they are less likely to use "don't know" as a response. The interviewer controls the sequencing of questions and can ensure that all respondents complete the questionnaire in the same order. Traditionally, the response rate to personal interviews has been much higher than that to mail surveys; the commonly accepted response rate is 80 to 85 percent. In recent years, however, increasing fear of urban crime and an increasing number of households with no one home during the day have tended to reduce the attractiveness of using personal interviews.

This impressive list of the advantages of personal interviews is offset by two disadvantages. The first disadvantage, high cost, results because the use of trained interviewers is expensive in terms of both money and time. The second, perhaps more critical, disadvantage involves the potential for **interviewer bias.** The interviewer should be a neutral medium through which questions and answers are transmitted. Interviewer bias occurs when the interviewer tries to adjust the wording of a question to "fit" the respondent or records only selected portions of the respondent's answers. Most often, however, interviewer bias results from the use of probes. *Probes* are follow-up questions used by interviewers to get respondents to elaborate on ambiguous or incomplete answers. In trying to clarify the respondent's answers, the interviewer must be careful not to introduce ideas that may then become part of the respondent's subsequent answer. For example, if a respondent in a survey of television viewing said that the major problem with current TV programming was excessive violence, the probe "Could you elaborate on what you mean by violence?" would be better than the probe "By violence do you mean murders, muggings, and rapes?" Interviewers must also be mindful of the feedback their verbal and nonverbal responses give to respondents. Smiling and nodding approvingly when a respondent fails to answer a question may lead the respondents to withhold responses to later questions.

The best protection against interviewer bias is highly motivated, well-paid interviewers who are trained to follow question wording exactly, to record responses accurately, and to use probes judiciously. Interviewers should also be given a detailed list of specifications—that is, instructions about how difficult or confusing situations are to be handled. Finally, interviewers should be closely supervised by the survey director. It should now be clear that the decision to use personal interviews is not one that survey researchers take lightly.

So far we have been describing the personal interview as a way of administering a highly structured questionnaire to an individual respondent. A frequently used variation of the personal interview is the *focused interview* (also called focus group). The focused interview is done in a group setting with the researcher trying to learn from the respondents more about the reasons for the attitudes or opinions that they hold. Focused interviews are used extensively in market research to determine consumers' reactions to current or new products or services. Focused interviews are increasingly being used as part of the strategic planning process by civic organizations and by churches. There is less of an emphasis in this approach on obtaining a quantitative summary of the views across all respondents. Instead, the goal is to obtain a qualitative description of the ideas that emerge from a guided group discussion.

TELEPHONE INTERVIEWS

Prohibitive travel costs and the difficulties involved in supervising interviewers when personal interviews are used have led many survey researchers to turn to telephone interviews. This method met with considerable criticism when it was first used because of serious limitations on the sampling frame of potential respondents. Many people have unlisted numbers, and the poor and those in rural areas were unlikely to have a phone. By 1979, however, more than 95 percent of all households had telephones, and techniques such as random-digit dialing have been developed to reach households with unlisted numbers. Telephone interviewing also provides access to dangerous neighborhoods, locked buildings, and respondents available only during evening hours. Interviews can be completed more quickly when contacts are made by phone, and interviewers can be better supervised when all interviews are conducted from one central location.

Of course, the telephone survey is not without its drawbacks. There is still a possible selection bias when respondents are limited to those people who have telephones, and the problem of interviewer bias remains. There is a limit to how long respondents are willing to stay on the phone, and the fact that responses are being given to a "faceless voice" may influence how people respond. In spite of these limitations, the high response rate and flexibility of the telephone interview make it the method of choice for nearly all brief surveys.

SURVEY RESEARCH DESIGNS

After investigators have decided who the respondents will be (sampling) and how to conduct the survey (survey method), one critical decision remains. This decision involves the selection of a research design, the overall plan by which the survey is administered. In making this decision, the survey researcher chooses among three general survey research designs: the cross-sectional design, the successive independent samples design, and the longitudinal design. As you probably suspect, there is no all-purpose research design to meet every survey need; the choice of design must be tailored to the objectives of the study.

CROSS-SECTIONAL DESIGN

The most commonly used survey research design is the **cross-sectional** (*one-shot*) **design.** If you make a cross-sectional cut through the middle of a banana, the sliced ends are circular. You can use the sliced ends to describe characteristics of the banana. Similarly, if you consider time to be the counterpart of the banana, a cross-sectional design slices a sample of the population *at one time*. Information is collected from this sample to serve as the basis for a description of the characteristics of the population. Jessor et al. (1980) used the cross-sectional design in their nationwide survey of drinking and marijuana use among teenagers. Their study illustrates that the cross-sectional design is not limited to the use of one sample and that the data collection period is not necessarily short. They made comparisons among different samples defined by age, gender, and ethnic group. Their survey took each respondent 45 minutes to complete, but the overall testing of respondents took over a month. In some studies it can take even longer.

The focus in a cross-sectional survey is on description—describing the characteristics of a population or the differences among two or more populations. Cross-sectional designs can also be used to assess interrelationships among variables within a population. This is what Jessor et al. (1980) did when they tried to determine what personality, social, and behavioral characteristics were most strongly related to marijuana use. They found that increased marijuana use was associated with several factors, such as lower expectations for academic achievement, greater tolerance of deviance, less compatibility between friends and parents, and a greater value placed on independence than on academic achievement. The three strongest predictors of marijuana use, however, were friends as models of marijuana use, the number of times drunk in the past year, and involvement in general deviant behavior. Thus marijuana use can be understood as a component of a larger behavior pattern and not as an isolated issue.

Cross-sectional surveys can be especially useful in epidemiology, the study of the incidence and prevalence of disease in a population. *Incidence* refers to the number of new cases of a disorder reported during a specific time period—a year, for example. *Prevalence* is the frequency of a disorder in a particular population. Seligman (1988) used such epidemiological studies to make a provocative argument about factors contributing to an increase in the occurrence of unipolar depression. The first step in his investigation was to determine whether there had, in fact, been a change in the occurrence of depression. Seligman used the lifetime prevalence of depression—the percentage of the population that has had the disorder at least once in their lifetime. In general, this is a cumulative statistic; if you look at the prevalence of broken legs, you find that it increases with age. As expected, the prevalence of depression increased from about 5 percent for those born around 1960 to about 9 percent for those born around 1945. For those born around 1925, however, the lifetime prevalence went down to 4 percent, and for those born around 1910 it went down to only 1 percent. After carefully tracking through possible artifacts in these results, Seligman concluded that there had been a genuine tenfold increase in the prevalence of unipolar depression since World War II. He went on to argue that the increase was attributable to an increasing emphasis on individualism and a decreasing emphasis on commitment to common values such as family and religion. Seligman's interpretation is one well worth considering, but the methodological point his study illustrates is that surveys can play a critical role in describing important epidemiological findings. Such findings can not only be used to test theoretical explanations of disorders such as unipolar depression but can also be helpful in identifying individuals or groups at risk for certain disorders.

Cross-sectional designs are ideally suited to the descriptive and predictive functions we have been discussing so far. Surveys are also used to assess changes in attitudes or behaviors over time and to determine the effect of some naturally occurring event, such as the passage of a law to raise the drinking age. For these purposes the cross-sectional design is not the method of choice. Rather, research designs are needed that systematically sample respondents across time. Two such designs are discussed in the next two sections.

SUCCESSIVE INDEPENDENT SAMPLES DESIGN

The **successive independent samples design** can be understood as a series of cross-sectional surveys in which the same questions are asked of each succeeding sample of respondents. This design is most appropriate when the major aim of the study is to describe changes over time in the attitudes or behaviors of members of a population. Campbell (1981) used the successive independent samples design in a series of national surveys that were done to assess changes in Americans' sense of well-being over a 20-year period. The studies were massive in scale. In each of five different years, over 2,000 people were interviewed in their homes and each interview lasted about an hour.

Studies of this kind are invaluable when discussion turns to the topics of the "good old days" or "the wonders of modern times." For instance, you may have heard someone say that people aren't so satisfied with life as they used to be. The data summarized in Table 4.1 show that people's reported satisfaction with a variety of areas of their lives changed little during the 1970s. This lack of change is remarkable, given the many changes in American society that occurred during this period. Consider, for example, the results of another survey measuring people's trust in government. Surveys were done in 1972 and 1978; the results are shown in Table 4.2. As these data suggest, Americans' attitudes clearly changed in at least one area—more were cynical in 1978 than in 1972. Such dramatic changes in attitude make it all the more surprising that Campbell's (1981) survey showed that people simply don't seem to be either more or less satisfied with their lives as a whole. Findings of this kind are typical of the provocative information that becomes available when the successive independent samples design is used.

The successive independent samples design has several limitations. The data given in Table 4.2 can be used to illustrate one of these limitations. Consider the change from 36 percent to 52 percent in the "cynical" category from 1972 to 1978. It is tempting to conclude that 16 percent of the population was added between 1972 and 1978 to the original 36 percent of Americans who were already cynical about government in 1972. We also might try to say that, of the 19 percent who were no longer "trusting," 16 percent were now cynical, 2 percent had mixed feelings, and 1 percent failed to answer. What we must

TABLE 4.1 MEAN SATISFACTION RATINGS IN VARIOUS DOMAINS OF LIFE*

Domain	1971	1978
Marriage	1.73	1.77
Family life	2.08	2.22
Health	2.22	2.28
Neighborhood	2.24	2.29
Friendships	2.26	2.33
Housework	2.29	2.65
Work	2.33	2.42
Life in the United States	2.39	2.38
Community	2.40	2.41
Housing	2.43	2.34
Standard of living	2.69	2.78
Amount of education	3.31	3.57
Savings	3.73	3.78
Life as a whole	2.45	2.46
Number of cases	(2146)	(3692)

* The mean values are based on a 7-point scale whereon 1 represents "completely satisfied" and 7 represents "completely dissatisfied." Data taken from Campbell (1981). Appendix Table 2.

remember, however, is that the people surveyed in 1978 were *not* the same people surveyed in 1972. It is possible (though unlikely) that all of them could have changed their views between 1972 and 1978. That is, the formerly cynical may now be mixed or trusting, the formerly trusting may now be mixed or cynical, and the formerly mixed may now be cynical or trusting. The extent to which individuals change categories can be determined only by testing the same individuals on both occasions. Given that you cannot determine who has changed or by how much, it is not surprising that it is difficult to use the successive independent samples design to ferret out the reasons for the changes you record.

A second problem with the successive independent samples design arises when samples are not representative of the *same* population. If Campbell had sampled affluent Americans in 1957 and poor Americans in 1978, his comparisons of the well-being of Americans over this time period would be meaningless. The affluent and poor samples illustrate the problem of *noncomparable successive samples.* Changes in the population across time can be described accurately only when the characteristics of the samples representing that pop-

TABLE 4.2 TRUST IN GOVERNMENT, 1972–1978*

	1972	1978
Cynical	36%	52%
Mixed	24%	26%
Trusting	38%	19%
Not answered	2%	3%
Number of cases	(2285)	(2304)

* Data taken from Campbell (1981), Appendix Table 8.

ulation are the same. Thus, it is important to check carefully to see if noncomparable successive samples are a problem in survey research that uses the successive independent samples design. There are sophisticated statistical procedures that can be used to try to unravel the problems of interpretation that arise because of noncomparable successive samples. The best solution to the problem of noncomparable successive samples is to avoid the problem.

One final problem with surveys based on successive independent samples arises when they are used to determine the effect of some naturally occurring event. For example, a survey of attitudes toward teenage drinking might be done before and after the passage of a law raising the legal drinking age, or a campus fraternity might sample students' attitudes toward the organization before and after a campaign publicizing the fraternity's activities. The major problem in this type of study is the high risk of confounding. We have already discussed one possible source of confounding: if the samples drawn before and after the event are not comparable, there is no way to attribute any obtained differences to the intervening event. Even when the samples *are* comparable, the threat of confounding is not eliminated. A dramatic accident involving teenage drunken driving may have been publicized at the same time as the new drinking law was passed. There would be no way to tell whether publicity surrounding this accident or the change in the drinking law caused any subsequent change in the respondents' attitudes toward teenage drinking. Fortunately, the problems of confounding by extraneous factors are not insurmountable; we discuss possible solutions to these problems in much greater detail in Chapter 11.

LONGITUDINAL DESIGN

The distinguishing characteristic of the **longitudinal design** is that the same sample of respondents is interviewed more than once. There are two principal advantages of the longitudinal design. First, the investigator can determine the direction and extent of change for individual respondents. This obviously makes it easier to answer questions about the reasons for attitude or behavior changes. Second, the longitudinal design is the best available survey research design when the effect of some naturally occurring event needs to be assessed. (For further discussion of assessing the effects of naturally occurring events, see Chapter 11). As mentioned previously, Cherlin et al. (1991) used the longitudinal design to investigate the effects of divorce on children in Great Britain and the United States. Over 17,000 British mothers who had had a child in the first week of March were interviewed in 1958. Almost 15,000 of these women were interviewed in 1965 when their children were 7 and again in 1969 when the children were 11. The original sample for the U.S. survey was done in 1976 and included 2,279 children aged 7 to 11 from 1,747 families. Follow-up interviews were done in 1981 in all families from the 1976 sample that had experienced a separation or divorce and in a randomly selected subsample of intact families. The distinguishing characteristic of the longitudinal design in both the British and the U.S. studies is the fact that the same individuals were surveyed in each successive phase of the study.

Longitudinal designs like that used in the Cherlin et al. (1991) study involve a massive effort. The potential power of such an undertaking, however, can be illustrated by describing just one aspect of Cherlin et al.'s (1991) findings. They differentiated three distinct sources that could contribute to differences in adjustment between children from families in which the parents have separated or divorced and children from intact families. The first source is growing up in a home with serious problems that can make normal development difficult; the second source is growing up in the midst of severe marital conflict; and the third source is making the difficult transition that occurs after the couples separate. Cherlin et al. (1991) argued that most research has focused on gathering data only after the separation has occurred. By using a longitudinal design that allowed them to gather data prior to the separation or divorce, Cherlin et al. (1991) were able to show that "Overall, the evidence suggests that much of the effect of divorce on children can be predicted by conditions that existed well before the separation occurred. These predivorce effects were stronger for boys than for girls" (p. 1388). One important implication of these findings is that children in troubled, intact families may require at least as much attention as those children who suffer the trauma of separation or divorce. More generally, the Cherlin et al. (1991) study illustrates how crucial the longitudinal design is in studying changes over time due to naturally occurring events.

One problem in a longitudinal design is that it can be difficult to obtain a sample of respondents who will agree to participate in a longitudinal study, which more often than not means a long-term study. In many studies the respondents may be asked to complete several lengthy surveys at regular intervals over a number of years. People are often hesitant to make the commitment of time necessary to complete such an extensive project.

Even when the respondents do agree to participate, there are further problems. You might think that this design solves the problem of noncomparable samples that can occur when successive independent samples are used. After all, how much more comparable can a sample be than one that is identical to the original sample? Unfortunately, successive samples in a longitudinal design are identical only if *all* members of the original sample are retained throughout the study. This is not likely to be the case. For example, in the Cherlin et al. (1991) study there were 17,414 mothers interviewed in the original 1958 sample. In 1965, 14,746 parents (usually mothers) were reinterviewed. Unless all the respondents in the original sample complete all phases of a longitudinal design, there is a possible problem due to *respondent mortality* (sometimes literal, but most often figurative). Respondent mortality is probably the most serious disadvantage of the longitudinal design. It is usually possible, however, to determine whether the final sample is comparable to the original sample in a longitudinal design, because the characteristics of nonrespondents in the follow-up phase are known (they were included in the original sample).

Problems also arise in a longitudinal design because the same respondents are interviewed more than once. One problem is that respondents may strive heroically to be consistent across interviews. This can be particularly troublesome if the study is designed to assess changes in respondents' attitudes. Although their attitudes have actually changed, people may report their original attitudes in an effort to appear consistent. Another problem is that the initial interview may sensitize respondents to the issue under investigation and make them more likely or less likely than they would otherwise have been to respond to the manipulation under investigation. For example, if a longitudinal design were used to test the effectiveness of TV political ads, people interviewed prior to the broadcast of the ads may pay more attention to the ads after the interview because participating in the survey piqued their interest in election issues. You might recognize that this is another illustration of reactive measurement—people reacting differently because they know they are being observed (see Chapter 3).

CORRESPONDENCE BETWEEN REPORTED AND ACTUAL BEHAVIOR

Regardless of how carefully survey data are collected and analyzed, the value of these data depends on the truthfulness of the respondents' answers to the survey questions. How willing should we be to believe that the survey responses validly reflect people's true thoughts, opinions, feelings, and behavior?

The question of the truthfulness of verbal reports has been debated extensively, and no clear-cut conclusion has emerged. Judd et al. (1991) note, however, that in everyday life we regularly accept the verbal reports of others as valid. If a friend tells us that he enjoyed reading a certain novel, we may ask why, but we do not usually question whether the statement accurately reflects our friend's feelings. However, in everyday life we also come across situations in which we *do* have reason to suspect the truthfulness of someone's statements. Generally we accept people's remarks at their face value unless we have reason to do otherwise. We should apply the same standards to the information we obtain from survey responses.

By its very nature, survey research involves reactive measurement. Respondents not only know that their responses are being recorded, but they may also suspect that their responses may serve as the basis for some social or political action. Hence the pressures are strong for people to respond as they "should" and not as they actually do believe. The term that is often used to describe these pressures is **social desirability.** For example, if respondents are asked whether they favor giving help to the needy, they may respond affirmatively because they believe that this is the most socially acceptable attitude to have. As suggested in Chapter 3, the best protection against reactive measurement is to be aware of its existence.

Sometimes it is possible to examine the accuracy of verbal reports directly by using archival data or unobtrusive measures (topics that are described more fully in Chapter 5). Judd et al. (1991) describe research by Parry and Crossley (1950) wherein responses obtained by experienced interviewers were subsequently compared with archival records of respondents kept by various agencies. Forty percent of respondents gave inaccurate reports to a question concerning contributions to United Fund (a charitable organization), 25 percent erred when reporting whether they had registered and voted in a recent election, and 17 percent misrepresented their age. A pessimist might find these figures disturbingly high, but an optimist would note that a majority of respondents' reports were accurate even when social desirability pressures were high, as in the question pertaining to charitable contributions.

Another source of evidence against which to compare the accuracy of verbal reports is direct observation of the respondents' behavior. The field experiment done by Latané and Darley (1970), described in Chapter 3, illustrates the problem. They found that bystanders are more likely to help a victim when the bystander is alone than when other witnesses are present. Subsequently, a second group of subjects was asked whether the presence of others would influence the likelihood that they would help a victim. They uniformly said that it would not. Research findings such as these should make us extremely cautious of reaching conclusions about people's behavior solely on the basis of verbal reports. Of course, we should be equally cautious of reaching conclusions about what people think solely on the basis of direct observation of their behavior.

One final point needs to be made about the usefulness of survey results. The process of doing a survey has much in common with the process of writing an essay. You often begin with a grand topic that must be focused so that it can be covered manageably. As you narrow your focus, you may sometimes have the feeling that your original topic has been lost or at least made trivial. No essay can capture all the aspects of a given topic, and no 20-item or even 200-item questionnaire can do so, either. Survey research, like the rest of the scientific enterprise, is built on faith that compiling reliable findings in a series of limited studies will eventually lead to increased understanding of the important broader issues we face.

TESTS

Students know a great deal about tests. Taking tests is a routine part of most undergraduate courses. Many students have a particular type of test that they prefer because they believe they perform better on it. Taking tests can also arouse emotional reactions from students, ranging from exhilaration to terror. One reason for these emotional reactions is that important decisions affecting students are based in part on test results—admission to college, passing or failing courses, admission to graduate or professional schools. This extensive experiential knowledge does not provide much insight, however, into the fundamental characteristics of a test or into the role tests play in psychological research. This section of this chapter is intended to provide a brief introduction to the use of tests in research.

There are several important similarities between the characteristics of tests and the characteristics of surveys. For example, sampling plays a critical role in tests as it does in surveys. Measurements made using surveys and tests, like all measurements in psychology, must be reliable and valid. There is, however, one salient difference between surveys and tests. When surveys are used, responses to predetermined questions are summed across the individuals in the sample to estimate the views of the population as a whole. When tests are used, on the other hand, the objective is to measure the performance of an individual relative to some criterion like the average score of people taking the test.

Our coverage of tests is organized in three sections. We first introduce three general types of tests. Next, we describe the role of sampling in the development and interpretation of tests. In the final section we describe ways to assess three key characteristics of a good test: reliability, validity, and fairness.

TYPES OF TESTS

Psychologists began to develop tests in response to practical concerns such as the identification of the mentally impaired, the assessment of students' progress in schools, and the clinical study of people who are emotionally disturbed. Three general types of tests have evolved from these concerns: aptitude tests, achievement tests, and personality tests (Anastasi, 1988). *Aptitude tests* are used to assess an ability or skill. For example, the verbal and quantitative tests on the Graduate Record Examination (GRE) are aptitude tests measuring two aspects of scholastic or academic abilities and skills. Aptitude tests are also used in employment settings. For example, mechanical aptitude tests and clerical aptitude tests are used to assess job applicants' aptitudes for positions requiring these skills. The purpose of aptitude tests is to provide one source of information that can be used to predict how likely it is that a person will succeed in an educational or employment setting.

Achievement tests are used to assess the level of mastery a person has achieved after completing a course of instruction or training. The tests given during and at the end of courses in college are types of achievement tests. Standardardized achievement tests are also used in the process of certification in many professions. A certified public accountant, for example, has passed an achievement test assessing mastery of the principles of accounting. The purpose of achievement tests is to determine whether a person can advance to further training or instruction or to a higher level of professional responsibility.

The distinction between aptitude tests and achievement tests is a useful one, but it is not a rigid one. Aptitude tests can be influenced by prior learning, and achievement tests can be used to predict a person's future performance. Anastasi (1988) provides a good description of the distinction between aptitude and achievement tests: "We might say that aptitude tests measure the effects of learning under relatively uncontrolled and unknown conditions, while achievement tests measure the effects of learning that occurred under partially known and controlled conditions" (p. 412).

The final type of test we will describe, a *personality test*, "most often refers to measures of such characteristics as emotional states, interpersonal relations, motivation, interests, and attitudes" (Anastasi, 1988, p. 17). One type of personality test, the self-report inventory, is very similar in physical structure to the questionnaires used in survey research. The tests consist of a carefully selected set of questions presented in a predetermined order, for which the person being tested usually provides written responses.

There are several hundred different personality tests. One of the most widely used is the Minnesota Multiphasic Personality Inventory (MMPI). The MMPI consists of over 500 statements like "When I get bored, I like to stir up some excitement," and "I do not tire quickly." The person responds to each statement by indicating if it is true or false. The content of the test items ranges over topics such as physical health, marriage and family issues, political and social attitudes, habits, and likes and dislikes.

The MMPI provides scores on several scales including depression, anxiety, schizophrenia, psychopathy, and social introversion. The test was originally developed to distinguish between normal individuals and those falling into certain diagnostic categories such as depression. The MMPI has also been used extensively in research examining general personality traits.

More generally, personality tests serve a critical function in research in the areas of personality, social, and clinical psychology. Paper-and-pencil personality tests may not look like technologically sophisticated instruments; but, when properly used, they can be powerful research tools.

ROLE OF SAMPLING IN TESTING

In our discussion of survey research we emphasized the importance of sampling, especially probability sampling. Representative samples are essential if the survey results found for the sample are to serve as a basis for a description of the population as a whole. Representative samples are most likely to be achieved when probability sampling is used. Sampling also plays a critical role in the development of tests. Tests are first and foremost instruments used to measure psychological concepts. It is important that tests, like all instruments in psychology, yield valid measurements. A valid test of mechanical aptitude, for example, should indicate a person's ability to work effectively with machines. In our later discussion of several key characteristics of tests, we will describe the role sampling plays in determining the validity of a test. In this section we will concentrate on the role of sampling in the interpretation of test scores.

Imagine that you were told you received a score of 30 on a recent test you took in your research methods class. What would knowing your score tell you about how well you had done on the test? Not much. If you knew there had been 50 possible points on the test, you could convert your score to a percentage (60%). Still, the percentage value would not allow you to know how well you had done. To interpret all test scores (whether they are expressed as raw scores or as percentages), we need a clearly defined frame of reference. The same score could indicate relatively good performance on a more difficult test or relatively poor performance on an easier test. One reasonable approach to this dilemma would be to determine a measure of central tendency (e.g., the mean) for the class's performance on the test. If the mean score on the test was 40, then you would know that you had performed less well than the average student. If the mean score had been 25, then your same test score of 30 would indicate better than average performance. Your research methods class would represent an accidental sample, but it still could reasonably be used by your professor as a basis of assigning grades for the test. When it comes to tests such as the GRE or the MMPI, however, interpretation of test scores must be based on a much more sophisticated frame of reference.

The process of developing tests like the GRE involves the careful selection of a normative or standardization sample which will serve as your frame of reference. It is essential that this sample is representative of those who will be taking the test being developed. For example, the normative sample for the GRE would be college students who plan to go on to graduate school. The normative sample for the depression scale of the MMPI would be individuals who were diagnosed with depression. The normative sample must be large enough so that it can be used to develop a distribution characterizing a wide range of performance on the test. The normative sample is then used to develop *derived scores* from the raw scores obtained by individual test takers. Derived scores are determined in a way very much like the one we described earlier in comparing your test score to the mean test score in your research methods class.

Two common derived scores used in standardized tests are percentile scores and standard scores. A **percentile score** is the percentage of people in the normative sample who scored below a given raw score. So, a person scoring at the 90th percentile would have obtained a raw score on the test below which 90 percent of the normative sample had scored. The second type of derived score, the standard score, is even more useful. A **standard score** expresses the distance of a given test taker's raw score from the mean score of the normative sample in standard deviation units. If the mean of the normative sample was 50 with a standard deviation of 10, then a raw score of 65 would correspond to a standard score of 1.5. GRE test scores are reported as standard scores with a mean of approximately 500 and a standard deviation of about 100. So, if you were told that your GRE verbal score was 700 you would know that you are 2.0 standard deviations above the mean of the normative sample.

Derived scores such as percentile scores and standard scores have two primary advantages over the use of raw scores. First, the derived scores allow evaluation of a person's performance relative to the known comparison provided by the normative sample. This comparison to the normative sample provides the point of reference that is needed to interpret an individual's raw test score. In this sense tests are almost always "graded on a curve." Second, derived scores can be used to compare an individual's performance on two different tests (such as the verbal and quantitative components of the GRE) even when the tests differ in terms of central tendency or units of measurement. In making these comparisons, however, it is essential that the normative samples of the two tests be representative of the same population as the people who will be taking the test. Comparing your verbal ability measured on a test normed for high school students with your quantitative ability measured on a test normed for graduate students would tell you very little about your relative strength in these two abilities. Knowing the normative sample for a test is essential for interpreting a score on that test.

KEY CHARACTERISTICS OF TESTS

By now you are becoming familiar with the idea that reliability and validity are vital characteristics of psychological measurement. Reliability and validity are equally important characteristics of tests. We will briefly describe in this section how the reliability and validity of a test can be determined. In addition, we will consider what it is that makes a test fair or unfair.

Reliable tests, like reliable observers or any other reliable measurements, are characterized by consistency. There are several ways to measure a test's reliability (see Anastasi, 1988). One common method is to compute a **test-retest reliability.** Usually, test-retest reliability involves administering the same test to a large sample of people at each of two different times. For a test to be reliable, people do not have to obtain identical scores on the two administrations of the test, but a person's relative position in the distribution of scores should be similar at the two test times. The consistency of this relative positioning is determined by computing a correlation coefficient using the two test scores for each person in the sample. (See Chapter 1 for an introduction of the concept of correlation and Appendix A for the computational procedures for a correlation coefficient.) A desirable value for test-retest reliability coefficients is in the range of .80 or above, but the size of the coefficient does depend on factors such as the types of items and the number of items.

Judd et al. (1991) have identified several factors that affect the reliability of a test. Within reasonable limits tests with more items will be more reliable than tests with fewer items. Tests will also generally be more reliable when there is greater variability on the factor being tested among those individuals being tested. Individuals who vary a great deal from one another are easier to differentiate reliably than are individuals who differ by only a small amount. For example, differentiating among the academic ability of a group drawn from the general student population would be easier than differentiating among a more homogeneous group of honor students. Finally, tests will be more reliable when the testing situation is free of distractions and when clear instructions are provided for completing the test.

The reliability of a test is easier to determine and to achieve than is the validity of a test. The definition of validity is straightforward—a valid test measures what it is intended to measure. Confirming that a test is valid is less straightforward. We will focus on construct validity which is just one of the many ways in which the validity of a test can be determined.

The **construct validity** of a test represents the extent to which the test measures the theoretical construct it is intended to measure. Quantitative reasoning, self-esteem, anxiety, and depression represent examples of theoretical constructs that have been measured using tests. One approach to determining the construct validity of a test begins by assessing the convergent validity of the test. Even stronger evidence for the construct validity of a test can be gained by assessing the discriminant validity of the test. These concepts can best be understood by considering an example.

Table 4.3 presents the hypothetical results of a test of the construct validity of a quantitative reasoning test. The parenthesized correlation coefficients presented on the diagonal represent the reliabilities of three measures obtained from giving two equivalent forms of three tests to the same students (quantitative reasoning, math grades, and verbal reasoning). Our focus now is on measuring the construct validity of the quantitative reasoning test. It is reasonable to expect that scores on the quantitative reasoning test should correlate with students' grades in math classes. The correlation of .60 between the quantitative reasoning test and math grades indicates that the two measures do correlate as expected. This finding provides evidence for *convergent validity;* the two tests converge as measures of quantitative reasoning.

The case for the construct validity of a test can be made even more strongly when the test is shown to have *discriminant validity.* As can be seen in Table 4.3, the correlations between quantitative reasoning and verbal reasoning (.15) and between math grades and verbal reasoning (.10) are low. These findings show that the quantitative test does not correlate with a test designed to measure another theoretical construct, namely, verbal reasoning. The low correlation between the quantitative reasoning test and the verbal reasoning test indicates that the two tests are measuring different constructs. Thus, there is evidence for discriminant validity of the quantitative reasoning test. The con-

TABLE 4.3 HYPOTHETICAL EXAMPLE ILLUSTRATING CONSTRUCT VALIDITY

	Test Form B		
Test Form A	Quantitative reasoning	Math grades	Verbal reasoning
Quantitative reasoning	(.90)	.60	.15
Math grades		(.80)	.10
Verbal reasoning			(.85)

struct validity of the quantitative reasoning test gains strong initial support in our example because there is evidence for both convergent validity and discriminant validity.

The last key characteristic of a test that we will consider is fairness. A fair test is one that is free of bias: each person taking the test has an equal opportunity to demonstrate the aptitude, achievement, or personality characteristic being assessed by the test. A fair test is intended to provide a level playing field for all those taking the test. It is possible for a test to be fair, however, and for there to be differences in the mean scores as a function of factors such as age, race, or gender. For example, men and women tend to have similar mean scores on the verbal GRE; but men tend to have higher mean scores than women do on the quantitative GRE. A similar pattern is shown on the SAT test. Brush (1991) has reported that the SAT test underpredicts the grades women achieve in college compared with those of men. He goes on to argue that "Thus an admissions process that gives the SAT significant weight will reject some women who would have done better than men who were accepted" (p. 409). The possibility of selection biases like this one provides strong motivation to make sure tests are as fair as possible to all those taking the tests.

One procedure intended to increase the fairness of a test is to conduct a sensitivity review of the test items. The sensitivity review follows a set of carefully written guidelines to ensure that tests reflect the multicultural nature of our society. The review is also intended to eliminate any items that might be offensive to major subgroups of those taking the test such as subgroups defined by age, disability, race, or gender. The sensitivity review does not guarantee that people in the designated subgroups will do well on the test. The sensitivity review does make it less likely that members of these subgroups will be distracted by language or content that they might find offensive or confusing.

USE OF SURVEYS AND TESTS IN CORRELATIONAL RESEARCH

Surveys and tests are useful research tools. In a broader sense, however, their use in research represents an excellent illustration of a more general approach called **correlational research.** Correlational research, unlike experimental research (see Chapter 6), does not involve the manipulation of independent variables. Instead, correlational research assesses the relationships among naturally occurring variables. The Levine (1990) study, described in Chapter 1, showing a relationship between the pace of life in a city and deaths in that city from heart disease is a good example of correlational research. The primary purpose of correlational research is to meet the second objective of scientific research, prediction. Correlational research seeks to identify predictive relationships based on the covariation (correlation) among the variables being studied. As we will see, once these predictive relationships have been established, they can be used in making a variety of important decisions.

CORRELATIONAL STUDIES

A common type of correlational study is one in which two or more sets of responses obtained as part of a survey or test are correlated with each other. For example, Lubin et al. (1988) investigated the relationship between measures of physical and psychological health in their survey of 1,543 adults living in the United States. They asked the respondents to provide self-ratings of physical health as well as to give information about such health-related factors as frequency of visits to a physician and the nature and frequency of any medications they were taking. The interviewers also collected demographic data (for example, occupation and religious affiliation of respondents) and data regarding the frequency of volunteer and social activities. Each of the respondents also was asked to complete a paper-and-pencil test measuring both positive affect (for example, happiness) and negative affect (for example, depression). Measures of psychological health and measures of physical health were found to be correlated. For instance, positive affect was positively correlated with self-ratings of physical health; frequency of volunteer activities correlated negatively with a measure of depression. The investigators suggested that correlational studies of this type can prove useful in the prediction of physical and psychological health-related problems.

A potential limitation of correlational studies involves interpretation of causal relationships. For instance, there is a strong and reliable correlation between educational level and happiness (Campbell, 1981). We could not, however, use this correlation alone to argue convincingly that increasing education causes increasing happiness. Increasing education *may* result in increasing happiness, but it is also possible that happier people do better in school and thus are more likely to continue. Another possibility is that those who are more financially well off are both happier and more likely to obtain more education. Sophisticated statistical procedures are available to discriminate among these possibilities. Discussion of these techniques used in the causal analysis of correlational studies goes beyond the scope of the present text (see Kenny, 1979; Judd et al., 1991).

One sophisticated statistical procedure that is used extensively in correlational studies is factor analysis. We will briefly describe factor analysis to give you some flavor of the potential power of correlational research. Anastasi (1988) provides a general definition of *factor analysis*: "a refined statistical technique for analyzing the interrelationships of behavior data . . . A major purpose of factor analysis is to simplify the description of behavior by reducing the number of categories from an initial multiplicity of test variables to a few common factors, or traits" (pp. 154–155). For example, the complexity of searching for correlations among variables is greatly reduced when the results of 300 tests can be summarized in terms of five or six common factors. As is the case with any powerful tool, factor analysis should be used cautiously and only after extensive training in its proper use.

Factor analysis can also be useful for providing feedback on tests and surveys. For example, students are sometimes asked to evaluate their professors using standardized teaching-evaluation instruments that contain many individual questions. Factor analysis can be used to analyze the results of the students' evaluations, and professors can be given feedback in terms of factor scores reflecting a small number of meaningful aspects of teaching such as Course Organization and Planning, Faculty/Student Interaction, Communication, and Course Workload. The use of factor scores for feedback on tests and surveys illustrates the principle that less can be more when it comes to useful information.

PREDICTIONS AND DECISIONS

The results of correlational research have implications for decision making. Predictive relationships that have been established in research studies can be used in making decisions about who should be admitted to college or graduate school or who should be admitted to a psychiatric hospital. Decisions such as these are rarely, if ever, based on a single source of information. Instead, several different measures are used in the decision process, with each having been shown to have some predictive value. In the graduate application process, for instance, GRE test scores, undergraduate grade-point average, letters of recommendation, and a personal essay all contribute to the admission committee's decisions. Similarly, decisions involving selections among applicants in more applied settings rely on the use of multiple predictors. Broach (1992) reported that predictions of performance by air traffic controllers in radar-based training after 1 or 2 years in that occupation were better when biographical data (such as age and prior experience) were included than when the predictions were based only on a civil service test. The use of several different predictors in developing an effective decision-making process follows a logic similar to that of the multimethod approach to research. The use of several different research methods to investigate a problem increases the likelihood of converging on a valid conclusion, and the use of several different predictors in a decision-making process increases the likelihood of making good decisions.

Meehl (1954) has studied a very important decision-making task in psychology. Clinical psychologists routinely face the challenge of having to identify the emotional disorders experienced by their clients. Meehl compared the accuracy of two different approaches to making these difficult decisions. Meehl called the first approach *clinical prediction* whereby the clinician reviews the available evidence pertinent to the case, including impressions the clinician forms from interviewing the client, and then makes a diagnosis of the disorder. Clinical prediction relies heavily on the personal and professional judgment of the clinician. Meehl referred to the second approach as *statistical prediction,* which involves the use of correlational research to develop statistical predictive relationships. The information about a given client is then entered into this predictive system, and a statistical prediction is made about which emotional disorder is most likely for this case. The distinguishing characteristic of statistical prediction is that it is based on empirical evidence rather than on the individual judgment of a clinician.

Meehl (1954) found that, in an absolute sense, neither clinical prediction nor statistical prediction was very accurate—a not surprising finding given the complexity involved in diagnosing emotional disorders. Meehl did find, however, that statistical prediction was more accurate than clinical prediction. Dawes (1988) has summarized a large body of research showing that statistical prediction outperforms clinical prediction for decisions ranging from whom to admit to graduate school to who is a good risk for a bank loan. Although evidence like that provided by Meehl (1954) and Dawes (1988) suggests that we should rely on statistical prediction whenever possible, it isn't practical to do so. Meehl (1992) has argued, "You couldn't choose a graduate school, buy a car, get married (or divorced), let alone invest money or vote for president, if you required all your choices to be derived rigorously from scientific proof" (p. 14). Empirical evidence simply is not available for many important decisions.

When we have no basis for making a statistical prediction, then we must make the best decision we can based on clinical prediction. Meehl (1992) argues, however, that when we *do* have evidence to serve as the basis for a statistical prediction, we are making an ethically questionable choice if we ignore this evidence and rely on clinical prediction. Our hope is that the knowledge you have gained about correlational research as a basis for predictions will allow you to make a more informed decision about how you make decisions.

SUMMARY

Survey research provides an accurate and efficient means of describing people's thoughts, opinions, and feelings. Surveys differ in purpose and scope, but they generally involve sampling, the procedure whereby results obtained with a carefully selected sample are used as a basis for describing the entire population of interest. Surveys also involve the use of a predetermined set of questions, generally in the form of a questionnaire. Survey research is typically not very effective for exploratory studies, but the greatest limitation of survey research is the problem of interpreting causal relationships.

Sampling is a procedure whereby a specified number of elements are drawn from a sampling frame that represents an actual list of the possible elements in the population. Our ability to generalize from the sample to the population depends critically on the representativeness of the sample, the extent to which the sample has the same characteristics as the population. Representativeness is best achieved by using probability sampling rather than nonprobability sampling. In simple random sampling, the most common type of probability sampling, every element is equally likely to be included in the sample. Stratified random sampling and cluster sampling provide alternatives when simple random sampling is not sufficient.

There are three general survey methods: mail surveys, personal interviews, and telephone interviews. Mail surveys avoid problems of interviewer bias and are especially well suited for examining personal or embarrassing topics. The problem of response bias is a serious limitation of mail surveys. Personal interviews and phone surveys usually have much higher response rates and provide greater flexibility. The phone survey is the method of choice for most brief surveys. Careful planning is required in preparing a questionnaire (see Appendix B).

The survey is administered according to an overall plan called a research design. There are three survey research designs: the cross-sectional design, the successive independent samples design, and the longitudinal design. Cross-sectional surveys focus on describing the characteristics of a population or the differences between two or more populations. Describing changes in attitudes or opinions over time requires the use of successive independent samples or longitudinal designs. The longitudinal design is generally preferred because it allows the assessment of changes for specific individuals and avoids the problem of noncomparable successive samples.

Survey results, like those of other verbal reports, can be accepted at face value unless there is reason to do otherwise. One such reason is the pressure on respondents to give socially desirable responses. People's behavior does not always conform to what they say they would do, so survey research will never replace direct observation. However, survey research does provide an excellent way to determine people's attitudes and opinions.

Tests bear several similarities to surveys, including the use of probability sampling and a standardized set of questions. Aptitude tests assessing abilities, achievement tests assessing levels of mastery, and personality tests assessing such characteristics as emotional states represent three general types of psychological tests. Derived scores such as percentile scores and standard scores are used to provide a frame of reference to interpret the raw scores obtained on tests. A good test must be reliable, valid, and fair. Test-retest reliability is one way to measure the reliability of a test; construct validity is one of many measures of the validity of a test. Fairness of a test is harder to measure, but no less important to achieve.

Surveys and tests are important tools in correlational research, which is intended to assess the covariation among naturally occurring variables. The goal is to identify predictive relationships by using correlations or more advanced techniques such as factor analysis. The results of correlational research also have implications for decision making.

KEY CONCEPTS

population
sampling frame
sample
element
representativeness
biased sample
nonprobability sampling
probability sampling
accidental samples
purposive sampling

simple random sampling
margin of error
stratified random sampling
cluster sampling
interviewer bias
cross-sectional design
successive independent samples design
longitudinal design
social desirability
percentile score
standard score
test-retest reliability
construct validity
correlational research

REVIEW QUESTIONS

1 What two characteristics do surveys have in common even when they differ widely in scope and purpose?
2 State two advantages and two limitations of the consistent use of the same phrasing and ordering of questions in a survey.
3 Give an example of a sampling plan that would be likely to result in each of the two sources of a biased sample.
4 What is the greatest danger when an accidental sample is used in survey research?
5 Explain the relationship between the size of a sample needed to ensure representativeness and the homogeneity of the population.
6 Why would a researcher choose to use stratified random sampling instead of simple random sampling?
7 When is cluster sampling likely to be used?
8 What are the strengths and weaknesses of a mail survey?
9 What procedures can be followed to enhance response rate in a mail survey?
10 What are the strengths and weaknesses of personal interviews?
11 Why does the use of probes increase the possibility of interviewer bias? How can this problem be avoided?
12 What advantages do phone surveys have over personal interviews?
13 What are the two most common purposes of a cross-sectional design?
14 Why must researchers be cautious in using successive independent samples to interpret changes in attitudes over time?
15 What are the strengths and weaknesses of a longitudinal design?
16 What general guideline that we follow in everyday life can be used in assessing the truthfulness of survey responses?
17 Explain how the objectives of surveys and tests differ.
18 Describe the nature of the psychological concepts that are measured by each of the three major types of tests: aptitude, achievement, and personality.
19 Describe the role of sampling in the development of a test.
20 What is the major advantage of using a derived score such as a percentile when reporting an individual's performance on a test?
21 What is one common technique for measuring the reliability of a test?
22 Identify three factors that affect the reliability of a test.
23 Explain the roles of convergent validity and discriminant validity in assessing the construct validity of a test.
24 Describe one procedure that can be used to assess the fairness of a test.
25 Describe the major purpose of correlational research, and briefly explain how correlational research is different from experimental research.

26 What role does factor analysis play in the interpretation of the results of correlational studies?

27 Distinguish between clinical prediction and statistical prediction as approaches to decision making.

CHALLENGE QUESTIONS

1 A survey researcher selected a random sample of households for a survey of consumer attitudes. In conducting the survey he often found that no one was home at the households he had selected. His solution to this problem was a simple one. He interviewed whichever next-door neighbor of the selected household happened to be home. Comment critically on the researcher's "solution" to his problem.

2 Two student researchers have been asked to do a survey to determine the attitudes of other students toward fraternities and sororities on campus. There are 2,000 students in the school. About 25 percent of the students belong to the Greek organizations and 75 percent do not. One researcher plans to draw a stratified random sample of 200 students: 100 from among those students who belong to Greek organizations and 100 from among the independent students. The second researcher plans to draw one simple random sample of 100 students from the campus as a whole. Comment critically on these two sampling plans. Finally, develop your own sampling plan if you decide that neither of the ones proposed so far is optimal.

3 A small national business manufactured and marketed a single product, Brand X. Members of the marketing department decided to do a mail survey of people who used Brand X to determine how satisfied they were with the product. They carefully selected a random sample of 100 people from the company's list of registered users of the product. Of the 30 people who returned the mail survey, 28 of them indicated that they were very pleased with the performance of Brand X. An advertising campaign was prepared in which the company boasted that 93 percent of those who use Brand X are very pleased with its performance. Explain what conditions would have to be met for this ad campaign to be defensible on the basis of the survey results, and explain why it is unlikely that these conditions would be met.

4 About a week before a national election a national survey company changed the way they conducted their surveys. Before the change, the company conducted "regular polls" using a sampling frame of registered voters. In the regular polls, the interviewers made three attempts to contact each person selected for the survey before dropping the person from the survey. After the change, the company conducted "tracking polls" using a sampling frame of "likely voters." The likely voters were selected on the basis of the characteristics of voters from the previous election—an election that had had a particularly low turnout rate. For the tracking polls, the interviewers tried only once to contact each person selected for the survey before dropping the person from the survey. The tracking poll results reported each day included the results of the three previous days' polling; the tracking polls were a rolling poll rather than the single sample that was the basis of the regular polls. The tracking polls attracted considerable attention because they showed that the gap between the two major candidates was smaller than it had been.

   A The smaller gap between the candidates that was indicated in the tracking polls could have resulted because the difference between the two candidates was actually getting smaller. Or, more undecided voters could have been committing to a candidate now that the election was getting so close with more of these undecided voters committing to the candidate who had been behind in the polls. It is possible, however, that the change from the regular polls to the tracking polls contributed to the change in the polling results. Identify what aspects of the use of tracking polls could have changed the polling results relative to the use of regular polls. Be sure to explain how these aspects of the tracking polls could have contributed to lessening the difference between the two candidates.

B Do the criticisms you raised about the tracking polls in part A of this problem assure that the reported results with the tracking polls do not validly reflect voters' preferences for the two candidates? Why or why not?

ANSWER TO CHALLENGE QUESTION 1

1 The interviewer's solution is likely to introduce a bias, thereby threatening the representativeness of the sample and the subsequent generality of any findings. Factors such as employment or socioeconomic status might make those who happen to be home systematically different from those who were originally selected for the sample who happened not to be available to be interviewed.

Chapter 5

Unobtrusive Measures of Behavior

Outline

OVERVIEW

The behavioral scientist generally learns about behavior through some form of direct observation (Chapter 3) or from data obtained through interviews, questionnaires, and tests (Chapter 4). In this chapter we consider some alternatives to these major approaches to the study of behavior. Although these alternative methods are often important in themselves, they also frequently provide a means of confirming the validity of conclusions reached on the basis of direct observation or surveys.

One major alternative is the examination of **physical traces** produced by persons engaged in some form of behavior. Consider, for example, the possibility that Latin Americans differ from North Americans in their concern for punctuality. Possible cultural differences in the importance of punctuality *could* be investigated by surveying people in both North American and Latin American countries as to how they feel about concerts or sporting events that begin later than the scheduled starting time. However, an alternative method would be to examine clocks in cities of North America and South America. It seems reasonable to assume that people's concern for time will be reflected in how accurately they set their clocks. In fact, researchers have found that public clocks (those located in banks) in a Brazilian city were less accurate than those in a similar-sized city in the United States (Levine, West, & Reis, 1980). Although there may be alternative explanations for this finding, differences in this physical-trace measure support the notion that cultural differences in concern for being on time do exist. You may remember from the discussion in Chapter 1 that Levine (1990) also used accuracy of public clocks to help define the "pace of life" of cities and countries around the world. Direct observation revealed that the walking speed of a country's citizens was correlated with the accuracy of the country's public clocks.

Archives constitute another important source of information about behavior. **Archival data** are obtained by inspecting the records and documents produced by society, as well as by analyzing reports in the media. For example, researchers have claimed that analyses of mortality data reveal a lower than expected frequency of deaths before important events, such as birthdays and religious holidays, and a higher than expected frequency of deaths after these important events. The general procedure behind studies investigating the relationship between death and important occasions is to examine archival data revealing the death dates of individuals in relation to certain important events (see, for example, Schulz & Bazerman, 1980). Three major positive events have been examined by researchers: birthdays, national elections, and religious holidays. For instance, one of the early studies to offer data supporting a death-dip hypothesis used birth dates and death dates of persons listed in the book *Four Hundred Notable Americans* (Schulz & Bazerman, 1980). The number of deaths in the month immediately prior to the month of an individual's birth was lower than what we would expect if chance alone was operating, thus giving credence to the death-dip hypothesis. According to Schulz and Bazerman a general explanation for this type of finding is that people are somehow able to prolong their lives or delay death until a certain event has been experienced. Exactly how one might do this is not particularly clear. One suggestion is that looking forward to a positive event creates a state of positive anticipation that precipitates beneficial neurochemical changes. Another possible explanation is that elderly persons are more likely to follow their health and medical regimens closely as an important date nears, so as to reduce the chances of dying before the event arrives.

In this chapter we present the rationale for using physical traces and archival data. Particular kinds of physical traces are identified and examples of their use in psychological studies are offered. Types of archives and the kinds of data that can be drawn from archival sources are also reviewed. Several important advantages of the use of physical traces or archival data are highlighted. There are some limitations and problems with these unobtrusive measures, and they, too, are discussed.

PHYSICAL TRACES

RATIONALE

As everyone who has read a few detective stories knows, examining physical evidence of past behavior can provide important clues to the characteristics (or even identity) of individuals, as well as information about the conditions under which an event occurred. The size of footprints in the ground says something about the size and age of the person who stepped there. The distance between footprints can indicate whether the person was walking or running. And so on. As we have already seen, physical evidence (in the form of clock settings) can be of value to the behavioral scientist. Physical traces (like the archival data that are discussed later in this chapter) are especially valuable because they provide nonreactive measures of behavior (Webb et al., 1981).

You will recall from Chapter 3 that a behavioral measure is reactive when the subjects' awareness of an observer's presence affects the measurement process. This is often the case when direct observations are made, and it is nearly always the case when surveys are conducted. Reactivity introduces the problem of response bias. Aware that their responses are being recorded, subjects may behave in a way that does not correspond to their normal behavior. Survey data are particularly susceptible to reactive effects, because respondents may give answers that they feel the researcher wants to hear or may answer in a way that makes them (the respondents) look good.

Physical-trace measures are unobtrusive (because they are obtained in the absence of the subject), so they are valuable alternatives to the reactive measures obtained via direct observation or surveys. Although a physical-trace measure might be the only measure of behavior in some studies, physical traces are more commonly used in combination with other measures. As we have emphasized previously, a research study can be strengthened considerably by including several different measures of behavior. A **multimethod approach** to hypothesis testing is recommended because it reduces the likelihood that research findings are due to some artifact of the measurement process (Webb et al., 1981). There are few (if any) perfect measures in the social sciences. Therefore, the results of a study must be carefully scrutinized to determine whether some characteristic of the measurement instrument (such as its reactivity) has contributed to the results. Even then, it is possible that some artifact has been overlooked. The most persuasive argument supporting the validity of a particular research hypothesis is one based on evidence obtained by applying a combination of measures.

Researchers investigating cultural differences in time perception used such a multimethod approach. They surveyed individuals living in Latin America and in the United States to find out how frequently their subjects were late for appointments and to discover their attitudes toward being late (Levine et al., 1980). Citizens of Brazil reported themselves more often late for appointments and expressed less regret at being late than did citizens of the United States. However, a bias in these responses could be present if people described themselves in a way that fit their cultural "image," rather than as they actually behaved. As already noted, however, the researchers also found that public clocks were less accurate in Brazil than in the United States. Further, the researchers observed that watches worn by people in the United States deviated less from the correct time (as reported by the telephone company) than watches worn by people in Brazil. The data obtained by examining public clocks and the watches worn by citizens of each country tended to confirm the validity of the survey responses and, in combination with the survey results, provided impressive evidence for the research hypothesis.

TYPES OF PHYSICAL TRACES

Physical traces are the remnants, fragments, and products of past behavior. Two broad categories of physical traces are use traces and products. *Use traces* are what the label implies—the physical evidence that results from use (or nonuse) of an item. Clock settings are an example of a physical-use trace. So are the remains of cigarettes in ashtrays and the marks made on school desks. *Products* are the creations, constructions, or other artifacts of earlier behavior. Anthropologists are often interested in the surviving products of ancient cultures. By examining the types of vessels, paintings, and other artifacts that remain, the anthropologist can often describe precisely the pattern of behavior exhibited in a setting that is thousands of years old. Psychologists may also examine physical products in order to describe behavior or to test hypotheses. Psychologists who study animal behavior, for instance, may learn about the behavior of different species by examining the types of nests that are constructed.

Use Traces An examination of physical evidence provides measures of both accretion and erosion (Webb et al., 1981). *Accretion measures* are based on the accumulation of material. Measuring the amount of litter, for example, would be taking an accretion measure. *Erosion measures* are obtained when the physical evidence is the result of selective wear. The degree to which a young child's dolls show signs of wear is an erosion measure that might indicate which dolls the child likes best. The distinction between accretion measures and erosion measures is not always so obvious. Settings of clocks, for instance, resist ready classification. Nevertheless, classifying physical-use traces in terms of accretion or erosion is often a meaningful description of physical traces, and the distinction calls our attention to two important dimensions of use traces.

Physical-use traces are also classified as either natural or controlled (planned). *Natural* use traces are produced without any intervention by the investigator. Their appearance is the result of naturally occurring events. *Controlled,* or planned, measures result to some degree from the intervention or manipulation of an investigator.

Friedman and Wilson (1975) employed both controlled and natural accretion measures to investigate college students' use of textbooks. They affixed tiny glue seals between adjacent pages of textbooks before the students purchased the books for a course. At the end of the semester the investigators obtained the books from the students and recorded how many seals in the textbooks had been broken and where the broken seals were located. This constituted a controlled accretion measure. The investigators also analyzed the frequency and nature of underlining in the textbooks, a natural accretion measure. Analysis of these physical-use measures indicated that students more often read (and presumably studied) the chapters that appeared early in the book than those appearing later in the book.

Table 5.1 contains examples of physical-use traces and the variables being measured. These measures either actually were used as part of a scientific study or represent suggestions by researchers of possible novel and nonreactive measures of behavior (see Webb et al., 1981). The examples given in Table 5.1 have been organized according to whether they are accretion or erosion measures and whether their use is natural or controlled. As you examine the contents of Table 5.1, try to think of other possible physical traces that could serve as measures of the variables listed.

Products Physical products have been examined less frequently in psychological studies than have physical-use traces. Nevertheless, this category of physical traces has been used in interesting and meaningful ways to test hy-

TABLE 5.1 EXAMPLES OF PHYSICAL-USE TRACES AND VARIABLES BEING MEASURED*

Trace	Variable
Natural accretion	
Inscriptions (graffiti) on walls of public restrooms	Sexual preoccupation
Radio dial settings	Popularity of radio stations
Fingerprints or smudges on pages of books	Book usage
Liquor bottles in trash cans	Alcohol consumption of households
Odometer readings in cars	Conservation of gasoline
Litter	Effectiveness of antilitter posters
Dust on books	Frequency or recency of use
Garbage	Food use and life-style
Locked/unlocked cars	Concern for property
Lengths of cigarette butts	Cultural differences in death rate due to cancer
Controlled accretion	
Glue seals broken (seals inserted prior to distribution)	Index of specific pages read
Nose prints on windows of museum exhibit (windows wiped clean each night)	Popularity (frequency) and age (height of prints) of viewers
Natural erosion	
Wear on floor or steps	Amount of foot traffic
Wear on library books	Frequency of use
Food consumed	Eating behavior
Spots (produced by rubbing) on statues or religious objects	Level of religious belief
Controlled erosion	
Wear on children's shoes (measured at two points in time)	Activity level of children
Removal of "tear-away" tags on ads or notices	Interest in notice
Wear on mats or other floor coverings placed in specific areas	Amount of foot traffic
Change in statues or objects coated with substances sensitive to touching	Superstitious behavior

* From Webb et al. (1981).

potheses about behavior. A particularly good example of the use of physical products is found in a study by Coren and Porac (1977). They investigated the extent of human right-handedness in various cultures since ancient times. To determine manual preference, they examined more than 12,000 works of art, including paintings, sculpture, and other products that spanned more than 50 centuries of human endeavor. The researchers recorded instances of unambiguous tool or weapon use depicted in the artworks. They looked for any differential trend in the depiction of right- or left-handers in different cultures and at different times in human history. No trend was evident. Rather, across many cultures and in every epoch, 93 percent of the artworks examined showed persons using their right hand. The results provide evidence for a physiological rather than a sociocultural theory of handedness.

Brandt (1972) points out that the products that people own harbor important clues to their life-style and behavior patterns. What personality differences, for instance, are reflected in the purchase of different models of cars or in the extras and options that are ordered with a car? Besides serving as a measure of social status or personality, the products a person owns can be used to assess the validity of certain kinds of verbal reports. Are individuals' statements about their attitude toward energy conservation, for instance, related to the kinds of products they own and use?

Mooney and Brabant (1987) cite data indicating that various kinds of greeting cards—for example, those celebrating birthdays or holidays, as well as those conveying sympathy—represent over half of all the personal mail moved annually by the U.S. Postal Service. It is not surprising, therefore, that this particular product of society has proved to be a veritable treasure trove for researchers investigating attitudes toward such social phenomena as drinking, aging, and death. Mooney and Brabant, for instance, randomly sampled birthday cards from fourteen retail outlets in a metropolitan area as part of a study of the deviant messages in interpersonal communications. The cards were classified according to various categories of deviant behavior (for example, making reference to obesity, violence, marital infidelity, or mental illness) as well as to a category of nondeviant behavior. Approximately 16 percent of the cards sampled contained some form of deviant message. Among the many differences noted between deviant and nondeviant cards was that deviant cards were more likely to present stereotypes, particularly of males, than were nondeviant cards. According to Mooney and Brabant, because cards containing deviant messages are the "moral opposite" of traditional birthday greetings, they likely signal a "unique moral order" between those involved, and, according to the authors, are perhaps appropriate when "you care enough to send the very worst" (p. 386).

PROBLEMS AND LIMITATIONS

Physical measures offer a researcher valuable and sometimes novel means to study behavior. And the measures available are limited only by the ingenuity of the investigator. However, the validity of physical traces must be carefully examined and verified through independent sources of evidence. Bias can be introduced in the way physical-use traces are laid down and in the manner in which traces survive over time. Does a well-worn path to the right indicate people's interest in objects in that direction or simply a natural human tendency to turn right? Is the setting of clocks a good measure of people's regard for punctuality, or do inaccurate clock settings indicate poor artisanship, inadequate maintenance, or irregular electrical service?

Problems associated with the analysis of physical traces are illustrated in a classic study of honesty carried out using the "lost-letter technique" (see Merritt & Fowler, 1948). We can consider the method as controlled accretion. The investigators dropped postcards and envelopes at various locations in cities of the East and Midwest. Two types of envelopes were discarded. One contained a written message, and the other contained a lead slug the size of a 50-cent piece. All the letters were addressed and bore proper postage, but no return address was shown. Although 85 percent of the "empty" envelopes were returned, only 54 percent of the envelopes with a slug found their way to a mailbox. Further, more than 10 percent of the envelopes with a slug were returned after having been opened.

Before the researchers could conclude that the return rates represented a valid measure of the public's honesty (or dishonesty), several possible biases associated with this physical trace had to be considered. Postcards, for instance, were less likely than sealed envelopes to be returned, but the fact that postcards are more easily disturbed by natural conditions no doubt contributed to this difference. On the other hand, envelopes with a slug are heavier and less likely to be blown away—and these were still less likely to be returned. Letters that were dropped in certain locations (for example, where many children are present) or at certain times of the day (for example, just before nightfall) are also likely to be "lost" for reasons other than the public's dishonesty or apathy.

Some of these possible biases associated with the lost-letter technique were avoided by the methods of dispersal used by the researchers, whereas others were checked via direct observation of a letter's fate. Observation of a sample of dropped letters revealed that a letter was picked up 90 percent of the time by the first person who saw it.

Whenever possible, supplementary evidence for the validity of physical traces should be obtained (see Webb et al., 1981). Alternative hypotheses for changes in physical traces must be considered, and data must be collected that allow different interpretations to be dismissed.

ARCHIVAL DATA

RATIONALE

When we were born, a record was made of our birth. Information on the birth record probably included the city and state in which we were born, the date and time of our birth, our parents' names, and our name. When we die, another record will be made. It will include such details as probable cause of death, date and time of death, and our age. In between these two events, innumerable records are made of our behavior. Physicians record visits. Hospitals keep a record of when we enter and when we leave. Schools record our grades and extracurricular activities. Businesses may record the number of times we are late or how often we fail to show up for work. Newspapers describe notable successes and failures. Local governments record when we get married and to whom, as well as when we buy a house and how much it costs. The federal government records, among other things, what we pay in income taxes.

Records are kept not only of individuals but also of countries, institutions, cities, and businesses. The gross national product of a country, its major exports and imports, the size of its navy, and the distribution of its population are but a few of the facts that are recorded. How much profit a company makes is part of its report to stockholders. Voting behaviors of state and federal legislators are recorded, as is the amount of money a city spends on social services. Analysis and interpretation of local and world events flood the media. The contents of the media and of documents and books (published and unpublished) are a source of information about current fads and prejudices, changing patterns of belief, and the ideas of important (and not so important) members of society.

Archives are records or documents recounting the activities of individuals or of institutions, governments, and other groups. As measures of behavior, archival data share some of the same advantages as physical traces. Archival measures are nonreactive and therefore provide an alternative to data collection via surveys. Like physical-trace measures, archival data can be used to check the validity of other measures and as a part of multimethod approaches to hypothesis testing. A nice illustration of the use of archival data in the context of a multimethod approach to hypothesis testing is Frank and Gilovich's (1988) investigation of the strong cultural association that exists between the color black and "badness," or evil.

As Frank and Gilovich point out, in vintage American Western movies you could always tell the good guys from the bad guys. The good guys, of course, wore white hats and the bad guys wore black hats. There is a strong cultural association between black and badness. We speak of people's being "blackballed," "blacklisted," "blackmailed," and a reputation's being "blackened." When terrible things happen it is a "black day." Black is seen in many cultures as the color of death. The good and bad sides of human nature are also contrasted using black-and-white images, as was illustrated by the characters of the famous *Star Wars* movie. Viewers of this movie (first of a classic trilogy) likely will remember the confrontation between the villain, Darth Vader (dressed completely in black), and the young hero, Luke Skywalker (dressed in white or light colors). Vader, unfortunately, had "gone over" to the dark side.

Frank and Gilovich wanted to find out if this strong cultural association between black and evil would affect the way people behave. Specifically, they asked whether professional sports teams that wear black uniforms are more aggressive than those that wear nonblack uniforms. Using archival data obtained from the central offices of the National Football League (NFL) and the National Hockey League (NHL), Frank and Gilovich analyzed penalty records of each major professional team in these sports between 1970 and 1986. Yards penalized were analyzed in the NFL, and minutes that a player was assigned to the penalty box were calculated in the NHL. These particular measures were deemed more appropriate given the study's hypothesis than was number of infractions. Penalties for overaggressiveness are generally more severe (in yards or minutes) than are those for simple rule violations. The operational definition of a "black uniform" was that the colored version of the team's uniform (the one used typically for away games in the NHL and for home games in the NFL) was more than 50 percent black. (An exception was made for the Chicago Bears of the NFL, who wear dark-blue uniforms but whose uniforms many people mistakenly remember as black.) According to the authors' hypothesis, teams wearing black should be penalized more than would be expected simply by chance. And they were. Thus, teams with black uniforms, such as Oakland, Chicago, and Cincinnati in the NFL, and Philadelphia, Pittsburgh, and Vancouver in the NHL, were reliably more aggressive than were many other teams.

What psychological processes might account for these effects? Frank and Gilovich suggest that both social-perception and self-perception processes are at work. They argue that others (specifically, referees) "see" players in black as more aggressive than players not wearing black (and therefore award more penalties to players in black), and that players themselves behave more aggressively when they put on black uniforms. As part of their multimethod approach to this issue, they provided support for these explanations in the form of data obtained from laboratory experiments. In one experiment, both college students and referees watched "staged" football games between teams wearing black or white uniforms and rated their aggressiveness. In a second study, students donned either black or white uniforms in anticipation of an athletic competition before choosing a game from a list of aggressive and nonaggressive games. In the first experiment, both referees and college students were more likely to rate a team wearing black as aggressive. The second experiment showed that subjects who donned black uniforms chose more aggressive games. By combining data obtained from archival analyses and laboratory experiments, the investigators provide an unusually strong case for their explanations of this interesting cultural phenomenon.

An examination of archival information may also provide a way to test the external validity of laboratory findings. Lau and Russell (1980) analyzed the contents of the sports pages in eight daily newspapers in order to test whether results obtained from laboratory-based experiments investigating *causal attributions* (the reasons people give for a certain outcome, or the cause they attribute the outcome to) were relevant to "real-world" settings. A major finding of attribution research is that people tend to make internal attributions (assuming that the outcome is due to some characteristic within themselves) for success and to make external attributions (assuming that the outcome is due to something beyond their control) for failure. Lau and Russell's analysis of explanations given by sportswriters or team members for the outcome of baseball and football games supported this conclusion that originally emerged from laboratory research. Specifically, they identified 594 explanations for success and failure involving 33 major sporting events. From the perspective of the winning team, 75 percent of the attributions were internal, whereas only 55 percent of the attributions of the losing team were internal.

Support for this laboratory-based attribution theory has also been obtained by analyzing letters and replies published in two widely syndicated newspaper advice columns: "Ann Landers" and "Dear Abby" (see Fischer, Schoeneman, & Rubanowitz, 1987; Schoeneman & Rubanowitz, 1985). The investigation was based on fifteen randomly selected columns of each adviser from 1980. The researchers, along with two-person teams of undergraduates trained for this task, first identified explanatory statements. The explanations were then coded according to whether the locus of the explanation was internal, that is, inherent to the subject, or external, implicating situations and circumstances. For one analysis, explanations were also coded in terms of temporal stability and controllability (see Fischer et al., 1987). A stable cause is one that is unchanging over time; an unstable cause is changeable. Attributions reflected controllable causes only when a subject was deemed capable of exercising control over them. One major finding of this archival study was that people view their own problems as the result of others' (external) invariable (stable) willful (controllable) tendencies. One letter-writer illustrated this attribution bias when she identified the source of her problematic vacations as follows: "Sydney is a drag on a trip [because] he has no interest in seeing new places or meeting new people" (Fischer et al., 1987, p. 461).

Other reasons for using archival data are to test hypotheses about previous behavior and to assess the effect of a natural treatment. It is possible, for instance, to obtain a measure of television-viewing habits by studying the water pressure records of a city (see Webb et al., 1981)! When a television show is watched by many of a city's residents, water pressure levels are found to fluctuate in accordance with the show. For example, in one city a "30-million-gallon effect" was found for half-time and end-of-game breaks in a Super Bowl game, whereas only a "15-million-gallon effect" was found at the end of a Presidential debate. Changes in level of water pressure presumably reflect trips that viewers make to get a drink of water or to use the toilet when a convenient break appears in a television show that they are watching. Archival records have played a central role in studies of the "home advantage" in sports competitions (see, for example, Courneya & Carron, 1992). The *home advantage* refers to the fact that in many sports competitions a team wins consistently more games played at home than it does games played away.

Natural treatments are naturally occurring events that have significant impact on society at large or on particular members. Because it is not always possible to anticipate these events, the investigtor who wishes to assess their impact must be prepared to use a variety of behavioral measures, including archival data. School records of absenteeism have been used as an indirect measure of health in a study investigating the effect of aircraft noise on children (see Cohen, Evans, Krantz, & Stokols, 1980). Assassinations of world leaders, drastic changes in the stock market, and the passage of new laws are examples of the kinds of events that may have important effects on behavior and that might be investigated using archival data.

Another reason for considering archival data as a behavioral measure is simply because archival data are so plentiful. We noted earlier the extensive records that society keeps on individuals, groups, and institutions. Through careful analysis of archival information, the industrious researcher can seek evidence to support numerous hypotheses. There are practical advantages as well. Archival data represent data that have already been collected; at times, initial summary descriptions may also be provided in archival records. Thus an extensive data-collection stage may be circumvented. Because archival information is frequently part of the public record and is usually reported in a manner that does not identify individuals, ethical concerns are less worrisome. One goal of this chapter is to alert you to the possible rich rewards of analyzing archival data in the context of psychological studies of behavior.

TYPES OF ARCHIVAL DATA

The sheer diversity and extent of archival sources make their classification rather arbitrary. One scheme is to distinguish between records that are continuously kept and updated, such as tax records and records of various government agencies, and those that are discontinuous or episodic (see Webb et al., 1981). Included in the latter category are sales records of business, absentee and tardiness records, and personal documents. These two types of records are often also distinguished by the degree of their availability for public inspection. Many continuous records, frequently referred to as *running records,* are kept by government agencies and are easily obtainable. Most discontinuous records of private institutions and businesses, however, are not open to public scrutiny or can be obtained only after many requests and considerable patience on the part of the researcher. Because of their continuous nature, running records are particularly useful in longitudinal studies or in the documentation of trends.

The news media are yet another important source of archival information. Both continuous and discontinuous records are published in newspapers and reported on television. The content of media reports is also a form of archival record and is subject to analysis. Earlier we described how the contents of sports pages were used to test a theory of causal attribution. The placement of "Found" advertisements in the Lost and Found section of a newspaper can be used to measure public altruism (see Goldstein, Minkin, Minkin, & Baer, 1978).

Phillips (1977) used running records of motor vehicle fatalities kept by the California Highway Patrol and a measure of suicide publicity derived from California newspapers to determine whether there is a significant suicidal component to motor vehicle fatalities. He hypothesized that a substantial number of deaths arising from motor vehicle accidents are actually the result of individuals using their cars to commit suicide. To test this hypothesis, Phillips investigated whether motor vehicle fatalities would, like suicides in general, increase after a well-publicized suicide story. Components of the publicity measure included the daily circulation of each newspaper and the number of days the newspaper carried the suicide story. This measure correlated significantly with changes in motor vehicle fatalities after each story. The number of motor vehicle fatalities increased significantly during the few days after a well-publicized suicide story, reaching a peak on Day 3. This result is shown in Figure 5.1. Changes in frequency were determined by comparing experimental periods (the week right after the story) with control periods that were free from suicide stories and were matched with the experimental periods in terms of day of the week, presence or absence of holidays, and time of the year. Phillips concluded that "suicide stories stimulate a wave of imitative suicides, some of which are disguised as motor vehicle accidents" (p. 1464).

Table 5.2 contains a list of selected sources of archival information and the nature of the data that might be obtained from them. The types of archival data shown in Table 5.2 have been rather arbitrarily classified as running records, those pertaining to the media, and "other records," including records of businesses, schools, and other private institutions. An examination of the sources described in Table 5.2 will introduce you to the variety of possible measures that can be obtained from archival sources. Then, following a brief discussion of content analysis of archival sources, we will review several specific illustrations of the use of archival data in the context of hypothesis testing.

CONTENT ANALYSIS

Although many sources of archival data can be identified, the usefulness of these sources depends ultimately on how their content is analyzed. In the simplest case, the analysis required may be minimal. Recording the votes of state legislators may be as simple as transcribing vote tallies found in legislative

FIGURE 5.1 Daily fluctuation in motor-vehicle accident fatalities for a 2-week period before, during (Day 0), and after publication of suicide stories. (From Phillips, 1977.)

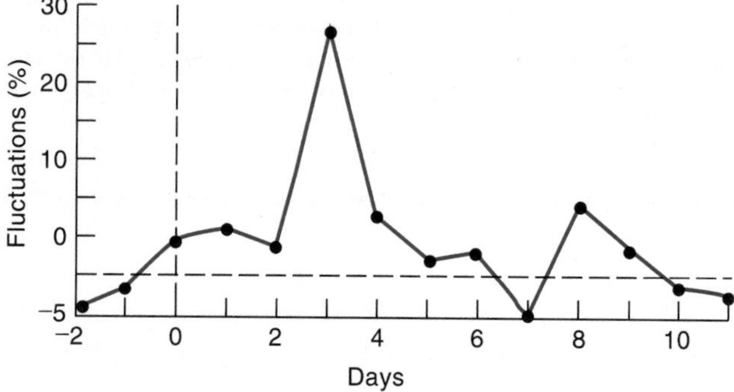

TABLE 5.2 SELECTED SOURCES OF ARCHIVAL INFORMATION AND ILLUSTRATIVE DATA FOR THREE TYPES OF ARCHIVES*

Source	Ilustrative data
Running records	
Congressional Record	Statements of position on particular issues
Telephone directories	Community ethnic group membership
Salaries of teachers or government employees	Community support
Government agency records (labor, commerce, agriculture departments)	Living trends
Judicial record	Uniformity in sentencing for antisocial behavior
Moody's Handbook	Corporate financial structure
Who's Who in America	Nature of cited accomplishments of successful people
Tax records	Regional differences in patterns of living
City budgets	Perceived value or extent of support of various activities
Media	
Society section of metropolitan newspaper	Upper-middle-class and lower-upper-class activities
Children's books on sale	Qualities of models (heroes and heroines)
Movie announcements in newspapers	Changing taboos and enticements
Want ads	Employer inducements
Obituary columns	Charity preferences
Published speeches	Political, social, economic attitudes
Newspaper headlines	Press bias
Other records†	
Absentee and tardiness records	Work habits or motivation
Military re-enlistment and longevity figures	Morale indicator
Pay increase and promotion lists	Perceived value of individuals to an organization
Number of people one supervises	Measure of management responsibility
Production and other output figures	Performance of individuals, departments, and so on
Sales contest records	Selling effectiveness, effectiveness of incentive plans
Sales slips at Delegates' Lounge bar in UN	Tension indicator
Peanut sales at ball games	Excitement indicator (greater after than before seventh inning)
Sales level of consumer goods	Effectiveness of display location, advertisement, or style of packaging
Air trip insurance figures	Public concern before and after air crashes
Sales of layettes by color (blue or pink)	Sex preference in different social classes
Sale price of autographs	Popularity indicator
Club membership list	Indicator of segment of society involved
Committee reports	Institutional modification attempts
Actuarial records: birth, baptismal, death records; marriage licenses	Comparative demographic data (occupation, religion, time of day, cause of death, and so on)
Cemetery documents, burial-lot records	Family membership

* Adapted from Brandt (1972).

† Institutions, businesses, hospitals, schools, and so on; may or may not be opened to public inspection.

documents. Similarly, determining the average sales figure for divisions of a corporation may be only a matter of adding and dividing sets of numbers provided by the corporation's accountant. In many cases, however, extracting relevant data from an archival source requires careful procedures and relatively complex analysis of the source's content. Furthermore, problems of sampling, reliability, and validity of measures must be addressed, just as these problems are addressed in situations where behavior is observed directly.

Content analysis is generally defined as any technique for making inferences by objectively identifying specific characteristics of messages (Holsti, 1969). Though it is associated primarily with written communications, content analysis may be used with any form of message, including television and radio programs, speeches, films, and interviews. Weigel, Loomis, and Soja (1980) used content analysis to study race relations as they are depicted on prime-time television. They analyzed the frequency of appearances of blacks and whites on evening television shows carried by all three major networks. In addition, they rated the quality of black-white and white-white interactions. Appearances by blacks involved less than 9 percent of human appearance time in programs and commercials, and, compared with white-white interactions, black-white interactions were relatively infrequent and more formalized when they did occur.

There are several discernible steps in conducting research using content analysis. First is the identification of a relevant archival source. What is relevant, of course, depends on the goals of the study and the questions the researcher is asking. In some cases merely a statement of the purpose of the study is sufficient to pinpoint an appropriate archival source. A researcher who sets out to study humor in tombstone messages, the manifest content of suicide notes, or race relations on television has already identified the general source for content analysis. In other situations the identification of relevant sources depends on the ingenuity of the researcher. Lau and Russell's (1980) choice of the sports page represented an appropriate and clever use of archival sources as a test of the external validity of laboratory findings related to attribution.

Having identified an archival source, the researcher must sample selections from this source appropriately. Sampling procedures similar to those described in previous chapters can be used. As is the case when behavior or events are sampled, the goal of sampling is to obtain a sample that is representative of all the data of interest. To investigate race relations on television, Weigel et al. (1980) videotaped a full week's broadcasts by the three major networks in the spring of 1978. Only programs with a story line, but all product commercials, were included in the sample. The decision not to use documentaries, news broadcasts, and sports shows reduced the sample of viewing time by about 20 percent. As always, the extent to which the results of an archival study can be generalized depends on the nature of the sample that is used.

The next step in performing a content analysis is *coding*. This step is similar to the scoring of narrative records (see Chapter 3) and requires that relevant descriptive categories and appropriate units of measure be defined (see Holsti,

1969). As with the choice of the archival source itself, what determines a relevant descriptive category is related to the goals of the study. This aspect of a content-analysis task can be illustrated by examining the categories used by Weigel et al. (1980) in their study of race relations. Four major categories were defined: (1) human appearance time, (2) black appearance time, (3) cross-racial appearance time, and (4) cross-racial interaction time. Each category was operationally defined. For instance, cross-racial interaction was defined as "the time during which black and white characters were engaged in active, on-screen interactions (talking, touching, or clear nonverbal communication)" (p. 886). The use of precise operational definitions permitted coders viewing the sample broadcasts to make reliable judgments of events.

In many content-analysis studies, the communication is written. The units of classification for quantitative analysis generally include single words, characters, sentences or paragraphs, themes, or particular items (Holsti, 1969). Lau and Russell (1980), for instance, determined the frequency of attribution statements that were categorized as either internal or external and were made by members of the winning or losing team. Another unit of measure often used when newspaper content is analyzed is that of space—for instance, number of column inches devoted to a particular topic. When television or radio broadcasts are studied, the unit of measure may be time. Such was the case for the study by Weigel et al. (1980). Both black appearances and black-white appearances were expressed in terms of the percentage of total human appearance time.

Qualitative measures are also occasionally used as part of content analysis. These qualitative assessments may be in the form of ratings. In addition to measuring time of cross-racial interactions on prime time television, Weigel et al. sought to determine the "degree to which cross-racial interactions on television were characterized by the conditions that promote friendliness and mutual respect in face-to-face encounters" (pp. 886–887). To do this, they developed a series of rating scales that emphasized the interpersonal dimensions found to be important in previous race-related research. Broadcasts videotaped a year earlier were used to define levels of the scales, and coders were trained in the use of the scales before real data were collected. As has been mentioned, the quality of black-white interactions, relative to white-white interactions, differed on several dimensions.

ILLUSTRATIVE USES OF ARCHIVAL DATA

Analysis of Communications Osgood and Walker (1959) compared the content of real suicide notes, simulated suicide notes (notes deliberately faked), and ordinary letters. Working under the assumption that language behavior changes as a function of heightened motivation, they suggested that suicide notes should differ from ordinary letters and faked notes in several ways. Specifically, the researchers hypothesized that, relative to other messages, suicide notes would show: (1) greater stereotypy (more repetitions, fewer modifiers, more familiar words and phrases); (2) greater disorganization of language (more grammatical errors, shorter units); (3) more frequent use of self-destructive motives (greater use of self-critical statements); and (4) more evidence of conflict (greater qualification of statements, more frequent use of constructions with "however," "but," and "if").

The investigators chose sixteen different measures to test their hypotheses regarding the content of these messages (for example, number of syllables per word and number of distress-expressing phrases). Many of these measures revealed significant differences between suicide notes and ordinary letters, lending support to three of the four major hypotheses. Interestingly, suicide notes did not show greater disorganization. When quantitative measures that were successful in distinguishing between suicide notes and ordinary letters were used to differentiate between faked and real suicide notes, the analysis correctly predicted the real suicide note in ten of thirteen matched pairs.

Analysis of Trends Over the years, women have frequently been underrepresented in businesses and professions. In the last few decades, however, significant attempts have been made to reduce any sex bias affecting hiring and promotion as well as entry into various professions. Scientific organizations, such as those in psychology, have taken steps to reduce discriminatory practices. The *APA Publication Manual* (American Psychological Association, 1983), for instance, includes specific guidelines for using nonsexist language in APA journals (see Appendix C of your textbook). The APA Ethics Code, which was discussed in part in Chapter 2, clearly promotes respect for people's rights and for the dignity of all individuals without regard to gender (as well as to other cultural, social, or physical factors). According to General Principle D of the Ethics Code, "Psychologists try to eliminate the effect on their work of biases based on these factors, and they do not knowingly participate in nor condone unfair discriminatory practices" (American Psychological Association, 1992a, p. 1600).

To what extent have psychologists been successful in reducing sex bias in their research activities? To attempt to answer this question, researchers reviewed nearly 5,000 scientific articles from eight psychology journals published between 1970 and 1990 (Gannon, Luchetta, Rhodes, Pardie, & Segrist, 1992). The journals were selected so as to represent various topic areas (developmental, abnormal, and so on) within psychology. With the exception of one journal that did not begin publication until 1978, the contents of all articles published in these journals in 1970, 1975, 1980, 1985, and 1990 were examined. Eight different variables were identified, and the contents of the articles were coded according to these variables. Among them were the sex of the first author, sex of the participants, the type of language (i.e., sexist or nonsexist) used, and the existence of generalizations based on gender (e.g., generalizations of results obtained from participants of one sex to both sexes).

The results of this trend analysis of sex bias in published psychology articles revealed that while "sexism has clearly diminished in the past two decades," there is "continued evidence of discriminatory practices" (p. 389). For example, on the positive side, significant increases between 1970 and 1990 in the percentages of articles with female first authors were found in nearly every journal, while the percentages of studies that had male-only participants declined significantly in most journals. In addition, sexist language in these psychology journals was all but totally eliminated by 1990. On the negative side, a substantial percentage of articles showing sex bias were still being published in 1990. An article was considered sex-biased "if participants included only one gender for no obvious reason or with no reason explicitly stated, if sexist language was used, or if the discussion section contained inappropriate generalizations" (p. 393). Under this definition, sex-biased studies averaged about 85 percent in 1970 and about 30 percent in 1990. As the authors indicated, the archival analysis revealed an obvious reduction in sex bias in psychological studies, but it is evident from the data that there is still room for improvement.

Assessing the Effect of a Natural Treatment A study investigating the effect of a natural treatment (one that we have mentioned previously) is that of Phillips (1977). In this study, the "treatment" was the publicity given by major newspapers to suicides, and the effect of this variable on motor-vehicle fatalities was assessed. In a subsequent study, Phillips (1978) used records of the U.S. National Transportation Safety Board (*Briefs of Accidents: U.S. Civil Aviation*) to show a relationship between well-publicized murder-suicides and changes in fatal aircraft accidents. This archival study revealed a sharp increase in multifatality crashes (implying both a murder and a suicide component) in the period following the widespread publicizing of a murder-suicide story. Interestingly, the peak increase in aircraft fatalities occurred on Day 3 following the story, just as was found when suicide stories were related to motor-vehicle fatalities (see Figure 5.1).

Yet another finding by Phillips (1983) is that homicides increased significantly following heavyweight championship prize fights during the period 1973–1978. At the time this study was conducted, daily counts of homicides in the United States for this 6-year period were publicly available from the National Center for Health Statistics. Particularly intriguing is the fact that deaths due to homicides peaked 3 days following the prize fight, as had been found in previous analyses of motor-vehicle and airplane fatalities following well-publicized suicide stories. According to Phillips, the heavyweight prize fights provoked a brief, sharp increase in homicides. As evidence that this effect is due to some type of modeling of aggression, Phillips carried out additional analyses showing that homicides increased with an increase in the level of publicity surrounding the event. He operationally defined level of publicity in terms of whether or not the fight was discussed on television network news. He found that the increase in homicides was significantly greater when the fight was given more publicity by being on the network news.

This series of studies by Phillips and his colleagues is an impressive demonstration of the use of archival data to provide external validity to the results of laboratory findings. Phillips noted that laboratory studies have shown that exposure to violent films and television produces brief increases in aggression by laboratory subjects. Often, however, neither the setting nor the nature of the violence studied (for example, hitting inflatable toys) is similar to that found in the real world. In contrast, studies using archival data, although lacking the rigorous control possible in the laboratory, provide evidence of what happens to people who are exposed to real media violence.

PROBLEMS AND LIMITATIONS

When discussing the validity of physical traces, we mentioned that biases may result from the way physical traces are established and from the manner in which they survive over time. These biases are referred to as selective deposit and selective survival, respectively, and they are no less a problem for archival records (see Webb et al., 1981). Either of these biases can impose severe limitations on the generality of research findings.

Problems of **selective deposit** arise when biases exist in the production of archival sources. An interesting example of selective deposit is that associated with suicide notes. We mentioned earlier the research of Osgood and Walker (1959), who performed a content analysis of suicide notes and compared real suicide notes to ordinary letters and to faked suicide notes. We might ask whether the thoughts and feelings expressed in suicide notes are representative of all suicides. It happens that fewer than a fourth of all suicides leave notes, so it is possible that those who do leave notes are not representative of no-note suicides (Webb et al., 1981).

Problems of selective deposit may also arise when individuals associated with archival sources have the opportunity to edit and alter records before they are permanently recorded. This is illustrated by legislators' use of the *Congressional Record.* Though the *Congressional Record* is ostensibly a spontaneous record of speeches and remarks made before the Congress, legislators actually have the opportunity to edit their remarks before they are published (Webb et al., 1981) and even to enter into the record documents and accounts that were never really read aloud. No doubt remarks that are, in hindsight, viewed as less than politically expedient are changed prior to publication in the *Congressional Record.* Researchers who use archival data must be aware of the biases that may enter in when an archive is produced. Consider, for example, what types of biases might cause selective recording of crime statistics, income expense accounts, or sales figures.

Problems associated with **selective survival** arise when records are missing or incomplete (something an investigator may or may not even be aware of). It is important to consider whether there are reasons to suspect systematic biases in the survival of certain records. Are documents missing that are particularly damaging to certain individuals or groups? Following a change of presidential administrations, are some types of archives destroyed or misplaced? Are "letters to the editor" representative of all letters that were received? Schoeneman and Rubanowitz (1985) cautioned that when analyzing the contents of advice columns, they could not avoid the possiblity of a preselection bias since advice columnists print only a fraction of the letters they receive. As one prominent group of researchers has commented, when one examines archival data, "the gnawing reality remains that archives have been produced for someone else and by someone else" (Webb et al., 1981, p. 140).

In addition to problems arising from selective deposit and survival, the researcher using archival sources must be aware of possible errors in the record keeping and changes over time in the manner in which the records were kept. It is important to demonstrate that the record keeping was relatively constant and stable over the period of the study. When running records are kept, there is always the possibility that the definitions of categories have been changed midstream. For example, had the U.S. National Transportation Safety Board made important changes in the definition of "noncommercial" aircraft during the period of Phillips' (1978) study, it would have seriously affected the statistics he used to implicate murder-suicides in aircraft fatalities.

Although archives represent nonreactive measures of behavior, their classification as such applies only to archival analysis; it does not imply that reactivity was not a problem when the archive was produced. Statements made by public figures and printed in newspapers or reported by other media must be evaluated for their reactive components. Politicians and others who are constantly exposed to media publicity no doubt learn how to "use" the media, and their public stance may not match their private views. Lau and Russell (1980) had to consider whether the public statements made by players and coaches about a team's performance were really the same as those they made in private. They concluded that differences between public and private statements of attribution no doubt existed but that these differences do not invalidate their generalization of laboratory findings to real-world settings. The only way to control for reactive effects in archival data is to be aware that they may exist and, when possible, to seek other forms of corroborative evidence.

Yet another problem in the analysis of archival data is identifying spurious relationships. A **spurious relationship** exists when evidence falsely indicates that two or more variables are associated. Such evidence may be the result of inadequate or improper statistical treatment. This problem may exist in studies showing a relationship between frequency of deaths and important occasions. Although many people appear to endorse the view that individuals can somehow prolong their life in order to experience certain important events, such as birthdays, Schulz and Bazerman (1980) reanalyzed data from several studies to show that supportive evidence may be the result of statistical artifacts—for example, the way in which the period of time before and after a death was measured. They applied a more sensitive measure to the archival data that had shown a death dip in the month prior to individuals' birthdays. They calculated the number of deaths in the 31-day period before and after individuals' birthdays. This measure should be more sensitive, because it classifies individuals who died in the same month of their birth but who died either before or after their birthday (except when they died exactly on their birthday). This reanalysis of the data eliminated any evidence for the death-dip hypothesis. These researchers also reanalyzed data from other studies supporting the death-dip and death-rise hypotheses and showed how statistical artifacts could account for the results. Although stating that "it has thus far been impossible to obtain the relevant data from archival records that would enable one to test the death-dip or death-rise hypothesis with respect to important positive events" (p. 260), Schulz and Bazerman suggested that supporting data "may well be within reach if we use the proper methodologies and carefully select important events" (p. 261).

Spurious relationships can also exist when variables are accidentally or coincidentally related. This is sometimes the case when changes in two variables are the result of another, usually unknown, third variable. For instance, it has been noted that ice-cream sales and the crime rate are positively correlated. However, before concluding that eating ice cream prompts people to commit crimes, it is important to consider the fact that both variables are affected by temperature; neither eating ice cream nor committing crime directly affects the other.

That Phillips' (1983) finding of a relationship between heavyweight prize fights and homicides in the United States is a spurious one has been the subject of several studies (e.g., Baron & Reiss, 1985). Some of the criticisms raised have to do with possible statistical artifacts in the complex analyses, while others suggest that important variables were not controlled. Baron and Reiss suggested that the third-day peak, which Phillips (1983) admitted he could not readily interpret, was quite possibly due to the occurrence of holidays or weekends near prize-fight dates or even to fluctuations in the unemployment rate.

There is no easy way to deal with spurious relationships except to gather, from independent sources, additional data that will help confirm a relationship and to subject the available archival data to more than one kind of analysis. Extensive reanalysis of Phillips' original data has tended to reaffirm a link between violence portrayed in the media and violence acted out in society (see Miller, Heath, Molcan, & Dugoni, 1991; Phillips & Bollen, 1985).

SUMMARY

The use of physical traces and archival data are important alternatives to direct observation and surveys. Physical traces are the remnants, fragments, and products of past behavior. Physical-use traces are based on the accumulation of evidence (accretion measures) or are the result of selective wear (erosion measures). Furthermore, use traces can either result naturally, without any intervention by the investigator, or be planned by the investigator. Physical traces may provide important nonreactive (unobtrusive) measures of behavior and can be used as the sole dependent variable or in combination with other measures of behavior. Multimethod approaches to the study of behavior are particularly recommended because they reduce the chance that results are due to some artifact of the measurement process. In obtaining physical traces, an investigator must be aware of possible biases in the way in which traces accumulate or survive over time.

Archival data are found in records and documents that recount the activities of individuals, institutions, governments, and other groups. These sources of information are valuable because they provide a way of investigating the external validity of laboratory findings, assessing the effect of a natural "treatment" (such as a political assassination), analyzing the content of communications, and describing trends. Archival records are nonreactive measures of behavior and, like physical traces, can be used in multimethod approaches to hypothesis testing. The analysis of archival data typically requires some form of content analysis, a process that can involve problems of sampling and coding that are not unlike those that arise in the analysis of narrative records (see Chapter 3). Problems of selective deposit and selective survival must be investigated when archival data are used, and evidence should be presented showing that spurious relationships have not been obtained.

KEY CONCEPTS

physical traces
archival data
multimethod approach
content analysis
selective deposit
selective survival
spurious relationship

REVIEW QUESTIONS

1 What characteristic of physical traces and archival data makes them especially attractive alternatives to the direct-observation and survey method of measuring?
2 Why are multimethod approaches to hypothesis testing recommended?
3 What are the different kinds of physical-trace measures used by psychologists, and in what ways do they differ?
4 What possible sources of bias exist when physical-use traces are the dependent variable in a research study, and how can the validity of these measures be verified?
5 Give four reasons for using archival data as an alternative to, or in conjunction with, direct observation and surveys.
6 What dimensions distinguish the various types of archival sources used by psychologists?
7 What three basic steps must be taken in any research in which content analysis is done?
8 Explain the role of precise operational definitions in content analysis, and give one example of a quantitative unit and one example of a qualitative unit of measurement in content analysis.
9 Identify and give an example of the problems that researchers must be aware of when they make use of archival sources.
10 Explain the two ways in which evidence indicating spurious relationships most often arises.

CHALLENGE QUESTIONS

1 Suggest *two* sources of archival data for *each* of the following variables. Be sure to specify an operational definition of each variable.
   A Public's interest in cultural events
   B Students' political attitudes
   C Community concern about crime
   D Amount of mobility in a corporation
   E Citizens' attitudes toward their schools
   F Ethnic grouping of neighborhoods
   G Current fads in dress

2 For *each* of the following archival sources, specify *two* kinds of data that might be useful in a psychological study. Once again, be sure to specify the operational definition that could be used for the variable you have identified.
   A Weekly news magazine
   B Television soap operas
   C Classified section of newspaper
   D Annual city budgets
   E Student yearbooks
   F List of donors to a university
   G Television commercials

3 A bright female graduate student in psychology has been offered a job with both *Newsweek* and *Time.* The salary offers of the two companies are basically the same, and it appears that both the working conditions and the job responsibilities are similar. To help her decide which job to accept, she resolves to determine whether one magazine has a better attitude toward women than the other. She appeals to you to help her with a content analysis of these two news magazines. What specific advice would you give her regarding each of the following steps of her content analysis?
   A Sampling
   B Coding
   C Reliability
   D Quantitative and qualitative measures

4 An educational specialist was convinced that schoolyard fights among young boys were more violent than those among young girls. To gather evidence relevant to her hypothesis, she checked the records at the nurse's office of her school. She found that, of the 100 injuries resulting from fights which were reported to the school nurse, 75 percent involved boys and only 25 percent involved girls. The investigator was convinced on the basis of these findings that her hypothesis was correct. Criticize this conclusion by showing how these very same findings *could result if exactly the opposite* of the investigator's hypothesis were true—namely, that fights among young girls are more violent. (Be sure to confine your answer to the adequacy of the data that the investigator has presented to support her conclusion.)

5 A researcher wishes to test the hypothesis that children attending private grade schools are not as "dirty-minded" as students attending public grade schools. He chooses two schools (one a parochial school and one public) that are located in the same neighborhood, approximately one mile apart. Both schools include grades 1 through 8. To test the hypothesis, the investigator decides to use measures both of natural accretion and of controlled accretion. Specifically, he operationally defines "dirty-mindedness" as the number of obscene words (from a predetermined list) that

are found in the restrooms of each school. The natural accretion measure is simply the number of new target words appearing on the walls of the restrooms at the end of each week. As a measure of controlled accretion, the investigator obtains permission from the school authorities to place pads of paper and pencils in the toilet stalls of the restrooms at each school. On each pad of paper is written "Leave me a note." At the end of each week the investigator replaces the pad with a fresh one and examines the pages that have been written on for the appearance of obscene words.

A Comment on possible problems of selective deposit and survival for the physical trace measures proposed in this study.

B Frame questions that might be asked concerning the external validity of this study.

C Suggest ways in which the investigator might use a multimethod approach to this problem.

ANSWER TO CHALLENGE QUESTION 1

The sources of archival data listed below for each of the variables represent only illustrations and not definitive answers. Operational definitions are only sketched here; they should be developed more fully through discussion in class.

A Public's interest in cultural events—attendance figures for theater and concerts in the past calendar year; membership lists of organizations that support cultural events

B Students' political attitudes—records of participation by students at local, state, and national conventions; membership lists of organizations that advocate political positions

C Community concern about crime—police records of all calls reporting "suspicious" activities in the community; sales records for locks, burglar alarms, and firearms

D Amount of mobility in a corporation—company records of average time spent by employees in various positions; company records with annual lists of promotions within the company

E Citizens' attitudes toward their schools—records of the election results for millage requests for schools, including number of millage votes that passed and number of times each had to come up for a vote; membership lists for parent-teacher organizations with the implication that active participation suggests positive attitudes

F Ethnic grouping of neighborhoods—analysis of the ethnic origins of the names in neighborhood phone directories; city licensing records for restaurants and food stores in the neighborhoods

G Current fads in dress—sales records for selected articles of clothing that typify a particular fad; magazine, newspaper, and television advertisements for clothing

Part

Experimental Methods

Chapter 6

Independent Groups Designs

Outline

OVERVIEW

Psychologists use the experimental method to construct artificial situations (usually in the laboratory) to isolate the process they want to investigate. For instance, no matter how long or how carefully you observed adult readers, you would be unlikely to be able to tell whether they were saying the words to themselves as they read silently. The process you were interested in would literally be unobservable. Haber and Haber (1982) constructed a situation in which they were able to make the unobservable available to inspection. The term they used for the unobservable process of talking to oneself while reading was "subvocal articulation." They gave college students two types of sentences to read, tongue-twisters (Francis Forbes' father fries five flounders) and control sentences that were not tongue-twisters (Mary Wright's uncle cooks red lobsters). The logic of their experiment was that, if the students *did* say the words to themselves as they read silently, the tongue-twister sentences would be harder to read and thus take longer to read than the control sentences. This is exactly what they found, so they concluded that we do "talk to ourselves" as we read. Haber and Haber never did observe subvocal articulation directly. They constructed a situation in which a difference in behavior occurred as a result of a process that they presumed was occurring, and the situation allowed this process to "show itself."

Much of the experimental research in psychology is like that illustrated in the study we have just described. Theoretical explanatory processes are proposed, experiments are done in which outcomes are predicted on the basis of these explanatory processes, and the outcomes of the experiments are used to make decisions about the existence of these unobservable theoretical processes.

The role of theories in psychological research was discussed in Chapter 1. In the next few chapters we will explore the use of the experimental method to test psychological theories.

In this chapter we will discuss the most commonly used experimental design when different conditions are administered to different groups of subjects—namely, the *random groups design*. The topics we will address include the underlying logic of this design, the procedures for forming random groups, the ways in which the external validity of experiments can be established, the challenges to internal validity that apply specifically to the random groups design, and the method used to identify a statistically significant effect in an experiment. We will then consider two alternative experimental designs involving independent groups: the matched groups design and the natural groups design. We will also describe special control and design problems that are applicable to the independent groups designs.

CHARACTERISTICS OF EXPERIMENTS

Up to this point we have been discussing research methods that serve primarily to fulfill the *descriptive* function of the science of psychology. Psychologists use observational methods to develop detailed descriptions of behavior, often in natural settings. Survey research methods allow psychologists to describe people's attitudes and opinions. The analysis of archival data provides a nonreactive means of obtaining converging evidence to enhance the validity of the descriptions of behavior that are based on observation and survey research. As essential as they are to the scientific study of behavior, descriptive methods are not sufficient. Psychologists seek to move beyond description to understanding—the *why* behind the *what* of behavior. As we mentioned in Chapter 1, scientific understanding is achieved when the causes of a phenomenon have been identified. The next four chapters focus on the best available research method for specifying *causal* relationships: the experimental method.

The distinction between experimental methods and descriptive research methods should not be drawn too sharply. Observation, survey research, and archival data can certainly contribute to our understanding of the causes of behavior. Field experiments and longitudinal designs in survey research clearly embody the principles of the experimental methods, although we have discussed them in the context of descriptive research methods. Similarly, experimental methods can be used effectively to develop accurate descriptions of behavior, especially when the methods are applied to practical research problems such as those involving the effectiveness of a behavior-modification program (see Chapter 10). Perhaps the best approach to research is the multimethod approach (see Chapters 1 and 5). If researchers reach comparable conclusions about a research question after using different methods to study it, our confidence in their conclusions increases. The conclusions are said to have *convergent validity*. Each method has different shortcomings, but the methods have complementary strengths that overcome these shortcomings. The experimental method, however, is especially effective in establishing cause-and-effect relationships.

An experiment involves the *manipulation* of one or more factors and measurement of the effects of this manipulation on behavior. The factors that the researcher controls or manipulates are called the **independent variables.** The measures that are used to assess the effect (if any) of the independent variables are called **dependent variables.** For example, students might be asked to listen to a tape of segments of either familiar or unfamiliar rock songs. Song segments would be played varying numbers of times, and the students' task would be to estimate how many times each segment had been played. In this experiment the familiarity of the songs would be the independent variable and the students' estimates of the songs' frequencies would be the dependent variable.

Four characteristics distinguish sound experiments from unsound experiments. Sound experiments are internally valid, reliable, sensitive, and externally valid. An *internally valid experiment* is one in which other plausible causes for the outcome that was obtained have been ruled out. The purpose of an experiment is to produce a difference in behavior; thus, a *reliable experiment* is one in which the obtained difference is likely to be found again if the experiment is repeated. Independent variables differ in terms of how large an effect they have on behavior. A *sensitive experiment* is one that is likely to detect the effect of an independent variable even when that effect is a small one. The findings of an *externally valid experiment* are generalizable to individuals, settings, and conditions beyond the scope of the specific experiment. Unfortunately, the four characteristics of a sound experiment cannot always be maximized simultaneously. For instance, the procedures that increase the sensitivity of an experiment can reduce its external validity. Nonetheless, the goal of the following chapters is to prepare you to conduct sound experiments, to interpret them appropriately, and to analyze them properly.

WHY PSYCHOLOGISTS CONDUCT EXPERIMENTS

A major purpose of conducting experiments is to provide an empirical test of hypotheses derived from psychological theories (see Chapter 1). If the results of the experiment are consistent with what is expected from the hypothesis, then the proposed explanation receives support. If the results are not what had been expected, then the proposed explanation may need to be modified and a new hypothesis developed to be tested in the next experiment. The process of conducting experiments to test a single hypothesis can be a long and painstaking one. Hypothesis testing is also not a process that provides definitive conclusions. It can thus be frustrating for a person who wants to know all the answers right away. The self-correcting nature of the interplay between experiments and proposed explanations, however, does provide a challenging and satisfying approach to understanding the causes of the way we think, feel, and behave.

Research by social psychologists on the topic of "social loafing" can serve as an illustration of the relationship between experiments and proposed explanations. Social loafing (see Figure 6.1) is the "tendency for people to exert less effort when they pool their efforts toward a common goal than when they are individually accountable" (Myers, 1990, p. 278). Latané, Williams, and Harkin (1979) demonstrated the phenomenon of social loafing by having six blindfolded subjects sit in a semicircle, with each person wearing a headphone through which the researchers played the sounds of people shouting. The subjects were instructed either to shout alone or to shout together with the others in the semicircle. The subjects who thought they were shouting alone shouted louder than the subjects who thought the other five were shouting with them, thus demonstrating social loafing.

One proposed explanation of social loafing is based on the idea of individual accountability. When we are less concerned that our work can be individually evaluated, we tend to make less of an effort. According to this proposed explanation, social loafing is presumed to occur because working in a group makes the individual's work less identifiable. To test this proposed explanation, Williams, Harkin, and Latané (1981) did another shouting experiment in which the independent variable was the presence or absence of a microphone on the

FIGURE 6.1 What effect does working in a group have on the individual efforts of these students who are participating in the annual Hope College "Pull"?

subjects. The experimenters compared the performance of subjects who were wearing individual microphones while they were shouting with those who were not wearing microphones. The microphones were intended to make the subjects aware that their individual performances were identifiable. The dependent variable was the measured loudness of shouting. The hypothesis tested in the experiment was that subjects who wear microphones will not exhibit social loafing; that is, they will shout as loudly alone as they will in a group. This was because their individual performance was identifiable. Subjects who were not wearing the microphones were expected to show social loafing by shouting more when alone than when in a group. The results were consistent with the hypothesis. Social loafing did occur when subjects did not wear microphones, and social loafing did not occur when subjects did wear individual microphones. This finding supports the proposed explanation that social loafing is due in part to a lessening of individual accountability in the group.

Besides providing empirical tests of proposed explanations derived from theories, experiments can be used to test the effectiveness of a treatment or program. Thomas (1992) describes how experiments were used to determine the effectiveness of some early medical treatments. Near the beginning of the nineteenth century, typhoid fever and delirium tremens were often fatal. The standard medical practice at that time was to treat these two conditions by bleeding, purging, and the administration of other, similar therapies. An experiment was performed to test the effectiveness of these standard treatments. One group was randomly assigned to receive the standard treatment, and a second group was randomly assigned to receive nothing but bed rest, good nutrition, and close observation. Thomas describes the results of this experiment as "unequivocal and appalling" (p. 9). The group given the standard medical treatment of the time did *worse* than the group left untreated. Experiments such as these contributed to the insight that many medical conditions are self-limited. They run their course, and patients recover on their own. Treating such conditions in the way they were treated in the early nineteenth century was worse than not treating them at all. As we will see in Chapters 10 and 11, well-conducted experiments can give us vital information about the effectiveness of treatments and programs in areas other than medicine. Experiments can thus serve a useful purpose not only in testing theories but also in making decisions in practical situations.

EXPERIMENTAL CONTROL

The primary reason that experiments are so effective for testing hypotheses is that they allow researchers to exercise a relatively high level of control. As we mentioned in Chapter 1, there are three aspects of control: *manipulation, holding conditions constant,* and *balancing*. These three aspects of control share a common objective: to meet the three conditions necessary for a causal inference (covariation, time order, and elimination of plausible alternative causes) and thereby to ensure the internal validity of the experiment. The covariation condition is met when we observe systematic changes in the dependent variable as a function of the manipulated independent variable. That is, when the experimenter changes the level of the independent variable, the subjects' responses as measured by the dependent variable also change. Because we manipulate the independent variable *before* measuring the changes in the dependent variable, the time-order condition is also met. Other factors that could influence the subjects' performance must be controlled either by holding them constant or by balancing in order to meet the third and most critical condition necessary for a causal inference: eliminating plausible alternative causes.

We can use another experiment that Williams et al. (1981) did on social loafing to illustrate the principles of control. The purpose of this experiment was to provide an additional test of the individual accountability explanation of social loafing. The dependent variable in this experiment was again how loudly the subjects shouted. They varied the accountability of the subjects by *manipulation* of the instructions they gave them. Their independent variable had three levels. The first set of instructions indicated that the experimenters could monitor each subject's shouting when the subject shouted alone but not when others were shouting (the "identifiable only when alone" group).The second set of instructions indicated that the experimenters were able to monitor each subject's shouting both when the subject shouted alone and in a group (the "always identifiable" group). The third set of instructions indicated that the experimenters could not monitor each subject's shouting either when the subject shouted alone or in a group (the "never identifiable" group). These manipulations involved deception because the experimenters could actually monitor shouting in all conditions. The results of the experiment showed that social loafing (louder shouting when alone than when in a group) occurred in the identifiable-only-when-alone group. In the always-identifiable group, there was a high and equal level of shouting whether the subjects shouted alone or in a group (no social loafing). In the never-identifiable group, there was a low and equal level of shouting whether the subjects shouted alone or in groups (subjects "loafed" even when alone). These results also support the individual-accountability explanation of social loafing.

The results of an experiment involving a manipulated independent variable are interpretable *only if* the independent variable is the only factor that differentiates the groups of the experiment. By *holding constant* other critical factors, Williams et al. made sure that the variable of the instructions given was the only factor that systematically varied across groups. For example, subjects in all three groups were tested in the same soundproof room. All of the subjects were blindfolded so they could not see each other, and they wore headsets over which the experimenters played loud shouting such that the subjects could not hear themselves shout. The instructions for all three groups included the same statement that the experimenters wanted the subjects to "make as much noise as you can." Only male subjects participated in this experiment, thereby holding the gender of the subjects constant. If the three groups had differed on a factor other than the instructional manipulation, then the results of the experiment would have been uninterpretable. For example, if the subjects in the always-identifiable group had not worn headsets while the subjects in the other two groups had worn them, then there would have been a **confounding** between the instructions and the wearing of the headset. A confounding arises when the independent variable of interest and a potential independent variable are allowed to covary. Holding the wearing of the headset constant avoided a confounding because a factor that does not change cannot possibly covary with the intended independent variable.

It is important to recognize, however, that we choose to control only those factors that we think might influence the behavior of interest. For instance, Williams et al. (1981) controlled what subjects could see by blindfolding them and what subjects could hear by having them wear headsets. The researchers held these conditions constant because they thought they were relevant to the phenomenon they were studying. They also held the setting constant by testing all their subjects in the same room, but it is unlikely that they monitored the room temperature to be sure that it stayed constant. The point of this brief discussion is that we control only those factors we believe are potentially relevant. Nevertheless, we should constantly remain alert to the possibility that there may be confounding factors in our experiments whose influence we had not anticipated.

The third aspect of control is *balancing*. For example, consider that you were going to perform an experiment and had two rooms available for testing. You could choose to control any potential effect of the testing room by using only one room, thereby holding this factor constant. Balancing gives you another option. You could use both rooms, but you would have to be sure that the same number of subjects was tested in each room in each of your experimental conditions. We will discuss a specific technique for carrying out this balancing later in this chapter. At this point it is important only that you recognize that balancing is a third effective control technique.

For factors such as testing rooms, the experimenter may use either balancing or holding conditions constant. However, balancing is the only control option for dealing with the characteristics of the subjects tested. Researchers have two types of designs from which to choose in dealing with these factors: the independent groups designs and the within-subjects designs. Both types of designs control factors that are not manipulated and that cannot be held constant by balancing the influence of these factors across the levels of the independent variable. In the **independent groups designs,** each group represents a different condition as defined by the level of the independent variable. The most common type of independent groups design is the **random groups design.** In this design, the groups are formed in such a way that they are presumed to be comparable at the start of the experiment. Then, if the groups perform differently, it is presumed that the independent variable is responsible. In Chapter 7 we will discuss the appropriate balancing techniques in within-subjects designs in which there is only one group of subjects, all of whom are given all the treatments in the experiment. In the present chapter, we will examine the most commonly used design involving independent groups of subjects, the random groups design.

RANDOM GROUPS DESIGN

RANDOM SELECTION VERSUS RANDOM ASSIGNMENT

The simplest experiments involve two *conditions.* That is, two levels of an independent variable are administered to subjects, and differences in the dependent variable between these two levels of the independent variable are used to measure the effect of the independent variable. In the independent groups design, each level represents a different group of subjects. In an experiment done by Loftus and Burns (1982), for example, one group of subjects was assigned to view a violent version of a film while a second group of subjects viewed a nonviolent version. Both groups were then tested for their memory of details included in the films. As we mentioned earlier, the logic of the design is straightforward. If the two groups are comparable on all important characteristics at the start of the experiment *and* if, in the experiment itself, the two groups are treated the same *except* for the level of the independent variable, then, if the two groups perform differently, the difference must be due to the independent variable.

In a *random groups design,* comparable groups are formed prior to the introduction of the independent variable. This is accomplished by sampling subjects in a way that ensures that each subject has an equal likelihood of being included in each group of the experiment. In practice, there are two ways to do this: random selection and random assignment. We discussed random selection procedures when we introduced survey research designs (see Chapter 4). Briefly, *random selection* involves drawing two or more random samples from the same population. Sampling theory assures us that, on the average, these randomly selected samples will not differ at the start of the experiment. In addition, we know that random samples, if sufficiently large, are representative of the population from which they were drawn. Thus random selection contributes to the internal validity of the experiment by balancing the differences among subjects across groups, and it enhances the external validity of the results by ensuring that the samples are representative.

Although random selection *could* be used to form comparable groups, it is used only rarely in psychology experiments. When descriptive research methods such as surveys are used, it is essential that the samples be representative of a well-defined population. After all, the goal of descriptive research is to describe a population by observing only a sample of it. In experiments, however, the emphasis is on identifying the independent variable as the source of the difference between otherwise comparable groups. Usually, populations of potential participants in psychology experiments are defined by convenience. For instance, human subjects are often students from introductory psychology courses who volunteer for experiments for extra course credit. Animal subjects are those that happen to be shipped to the researcher by the supplier. Although you could form comparable groups by randomly selecting subjects, the procedure would be time-consuming and impractical. And you would not enhance the external validity of your experiment by drawing random samples from ill-defined populations such as students who happened to be taking introductory psychology. The most common solution to the problem of forming comparable groups is to *assign* subjects randomly to the conditions of the experiment.

A closer look at the details of the Loftus and Burns experiment will illustrate both the procedures of **random assignment** and the power of the random groups design. Their experiment concerned the effect of viewing a violent scene on a person's memory for information that was processed seconds before the individual witnessed the mentally shocking event. The experiment was done at the University of Washington, and 226 students volunteered to participate in order to fulfill a course requirement. The students participated in small groups, and each small group was randomly assigned to view one of two films. Approximately half of the subjects (115) were assigned to view a violent version of a film. Near the end of the film, these subjects saw a robber, while running to a getaway car, turn and fire a shot toward two men who were pursuing him. The shot hit a boy in the face, and the boy fell bleeding to the ground. The other half of the subjects viewed a nonviolent version of the film that was identical to the violent version until just before the shooting. At this point in the film, the camera switched back to inside the bank, where the subjects saw the bank manager telling the customers and employees what happened and asking them to remain calm. The two versions of the film (violent and nonviolent) represent the levels of the independent variable in the experiment.

After viewing the film, subjects in both groups were asked to answer twenty-five questions about events in the film. One question was critical: It asked for the number on the football jersey worn by a boy playing in the parking lot outside the bank. The boy wearing the jersey was visible for 2 seconds during the film—the 2 seconds before the shooting (violent version) or the 2 seconds before the scenes back in the bank (nonviolent version). The dependent variable was the percentage of subjects who correctly recalled the jersey number. The results were clear-cut: just over 4 percent of the subjects correctly recalled the number in the violent condition, whereas nearly 28 percent did so in the nonviolent condition.

The major benefit of randomly assigning subjects to groups is to balance the characteristics of the subjects in the two groups. These two random samples of over a hundred subjects are unlikely to differ, on the average, in memory ability, in attentiveness, or in any other way that might influence their performance on the memory test. Thus, if they had seen the same version of the film, their performance would not have been expected to differ. Moreover, it is important to remember that random assignment was not the only method of control used in the Loftus and Burns experiment. For instance, the equipment used to present the films, the quality of the films, the instructions given prior to showing the films, the tone of voice used by the experimenter in giving these instructions, and any other factors that could be controlled by being held constant were identical in the two conditions of the experiment. Because the subjects' performances *did* differ, and because other potential causal factors were controlled, we conclude that the different versions of the film caused the difference in test performance.

The balancing accomplished through random assignment applies to factors other than the characteristics of the subjects. It is unlikely, for example, that Loftus and Burns were able to hold the temperature of the room constant during the various showings of the films. These variations in room temperature would threaten the internal validity of the experiment only if they systematically covaried with the levels of the independent variable, the two types of films. The random assignment of small groups of subjects to the two film conditions makes it unlikely that the room was consistently warmer or colder when the violent film was shown. Thus, although most of us associate the concept of control with holding conditions constant, the balancing accomplished through random assignment is an equally effective control technique. The most common procedure for carrying out random assignment, **block randomization,** is described in Box 6.1 (p. 186).

ESTABLISHING EXTERNAL VALIDITY

As we have already mentioned, random assignment, not random selection, is the most commonly used procedure for carrying out a random groups design. And random assignment alone is not sufficient to ensure that the results can be generalized beyond the particular subjects who happened to participate in the experiment. How, then, do we establish the external validity of experiments?

One answer to this question is a bit unsettling, at least initially. For some experiments we do not establish external validity. Mook (1983) has argued that, when the purpose of an experiment is to test a specific hypothesis derived from a psychological theory, the question of the external validity of the findings is irrelevant. An experiment is often done to determine whether subjects *can* be induced to behave in a certain way. The question whether subjects *do* behave that way in their natural environment is secondary to the question raised in the experiment. The issue of the external validity of experiments is not a new one, as reflected in the following statement by Riley (1962, p. 413):

> In general, laboratory experiments are not set up to imitate the most typical case found in nature. Instead, they are intended to answer some specific question of interest to the experimenter.

There are occasions, however, in which it *is* critical to obtain results that can be generalized beyond the boundaries of the experiment itself. It is important in these instances to obtain representative data on all dimensions on which we wish to generalize. In experiments of this type, random selection of subjects is preferable to random assignment. Keep in mind, however, that random selec-

BOX 6.1

BUILDING BLOCKS OF RANDOM ASSIGNMENT

Picture a researcher who is preparing to conduct a random groups design experiment. Now envision a long line of participants outside the door to the laboratory. As each participant gets to the door, he or she must be assigned to one of the conditions of the experiment. This long line never actually forms because human participants usually make an individual appointment to come to the laboratory at a prearranged time, and animal participants are brought from the animal room to the laboratory one at a time. Nonetheless, the image of the long line of participants gives you a good way to think about the process of assigning subjects to conditions over the course of the entire experiment. One way to assign participants to conditions would be to use simple random assignment, with each individual independently randomly assigned to a condition. When the experiment to be performed called for only two conditions, a simple coin toss or odd-even roll of a die would suffice to assigning subjects to a condition. Another alternative would be to use the Table of Random Numbers in Appendix A and assign odd-numbered entries to one group and even-numbered entries to the other group.

There is one minor problem with the use of simple random assignment. The different groups in the experiment are unlikely to come out with equal numbers of subjects. This problem of unequal numbers in each group becomes especially troublesome when you have five or six different conditions in the experiment. There is an advantage to having equal sample sizes in each group of a random groups design. Because the number of observations contributing to a descriptive statistic influences the reliability of that measure, and because you will be comparing such descriptive statistics across the groups in your experiment, the measures taken in each group should be based on the same number of observations. With small numbers of conditions and large samples within each condition, this concern with equal-sized groups is a very minor one. For example, in the study done by Loftus and Burns, two groups, of 115 and of 111 subjects, were tested. These two sample sizes clearly provide equally reliable estimates of performance. As the number of conditions increases and the sample size within each condition decreases, however, it becomes more critical that the groups contain equal numbers of subjects. Fortunately, a technique is available for randomly assigning subjects to groups in such a way that the groups will be of equal size. This technique is called *block randomization.*

A block in a block-randomized schedule is made up of a random order of the conditions of the experiment. If our experiment involved five conditions (A, B, C, D, and E), then the first five subjects in our fictitious line outside the laboratory would constitute the first block, and one of these five individuals would be assigned to each of the five conditions.The next five individuals would make up the second block, and each of them would similarly be randomly assigned to one of the five conditions. In block randomization, one subject is assigned to *each* group before a second subject is assigned to *any* group. There are as many blocks in the block-randomized schedule as there are subjects in each group of the experiment. For example, if we wanted to have twenty subjects in each of five groups, then there would be twenty blocks in our block-randomized schedule. Each block would be formed using the Random Number Table in Appendix A. We would assign each condition a number, such as A = 1, B = 2, C = 3, D = 4, and E = 5, and then enter the

Random Number Table. If the sequence in the random number table were 1-4-1-9-4-6-2-5-9-0-3-6, then (ignoring repeated numbers and numbers higher than 5) the first block in our schedule would be A-D-B-E-C. Thus the first participant would be tested in Group A, the second in Group D, and so on. We form each successive block in the same way. The result is a schedule by which we can randomly assign each subject in the long line outside our laboratory to a condition and end up with equal numbers of subjects in each group.

The table in this box shows a partially completed portion of a block-randomized schedule. Each subject is given a number, which also appears on any data sheets for that subject in the experiment. In this way, the subject can be identified while the confidentiality of the subject's data is maintained. The subject's name is recorded so that the experimenter can be sure not to test the same person more than once. If a subject begins the experiment but fails to complete it successfully, the subject's name will appear on the block sheet under the column "Dropped subject," and the reason why the subject did not complete the experiment will be recorded on the back of the block sheet. (See the section on challenges to internal validity later in this chapter for a discussion of the problem of subject loss.) The dropped subject will be replaced by the next subject who comes to the laboratory. The block sheets contain a vital record of the sequence in which subjects were tested. It should be carefully prepared before beginning the experiment and followed closely throughout the experiment. It represents one of the basic building blocks of a good experiment.

Subject	Name	Condition	Dropped subject
1	J. Swim	A	
2	D. DeWolff	D	
3	D. Morier	B	
4	J. Gentile	E	E. Greij
5	R. Cutler	C	
6		D	
7		B	
8		E	
9		C	
10		A	
11		E	
12		C	
13		D	
14		A	
15		B	
16		E	
17		B	
18		D	
19		C	
20		A	

tion of subjects ensures only that we can generalize our results to the population from which we drew our subjects. If we also want to generalize our results to specific settings, for example, we must be equally careful to select a representative sample of settings in our experiment. The general rule is a simple one. The results of our experiment can be generalized on any dimension on which we have included a representative sample.

External validity is not likely to be established on the basis of the results of a single experiment. Replication plays a key role in establishing external validity. **Replication** means repeating all of the procedures used in a particular experiment in order to determine whether the same results will be obtained a second time. Most replications are done when an initial finding is unexpected or is judged to be especially important. Typically, a replication is said to have occurred if the effect of the independent variable is present in both the original study and in the replication study.

An exact replication is almost impossible to carry out. The subjects tested in the replication will be different from those tested in the original study, and the experimenters are often different. Partial replications, however, are commonly done as a routine part of the process of investigating the conditions under which a phenomenon occurs. Hendrick (1990) has identified several characteristics that can be varied when a partial replication is done. These include subject characteristics, the general physical setting of the experiment, characteristics of the experimenters doing the testing, task characteristics, and the nature of the instructions. Partial replications can be very useful in establishing the external validity of a finding. When the same basic experiment is done in both a large metropolitan public university and in a small rural private college, the subjects and the settings in the experiments are very different, and so the two experiments represent partial replications. If the same results are obtained in these partial replications of the experiment, we can be confident that the findings are not peculiar to the particular type of subject tested or to the particular setting in which the test took place. The dimensions that are not replicated across the two experiments provide the basis for increased external validity. Notice that neither experiment alone has external validity; it is the findings that occur in both experiments that have external validity.

It would be virtually impossible to establish the external validity of each finding in psychology by performing partial replications across each of the dimensions over which we would want to generalize (e.g., subjects, settings, tasks, and so on). Questions can arise, however, about the external validity of psychological research findings when there is little direct empirical evidence to use as a basis for making generalizations. Most studies in psychology involve college students who participate in experiments as part of their introductory psychology course. Dawes (1991), among others, has argued that college students are a select group who may not always be a good basis on which to build general conclusions about human behavior and mental processes. For example, Dawes argues that the college environment tends to protect students from external problems, thereby enhancing their sense of being in control of their lives. People living outside the college environment may not have the same sense of control that college students do. Thus, research on locus of control done with college students may not generalize to people living outside the college environment. In general, the arguments raised by Dawes and others should lead us to exercise care in generalizing conclusions from studies using college students as subjects.

Although we should take arguments like those of Dawes seriously, we should not let them immobilize us. Underwood and Shaughnessy (1975) have argued that the burden of proof regarding questions of external validity rests with the person claiming we should not generalize. These two researchers begin with a *continuity assumption* that asserts that we should assume that behavior is relatively continuous across time, subjects, and settings unless we have reason to assume otherwise. Researchers use the continuity assumption as an initial basis for generalization. For instance, most experiments are carried out in individual laboratory rooms, but we would not be likely to argue that the results of the experiment therefore apply only to those particular rooms. Similarly, the particular subjects tested in an experiment are considered, according to the continuity assumption, to be generally representative of other, similar individuals who might have been tested.

The continuity assumption is not a call to blind faith. The boundaries of the continuity assumption are set by consensus of the research community. The research community may agree, for example, that introductory psychology students who volunteer for experiments are representative of college students in general but not of young children or of the elderly. There is always a technique available, however, to test the limits of the continuity assumption when serious challenges are raised regarding the external validity of findings. The technique involves doing a partial replication including the dimension on which the generalization has been challenged as an independent variable. For example, Singer (1982) noted that most studies conducted on reading comprehension in the past decade had been based on reading in the laboratory. He was concerned that laboratory reading might involve goals or techniques different from those used in natural reading, and so he conducted an experiment in which he asked subjects who had not read a particular newspaper article before to read it in the laboratory. These subjects were then given a memory test that was also given to subjects who had read the article *outside* the laboratory. The two groups performed similarly on the tests, leading to Singer's conclusion: "These effects, coupled with the similarity of the natural and laboratory readers, provide reassurance that it is reasonable to treat laboratory reading as an approximation of natural reading" (p. 331). Such direct tests of the continuity assumption represent perhaps the best way to establish the external validity of research findings.

CHALLENGES TO INTERNAL VALIDITY

Balancing Nuisance Factors A number of factors in an experiment may vary as a result of practical considerations in carrying out the study. For example, in order to complete an experiment more quickly, a researcher might decide to have several different experimenters test small groups of participants. The sizes of the groups and the experimenters themselves become potentially relevant variables that could confound the experiment if their effects are not somehow balanced across conditions. If all the subjects in the experimental group are tested by one experimenter and all those in the control group are tested by another experimenter, for example, differences between the experimenters would confound the intended independent variable.

Potential independent variables that are not directly of interest to the researcher but serve only as vexing sources of confounding can be called **nuisance factors.** But don't let the term fool you! An experiment confounded by such nuisance factors is no less confounded than if the confounding factor were of considerable inherent interest. For instance, if all the small groups in one condition of the experiment included two or three subjects, while all those in another condition included eight or nine subjects, any difference between these two conditions *could* result from the influence of the different group sizes on subjects' performance. Evans and Donnerstein (1974) studied a similar nuisance factor, specifically, differences between subjects who volunteer early in the term, on the one hand, and those who volunteer late in the term on the other. Their results indicated that those who volunteer early are more academically oriented and are more likely to have an internal locus of control (to emphasize their own responsibility for their actions rather than to emphasize external factors). These findings suggest it would not be wise to test a control group at the end of the term if the subjects in the other conditions of the completed experiment had been tested in the first half of the term.

Fortunately, block randomization provides an easy and effective way to balance nuisance factors (see Box 6.1). All that is required is that entire blocks be tested at each level of the nuisance variable. Normally, the blocks of a block-randomized schedule are tested sequentially—the first block, then the second block, and so on. It is possible, however, to balance the possible effects of nuisance variables by assigning different blocks to each of the levels of the nuisance variable. For example, if there were four different experimenters, entire blocks of the block-randomized schedule would be assigned to each experimenter. Because each block contains all the critical conditions of the experiment, this strategy guarantees that each condition has been tested by each experimenter. We would probably assign the same number of blocks to each experimenter, but this is not essential. What is essential is that whole blocks be tested at each level of the nuisance factor. The balancing act can become a bit tricky when there are several nuisance factors, but careful advance planning can avoid confounding by such factors.

Even when their potential effects have been neutralized through balancing, nuisance factors affect the sensitivity and external validity of an experiment. For example, if five different experimenters test an equal number of subjects in each of two conditions, the experiment will be free of confounding due to the differences across experimenters. The performance of the subjects *within* each condition, however, is likely to vary more than if one experimenter had tested all the subjects. Subjects are likely, after all, to respond differently to the different experimenters, even when the experimenters try to treat all subjects within a condition the same way. This increased variation within each group makes it harder to detect differences between the groups, thus reducing the sensitivity of the experiment. If a difference is obtained between the two conditions, however, this finding has greater external validity than it would have had if only one experimenter had done the testing.

The general principle that emerges is that controlling nuisance factors by holding them constant leads to more sensitive experiments with less external validity, whereas controlling nuisance factors by balancing leads to lower sensitivity but increased external validity. Both balancing and holding nuisance factors constant are equally effective, however, in meeting the primary objective of a sound experiment: ensuring that the experiment is internally valid.

Subject Loss Internally valid experiments involving the random groups design need not only to start with comparable groups but also to end with comparable groups. When subjects begin an experiment but fail to complete it successfully, the internal validity of the experiment is threatened. There are two types of subject loss, mechanical and selective. Only selective subject loss poses a threat to internal validity (Underwood & Shaughnessy, 1975). **Mechanical subject loss** occurs when a subject fails to complete the experiment because of an equipment failure (in this instance the experimenter is considered part of the equipment). If a light bulb burns out, or if someone inadvertently interrupts an experimental session, or if the experimenter reads the wrong set of instructions, the subject who was being tested represents a mechanical subject loss. Mechanical loss is unrelated to any characteristic of the subject, so it should not lead to systematic differences between the characteristics of the subjects who successfully complete the experiment in the various conditions of the experiment. When mechanical subject loss occurs, the name of the dropped subject and the reason for the loss are recorded on the block-randomized schedule. The lost subject is then simply replaced by the next subject tested.

Selective subject loss is a far more serious matter. **Selective subject loss** occurs when subjects are lost differentially across the conditions of the experiment and some characteristic of the subject that is related to the outcome of the study is responsible for the loss. Selective subject loss destroys the equivalence of groups that is essential to the random groups design and can thus render the experiment uninterpretable. This problem can arise in a variety of experimental situations—physiological studies involving surgical or drug treatments, memory experiments testing retention over days or weeks, and longitudinal designs in survey research (see Chapter 4). For our purposes, the problems associated with selective subject loss can be illustrated by considering a fictitious but realistic example.

Assume that the directors of a local fitness center decide to do an experiment to test the effectiveness of a one-week fitness program they have developed. They identify eighty people who are willing to volunteer for the experiment, and they randomly assign forty to each of two groups. Members of the control group are simply asked to come to the center on Friday. When they arrive, they are given a fitness test. Those in the experimental group participate in a vigorous fitness program for one week prior to the Friday test. All forty control subjects are given the fitness test, but only twenty-five of the experimental subjects stay with the rigorous fitness program for the full week, and only these twenty-five people are given the test. The average fitness score is significantly higher for the experimental group, leading the directors of the fitness center to insert in the brochure describing their program the following claim: "A scientifically based research study has shown that our program leads to better fitness."

Is the fitness center's claim justified? Not on the basis of the study we have described. This example perfectly fits the criteria for selected subject loss. The loss occurred differentially across conditions in that subjects were lost only from the experimental group. The problem is *not* that the groups ended up different in size. If twenty-five people had been randomly assigned to the experimental group and forty to the control group, and all subjects had completed the experiment, the results would have been interpretable (although the results in each group would have had slightly different reliabilities). The problem is that the twenty-five experimental subjects who were given the fitness test are not likely to be comparable to the forty control subjects. In addition to occurring differentially, the loss is traceable to a characteristic of the subjects—their original level of fitness—and this characteristic is relevant to the outcome of the study. It is reasonable to expect that only the more fit experimental subjects could complete the rigorous program. Accordingly, their final fitness scores might have been higher even if they had not taken the fitness program!

If selective subject loss is not identified until after the experiment is completed, little can be done except to chalk up the experience of having conducted an uninterpretable experiment. Some preventive steps can be taken, however, if the researcher realizes in advance that selective loss may be a problem. One alternative is to administer a pretest and screen out subjects who are likely to be lost. In our example, an initial test of fitness could have been given, and only those subjects who scored above some minimal level allowed into the experimental and the control groups. The cost associated with this alternative is decreased external validity because the results could be generalized only to people above the minimal fitness level. However, an interpretable study of limited external validity is still preferable to an uninterpretable study.

The second way to minimize the risk of selective subject loss also involves a pretest. Here all subjects are given the pretest but are then simply randomly assigned to one of the conditions. Then, if a subject is lost from the experimental group, a subject with a comparable pretest score is dropped from the control group. In a sense, this approach tries to restore the comparability of the groups, but once again, the cost of this approach is decreased external validity. The advantage of this approach is that external validity is lost only if selective subject loss *does* occur. When a pretest is used in this situation, it is essential that it be a measure of the dimension responsible for the loss. For instance, a pretest of visual acuity could not be used to restore the comparability of groups in our fitness example.

IDENTIFICATION OF STATISTICALLY SIGNIFICANT EFFECTS

The purpose of an experiment is to determine whether an independent variable has had an effect on behavior. Evidence for an effect is found when the different levels of the independent variable are associated with differences in the dependent variable. Another way to say this is to say that there are differences in the dependent variable across the levels of the independent variable. If these differences are to be attributable to the independent variable, however, control techniques must be properly implemented to ensure the internal validity of the experiment. And even when this has been accomplished, a problem remains. As we described earlier, the use of balancing to control the individual differences among subjects does not eliminate these individual differences—balancing only distributes the differences equally across the levels of the independent variable. Because of the presence of individual differences, the differences in the dependent variable across levels of an independent variable may or may not reasonably be attributed to the effect of the independent variable. We will illustrate this problem and its solution by focusing on the procedures and results of an experiment from a classic series of studies by Asch (1951, 1955) on conformity to group pressure.

The task in Asch's experiments was a simple one. Male subjects were shown two cards. The first card contained one line, called *the standard.* The second card contained three lines of different lengths, only one of which matched the standard. The subject's task was to select the line that matched the standard. Eighteen tests of this kind were given to each subject. During a test session there were varying numbers of other men present. These men were introduced to the subject as fellow participants in the experiment, but they were actually working as confederates (see Chapter 3 for a definition of *confederates*) of the experimenter. These confederates responded with the same incorrect responses on twelve of the eighteen trials. Thus the independent variable was the number of confederates present, and there were seven levels of this variable (0, 1, 2, 3, 4, 8, and 16). Subjects were randomly assigned to a group representing one of these seven levels. The dependent variable was the number of trials (out of the twelve possible on which the confederates gave incorrect responses) on which the subject conformed to group pressure by choosing the incorrect response instead of what was obviously the correct choice.

Two questions were addressed in Asch's experiment. First, would subjects conform? That is, would they choose the incorrect line more in the conditions when others were present than when they were alone? Second, would conformity increase with increasing size of the incorrect majority? Asch conducted a properly controlled experiment, so it is possible to use the results of the study to answer these two questions.

The first and most important step in analyzing an experiment is to summarize the results using an appropriate descriptive statistic. The most commonly used descriptive statistic in psychology experiments is the mean. The mean number and the range of errors for the subjects who had been randomly assigned to each of the seven groups in the Asch experiment are presented in Table 6.1. The results seem clear. Fewer errors, on the average, were made

TABLE 6.1 MEAN NUMBERS OF ERRORS AS A FUNCTION OF THE SIZE OF THE DISSENTING MAJORITY

	Size of dissenting majority						
	0	1	2	3	4	8	16
Mean number of errors	0.08	0.33	1.53	4.00	4.20	3.84	3.75
Range of errors	0–2	0–1	0–5	1–12	0–11	0–11	0–10

Adapted from Asch (1951).

when the subjects were alone than when they were confronted with the incorrect responses of other "subjects," and mean errors increased with increasing size of the dissenting majority, at least up to groups of four.

Descriptive statistics alone are not sufficient, however, to provide definitive answers to the two questions that Asch's experiment addressed. The problem rests with the nature of the control provided by balancing through random assignment. Random assignment (and random selection, for that matter) do not eliminate the differences among subjects. They simply distribute these differences equally across the groups in the experiment. That is, the differences among subjects are not allowed to vary systematically *across* groups.

The nonsystematic variation due to differences among subjects *within* each group is called *error variation*. The individual differences within each group are reflected in the range of errors presented in the second row of Table 6.1. Even with a dissenting majority of sixteen, at least one subject made no errors, while another subject made ten errors. The problem confronting the researcher is that, because individual differences among subjects are balanced and not eliminated, the means of the groups in the experiment may differ even if the independent variable has had no effect. Thus, by themselves, the results of the best-controlled random groups design experiment do not permit a definite judgment about whether the "treatment" was effective.

A good way to determine whether the differences obtained in an experiment are reliable would be to replicate the experiment and see if the same outcome is obtained. But replication is a cumbersome and inefficient solution to the problem for experiments as extensive as Asch's. Participants for experiments are a scarce resource, and each replication costs us a study that could be done to ask new and different questions about behavior. (As we discussed earlier when we described ways to establish external validity, the problem is not quite so severe as the previous statement implies, because partial replication usually occurs in the natural course of research on a topic. For example, subsequent experiments that were done to locate the basis of conformity in the Asch experiment included at least some conditions from the original study.) In any case, some alternative to replication is needed to determine whether the differences obtained in a single experiment are larger than would be expected on the basis of error variation alone.

Inferential statistics provide a means of testing whether the differences in a dependent variable that are associated with various conditions of an experiment should be attributed to an effect of the independent variable. The most commonly used inferential statistic in psychology experiments—the analysis of variance—is discussed in Chapter 9. Here, we briefly describe the underlying logic of all inferential tests, a logic that unfortunately is not always intuitively clear.

Statistical inference is inductive and indirect. It is inductive because we draw *general* conclusions about populations on the basis of the *specific* samples that we test in our experiments. Statistical inference is indirect because it begins by assuming the null hypothesis. As the name implies, the **null hypothesis** is the assumption that the independent variable has had *no* effect. Once we make this assumption, we can use probability theory to determine the likelihood of our obtaining the difference that we did obtain in our experiment if the null hypothesis were true (if the independent variable had no effect). If this likelihood is small, we reject the null hypothesis and conclude that the independent variable *did* have an effect. Outcomes that lead us to reject the null hypothesis are called **statistically significant.** By this we mean only that the difference we have obtained in our experiment is larger than would be expected if error variation alone were responsible for the outcome.

Perhaps you can appreciate the process of statistical inference by considering the following dilemma. A friend offers to toss a coin with you to see who pays for the meal you just enjoyed at a restaurant. Your friend happens to have a coin ready to toss. Now it would be convenient if you could *directly* test whether your friend's coin were biased. The best you can do, however, is to test your friend's coin *indirectly* by assuming that it is not biased and seeing if you consistently get outcomes that differ from the expected 50–50 split of heads and tails. If the coin does not exhibit the ordinary 50–50 split, you might surmise that your friend is trying, by slightly underhanded means, to get you to pay for the meal. Similarly, researchers would like to test any obtained difference directly for significance, but the best they can do is to compare their outcome with the expected outcome of no difference. The key to understanding null-hypothesis testing is to recognize that *we can use the laws of probability to estimate the likelihood of an outcome only when we assume that chance factors are the sole cause of that outcome.*

As we have said, a statistically significant outcome is one that has only a small likelihood of occurring if the null hypothesis is true. But just how small is small enough? Although there is no definitive answer to this important question, the consensus among members of the scientific community is that outcomes associated with probabilities of less than 5 times out of 100 (or .05) if the null hypothesis were true are judged to be statistically significant. The probability that we elect to use to indicate that an outcome is statistially significant is called the **level of significance.** The level of significance is indicated by the Greek letter α (alpha). Thus we speak of the .05 level of significance, the .10 level, or the .01 level, which we report as $\alpha = .05$, $\alpha = .10$, or $\alpha = .01$.

You must choose the level of significance *before* you begin your experiment, not after you have done the statistical analysis. This procedure allows you to avoid the temptation of using the probability of the obtained outcome as the level of significance you *would have chosen.* The level of significance is like a pregnancy test—just as you are either pregnant or not pregnant, an outcome is either statistically significant or it isn't. An outcome can't be a little bit statistically significant! Strictly speaking, there are only two conclusions possible when you do an inferential statistics test: you either reject the null hypothesis or you fail to reject the null hypothesis. There are, however, alternatives to tests of statistical significance that can be used to assess the impact of an independent variable (see measure of effect size in Chapter 9).

When we take a strict approach to null-hypothesis (H_0) testing, we are essentially acknowledging the fact that it is impossible to prove that something does not exist. For example, if we were to propose that there was a monster in Lake Michigan, you would be unable to prove to us that this was not so. Putting ecological considerations aside for the moment, you might drain Lake Michigan to show that no monster is there but we could simply assert that the monster dug into the bed of the lake. You might then begin to dredge the lake, and if you still came up with no monster we could argue that our monster is digging faster than you are dredging. Becoming more desperate, you might fill the lake with explosives and if after detonating them, you found no remains of the monster we could calmly propose that our monster is impervious to explosives. So long as we were free to add characteristics to our monster, there is no test that you could perform that would convincingly show that the monster does not exist. Practically speaking, however, if we continued to believe in our monster after reasonable efforts had failed to yield evidence of its existence, we would be judged unreasonable and would lose credibility with other members of the community.

A similar practical problem faces the community of researchers in psychology. Although we recognize the logical impossibility of proving that H_0 is true, we also must have some method of deciding which independent variables are not worth pursuing. Most often, experiments are done to show that an independent variable causes a change in behavior. We should not get too discouraged, however, if the particular independent variable we are studying does not produce a statistically significant difference in our experiment. The discipline of psychology also progresses by identifying factors that do *not* influence behavior. Somewhat ironically, the standards for experiments that show that an independent variable is irrelevant are even higher than the standards for those that show that the independent variable is relevant. This is understandable when you recognize that experiments showing differences are likely to be subject to replication, whereas experiments finding no effects may discourage investigators from pursuing those avenues of investigation any further. All too often, however, after failing to reject H_0, researchers do a small (and insensitive) "replication" to confirm their original conclusion. If anything, the second experiment should be more sensitive than the first if it is to strengthen the conclusion that the independent variable has had no effect (Tversky & Kahneman, 1971).

Yeaton and Sechrest (1986, pp. 836–837) argue persuasively that findings of no difference (those that would lead us to accept the null hypothesis) are especially critical in applied research. They cite several questions to illustrate their point: "Does Agent Orange increase the risk of health problems? Are the pollutants in Love Canal associated with an increased risk of genetic defects? Are children who are placed in day-care centers as intellectually, socially, and emotionally advanced as children who remain in the home? Is a new, cheaper drug with fewer side effects as effective as the existing standard in preventing heart attacks? Does saccharin increase one's risk of developing bladder cancer?" These important questions clearly illustrate situations in which accepting the null hypothesis involves more than a theoretical issue—life and death consequences rest on making the correct decision. As a community, we need some way to assure ourselves that some monsters are just not worth searching for.

There is a troublesome aspect to the process of statistical inference. No matter what decision you reach and no matter how carefully you reach it, there is always some chance that you are making an error. The two possible "states of the world" and the two possible decisions an experimenter can reach are listed in Table 6.2. The independent variable either does or does not have an effect on behavior. The two possible correct decisions the researcher can make are represented by the upper-left and lower-right cells of the table. If the independent variable does have an effect, the researcher should reject the null hypothesis; if it does not, the researcher should fail to reject the null hypothesis.

The two potential errors are represented by the other two cells of Table 6.2, and these two types of errors have the highly descriptive names of Type I error and Type II error. These errors arise because of the probabilistic nature of statistical inference. When we decide that an outcome is statistically significant because its probability of occurring under the null hypothesis is less than .05, we acknowledge that in 5 times out of every 100 tests, the outcome *could* occur even if the null hypothesis were true. The level of significance, therefore, represents the probability of making a *Type I error:* rejecting the null hypothesis when it is true. The probability of making a Type I error can be reduced simply by making the level of significance more stringent, perhaps .001. The problem with this approach is that it increases the likelihood of making a *Type II error:* failing to reject the null hypothesis when it is false.

The problem of Type I errors and Type II errors should not immobilize us. But it should help us understand why researchers rarely use the world *prove* when they describe the results of an experiment that involved inferential statistics. Instead, they describe the results as "consistent with the hypothesis," or "confirming the hypothesis," or "supporting the hypothesis." These more

TABLE 6.2 POSSIBLE OUTCOMES OF DECISION-MAKING WITH INFERENTIAL STATISTICS

	States of the world	
	Null hypothesis is false	Null hypothesis is true
Reject null hypothesis	Correct decision	Type I error
Fail to reject null hypothesis	Type II error	Correct decision

tentative statements are a way of indirectly acknowledging that the possibility of making a Type I error or a Type II error always exists. The .05 level of significance represents a compromise position that allows us to strike a balance and avoid making too many of either type of error. The problem of Type I errors and Type II errors also reminds us that statistical inference can never replace replication as the ultimate test of the reliability of an experimental outcome. In spite of its limitations, however, statistical inference is an essential tool for the analysis of experiments.

Like any tool, statistical inference can be and often is misused. At times, researchers seem to forget that the statistical significance of a finding does nothing to enhance the internal validity of the experiment. Although we might be tempted to accept an interpretation if it is based on a "statistically significant" finding, we must remember that our ability to draw appropriate conclusions depends, most of all, on the internal validity of the study. And internal validity, as we have seen, depends mainly on whether the investigator has been able to exert enough control to eliminate alternative explanations. In other words, confounded experiments can easily produce statistically significant outcomes.

This brief introduction to inferential statistics is intended to show how closely the analysis of an experiment is tied to the questions and hypotheses that motivated the investigator to perform the experiment in the first place. Statistical analysis is not a necessary evil in experimentation; it is a critical step on the path from asking a research question to answering it.

ALTERNATIVE INDEPENDENT GROUPS DESIGNS

MATCHED GROUPS DESIGN

The random groups design is by far the most common variant of the independent groups design. To function effectively, however, the random groups design requires samples of sufficient size to guarantee that individual differences among subjects will average out across groups. The number of subjects required for a sufficient sample size cannot be specified exactly because the required number increases as the heterogeneity of the population from which the subjects are drawn increases. However, we can be relatively confident that, when small numbers of subjects are tested from heterogeneous populations, random assignment will not suffice to balance the differences among subjects. This is exactly the situation researchers face in several areas of psychology. For example, some developmental psychologists study newborn infants; others study elderly people. These psychologists often have available only limited numbers of subjects, and both newborns and the elderly certainly represent diverse populations.

One alternative that researchers have in this situation is to administer all the treatments to all the subjects, using the within-subjects designs that we will discuss in the next chapter. Some independent variables require separate groups of subjects for each level, however, and for these variables the within-subjects designs are of no use. For instance, when the effects of participation in a special program for senior citizens are being assessed, a separate control group that does not participate in the program is essential. The matched groups design is a viable alternative when neither the random groups design nor the within-subjects designs can be used effectively.

The logic of the **matched groups design** is simple and compelling. Instead of trusting randomization in the formation of comparable groups, the researcher makes the groups equal by matching subjects. One approach to accomplishing the matching that is used in research with animals is the *split-litter technique.* Offspring from the same litter are randomly assigned to different conditions. The genetic similarity of the offspring constitutes the basis for the matching. The different experimental groups are expected to be comparable initially even if there are relatively few subjects in each group. A similar approach to the matched groups design is used when identical twins are the subjects. Since identical twins are monozygotic (developed from a single zygote), their genetic makeup is the same. Thus, if one in each set of pairs of twins is assigned to one of two experimental groups, the groups should be comparable. Studies involving identical twins have been critical in research examining whether intellectual abilities (i.e., IQ) are influenced more by heredity or by environment.

Most uses of the matched groups design do not involve the split-litter technique or the testing of identical twins. Instead, a pretest task is used to match subjects. The challenge in this approach to the matched groups design is *to select a pretest task* (also called a *matching task*) *that equates the groups on a dimension that is relevant to the outcome of the experiment.* We discussed a similar problem earlier in this chapter when we described techniques to deal with the problem of subject loss. We noted then that it is of little help to match subjects on visual acuity if the experiment is designed to test the subjects' physical fitness. Similarly, the matched groups design is useful only when a good matching task is available.

Researchers have three options when selecting a matching task. The most widely preferred option is to match subjects on the same task that will be used in the experiment itself. If the dependent variable in the experiment will be blood pressure, subjects should be matched on blood pressure. The matching is accomplished by measuring the blood pressure of all subjects and then forming pairs or triples or quadruples of subjects (depending on the number of conditions in the experiment) who have identical or similar blood pressures. After these matched sets are formed, the investigator must assign subjects randomly to the conditions of the experiment in order to balance individual differences other than those included in the matching task.

In some experiments, the experimental task cannot be used as the matching task. For example, if the experiment involved various approaches to solving a puzzle and a pretest were given to see how long it took subjects to solve the puzzle, their learning the solution to the puzzle during the pretest would make it impossible to observe differences in the speed with which the same problem could be solved in the experiment itself. After having experience with the puzzle in the pretest, all subjects might solve the puzzle very quickly. The next best alternative to using the experimental task as the matching task is to use a task from the same class as the experimental task. In our problem-solving experiment, subjects could be matched on their performance solving a different puzzle from the experimental puzzle, so long as it had been shown that performance on the experimental puzzle correlated with performance on the matching puzzle. The least preferred alternative is to use a task from a class different from the experimental task. For our problem-solving experiment, subjects could be matched on some test of general ability, such as an intelligence test. Once again, to be useful, this general matching task must correlate with performance on the experimental task.

The matched groups design is not without problems. It is often difficult to find appropriate matches for all subjects. Even when matched sets of subjects can be obtained, the matching process may so severely restrict the people included in the study that the groups may no longer be representative of the general population. For example, in an experiment aimed at comparing the emotional disorders of college students with those of elderly people who matched the college students in general health and amount of education, the researcher would be studying a very unrepresentative group of the elderly population.

A more serious problem with matching, however, is that the matching task ensures comparable groups *only* on the dimension measured by the matching task. There are many potentially relevant characteristics of the subjects in addition to those assessed by the matching task. The groups must also be comparable on these other characteristics if any differences that emerge between groups are to be attributed solely to the effect of the independent variable. Random assignment bears the burden of balancing these additional factors, and, as we mentioned at the beginning of this section, we turn to the matched groups design when we fear that randomization may not be sufficient to accomplish this balancing. In spite of potential problems, the matched groups design is a better alternative than the random groups design when only a small number of subjects is available for an experiment that requires separate groups for each treatment, and when a good matching task is available.

NATURAL GROUPS DESIGN

So far we have been considering individual differences among subjects as a potential source of confounding that must be neutralized in our experiments. In many areas of psychology—such as personality research, abnormal psychology, and social psychology—individual differences represent much more than a source of confounding and error variation. The characteristics that subjects bring with them to the laboratory (called *subject variables*), such as their gender, their degree of intraversion-extraversion, or their aggressiveness, are important variables in many areas of psychology. Subject variables are different from manipulated independent variables because researchers *select* the levels of subject variables. They do so, however, to determine systematic relationships between the subject variables and other aspects of behavior. As such, subject variables are usually treated as if they were independent variables. To differentiate experiments involving subject variables from those involving manipulated independent variables, we refer to the former as **natural groups designs.**

The natural groups design can also be used in situations where ethical and practical constraints limit the scope of problems that can be studied by directly manipulating independent variables. No matter how interested we might be in the effects of traumatic events such as major surgery on subsequent depression, we could not ethically perform major surgery on a randomly selected group of introductory psychology students and then compare this group with another group on whom we had *not* performed surgery! Similarly, if we were interested in the relationship between divorce and emotional disorders, we could not randomly assign some people to get divorced. By using the natural groups design, however, we can compare people who have had surgery with those who have not. Similarly, people who have chosen to divorce can be compared with those who have chosen to stay married. The intent of these studies is to determine whether these natural treatments result in other systematic differences between the groups. For example, studies have shown that people who are separated or divorced are much more likely to receive psychiatric care than are those who are married, widowed, or have remained single (Bloom, Asher, & White, 1978). The natural groups design essentially involves looking for correlations between subjects' characteristics and their performance. Because of this, these designs are also called *correlational research* (see also Chapter 4).

Natural groups designs are highly effective in meeting the first two objectives of the scientific method—description and prediction. Unfortunately, serious problems can arise when the results of these designs are used as a basis for causal inference. People have a tendency to conclude that all three conditions for a causal inference have been met when really only the first condition, covariation, has been met. For instance, the finding that divorced persons are more likely than married persons to receive psychiatric care shows that these two factors covary. This result could be taken to mean that divorce causes emotional disorders that lead to the need for psychiatric care. Before reaching this conclusion, however, we must assure ourselves that the time-order condition for a causal inference has been met—namely, that divorce *preceded* the emotional disorder. Demonstrating covariation does nothing to specify the *direction* of the causal relationship. Perhaps those who suffer from emotional disorders are more likely to get divorced because of the strain placed on the relationship by the disorder or because the emotional disorder contributed to their marrying unwisely in the first place.

The most critical problem in drawing causal inferences based on the natural groups design is in meeting the third condition for demonstrating causality: eliminating plausible alternative causes. As you might suspect, this problem arises because the experimenter has far less control in the natural groups design. The subject variables being studied in the natural groups design are usually confounded. For example, intraverts and extraverts differ with respect to a number of characteristics other than their degree of introversion. For example, extraverts are apt to prefer excitement and practical jokes but not like quiet reading, while introverts generally show the opposite pattern. The manipulation done "by nature" is rarely the controlled type we have come to expect in establishing the internal validity of an experiment. The most effective approach to the problem of confounding in the natural groups design is *to study subject variables in combination with independent variables that can be manipulated.* We will be discussing the procedures for experiments involving more than one independent variable in Chapter 8. We will resume our discussion of the natural groups design in Chapter 8 after we have covered the basics of complex designs. For now, it is sufficient for you to recognize that drawing causal inferences based on the natural groups design is a treacherous enterprise.

SPECIAL CONTROL AND DESIGN PROBLEMS

PLACEBO CONTROL AND DOUBLE-BLIND EXPERIMENTS

Additional problems of control may arise in psychology experiments because of expectations held by both subjects and experimenters. In our discussion of the problem of reactivity in observational research (see Chapter 3), we introduced the concept of **demand characteristics** (Orne, 1962). As you may remember, Orne used the term to refer to the cues and other information used by subjects to guide their behavior in a psychological study. For example, if subjects know that they have been given alcohol, they may expect certain effects, such as relaxation or giddiness. In addition to the problems posed by subjects' expectations, there are also problems traceable to the expectations of the experimenters. These expectations may lead the experimenters to treat subjects differently in the different groups of the experiment in ways other than those required to implement the independent variable. The experimenters' observations may also be biased by their knowing which treatment the subject has received. Continuing with our alcohol experiment example, experimenters might read the instructions more slowly to subjects who have been given alcohol. The experimenters might also be more likely to notice any unusual motor movements or slurred speech among the "drinkers." The general term used to describe these biases is **experimenter effects** (Rosenthal, 1963).

The problems of demand characteristics and experimenter effects can never be eliminated, but their effects can be greatly diminished by using sound research methods. Every effort must be made to ensure that the only systematic difference in the way subjects are treated across the groups of the experiment is traceable to the independent variable of interest. The more mechanized the procedures for administering instructions and recording results, for example, the less likely it is that problems with experimenter effects will arise.

One approach to these problems is to do an experiment to see just how serious the problems are. Intons-Peterson (1983) directly manipulated experimenters' expectations to determine the effects of these expectations on the subjects' responses in a number of different tests that the experimenters were administering. In one experiment, imaginal and perceptual scanning of maps were compared. Subjects were asked to estimate the distances between two cities either while looking at a map or while imagining the map. One group of experimenters was led to believe that the subjects' estimates would be more accurate when they were imagining the map. Other experimenters were led to expect better estimates when the subjects were looking at the map. Sure enough, the subjects' estimates varied with the experimenters' beliefs; that is, whichever estimates the experimenter expected to be more accurate were more accurate!

Special research designs are available to control for both demand characteristics and experimenter effects. The first research design involves the use of **placebo control** groups. A *placebo* (from the Latin word meaning "I shall please") is a substance that looks like a drug or other active substance but is actually an *inert,* or inactive, substance. Pishkin and Shurley (1983) used a placebo control group to demonstrate the effectiveness of two drugs, doxepin and hydroxyzine, in reducing the arousal levels of psychiatric patients in response to the stress of failure on a cognitive task. The placebo subjects were given capsules identical to those used to administer the two drugs, but the placebo capsules contained only lactose, a sugar found in milk. Because no subject in the placebo control group realized that the pill she or he was taking contained no medicine, all the groups had the same "awareness" of taking a drug, and any differences between the experimental groups and the placebo control group could legitimately be attributed to an effect of the drug the experimental subjects took. Placebo control groups are often used in psychotherapy research to control for the nonspecific components of the therapy situation, such as time spent with the therapist and the client's expectations of improvement. Placebo control groups in psychotherapy research generally receive treatment that is considered "theoretically inert" in that no specific procedure related to the psychotherapy is included (O'Leary & Borkovec, 1978).

Placebo control groups are typically used in combination with a second research design that even more effectively controls for demand characteristics and experimenter effects. This second design is called a **double-blind experiment** because both the subject and the observer are kept unaware of (blind to) what treatment is being administered. In an experiment such as the Pishkin and Shurley (1983) study, two researchers would be needed to accomplish the double-blind control. The first researcher would prepare the drug capsules and code each capsule in some way; the second researcher would distribute the drugs to the subjects, recording the code for each drug as it was given to a subject. Hence there would be a record of which drug each subject received, but neither the subject nor the experimenter who actually administered the drugs would know which treatment the subject had received.

TESTING INTACT GROUPS

Sometimes noncomparable groups are formed even when random assignment appears to have been used. This occurs when intact groups (and not individual subjects) are randomly assigned to the conditions of an experiment. *Intact groups* are those that were formed prior to the start of the experiment. For example, the different sections of an introductory psychology class are intact groups. If a researcher were to assign different sections randomly to the different conditions in the experiment, it would be highly likely that the experiment would be confounded by differences in the characteristics of the subjects in the different groups. The introductory psychology classes were not formed randomly. They probably meet at different times of the day, have different instructors, and exhibit any number of other factors influencing the choices students made to be in their section rather than in one of the others. Random assignment of such intact groups to experimental conditions is simply not sufficient to balance the differences among the intact groups that are almost guaranteed to confound the independent variable under investigation.

The solution to this problem is simple—do not use intact groups in an independent groups design. Sometimes practical constraints may force you to test intact groups in what is called the *nonequivalent control group design* (see Chapter 11). In such situations, however, it is essential that some effort be made to show that the groups are comparable on dimensions that might be critical to the outcome of the experiment. For example, if you were doing a problem-solving experiment, the least you would need to do is to administer a pretest of general problem-solving ability to both groups to show that the groups were comparable on this critical dimension. It is far better, however, to avoid, whenever possible, the use of intact groups.

REGRESSION TO THE MEAN

The final design problem we will describe is called *regression to* (or *toward*) *the mean*. It is a problem that corresponds somewhat to several everyday expressions. We often refer to the "law of averages," or we say that "things will even out," or that "we are due" for a good day after a string of bad ones. Each of these sayings expresses the idea that extreme experiences tend to be balanced by less extreme experiences. Cook and Campbell (1979) provide a somewhat more formal analogy but one that still makes reference to students' common experience. They suggest that you consider your own experience in taking classroom tests. Sometimes you do more poorly than you expected because you lost some sleep, because you misread some questions, or because your instructor happened to ask several questions on a portion of the text you had not studied. If you took another version of the test the next day, your score would probably be higher, even without additional study, because it is unlikely that all the negative factors affecting the first test would "gang up on you" again during the second test.

In general, a test score or a subject's score on an experimental task is made up of two components: (1) the true score, reflecting what the test is validly measuring and likely to be stable from one measurement to the next, and (2) the error component, reflecting random error and unlikely to be stable from one time to another. The error component includes nonsystematic factors such as lack of sleep and question wording that affect the measurement. This error component is what "averages out" from one measurement to another. Those who have extremely high scores on the first test are likely to score lower on a second test simply because their error component is likely to be less extreme and closer to the average. The complement is true for those with extremely low scores on the first test. Hence, the name given to this phenomenon is **regression to the mean.** The less reliable the test, the more regression to the mean will occur.

Regression to the mean plays a role in experiments when subjects are selected because of their extreme scores on a pretest. For example, students scoring the highest and lowest on a reading test might be selected. In the experiment, a reading enhancement program would be given to those scoring lowest; those scoring highest would serve as the control group. On the surface this seems to be a stringent test because you are using the best readers as the standard for determining the effectiveness of the program. In fact, this is not a good test at all; the poorest readers are likely to do better on a subsequent test even if they didn't have the program. Similarly, the best readers are likely to do worse. Both of these changes reflect the effects of regression to the mean.

The moral of this story about regression to the mean is a simple one. If you have a treatment that is intended only for subjects at one extreme (such as a program to help poor readers), form both an experimental group and a control group from these extreme subjects so that the control group can serve as a check on regression to the mean. If you want to show that the effect appears for one extreme and not for the other, you will need four groups, with half of each extreme randomly assigned to receive the treatment. Designs of this type will be explained more fully in Chapter 8. In most instances, however, these special conditions do not apply, and the best way to test the effectiveness of a treatment is to use the random groups design. This approach offers the greatest external validity with the fewest threats to internal validity.

SUMMARY

Experimental research allows us to observe the unobservable. Predictions based on proposed explanatory processes can be either confirmed or refuted by experimental outcomes. Sound experiments are internally valid, reliable, sensitive, and externally valid. A major purpose of experiments is to test hypotheses derived from theories, but experiments can also be useful in testing the effectiveness of treatments or programs in applied settings. The experimental method is ideally suited to identifying cause-and-effect relationships when the control techniques of manipulation, holding conditions constant, and balancing are properly implemented. In this chapter we have focused on the application of these control techniques in experiments in which different groups of subjects are given different treatments represented by the levels of the independent variable. In the most common design of this type, the random groups design, the groups are formed in such a way that they are comparable at the start of the experiment. If they perform differently, it is presumed that the independent variable is responsible.

Random assignment, not random selection, is the most common means of forming comparable groups. By distributing subjects' characteristics equally across the conditions of the experiment, random assignment is an attempt to ensure that the differences among subjects are balanced. The most common technique for carrying out random assignment is block randomization.

Random assignment contributes to the internal validity of an experiment, but external validity must be established in some other way. One approach to enhancing external validity is to select representative samples of *all* dimensions on which you wish to generalize. Replication serves primarily as a check on the reliability of experimental finding, but replication also plays a key role in establishing external validity. When we obtain the same outcomes in two partial replications of the same experiment done in two widely different settings with different subjects, our confidence in the external validity of that finding increases. A partial replication, including the dimension on which you want to generalize as an independent variable, is perhaps the best way to establish external validity.

Nuisance factors, such as different rooms or different experimenters, must not be allowed to confound the independent variable of interest. Even when such nuisance factors are controlled, however, they can contribute to the sensitivity and external validity of an experiment. Holding nuisance factors constant increases sensitivity and decreases external validity, whereas balancing nuisance factors decreases sensitivity and increases external validity. A more serious threat to the internal validity of the random groups design is involved when subjects fail to complete the experiment successfully. Selective subject loss occurs when subjects are lost differentially across the conditions and some characteristic of the subject that is related to the outcome of the experiment is responsible for the loss. We can help prevent selective loss by restricting subjects to those likely to complete the experiment successfully, or we can compensate for it by selectively dropping comparable subjects from the group that did not experience the loss.

An independent variable has had an effect on behavior when differences in the dependent variable occur across the levels of the independent variable. The identification of such differences begins with a summary of descriptive statistics (usually the mean) in a table or a figure. Because differences in the dependent variable can arise because of error variation alone, confirmation of a statistically significant effect of an independent variable requires the use of inferential statistics. The inductive and indirect process of null-hypothesis testing provides a set of guidelines for deciding on the statistical significance of a finding. By agreeing on the level of significance (usually $\alpha = .05$), we can determine whether a difference occurs *less* frequently than we would judge to be the result of *error variation* (chance factors) alone. The reality of Type I error and Type II error prevent null-hypothesis testing from ever replacing replication; replication remains the ultimate test of the reliability of a research finding.

The matched groups design is an alternative to the random groups design when only a small number of subjects is available along with a good matching task and when the experiment requires separate groups for each treatment. The biggest problem with the matched groups design is that the groups are equated *only* on the characteristic measured by the matching task. In the natural groups design, researchers select the levels of independent variables (usually subject variables) and look for systematic relationships between these independent variables and other aspects of behavior. Essentially, the natural groups design involves looking for correlations between subjects' characteristics and their performance. Such correlational research designs pose problems in drawing causal inferences.

Demand characteristics and experimenter effects can be minimized through the use of proper experimental procedures, but they can best be controlled by using placebo control and double-blind procedures. Testing intact groups and regression to the mean are two easily avoidable threats to the internal validity of experiments involving the independent groups design.

KEY CONCEPTS

independent variables
dependent variables
confounding
independent groups designs
random groups design
random assignment
block randomization
replication
nuisance factors
mechanical subject loss
selective subject loss
inferential statistics
null hypothesis
statistically significant
level of significance
matched groups design
natural groups designs
demand characteristics
experimenter effects
placebo control
double-blind experiment
regression to the mean

REVIEW QUESTIONS

1 What role do manipulation, holding conditions constant, and balancing play in ensuring the internal validity of an experiment?
2 Briefly outline the logic of the independent groups design.
3 Distinguish between random selection and random assignment in terms of their use in carrying out the random groups design.
4 Briefly describe the procedures you would follow in order to use block randomization to assign subjects in an experiment involving four different groups.
5 Describe the role of replication in establishing the external validity of a research finding.

6 How are nuisance factors balanced in the random groups design? What impact do nuisance factors have on the sensitivity and external validity of an experiment?
7 What preventive steps can a researcher take when he or she anticipates that selective subject loss may pose a problem in an experiment?
8 Why is statistical inference said to be inductive and indirect?
9 Distinguish between Type I error and Type II error in statistical significance, and explain the role that level of significance (α) plays in influencing the likelihood of making each of these two types of error.
10 What is the logic of the matched groups design? When is it most likely to be used? What three options do researchers have in selecting a matching task?
11 How do subject variables differ from manipulated independent variables?
12 Why is drawing causal inferences on the basis of the natural groups design so difficult?
13 Why should the use of intact groups be avoided in the independent groups design?
14 Briefly explain the problem of regression to the mean, and outline at least one approach to dealing with this problem when testing extreme groups.

CHALLENGE QUESTIONS

1 Consider a random groups design experiment involving one independent variable. Specifically, the independent variable is Rate of Presentation and it is manipulated at four levels (Very Fast, Fast, Slow, and Very Slow).

A Use the following set of random numbers to prepare a block randomization schedule such that there will be four participants in each of the four conditions. Select a random order from each of the four rows of the numbers from 1 to 16.

15-8-11-14-9-4-12-10-13-7-16-1-3-2-5-6
10-3-4-16-7-8-9-13-2-1-6-12-5-11-15-14
11-8-12-2-16-10-14-3-15-7-4-6-5-1-13-9
11-9-14-15-16-4-3-8-5-13-2-6-1-10-7-12

B The experimenter is considering restricting participants to those who pass a stringent reaction time test so as to be sure that they will be able to perform the task successfully with the Very Fast presentation rate. Explain what factors the experimenter should consider in making this decision, being sure to describe clearly what risks, if any, are taken if only this restricted set of participants is tested.

C The experimenter discovers that it will be necessary to test participants in two different rooms. How should the experimenter arrange the testing of the conditions in these two rooms so as to avoid possible confounding by this nuisance factor?

2 A researcher was conducting a series of experiments on the effects of external factors on people's persistence in exercise programs. In one of these experiments, the researcher manipulated three types of distraction while subjects walked on a treadmill. The three types of distraction were: concentrating on one's own thoughts, listening to a tape of music, and watching a video of people engaging in outdoor recreation. The dependent variable was how strenuous the treadmill exercise was at the time the subject decided to end the session (the incline of the treadmill was regularly increased as the person went through the session, thereby making the exercise increasingly strenuous). In an introductory psychology course, 120 students volunteered to partici-

pate in the experiment, and the researcher randomly assigned forty students to each of the three levels of the distraction variable.

After only 2 minutes on the treadmill each subject was given the option to stop the experiment (this option came before any of the subjects could reasonably be expected to be experiencing fatigue). Data for the subjects who decided to stop after only 2 minutes were not included in the analysis of the final data. Twenty-five subjects who were concentrating on their own thoughts completed the experiment; thirty subjects in the music condition completed the experiment; and forty subjects in the video group completed the experiment. The mean strenuousness score was highest for the concentration group, next highest for the music group, and lowest for the video group. These results did not support the researcher's prediction that persistence would be highest in the video group.

A What methodological problem may threaten the internal validity of this experiment? What factors indicate that this problem occurred?

B Assume that a pretest measure was available for each of the 120 subjects and that the pretest measured the degree to which each subject was likely to persist at exercise. Describe how you could use these pretest scores to confirm that the problem you identified in part A had occurred.

3 Psychologists have identified one source of conflict that occurs when our ideal self does not conform to how we actually perceive ourselves as being. An experiment was done to see if alcohol would have an especially strong effect on our perception of ourselves when such a conflict between our real and ideal selves was present. Specifically, the hypothesis was that alcohol would cause subjects to see themselves in a more favorable light, thereby reducing the discrepancy between their real and ideal selves. There were four conditions in the experiment. For two of the groups there was low conflict between their real and ideal selves. One of these groups was given alcohol, and one was not. In the other two groups there was high conflict between their real and ideal selves. Again, one of these groups received alcohol, and one did not. Twenty subjects participated in each of the four groups. The dependent variable was the subjects' mean rating of how favorable their perception was of their real self. An experimenter was present with each subject to give instructions for the experiment and to monitor the subjects while they completed their ratings. Explain why it would be essential to use placebo control and double-blind procedures in this experiment.

4 A certain social worker was interested in reducing the amount of prejudice expressed by the members of the community in which she worked. She designed what she thought was an effective program for changing people's prejudicial attitudes. She decided to test her program in the most stringent way she knew. On the basis of a pretest measure of attitudes, she selected the ten most prejudiced people in her community (these people had a mean prejudice score of 9 on the 10-point paper-and-pencil test of prejudice that the investigator had quickly prepared for the purpose of selecting the most prejudiced people). She also selected the ten least prejudiced people (they had a mean prejudice score of 1.0 on her pretest). She administered her program to the ten most prejudiced people for a month and then tested all twenty people again. She found that the mean prejudice score for the ten most prejudiced was now 7.5 and that for the ten least prejudiced it was 1.5. Because she had reduced the difference between the least and most prejudiced groups by 25 percent, she decided that her program was highly successful.

A Explain why you would be hesitant to accept this conclusion. Be sure to explain the role of the reliability of the pretest in this problem.

B Describe how the investigator should have tested her program.

ANSWERS TO CHALLENGE QUESTION 1

A Assigning the numbers 1 to 4 to the respective conditions Very Fast to Very Slow, and following the random number sequences (across the rows), the order of the four conditions in each of the four blocks would be

Block 1	Very Slow, Very Fast, Slow, Fast
Block 2	Slow, Very Slow, Fast, Very Fast
Block 3	Fast, Slow, Very Slow, Very Fast
Block 4	Very Slow, Slow, Fast, Very Fast

B The investigator is taking a reasonable step to avoid selective subject loss, but restricting participants to those who pass a stringent reaction time test entails the risk of decreased external validity of the obtained findings.

C The rooms can be balanced by assigning entire blocks from the block-randomized schedule to be tested in each room. Usually, the number of blocks assigned to each room is equal, but this is not essential. For effective balancing, however, several blocks should be tested in each room.

Chapter 7

Within-Subjects Designs

Outline

OVERVIEW

As we have repeatedly emphasized, the experimental method involves administering at least two treatments to subjects to determine their differential influence, if any, on behavior. Thus far we have considered experimental designs in which each treatment is administered to a separate group of subjects. These independent-groups designs (random groups, matched groups, and natural groups) are powerful tools for studying the effects of a wide range of independent variables. There are times, however, when it is inefficient to give a different treatment to each of several separate groups of subjects. In such circumstances, it is still possible to do an interpretable experiment by administering all the treatments to each subject. In a sense, the experiment is done within each subject, so these designs are called **within-subjects designs.**

We begin this chapter by exploring the reasons why a researcher might choose a within-subjects design. We next examine the problem of practice effects in the within-subjects designs. Practice effects arise because subjects undergo changes as they are repeatedly tested. Subjects may improve with practice, for example, because they learn more about the task or because they become more relaxed in the experimental situation. They also may get worse with practice—for example, because of fatigue or reduced motivation. Unless these practice effects are balanced across the conditions of the experiment, the independent variable of interest will be confounded by the practice effects and the experiment will be uninterpretable. This chapter discusses various techniques for accomplishing this balancing. We will conclude this chapter by describing potential limitations of the within-subjects designs.

REASONS FOR USING WITHIN-SUBJECTS DESIGNS

There are at least five reasons why a researcher might choose a within-subjects design. First, the within-subjects designs require fewer subjects, so they are ideal for situations in which only a small number of subjects is available. The within-subjects designs are especially useful when no acceptable matching task exists with which to equate small independent groups of subjects.

The second reason for choosing a within-subjects design applies even when sufficient numbers of subjects are available for an independent-groups design. A researcher might choose to use a within-subjects design for the sake of convenience or efficiency. For example, Posner (1973) describes a series of experiments dealing with the cognitive processes that are required to identify individual letters while reading. In one of these experiments, the investigators measured how long it took subjects to decide whether two briefly presented letters had the same name. There were two conditions in the experiment: either the two presented letters were physically identical (*AA*) or they had the same name but were physically different (*Aa*). Even though the subjects' task was the same in the two conditions (to decide whether the two letters had the same name), the researchers found that subjects could respond 80 milliseconds faster when the letters were physically identical than they could when the letters had only their name in common. Each trial in this experiment required only a few seconds to complete. They could have tested separate groups of subjects for each of the two conditions, but this approach would have been horribly inefficient. It would have taken more time to instruct subjects regarding the nature of the task than it would to do the task itself. A within-subjects design in which each subject was tested on both types of pairs of letters provided the experimenters with a far more efficient way to answer their research question.

The third reason for choosing a within-subjects design is that experiments done using within-subjects designs are generally more sensitive than those done using independent-groups designs. The *sensitivity* of an experiment refers to the extent to which it is able to detect differences in the dependent variable as a function of the independent variable. In within-subjects designs, the investigator is trying to detect differences in the performance of the same subject under different conditions. In independent-groups designs, researchers are trying to detect differences in the performance of different subjects under different conditions. Because subjects vary from themselves less than they do from other subjects, the error variation in within-subjects-designs experiments is likely to be less than the error variation in independent-groups-designs experiments. This lower variability in within-subjects-designs experiments is what makes them more sensitive. The increased sensitivity of within-subjects designs is especially attractive to researchers who are studying independent variables that have small effects on behavior.

The fourth reason for choosing a within-subjects design is that some areas of psychological research require its use. When the research question involves studying changes in subjects' behavior over time, such as in a learning experiment or in a longitudinal design (see Chapter 4), a within-subjects design is needed. Further, whenever the experimental procedure requires that subjects compare two or more stimuli relative to one another, a within-subjects design must be used. For example, a within-subjects design would have to be used if a researcher wanted to measure the minimum amount of light that must be added before subjects could detect that a spot of light had become brighter. It would also be called for if a researcher wanted subjects to rate the relative attractiveness of a series of photographs. In general, the research areas of psychophysics (illustrated by the light-detection experiment) and scaling (illustrated by the ratings of attractiveness) rely heavily on within-subjects designs.

A fifth reason for using the within-subjects designs is that the same independent variable can have different effects when the independent variable is investigated in an independent-groups design and in a within-subjects design. Grice and Hunter (1964) studied the effect of two different intensities of a sound as conditioned stimuli in a classical conditioning experiment. Classical conditioning involves the pairing of a neutral stimulus, called the *conditioned stimulus (CS),* with a stimulus that reliably elicits a response from the organism, called the *unconditioned stimulus (UCS).* As you may remember, Pavlov used classical conditioning to train dogs to salivate to a sound (e.g., the noise of a metronome) by pairing sound as a CS with food as a UCS.

Grice and Hunter found that in general, a more intense CS leads to stronger classical conditioning. But they also found that the effect of the intensity is much greater when the subjects receive both intensities in a within-subjects design than when they receive only one intensity in an independent-groups design. Grice and Hunter developed a theoretical explanation of the different effects of CS intensity based on the concept of adaptation level. For our purposes, the main point of their experiment is that an independent variable may have different effects on behavior depending on the design used. Although this may be disconcerting to an investigator, the Grice and Hunter study illustrates that variations in experimental designs can form the basis of discoveries that advance our understanding of psychological processes.

STAGE-OF-PRACTICE EFFECTS

At first glance, the within-subjects designs might appear far superior to the independent-groups design. The within-subjects designs require fewer subjects than do the independent-groups designs, and experiments can usually be completed more quickly when the within-subjects designs are used. In addition to their greater efficiency, the within-subjects designs offer another advantage—the problem of confounding the conditions of the experiment with the characteristics of the subjects within each condition is avoided. The same subjects are tested in all conditions of a within-subjects design, so it is impossible to end up with brighter, more aggressive, or more anxious subjects in one condition than in another condition. Stated formally, there can be no confounding by subject variables in the within-subjects designs.

The apparent elegance of the within-subjects designs vanishes, however, when we realize that these designs require that the same subject must be tested more than once. Subjects may change across repeated testings even if all tests are done under the same conditions. That is, subjects may get better and better at doing a task if a skill is being developed, or they may get worse and worse at the task because of such factors as fatigue and boredom. The repeated testing of each subject in the within-subjects designs gives the subjects practice with the experimental task. The changes subjects undergo with repeated testing are called **stage-of-practice effects** or just *practice effects.*

These changes with repeated testing are also sometimes called *progressive error,* and they can be understood as temporary subject variables—temporary changes in the characteristics of the subject. In the random-groups design, the individual differences among subjects (subject variables) contribute to the error variation in the experiment. This error variation is balanced by randomly assigning subjects to groups. Similarly, the temporary changes subjects undergo in a within-subjects design contribute to progressive error. Progressive error (or stage-of-practice effects) must also be balanced if a within-subjects-design experiment is to have internal validity. We describe techniques for doing this balancing in this chapter.

Wortman and Loftus (1981) describe a series of experiments that illustrate what happens when stage-of-practice effects are not balanced. Several hundred children from 3 to 10 years of age were tested to determine whether children perceive colors as adults do. The children were told to arrange fifteen colored caps in a specific order. The fifteen caps represented various shades of one color, such as red or blue, and several different colors were tested. In early published reports, 50 percent of 3-year-olds made errors on the color blue, whereas only 11 percent of 10-year-olds did so. This suggested that the ability to detect differences in the color blue increased with age. But careful examination of the procedures revealed a serious problem: The early investigators had always tested the color blue last. These investigators failed to consider that children, especially young children, quickly become bored with a repetitive task and begin to make mistakes. When a second group of researchers repeated the experiment, they balanced for practice effects by administering the color tests in different orders. The younger children continued to make the most errors on colors tested last, but there were no consistent differences in errors made on the color blue (or on any other color) as a function of age. If the second group of researchers had not done experiments to balance practice effects, we might still be trying to explain why 3-year-olds have trouble seeing the color blue!

BALANCING STAGE-OF-PRACTICE EFFECTS

There are two types of within-subjects designs. In the **complete within-subjects design,** practice effects are balanced by administering the conditions several times to each subject, using different orders each time, such that the results for each subject are interpretable. In the **incomplete within-subjects design,** each condition is administered to each subject only once and the order of administering the conditions is varied across subjects, such that practice effects can be neutralized by combining the results for all subjects. The specific techniques for balancing practice effects in the two within-subjects designs are different, so we will discuss the two designs separately.

COMPLETE WITHIN-SUBJECTS DESIGN

Does one side of your face express emotion more intensely than the other side? Sackheim, Gur, and Saucy (1978) used a within-subjects design to attempt to answer this question. Earlier research had shown that subjects given photographs depicting posed facial expressions of six basic human emotions (happiness, surprise, fear, sadness, anger, and disgust) could readily and accurately identify the expressed emotion. Sackheim and coworkers took advantage of a technique developed in earlier work on facial recognition whereby a full photograph of a face can be constructed using only one side of a person's face. The technique involves developing both a photograph of a full face and a photograph of its mirror image. These two photographs are then split down the middle and two composite photographs are made—one from the two versions of the left side of the face and one from the two versions of the right side. Illustrative photographs are presented in Figure 7.1. In the center is a photograph of a person expressing disgust. The two composite photographs made from the center photograph are presented on either side of the original.

Subjects were shown slides of photographs like those in Figure 7.1 and were asked to rate each slide on a 7-point scale indicating the intensity of the expressed emotion. The slides were presented individually for 10 seconds, and subjects were then given 35 seconds to make their rating. To increase the

FIGURE 7.1 (a) Left-side composite, (b) original, and (c) right-side composite of the same face. The face is expressing disgust. (From Sackheim et al., 1978.)

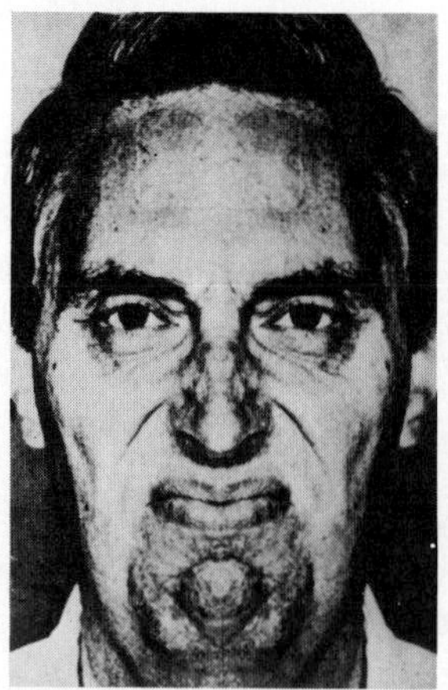

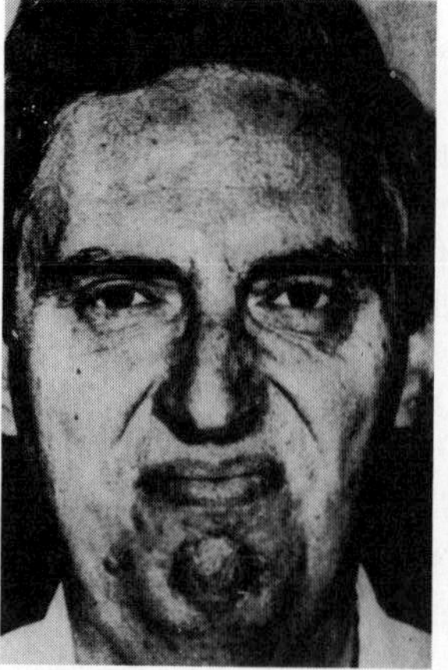

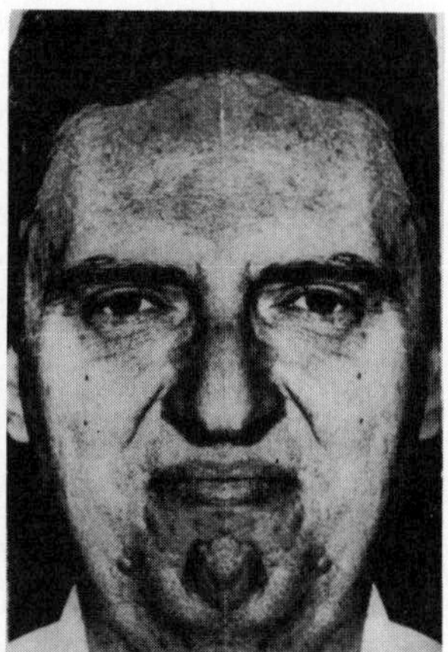

external validity of their experiment, the investigators had photographs of fourteen different people depicting the six identifiable emotions and one neutral expression. The critical independent variable in the experiment, however, was the *version* of the photograph (left composite, original, or right composite). Each subject rated fifty-four slides: eighteen left composites, eighteen originals, and eighteen right composites.

Does one of the two composites in Figure 7.1 look more disgusted than the other? Subjects' ratings of emotional intensity were consistently higher for the left composite than for the right composite. Sackheim et al. interpreted these findings in terms of hemispheric specialization of the brain. In general, the left hemisphere controls the right side of the body and the right hemisphere controls the left side of the body. Thus, the left composite reflects control by the right hemisphere, and the right composite reflects control by the left hemisphere. The higher ratings of emotional intensity for the left composite photographs suggest that the right hemisphere may be more heavily involved than the left hemisphere in the production of emotional expression.

The interpretation of the differences in mean ratings assigned to the three versions of the photographs depends critically on the order in which the slides were presented to subjects. If all the original versions were presented first, followed by all the right composites, then by all the left composites, higher ratings for the slides shown at the end of this long sequence may reflect the intensity of the subjects' boredom and fatigue rather than the intensity of the emotions actually depicted in the photographs. The problem is the same as the one we described earlier in the experiments dealing with children's perception of color. If you imagine yourself in this experiment making a rating for each of the slides in this long sequence, you will get a sense of what we mean by practice effects. Surely your attention, motivation, and experience in rating the emotionality of photographs will change as you work through the sequence of slides. Sackheim et al. used balancing techniques specifically developed for use in the complete within-subjects design to ensure that each of the three versions of the photographs was equally likely to appear at any point in the long series of slides.

In the complete within-subjects design, subjects are given each treatment enough times to balance stage-of-practice effects for each subject. Of course, this is possible only when each treatment can be administered more than once. When the task is simple enough and not too time-consuming (such as judging the emotional intensity of photographs), it is often possible to give one subject several experiences with each treatment. In fact, in some complete within-subjects designs, only one or two subjects are tested and each subject experiences literally hundreds of trials. More commonly, however, researchers use procedures like those used by Sackheim et al. That is, several subjects are tested, and each subject is given each treatment only a relatively small number of times. Researchers have two choices in deciding how to arrange the order in which the treatments in a complete within-subjects design are administered: block randomization and ABBA counter-balancing.

Block Randomization The first option for balancing practice effects in the complete within-subjects design represents a new use of a familiar technique. We introduced block randomization in Chapter 6 as an effective technique for assigning subjects to conditions in the random groups design. Block randomization can also be used to order the conditions for each subject in a complete within-subjects design. For instance, Sackheim et al. administered each of the three versions of their photographs (left composite, original, and right composite) eighteen times to each subject. The sequence of trials shown in Table 7.1 illustrates how block randomization could be used to arrange the order of the three conditions in their experiment. The sequence of fifty-four trials is broken up into eighteen blocks of three. Each block contains the three conditions of the experiment in random order. In general, the number of blocks in a block-randomized schedule is equal to the number of times each condition is administered, and the size of each block is equal to the number of conditions in the experiment.

If a subject rated the photographs following the sequence in the block-randomized schedule shown in Table 7.1, it is unlikely that changes in the subject's attention, motivation, or experience with rating photographs would affect any one of the conditions more than any other. The practice effects can reasonably be expected to "average out" over the three experimental conditions. Determining the average position of each of the three conditons in the block-randomized sequence gives a rough indication of the balancing of practice effects. This can be done by summing the trial numbers on which each condition appears and dividing by 18. For instance, the original photographs appeared on trials 1, 5, 8, 11, 13, 18, 21, 24, 27, 28, 33, 34, 39, 40, 44, 48, 49, and 53. The average position of the original photographs, therefore, was 27.6. The corresponding values for the left and right composite photographs are 27.7 and 27.2, respectively.

As you may have already recognized, block randomization requires several repetitions of each condition before practice effects can be expected to average

TABLE 7.1 BLOCK-RANDOMIZED SEQUENCE OF TRIALS IN AN EXPERIMENT WITH THREE CONDITIONS ADMINISTERED EIGHTEEN TIMES EACH

Trial	Cond.	Trial	Cond.	Trial	Cond.	Trial	Cond.	Trial	Cond.	Trial	Cond.
1	0	10	L	19	R	28	O	37	L	46	R
2	L	11	O	20	L	29	L	38	R	47	L
3	R	12	R	21	O	30	R	39	O	48	O
4	R	13	O	22	L	31	R	40	O	49	O
5	O	14	L	23	R	32	L	41	R	50	R
6	L	15	R	24	O	33	O	42	L	51	L
7	R	16	R	25	R	34	O	43	R	52	R
8	O	17	L	26	L	35	R	44	O	53	O
9	L	18	O	27	O	36	L	45	L	54	L

Note: The conditions are the three versions of the photographs used by Sackheim et al. (1978): L = left composite; O = original; R = right composite.

out. We should not expect practice effects to be balanced after two or three blocks—any more than we would expect sample sizes of two or three in the random-groups design to equate the characteristics of subjects across groups. Fortunately, a technique is available to balance practice effects when it is not possible to administer each condition often enough for the averaging process of block randomization to work effectively.

ABBA Counterbalancing In its simplest form, ABBA counterbalancing can be used to balance practice effects in the complete within-subjects design with as few as two administrations of each condition. **ABBA counterbalancing** involves presenting the conditions in one sequence followed by the opposite of that same sequence. Its name describes the sequences when there are only two conditions (A and B) in the experiment, but ABBA counterbalancing is not limited to experiments with just two conditions. Sackheim et al. could have presented the versions of their photographs according to the sequence outlined in Table 7.2.

Note that the order of the three conditions on the first three trials is simply reversed for trials 4 to 6. The values in the first row show the hypothetical amount of practice effects that would be added on each trial of the ABBA sequence when practice effects are linear. When practice effects are linear, the same amount is added to or subtracted from performance on each successive trial. In our example, practice effects add one unit to performance on each trial. If you add up the practice effects for each condition, you will see that all the totals are the same, namely, 5. The left composite condition gets the least and the greatest influence from practice effects, while the right composite condition gets two intermediate amounts. The ABBA cycle can be applied with any number of conditions and can be repeated any number of times. It balances practice effects even more effectively with larger numbers of repetitions of the cycle. Usually, however, ABBA counterbalancing is used when the number of conditions and the number of repetitions of each condition are relatively small.

Although ABBA counterbalancing provides a simple and elegant means to balance practice effects, it is not without limitations. ABBA counterbalancing is most effective when practice effects are linear. When practice effects for a task involve abrupt initial changes followed by relatively little change thereafter, ABBA counterbalancing is ineffective, especially if only one ABBA cycle is used. This is illustrated in the last row of Table 7.2. The left composite receives

TABLE 7.2 ABBA COUNTERBALANCED SEQUENCE OF TRIALS IN AN EXPERIMENT WITH THREE CONDITIONS (LEFT COMPOSITE, ORIGINAL, AND RIGHT COMPOSITE)

	Trial 1	Trial 2	Trial 3	Trial 4	Trial 5	Trial 6
Condition	Left	Original	Right	Right	Original	Left
Practice effect (linear)	+0	+1	+2	+3	+4	+5
Practice effect (nonlinear)	0	+6	+6	+6	+6	+6

only six hypothetical units of practice effects, and the other two conditions receive twelve units each. When practice effects of this type are anticipated, researchers often ignore performance on the early trials and wait until the practice effects reach a "steady state." Even in these situations, however, researchers still use either block randomization or ABBA counterbalancing to balance possible practice effects.

Achieving a stable baseline before beginning the experiment offers an advantage beyond that of increasing the likelihood that the balancing techniques will be effective. Practice effects add variability to performance within each condition, thereby reducing the sensitivity of the experiment. Thus, when practice effects are minimized, the sensitivity of the experiment is increased. The counterpart to this in the random-groups design is testing subjects from homogeneous rather than heterogeneous populations. It is important to recognize, however, that the internal validity of an experiment takes precedence over its sensitivity. So long as appropriate balancing techniques have been used, the internal validity of a complete within-subjects-design experiment is ensured.

A second limitation of ABBA counterbalancing is the problem of anticipation effects. **Anticipation effects** occur when a subject develops expectations about which condition should occur next in the sequence. The subject's response to that condition may then be influenced more by this expectation than by the actual experience of the condition itself. For example, consider a time-perception experiment in which the subject's task is to estimate the length of time that has passed between when the experimenter said "Start" and when the experimenter said "Stop." (Of course, subjects have to be prevented somehow from marking off time during the interval by counting or rhythmically tapping.) If the time intervals in such an experiment are 12, 24, and 36 seconds, then one possible ABBA sequence of conditions could be 12-24-36-36-24-12. If this cycle were repeated several times, subjects would very likely recognize the pattern and expect a series of increasing and then decreasing intervals. Their time estimates might soon begin to reflect this pattern rather than their perception of each independent interval.

Anticipation effects do not usually pose a serious problem, because the ABBA cycle is not repeated enough times to allow subjects to recognize the pattern. The possibility that subjects might recognize the pattern can be reduced even further by using a random sequence of the conditions for the first half of the ABBA cycle. In the time-perception experiment, the ABBA pattern of 24-36-12-12-36-24 would be less likely to be detected than the pattern of 12-24-36-36-24-12. In general, however, ABBA counterbalancing should not be used if anticipation effects are likely.

An Illustration: Measuring a Difference Threshold The complete within-subjects design, like all experimental designs, is used primarily to implement an independent variable in order to determine its effect on the dependent variable. The Sackheim et al. experiment testing the effect of the different photographs of faces expressing emotion illustrates this primary use of the complete within-subjects design. It is also possible, however, to use the complete within-subjects design to make measurements that are essential in certain areas of research in psychology, such as psychophysics. *Psychophysics* is an area of research that seeks to quantify precisely the relationship between stimulation, measured in physical units, and the psychological sensation experienced in response to that stimulation. For example, how many grams would you need to add to a tin can before you noticed that the can was heavier? Or how much would you need to turn up your stereo before you roommate noticed that it was louder?

How much a physical stimulus must change before we can detect the change is called the *difference threshold* or the *just noticeable difference (JND)*. To measure a difference threshold, we need to use the complete within-subjects design. The psychophysical method that is often used to determine a difference threshold is the method of constant stimuli. In this method, an observer is asked to compare a series of comparison stimuli to a standard, making a separate judgment for each comparison stimulus. In a weight-discrimination experiment, for example, a standard weight of 100 grams could be used with comparison stimuli ranging from 75 to 125 grams in 5-gram increments. For each experimental trial, the standard stimulus is presented along with one of the eleven comparison stimuli (one of the comparison stimuli is 100 grams, the same weight as the standard). The observer is asked to judge whether the comparison stimulus is lighter or heavier than the standard. Block randomization in the complete within-subjects design would be used to determine the order of presenting the comparison stimuli on each experimental trial. Practice effects should be well-balanced after several trials on which each comparison stimulus is presented once.

Data collected from one student who had gone through a series of ten trials, making comparisons of a 100-gram standard to eleven comparison stimuli, are presented in Figure 7.2. The percentage of times the student responded "heavier" for the ten presentations of each comparison weight is plotted as a function of the weights of the comparison stimuli. The difference threshold, or just noticeable difference, is defined as that increment or decrement in weight that the student could detect 50 percent of the time. The first step in determining a difference threshold is to compute the *interval of uncertainty:* the difference between the weights corresponding to the points at which the subject responded "heavier" 75 percent and 25 percent of the time, respectively. The difference threshold is then computed by taking one-half of the interval of uncertainty. For the results plotted in Figure 7.2, we obtained a difference threshold of 5 grams.

The major point of this illustration is that the measurement of important concepts in psychology, like a difference threshold, requires doing a small experiment using the complete within-subjects design for each subject whose threshold you wish to measure. Many experiments investigating the phenomena of sensation and perception make use of within-subjects designs. This illustration also demonstrates that our sensory capacities are quite impressive.

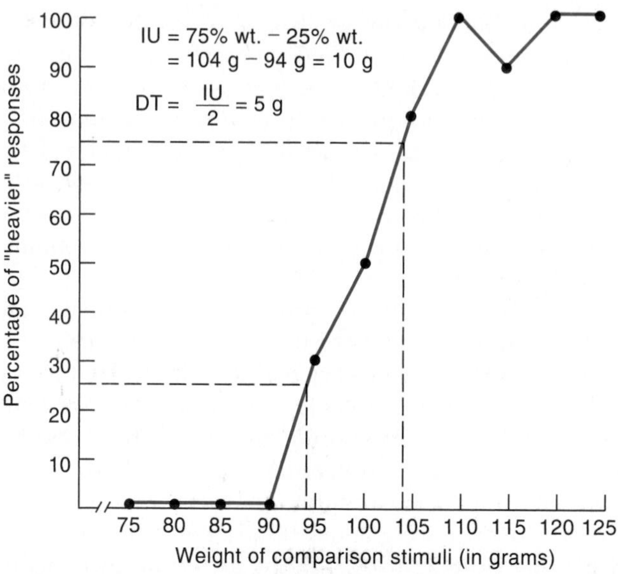

FIGURE 7.2 Graphic illustration of the computation of a difference threshold based on a subject's responses in a weight-discrimination experiment.

The difference threshold of 5 grams shown in Figure 7.2 represents the student's ability to detect a change in weight of less than 0.2 ounces against a background of 3.5 ounces (100 grams). The complete within-subjects design is essential in making such precise measurements possible in psychology.

INCOMPLETE WITHIN-SUBJECTS DESIGN

In the incomplete within-subjects design, each subject is given each treatment only once. For any given subject, therefore, any differences produced by the independent variable are uninterpretable. The levels of the independent variable of interest are perfectly confounded with the ordinal position in which those levels appeared. For instance, the first subject in an incomplete within-subjects-design experiment might be tested first in the experimental condition and second in the control condition (i.e., E, then C). Any differences in the subject's performance between the experimental and control conditions could be due to the effect of the independent variable or to the practice effects of the order in which the conditions were administered. To break this confounding of ordinal position and the independent variable, we must administer different orders of the conditions to different subjects. For example, we could administer the conditions of our incomplete within-subjects-design experiment to a second subject in a different order, testing the control condition first and the experimental condition second (i.e., C, then E). In this way, we could balance the effects of ordinal position across conditions. The effects of ordinal position represent the practice effects that must be balanced in the incomplete within-subjects design.

To illustrate the techniques for balancing practice effects in the incomplete within-subjects design, we will use an experiment by Erber (1991) on the effects of people's moods on their perceptions of other people. There were two stages in this experiment. In the first stage, subjects were asked to read *one* of three stories about events in the life of a young female artist. These stories were previously shown to be effective in inducing positive, neutral, or negative moods in subjects. The story for the positive-mood condition included several events culminating in the artist's receiving a scholarship to college. The neutral-mood story described how the artist decided which college to attend. The negative-mood story described how the artist was overcome by a rare disabling illness at the end of her first year in college. (In the first stage, the independent variable of mood is manipulated *between* subjects, that is, each subject is in only one mood group).

After reading one of these stories, the second stage of the experiment began. Subjects were asked to participate in what they believed to be a separate experiment, one in which they were asked to rate the likelihood of a person's engaging in a particular behavior (welcoming a friend with a hug, getting depressed over the weather, and so on). Various individuals were described to the subjects, and then the subjects were asked to rate the likelihood of various behaviors. The subjects were introduced to the four individuals whose behavior they would be asked to judge by way of brief written descriptions. For reasons that will become apparent, the descriptions were based on somewhat contradictory traits. Each of the four "target people" was described as either moody and warm; pessimistic and understanding; unselfish and unsociable; or trustworthy and possessive. The incomplete within-subjects design was used to implement the independent variable of the target person in the second stage of the experiment. That is, each subject rated all four target persons once.

Before describing the techniques that can be used to balance practice effects for an independent variable in the incomplete within-subjects design, we will take a brief look at the results of the Erber study. The dependent variable in this study was the subjects' ratings of the likelihood that the target people would engage in certain behaviors as a function of the subjects' mood. Because the target people were described using both a positive (e.g., warm) and a negative (e.g., moody) trait, the researchers wanted to see if the subjects' mood would determine which of the two traits affected the rating. The subject's task was to rate how likely it was for someone described as "warm and moody" to engage in positive behavior, such as "welcoming a friend with a hug," or in negative behavior, such as "getting depressed over the weather." Welcoming someone with a hug is something a "warm" person might do, while getting depressed is something a "moody" person is more likely to do.

Erber found that if a subject was in a positive mood, then a "warm and moody" person was rated as more likely to engage in positive behavior (e.g., welcoming with a hug) than in negative behavior (e.g., getting depressed over the weather). If the subject was in a negative mood, the same "warm and moody" individual was rated more likely to engage in negative behavior than in positive behavior. The effect of mood on ratings of negative behaviors was larger than was the effect of mood on ratings of positive behaviors. These findings (along with other findings reported in the study) indicate that mood can influence the way we perceive other people in important ways. One such influence, Erber argues, is that negative affect may facilitate negative stereotypic responses by increasing the accessibility of negative information about others: In other words, if you're in a bad mood, you're more likely to accentuate someone's negative traits!

We turn now to the balancing techniques that are used in the incomplete within-subjects design. The general rule for balancing practice effects in the incomplete within-subjects design is a simple one: *Each condition of the experiment must appear in each ordinal position equally often.* Several techniques are available for satisfying this general rule. These techniques differ in what additional balancing they accomplish, but so long as the techniques are properly used, the basic rule will be met and the experiment will be interpretable.

All Possible Orders The preferred technique for balancing practice effects in the incomplete within-subjects design is to use all possible orders of the treatments. Each subject is randomly assigned to one of the orders. With only two treatments there are only two possible orders (AB and BA); with three treatments there are six possible orders (ABC, ACB, BAC, BCA, CAB, CBA). In general, there are $N!$ (which is read "N factorial") possible orders with N treatments, where $N!$ equals $N(N-1)(N-2)\cdots(N-[N-1])$. The number of required orders increases dramatically with increasing numbers of treatments. For instance, for only five treatments there are 120 possible orders. Because of this, the use of all possible orders is usually limited to experiments involving four or fewer conditions.

The twenty-four sequences that would be required to use all possible orders to balance the effects of ordinal position for the four descriptions of the target people in the Erber (1991) experiment are presented in the left half of Table 7.3. Using all possible orders certainly meets the general rule of ensuring that all conditions appear in each ordinal position equally often. The first ordinal position shows this balancing most clearly: The first six sequences begin with the Moody-Warm (M) target, and each succeeding set of six sequences begins with one of the other three targets. The same pattern applies at each of the four ordinal positions. The use of all possible orders also provides two other potentially useful types of balancing. First, careful examination of the twenty-four sequences reveals that each condition precedes and follows every other condition equally often. For instance, the Unselfish-Unsociable target (U) precedes the Trustworthy-Possessive target (T) six times, and the reverse order (TU) also appears six times. Second, each condition precedes and follows every other

TABLE 7.3 ALTERNATIVE TECHNIQUES TO BALANCE PRACTICE EFFECTS IN AN INCOMPLETE WITHIN-SUBJECTS-DESIGN EXPERIMENT WITH FOUR CONDITIONS

All possible orders								Selected orders							
								Latin Square				Random starting order with rotation			
Ordinal position				Ordinal position				Ordinal position				Ordinal position			
1st	2d	3d	4th	1st	2d	3d	4th	1st	2d	3d	4th	1st	2d	3d	4th
M	P	U	T	U	M	P	T	M	P	U	T	P	U	T	M
M	P	T	U	U	M	T	P	P	T	M	U	U	T	M	P
M	U	P	T	U	P	M	T	T	U	P	M	T	M	P	U
M	U	T	P	U	P	T	M	U	M	T	P	M	P	U	T
M	T	P	U	U	T	M	P								
M	T	U	P	U	T	P	M								
P	M	U	T	T	M	P	U								
P	M	T	U	T	M	U	P								
P	U	M	T	T	P	M	U								
P	U	T	M	T	P	U	M								
P	T	M	U	T	U	M	P								
P	T	U	M	T	U	P	M								

Note: The four conditions are identified by the first letter of the first adjective describing each of the four target people in the Erber (1991) experiment: Moody-Warm (M), Pessimistic-Understanding (P), Unselfish-Unsociable (U), and Trustworthy-Possessive (T).

condition equally often at each ordinal position. That is, the orders UT and TU appear exactly twice in ordinal positions 1 and 2, 2 and 3, and 3 and 4.

There is one other issue that must be addressed in deciding to use all possible orders. For this technique to be effective, it is essential that at least one subject be tested with each of the possible orders of the conditions. Therefore, the use of all possible orders requires at least as many subjects as there are possible orders. That is, if there are four conditions in the experiment, you must test twenty-four subjects (or forty-eight or seventy-two or some other multiple of twenty-four). This restriction makes it very important that you have a good idea of the number of potential subjects *before* you begin to test the first subject.

Selected Orders The preferred method for balancing practice effects in the incomplete within-subjects design is to use all possible orders. There are times, however, when the use of all possible orders is not practical. For example, if we wanted to use the incomplete within-subjects design to study an independent variable with seven levels, we would need to test 5,040 subjects if we used all possible orders—one subject for each of the possible orders of the seven conditions (7! orders). We obviously need some alternative to using all possible orders if we are to use the incomplete within-subjects design for experiments with five or more conditions.

Practice effects can be balanced by using just *some* of all the possible orders. The number of selected orders will always be equal to some multiple of the number of conditions in the experiment. For example, to do an experiment with one independent variable with seven levels, we need to select seven, fourteen, twenty-one, twenty-eight, or some other multiple of seven orders to balance practice effects. The two basic variations of using selected orders are illustrated in the right half of Table 7.3. To allow you to compare the types of balancing more directly, we have illustrated the techniques for selected orders with the four-level independent variable from Erber's (1991) experiment that we described in the previous section.

The first type of balancing using selected orders is called the *Latin Square.* In a Latin Square, each condition appears at each ordinal position once (the essential characteristic to meet the general rule for balancing practice effects), but each condition also precedes and follows each other condition exactly once. The only difference between using all possible orders and using a Latin Square is that in the Latin Square, each condition does not precede and follow every other condition equally often at each ordinal position. For instance, in the Latin Square shown in Table 7.3, the orders UT and TU both appear, but UT appears only in ordinal positions 3 and 4 whereas TU appears only in positions 1 and 2. One procedure for constructing Latin Squares is illustrated in Box 7.1.

The second balancing technique using selected orders requires you to begin with a random order of the conditions and to rotate this sequence systematically with each condition moving one position to the left each time (see the example given in Table 7.3). When a random starting order with rotation is used, practice effects are balanced because each condition appears in each ordinal position. The systematic rotation of the sequences means that each condition always follows and always precedes the same other conditions. For example, in the illustration in Table 7.3, condition M always precedes condition P and follows condition T. Therefore, each condition does not precede and follow every other condition, as is true with the Latin Square technique.

The characteristics of the three balancing techniques in the incomplete within-subjects design are summarized in Table 7.4. The use of all possible orders, the Latin Square, and random starting orders with rotation are equally effective in balancing practice effects because all three techniques ensure that each condition appears in each ordinal position equally often. Regardless of which technique one uses to balance practice effects, the sequences of conditions should be fully prepared prior to testing the first subject, and subjects should be *randomly* assigned to these sequences. The additional characteristics present with the use of all possible orders are especially helpful when it becomes necessary to track down possible interpretive problems in the incomplete within-subjects design. We will discuss these possible interpretive problems later in this chapter.

The Problem of Irreversible Tasks Sharma and Moskowitz (1972) asked subjects to come to their laboratory on four different days. Each day the subjects were given twenty minutes to smoke two cigarettes that contained one of four dose levels of marijuana—a placebo control (0) and doses of 50, 100, and 200

BOX 7.1

SQUARING OFF AGAINST LATIN SQUARES

There is a simple procedure to follow when generating Latin Squares based on an even number of conditions. It is only slightly more complicated when there is an odd number of conditions.

First, let us outline the procedure when there is an even number of conditions in your experiment. Follow these steps:

1 Randomly order the conditions of your experiment. The number of conditions that you have is designated *N*. The size of the square will be *N* × *N*. (At this time we are considering only situations where *N* is even.) Number your randomly ordered conditions 1 through *N*. For example, suppose there are six conditions in your experiment that when randomly ordered, appear as White, Yellow, Blue, Green, Red, and Purple. Assign White the number 1, Yellow the number 2, and so on. We are looking to build a square that is 6 × 6.

2 To generate the first row of your square, use the following rule:

1, 2, *N*, 3, *N* − 1, 4, *N* − 2, 5, *N* − 3, 6, *N* − 4, 7, and so on.

In our example, the first row is 1–2–6–3–5–4, or White–Yellow–Purple–Blue–Red–Green.

3 The second row is generated by adding 1 to each number in the first row with the understanding that 1 added to *N* equals 1. For our example, the second row is 2–3–1–4–6–5. Thus, condition 2 appears first, condition 3 appears second, and so on.

4 The third row is generated by adding 1 to each number in the second row (and *N* + 1 = 1). The example third row is 3–4–2–5–1–6.

5 Similar steps are followed until *N* rows are completed. The Latin Square for our example is:

1(W)	2(Y)	6(P)	3(B)	5(R)	4(G)
2(Y)	3(B)	1(W)	4(G)	6(P)	5(R)
3(B)	4(G)	2(Y)	5(R)	1(W)	6(P)
4(G)	5(R)	3(B)	6(P)	2(Y)	1(W)
5(R)	6(P)	4(G)	1(W)	3(B)	2(Y)
6(P)	1(W)	5(R)	2(Y)	4(G)	3(B)

6 Subjects are assigned randomly to rows of the Latin Square with the restriction that each row be used an equal number of times. Thus, the total number of subjects must be a multiple of *N*.

When there is an odd number of conditions, two squares must be constructed. The first square is generated according to the steps outlined above. The second square is generated by reversing the rows in the first square. The squares are then joined so that the original *N* × *N* square is now *N* × 2*N* in size. For example, if *N* = 5, then we are looking to build a 5 × 10 square. Suppose we have five conditions that when randomly arranged and numbered yield: 1 = Red, 2 = Blue, 3 = Purple, 4 = White, 5 = Yellow. The Latin Square we would generate is:

1(R)	2(B)	5(Y)	3(P)	4(W)	4(W)	3(P)	5(Y)	2(B)	1(R)
2(B)	3(P)	1(R)	4(W)	5(Y)	5(Y)	4(W)	1(R)	3(P)	2(B)
3(P)	4(W)	2(B)	5(Y)	1(R)	1(R)	5(Y)	2(B)	4(W)	3(P)
4(W)	5(Y)	3(P)	1(R)	2(B)	2(B)	1(R)	3(P)	5(Y)	4(W)
5(Y)	1(R)	4(W)	2(B)	3(P)	3(P)	2(B)	4(W)	1(R)	5(Y)

As when an even number of conditions is used, subjects are assigned randomly to the rows of the square, with each row used the same number of times.

units (1 unit = 1 μg/kg of body weight). The doses reflected the amount of tetrahydrocannabinol (THC; the active agent in marijuana) in the two cigarettes combined. The experiment involved the incomplete within-subjects design, so each subject was given each dose once. The order of the doses across subjects was determined using a Latin Square. Immediately after the subjects smoked the two cigarettes, they were tested on an autokinetic illusion task. In this task

TABLE 7.4 CHARACTERISTICS OF ALTERNATIVE TECHNIQUES TO BALANCE PRACTICE EFFECTS IN THE INCOMPLETE WITHIN-SUBJECTS DESIGN

All possible orders

1. Each condition appears at every ordinal position equally often.
2. Each condition precedes and follows every other condition equally often.
3. Each condition precedes and follows every other condition equally often at every ordinal position.

Latin square

1. Each condition appears at every ordinal position equally often.
2. Each condition precedes and follows every other condition equally often.

Random starting order with rotation

1. Each condition appears at every ordinal position equally often.

the subject is placed in a darkened room and asked to focus on a pinpoint of light. The illusion that subjects often experience in this situation is that the pinpoint of light appears to move, even though it is really stationary. Sharma and Moskowitz found that the degree of the autokinetic illusion—that is, the degree of apparent movement—increased with increasing doses of marijuana. Such an outcome indicates that there may be hazards associated with driving a car or flying an airplane at night under the influence of marijuana, especially at relatively high doses.

The task designed to measure the autokinetic illusion can be given repeatedly to subjects without their "mastering" it. Subjects will continue to experience the illusion even after being tested several times. Therefore, Sharma and Moskowitz needed to balance practice effects only for the marijuana variable.

Consider, however, how the situation would change if Sharma and Moskowitz had been interested in the effects of marijuana on people's ability to learn and remember new information. One way to carry out such an experiment would be to give each subject a different list of words to learn under each dose of marijuana. A different list of words would be needed each time because a memory task of this type is an **irreversible task**—one that cannot be administered more than once without risking that the subject will master the task. Once subjects master the task, their performance under subsequent conditions is not likely to vary. In a sense, irreversible tasks result in a "ceiling effect" (see Chapter 8) for all conditions after the first one under which the task has been performed.

The solution to the problem of irreversible tasks is outlined in Table 7.5. The solution requires two steps. The first step is to balance practice effects for (in our case) the marijuana variable. A random starting order with rotation has been used to accomplish the balancing of the four dose levels (0, 50, 100, and 200 units). Only four subjects are needed to do this balancing, and the sequences for these four subjects appear in the upper-left quadrant of the table. Because each dose appears with each list exactly once, the marijuana variable is also balanced for the possible effects of the list variable.

A problem would arise, however, if the researcher were to try to assess

TABLE 7.5 BALANCING EXPERIMENTS WITH IRREVERSIBLE TASKS IN THE INCOMPLETE WITHIN-SUBJECTS DESIGN

	Ordinal position					Ordinal position			
	1st	2d	3d	4th		1st	2d	3d	4th
	List					List			
Subject	A	B	C	D	Subject	B	C	D	A
1	050	200	000	100	5	050	200	000	100
2	200	000	100	050	6	200	000	100	050
3	000	100	050	200	7	000	100	050	200
4	100	050	200	000	8	100	050	200	000

	Ordinal position					Ordinal position			
	1st	2d	3d	4th		1st	2d	3d	4th
	List					List			
Subject	C	D	A	B	Subject	D	A	B	C
9	050	200	000	100	13	050	200	000	100
10	200	000	100	050	14	200	000	100	050
11	000	100	050	200	15	000	100	050	200
12	100	050	200	000	16	100	050	200	000

Note: The numbers 000, 050, 100, and 200 refer to dose levels.

differences among the four lists. The lists for the first four subjects are perfectly confounded by the ordinal position variable. The confounding of lists and ordinal position can be overcome by taking the second step in dealing with the problem of irreversible tasks. In general, this second step requires testing additional subjects so that the list variable and the ordinal position variable are also balanced. In our example, twelve additional subjects would need to be tested, with the order of the lists systematically rotated for each successive set of four subjects. This is illustrated in Table 7.5. Each quadrant of the table includes the same order of the marijuana doses. The list order for each group of four subjects is different, however. The order of the lists has been determined using a random starting order with rotation. The two-step process of balancing in experiments involving irreversible tasks ensures that each of three variables (independent variable of interest, stage of practice, and task) are balanced for the other two. Thus, the effects of all three variables are interpretable.

LIMITATIONS OF THE WITHIN-SUBJECTS DESIGNS

The first obvious limitation of the within-subjects designs is that they cannot be used to study subject variables such as age and gender. It is unlikely that any such subject characteristics could be successfully balanced. A 40-year-old person cannot be 20 years old, then 60 years old, and then 40 years old again (though we've all known people who *act* that way!). Within-subjects designs *can* be used effectively, however, in combination with subject variables in a complex design (see Chapter 8). Second, within-subjects designs are not appropriate when the levels of the independent variable represent an unfolding sequence of successive events. A study of brain lesions would require controls such as Anesthesia Only and a Sham-Operated condition, and the sequential nature of these treatments seems to demand separate groups. That is, an animal could not be tested in the Anesthesia Only group once the animal was lesioned. Third, experiments in which each condition takes a great deal of time to implement are not likely to be suitable for within-subjects designs. If the treatment involved participation in a year-long program, one ABBA sequence in the complete within-subjects design would take four years! It is unlikely that the random-groups design will be completely replaced by the within-subjects designs. In the next section, we introduce a fourth and final limitation of within-subjects designs—the problem of differential transfer.

DIFFERENTIAL TRANSFER

The most consistent and vocal critic of within-subjects designs has been E. C. Poulton (1973, 1975, 1982; Poulton & Freeman, 1966). While conceding that balancing techniques control practice effects, Poulton has argued that they do not eliminate a more serious problem. This problem arises when performance in one condition differs depending on which of two other conditions precedes it. We call this **differential transfer.**

Consider a problem-solving experiment in which two types of instructions are being compared in an incomplete within-subjects design. One set of instructions (A) is expected to enhance problem solving, whereas the other set of instructions (B) serves as the neutral control condition. It is reasonable to expect that subjects tested in the order AB will be unable or unwilling to abandon the approach outlined in the A instructions when they are supposed to be following the B instructions. Giving up the "good thing" subjects had under instruction A would be the counterpart of successfully following the admonition "Don't think of pink elephants!" When subjects fail to give up the instruction from the first condition (A) when they are supposed to be following instruction B, any difference between the two conditions is reduced. For those subjects, after all, condition B was not really tried.

In general, the presence of differential transfer threatens internal validity. It also tends to underestimate differences between the conditions and thereby reduces the external validity of the findings. Thus the within-subjects design should not be used when differential transfer may arise. Differential transfer is sufficiently common with instructional variables to advise against the use of within-subjects designs for these variables (Underwood & Shaughnessy, 1975). Unfortunately, differential transfer can arise in any within-subjects design. For instance, the effect of 50 units of marijuana may be different if administered after the subject has received 200 units than if admininistered after the subject has received the placebo. There are ways, however, to determine whether differential transfer is likely to have occurred.

DOCUMENTING DIFFERENTIAL TRANSFER

The first method for documenting differential transfer can be applied when all possible orders have been used to balance practice effects and when several subjects have been tested with each of the possible orders. Table 7.6 presents the sequences for twenty-four subjects who were each tested once with each of three doses of marijuana. Because all possible orders were used, each dose level precedes and follows each other dose level at each ordinal position. The orders have been repeated four times, so there are eight measurements when the 100-unit dose follows the 0-unit dose and eight measurements when the 100-unit dose follows the 50-unit dose. If differential transfer has occurred, the average performance for the 100-unit dose will differ in these two situations. That is, the 100-unit dose will have had a different effect when it followed the 50-unit dose from when it followed the 0-unit dose. Of course, similar tests would have to be done for the 0-unit and the 50-unit doses before the search for differential transfer would be complete.

There are alternative methods available to document differential transfer when all possible orders have not been used to balance practice effects. Poulton (1982) maintains that the best way to determine whether differential transfer is a problem is to do two separate experiments. The same independent variable would be studied in both experiments, but a within-subjects design would be

TABLE 7.6 DOCUMENTING DIFFERENTIAL TRANSFER WHEN ALL POSSIBLE ORDERS HAVE BEEN USED TO BALANCE PRACTICE EFFECTS

	Ordinal position				Ordinal position		
Subject	1st	2d	3d	Subject	1st	2d	3d
*1	0	50	100	*13	0	50	100
**2	0	100	50	**14	0	100	50
**3	50	0	100	**15	50	0	100
*4	50	100	0	*16	50	100	0
5	100	0	50	17	100	0	50
6	100	50	0	18	100	50	0
*7	0	50	100	*19	0	50	100
**8	0	100	50	**20	0	100	50
**9	50	0	100	**21	50	0	100
*10	50	100	0	*22	50	100	0
11	100	0	50	23	100	0	50
12	100	50	0	24	100	50	0

Note: The text refers to eight measurements when the 100-unit dose follows the 50-unit dose. These sequences are marked with one asterisk (*). The eight measurements when the 100-unit dose follows the 0-unit dose are marked with two asterisks (**).

used in one experiment and a random-groups design in the other. The random-groups design cannot possibly involve differential transfer because each subject is tested in only one condition. Thus, the logic of Poulton's recommended approach is that, if the within-subjects design shows the same effect as that shown in a random-groups design, differential transfer is not a problem. If the two types of design show different effects for the same independent variable, however, differential transfer is likely to be guilty of producing the different outcome in the within-subjects design. When differential transfer does occur, the results of the random-groups-design experiment should be used to provide the best description of the effect of the independent variable.

Perhaps the most efficient way to follow Poulton's advice is to do experiments involving a relatively large incomplete within-subjects design. For example, if forty-eight subjects were tested in a four-condition experiment with all possible orders of the conditions, there would be twelve subjects tested in each of the four conditions at the first stage of practice. So long as subjects have been randomly assigned to sequences, the incomplete within-subjects design contains a random-groups design at the first stage of practice. The results for the first stage can then be compared with the overall results to achieve the comparison Poulton recommends between the random-groups design and the within-subjects design for the same independent variable.

SUMMARY

Within-subjects designs provide an effective and efficient way to conduct an experiment by administering all the treatments in the experiment to each subject. Within-subjects designs are useful when only very few subjects are available or when an independent variable can be studied most efficiently by testing fewer subjects several times. The area of psychological research (e.g., psychophysics) may also require the use of within-subjects designs. Finally, within-subjects designs may be used when a more sensitive experiment is required or when a comparison of the effect of an independent variable needs to be made by using both the random-groups design and the within-subjects design.

For any within-subjects-design experiment to be interpretable, however, stage-of-practice effects must be balanced. Practice effects are changes that subjects undergo because of repeated testing. In the complete within-subjects design, practice effects are balanced for each subject. In the incomplete within-subjects design, each subject receives each treatment only once, and the balancing is accomplished across subjects.

Block randomization and ABBA counterbalancing can be used to balance practice effects in the complete within-subjects design. ABBA counterbalancing should not be used, however, if practice effects are expected to be nonlinear or if anticipation effects are likely. Alternative techniques for balancing practice effects in the incomplete within-subjects design involve either the use of all possible orders or selected orders (the Latin Square and rotation of a random starting order). When irreversible tasks are used, three independent variables must be balanced (the independent variable of interest, stage of practice, and the task variable). The most serious problem in any within-subjects design is differential transfer—when performance in one condition differs depending on which of two other conditions it follows. Procedures for detecting the presence of differential transfer are available, but there is little that can be done to salvage a study in which it occurs. In an incomplete within-subjects design, however, it is possible to analyze the results of the random-groups design included at the first stage of practice if differential transfer arises in the experiment as a whole.

KEY CONCEPTS

within-subjects designs
stage-of-practice effects
complete within-subjects design
incomplete within-subjects design
ABBA counterbalancing
anticipation effects
irreversible task
differential transfer

REVIEW QUESTIONS

1 For what five reasons might a researcher choose to use a within-subjects design?
2 Distinguish between the complete within-subjects design and the incomplete within-subjects design.
3 What options do researchers have in balancing practice effects in the complete within-subjects design?
4 Under what two circumstances would you recommend against the use of ABBA counterbalancing to balance practice effects in the complete within-subjects design?
5 What measurement purpose do complete within-subjects designs serve in certain areas of research in psychology such as psychophysics?
6 State the general rule for balancing practice effects in the incomplete within-subjects design.
7 What techniques can be used to balance practice effects in the incomplete within-subjects design? Which technique is preferred? Why?
8 Explain what is meant by an irreversible task. What additional balancing procedures must be used when an irreversible task is used in the incomplete within-subjects design along with another independent variable of interest?
9 For which types of independent variables is the within-subjects design unlikely to prove useful?
10 Describe how researchers can document differential transfer in an incomplete within-subjects design.

CHALLENGE QUESTIONS

1 The following problems represent different situations in the within-subjects design in which stage-of-practice effects need to be balanced.
   A Consider a complete within-subjects design experiment involving one independent variable. The independent variable has three levels (Low, Medium, and High). You

are to prepare an order for administering the conditions of this experiment so that the independent variable is balanced for stage of practice. You are first to use block randomization to balance the variable and then to use ABBA counterbalancing to balance the variable. Each condition should appear twice in the order you prepare. Use the two rows of random numbers between 1 and 16 in doing your block randomization; each row should be used for one random order of the three conditions.

15-8-11-14-9-4-12-10-13-7-16-1-3-2-5-6
10-3-4-16-7-8-9-13-2-1-6-12-5-11-15-14

B Consider an experiment to be done using the incomplete within-subjects design. One independent variable is to be manipulated at six levels (A, B, C, D, E, and F). Present a table showing how you would determine the order of administering the conditions to the first six subjects of the experiment. Be sure that practice effects are balanced for these subjects.

2 Consider an experiment in which the incomplete within-subjects design is used to manipulate an environmental variable, room temperature. There are three levels of the variable (60, 65, and 70 degrees). The dependent variable of interest is the amount of time taken to solve a list of word problems. Thus three different word problem lists are required (designated as Lists A, B, and C). Present a table showing how you could administer the conditions of the experiment in order to determine the effect of the three independent variables: room temperature, stage of practice, and list. You have only *nine* people available for participants, but previous research indicates that you need not be concerned with problems of differential transfer.

3 The following table represents the order of administering the conditions to participants in an incomplete within-subjects design in which the independent variable was the difficulty of the task given to the participant (High, Medium, or Low Difficulty). The values in parentheses represent the number correct for each participant in each condition. Use this table, when necessary, to answer questions that follow.

Participant	Order of Conditions		
1	High (2)	Medium (9)	Low (9)
2	Medium (3)	Low (5)	High (7)
3	Low (4)	High (3)	Medium (5)
4	High (6)	Low (10)	Medium (8)
5	Medium (7)	High (8)	Low (6)
6	Low (8)	Medium (4)	High (4)

A What method was used to balance the stage-of-practice effects?

B Identify two ways in which this experiment would be improved if the experimenter used the same balancing technique but tested twenty-four participants rather than six.

4 The pursuit rotor is a test of perceptual-motor coordination. It involves a turntable with a disk about the size of a dime embedded in it. The subject is given a pointer and is asked to keep the pointer on the disk while the turntable is rotating. The dependent variable is the percentage of time on each trial that the subject keeps the pointer on the disk. Learning on this task is linearly related to trials over many periods of practice, and the task generally takes a long time to master. A researcher wants to study the influence of time of day on the performance on this task with four different times (10 A.M., 2 P.M., 6 P.M., and 10 P.M.). The subjects will receive a constant number of trials under each of the four conditions, and subjects will be tested on one condition per day over four consecutive days. The researcher has ninety-six subjects available.

A What design is being used for the time-of-day variable in this experiment?

B What technique for balancing stage-of-practice effects would be the best one to use in this situation if the researcher wants to be able to test for the possibility of differential transfer?

C What research design is included in the first stage of practice of this experiment? How could the researcher use the results of the design in the first stage of practice as an indication of whether differential transfer had occurred?

ANSWER TO CHALLENGE QUESTION 1

A Assigning the values 1, 2, and 3 to the Low, Medium, and High conditions, respectively, and using the accompanying random numbers, the block-randomized sequence is Low–High–Medium–High–Medium–Low. One possible ABBA counterbalanced sequence is Low–Medium–High–High–Medium–Low.

B Because there are six conditions, all possible orders is not feasible. Therefore, either a Latin Square or a random-starting order with rotation is needed to balance practice effects. A possible set of sequences using rotation is:

	Position					
Subject	1st	2nd	3rd	4th	5th	6th
1	B	D	E	C	A	F
2	D	E	C	A	F	B
3	E	C	A	F	B	D
4	C	A	F	B	D	E
5	A	F	B	D	E	C
6	F	B	D	E	C	A

Chapter 8

Complex Designs

Outline

OVERVIEW

In the last two chapters we described the basic designs that psychologists use to study the effect of an independent variable. We discussed how an independent variable could be implemented by administering each treatment to a separate group of subjects (Chapter 6) or by administering all the treatments to each subject (Chapter 7). We limited our discussion in these two chapters to experiments involving only one independent variable. We did this primarily because we wanted you to concentrate on the characteristics of each research design. Experiments involving only one independent variable are not, however, the most common type of experiment in current psychological research. Instead, researchers most often use **complex designs** in which two or more independent variables are studied simultaneously in one experiment.

Johnson, Petzel, Hartney, and Morgan (1983) used a complex design to compare the memory performance of depressed and nondepressed people. Specifically, these investigators were testing the hypothesis that depressed individuals would be more likely to remember tasks they had *not* completed, whereas nondepressed individuals would be more likely to remember tasks they *had* completed. If depressed people do tend to dwell on the negative, this tendency may contribute to sustaining their depression. In the experiment, groups of depressed and nondepressed subjects were asked to do twenty tasks, ten of which were interrupted by the experimenter before they were completed. After the last task, the subjects were asked to recall the names or descriptions of as many tasks as they could.

As indicated in the following diagram, this experiment involved four conditions: Completed and Uncompleted tasks for Depressed and for Nondepressed subjects.

Type of subject	Type of task	
	Completed	Uncompleted
Depressed		
Nondepressed		

In a complex design such as this one, the levels of each of the two independent variables are combined factorially. *Factorial combination* involves pairing each level of one independent variable with each level of a second independent variable. Factorial combination makes it possible to assess the effect of each independent variable alone (*main effect*) *and* the effect of the two independent variables in combination (*interaction*). For example, Johnson et al. found, as they had predicted, that depressed subjects recalled more uncompleted than completed tasks and that nondepressed subjects recalled more completed than uncompleted tasks. The task variable, then, had opposite effects on depressed and nondepressed subjects. This type of effect, called an *interaction effect,* can be discovered only when two or more independent variables are included in the same experiment. In general, an **interaction** occurs when the effect of one independent variable differs depending on the level of a second independent variable. The procedures for producing and interpreting interactions are the subject of the present chapter.

We begin with a review of a set of guidelines for identifying or selecting an experimental design. The major advantages of using a complex design are then briefly introduced, along with the basic concepts of main effects and interactions. Next, we examine the nature of interactions in the simplest of complex designs, the 2 $\times$ 2 design. We also discuss designs having more than two levels of each of two independent variables and designs having more than two independent variables. Special attention is given to the problems of interpretation that complex designs pose and to the role of interactions when implementing the natural-groups design (see Chapter 6).

INTRODUCTION TO COMPLEX DESIGNS

GUIDELINES FOR IDENTIFYING AN EXPERIMENTAL DESIGN

As we have already mentioned, an experiment involving a complex design is one in which more than one independent variable is being studied. Each independent variable in a complex design must be implemented using either a within-subjects or an independent-groups design according to the procedures described in the previous two chapters. Before examining complex designs themselves, we need to review briefly the characteristics of the various experimental designs that can be used to study a single independent variable. You will be better able to understand descriptions of complex designs if you can quickly and accurately identify the independent variables, their levels, and the design used to implement each independent variable. Similarly, your ability to carry out your own experiments using complex designs will be enhanced if you can confidently select the most appropriate design for each independent variable in which you are interested.

The flow diagram in Figure 8.1 summarizes the distinctions among experimental designs by taking you through a series of questions. The diagram will probably prove most useful to you when you are reading about a particular experiment in either your text or a journal article. As you identify each independent variable in the experiment you are reading about, you can track the variable through Figure 8.1 to determine what design has been used to implement the independent variable. The first question at the top of the diagram is the most critical one. The answer to this question (number of levels of the independent variable administered to each subject) determines whether the independent-groups or the within-subjects design has been used. Answering the subsequent questions for the independent-groups designs will allow you to identify the particular type of design by examining the procedures whereby the groups were formed. For the within-subjects designs, we have included questions to help you identify which balancing technique has been used.

Complex designs require that you go through the diagram as many times as necessary to identify the design for each independent variable in the experiment. In a complex design, the two or more independent variables need not be implemented in the same way. In the Johnson et al. (1983) study, the type of subject (Depressed versus Nondepressed) represented a natural-groups design, whereas the type of task (Completed versus Uncompleted) was manipulated using the within-subjects design. When the independent variables in a complex design are implemented using different designs for each independent variable, the experiment is sometimes described as a **mixed design.** Choosing a label to describe the design of the experiment as a whole is less critical than knowing that you must identify the type of design used for *each* independent variable in an experiment.

ADVANTAGES OF COMPLEX DESIGNS

Resolving Contradictions When only one independent variable is manipulated in an experiment, it is essential that all other potential independent variables be controlled by holding them constant or by balancing them across conditions. A problem can arise, however, if two researchers choose to hold the same potential independent variable constant at different levels in their respective experiments. For example, two memory researchers might be studying the relative effectiveness of two different learning strategies (A and B). These two strategies would represent the levels of the manipulated independent variable in both experiments. One potential independent variable that would clearly need to be controlled in these experiments is the difficulty of the

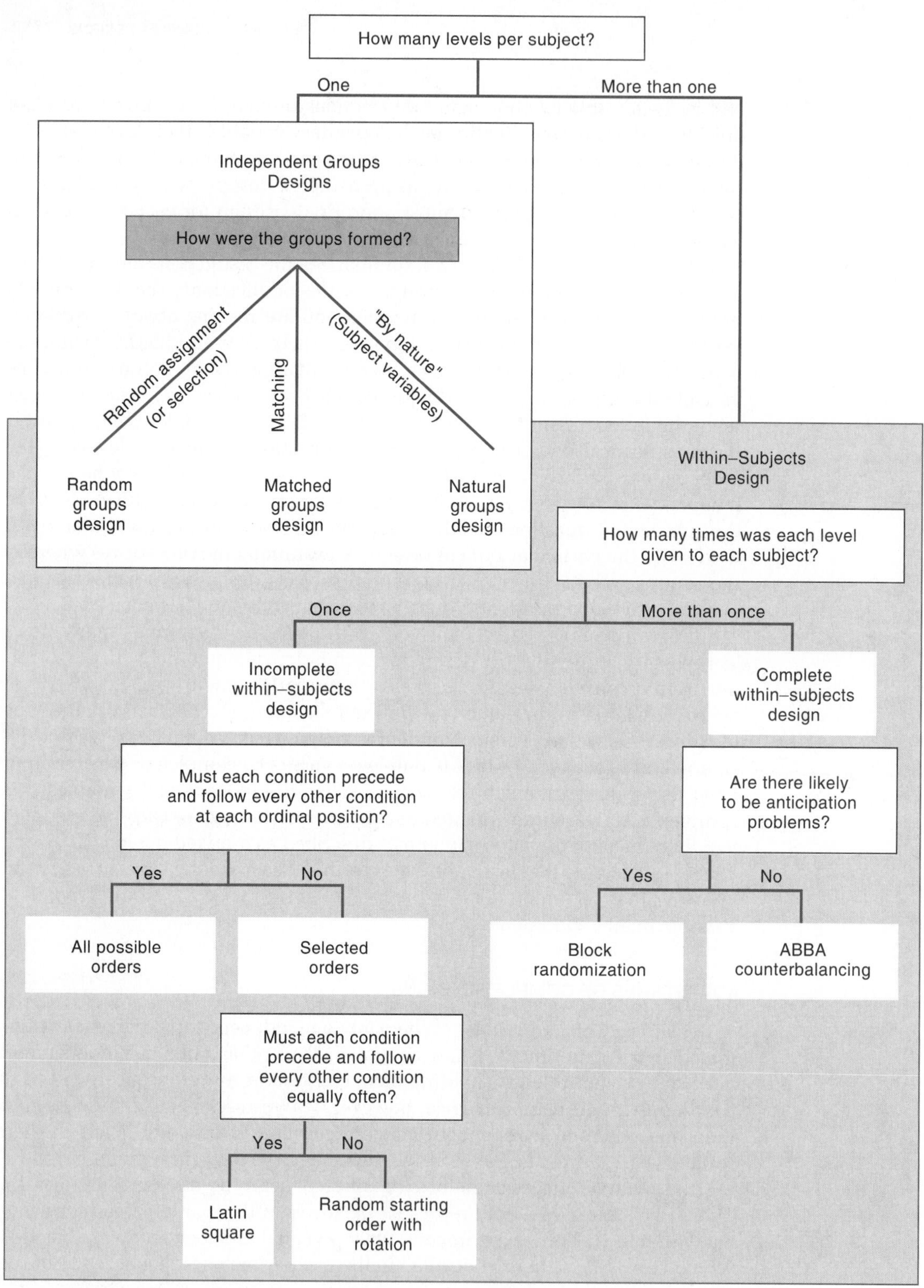

How many levels per subject?
One
More than one
Independent Groups Designs
How were the groups formed?
Random assignment (or selection)
Matching
"By nature" (Subject variables)
Random groups design
Matched groups design
Natural groups design
WIthin–Subjects Design
How many times was each level given to each subject?
Once
More than once
Incomplete within–subjects design
Complete within–subjects design
Must each condition precede and follow every other condition at each ordinal position?
Yes
No
All possible orders
Selected orders
Are there likely to be anticipation problems?
Yes
No
Block randomization
ABBA counterbalancing
Must each condition precede and follow every other condition equally often?
Yes
No
Latin square
Random starting order with rotation

material to be learned. The first researcher might decide to control the level of difficulty of the material by giving subjects in both conditions relatively easy textbook passages to learn. The second researcher, who is equally concerned with the problem of controlling the difficulty of the material, might decide to give subjects in both conditions relatively hard textbook passages to learn. It would not be surprising if these two researchers obtained different results. One such possible outcome is illustrated in the following diagram:

	Learning strategy	
Passage difficulty	A	B
Easy (Researcher 1)	50	50
Hard (Researcher 2)	25	10

The first researcher found that the two learning strategies are equally effective, while the second researcher found that strategy A is more effective than strategy B! Why couldn't these two researchers replicate each other's findings?

At first, we might try to account for the different outcomes in the two experiments by focusing on the difficulty of the textbook passages. We could argue that the two strategies are equally effective for learning easy textbook passages, but strategy A is better for learning hard passages. This argument would not be convincing, however, unless the two types of passages represented the only independent variable that was held constant at two different levels in the two experiments. This seems highly unlikely. For example, the passages may very well have been studied for different lengths of time in the two experiments, the passages were probably on different topics, and the experimenters and subjects in the two experiments were undoubtedly different. Clearly, the difficulty of the passages is not the only factor that *could* be responsible for the different effects of the strategy variable in the two experiments.

The best way to identify which factor is responsible for the discrepant findings is to *use a complex design in which you manipulate the factor you think is responsible along with the strategy variable in the same experiment.* The use of a complex design to resolve discrepant findings follows a logic similar to the logic of doing a partial replication to establish the external validity of a finding (see Chapter 6). In both cases, you are examining whether the effect of the independent variable of interest depends upon a second independent variable; in this case, the variable of interest is the learning strategy, and the second independent variable is the difficulty of the passage. In an experiment in which the strategy variable and the passage-difficulty variable were both manipulated, there would be four conditions in a complex design. Both easy and hard

FIGURE 8.1 Flowchart for identifying experimental designs.

passages would be tested under both strategies. Two possible outcomes of such an experiment are shown in the following diagram. The pattern of results outlined in Outcome 1 has the same form as the original discrepancy between the outcomes in the two separate experiments involving *only* the strategy variable. That is, the strategies are equally effective for easy material, and strategy A is better for hard material. If you obtain this outcome, you can be confident that the difficulty of the text was responsible for the different effects of the strategy variable in the two original experiments.

The situation would be very different, however, if you were to obtain results in your new experiment like those in Outcome 2. The pattern of results in Outcome 2 is *not* like the original pattern distinguishing the two experiments. The strategy variable has had no effect with either the easy or the hard text material. Because the strategy variable has the same effect with both types of material, differences in degree of difficulty between the materials in the two original experiments cannot be responsible for the different outcomes in those experiments. You must select another variable that you "suspect" and manipulate *it* along with the strategy variable. Both trial and error and the guidance of theory are involved in the selection of the variable. The process can be a painstaking one, but complex designs are extremely useful in tracking down the reasons for the seemingly contradictory finding that the same independent variable has had different effects in two different experiments.

	Outcome 1		Outcome 2	
Passage difficulty	Strategy A	Strategy B	Strategy A	Strategy B
Easy	50	50	50	50
Hard	25	10	15	15

Testing Theories In Chapter 1 we described the critical role that theories play in the scientific method. In Chapter 6 we described how experiments are used to test hypotheses derived from psychological theories. Complex designs greatly enhance the researcher's ability to test theories. For instance, the optimal arousal theory of motivation predicts that performance will be best when our arousal level is moderate—neither too low nor too high. If you have ever had to perform in either an athletic or an artistic event, you have some sense of what is meant by optimal arousal. Your performance is not likely to be at its best if your arousal level is too low (you don't care how well you do) or too high (you are scared out of your wits). The optimal arousal theory further predicts that the level of arousal that is best depends on the complexity of the task to be performed. Specifically, the theory predicts that higher arousal levels will lead to better performance on simple or well-learned tasks but lower arousal levels will lead to better performance on complex tasks. You would probably be able to do simple arithmetic problems at a high arousal level, but the same arousal level would probably be disastrous if you were solving differential equations. Our focus for now is not on the details of optimal arousal theory but on the use of complex designs to test predictions derived from such a theory.

If we were to test the prediction that optimal arousal varied with task complexity, we would need to manipulate two independent variables: arousal level (high or low) and task complexity (simple or complex). Our experiment would therefore have four conditions.

	Arousal level	
Task complexity	High	Low
Simple	50	35
Complex	10	25

The dependent variable entered in the body of our table is the mean number of tasks completed correctly in each of the four conditions. As you can see, the effect of arousal level depended on the level of task complexity—an interaction occurred. For the simple task, high arousal led to better performance; for the complex task, low arousal led to better performance. This hypothetical but reasonable outcome supports the prediction derived from optimal arousal theory.

As in the example we just described, complex designs are often used to test a predicted interaction of two independent variables. In any complex design, however, it is also possible to test predictions regarding the overall effect of each independent variable in the experiment. The overall effect of an independent variable in a complex design is called a **main effect.** The following diagram contains the same information we used to examine the interaction of task complexity and arousal level.

	Arousal level		
Task complexity	High	Low	Main effect of task complexity
Simple	50	35	42.5
Complex	10	25	17.5
Main effect of arousal level	30	30	

In addition, the means for the main effect of task complexity are presented in the far right-hand column, and the means for the main effect of arousal level are presented in the bottom row. These means were obtained by averaging the two entries in each respective row or column of the table.[1] For example, the

[1]The simple averaging of the values within each row and column to obtain the means for the main effects is possible *only* when there are equal numbers of subjects contributing to each mean in the table. For procedures to use when the cells of the table involve different sample sizes, see Keppel (1991).

mean for simple tasks (42.5) was obtained by averaging the two values for high and low arousal level: (50 + 35)/2. The means for the main effects represent the overall performance at each level of each individual variable *collapsed across* (averaged over) the levels of the other independent variable.

Analysis procedures for determining the statistical significance of the interaction and main effects will be described in Chapter 9. For now, we need only note that the interpretation of main effects is critically dependent on whether an interaction is or is not present. For instance, the main effect of arousal level in the preceding table indicates no effect of this variable (the means for the high and low arousal levels are both 30). The absence of a main effect of arousal level, however, is totally determined by the equal and opposite effects of arousal level at the two levels of task complexity. The main effect of this variable was nonsignificant, but it would clearly be inappropriate to conclude that arousal level had no effect. Instead, the *interaction* of arousal level and task complexity indicates that the effect of arousal level *depends* on the complexity of the task. In general, main effects should be interpreted with caution whenever an interaction is present in the experiment. When no interaction occurs, the main effects of each independent variable can be interpreted as though they had been manipulated in two separate experiments, each of which involved only one independent variable.

THE NATURE OF INTERACTIONS

THE 2 × 2 DESIGN

The simplest possible experiment involves one independent variable manipulated at two levels. Similarly, the smallest possible complex design involves two independent variables, each of which is manipulated at two levels. Complex designs are identified by specifying the number of levels of each of the independent variables in the experiment. A 2 × 2 (which is read "2 by 2") design, then, identifies the most basic complex design. The number of conditions in a complex design can be determined by multiplying the number of levels of the independent variables. For instance, there are four conditions in a 2 × 2 design, eight conditions in a 4 × 2 design, and twelve conditions (and three independent variables) in a 3 × 2 × 2 design. As we mentioned earlier, a complex design can be used to identify interactions between independent variables. The nature of an interaction is essentially the same in all complex designs, but an interaction can be seen most easily in a 2 × 2 design. We will now consider one such experiment.

Cross-racial evaluations of performance is a research topic of both theoretical and practical importance. When given comparable information about a white and a black applicant for a job, for instance, do evaluators rate the candidate of their own race (in-group) more favorably than the candidate of the other race (out-group)? Hass, Katz, Rizzo, Bailey, and Eisenstadt (1991) used a 2 ×

2 design to investigate cross-racial evaluations. The subjects in the experiment (all of whom were white) were told by a white female experimenter that the researchers were developing a new quiz game for college students called Trivia Challenge.

The subjects were tested in groups of from three to five, but one member of the group was always a confederate of the experimenter. The race of the captain was the first independent variable. The two levels were black and white captains. The experimenter made sure that an election among the group members always resulted in the confederate's being selected as the captain of the group. The captain selected the questions that the group had to answer in the quiz game. The nature of these questions defined the second independent variable in the experiment. It also had two levels. In the success conditions, the captain selected easy questions and the group easily reached the criterion for correct answers in the allotted time. In the failure condition, the captain selected questions of such difficulty that the group failed to meet the criterion. Groups of subjects were randomly assigned to the four groups formed by the factorial combination of the race of the captain and the outcome.

After the quiz game, subjects completed a questionnaire that included several items requiring them to evaluate the captain of their group. The responses to these questions were combined into an overall evaluation score, with higher scores indicating more favorable evaluations of the captain. The mean evaluation scores for the four conditions of the experiment are presented in Table 8.1.

For our purposes, the most important aspect of Table 8.1 is that it reflects an interaction between the two independent variables, race of the captain and outcome. If only successful outcomes had been tested in the experiment, we would have concluded that white subjects evaluate black captains more favorably than they do white captains. If only outcomes involving failure had been tested, on the other hand, we would have concluded that white subjects evaluate white captains more favorably than they do black captains. What the results in Table 8.1 indicate is that the effect of the race of the captain depends on the type of outcome. As you may have suspected, however, statistical analysis is required before we can conclude with confidence that an interaction has occurred (see Chapter 9). For now, it is sufficient if you recognize that, when our conclusion about the effect of one independent variable changes as we

TABLE 8.1 EXAMPLE OF A 2 × 2 DESIGN WITH AN INTERACTION
Mean Evaluation Scores for Captains in Each Group

	Race of captain	
Outcome	Black	White
Success	309.6	280.9
Failure	155.3	196.1

Adapted from Hass et al. (1991).

move across the levels of the second independent variable, an interaction is likely.

When one independent variable interacts with a second independent variable, the second independent variable must interact with the first one. For example, we described the interaction in Table 8.1 by stating that the effect of the race of the captain varies with the type of outcome. The reverse is also true; the effect of the type of outcome varies with the race of the captain. Black captains were evaluated more favorably than white captains in the success condition, but white captains were evaluated more favorably than black captains in the failure condition. Hass et al. chose to describe the interaction by emphasizing that the evaluation of the black captains was more extreme than was the evaluation of the white captains (the black captains evaluation was more positive with success and more negative with failure). How you choose to describe the results of an interaction depends on which aspect of the interaction you want to emphasize. For example, Hass et al. emphasized the more extreme ratings given to the black captains because they were testing the hypothesis that cross-race evaluation leads to more polarized (more extreme) responses for out-group members than for in-group members.

Mastering the concept of an interaction requires practice in identifying the various types of outcomes that can arise in a complex design. Therefore, we will conclude this section on the 2 × 2 design with an exercise that will give you an opportunity to identify main effects and interactions using only descriptive statistics. Inferential statistics would be required to confirm the statistical significance of any obtained effects, but the effects themselves can best be seen in a table or graph of the means for the conditions of the experiment.

There are three common ways to report a summary of the descriptive statistics in a complex design: tables, bar graphs, and line graphs. The procedures for preparing such tables and figures and the criteria for deciding to use each type of presentation are described in Appendix C. In general, tables can be used for any complex design and are most useful when the exact values for each condition in the experiment need to be known. Bar graphs and line graphs, on the other hand, are especially useful for showing patterns of results without dwelling on the exact values. Line graphs are particularly useful for depicting the results of complex designs because an interaction can be seen so readily in a line graph. *Nonparallel lines in the graph suggest an interaction; parallel lines suggest no interaction.*

When the results of a 2 × 2 design are summarized in a table, it is easiest to assess the presence or absence of an interaction by using the subtraction method. One determines the differences between the means in each row (or column) of the table and then compares these differences. If the differences are different, an interaction is likely. The mechanics of the subtraction method can best be illustrated by examining an actual research example.

The following table presents the results of the Johnson et al. (1983) study we described earlier. The dependent variable entered in the table is the mean number of correctly recalled tasks out of a possible 10.

Type of subject	Type of task	
	Completed	Uncompleted
Depressed	6.75	7.85
Nondepressed	7.70	6.70

As we mentioned earlier, Johnson et al. did obtain an interaction when they analyzed their recall results. The subtraction method can be used to indicate the presence of this interaction. In the first row of the table (for depressed subjects), the difference between the mean recall of uncompleted tasks and that of completed tasks is 1.10 (7.85 − 6.75). For nondepressed subjects, on the other hand, computing the difference in the same direction results in a value of −1.00 (6.70 − 7.70). Applying the subtraction method reveals that the mean differences in the two rows of the table are different, thereby indicating that an interaction is present. In applying the subtraction method, it is essential that the differences be determined in the same direction (for example, uncompleted tasks − completed tasks) and that the sign of the obtained difference be carefully noted. You can practice applying the subtraction method by determining the mean differences in the two columns of the Johnson et al. table. For more practice, see Box 8.1.

BEYOND THE 2 × 2: TWO ILLUSTRATIONS

The opportunity to identify an interaction makes the 2 × 2 design more useful analytically than designs involving only one independent variable. Nonetheless, the 2 × 2 design barely scratches the surface when it comes to tapping the potential of complex designs. The 2 × 2 design can be extended in one of two ways. Additional levels of one or both of the independent variables can be included in the design, yielding designs such as the 3 × 2, the 3 × 3, the 4 × 2, the 4 × 3, and so on. Or additional independent variables can be studied in the same experiment with the number of levels of each variable ranging from 2 to some unspecified upper limit. The addition of a third or fourth independent variable yields designs such as the 2 × 2 × 2, the 3 × 3 × 3, the 2 × 2 × 4, the 2 × 3 × 3 × 2, and so on. It is obviously not feasible to illustrate each possible complex design. It is also not necessary. One illustration of each of the two types of extensions of the 2 × 2 should suffice.

What Was That Number? Hinrichs and Novick (1982) used a 2 × 4 design to investigate the way people remember the order of a string of unrelated digits. Memory researchers have consistently found that serial recall of unrelated strings of digits, letters, or words follows a familiar pattern called the *serial position curve* (Zechmeister & Nyberg, 1982). Recall of the first few items in a string is best and recall of the last few items in the string is almost as good, but recall of items from the middle of the string is much poorer. Although the serial position curve is one of the most reliable phenomena of human memory,

BOX 8.1

HERE AN INTERACTION, THERE AN INTERACTION, EVERYWHERE AN INTERACTION

In the spirit of practice makes perfect, let us now turn our attention to the exercise we have prepared to help you learn to identify interactions. Your task is to identify main effects and interactions in each of six complex design experiments (A through F). In each table or graph in this box, you are to determine whether the effect of each independent variable differs depending on the level of the other independent variable. In other words, is there an interaction? After checking for the interaction, you can also check to see whether each independent variable produced an effect when collapsed across the other independent variable. That is, is there a main effect of one or both independent variables? The exercise will be most useful if you also practice translating the data presented in a table (Figure 8.2) into a graph and those presented in graphs (Figures 8.3 and 8.4) into tables. The idea of the exercise is to become as comfortable as you can with the various ways of depicting the results of a complex design.[2]

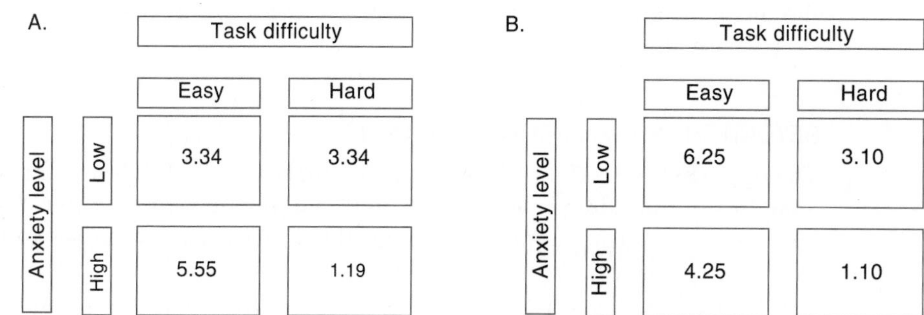

A.

Anxiety level	Task difficulty: Easy	Task difficulty: Hard
Low	3.34	3.34
High	5.55	1.19

B.

Anxiety level	Task difficulty: Easy	Task difficulty: Hard
Low	6.25	3.10
High	4.25	1.10

FIGURE 8.2 Mean number of correct responses as a function of task difficulty and anxiety level.

Hinrichs and Novick wondered whether our memory for a sequence of numbers would *always* conform to this pattern.

Hinrichs and Novick (1982) distinguished between two different ways in which we use numbers. We sometimes use them as arbitrary strings, as is the case with telephone numbers. In this instance, Hinrichs and Novick argued, it would be reasonable to expect a person's memory for the number string to follow the serial position effect. Most of the time, however, we use numbers to reflect amounts or magnitudes, as when a number indicates the cost of a new car. In this case, Hinrichs and Novick expected the number to be remembered not as a string of unrelated digits but as an approximate amount. That is, the first digit should be remembered best, with each successive digit being less critical and thus less likely to be remembered. For example, the digit string 8362 would need to be remembered exactly if it were a phone number, but remembering 8,300 would be close enough if the original number was intended

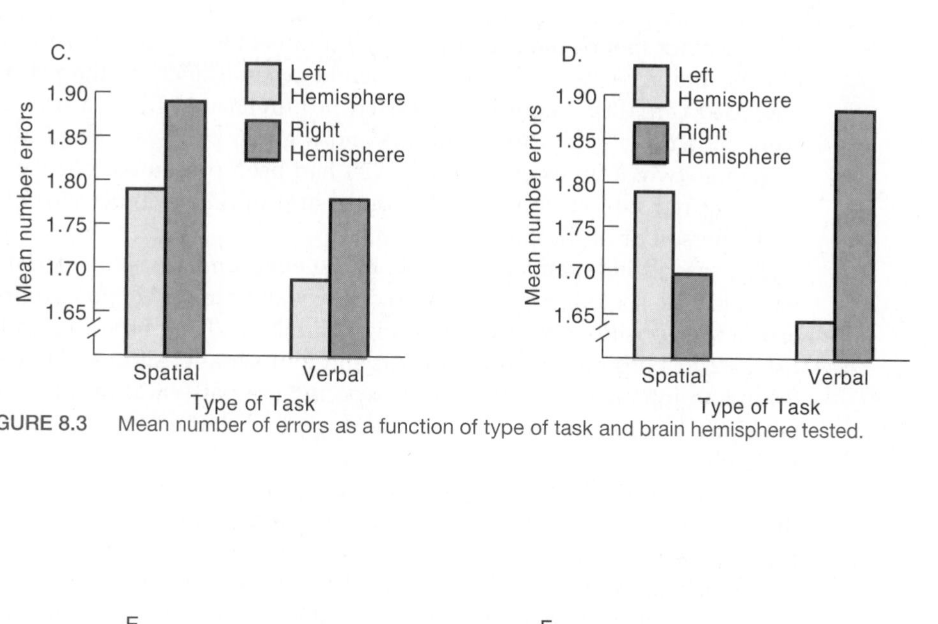

FIGURE 8.3 Mean number of errors as a function of type of task and brain hemisphere tested.

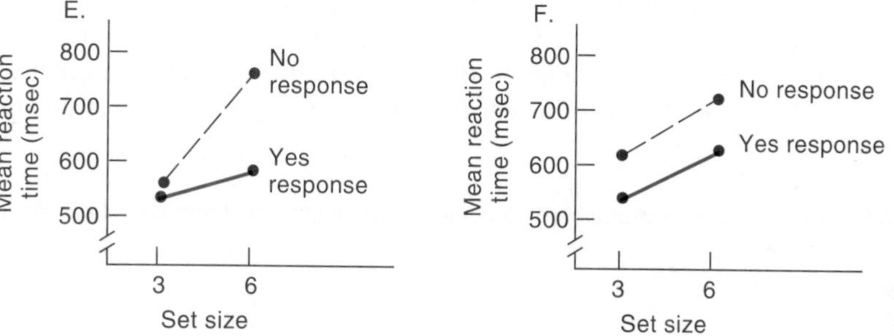

FIGURE 8.4 Mean reaction time as a function of set size and response type.

[2]Answer key for exercises in this box: An interaction occurs in A, D, and E.

to reflect the price of a car. When numbers reflected amounts, Hinrichs and Novick saw no reason why the serial recall of the digits should show a serial position curve.

The experiment Hinrichs and Novick did closely followed the logic described in the preceding paragraph. They manipulated two independent variables, using the within-subjects design for both. The first independent variable in their experiment was the type of list subjects were asked to learn. Half of the lists that subjects were asked to learn consisted of thirty 4-digit numbers, each paired with a person's name. Subjects were told to consider the numbers the 4-digit extensions of campus phone numbers for a group of thirty students.

For the other half of the lists, the 4-digit numbers were paired with the names of cars, and subjects were told to remember the numbers as the prices of new and used cars they might be interested in purchasing. In both lists, the pairs were shown for study for 5 seconds and a given pair was tested after either zero, one, two, four, or eight other pairs had been presented. The test for both lists required subjects to respond with the appropriate number when the name of the person or of the car was presented.

The second independent variable in the experiment was the serial position variable. The accuracy of subjects' recall was determined for the digits at each of the four positions within the 4-digit numbers. Thus Hinricks and Novick used a 2 × 4 design (two types of lists and four serial positions). They expected to find an interaction. That is, they expected the pattern of recall across serial positions to differ depending on the type of list the subject was trying to remember.

The proportion of digits recalled correctly at each serial position for the two different lists is presented in Figure 8.5. As predicted by Hinrichs and Novick, recall was best for serial positions 1 and 4 when the list was "phone numbers"—the serial position curve appeared. For the "prices" list, however, recall systematically decreased across serial positions, at least across the first three positions. As we previously mentioned, the appearance of nonparallel lines in a line graph like that shown in Figure 8.5 suggests that an interaction has occurred. The interaction can also be verified by applying the subtraction method to deter-

FIGURE 8.5 Illustration of an interaction in a complex design (2 × 4). (From Hinrichs & Novick, 1982).

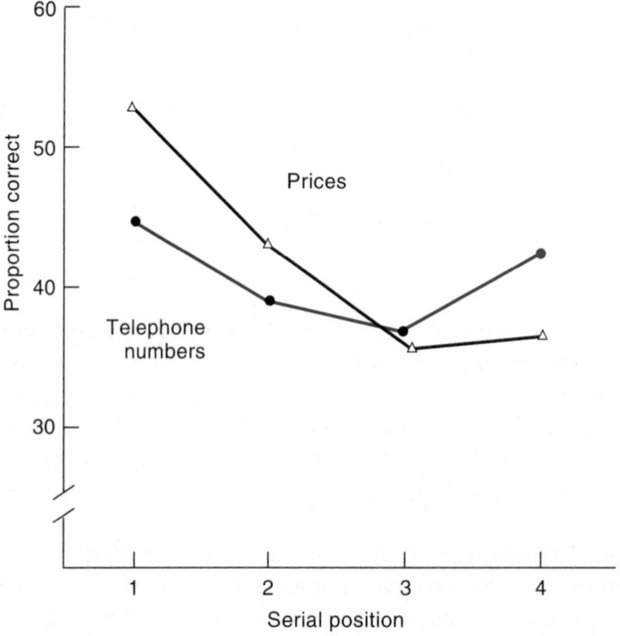

mine the differences between the points plotted above each serial position. The prices list led to higher recall for serial positions 1 and 2 but to lower recall for serial positions 3 and 4. The different patterns of recall across serial positions for the two types of lists confirm that our memories for numbers differ depending on what those numbers represent.

The experiment by Hinrichs and Novick illustrates an intriguing fact about human memory. For our purposes, however, their experiment also illustrates that the concept of an interaction can be extended to complex designs beyond the 2 × 2. You should now be beginning to see how complex designs allow psychologists to test predictions that specify how two independent variables can work together to produce an interaction.

The power and complexity of complex designs increase substantially when the number of independent variables in the experiment increases from two to three. In the two-factor design there can be only one interaction, but in the three-factor design each independent variable can interact with each of the other two independent variables and all three independent variables can interact together. Thus the change from a two-factor to a three-factor design introduces the possibility of obtaining four different interactions. If the three independent variables are symbolized as A, B, and C, the three-factor design allows a test of the main effects of A, B, and C; the two-way interactions of A × B, A × C, B × C; and the three-way interaction of A × B × C. The efficiency of an experiment involving three independent variables is remarkable. We would have to perform three experiments involving two variables at a time (A and B, A and C, and B and C) in order to assess the three main effects and the three two-way interactions that we can examine in a single three-factor design. Furthermore, we can assess the simultaneous interaction of all three independent variables *only* by including all three variables in the same experiment.

We Don't All Think Alike When a college student reads the words *cat* and *robin*, there is good reason to believe that the student automatically also registers the concepts "animal" and "bird" in memory. The student may not be consciously aware of her or his spontaneous production of these concept labels, but memory research suggests that they do occur. For example, suppose a college student in a free-recall experiment was asked to memorize a list of conceptually related words (such as *cow, green, sparrow, blue, horse, robin*). In free-recall experiments, words are presented one at a time for a brief period of study. After the last word is presented, the subject recalls as many words as possible in any order. The student's subsequent recall of related words would be greater than it would be if he or she were asked to memorize a comparable list of words that were not conceptually related. Presumably, what makes the former task easier is that implicit category labels serve to organize the conceptually related list.

However, conceptually related items do not always facilitate memory performance. In a paired-associate task, the subject must learn to give a specific response whenever a cue word is given. For instance, for the pair *mother-picnic,* the subject would have to learn to respond with the word *picnic* whenever the word *mother* was shown. When a paired-associate list contains several conceptually related items with different instances of two categories forming the pairs (*ocean-tea, lake-milk, river-coffee*), learning is often slower than when no conceptual relationships exist among pair members. This interfering effect of conceptual relationships in the paired-associate task, like the facilitating effect of such relationships in the free-recall task, is traceable to the automatic and implicit occurrence of category labels to category instances.

The preceding brief summary of research on conceptual relatedness aptly characterizes one important aspect of the thinking of typical college students—at least their thinking in memory researchers' laboratories. But what about adults who are mentally impaired? Do the mentally impaired think in the same way as college students but not as efficiently? Or do mentally impaired adults think in ways different from typical college students? Wallace and Underwood (1964) used a complex design involving three independent variables to address one question about the thinking of mentally impaired adults: whether they spontaneously produce category labels when they come across category instances.

The overall design of Wallace and Underwood's (1964) experiment was 2 × 2 × 2. There were two different types of subjects (college students and mentally impaired young adults), two different types of memory tasks (free-recall and paired-associate), and two different types of lists for each task (conceptually related and conceptually unrelated). There were thus eight conditions in the experiment, and a separate group of twenty subjects participated in each of the eight groups. On the basis of the research we have already summarized, Wallace and Underwood expected that the college students would do better with the conceptually related list in the free-recall task but worse with the conceptually related list in the paired-associate task. Wallace and Underwood went on to argue, however, that the mentally impaired adults would *not* spontaneously think of the category labels. Thus, the mentally impaired adults were expected to perform equally well on the conceptually related and the conceptually unrelated lists in both the free-recall and the paired-associate tasks.

The outcome of an experiment involving three independent variables can be summarized by using a two-panel graph like that shown in Figure 8.6. The performance of the college students is presented in the left panel and that of the mentally impaired adults in the right panel. As expected, the college students did better with conceptually related lists in the free-recall task but worse with conceptually related lists in the paired-associate task. The pattern shown for the mentally impaired adults in the right panel is very different: Conceptual relatedness has little or no effect in either the free-recall or the impaired-associate task. You may have recognized that the graph in the left panel reflects an interaction of conceptual relatedness and task. The right panel reflects no such interaction. The findings depicted in Figure 8.6 represent a specific example of a triple interaction involving three independent variables. In general, when the interaction of two independent variables differs depending on the level of a

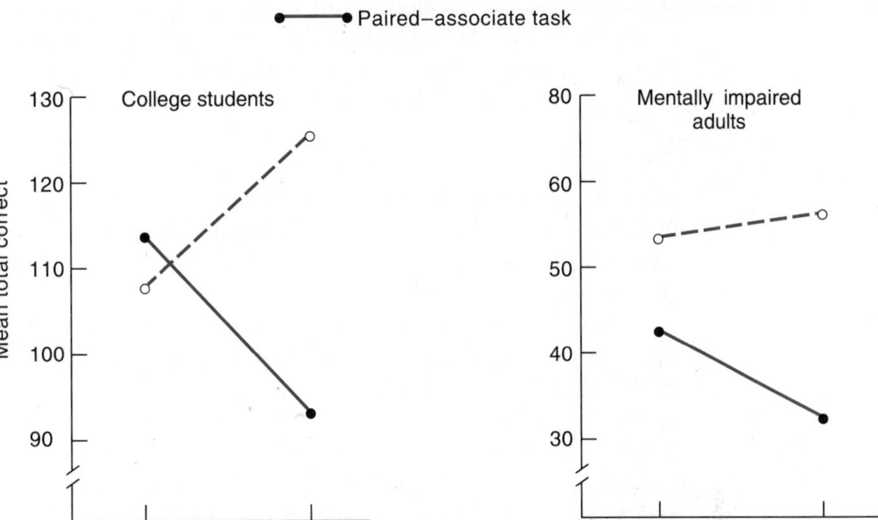

FIGURE 8.6 The results of a complex design involving three independent variables in which there was a triple interaction. (From Wallace & Underwood, 1964).

third independent variable, there is evidence of a triple interaction. The description of this one experiment only hints at the power and complexity of experiments involving three independent variables. For now, however, we will turn to a discussion of the interpretation of interactions.

INTERPRETING INTERACTIONS

EXTERNAL VALIDITY OF FINDINGS

In Chapter 6 we discussed at some length the procedures for establishing the external validity of a research finding when an experiment involves only one independent variable. We noted at that time that partial replication was the primary means by which external validity could be established. We can now examine the role of complex designs in establishing the external validity of a finding. As you might have suspected, the presence or absence of an interaction is critical in determining the external validity of the findings in a complex design.

When a complex design is used and when no interaction occurs, we know that the effects of each independent variable can be generalized across the levels of the other independent variable. For instance, Dittmar, Berch, and Warm (1982) tested hearing and deaf subjects in a vigilance task that required subjects to detect intermittent blips on a radar screen. They found that performance did decline across three 15-minute vigilance periods, but the decline occurred at approximately the same rate for hearing and deaf subjects. That is, there was no interaction of the subject variable (hearing or deaf) and the period variable. Thus, declining performance in a vigilance task can be generalized to both hearing and deaf people. This same generalization across types of subjects could have been made on the basis of the continuity assumption (see Chapter 6) if only deaf subjects or only hearing subjects had been tested. That is, we could have argued that there would be no reason to expect that deaf subjects' performance would decline but that of hearing subjects would not. The inference is far less risky, however, when it is based on the empirical finding of the absence of an interaction.

Of course, the absence of an interaction in a complex design does not establish the external validity of a finding beyond the boundaries that were included in the experiment. For example, the absence of an interaction of the subject variable and periods in the vigilance task does not allow us to conclude that detection performance would decline at the same rate if young children or trained observers were tested. Similarly, we do not know whether the same decline across periods would occur if there were short breaks after each observation period. We must also exercise caution in making generalizations based on the *absence* of an interaction. This situation involves problems associated with the failure to reject the null hypothesis, such as the sensitivity of the experiment to detect any interaction that might be present (see Chapter 6).

As we have seen, the absence of an interaction increases the external validity of the effects of each independent variable in the experiment. Perhaps more important, the presence of an interaction specifies *limits* on the external validity of a finding. When they tested college students, Wallace and Underwood (1964) found that there was an interaction between the conceptual relatedness of the material to be remembered and the type of memory test. This interaction clearly sets limits on the external validity of the nature of the effects of conceptual relatedness on memory. Given this finding, the best way to respond to someone's query regarding the general effect of conceptual relatedness on memory is to say "it depends." The presence of the interaction limits external validity but also specifies what those limits are. The limits on the external validity of a finding are greatest when a disordinal interaction occurs. In a *disordinal interaction,* the effects at different levels of the second independent variable are opposite in direction. When Wallace and Underwood found that conceptual relatedness enhanced performance on a free-recall test and interfered with performance on a paired-associate test, they obtained a disordinal interaction. They could reach no general conclusion regarding the effect of conceptual relatedness; their conclusions had to be specific to the particular type of memory test that had been used.

IDENTIFYING RELEVANT INDEPENDENT VARIABLES

One of the primary tasks facing researchers who use the experimental method is identifying relevant and irrelevant independent variables. A **relevant inde-**

pendent variable is one that has been shown to influence behavior; an *irrelevant independent variable* is one that has been shown *not* to influence behavior. Identifying factors that do affect behavior and those that do not is essential both for developing adequate theories to explain behavior and for designing effective interventions to deal with problems in applied settings such as schools, hospitals, and factories (see Chapters 10 and 11).

If independent variables did not interact with one another, the task of identifying relevant independent variables would be a long one, but not a particularly challenging one. Each independent variable would simply be manipulated across a wide range of levels in separate single-factor experiments. The variables would be classified as either relevant or irrelevant depending on whether or not they produced a significant difference in the dependent variable. Independent variables do interact, however, and we must adjust our definition of relevant and irrelevant independent variables accordingly.

Thousands of children in the United States receive drug treatment for hyperactivity every year. A reasonable question is whether dosage of the drugs is a relevant independent variable in determining the effectiveness of treatment. A hypothetical but typical experiment that could be done to address this question might include two dose levels (low and high) and three types of tasks (easy, moderate, and difficult). One possible outcome of such an experiment is summarized in the following table, with the dependent variable being the percent correct performance in each condition.

	Dose level		
Type of task	Low	High	Overall mean
Easy	75	90	82.5
Moderate	70	70	70.0
Difficult	65	50	57.5
Overall mean	70.0	70.0	

The overall means for the main effect of dose level are identical, and this information could mistakenly be used to argue that dose level was an irrelevant independent variable. By now you recognize, however, that the dose level produced different effects depending on the difficulty of the task to be performed. For difficult tasks a low dose is better, for moderate tasks there is no effect of dose level, and for easy tasks a high dose is better. Dose level is a relevant independent variable because it enters into a significant interaction with the difficulty variable. In general, a relevant independent variable is one that influences behavior directly (results in a main effect) or produces an interaction when studied in combination with a second independent variable.

The knowledge that interactions of independent variables can occur in complex designs should make us cautious about identifying any independent variable as irrelevant solely on the basis of having found that the independent variable failed to produce an effect in a single-factor experiment. It is always possible that some factor that was held constant in the experiment would have resulted in an interaction if it had been manipulated along with the original independent variable. (Imagine what would have happened if our hypothetical experiment testing the effects of drug doses had been done using only problems of moderate difficulty.) Theories about the processes underlying behavior help us to deal effectively with interactions (Underwood & Shaughnessy, 1975). For now, it is best if you avoid being dogmatic about identifying any independent variable as irrelevant.

CEILING AND BASEMENT EFFECTS

Consider the results of an experiment investigating the effects of increasing amounts of practice on performance on a physical-fitness test. There were six groups of subjects in this fictitious experiment. Subjects were given either 10, 30, or 60 minutes to practice, doing either easy or hard exercises, just prior to taking a fitness test using one of these types of exercises. The dependent variable was the percentage of the assigned number of exercises that each subject was able to complete in a 15-minute test period. Hypothetical results of the experiment are presented in Figure 8.7.

The pattern of results in Figure 8.7 looks like a classic interaction; the effect of practice time was different for the easy and for the hard exercises. Test performance improved with increasing amounts of practice for the hard exercises, but it leveled off after 30 minutes of practice with the easy exercises. If a standard analysis of variance were applied to these data, the interaction effect

FIGURE 8.7
Illustration of a ceiling effect.

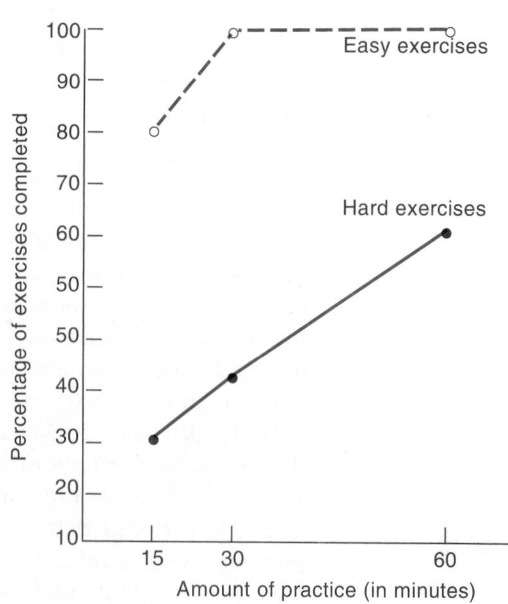

would very likely be statistically significant. Unfortunately, this interaction would be essentially uninterpretable. For those groups given practice with the easy exercises, performance reached a maximum after 30 minutes of practice, so no improvement beyond this point could be shown in the 60-minute group. Even if the subjects given 60 minutes of practice had further benefited from the extra practice, the experimenter could not measure this improvement on the chosen dependent variable.

The preceding experiment illustrates the general measurement problem referred to as a **ceiling effect.** Whenever performance reaches a maximum in any condition of an experiment, there is danger of a ceiling effect. The corresponding name given to this problem when errors are used to measure performance is a **basement effect** (or floor effect). In general, one can avoid ceiling and basement effects by selecting dependent variables that allow ample "room" for performance differences to be measured across conditions. For example, in the fitness experiment it would have been better to test subjects with a greater number of exercises than anyone could be expected to complete in the time allotted for the test. The mean number of exercises completed in each condition could then be used to assess the effects of the two independent variables without the danger of a ceiling effect.

INTERACTIONS AND THE NATURAL-GROUPS DESIGN

The natural-groups design, which we described briefly in Chapter 6, is one of the most popular research designs in psychology. Groups of subjects are formed by selecting individuals who differ on some characteristic such as gender, introversion-extraversion, or aggressiveness. Researchers then look for systematic relationships between these subject variables and other aspects of behavior. The natural-groups design is an effective one for establishing correlations between subjects' characteristics and their performance. As we also noted in Chapter 6, however, the natural-groups design is perhaps the most challenging design when it comes to drawing conclusions about cause and effect.

The difficulty in interpreting the natural-groups design arises when we try to conclude that differences in performance are *caused* by the characteristics of the subjects we used to define the groups. For instance, consider an experiment in which subjects are selected because of their musical training. One group of subjects includes people with ten or more years of formal musical training, and one group includes people with no formal training. Both groups are tested on their ability to remember the musical notation for simple ten-note melodies. The results of these tests show that those with musical training perform far better than those without such training.

We can conclude on the basis of these results that memory for simple melodies varies with (is correlated with) amount of musical training. But we cannot conclude that the superior memory performance was *caused* by the musical training. Why not? There are probably many ways in which people with ten years of musical training differ from those without such training other than the characteristic of amount of training. The groups may differ in amount and type of general education, family background, socioeconomic status, and amount and type of experience they have had listening to music. Those with musical training may have generally better memories than those without such training, and their superior memory for musical notation of simple melodies may reflect this general memory ability. Finally, those who sought out musical training may have done so because they had a special aptitude for music. Accordingly, they might have done better on the memory-for-melodies task even if they had not had any musical training. In short, there are many possible causes other than musical training for the difference in memory performance that was observed.

There is a potential solution to the problem of drawing causal inferences based on the natural-groups design (Underwood & Shaughnessy, 1975). The key to this solution is to develop a theory regarding the critical subject variable. For example, Halpern and Bower (1982) were interested in how memory for musical notation differs between musicians and nonmusicians. Halpern and Bower developed a theory of how musical training would influence the cognitive processing of musical notation by those who had such training. Their theory was based on a memory concept called "chunking." You can get some sense of the memory advantage provided by chunking if you imagine trying to memorize the following strings of letters: IBMTWASOSUSAUSSR versus IBM-TWA-SOS-USA-USSR.

Halpern and Bower argued that musical training led musicians to "chunk" musical notation into meaningful musical units, thereby reducing the amount of information they needed to remember in order to reproduce the notation for a simple melody. If this process were responsible for the difference between the memory performance of musicians and nonmusicians, then the difference should be greater for melodies with good musical structure than for those with poor musical structure.

Halpern and Bower chose to manipulate the independent variable of musical structure to test their theory. To do this, they used three different types of melodies to test their groups of musicians and nonmusicians. They prepared sets of simple melodies whose notations had similar visual structures but that were either good, bad, or random in musical structure. The critical test was whether they would obtain an interaction of the two independent variables. Specifically, they expected that the difference in memory performance between musicians and nonmusicians would be largest for the melodies exhibiting good structure, next largest for the melodies exhibiting bad structure, and smallest for the random melodies. The results of Halpern and Bower's experiment conformed exactly to these expectations.

The obtained interaction allowed Halpern and Bower to rule out many alternative hypotheses for the difference in memory performance between musicians and nonmusicians. Such characteristics as amount and type of general education, socioeconomic status, and family background are not likely to explain why there is a systematic relationship between the structure of the melodies and the size of the difference in memory performance between musicians and nonmusicians. The interaction makes such simple correlational explanations much less plausible.

There are several steps that the investigator must take in carrying out the general procedure for drawing causal inferences based on the natural-groups design. The first step is to develop a theory explaining why a difference should occur in the performance of the groups that have been differentiated on the basis of a subject variable. The second step is to select an independent variable that can be manipulated and that is presumed to influence the likelihood that this theoretical process will occur. This independent variable is then applied to both natural groups. The most critical aspect of the recommended approach is to continue to strive to produce an interaction between the manipulated variable and the subject variable. The approach can be strengthened even further by testing predictions of interactions of three independent variables: two manipulated independent variables and the subject variable (see, for example, Anderson & Revelle, 1982).

INTERPRETING THE RESULTS OF COMPLEX DESIGNS

A more complete description of the procedures for analyzing the results of a complex-design experiment are provided in Chapter 9. We will conclude this chapter, however, with a brief description of how the results of a complex-design experiment are interpreted. The interpretation of a complex design differs depending on whether an interaction is or is not obtained in the experiment. Table 8.2 provides guidelines for interpreting a complex-design experiment when an interaction does occur and when one does not. We will track through Table 8.2 twice, once describing an experiment in which there is no interaction and once describing a study in which there is an interaction.

TABLE 8.2 GUIDELINES FOR THE ANALYSIS OF A TWO-FACTOR EXPERIMENT

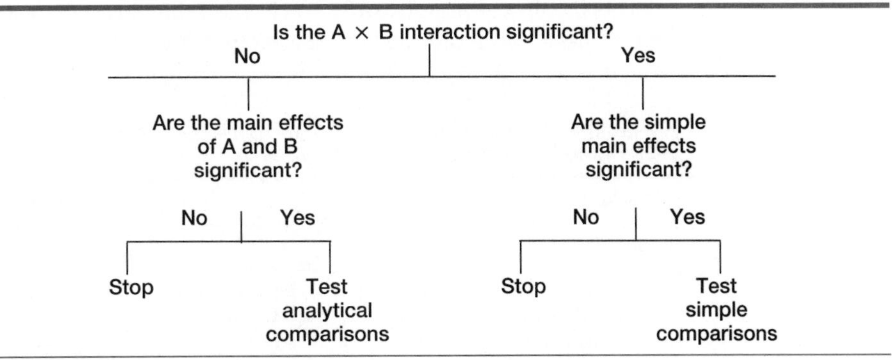

ANALYSIS OF A COMPLEX DESIGN WITH NO INTERACTION

Earlier we described a study by Dittmar et al. (1982), who used a 3 × 3 design to test whether people who are deaf perform better on a visual-vigilance task than people who can hear. As you may remember, a visual-vigilance task requires a person to detect intermittent visual signals such as blips on a radar screen for a long period of time. Dittmar et al. expected that deaf people would have an advantage on such a task because their deafness would keep them from being distracted. The deaf subjects who participated were offered a prize if their vigilance performance was the best in their group. To assess the possible effect of the prize as an incentive, two additional groups of hearing subjects were tested, one offered a prize and one not. These three groups represent the levels of the first independent variable in the experiment. The subjects were all tested in a 45-minute session divided into three continuous 15-minute periods, and these three periods were the levels of the second independent variable.

The mean percentage of correct detections across the three periods for the three different groups of subjects is presented in Table 8.3. The same data are depicted graphically in Figure 8.8. The interaction, or more accurately the lack of an interaction, can best be seen in Figure 8.8. Although the three lines in the figure are not perfectly parallel, the mean percentage of correct detections appears to decrease in all three groups at approximately the same rate.

The guidelines for the analysis of a complex design listed in Table 8.2 suggest that, when the interaction effect is not significant, the next step is to examine the main effects of each independent variable. This can be done most easily by referring to the data in Table 8.3. By collapsing across the three vigilance periods, we can obtain the means for the main effect of the group variable. These means are 86.0, 81.7, and 78.3 for the Deaf, Hearing—Prize, and Hearing—No Prize groups, respectively. The overall analysis of the group main effect was statistically significant. As indicated in Table 8.2, the source of a significant main effect can be specified more precisely by performing analytical comparisons (see Chapter 9). For example, a comparison of performance in the Hearing—Prize and Hearing—No Prize groups (81.7 and 78.3) was not statistically significant, but the average performance of the two groups of hearing subjects (80.0) was significantly lower than the performance of the deaf subjects (86.0). These two analytical comparisons allow us to confirm that deaf subjects

TABLE 8.3 MEAN PERCENTAGE OF CORRECT DETECTIONS ACROSS THREE PERIODS OF A VIGILANCE TASK FOR DEAF AND HEARING SUBJECTS

	Period		
Group	1	2	3
Deaf	95	85	78
Hearing—Prize	93	82	70
Hearing—No Prize	93	74	68

Adapted from Dittmar et al. (1982).

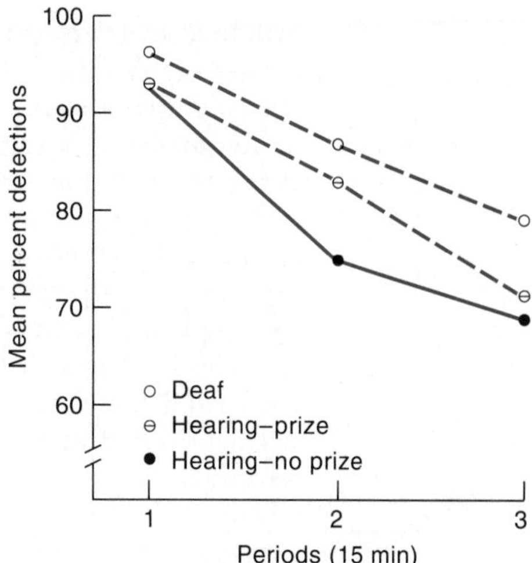

FIGURE 8.8
Results of a 3 × 3 complex design in which there was no interaction effect but there were two main effects. (Adapted from Dittmar et al., 1982.)

were better at the vigilance task than hearing subjects and that the offer of a prize did not affect the vigilance performance.

A similar approach would be followed in assessing the main effect of the period variable. By collapsing across the three groups of subjects, we obtain the means 93.7, 80.3, and 72.0 for the main effect of the period variable. The main effect of this variable was statistically significant. Analytical comparisons could then be used to determine whether the decreases over each successive period (93.7 to 80.3 and 80.3 to 72.0) were significant. The analysis of Dittmar et al.'s vigilance experiment illustrates that much can be learned from a complex design even when there is no interaction. We turn now to the analysis of an experiment that *does* contain an interaction.

ANALYSIS OF A COMPLEX DESIGN WITH AN INTERACTION

One of the many approaches psychologists have tried to use to understand depression is based on investigating the differences between the thought patterns of depressed and nondepressed people. One aspect of this cognitive approach to depression deals with attributions, the causal explanations we use to try to account for our own behavior and the behavior of others. For example, nondepressed people tend to overestimate how much control they have over their lives, while depressed people, more realistically, estimate that they have less control (Bootzin, Acocella, & Alloy, 1993). According to the cognitive approach, this tendency toward less optimistic thinking on the part of depressed people may be critically involved in causing the onset of depression, maintaining depression once it occurs, and alleviating depression by changing to a more optimistic way of thinking. The Johnson et al. (1983) study with which we began this chapter fits well into the cognitive perspective—depressed subjects were more likely to remember unfinished than finished tasks. The study we will be using to illustrate the interpretation of the results of a complex design with an interaction represents another of the many experiments investigating the cognitive bases of depression.

Rodman and Burger (1985) investigated a particular phenomenon called the *defensive attribution effect.* In previous experiments, nondepressed subjects read a description of an accident in which a person suffered mild or severe consequences. These nondepressed subjects attributed more responsibility to the perpetrator in the severe than in the mild accident condition. One interpretation of this phenomenon is that people do not want to attribute the cause of a severe accident to chance. If they did attribute the accident to chance, they would be increasing the perceived possibility that they could be involved in a severe accident. Their attribution of greater responsibility to the perpetrator in the severe accident is a defensive attribution, protecting them against a greater likelihood of future severe accidents. Rodman and Burger reasoned that depressed people might be less likely to show this type of defensive attribution effect because their negative thinking would lead them to be less self-protective. Stated more formally, they tested the hypothesis that the defensive-attribution effect would decrease as a person's level of depression increased.

Rodman and Burger tested fifty-six college students in a 2 × 3 design. The first independent variable was the severity of the described accident (severe and nonsevere), and this was manipulated using the random-groups design. The natural-groups design was used for the second independent variable; students were selected on the basis of their scores on a paper-and-pencil test of depression to represent nondepressed, slightly depressed, and mildly depressed subjects. The dependent variable was a single item on a longer questionnaire that asked subjects to divide 100 percent among four potential sources of responsibility: each of the three drivers in the accident and "uncontrollable circumstances." The defensive-attribution effect would be reflected in a larger value assigned to uncontrollable circumstances for the nonsevere than for the severe accident. The mean percentage values for this uncontrollable factor for each of the six conditions are presented in Table 8.4.

As Rodman and Burger had predicted, there is an apparent interaction; as degree of depression increases, the differences between the percentage values for severe and nonsevere accidents change. Nondepressed subjects show the

TABLE 8.4 MEAN PERCENTAGE OF RESPONSIBILITY ATTRIBUTED TO UNCONTROLLABLE CIRCUMSTANCES

	Degree of depression		
Type of accident	Nondepressed	Slightly depressed	Mildly depressed
Severe	7.00(9.2)	14.00(16.1)	16.90(16.0)
Nonsevere	30.50(22.2)	16.50(12.7)	3.75(3.5)

Note: Standard deviations appear in parentheses. Adapted from Rodman and Burger (1985).

defensive-attribution effect and mildly depressed subjects do not. Analysis of these results confirmed that the interaction was statistically significant.

Once we have confirmed that there is an interaction of two independent variables, we must locate more precisely the source of that interaction. As outlined in Table 8.2, there are statistical tests specifically designed for tracing the source of a significant interaction. These tests are called *simple main effects* and *simple comparisons* (see Keppel, 1991).

A **simple main effect** is the effect of one independent variable at *one* level of a second independent variable. In fact, one definition of an interaction is that the simple main effects in an experiment are different. We can illustrate the use of simple main effects by returning to the results of the Rodman and Burger experiment. There are *five* simple main effects in Table 8.4: the effect of the type of accident at each of the three degrees of depression and the effect of the degree of depression at each of the two types of accident. Rodman and Burger predicted that the defensive-attribution effect (the difference between the means for severe and nonsevere accidents) would decrease as severity of depression increased. Therefore, they chose to test the simple main effects of type of accident at each of the three levels of depression. They found, as predicted, that the simple main effect of type of accident was statistically significant for nondepressed subjects, but the simple main effects of type of accident for the slightly depressed and for the mildly depressed subjects were not statistically significant.

Simple comparisons are analytical comparisons done on simple main effects rather than on the overall main effect. Simple comparisons are not necessary when the simple main effect has only two levels, as was the case for the simple main effects of type of accident at each degree of depression. If Rodman and Burger had tested the simple main effects of degree of depression at the two types of accident, these simple main effects likely would have been statistically significant. Once again, finding significant simple main effects does not tell us the source of these omnibus effects. Simple comparisons must be done. For example, one way to break down the simple main effect of degree of depression for the nonsevere accident would be to use a simple comparison that contrasts the average of the two depressed groups to the mean for the nondepressed group. This comparison would be testing the effect of depression versus nondepression. A second simple comparison could then be made between the means of the slightly depressed group (16.50) and the mildly depressed group (3.75). Remember, these analyses are called *simple comparisons* because they break down a simple main effect which is the effect of one independent variable at only one level of a second independent variable.

When students are introduced to the analysis of simple main effects and simple comparisons, they sometimes tend to overuse them. That is, the students analyze all possible simple main effects and every conceivable simple comparison. More often than not, this "barrage" approach to the analysis of a complex design that involves an interaction leads to utter confusion. Usually a researcher selects one set of simple main effects to break down a significant interaction. This choice is based on the rationale behind the predicted interaction and is not a "fishing expedition". With experience, students also can learn to use these powerful analytical tools effectively and judiciously.

Once an interaction has been thoroughly analyzed, researchers can also examine the main effects of each independent variable. As we mentioned earlier in this chapter, however, the main effects are of much less interest when we know that an interaction is significant. For instance, once we know that the effect of the type of accident varies depending on the degree of depression, we have not added much when we learn that, overall, the nonsevere accident led to a higher mean percentage than did the severe accident. Nonetheless, there are experiments in which the interaction and the main effects are all of interest. In such cases, the guidelines in Table 8.2 can be followed to track down all sources of systematic variation in a complex design.

SUMMARY

A complex design is one in which two or more independent variables are studied in the same experiment. A complex design involving two independent variables allows one to determine the overall effect of each independent variable (the main effect of each variable). More important, complex designs can be used to reveal the interaction of two independent variables that exist when the effect of each independent variable depends on the level of the other independent variable. Complex designs are essential to resolve contradictions that arise when two experiments involving the same independent variable result in different findings. Investigators can trace the source of the contradictory findings by using a complex design in which both the original independent variable and the independent variable that is presumed to be responsible for the discrepant findings are manipulated in the same experiment. Complex designs also play a critical role in the testing of predictions derived from psychological theories.

The smallest possible complex design is the 2 × 2 design, in which two independent variables are both studied at two levels. The analytical power of complex designs increases when additional levels of one or both of the independent variables are included in the design, yielding designs such as the 3 × 2, the 3 × 3, the 4 × 2, the 4 × 3, and so on. Additional independent variables can also be included to yield designs such as the 2 × 2 × 2, the 3 × 3 × 3, and so on. Experiments involving three independent variables are remarkably efficient. They allow determination of the main effects of each of the three variables, the three two-way interactions of the three independent variables, and the simultaneous interaction of all three variables.

When a complex design is used and no interaction occurs, we know that the effects of each independent variable can be generalized across the levels of the other independent variable(s). When an interaction does occur, however, limits on the external validity of a finding can be clearly specified. Disordinal interactions place the greatest limits on the external validity of a finding in that the effects of one independent variable at different levels of a second independent variable are opposite in direction. The possibility of interactions requires that we expand the definition of a relevant independent variable to include those that influence behavior directly (produce main effects) and those that produce an interaction when studied in combination with another independent variable.

Interactions that may arise because of measurement problems such as ceiling or basement effects must not be confused with interactions that reflect the true combined effect of two independent variables. Interactions can also be most helpful in solving the problem of drawing causal inferences based on the natural-groups design.

The interpretation of the results of complex designs with two independent variables involves three potential sources of systematic variation. Each independent variable can produce a significant main effect, and the two independent variables can combine to produce a significant interaction. Interactions can be initially identified by using the subtraction method when the descriptive statistics are reported in a table or by the presence of nonparallel lines when the results appear in a line graph. If the interaction does prove to be statistically significant, we can interpret the results by examining simple main effects and simple comparisons. When no interaction arises, we interpret the main effects of each independent variable, using analytical comparisons when necessary.

KEY CONCEPTS

complex designs
interaction
mixed design
main effect
relevant independent variable
ceiling (basement) effect
simple main effect
simple comparisons

REVIEW QUESTIONS

1 Explain how a complex design can be used to resolve contradictions that arise when two researchers obtain different results after manipulating the same independent variable in their respective single-factor experiments.
2 Use an example to illustrate how a complex design can be used to test predictions derived from a psychological theory.
3 How is the interpretation of a main effect influenced by the presence or absence of an interaction in a complex design?
4 Use the Hass et al. cross-racial evaluation experiment to illustrate that there is one possible interaction in a 2 × 2 design but that there are *two* possible ways to describe the interaction.
5 Describe the method you would use to decide whether an interaction was present in a table showing the results of a 2 × 2 complex design.
6 Describe the pattern in a line graph that indicates the presence of an interaction in a complex design.

7 In what two ways can the basic 2 × 2 design be expanded to create more extensive complex designs?
8 How is the external validity of the findings in a complex design influenced by the presence or absence of an interaction?
9 Why must we be cautious in making generalizations based on the absence of an interaction in a complex design?
10 What expansion in the definition of a relevant independent variable is required by the use of complex designs?
11 What potential solution is there for the problem of drawing causal inferences on the basis of the natural-groups design?
12 Describe the steps in the analysis of a complex design involving two independent variables when there is an interaction and when there is not an interaction.

CHALLENGE QUESTIONS

1 Consider an experiment in which two independent variables have been manipulated. Variable A has been manipulated at three levels, and Variable B has been manipulated at two levels.

A Draw a graph showing an effect of Variable B, no effect of Variable A, and no interaction between the two variables.
B Draw a graph showing no effect of Variable A, no effect of Variable B, but an interaction between the two variables.
C Draw a graph showing an effect of Variable A, an effect of Variable B, *and* no interaction between the A and B variables.

2 A researcher has used a complex design to study the effects of training (untrained and trained) and problem difficulty (easy and hard) on subjects' problem-solving ability. The researcher tested a total of eighty subjects, with twenty subjects randomly assigned to each of the four groups resulting from the factorial combination of the two independent variables. The data presented below represent the percentage of the problems that subjects solved in each of the four conditions.

	Training	
Problem difficulty	Untrained	Trained
Easy	90	95
Hard	30	60

A Is there evidence of a possible interaction in this experiment?
B What aspect of the results of this experiment would lead you to be hesitant to interpret an interaction if one were present in this experiment?
C How could the researcher modify the experiment so as to be able to interpret an interaction if it should occur?

3 A psychologist is interested in whether older people suffer a deficit with respect to their reaction time in processing complex visual patterns. He selects a random sample of 65-year-old people and another random sample of young adults (such as college students). He tests both groups of fifty people in the same reaction time task. He

presents a simple figure to each subject, then a complex pattern, and asks the subject to indicate as quickly as possible whether the simple figure is present in the complex pattern. Subjects are timed only for their reaction to the complex patterns. This test is called an embedded figures test. As he had expected, the mean reaction time for the older adults was markedly longer than that for the young adults. By any standard the results were statistically significant.

A Explain what minimal set of conditions the psychologist would have to include in his experiment before he could conclude that older adults suffered a deficit in their processing of *complex* visual patterns. That is, state what additional reaction time test must be given to both groups. Finally, describe an outcome of the test you propose which would support his position and one which would lead you to question his conclusion.

B Recognizing that his original study is flawed, the psychologist tries to use post hoc matching to try to equate his two groups. He decides to match on general health (i.e., the better your general health, the faster your reaction time). Although he cannot get an exact matching across groups he does find that when he looks only at the fifteen healthiest older adults, their reaction times are only slightly longer than the mean for the college students. Explain how this outcome would change the psychologist's conclusion concerning the effect of age on reaction time. Could the psychologist reach the general conclusion that older adults do not suffer a deficit in reaction time in this task? Why or why not?

ANSWER TO CHALLENGE QUESTION 1

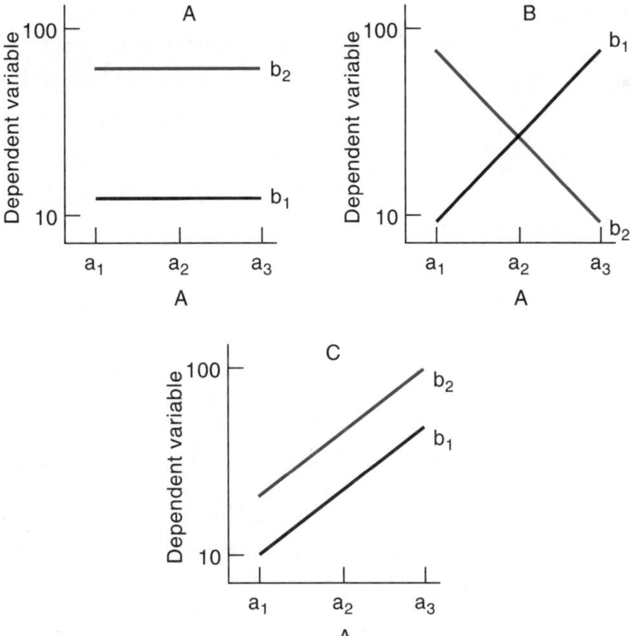

Chapter 9

Analysis of Experiments

Outline

OVERVIEW

The analysis and interpretation of the results of an experiment would be straightforward and relatively simple if it were not for error variation. We could examine the means directly and interpret any differences between the means. Error variation, however, is present in every experiment. In the independent-groups designs, error variation is the result of the individual differences among subjects that are balanced across groups. In the within-subjects designs, error variation arises because of the different effects the conditions have on individual subjects. Because of the presence of error variation, we know that the means could differ even if the independent variable had no effect. A statistically significant difference is one that is larger than would be expected on the basis of error variation alone. The process of null hypothesis testing (described in Chapter 6) provides a means of deciding how unlikely a difference needs to be in order to be statistically significant. The probability of the obtained difference must be less than the level of significance (*alpha*).

To test a null hypothesis, it is necessary to compute a statistic that reflects both the effect of the independent variable and the amount of error variation in the experiment. The most commonly used inferential statistic in the analysis of experiments is the analysis of variance. In this chapter we will provide an introduction to the analysis of variance procedures used to analyze experiments involving the random-groups design, within-subjects designs, and complex designs. Our approach will be to emphasize the conceptual rather than the computational aspects of the analysis of variance. Our goal is to help you develop an understanding of the role of the analysis of variance in the *inter-*

pretation of the results of an experiment. (Detailed descriptions of the analysis procedures are provided in Appendix A.)

The likelihood of obtaining a statistically significant effect in an experiment is influenced by the sensitivity of the experiment and the power of the statistical test used to analyze the results. More powerful statistical tests are more likely to detect the presence of an effect of an independent variable—even if the effect is only a small one. We will describe in this chapter the primary factors affecting the power of a statistical test. We will also describe the procedures used to measure the size of an effect of an independent variable. A calculation of an effect size provides an estimate of the extent of the impact of an independent variable. Measures of effect size complement tests of statistical significance which verify that an effect exists. Finally, we will introduce meta-analysis as a means of interpreting the results of more than one experiment.

ANALYSIS OF THE RANDOM-GROUPS DESIGN

There are two sources of variation in any random-groups experiment. First, variation *within each group* can be expected because of the individual differences among the subjects who have been randomly assigned to that group. As we have already mentioned, however, in a properly conducted experiment the differences within each group should represent only error variation because all the subjects in the group have been treated in the same way. The second source of variation in the random-groups design is variation *between the groups.*

If the null hypothesis is true, the nonsystematic variation among the means of the groups can also be attributed to error variation. Remember, when the null hypothesis is true, the performance in each group reflects the same underlying population, and thus the average performance in each group should be the same as the average performance in every other group. If several random samples are drawn from the same population, however, we cannot expect the means of these samples to be identical. Fluctuations produced by chance make it likely that the means for the different random samples will vary somewhat. Thus the variation among the group means, under the condition that the null hypothesis is true, provides a second estimate of error variation. If the null hypothesis is true, this estimate of error variation between groups should be comparable to the earlier estimate we described of error variation within groups.

Now suppose that the null hypothesis is false. That is, suppose that the independent variable has had an effect. In that case, there will be systematic differences across the groups of the experiment. This systematic variation will be *added to* the differences in the group means that always result from error variation.

THE *F*-TEST

We are now in a position to develop a statistic that will allow us to tell whether the variation due to our independent variable is larger than would be expected on the basis of error variation alone. This statistic is called the *F-test*; it is named after Ronald Fisher, the statistician who developed the test. The conceptual definition of the ***F*-test** is as follows:

$$F = \frac{\text{variation between groups}}{\text{variation within groups}}$$

$$= \frac{\text{error variation} + \text{systematic variation}}{\text{error variation}}$$

If the null hypothesis is true, there is no systematic variation and the resulting *F*-ratio has an expected value of one. As the extent of the systematic variation increases, however, the expected size of the *F*-ratio becomes greater than 1.00.

The analysis of experiments would be easier if we could isolate the systematic variation produced by the independent variable. Unfortunately, the systematic variation between groups comes in a "package" along with error variation. Consequently, the *F*-ratio may sometimes be larger than 1.00 simply because our estimate of error variation between groups happens to be larger than our estimate of error variation within groups. This problem becomes less and less likely to arise with increasingly larger *F*-ratios, but we are still faced with a nagging question: How much greater than 1.00 does the *F*-ratio have to be before we can be relatively sure that it reflects systematic variation? Our discussion of null-hypothesis testing in Chapter 6 provides one answer to this question. To be statistically significant, the *F*-ratio needs to be large enough so that its probability of occurring if the null hypothesis were true is less than our chosen level of significance, usually .05.

Having described the general principles of the analysis of variance, we are now ready to consider the application of these principles to the interpretation of the results of a specific experiment. One of many illusions used to study cues for depth perception is the Ponzo illusion. This illusion involves presenting two equal-sized bars on a background suggesting depth (see Figure 9.1) with one bar appearing closer than the other. The illusion results because we see the more distant bar as larger than the closer bar even if the two bars are the same size. An experiment was done in a research methods class testing to see if the size of the illusion would vary if the background surrounding the two bars was varied.[1] Three different backgrounds were used. They are illustrated in the panels of Figure 9.2: a clear background (C) with only the two bars on the screen (upper left panel); a line background (L) that included twelve diagonal lines randomly arranged on the screen (lower left panel); and the tunnel background (T) typically used to test for the Ponzo illusion (lower right panel).

Twenty undergraduate students were randomly assigned to each of the three

[1] We thank Tom Ludwig of Hope College for writing the software for this experiment, including the design of the stimulus backgrounds and the control of the stimulus presentation.

FIGURE 9.1 An illustration of the Ponzo illusion.

background conditions. The subjects' task in each condition was to lengthen or shorten Bar A until it was exactly the same length as Bar B. When the subjects judged that the two bars were equal, they pressed the F key on a computer keyboard to indicate they were finished for that trial. The subjects were then given feedback on a screen like that in the upper right panel of Figure 9.2. For example, a subject's adjusted Bar A appears to the left of the comparison bar showing the actual length of Bar B. In this example, there is a considerable difference between the subject's judged length of Bar B and its actual length. Overestimating the length of Bar B is evidence of the Ponzo illusion. The dependent variable was the difference between the length of Bar A minus Bar B expressed as a percentage of the length of Bar B. All subjects were given eight test trials with feedback on the adjustment task. The mean percent error for the 20 subjects averaged across the eight trials in the three groups was 25.3 in the tunnel group, 7.3 in the line group, and 6.5 in the clear group.

The first step in the analysis of any experiment is to state the research question the analysis is intended to answer. Typically, this takes the form of "Did the independent variable have any overall effect on performance?" In our illusion experiment this question would read "Did varying the background have any effect on the percent error subjects made in adjusting the bar?" Once the research question is clear, the next step is to develop a null hypothesis for the analysis.

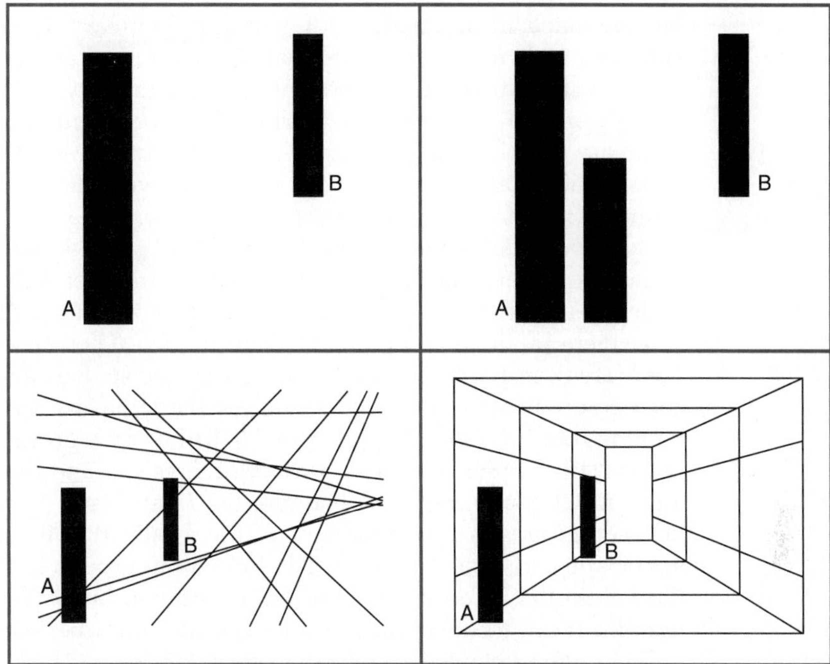

FIGURE 9.2 Illustrations of the conditions in an experiment testing the Ponzo illusion.

The initial overall analysis of the experiment is called an **omnibus F-test.** The null hypothesis for such omnibus tests is that all the group means are equal. The formal statement of a null hypothesis (symbolized as H_0) is always made in terms of population characteristics. These population characteristics are indicated by Greek letters, and the population mean is symbolized as μ (mu). We can use a subscript for each mean in the illusion experiment to reflect the background for that group. Our null hypothesis then becomes

$$H_O: \mu_T = \mu_L = \mu_C$$

The alternative to the null hypothesis, of course, is that the means for all the groups are not equal. If the background does have an effect (i.e., if the background produces systematic variation), we will be led to reject the null hypothesis.

ANALYSIS OF VARIANCE SUMMARY TABLE

The next step is to carry out the necessary computations to obtain the estimates of variation that make up the numerator and denominator of the *F*-ratio. Computing *F*-ratios is best done using a computer (the procedures for doing computer analyses are described in Appendix A). The results of the computations are presented in an Analysis of Variance Summary Table. Table 9.1 is the summary table for the omnibus analysis of the illusion experiment.

We will examine the components of the summary table before looking at the outcome of the *F*-test for the illusion experiment. The left column of a summary table lists the sources of variation. In this case the independent variable of background is a source of variation between the groups and the within-groups differences provide an estimate of error variation. The total variation in the experiment is the sum of the variation between and within the groups. The next column is the degrees of freedom (*df*). In general, the statistical concept of degrees of freedom is defined as the number of entries of interest minus one. Since there are three backgrounds, there are two *df* between groups (3 - 1 = 2). There are twenty subjects within each group and so there are nineteen *df* within each group. Because all three groups are the same size we can determine the within-groups *df* by multiplying the *df* within each group by the number of groups (19 × 3) for 57 *df*. The sums of squares (SS) and the mean square (MS) are computational steps in obtaining the *F*-ratio (see Appendix A). The MS between groups is the numerator of the *F*-ratio that is an estimate of both systematic and error variation. The MS within groups is the denominator of the *F*-ratio that is an estimate of error variation only. We are now ready to examine the outcome of the *F*-test for our illusion experiment.

The *F*-ratio obtained in this analysis is $F(2,57) = 22.42$. The probability of obtaining an *F*-ratio as large as 22.42 if the null hypothesis is true is .0001. (The probability associated with an *F*-ratio is typically provided as part of the printout of a computer analysis.) The obtained probability of .0001 is clearly less than the level of significance ($\alpha = .05$), so we reject the null hypothesis and conclude that the overall effect of the background is statistically significant.

Just what have we learned when we find a statistically significant outcome in an omnibus analysis of variance? In one sense, we have learned something very important. We are now in a position to state with confidence that manipulation of the independent variable produced a change in performance. In another sense, merely knowing that our outcome is statistically significant tells us nothing about the *nature* of the effect of the independent variable. The descriptive statistics (in our example, the mean percent error for the three background groups: T = 25.3, L = 7.3, and C = 6.5) are the basis for our description of the nature of the effect. For example, if the mean percent error had been largest with the clear background and smallest with the tunnel background, the results could also have been statistically significant but in the opposite

TABLE 9.1 ANALYSIS OF VARIANCE SUMMARY TABLE

Source of variation	df	SS	MS	F	P
Between groups (Background)	2	4,519.8	2,259.9	22.42	.0001
Within groups (Error Variation)	57	5,745.6	100.8		
Total	59	10,265.4			

direction, leading to a very different conclusion from the one we draw from the actual means. The point is that you should never try to interpret a statistically significant outcome without referring to the corresponding descriptive statistics.

Knowing that the omnibus test is statistically significant also does not tell us the *source* of the significant effect. All we know is that there is systematic variation somewhere in our experiment. On the basis of the omnibus test, we can only respond to a person who asked "What happened in your experiment?" by saying "Something." This response is not very satisfying and would almost surely prompt the exasperated query, "Yes, but what?" Fortunately, there are analysis techniques that allow us to locate more specifically the sources of systematic variation in our experiments. These techniques are called *analytical comparisons,* and they are linked directly to the hypotheses that led the researcher to do the experiment in the first place.

ANALYTICAL COMPARISONS

We did not perform the Ponzo illusion experiment simply to find out whether something would happen if the backgrounds were manipulated. Instead, at least two specific questions were addressed in the experiment. Would the tunnel background lead to a larger illusion than that created by the other two backgrounds? And would the illusion differ in size for the line and for the clear backgrounds? **Analytical comparisons** are a way to translate these research questions into a form that will allow us to locate a specific source of systematic variation in our experiment. We will illustrate this process with the two research questions we just posed about the illusion experiment.

The first step in doing an analytical comparison, like the first step in doing an omnibus analysis, is to state the null hypothesis for the analysis. The verbal statement of the null hypothesis for the first research question is as follows: The mean for the group of subjects who see the tunnel background is equal to the mean for the two groups who see either the line or the clear background. More formally, the null hypothesis is

$$H_O\colon \mu_T = \frac{\mu_L + \mu_C}{2}$$

Using the computational procedures outlined in Appendix A, we can compute a mean square for this particular comparison. The mean square for the comparison reflects a combination of error variation and systematic variation due to this specific comparison. An *F*-ratio can then be formed with the comparison mean square in the numerator and the mean square within groups in the denominator as an estimate of error variation alone. Because this analytical comparison essentially involves the contrast between two means (subjects in the tunnel group and subjects in the other two background groups), it has only 1 degree of freedom. We then determine the probability of the resulting *F*-ratio by using the same procedures we described earlier for omnibus *F*-tests. We compare this obtained probability with the level of significance to decide whether the comparison has resulted in a statistically significant outcome.

The computations for the first analytical comparison in the illusion experiment result in $F(1,57) = 21.8$ with a $p = .0001$. The obtained p is less than the conventional .05 level of significance, and so the analytical comparison is statistically significant. This outcome allows us to state with confidence that one source of systematic variation in the illusion experiment was that subjects in the tunnel group performed differently from subjects who saw the other two backgrounds. Because the mean percent error for subjects in the tunnel group (25.3) was higher than that for subjects in the other two groups combined (6.9), we can conclude that the illusion was larger in the tunnel group than the combined illusion in the other two groups. A second analytical comparison was done comparing the mean percent error in the line and clear groups. The resulting $F(1,57) = .92$ indicated that there was not a statistically significant difference in the size of the illusion for these two groups. These conclusions based on the analytical comparisons are much more useful than the general conclusion (based on the omnibus test) that something happened in the experiment.

ANALYSIS OF WITHIN-SUBJECTS DESIGNS

The analysis of within-subjects design experiments involves the same general procedures used in the analysis of independent-groups design experiments. The principles of null-hypothesis testing are applied to determine whether the differences obtained in the experiment are larger than would be expected on the basis of error variation alone. The analysis begins with an omnibus analysis of variance to determine whether the independent variable has produced any systematic variation. Should this omnibus analysis prove statistically significant, analytical comparisons can be made to find the specific source of the systematic variation. Because we have already described the logic and procedures for this general analysis plan in the context of the random-groups design, we will focus in this section on the analysis procedures specific to within-subjects designs.

ESTIMATING ERROR VARIATION

One distinctive characteristic of the analysis of within-subjects designs is the way in which error variation is estimated. In random-groups designs individual differences among subjects that are balanced across groups provide the estimate of error variation that becomes the denominator of the *F*-ratio. Since subjects participate in only one condition in these designs, differences among subjects cannot be eliminated—they can only be balanced. In within-subjects designs, on the other hand, there is systematic variation among subjects. Some subjects consistently perform better across conditions, and some subjects consistently perform worse. Because each subject participates in each condition of within-subjects designs, differences among subjects contribute equally to the mean performance in each condition. Accordingly, any differences among the means for each condition in within-subjects designs *cannot* be the result of systematic differences among subjects. In within-subjects designs, however, differences among subjects are not just balanced—they are actually eliminated from the analysis. The ability to eliminate systematic variation due to subjects in within-subjects designs makes these designs generally more sensitive than random-groups designs.

If differences among subjects cannot be the basis of estimating error variation in within-subjects designs, how do we get an estimate that involves only error variation in these designs? The source of error variation in the within-subjects designs is the differences in the ways the conditions affect different subjects. Perhaps the best way to describe the way we get these estimates is to say that we do it "by default." We first determine how much total variation there is in our experiment. Then we subtract the two potential sources of systematic variation: the independent variable and subjects. The remainder is called **residual variation,** and it represents our estimate of error variation alone.[2] As was the case in the random-groups design when we used variation within groups as our estimate of error variation alone, residual variation serves as the denominator for the *F*-ratio in within-subjects designs. Before we go into more detail regarding the use of the *F*-ratio in the analysis of within-subjects designs, we need to outline the procedures used to describe the effects of an independent variable in within-subjects designs.

DETERMINING THE EFFECT OF THE INDEPENDENT VARIABLE

The first step in analyzing an experiment is preparing a matrix summarizing performance in each condition of the experiment. In random-groups designs, this means simply listing the scores of the subjects tested in each of the conditions of the experiment and then summarizing these scores with some descriptive statistic such as the mean. Similarly, in within-subjects designs, we prepare a matrix in which the scores for each subject in each condition of the experiment are listed.

An example of such a matrix appears in Table 9.2. The data represent performance of the five subjects tested in a time-perception experiment done as a classroom demonstration of a within-subjects design. The purpose of the experiment was not to test the accuracy of subjects' time estimates compared with the actual interval lengths. Instead, the purpose of the experiment was to determine whether subjects' estimates of time increased systematically with increasing lengths. In other words, could subjects discriminate between intervals of different lengths? Each subject was tested on all four interval lengths

[2] The residual variation can, of course, be computed directly. It reflects the interaction effect of the independent variable and subjects. For a more complete discussion of residual variation and why it is an estimate of error variation alone, see Keppel (1991).

TABLE 9.2 DATA MATRIX AND ANALYSIS OF VARIANCE SUMMARY TABLE FOR A WITHIN-SUBJECTS DESIGN EXPERIMENT

Data matrix				
	Interval length			
Subject	12	24	36	48
1	13	21	30	38
2	10	15	38	35
3	12	23	31	32
4	12	15	22	32
5	16	36	69	60
Mean	12.6	22.0	38.0	39.4

(12, 24, 36, and 48 seconds). If the incomplete within-subjects design had been used, the matrix shown in this table would have been prepared by "unraveling" the different sequences in which the subjects had been tested so that the results for each subject were in the same order. For example, the first subject might have received the intervals in the order 12-24-36-48 while the second subject received them in the order 24-36-48-12. The time estimates for each interval for the first subject could be placed directly in Table 9.2. The estimates for the second subject, however, would have to be rearranged so that they would be listed in Table 9.2 in the proper order. In fact, the complete within-subjects design was used for this experiment, so the preparation of the data matrix is a bit more involved.

Each of the four interval lengths was tested six times in the experiment, and block randomization was used to determine the order in which the intervals were presented. Thus, each subject provided twenty-four time estimates, six estimates for each of the four interval lengths. Any one of the six estimates for a given time interval is contaminated by practice effects, so some measure that combines information across the six estimates is needed. Typically, the mean across the six estimates for each interval for each subject would be used to provide a single estimate of performance in each condition. As you may remember, however, the mean is influenced by extreme scores; it is quite possible that subjects gave extreme estimates of the time intervals for at least one of the six tests of each interval. Thus, the median of the six estimates probably provides the best measure to reflect the subjects' estimates of the time intervals. It is these median estimates (rounded to the nearest whole number) that are listed in Table 9.2. For example, the six estimates for the 24-second interval across the six blocks by Subject 3 can be found in Table 9.3. These estimates are: 23, 24, 26, 19, 18, and 23. The median of these six estimates is 23 and that is the value listed in Table 9.2 for Subject 3 for the 24-second interval.

Once the problem of obtaining an individual score to reflect performance by each subject in each condition has been solved, the next step is to summarize

TABLE 9.3 PROCEDURES FOR PREPARING DATA MATRIX FOR DETERMINING THE EFFECT OF THE INDEPENDENT VARIABLE IN THE COMPLETE WITHIN-SUBJECTS DESIGN

	Block 1				Block II				Block III				Block IV				Block V				Block VI			
Trial	1	2	3	4	5	6	7	8	9	10	11	12	13	14	15	16	17	18	19	20	21	22	23	24
Subject	48	36	12	24	24	48	12	36	12	48	24	36	36	48	12	24	24	12	36	48	12	24	48	36
1	33	35	13	20	10	15	8	20	8	23	15	17	12	17	6	8	10	7	15	17	13	22	44	25
2	45	35	10	15	10	25	5	15	5	15	10	15	10	15	5	15	10	10	15	20	10	15	25	40
3	25	32	10	23	24	34	10	30	13	38	26	30	22	31	10	19	18	16	27	34	15	23	40	30
4	35	25	15	15	15	25	10	20	10	25	15	20	15	25	10	15	15	10	25	25	10	15	30	20
5	69	60	15	41	30	40	10	47	10	35	15	30	20	35	10	15	25	10	35	53	17	32	78	51

the results across subjects, using an appropriate descriptive statistic. (From this point on, by the way, the procedures for the analysis of the complete and the incomplete within-subjects designs are identical.) The mean estimates across subjects for each of the four intervals are listed near the bottom of Table 9.2. Even though the data for only five subjects are included in the table, these mean estimates are reasonably accurate reflections of the actual interval lengths, at least for intervals up to 36 seconds. The collective judgments of this small group of undergraduates provide a fair approximation to a stopwatch. The focus of the analysis, however, was on whether the subjects could discriminate intervals of different lengths. As you have probably already realized, we cannot confirm the subjects' ability to discriminate intervals of varying lengths until we know that the mean differences in Table 9.2 are greater than would be expected on the basis of error variation alone.

The null hypothesis for an omnibus analysis of variance for the data in Table 9.2 is that the mean estimates for each interval are the same. To form an F-ratio to test this null hypothesis, we need an estimate of error variation plus systematic variation (the numerator of an F-ratio). The variation among the mean estimates across subjects for the four intervals provides the information we need for the numerator. Even if these five subjects had been tested on only one interval length several times, we would not expect their mean estimates to be identical. Thus, we know the mean estimates we have for each level of the interval variable reflect error variation. We also know, however, that if the different interval lengths *did* systematically affect the subjects' judgments, then the mean estimates for the intervals would reflect this systematic variation. To complete the F-ratio, we also need an estimate of error variation alone (the denominator of the F-ratio). We described earlier how residual variation provides an estimate of error variation alone in the within-subjects designs.

The analysis of variance summary table in Table 9.4 lists the four sources of variation in the analysis of a within-subjects design with one manipulated independent variable. Reading from the bottom of the summary table up, these sources are (1) total variation, (2) residual variation, (3) variation due to interval

TABLE 9.4 ANALYSIS OF VARIANCE SUMMARY TABLE FOR A WITHIN-SUBJECTS DESIGN

Source of Variation	df	SS	MS	F	p
Subjects	4	1553.5	—	—	—
Interval Length	3	2515.6	838.5	15.6	.0004
Residual (error variation)	12	646.9	53.9		
Total	19	4716.0			

length (the independent variable), and (4) subject variation. The values in the summary table were computed using a statistical software package. Our focus now is on interpreting the information in the summary table.

As in any summary table, the most critical pieces of information are the *F*-ratio for the effect of the independent variable of interest and the probability associated with that *F*-ratio under the null hypothesis. The important *F*-ratio in Table 9.4 is the one for interval length. The numerator for this *F*-ratio is the mean square (MS) for interval length; the denominator is the residual MS. There are four interval lengths, so there are 3 degrees of freedom (df) for the numerator. There are 12 df for the residual variation. We can obtain the *df* for the residual variation by subtracting the *df* for subject and for interval length from the total *df* (19 − 4 − 3 = 12). The obtained *F* of 15.6 has a probability under the null hypothesis of .0004, which is less than the .05 level of significance. So we reject the null hypothesis and conclude that the interval length was a source of systematic variation. The subjects' estimates did differ systematically as a function of interval length.

This omnibus analysis of variance would almost certainly be followed by analytical comparisons (such as comparing the mean for each interval to the mean for the succeeding interval) to determine more exactly that mean estimates increased with increasing interval lengths. Once again, the logic of these analytical comparisons corresponds to the logic we discussed earlier in this chapter when we considered analytical comparisons in the random-groups design. In most instances, the residual MS can be used as an estimate of error variation alone in computing the *F*-ratios for the analytical comparisons. (See Keppel [1991], however, for a discussion of the complications that can arise in doing analytical comparisons in within-subjects designs.)

ANALYSIS OF COMPLEX DESIGNS

LOGIC OF ANALYSIS PLAN

The analysis of complex designs builds on the logic used in the analysis of experiments with only one independent variable. The first step in analyzing such single-factor experiments is to perform an omnibus *F*-test to determine whether the independent variable has produced any systematic variation. If the omnibus test is statistically significant, analytical comparisons can be used to pinpoint more precisely the source of the systematic variation.

The tracking of sources of systematic variation applies equally to the analysis of complex designs that involve more than one independent variable. The same basic tool—the analysis of variance—can be used for complex designs. In complex designs with two independent variables, however, there are three potential sources of systematic variation. Each independent variable can produce a main effect, and the two independent variables can combine to produce an interaction effect.

We will use a hypothetical experiment to illustrate an analysis plan for a complex design. The experiment involved a 3 × 3 design with nine groups of subjects. Children of three different ages (4, 5, and 6) were tested under one of three conditions (Alone, With a Parent, and With Another Child). The dependent variable in the experiment was the amount of time the child spent playing with novel (compared with familiar) toys. There were ten children of each age tested under each of the three conditions, so there were ninety subjects in the experiment, ten subjects in each of the nine conditions. Table 9.5 shows the mean times children in each group spent playing with novel toys. An analysis of variance summary table for this complex design is presented in Table 9.6.

Let's look first at the analysis of variance summary table. There are three potential sources of systematic variation in this experiment: the main effect of age, the main effect of condition, and the interaction between age and condition. The summary table indicates the degrees of freedom (*df*) for each of these effects. For the main effects, the degrees of freedom are equal to the number of levels of the independent variable minus one. Since there are three levels for both age and condition, the degrees of freedom for both main effects is 2. The degrees of freedom for the interaction is obtained by multiplying the degrees of freedom for each independent variable entering into the interaction. Thus, there are 4 degrees of freedom for the Age × Condition interaction (2 × 2 = 4). The degrees of freedom for the Mean Square Within Groups (the estimate of error variation for all three effects in the complex design) is obtained by multiplying the degrees of freedom within each group times the number of groups. In our example, there are ten subjects in each group and therefore 9 degrees of freedom within each group. Because there are nine groups in the experiment, there are 81 df within groups. The three *F*-tests entered in the summary table were computed by dividing the mean square (MS) within

TABLE 9.5 TABLE OF MEAN TIMES (IN MINUTES) SPENT PLAYING WITH NOVEL TOYS IN A 3 × 3 DESIGN

	Age			
Condition	4	5	6	Means for main effect of condition
Alone	5	5	10	6.7
With a parent	15	25	35	25.0
With another child	10	15	15	13.3
Means for main effect of age	10.0	15.0	20.0	

TABLE 9.6 ANALYSIS OF VARIANCE SUMMARY TABLE FOR A 3 × 3 DESIGN

Source of variation	df	MS	*F*	*p*
Age (A)	2	35	3.5	.03
Condition (B)	2	92	9.2	.0005
Age × condition (A × B)	4	48	4.8	.002
Error variation within groups	81	10		
Total	89	—		

groups into the mean square for age, for condition, and for the interaction. (The mean squares were computed using procedures for complex designs described in Appendix A.) The probabilities for each of the *F*-tests were determined using the value of *F* and the appropriate degrees of freedom for each effect (2 and 81 for the two main effects and 4 and 81 for the interaction).

The information in the analysis of variance summary table is useful only in conjunction with the means reported in Table 9.5. The statistically significant *F*-test for the interaction indicates that the patterns across age differ for the three conditions. That is, the table of means indicates a larger increase across age in the time spent playing with a novel toy when the child is with a parent than when the child is either alone or with another child. The interaction can be seen clearly in the pattern of nonparallel lines shown in Figure 9.3. The means for the main effects of age and of condition on the outside of the table also appear to differ, and these apparent differences are supported by the statistically significant *F*-test for each main effect.

The three *F*-tests in the summary table represent the counterpart of the omnibus *F*-tests we described when discussing the analysis of experiments with only one independent variable. In a complex design, just as in a single-factor design, follow-up analyses are needed to interpret the initial omnibus tests. The analysis plan for complex designs differs depending upon whether a statistically significant interaction is present. Since there is an interaction in our example, we will continue to use this experiment to illustrate an analysis plan when an interaction is present.

ANALYSIS WITH INTERACTION

When an interaction is present in a complex design, the first step in tracking down the source of the interaction is to test the simple main effects. As we discussed in Chapter 8, a **simple main effect** is the effect of one independent variable at one level of a second independent variable. The first row in Table 9.5 is the basis for computing the simple main effect of age at the Alone level of the condition variable. There are three simple main effects of age (one for Alone, one for With a Parent, and one for With Another Child) and three simple

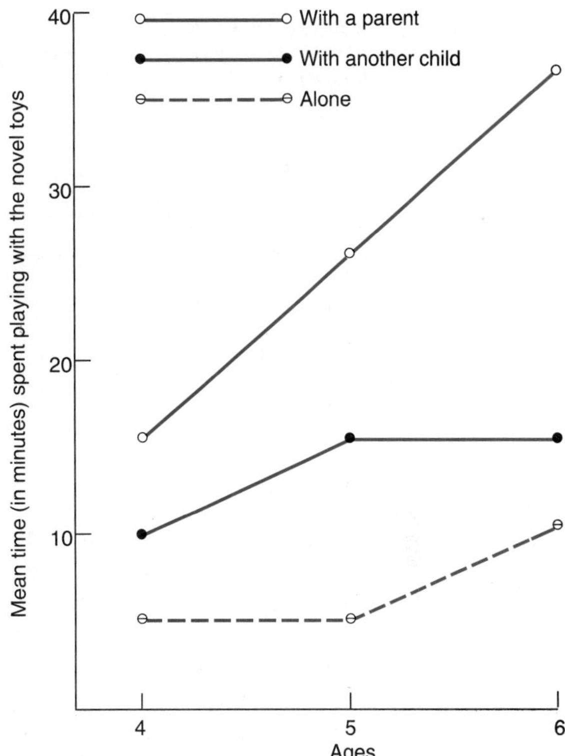

FIGURE 9.3
This graph shows results of complex design involving two independent variables, each with three levels.

main effects of condition (one for age 4, one for 5, and one for 6). To illustrate the use of simple main effects, we will focus on the three simple main effects of age. A separate *F*-test can be computed for each of the simple main effects. When these computations were done, the only simple main effect that was statistically significant was the effect of age when the child was with a parent. The mean differences for the simple main effects for age when a child was alone or with another child were not large enough to be statistically significant.

After identifying which of the simple main effects is statistically significant, it is time to compute simple comparisons. **Simple comparisons** represent a more analytical breakdown of the simple main effect. For example, simple comparisons could be done in our example experiment to determine whether the mean times spent playing with the novel toys were greater for the 5-year-olds than for the 4-year-olds when they were with a parent. Similarly, the 5- and 6-year-olds who were with a parent could be compared using a simple comparison. The analysis of simple main effects using simple comparisons is, as always, guided by the questions the researcher is trying to investigate. The analysis of simple main effects and simple comparisons can be powerful tools in helping us understand the results of a complex design involving an interaction.

When the interaction is significant

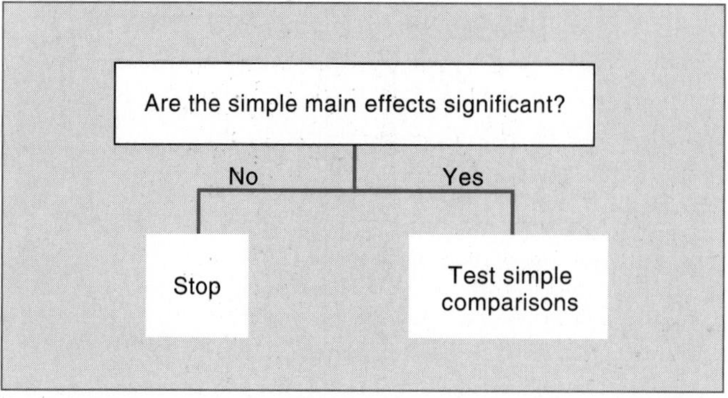

ANALYSIS WITH NO INTERACTION

As we have just seen, the analysis of the interaction is the focus of an analysis plan for a complex design in which an interaction is present. The analysis plan takes a different course when there is no interaction. In the absence of an interaction, a complex design represents two experiments, each testing the effects of one of the independent variables. If there had not been an interaction in our experiment testing children of different ages under three different conditions, then we would have essentially been doing one experiment testing the effect of age and another testing the effect of conditions. The effects of each of these independent variables alone are indicated by the main effects of each variable.

When there is no interaction, the first step in the analysis plan is to determine whether the main effects are statistically significant. If the main effect of either independent variable is statistically significant and if the independent variable

When the interaction is not significant

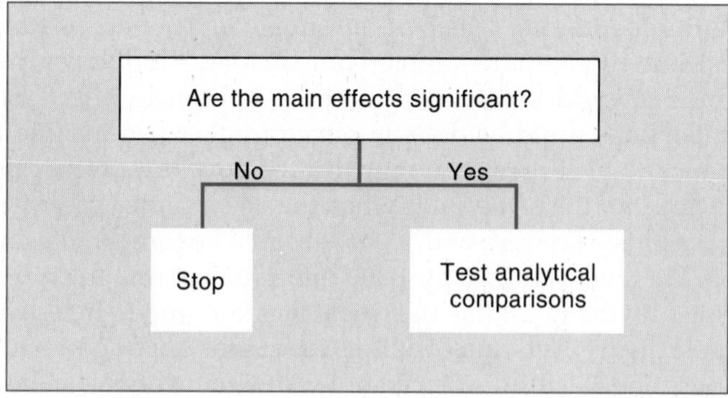

has more than two levels, then the next step in the analysis plan is to perform analytical comparisons. These analytical comparisons are used in the same way for a main effect in a complex design as they are used in the analysis of single-factor experiments. The key to understanding the analysis of complex designs is to remember that the choice of an analysis plan hinges on the presence or absence of an interaction.

POWER AND EXPERIMENTS

Up to this point, we have been considering the role of statistical inference and the use of analysis of variance in the interpretation of the results of different types of experimental designs. Outcomes designated *statistically significant* are those that are considered reliable—likely to occur if the same experiment is repeated. You may even have the impression that statistical significance is related *only* to the issue of the reliability of experiments.

Statistical significance also plays a critical role in another important characteristic of experiments. In planning experiments, researchers must consider the *sensitivity* of the experiment. The **sensitivity** of an experiment is the likelihood that it will detect an effect of the independent variable if the independent variable does, indeed, have an effect. For example, we have noted that within-subjects designs are generally more sensitive than between-subjects designs. An experiment is said to have sensitivity; a statistical test is said to have *power.* The **power** of a statistical test is the probability that the null hypothesis will be rejected when it is false. You may remember our discussion of Type I and Type II errors (see Chapter 6). We defined a Type II error as the probability of failing to reject the null hypothesis when it is false. Power can also be defined as $1-\beta$ (the probability of a Type II error). Cohen (1992) provides a brief introduction to power, and Cohen (1988) provides a more thorough introduction. It is important to be aware before beginning to collect data in an experiment of the factors that affect the power of the statistical test that will be used to analyze the data once they have been collected.

Keppel (1991) provides an excellent description of the factors affecting the power of a statistical test like the analysis of variance. The power of a statistical test is determined by the interplay of three factors: the level of significance, the size of the treatment effect, and the sample size. Keppel goes on to argue, however, that for all practical purposes sample size is the primary factor that researchers can use to control power. He describes how to use power charts to select an appropriate sample size for a given level of power with a certain level of significance and with an expected treatment effect that is either small, medium, or large. (We will describe the nature of small, medium, and large effects when we describe the measurement of effect sizes in the next section.) The differences in sample size that are needed to detect effects of different sizes can be dramatic. Cohen (1988) reports the sample sizes that are needed for an independent-groups design experiment with one independent variable manipulated at three levels. It takes a sample size of 30 to detect a large treatment effect; it takes a sample size of 76 to detect a medium treatment effect; and it takes a sample size of 464 to detect a small treatment effect. It thus takes over fifteen times more subjects to detect a small effect than it does to detect a large effect! We now turn to the procedures used to measure the size of a treatment effect.

MEASURING EFFECT SIZE

One limitation of statistical tests (like the analysis of variance) used to determine statistical significance is that they are sensitive not only to the size of the effect of the independent variable but also to the sample size used in the experiment. For an independent variable that has an effect of a given size, the size of the *F*-ratio will be larger the larger the sample size in the experiment. Because of this positive correlation between the power of a statistical test and the sample size of an experiment, it is not possible to use statistical significance alone as a measure of the size of the effect of an independent variable. What is needed to measure **effect size** is an indicator that reflects the strength of the relationship between the independent and the dependent variables *and* is independent of sample size. There are several measures of effect size that meet these criteria (Keppel, 1991). The computation of effect size goes beyond the scope of this text, but it will be useful for you to have some idea of the nature of measures of effect size.

In general, the measures of effect size in experimental research reflect the differences between the means for the levels of the independent variable relative to the within-group standard deviation. This measure of effect size is called *d*. Cohen (1992) has provided a useful scale of effect sizes with three values—small, medium, and large. Cohen (p. 156) describes the rationale for his scale of effect size (ES) as follows: "My intent was that medium ES represent an effect likely to be visible to the naked eye of a careful observer. (It has since been noted in effect-size surveys that it approximates the average size of observed effects in various fields.) I set small ES to be noticeably smaller than medium but not so small as to be trivial, and I set large ES to be the same distance above medium as small was below it. Although the definitions were made subjectively, with some minor adjustments, these conventions . . . have come into general use." Each of these values on the scale can be expressed in quantitative terms; for example, a medium effect for a two-group experiment is a *d* of .50, while a small and large effect are *d*s of .20 and .80, respectively.

Chow (1988) describes several advantages of using measures of effect size in addition to using tests of statistical significance. Tests of statistical significance give only an indication of the presence or absence of an effect of an independent variable. Measures of effect size provide more information in that they allow a ranking of the results of experiments in terms of the amount of variance accounted for by the independent variable. Measures of effect size are also useful in meta-analysis (see next section of this chapter), which attempts to summarize a series of experiments that have included the same independent variable or dependent variable. The use of measures of effect size allows those doing a meta-analysis to make a quantitative comparison of the outcomes of two or more studies. This comparison is especially important in applied research examining the effectiveness of treatments like an educational innovation or a new approach to psychotherapy. Measures of effect size can also be averaged to provide an estimate of the overall effect size of an independent variable across a series of experiments.

Chow goes on to argue, however, that measures of effect size and tests of statistical significance are complementary. Measures of effect size are more informative in helping researchers determine the substantive importance of experimental outcomes (see Chapter 10 for a discussion of clinical significance). When an experiment is being done to test predictions derived from a theory, however, the size of the effect of an independent variable is less critical. In fact, as tests of a theory become more sophisticated, it is likely that small effects will be more critical. Tests of statistical significance alone are useful when experiments are done to test theories in order to confirm that an effect is present.

META-ANALYSIS: BEYOND A SINGLE EXPERIMENT

Throughout the sections of the text dealing with experimental designs, we have concentrated on the building blocks of experimental research—individual experiments. This concentration has been appropriate. Without individual experiments that are interpretable and that yield reliable results, there would be no foundation on which to build general principles of psychology. If we focused only on individual building blocks, however, we would not be able to see the general structure that was made from the building blocks. We can only discern overall structure by considering the relationships among individual blocks. Similarly, general principles of psychology can be discerned only by looking at the relationships among the results of many individual experiments. As we described in Chapter 1, theories serve the primary function of guiding researchers in organizing the results of individual experiments. In this section we describe a valuable tool, meta-analysis, that can make it easier to summarize the results of experiments investigating the same independent variable or dependent variable.

Meta-analysis is the analysis of the results of several independent experiments. In any experiment, the unit of analysis is the responses of individual subjects. In a meta-analysis, the unit of analysis is the results of individual experiments. These results are summarized using measures of effect size like those described in the previous section. Meta-analyses are used to answer questions like, Are there gender differences in conformity? What are the effects of class size on academic achievement? Is cognitive therapy effective in the treatment of depression? The results of individual experiments, no matter how well done, are not likely to be sufficient to provide answers to questions about such important general issues. We need to consider a body of literature pertaining to each issue.

Prior to the use of meta-analysis, the results of previous research on a particular topic were summarized using some form of narrative review. These reviews were typically published in the *Psychological Bulletin.* The reviewers were often experts in the area of research under investigation. After reading and thinking about the relevant studies, the reviewers would draw conclusions that they thought were supported by the evidence. Meta-analysis is not intended to replace these narrative reviews; instead, it is meant to strengthen the evidence used to reach conclusions. For example, previously reviewers would tally the number of experiments that did or did not show a statistically significant effect of an independent variable. This "voting method" was a crude measure of the effect of the independent variable. Meta-analysis allows for the actual measurement of the mean and standard deviation of the effect sizes for a given independent variable across experiments. This procedure is especially helpful when the area under investigation involves applied questions such as the effectiveness of a certain type of psychotherapy. The use of meta-analysis, however, has also been helpful in reviews of basic research. Using meta-analysis, reviewers have identified overall trends in research areas even though some studies showed statistically significant results and other studies showed results that were not statistically significant.

Meta-analysis involves a sophisticated set of statistical procedures that help summarize the results of many studies. These sophisticated statistical techniques are useful only insofar as the data being analyzed have been gathered in appropriate ways. For example, just which experiments are going to be included in the analysis? Will only experiments reported in journals with high editorial standards be included, or will the analysis include research reports that have not undergone editorial review? In general, the methodological soundness of the experiments included will determine the value of the meta-analysis. Judd et al. (1991) provide a more complete description of the proper procedures for conducting a meta-analysis.

We will conclude this section on meta-analysis by describing an illustration of its use. Greenberg, Bornstein, Greenberg, and Fisher (1992) did a meta-analysis to try to summarize the results of empirical studies on the efficacy of antidepressant medications. In order to try to reduce the effects of bias in clinician's ratings of effectiveness, Greenberg et al. (1992) included only studies in which standard antidepressents were used as a control condition along with a placebo control in tests of the effectiveness of newer antidepressants. Their meta-analysis included twenty-two studies that met their criteria. Overall, the effect sizes in the studies they reviewed were modest and smaller than those obtained in earlier reviews in which the standard antidepressants were the experimental treatment instead of a control comparison condition. This brief description does not do justice to the scope and richness of the meta-analysis done by Greenberg et al. (1992). We hope it gives you some appreciation of how valuable meta-analysis can be in answering important questions faced by researchers and practitioners.

SUMMARY

The analysis of experiments includes the use of a test to determine whether the results of the experiments are statistically significant. The analysis of variance is one test frequently used for this purpose. An *F*-ratio reflects both systematic variation due to the independent variable and error variation. The estimate of error variation is different in the random-groups design and in the within-subjects designs. The structure of the analysis of variance summary table and the interpretation of omnibus *F*-ratios and analytical comparisons are similar for the two designs.

The analysis of complex designs includes the interpretation of interactions, main effects, simple main effects, and simple comparisons. The analysis plan for a complex design varies depending on whether an interaction is obtained. When an interaction is present, simple main effects and simple comparisons can be used to locate the source of the interaction. In the absence of an interaction, the main effects represent two separate experiments, and analytical comparisons can be used to analyze a statistically significant main effect more thoroughly.

The power of a statistical test plays a critical role in influencing whether a statistically significant effect is obtained in an experiment. The level of significance, the size of the treatment effect, and sample size affect the power of a test. The factor affecting power that researchers have most control over is sample size. Measures of effect size complement the information derived from a test of significance. Effect size is especially useful in applied research and in meta-analysis. Meta-analysis provides a quantitative summary of the results of more than one experiment on an important research problem.

KEY CONCEPTS

F-test
omnibus F-test
analytical comparisons
residual variation
simple main effect
simple comparisons
sensitivity
power
effect size
meta-analysis

REVIEW QUESTIONS

1 What are the two sources of variation in the analysis of a random-groups experiment, and what does each of these sources estimate?
2 Why is it critical to refer to the descriptive statistics when interpreting a statistically significant *F*-ratio?

3 Explain what information is added beyond that provided in an omnibus test when analytical comparisons are used in the analysis of an experiment.
4 Explain the different roles played by systematic differences across subjects in the analysis of random-groups designs and within-subjects designs. Include in your explanation the role of this factor in the likely differences in sensitivity of the two types of design.
5 Outline the procedures that are used to determine whether an independent variable has had a statistically significant effect in a within-subjects design experiment.
6 What values are used for the numerator and denominator of the *F*-ratio for the omnibus analysis of a within-subjects design?
7 Outline the steps in the analysis plan for a complex design with two independent variables when there is an interaction and when there is not an interaction.
8 What three factors determine the power of a statistical test? Which factor is the primary one that researchers can use to control power?
9 Describe three advantages of using measures of effect size in addition to using tests of statistical significance.
10 What is the unit of analysis in a meta-analysis?

CHALLENGE QUESTIONS

1 An experiment was done comparing the effectiveness of three methods of instruction for vocabulary acquisition and an uninstructed control condition. The independent groups design was used for the experiment. Thus there were four groups. The three experimental methods were: studying a synonym of the to-be-learned word (Synonym Method), studying a dictionary definition of the to-be-learned word (Definition Method), and studying the to-be-learned word in the context of a literary passage (Passage Method). The researcher expected all three experimental methods to be better than the uninstructed control group (Control Method), but the Passage Method was expected to be the best of all. The test given to all participants was a vocabulary usage test in which the participants had to select one sentence from a set of three for which the vocabulary word was appropriate. The values presented below are the mean numbers correct, out of a possible twenty, on this test for each of the four groups. There were twenty-five participants randomly assigned to each group. The omnibus *F*-test for this experiment was $F(3, 96) = 5.33, p = .01$.

Control	Synonym	Definition	Passage
10.2	13.4	14.2	13.5

A Is the omnibus *F*-test in this analysis statistically significant? Be sure to provide the evidence on which you base your decision.
B Present the null hypothesis to be tested for an analytical comparison to determine whether the average of the three experimental conditions exceeds the performance in the control condition.

2

Subject	UNF	SYL	FREQ	FREQ	SYL	UNF
1	33	15	23	17	17	44
2	45	25	15	15	20	25
3	25	34	38	31	34	40
4	35	25	25	25	25	30
5	69	40	35	25	53	78
6	65	25	15	25	20	35
7	35	25	25	25	35	45
8	45	35	35	45	40	45
9	50	30	27	30	37	42
10	70	55	40	50	50	55

The foregoing table indicates the order in which the three conditions of a complete within-subjects design experiment were administered to each of the ten participants. The experiment was a time perception experiment, and the independent variable was the nature of the activity in which the participant was engaged while the to-be-judged interval passed. Unbeknown to the participant, the interval was always the same length: 48 seconds. Six such intervals were presented, and the data shown represent the judged length of the intervals for each participant. During two of the intervals the participant did nothing [Unfilled (UNF) Intervals]; during two of the intervals the participant classified each word on a list as to the number of syllables in the word [Syllables (SYL) Intervals]; and during two of the intervals the participant classified each word as to its frequency of usage in printed English [Frequency (FREQ) Intervals]. You are to use these data to carry out the following analyses.

A Present the values you would use to describe the overall effect of the Interval Activity variable on the mean judged length of the interval. You are to include a verbal description of the effect along with the descriptive statistics that are the basis for your description.

B Indicate any analytical comparisons you would do to locate the source of the overall effect of the Interval Activity variable. Be sure to explain why you would make each comparison.

C For how many individual participants does the overall pattern of the results hold? Of what value is this type of information?

3 A developmental psychologist was interested in assessing the effects of support given to a spouse on the parenting competence of the mothers and fathers of young children. The psychologist had been able to code the data from a home observation study such that she had reliable and valid measures of spousal support (the extent to which a husband and wife supported each other in parenting) and of parental competence. She classified the parents she had studied into three groups (Low, Moderate, and High Spousal Support). She expected to find that amount of spousal support would have no effect on mothers. For fathers, however, she expected a substantial effect of spousal support with increasing spousal support leading to increasing parental competence. She also expected that mothers would show higher overall parenting competence than fathers. The two independent variables in this complex design were gender of parent (Mother and Father) and Spousal Support (Low, Moderate, High). The dependent variable was parenting competence measured on a 50-point scale. There were 120 subjects, 20 mothers and 20 fathers in each of the spousal support groups. The mean parenting competence scores for each condition are presented below.

	Spousal support		
Gender of Parent	Low	Moderate	High
Mother	40	40	40
Father	15	25	35

A Complete the ANOVA Summary Table below, using only sources of variation and degrees of freedom.

Source of Variation	*df*	
________________	______	$p<.05$
________________	______	$p<.05$
________________	______	$p<.05$
________________		
________________		

B Was there a statistically significant interaction in this experiment? Be sure to state specifically the evidence you used to reach your conclusion.
C Was the pattern of results of this experiment consistent with the pattern predicted by the researcher? Why or why not?
D What means would you use to describe the main effect of the Spousal Support variable?
E Why would you be cautious in interpreting the main effects in this experiment?
F What analysis plan would you follow to complete the analysis of this experiment?

ANSWER TO CHALLENGE QUESTION 1

A The omnibus *F*-test in this analysis, $F\ (3, 96) = 5.33$, is statistically significant. The *p* value of .01 for the obtained *F* is less than the conventional level of significance of .05.
B The null hypothesis for the comparison of the three experimental groups to the control group is:

$$\mu\ \text{control} = \frac{\mu\text{syn} + \mu\text{def} + \mu\text{pass}}{3}$$

Part

IV

Applied Research

Chapter 10

Single-Case Research Designs

Outline

OVERVIEW

What do Sigmund Freud and B. F. Skinner have in common? They are, of course, among the best-known psychologists of the twentieth century. However, having made this point, many may find it difficult to identify significant commonalities between these two psychologists. Freud introduced psychoanalysis. If we were to use the psychoanalyst's technique of free association, the mention of Freud would likely bring to mind concepts such as "unconscious motives," "defense mechanisms," and "Freudian slips." Skinner developed the experimental analysis of behavior. Associations to Skinner's name are likely to include terms like "behaviorism," "reinforcement," and *Walden Two.* Freud and Skinner did share a methodology: They based their research on the study of single subjects. And there the similarity ends!

Thus far in this book, we have emphasized *group methodology*—research designed to examine the average performance of one or more groups of subjects. This was particularly evident in the last few chapters, in which experimental methods were examined. This emphasis on group methodology is warranted given the nomothetic nature of the science of psychology, and it reflects well the activities of researchers in this field. The most common research design in psychological research is one involving many subjects, whose behavior is observed following one or more experimental treatments. A decision about the effectiveness of an independent variable is made when other potential independent variables have been controlled either within or between groups of subjects.

In this chapter you are introduced to an alternative methodology. The distinctive characteristic of this approach is its emphasis on a single subject or, at most, a few subjects (see, for example, Kratochwill & Levin, 1992). The approach is sometimes called "small *n* research." We have chosen the name *single-case research design* to identify this general approach to psychological research. Single-case designs have been used since scientific psychology began in the nineteenth century. Psychophysical methods, which were briefly introduced in Chapter 7, had their origin in the work of Gustav Fechner and were described in his 1860 book, *Elemente der Psychophysik*. Fechner, and countless other psychophysicists since, relied on data obtained through experiments with single subjects. Most students of psychology know that Hermann Ebbinghaus initiated the scientific study of human memory with the publication, in 1885, of his monograph on memory. Ebbinghaus was both subject and experimenter; over a period of many months he learned and then attempted to relearn hundreds of series of nonsense syllables. His data provided psychologists with the first systematic evidence of forgetting as a function of the time since the original learning (see, for example, Zechmeister & Nyberg, 1982). Closer to the present, Linton (1978) examined the retention of everyday events over a 6-year period by testing a single subject, herself.

In this chapter we discuss two specific single-case research methodologies. The first is the case study method. This approach, used by Freud and other psychoanalysts, is often thought of as a methodology used mainly by clinical psychologists, but as you will see, psychologists from other branches of psychology also make use of this important method. Case studies, frequently the source of valuable hypotheses about behavior, can be an important complement to more rigorously controlled approaches to understanding behavior. Both the advantages and the disadvantages of the case study method will be reviewed. The second single-case methodology to be discussed is derived from Skinner's experimental analysis of behavior. Techniques derived from laboratory studies of animal and human behavior have been found effective in managing behavior in numerous applied situations, including schools, the home, hospitals, and businesses. Single-case experimental designs, also frequently called "$N = 1$ experimental designs," are characteristic of the approach called *applied behavior analysis*. The rationale behind this approach will be discussed, and specific illustrations of the more common $N = 1$ experimental designs will be given. $N = 1$ experimental designs represent a special case of the within-subjects design introduced in Chapter 7.

THE CASE STUDY METHOD

CHARACTERISTICS

A **case study** is an intensive description and analysis of a single individual. The "data" for a case study may be obtained from several different sources, including naturalistic observation (Chapter 3), interviews and psychological tests (Chapter 4), and even archival records (Chapter 5). A case study occasionally describes the application and results of a particular "treatment," as, for example, when a new therapeutic technique is used to treat an emotionally disturbed person. However, in the context of a case study, treatment variables are rarely varied systematically in an effort to control extraneous variables, and several different treatments are often applied simultaneously. The case study method can be contrasted with "$N = 1$" approaches, which are based exclusively on experimental methods. Although most closely associated with the field of clinical psychology, the case study method has been used by child psychologists, memory researchers, and animal behaviorists, as well as by researchers in fields such as anthropology, criminology, and sociology.

In actual practice, the form and content of case studies are extremely varied. Published case studies may be only a few printed pages long or may fill a book. Kirsch (1978) described an attempt to implement "self-management training" with a woman experiencing low self-confidence and social inhibition. The case study, describing her treatment during nine therapy sessions and a 5-month follow-up, was presented in just four pages of one issue of the journal *Psychotherapy: Theory, Research and Practice.* In another case study, the personality psychologist Gordon W. Allport described the relationship between a mother and son as revealed in 301 letters that the mother wrote to friends. First reported in two consecutive issues of the *Journal of Abnormal and Social Psychology* (1946, Vol. 41, Nos. 3 and 4), this classic case study was published in 1965 as a 223-page book under the title *Letters from Jenny.*

The cognitive psychologist Ulric Neisser (1981) presented a case study based on John Dean's memory for events and conversations surrounding the Watergate scandal. Dean was President Richard Nixon's legal counsel. In his testimony before the Senate Watergate Investigating Committee, Dean demonstrated an apparent ability to recall literally dozens of episodes that occurred during a several-year period prior to the Watergate investigation. Neisser compared Dean's memory for conversations with tape recordings of the actual conversations that had been secretly recorded in Nixon's Oval Office (published as *The Presidential Transcripts*). Although Dean's testimony was basically accurate, Neisser was able to show that his memory underwent systematic distortion. This 21-page case study appeared in the journal *Cognition.*

Many aspects of the case study method make it a unique means of studying behavior. It differs somewhat from more experimental approaches in terms of its goals, the methods used, and the types of information obtained (see Kazdin, 1980b). For example, the case study method is often characterized as "exploratory" in nature and a source of hypotheses and ideas about behavior (Bolgar, 1965). Experimental approaches, on the other hand, are frequently viewed as opportunities to test specific hypotheses. The case study method has sometimes been viewed as antagonistic to more controlled methods of investigation. A more appropriate perspective is suggested by Kazdin (1980b), who sees the case study method as interrelated with and complementary to other research methods in psychology.

The case study method offers both advantages and disadvantages to the research psychologist (see, for example, Bolgar, 1965; Hersen & Barlow, 1976; Kazdin, 1980b). Before reviewing its advantages and disadvantages, however, let us illustrate the method with a summary of an actual case study reported by Kirsch (1978), which was mentioned earlier. It is important that you read this slightly abbreviated version of a case study carefully because we will make reference to it when discussing the advantages and disadvantages of the methodology.

CAN CLIENTS BE THEIR OWN THERAPISTS? A CASE STUDY ILLUSTRATION

This article reports on the use of Self-Management Training (SMT), a therapeutic strategy which capitalizes on the advantages of brief therapies, while at the same time reducing the danger of leaving too many tasks not fully accomplished. . . . The essence of this approach involves teaching the client how to be his or her own behavior therapist. The client is taught how to assess problems along behavioral dimensions and to develop specific tactics, based on existing treatment techniques, for overcoming problems. As this process occurs, the traditional client-therapist relationship is altered considerably. The client takes on the dual role of client and therapist, while the therapist takes on the role of supervisor.

The Case of Susan

Susan, a 28-year-old married woman, entered therapy complaining that she suffered from a deficient memory, low intelligence, and lack of self-confidence. The presumed deficiencies "caused" her to be inhibited in a number of social situations. She was unable to engage in discussions about films, plays, books, or magazine articles "because" she could not remember them well enough. She often felt that she could not understand what was being said in a conversation and that this was due to her low intelligence. She attempted to hide her lack of comprehension by adopting a passive role in these interactions and was fearful lest she be discovered by being asked for more of a response. She did not trust her own opinions and, indeed, sometimes doubted whether she had any. She felt dependent on others to provide opinions for her to adopt.

Administering a Wechsler Adult Intelligence Scale (WAIS), I found her to have a verbal IQ of about 120, hardly a subnormal score. Her digit span (scale score = 12, raw score = 13) indicated that at least her short-term memory was not deficient. The test confirmed what I had already surmised from talking with her: that there was nothing wrong with her level of intelligence or her memory. After discussing this conclusion, I suggested that we investigate in greater detail what kinds of things she would be able to do if she felt that her memory, intelligence, and level of self-confidence were sufficiently high. In this way, we were able to agree upon a list of behavioral goals, which included such tasks as stating an opinion, asking for clarification, admitting ignorance of certain facts, etc. During therapy sessions, I guided Susan through overt and covert rehearsals of anxiety-arousing situations . . . structured homework assignments which constituted successive approximations of her behavioral goals, and had her keep records of her progress. In addition, we discussed negative statements which she was making to herself and which were not warranted by the available data (e.g., "I'm stupid"). I suggested that whenever she noticed herself making a statement of this sort, she counter it by intentionally saying more appropriate, positive statements to herself (e.g., "I'm not stupid—there is no logical reason to think that I am").

During the fifth session of therapy, Susan reported the successful completion of a presumably difficult homework assignment. Not only had she found it easy to accomplish, but, she reported, it had not aroused any anxiety, even on the first trial. . . . It was at this point that the nature of the therapeutic relationship was altered. During future sessions, Susan rated her progress during the week, determined what the next step should be, and devised her own homework assignments. My role became that of a supervisor of a student therapist, reinforcing her successes and drawing attention to factors which she might be overlooking.

After the ninth therapy session, direct treatment was discontinued. During the following month, I contacted Susan twice by phone. She reported feeling confident in her ability to achieve her goals. In particular, she reported feeling a new sense of control over her life. My own impressions are that she had successfully adopted a behavioral problem-solving method of assessment and had become fairly adept at devising strategies for accomplishing her goals.

Follow-up

Five months after termination of treatment, I contacted Susan and requested information on her progress. She reported that she talked more than she used to in social situations, was feeling more comfortable doing things on her own (i.e., without her husband), and that, in general, she no longer felt that she was stupid. She summarized by saying: "I feel that I'm a whole step or level above where I was."

I also asked her which, if any, of the techniques we had used in therapy she was continuing to use on her own. . . . Finally, she reported that on at least three separate occasions during the five-month period following termination of treatment, she had told another person: "I don't understand that—will you explain it to me?" This was a response which she had previously felt she was not capable of making, as it might expose her "stupidity" to the other person.

Three months after the follow-up interview, I received an unsolicited letter from Susan (I had moved out of state during that time), in which she reminded me that "one of [her] imaginary exercises was walking into a folk dancing class and feeling comfortable; well, it finally worked."*

ADVANTAGES OF THE CASE STUDY METHOD

Sources of Ideas about Behavior The "power" of the case study method, according to Bolgar (1965), "lies in its ability to open the way for discoveries" (p. 30). It acts as a breeding ground for hypotheses that may subsequently be pursued with more rigorous methodologies. This aspect of the case study method was acknowledged by Kirsch (1978) in discussing the successful psychotherapy with the women named Susan (see above). He stated that the "conclusions [of this study] share the limitations of any inferences drawn from case study material. At this point they should be viewed as tentative. It is hoped that the utility of [this technique] will be established by more controlled research" (p. 305). The case study method is a natural starting point for a researcher who is entering an area of study about which relatively little is

* *Source:* Kirsch, I. Teaching clients to be their own therapists: A case-study illustration. *Psychotherapy: Theory, Research, and Practice*, 1978, *15*, 302–305. (Reprinted by permission.)

known. In psychology, the development of psychoanalytic theory stands as a classic example of hypothesis formation based on the case study method.

Opportunity for Clinical Innovation The case study method provides an opportunity to "try out" new therapeutic techniques or to attempt unique applications of existing techniques. In this way it offers an opportunity for clinical innovation. The use of self-management training (SMT) in psychotherapy changes the typical client-therapist relationship. The approach is based on teaching clients to be their own therapists—in other words, to identify problems and design behavioral techniques for dealing with them. The client is both client and therapist, while the therapist acts as supervisor (see above). In a similar vein, Van Nuys (1975) used the case study method to call attention to the wording of hypnotic suggestions in helping a woman stop smoking. Information gained from this case study may provide guidance to other therapists who use hypnosis as a psychotherapeutic technique.

Method to Study Rare Phenomena Certain events appear so infrequently in nature that it is possible to describe them only through the intensive study of single cases. An interesting example is a case study prepared by the Russian psychologist A. R. Luria that describes a man with a nearly perfect memory. This case study was published as a book entitled *The Mind of a Mnemonist* (1968). In it Luria details at length the nature of this man's memory and the effect his prodigious ability to remember had on events in his life and on his personality. The case study material was based on more than 30 years of observation and informal experiments. Luria reported that the subject's use of visual imagery not only helped him to remember but also allowed him to exercise an amazing control over his body. He could increase his heart rate from a resting rate of 70–72 beats a minute to a rate approaching 100 beats per minute simply by imagining that he was running to catch a train!

Challenge to Theoretical Assumptions A theory that all Martians have three heads would quickly collapse if a reliable observer spotted a Martian with only two heads. The case study method can often advance scientific thinking by providing a "counterinstance": a case that violates a general proposition or universally accepted principle (Kazdin, 1980b). Consider the idea that the mind is unitary, that human consciousness is inseparable. This view was challenged when surgeons who were trying to control a patient's epileptic seizures performed an operation that involved severing the corpus callosum, the brain pathway connecting the two cerebral hemispheres. The result was an individual who had, in fact, a "split brain." Normal conscious unity was disrupted, producing, in the words of one researcher, a "patient with two minds" (Gazzaniga, 1972, p. 311). Although he behaved normally, careful testing of the split-brain patient revealed peculiar aspects of his cognitive functioning. It is possible for the right brain (mind?) to know something that the left brain (mind?) does not, and vice versa.

Tentative Support for a Psychological Theory Few researchers would accept the results of a case study as conclusive evidence for a particular hypothesis (see the treatment of disadvantages of the case study method that follows). The results of a case study generally must be viewed as tentative and must await investigation via more carefully controlled procedures before they are accepted by the scientific community. Nevertheless, the outcome of a case study can sometimes provide important evidence in support of a psychological theory. As an illustration, we can take another example from the memory literature.

In 1968 Atkinson and Shiffrin proposed a model of human memory that was to have considerable influence on research in this field. The model, which was based on principles of information processing, described both a short-term memory (STM) system and a long-term memory (LTM) system. Human memory, in other words, should be thought of as containing at least two structures, each with different characteristics and functions. STM was identified with "working memory" and represented the locus of conscious rehearsal and elaboration of information. It was the kind of memory we might use when looking up a telephone number and "holding" it until we had dialed it correctly. Information in LTM did not have to be actively processed in order to be remembered; rather, information in this memory system was stored on a relatively permanent basis, from whence it could be retrieved and brought into conscious memory (into STM).

Although results of numerous experiments provided evidence for this dual nature of our memory, Atkinson and Shiffrin considered the results of several case studies as "perhaps the most convincing demonstrations of a dichotomy in the memory system" (p. 97). These case studies involved patients who had been treated for epilepsy via surgical removal of parts of the brain within the temporal lobes, including a subcortical structure known as the *hippocampus*.

Of particular importance to Atkinson and Shiffrin's theory was the case study of a patient known as H. M. (see Scoville & Milner, 1957). Following the brain operation, H. M. was found to have a disturbing memory deficit. Although he could carry on a normal conversation and remember events for a short period of time, H. M. apparently could not put new information into long-term memory. He could not remember day-to-day events. He was able to read the same magazine over and over again without finding its contents familiar. It looked as though H. M. had an intact short-term memory system but could not get information into a long-term memory system. Subsequent testing of H. M. and patients with similar memory deficits has shown that the nature of this memory problem is more complex than originally suggested (see Zechmeister & Nyberg, 1982), but the case study of H. M. continues to be important whenever theories of human memory are discussed (for example, see Squire, Knowlton, & Musen, 1993).

Complement to the Nomothetic Study of Behavior Psychology is a **nomothetic** discipline. This means that psychology (like science in general) seeks to establish broad generalizations, universal "laws" that will apply to a wide population of organisms. As a consequence, psychological research is often characterized by studies that involve large numbers of subjects and that seek to determine the "average" or typical performance of a group (see especially Chapters 6–9). This average may or may not represent the value of any one individual in the group. Rather, a researcher hopes to be able to predict, on the basis of this mean performance, what organisms will be like "in general."

Some psychologists, notably Allport (1961), argue that a nomothetic approach is inadequate—that the individual is more than what can be represented by the collection of average values on various dimensions. Allport argues that the individual is both unique and *lawful* (operates in accordance with internally consistent principles) and that the study of the individual (**idiographic** research) is an important goal. The need for an idiographic approach can be illustrated by the task confronting the clinical psychologist. As Allport points out, the clinician's goal "is not to predict the aggregate, but to foretell 'what any one man will do.' In reaching this ideal, actuarial predictions may sometimes help, universal and group norms are useful, but they do not go the whole distance" (p. 21). Allport suggests that our approach to understanding human nature should be neither exclusively nomothetic nor exclusively idiographic but should represent an "equilibrium" between the two. At the very least the idiographic approach, as represented by the case study method, permits the kind of detailed observation that has the power to reveal various nuances and subtleties of behavior that a "group" approach may miss.

DISADVANTAGES OF THE CASE STUDY METHOD

Difficulty of Drawing Cause-Effect Conclusions As we saw in Chapter 1, it is a goal of science to discover the causes of phenomena—to reveal in an unambiguous manner the specific factors that produce a particular event. The nature of the case study method is such that cause-effect conclusions can rarely be drawn on the basis of the results that are obtained. The major limitation of the case study method in this regard is its failure to control extraneous variables. Numerous plausible hypotheses are generally present to "explain" behavior change.

Consider, for instance, the treatment of Susan through SMT reported by Kirsch (1978). Although Susan apparently benefited from the SMT therapy, can we be sure that this particular factor accounted for her improvement? Many illnesses and certainly numerous emotional disorders are known to subside spontaneously. That is, over the course of time a certain number of people generally report a decrease in symptoms and an overall improvement. The case study method generally does not permit one to dismiss the hypothesis that improvement would have been observed even if the specific treatment had never been administered. In addition, numerous aspects of the situation may be seen as responsible for Susan's improvement. Her care was in the hands of a "clinical psychologist" who assured her that she should not trust her own feelings and discussed with her the reasons for these feelings. The "insight" provided by a professional therapist may be sufficient to change Susan's attitudes toward herself. The therapist also asked Susan, as part of her therapy, to rehearse anxiety-arousing situations covertly and overtly. This technique is similar to rehearsal desensitization, which may be an effective therapeutic treatment in itself (see Rimm & Masters, 1979).

The fact that several "treatments" were used simultaneously makes it difficult to argue conclusively that the SMT therapy "caused" Susan's improvement. As we have seen, Kirsch himself was sensitive to the limitations of his results and suggested that the inferences drawn from his study should be considered tentative until they were investigated more rigorously.

Sources of Bias in Interpretation The "outcome" of a case study often depends on inferences drawn by a researcher who is both participant and observer (see Bolgar, 1965). A therapist is an observer but is also certainly a participant in the therapeutic process. Problems of observer bias can arise in the context of the case study as they do in other types of observation (see Chapter 3). In the absence of observable measures, the outcome of a case study may be based mainly on the "impressions" of the observer (see Hersen & Barlow, 1976). Kirsch (1978) described the patient Susan's "feelings" about her ability to achieve her goals and told how she reported a "sense of control" over her life. He stated that his "impressions are that she successfully adopted a behavioral problem-solving method of assessment and had become fairly adept at devising strategies for accomplishing her goals" (p. 304). Interpretation of an outcome solely on the basis of the subjective impressions of the observer can be seen as a serious weakness in the case study method.

Possible Biases in Data Collection The material of a case study often includes several kinds of information, some of it obtained from personal documents and psychological tests. Each of these sources of information must be carefully examined for possible biases. Archival records, as we have described in Chapter 5, are open to several sources of bias. Further, when information is based on self-reports, there is always the possibility of distortion or falsification. Such was a possibility (although not necessarily a significant one) in the case of Susan's treatment. We have no way of knowing whether the patient's self-reports of improvement were exaggerated or even false.

Reports of even the most intelligent and well-intentioned individuals are susceptible to biases and reconstructions, especially when memory for remote events is concerned. Consider the following excerpt from a self-analysis by the well-known personality psychologist Alfred Adler (1973, pp. 179–180):

> Shortly after I went to a board[ing] school. I remember that the path to the school led over a cemetery. I was frightened every time and was exceedingly put out at beholding the other children pass the cemetery without paying the least attention to it, while every step I took was accompanied by a feeling of fear and horror. Apart from the extreme discomfort occasioned by this fear I was also annoyed at the idea

of being less courageous than the others. One day I made up my mind to put an end to this fear of death. Again (as on my first resolve), *I decided upon a treatment of hardening* (Proximity of death!). I stayed at some distance behind the others, placed my school-bag on the ground near the wall of the cemetery and ran across it a dozen times, until I felt that I had mastered the fear. After that, I believe, I passed along this path without any fear.

Thirty years after that I met an old schoolmate and we exchanged childhood reminiscences of our school days. It happened to occur to me that the cemetery was no longer in existence and I asked him what had happened to it remembering the great uneasiness it had at one time caused me. Astonished, my former schoolmate who had lived longer in that neighborhood than I had, insisted that *there never had been a cemetery* on the way to our school. Then I realized that the story of the cemetery had been but a poetic dress for my longing to overcome the fear of death.

Problem of Generalizing from a Single Individual As Bolgar (1965) has stated, "Much of the criticism leveled against the case study method of research is based on the accepted canon that it is impossible to generalize from one case" (p. 30). As Kazdin (1980b) notes, however, the ability to generalize from a single case depends on the degree of variability in the population from which the case was selected. Psychologists who study visual perception are often able to make wide generalizations based on the study of one individual. The assumption is that visual systems in humans are very similar and are related to the biological makeup of all humans. When significant variability exists among individuals, as would be the case when measures are made of learning and memory, emotionality, or personality, it becomes impossible to claim that what is observed in one individual will hold for all individuals. Even if we accept the validity of Kirsch's (1978) conclusion regarding the effectiveness of the SMT technique of psychotherapy, we do not know whether this particular treatment would be as successful for other individuals who might differ from the patient Susan in any of numerous ways, including intelligence, age, family background, and gender.

THE CASE STUDY METHOD: FINAL COMMENTS

Kazdin (1980b) points out that case studies sometimes offer "dramatic" demonstrations of "new" or "unusual" findings or provide evidence for "success" of a particular treatment. These reports are often highly persuasive. Everyday examples are found in the media and in advertisements for various products. How many people with receding hairlines can resist the example of a formerly bald man who is shown to have grown an amazing amount of hair in the span of a few weeks! The persuasive value of case study examples are both an asset and a liability to the scientific community. Demonstrations of new or unusual findings based on a case study may lead scientists to rethink their original theoretical assumptions or may lead them into new and fruitful avenues of research. However, the results of case studies are often accepted by nonscientists with little regard for the limitations of such evidence. This is particularly likely when individuals are in a position to identify with the subject of the case study.

A person who suffers from a life-threatening illness may see more than a ray of hope in the results of a dramatic "new cure" based on treatment of an individual with the same illness. If this treatment worked for him, why wouldn't it work for me? For people who have (or think they have) few alternatives, this grasping at straws may not be totally unreasonable. Nevertheless, too often people do not consider (perhaps they do not want to consider) the reasons why a particular treatment would *not* work for them. They fail, in other words, to recognize the limitations of the case study method. This may have unfortunate consequences. For example, during the early 1980s there was considerable controversy surrounding the supposed cancer-curing drug Laetrile (see Sun, 1981). Few respectable scientists or medical researchers considered this drug, which was made from apricot pits, to be beneficial in the treatment of cancer. Positive results, however, based on individual "case studies," were presented as evidence by advocates of the drug. Largely because of public (not scientific) pressure, the government carried out systematic tests of the drug under controlled conditions. No beneficial effect of the drug was found. As others have commented, by using Laetrile instead of traditional therapies, many patients may have postponed or interrupted valid courses of treatment and thus contributed to the spread of their cancer.

A BRIEF INTRODUCTION TO EXPERIMENTAL ANALYSIS OF BEHAVIOR

Behaviorism, or behavior theory, was officially launched in 1913 with the publication of John B. Watson's article "Psychology as the Behaviorist Views It." Watson argued that psychology would be able to take its place among the natural sciences, such as chemistry and biology, only when it abandoned subjective methods of inquiry, such as introspection, and emphasized observable behavior instead. As the behaviorist viewed it, psychology's goal should be the prediction and control of behavior.

A particularly important form of behaviorism that emerged in the 1930s is that associated with B. F. Skinner. Skinner's approach is synonymous with what is called an *experimental analysis of behavior*. It presents a unique behavioral view of human nature that not only contains prescriptions for the way psychologists should do research but also has implications for the way society should be organized. Several of Skinner's books, including *Walden Two* and *Beyond Freedom and Dignity,* describe how the principles of behavior control that have been and will be derived from an experimental analysis of behavior can be put to work improving society. In the experimental analysis of behavior, all behaviors can be classified as one of two types: respondent and operant (Reynolds, 1968). A response that is *elicited* naturally by an environmental event is a **respondent.** It is usually an innate reflex. Examples of respondents are the withdrawal of a hand from a hot stove, salivation in response to dry food placed in the mouth, the startle response made to a loud noise, and constriction of a pupil in response to a bright light. Respondents are clearly adaptive and help to ensure the safety and survival of an organism. That your eyelid closes "automatically" when a puff of air hits the eye serves to protect the eye from damage due to objects carried in the air.

Although it is clearly important, respondent behavior represents only a small part of all human behavior. Most human behaviors are classified as **operants.** These are responses that operate directly on the environment (Skinner, 1937). Operants have no identifiable eliciting stimulus; their "cause" is within the organism (Reynolds, 1968). Consequently, operants are said to be *emitted* by an organism rather than elicited by an environmental stimulus. Behaviors that we normally view as "voluntary" are operants. Walking, talking, sitting, jumping, standing, and hitting are good examples. Research methods employed in the experimental analysis of behavior are those associated with respondent and operant conditioning.

Psychology students are usually introduced to respondent conditioning through the work of the Russian physiologist I. P. Pavlov. He carried out the first systematic experiments using respondent conditioning, which is also known as Pavlovian or (most frequently) classical conditioning. Pavlov showed that an originally "neutral" event, such as the sound of a metronome, will, after being repeatedly presented prior to a dog's receiving food, cause the animal to salivate. Many everyday behaviors are the product of respondent conditioning. Salivation at the thought of biting into a juicy lemon or at the sight of a steak frying on the grill, crying at a sad movie, feeling anxious in front of a group of people—all are likely to have their basis in respondent conditioning.

Operant conditioning is the process by which behavior is modified by its consequences. Changes in behavior are usually measured in terms of frequency of responding, although other measures (such as duration or latency) may be used. Thus, rate of responding is a major dependent variable in operant conditioning. The task of the operant researcher is to relate changes in rate of responding to changes in the environment. Generally, an increase in rate of responding is brought about by a procedure known as *reinforcement.* The giving of "rewards" (such as praise, candy, flowers, ribbons, or high grades) following a response is one way to increase the subject's rate of responding. Decreases in rate of responding are brought about by a procedure known as *punishment.* One way to punish an organism is to follow a response with an aversive (repugnant) event. The laboratory rat that is shocked when it presses a bar will soon stop bar pressing. Another way to use punishment is, following a response, to remove something that an organism would normally want. The parent who takes away the keys to the family car after a teenager gets a traffic ticket and the teacher who denies recess privileges to students who misbehave are using this form of punishment.

In conducting the experimental analysis of behavior, experimenters frequently make observations on single subjects. As we said earlier, it is often the case in the experimental analysis of behavior (unlike the group methodologies discussed in previous chapters) that $N = 1$. Experimental control is demonstrated by arranging experimental conditions such that the individual's behavior changes systematically with the manipulation of an independent variable. As Skinner (1966, p. 21) commented,

> instead of studying a thousand rats for one hour each, or a hundred rats for ten hours each, the investigator is likely to study one rat for a thousand hours. The procedure is not only appropriate to an enterprise which recognizes individuality, it is at least equally efficient in its use of equipment and of the investigator's time and energy. The ultimate test of uniformity or reproducibility is not to be found in the methods used but in the degree of control achieved, a test which the experimental analysis of behavior usually passes easily.

There is a minimum of statistical analysis. Conclusions regarding the effect of an experimental variable are made by visually inspecting the behavioral record in order to observe whether behavior changes systematically with the introduction and withdrawal of the experimental treatment.

APPLIED BEHAVIOR ANALYSIS

HISTORICAL BACKGROUND

Kazdin (1978a), in his *History of Behavior Modification*, points out that it was during the 1950s and early 1960s, about two decades after Skinner's seminal work, that researchers began to extend operant conditioning research to humans. The principles of behavior control based on the experimental analysis of behavior, which had been so successfully explored with nonhuman subjects such as rats and pigeons, began to be applied to human behavior. Numerous studies showed how operant techniques could be successfully employed to shape the behavior of psychotic individuals, normal and mentally impaired children and adults, individuals diagnosed as schizophrenic, stutterers, psychiatric patients, children with learning problems, and many others. At this same time, extensions of operant research were being promoted in education. Skinner (1958) advocated the use of teaching machines. Based on operant principles of immediate and positive reinforcement, these machines permitted students to work at their own pace and to master complex material by progressing in small steps that reduced, if not eliminated, the probability of errors. In 1967, The Society for the Experimental Analysis of Behavior voted to sponsor a journal which would publish studies on applications of behavior modification (see Bailey, 1987). In 1992, the *Journal of Applied Behavior Analysis* marked its 25th anniversary.

One of the most influential developments during this period was the successful design and implementation of **token economies** (Kazdin, 1978a). Tokens are conditioned reinforcers. They achieve their "value" by being paired with a variety of positive reinforcers, such as food, candy, activities, and privileges. The tokens themselves may be plastic discs, paper stars, or even tally marks on a chart. In a token economy, tokens act like money does in our economic system. Behaviors are reinforced by paying out tokens, which can then be used to "purchase" desired reinforcers. A token economy can be (and has been) implemented on entire psychiatric wards in hospitals, in classrooms, and in numerous other settings (see Kazdin, 1982b; Kazdin & Bootzin, 1972, for evaluative reviews).

The application of learning-conditioning principles to clinical populations is called **behavior therapy,** a term that was first used synonymously with the term **behavior modification** (Wilson, 1978). Behavior-therapy approaches grew rapidly in the 1960s. To many, they offered an important alternative to traditional psychodynamic approaches to understanding and treating psychopathology. The psychodynamic perspective is a collection of theories and therapies that have in common a "concern with the dynamics, or interaction, of forces lying deep within the mind" (Bootzin, Acocella, & Alloy, 1993). Behavior, in this view, is often determined unconsciously by inner forces that have been affected by early-childhood experiences. Freud's psychoanalytic theory is particularly representative of this approach. Behavior therapy, with its emphasis on observable behavior rather than hypothesized inner forces, was seen by many as a more effective approach to clinical treatment than that based on the psychodynamic model. For example, by conceptualizing self-stimulatory behaviors, such as prolonged body rocking, gazing at lights, or spinning, that often characterize so-called autistic children, as operant behaviors, clinicians and teachers may be able to control their frequency of occurrence (see Lovaas, Newsom, & Hickman, 1987). In applied behavior analysis, the methods that are developed within an experimental analysis of behavior are applied to socially relevant problems.

SINGLE-CASE (N = 1) EXPERIMENTAL DESIGNS

The use of single subjects, which we have seen is often characteristic of the experimental analysis of behavior, is also a hallmark of an applied behavior analysis. Like its classic cousin, the case study, the **single-case experiment** typically focuses on an examination of behavior change in one individual. This methodology can be extended, however, to treatments applied to single groups of individuals as well (Kazdin, 1980b). Single-case experiments differ from the traditional case study method in that they systematically contrast conditions within an individual whose behavior is being continuously monitored. Consequently, single-case experimental designs are an important alternative to the relatively uncontrolled case study method (Kazdin, 1982a).

For certain kinds of applied research, $N = 1$ experimental designs may be more appropriate than designs based on multiple-group methodology (see Hersen & Barlow, 1976). This is likely to be true when research is directed toward changing the behavior of specific individuals. For example, the average response of a group of subjects will not necessarily be the same as the response of any one individual in the group. Therefore, the outcome of a group experiment may lead to recommendations about what treatments "in general" should be applied to modify behavior, but it is not possible to say what the effect of that treatment will be on any particular individual. As Kazdin (1982a) commented, "Perhaps the most obvious advantage [of single-case experimental designs] is that the methodology allows investigation of the individual client and experimental evaluation of treatment for the client" (p. 482).

Another disadvantage of multiple-group methodology, particularly in the context of clinical research, is that ethical problems arise when a potentially beneficial treatment is withheld from subjects in order to provide a control group that satisfies the requirements of internal validity. Because single-case experimental designs contrast conditions of No Treatment and Treatment within the same individual, this problem can be avoided. Moreover, investigators doing clinical research often find it difficult to gain access to enough clients to do a group experiment. For instance, a clinician may be able to identify from a list of clients only a few individuals experiencing claustrophobia (excessive fear of enclosed spaces). The single-case experiment provides a practical solution to the problem of investigating cause-effect conclusions when only a few subjects are available.

The first stage of a single-case experiment is usually an observation stage, or **baseline stage.** During this stage a record is made of the individual's behavior prior to any intervention. A typical measure is frequency of behavior per some unit of time, such as a day, an hour, or another recording interval. An applied researcher might record the number of times during a 10-minute interview that an excessively shy child makes eye contact, the number of headaches reported each week by a depressed migraine sufferer, or the number of verbal pauses per minute made by a chronic stutterer. The baseline record provides information about what behavior would be like if treatment were not provided (Kazdin, 1978b).

Once behavior is shown to be relatively stable—that is, it exhibits little fluctuation between recording intervals—an intervention is introduced. Behavior immediately following an intervention is contrasted with that seen during baseline performance. The effect of a behavioral intervention is typically evaluated by visual inspection of the behavioral record. How did behavior change, in other words, following the experimental treatment? Traditionally, tests of statistical significance have not been used, although there is some controversy surrounding this aspect of single-case methodology (Kratochwill & Brody, 1978). Later in this chapter we will discuss some of the problems that arise when visual inspection is used to determine whether a treatment was effective.

Another approach to treatment evaluation is to assess the **clinical significance** of an experimental result. Information, for instance, about the strength of a treatment—how likely it is to improve the life of a client in a real-world setting—is often more important for the applied researcher than a treatment's statistical significance or even its "obvious" effect on behavior as contrasted with baseline performance (Yeaton & Sechrest, 1981). Two methods for determining clinical significance of a treatment are social comparison and subjective evaluation (Kazdin, 1977; 1982a). In a **social comparison** approach to clinical significance, the researcher compares the behavior of a client after treatment with the behavior of a "normal" group of subjects. For example, following treatment aimed at reducing the aggressive behavior of a child in a classroom, a researcher may compare the treated child's behavior with that of children who are not normally aggressive. A **subjective evaluation** approach uses the judgments of people who have contact with the client to help decide whether a treatment has been effective. Family members, teachers, friends, and staff members in a hospital might be asked, for example, whether the behavior of the individual after treatment is perceptibly different from the behavior before treatment.

Although there are numerous design possibilities for the researcher who uses a single-case experimental design (Hersen & Barlow, 1976; Kazdin, 1980a), the most commonly employed are the ABAB and multiple-baseline designs (Kazdin, 1978b).

SPECIFIC EXPERIMENTAL DESIGNS

The ABAB Design The **ABAB design** seeks to confirm a treatment effect by demonstrating that behavior changes systematically with alternating conditions of No Treatment and Treatment. An initial baseline stage (A) is followed by a treatment stage (B), next by a return to baseline (A), and then by another treatment stage (B). Because treatment is removed during the second A stage, and any improvement in behavior is likely to be reversed at this point, this design is also called a *reversal design*. The researcher using the ABAB design observes whether behavior changes immediately upon introduction of a treatment variable (first B), whether behavior reverses when treatment is withdrawn (second A), and whether behavior improves again when treatment is reintroduced (second B). When variations in behavior follow the introduction and withdrawal of treatment in this way, there is considerable evidence supporting the conclusion that the treatment caused behavior change.

Horton (1987) used an ABAB design to assess the effects of facial screening on the maladaptive behavior of a severely mentally impaired 8-year-old girl. Facial screening is a mildly aversive technique involving the application of a face cover (for example, a soft cloth) contingent on the appearance of the undesirable behavior. Previous research had shown this technique to be effective in reducing the frequency of self-injurious behaviors such as face slapping. Horton sought to determine whether it would reduce the frequency of spoon banging by his young subject at mealtime. The spoon banging prevented the girl from dining with her classmates at the school for exceptional children which she attended. The banging was disruptive not only because of the noise but because it often led her to fling food on the floor or resulted in her dropping the spoon on the floor.

A clear definition of spoon banging was made to distinguish it from normal scooping motions. Then, a paraprofessional was trained to make observations and to administer the treatment. A frequency count was used to assess the magnitude of spoon banging within each 15-minute eating session. During the initial, or baseline, period the paraprofessional recorded frequency and, with each occurrence of the response, said "no bang," gently grasped the subject's wrist, and returned her hand to her dish. The procedure was videotaped, and an independent observer viewed the films and recorded frequency as a reliability check. Interobserver reliability was approximately 96 percent. The baseline was conducted for 16 days.

The first treatment period began on Day 17 and lasted for 16 days. Each time spoon banging was observed, the paraprofessional continued to give the corrective feedback of "no bang" and returned the girl's hand to her dish. However, the paraprofessional also pulled a terry-cloth bib over the subject's entire face for 5 seconds. Release from facial screening was contingent on the subject's not banging for 5 seconds. The first treatment phase was followed by a second baseline period and another treatment phase. Posttreatment observations were also made at 6, 10, 15, and 19 months.

Figure 10.1 shows changes in the frequency of the mentally impaired girl's spoon-banging behavior as a function of alternating baseline and treatment phases. Facial screening was not only effective in reducing this behavior during treatment phases; follow-up observations revealed that the target behavior was still absent months later. Following the final treatment phase, the girl no longer required direct supervision during mealtime at either school or home and was permitted to eat with her peers. The facial-screening technique was a successful procedure for controlling the maladaptive behavior of the young child when other, less intrusive procedures had failed. Because only one treatment was administered, and because visual inspection revealed that behavior changed systematically with the introduction and withdrawal of treatment, it can be

FIGURE 10.1 Frequency of spoon-banging responses across baseline, treatment, and follow-up phases of study. (Adapted from Horton, 1987).

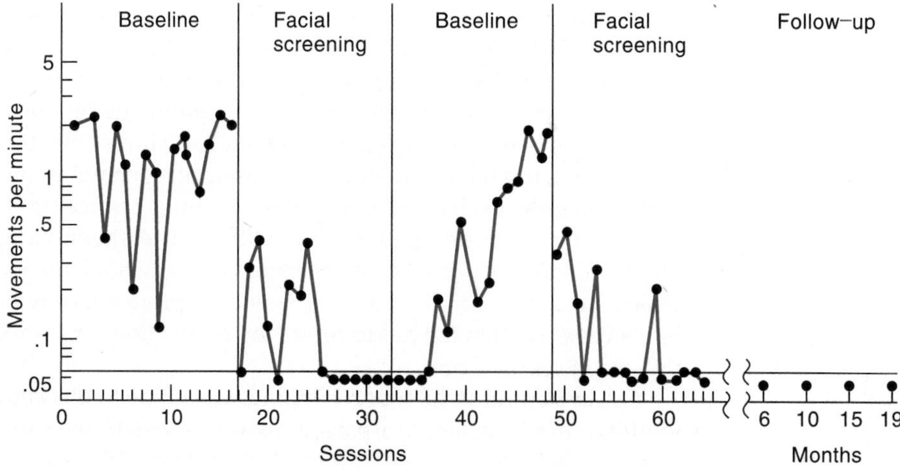

concluded that application of an aversive stimulus was responsible for eliminating spoon banging.

A major methodological problem that sometimes arises in the context of an ABAB procedure can be illustrated by looking again at the results of the Horton (1987) study shown in Figure 10.1. In the second baseline stage, when application of the facial screening was withdrawn, spoon banging increased in frequency. That is, the improvement observed under the preceding treatment stage was reversed. What if behavior was not found to change when the treatment was withdrawn? What can be concluded? Behavior in a second baseline stage may not revert to what it was during the initial baseline period, and when that occurs it raises serious problems of interpretation.

One reason why improvement in behavior may not reverse is that the behavior that is the focus of treatment would not logically be expected to become worse once improvement was observed. This might be the case if treatment involved training an individual in a new skill. Once the skill is acquired, it cannot reasonably be expected to be unlearned. The solution to this problem is one of foresight. That is, the ABAB design should not be used when the target behavior could not logically be expected to show reversal when treatment is withdrawn.

Given that the experienced researcher is likely to avoid using an ABAB design in situations wherein behavior would not be expected to reverse, the failure to observe a reversal of performance is probably due to one of two factors. One possibility is that a variable other than the treatment variable was responsible for the improvement in behavior in the first shift from baseline to treatment stages. For example, the subject may receive increased attention from staff or friends during treatment. This increased attention—rather than the treatment—may produce an improvement in behavior. If the attention persists even though the specific treatment is withdrawn, the behavior change is likely to persist as well. It is also possible that, although the treatment caused behavior to improve, other variables "took over" to control the new behavior. Again, we might consider attention as a variable having an effect on behavior. When family and friends witness a change in behavior, they may pay increased attention to the subject. Positive reinforcement in the form of attention may maintain the behavior change that was initiated by the treatment.

In either case, when improvement in behavior does not reverse, it is not clear whether the experimental treatment or some other factor led to the initial behavior change (Kazdin, 1980a). The solution to this set of circumstances is to examine the situation carefully in hopes of finding variables that might be confounding the treatment variable or to replicate the procedure with the same subject or with different subjects (Hersen & Barlow, 1976).

From an applied researcher's point of view, in some situations there is also an ethical problem in using the ABAB design. As you might imagine, the withdrawal of a beneficial treatment may not be justified in all cases. For example, although spoon-banging behavior would not be considered life-threatening or exceptionally debilitating, other kinds of behavior might be, and it would not be ethical in these cases to remove or even suspend treatment once a positive effect was observed. Some autistic children exhibit self-injurious behaviors such as head banging or face slapping. If a clinical researcher succeeded in reducing the frequency of such behavior, it might be considered unethical to withdraw treatment to meet the requirements of an experimental design. Fortunately, there are other single-case experimental designs that do not involve withdrawal of treatment and that may be appropriate in such situations.

The Multiple-Baseline Design The **multiple-baseline design** demonstrates the effect of a treatment by showing that behaviors in more than one baseline change as a consequence of the introduction of a treatment. There are several variations on the multiple-baseline design, depending on whether multiple baselines are established for different individuals, for different behaviors in the same individual, or for the same individual in different situations. In each case, the conclusion that an experimental variable produced a reliable effect rests on the demonstration that behavior changed only when the experimental variable was introduced. Although they sound complex, multiple-baseline designs are frequently used and easily understood. Let us refer to a specific example of each type from the applied research literature.

A *multiple-baseline design across subjects* is a procedure wherein more than one individual is observed simultaneously. Specifically, baselines are first established for different individuals. When the behavior of each individual has stabilized, an intervention is introduced for one individual, then for another individual, later for another, and so on. That is, the experimental treatment is introduced at a different time for each subject. If the treatment is responsible for changing behavior, then an effect in the behavioral record will be seen immediately following the application of the treatment in each individual.

An interesting example of the use of a multiple-baseline design across subjects is from a study by Allison and Ayllon (1980). Their study also illustrates how an applied-behavior analysis can be employed in the area of sports psychology. This field involves the application of psychological principles to the improvement of recreation and sports (see, for example, Browne & Mahoney, 1984). Specifically, Allison and Ayllon investigated the effect that a coaching method based on several behavioral techniques had on the acquisition of specific football, tennis, and gymnastic skills. To evaluate this new coaching method, they used a multiple-baseline design. Although their investigation was successful in each sport, we will examine the effects of behavioral coaching only as it was applied to the acquisition of a football skill.

The subjects in this experiment were second-string members of a citywide football program chosen because they "completely lacked fundamental football skills" (Allison & Ayllon, 1980, p. 299). The skill to be acquired was blocking, which was defined operationally in terms of eight elements, ranging from the body's first being behind the line of scrimmage to maintaining body contact until the whistle was blown. Behavioral coaching involved specific procedures implemented by the team coach. The procedures included systematic verbal feedback, positive and negative reinforcement, and several other behavioral techniques. The experimenter first established baselines for several different members of the football team under "standard coaching" conditions. In this procedure, the coach used verbal instructions, provided occasional modeling or verbal approval, and, when execution was incorrect, "loudly informed the player and, at times, commented on the player's stupidity, lack of courage, awareness, or even worse" (p. 300). In short, an all-too-typical example of negative coaching behavior.

The experimenter and a second, reliability observer made observations of the frequency of correct blocks made in sets of ten trials. Behavioral coaching was begun, in accordance with the multiple-baseline design, at different times for various football players. Results of this intervention are shown in Figure 10.2. Across four individuals, behavioral coaching was shown to be effective in increasing the frequency of correctly executed blocks. Observer agreement

FIGURE 10.2 Multiple baselines showing percentage of football blocks executed correctly by four players as a function of standard coaching and behavioral coaching. (From Allison & Ayllon, 1980).

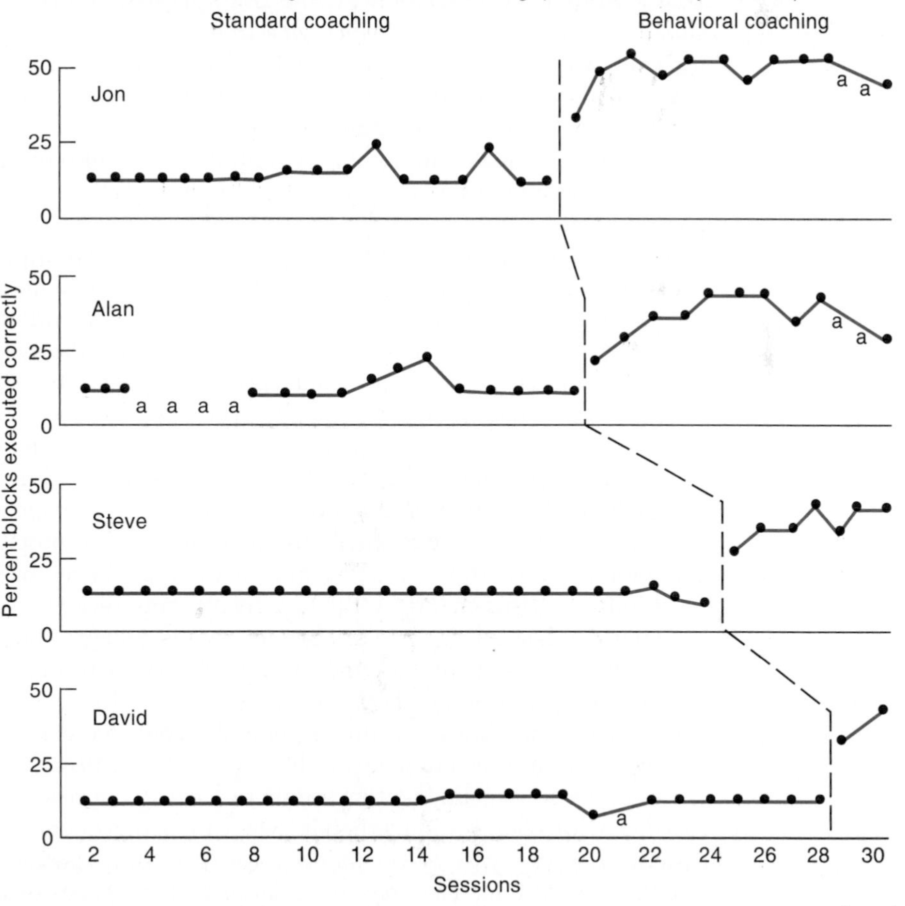

on blocking performance ranged from 84 to 94 percent, indicating that the observation of behavior change was reliable. The skill execution changed for each player at the point where behavioral coaching was introduced. Thus it can be argued that this method caused the change in each player's performance.

When two or more baselines are established by observing different behaviors in the same individual, the design is called a *multiple-baseline design across behaviors.* A treatment is directed first at one behavior, then at another, and so on. A causal relationship between treatment and behavior is assumed if each behavior responds directly to treatment. For example, Bornstein, Bellack, and Hersen (1977) successfully treated an 8-year-old elementary-school girl who was judged to be excessively shy, unassertive, and passive. Multiple baselines were established for behaviors of eye contact, number of requests, and loudness of speech. Intervention consisted of prompting, feedback, and modeling of behaviors and was instituted at different times across behaviors. An inspection of the behavioral record showed that the different behaviors changed immediately after introduction of the new intervention.

The third major variation on the multiple-baseline design is that across situations. In a *multiple-baseline design across situations,* baselines are established for a behavior in different situations. For example, a researcher might establish baselines showing frequency of a target behavior in the clinic and frequency of this same behavior in the home. As with other variations of this design, the treatment is applied at different times and the behavioral records are examined to determine whether behavior changes systematically with the introduction of treatment.

VanBiervliet, Spangler, and Marshall (1981) used a multiple-baseline design across situations to demonstrate how changes in the way meals are served can influence the frequency of mealtime language of institutionalized mentally impaired persons. The investigators suggested that the typical institutional method of serving meals does not encourage peer interaction and that an alternative procedure, serving "family style," would increase verbal interactions. Baselines for frequency of verbalizations of five residents were made for three different situations (actually, three meals)—dinner, lunch, and breakfast. An analysis of behavior change both in terms of the average number of vocalizations made by the five residents and in terms of an examination of individual behavioral records showed that frequency of verbal behavior increased at each meal following this change in the way meals were served.

Often the first question to arise when one is doing a multiple-baseline experiment is "How many baselines do I need?" As with many other aspects of single-case methodology, there are no hard-and-fast rules. The bare minimum is clearly two baselines, but this is generally considered inadequate. Three to four baselines are recommended (Hersen & Barlow, 1976).

Because a convincing demonstration of a treatment rests on the observation that behavior changes immediately when the experimental variable is introduced, problems arise when changes are seen in a baseline *before* an experimental intervention. This may occur in any of the types of multiple-baseline designs we have considered, and the reasons are not always clear. When changes in baseline performance occur prior to an experimental intervention, it is often difficult to draw a conclusion about the efficacy of the experimental treatment. However, the multiple-baseline design can still be interpreted with some confidence when preintervention changes appear in only one of several baselines that are being recorded—so long as plausible explanations for the baseline change, explanations based on procedural or situational variables, are available. For instance, Kazdin and Erickson (1975) used a multiple-baseline design across subjects to develop responsiveness to instructions in severely mentally impaired individuals. Subjects who followed instructions were reinforced with candy-coated cereal and praise, and this intervention was introduced in each of four small groups at different points in time. Performance changed directly with the application of the positive reinforcement procedure in three groups, but not in the fourth. In this group, which had the longest baseline, behavior gradually improved prior to the intervention. The researchers reasonably suggested that this occurred because subjects in this group saw other patients comply with instructions and then imitated the treated subjects' behavior.

Another problem sometimes seen in the context of a multiple-baseline design occurs when changes in one behavior generalize to other behaviors or situations. For example, when VanBiervliet et al. (1981) successfully increased the degree of verbal interaction of mentally impaired persons at a dinner meal, we might not have been totally surprised if the residents increased their amount of talking at other meals. Once behavior at dinner was changed, at other meals the sight of food being served or the act of sitting down beside an acquaintance might prompt an increased level of verbal interaction. Such generalization effects were not seen, however, so the effect of the mealtime variable was clearly demonstrated.

To circumvent possible problems, we must again bring foresight to bear. If altering the behavior of one individual is likely to affect the behaviors of others, if behavior in one situation is likely to influence behavior in another situation, or if changing one type of behavior is likely to affect other behaviors, then multiple-baseline designs should not be used (Kazdin, 1980a). As we have noted, unless behavior improves directly following an experimental intervention, concluding that the treatment variable was effective is problematic. Unfortunately, anticipating when changes will occur simultaneously in more than one baseline is not always easy, but these problems appear to be relatively infrequent exceptions to the effects usually seen in a multiple-baseline design (Kazdin, 1980a).

PROBLEMS AND LIMITATIONS COMMON TO ALL SINGLE-CASE DESIGNS

Increasing or decreasing baseline trends, or excessive variability, in behavioral records can make it difficult to evaluate the effects of an intervention. An ideal baseline record and response to an intervention are shown in panel A of Figure

10.3. Behavior during baseline is very stable, and behavior changes immediately following the introduction of treatment. If this were the outcome of the first stages of either an ABAB or a multiple-baseline design, we would be headed in the direction of showing that our treatment is effective in modifying behavior. However, consider the baseline and treatment stages shown in panel B of Figure 10.3. The baseline shows extreme variability, and, although behavior appears to increase in frequency following an intervention, it is difficult to know whether the treatment produced the change or behavior just happened to be on the upswing. In this case it would be hard to decide whether our intervention successfully changed behavior.

There are several approaches to the problem of excessive baseline variability. One approach is to look for variables in the situation that might be producing the variability and that we might be able to remove. The presence of a particular staff member, for instance, might be causing changes in the behavior of a psychiatric patient. Another approach is to "wait it out"—to continue taking baseline measures until behavior stabilizes. It is, of course, not possible to predict *when* and *if* this might occur, but introducing an intervention before behavior has stabilized would jeopardize a clear interpretation of the experimental outcome. Another approach is to average data points. By charting a behavioral record using averages of several points, we can sometimes reduce the "appearance" of variability (Kazdin, 1978b).

Another problem arises when the baseline record shows an increasing or a decreasing trend. In panel C of Figure 10.3, we see how behavior might change following an intervention when the initial baseline stage was characterized by

FIGURE 10.3 Examples of behavioral records showing possible relationships between baseline and intervention phases of a behavior modification program.

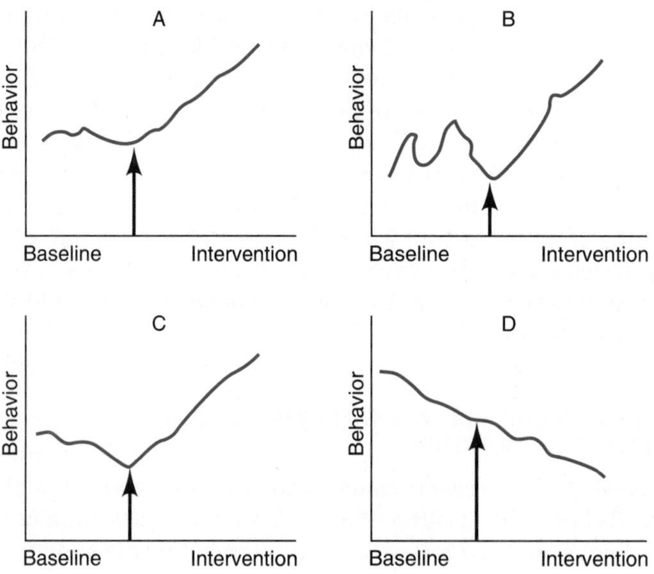

a reduction in frequency of behavior. If the goal of the intervention was to increase frequency of behavior, the change described in panel C offers little problem of interpretation. An intervention that reversed the decreasing trend can be taken as evidence that the treatment was effective. However, should the goal of intervention be to *reduce* frequency of behavior, it would be difficult to know whether the decrease in frequency of behavior following the intervention is due to the intervention or to continuation of a trend. This situation is illustrated in panel D. Here we see a decreasing trend in the baseline stage and continued reduction of frequency in the treatment stage. It is difficult in this case to know whether the experimental treatment had an effect. Generally speaking, when an intervention is expected to have an effect in the same direction as a baseline trend, the effect must be very marked in order to conclude that behavior was modified by the application of a treatment (Kazdin, 1978b). Moreover, because a treatment effect in a single-case design is usually judged by visually inspecting the behavioral record, in cases where baseline trends are evident it is often difficult to say what a "marked" change in the behavioral record is (see, for example, Parsonson & Baer, 1992). In such cases other means of evaluation, such as social comparison or subjective evaluation, should be employed.

When an effect is demonstrated using an $N = 1$ design, a frequent criticism is that external validity is limited. In other words, the $N = 1$ experiment appears to have the same limitation as the traditional case study method. Because each person is unique, it can be argued that there is no way of knowing whether the effect of a particular intervention will generalize to other individuals. There are several reasons why this problem may not be as serious as it seems. First, the types of intervention used in single-case studies often produce dramatic and sizable changes in behavior (Kazdin, 1978b). Consequently, these types of treatments are often found to generalize to other individuals. Other evidence for the generality of effects based on single-case studies comes from the use of multiple-baseline designs. A multiple-baseline design across subjects, for example, is often able to show that a particular intervention was successful in modifying the behavior of *several* individuals. Similarly, multiple baselines across situations and behaviors attest to the external validity of a treatment effect.

A treatment effect can also be shown to generalize to other individuals when a "single group" of subjects is used in a single-case experiment. As was mentioned before, the procedures associated with single-case designs are sometimes used with small groups of individuals as well. We have already seen two examples of this. VanBiervliet et al. (1981) showed that changes in a mealtime procedure were effective in increasing the average frequency of verbalizations of five mentally impaired individuals who were treated simultaneously. Similarly, Kazdin and Erickson (1975) found that positive reinforcement improved responsiveness to instructions in small groups of mentally impaired individuals. In both these experiments, the researchers were able to demonstrate that an experimental treatment was effective for a small group of subjects as well as for individuals in the group. In other words, an effect was replicated several times across members of a group each time an experimental manipulation was introduced. Such studies offer impressive evidence for both internal and external validity.

One limitation of the $N = 1$ methodology is not easily dismissed, and it illustrates again the lesson that no one research methodology is able to provide all the answers to questions that psychologists ask. The $N = 1$ experiment is usually not appropriate for examining the effect of interactions among variables. Although a single-case design can provide evidence of the effect of one variable (a main effect) by showing, for example, that behavior changes between conditions of No Treatment and Treatment, it is difficult to examine adequately the differential effect of *combinations* of various levels of experimental variables. It was pointed out in Chapter 8 that, when a subject variable is investigated, any "effect" of that variable must be considered essentially the same as correlational evidence. Therefore, when subject variables are of concern, it is best to do a factorial design that combines levels of the subject variable and levels of a manipulated variable. The subject variable and the manipulated variable may work together to produce an interaction. This interaction effect may offer crucial information about what characteristics of the subject are important in producing an effect of the treatment variable on the dependent variable. Or it may demonstrate under what conditions a difference between levels of the subject variable will be found. Questions about interactions between treatment variables and subject variables are not easily answered using single-group methodology (Kazdin, 1982a). In this situation, a between-groups design is most appropriate. The experienced research psychologist realizes that there are problems and limitations associated with most methodologies. The methodology best suited to answering a particular question should be used. And, as we have stated previously, when possible, multimethod approaches to data collection are recommended.

SUMMARY

Two important single-case research designs are the case study and the single-case experiment, or $N = 1$ design. The case study method can be an important source of hypotheses about behavior, can provide an opportunity for clinical innovation (for example, trying out new approaches to therapy), can permit the intensive study of rare phenomena, can challenge theoretical assumptions, and can provide tentative support for a psychological theory. The intensive study of individuals that is the hallmark of the case study method is called idiographic research, and it can be viewed as complementary to the nomothetic inquiry (seeking general laws or principles) that is also characteristic of psychology. Problems arise when the case study method is used to draw cause-effect conclusions, or when biases of interpretation or in the collection of data are not identified. The case study method also suffers from a lack of generalizability. How do we generalize on the basis of studying a single individual? Moreover, the "dramatic" results obtained from some case studies, though they may give scientific investigators important insights, are frequently accepted as valid by nonscientists who are not aware of the limitations of this method.

Behaviorism is an approach to the study of psychology that emphasizes the study of observable behavior under strictly controlled conditions. The behaviorism of B. F. Skinner is called the experimental analysis of behavior. Research methods associated with this approach are those of respondent and operant conditioning. Applied behavior analysis seeks to apply principles derived from an experimental analysis of behavior to socially relevant problems. The major methodology of this approach is the single-case experiment, or $N = 1$ design. Although there are many kinds of $N = 1$ designs, the most common are the ABAB design and the multiple-baseline design. An important consideration in applied behavior analysis is obtaining evidence for the clinical significance of a treatment—that is, how likely a treatment is to modify the behavior of a client in a real-world setting.

An ABAB design, or reversal design, allows a researcher to confirm a treatment effect by showing that behavior changes systematically with conditions of No Treatment (baseline) and Treatment. Methodological problems arise in this design when behavior that changed during the first treatment (B) stage does not reverse when treatment is withdrawn during the second baseline (A) stage. When this occurs, it is difficult to establish that the treatment variable, rather than some other variable, was responsible for the initial change. One may encounter ethical problems when using the ABAB design if a treatment that has been shown to be beneficial is withdrawn during the second baseline stage.

A multiple-baseline design demonstrates the effectiveness of a treatment by showing that behaviors across more than one baseline change as a consequence of the introduction of a treatment. Baselines are first established across different subjects, across behaviors in the same subject, or across situations. Methodological problems arise when behavior does not change immediately with the introduction of a treatment or when a treatment effect generalizes to other subjects, other behaviors, or other situations.

Problems of increasing or decreasing baselines, as well as excessive baseline variability, sometimes make it difficult to interpret the outcome of single-case designs. The problem of excessive baseline variability can be approached by seeking out and removing sources of variability, by extending the time during which baseline observations are made, or by averaging data points to remove the "appearance" of variability. Increasing or decreasing baselines may require the researcher to obtain other kinds of evidence for the effectiveness of a treatment—for example, measures of social comparison or subjective evaluation. Finally, the $N = 1$ design is often criticized for its lack of external validity. However, because treatments typically produce substantial changes in behavior, these changes can often be easily replicated in different individuals. The use of "single groups" of subjects can also provide immediate evidence of generality across subjects. The fact that the $N = 1$ design usually is not appropriate for testing the possible interactions of variables emphasizes the importance of selecting the research methodology that is most relevant to answering the particular question under investigation.

KEY CONCEPTS

case study
nomothetic approach
idiographic approach
behaviorism
respondent
operants
token economies
behavior therapy
behavior modification
single-case experiment
baseline stage
clinical significance
social comparison
subjective evaluation
ABAB design (reversal design)
multiple-baseline design (across subjects, across behaviors, across situations)

REVIEW QUESTIONS

1 Cite and give an example of the advantages of the case study method.
2 Distinguish between a nomothetic and an idiographic approach to research.
3 Cite and give an example of the disadvantages of the case study method.
4 What is the major limitation of the case study method in drawing cause-effect conclusions?
5 Under what conditions might an $N = 1$ design be more appropriate than a multiple-group design?
6 Distinguish between baseline and intervention stages of an $N = 1$ experimental design.
7 How does clinical significance differ from statistical significance? Explain how clinical significance can be evaluated.
8 Why is an ABAB design also called a *reversal design*?
9 What major methodological problems are specifically associated with an ABAB design?
10 Outline the general rationale behind all the major forms of multiple-baseline designs.
11 What major methodogical problems are specifically associated with multiple-baseline designs?
12 What major methodological problems are inherent in all $N = 1$ experimental designs?
13 What answers are given to the frequent criticism that $N = 1$ experimental designs lack external validity?
14 What types of research questions are not easily answered using single-case ($N = 1$) experimental designs?

CHALLENGE QUESTIONS

1 A case study showing how "mud therapy" was successful in treating an individual exhibiting excessive anxiety was reported in a popular magazine. The patient's symp-

toms included having trouble sleeping, loss of appetite, extreme nervousness when in groups of people, and general feelings of arousal that led the individual always to feel "on edge" and fearful. The California therapist who administered the mud therapy was known for this treatment, having appeared on several TV talk shows. He first taught the patient a deep relaxation technique and a "secret word" to repeat over and over in order to block out all disturbing thoughts. Then the patient was asked to lie submerged for two hours each day in a special wooden "calm tub" filled with mud. During this time the patient was to practice the relaxation exercises and to concentrate on repeating the secret word whenever the least bit of anxiety was experienced. The therapy was very costly, but after six weeks the patient reported to the therapist that he no longer had the same feelings of anxiety that he had had before. The therapist pronounced him cured and attributed the success of the treatment to immersion in the calming mud. The conclusion drawn by the author of the magazine article describing this therapy was that "it is a treatment that many people could benefit from." On the basis of your knowledge of the limitations of the case study method, answer the following questions:

A What possible sources of bias were there in the study?

B What alternative explanations can you suggest for the successful treatment?

C What problem arises from studying only one individual?

2 A 5-year-old child frequently gets skin rashes, and the mother has been told by her family doctor that the problem is due to "something" that the child eats. The doctor suggests that she "watch carefully" what the child eats. The mother decides to approach this problem by recording each day whether the child has a rash and what the child has eaten the day before. She hopes to find some relationship between eating a particular food and the presence or absence of the rash. Although this approach might help discover a relationship between eating certain foods and the appearance of the rash, a better approach might be one based on the logic and procedures associated with $N = 1$ designs. Explain how the mother might use such an alternative approach. Be specific and point to possible problems that may arise in this application of behavioral methodology.

3 During the summer months you find employment in a camp for mildly mentally impaired children. As a counselor you are asked to supervise a small group of children, as well as to look for ways to improve their attention to various camp activities that take place indoors (for example, craft making and sewing). You decide to explore the possibility of using a system of rewards (M & M candies) for "time on task." You realize that this behavior must be shaped before it can be maintained through some schedule of reinforcement. Furthermore, you realize that the camp director will want evidence of the effectiveness of your intervention strategy as well as some assurance that it will work with other children in the camp. Therefore you are to:

A Plan an intervention strategy based on operant principles that has as its goal an increase in the time children spend on a camp activity.

B Explain what behavioral records you will need to keep and how you will determine whether your intervention has produced a change in the children's behavior. You will need, for example, to specify exactly when and how you will measure behavior, as well as to justify your use of a particular design to carry out your "experiment."

C Describe the argument you will use to convince the director that your intervention strategy (assuming that it works) will work with other, similar children.

4 A schoolteacher asks your help in planning a behavioral intervention that will help manage the behavior of children in the classroom. Many of the children do not stay at their desks when asked to do so, do not remain quiet during "quiet times," and exhibit other behaviors that disrupt the teaching environment. Explain how a token economy might be established to help control the children's behavior. Identify what the tokens are and what specific things might be "purchased" with the tokens. Also explain under what conditions the tokens will be awarded (the contingencies of reinforcement). Finally, explain how an ABAB $N = 1$ experimental design could be used with this group of children in order to demonstrate the effectiveness of the intervention.

ANSWER TO CHALLENGE QUESTION 1

1 A One source of bias in this case study was that the same individual served as therapist and as researcher with the commensurate problems of observer bias. A second source of bias is that the therapist based his conclusion solely on the self-reports of the patient.

B The successful treatment may have resulted from: the relaxation technique alone; the use of the "secret word" in the face of anxiety; attention the patient received from the therapist; or even the high cost of the treatment.

C The major problem that arises from studying one individual is a potential lack of external validity.

Chapter 11

Quasi-Experimental Designs and Program Evaluation

Outline

OVERVIEW

In the most general sense, an experiment is a test; it is a procedure used to find out something not presently known. In this sense we experiment when we add new ingredients to the chili in order to see whether they improve its taste. We experiment with new ways to catch fish by changing the lures we use. We experiment by driving a different route in order to find a quicker way to commute to work. As you have seen, however, in the conduct of psychological research, experiments are usually carried out in order to discover the causes of a phenomenon. Experimental methods, unlike other research techniques such as observation and surveys, are viewed as the most efficient way to determine causation. Indeed, in one way or another, discussions found in Chapters 6 through 10 have emphasized experimental methods in psychological research.

By now you probably appreciate the complexity of the task facing the researcher who seeks to understand a phenomenon by discovering what caused it. In this chapter we continue our discussion of experimental methods, but we focus on experiments as they are often conducted in natural settings. You will see that the task of drawing cause-effect conclusions often becomes even more difficult, and that new problems arise, when an investigator leaves the confines of the laboratory to experiment in natural settings.

There are numerous reasons why experiments are carried out in natural settings. One important reason (mentioned in Chapter 6) is to test the external validity of a laboratory finding. Other reasons for doing field experiments are likely to be associated with attempts to improve conditions under which people live and work. The government may experiment with a new tax system or a new method of training military enlistees. Schools may experiment by changing lunch programs, after-school care, or curricula. A business may experiment with new product designs, methods of delivering employee benefits, or flexible work hours. In these cases, as is true in the laboratory, it is important to determine whether the "treatment" caused a change. Did a change in the way patients are admitted to a hospital emergency room cause patients to be treated more quickly and efficiently? Did a college energy conservation program cause a decrease in energy consumption?

Knowing whether a treatment was effective permits us to make important decisions about continuing the treatment, about spending additional money, about investing more time and effort, or about changing the present situation on the basis of our knowledge of the results. Research that seeks to determine the effectiveness of changes made by institutions, government agencies, and other units of society is one goal of the discipline of **program evaluation.**

In this chapter we discuss the problems of conducting experiments in natural settings. We describe obstacles to doing true experiments in such settings, and we discuss ways of overcoming these obstacles so that true experiments are done whenever possible. Nevertheless, true experiments are sometimes not feasible outside the laboratory. In these cases, experimental procedures that only approximate the conditions of laboratory experiments must be considered. We discuss several of these "quasi-experimental" techniques. The problems attendant on quasi-experimentation make us realize the value of true experiments, so we briefly consider alternatives to quasi-experiments in natural settings. One such alternative is the extension of single-case experimental designs (which we discussed in Chapter 10) to research in natural settings. We conclude the chapter by providing a brief introduction to the logic, procedures, and limitations of program evaluation.

DIFFERENCES BETWEEN LABORATORY EXPERIMENTS AND EXPERIMENTS IN NATURAL SETTINGS

There are some important considerations to keep in mind as we discuss experimentation in natural settings. Experimentation outside the confines of the psychology laboratory is likely to differ from laboratory research in a number of significant ways. Not every experiment in a natural setting differs from laboratory experiments in all of these ways, of course. But when considering research in a natural setting, it is important to weigh the following points.

CONTROL

More than anything else, the scientist is concerned with control. Only by controlling those factors that are assumed to influence a phenomenon can one make a decision about causation. As you have seen in previous chapters, control takes several forms. The assignment of subjects to conditions of an experiment is a method of control used to balance subject characteristics in treatment and no treatment conditions. Other factors that are likely to influence a phenomenon may be controlled by holding them constant.

In a natural setting, a researcher may not always have the same degree of control over conditions of an experiment or over assignment of subjects as in a laboratory. A field experiment may have to be conducted according to the availability of subjects or at the discretion of an administrator or government official. Natural settings place various restrictions on an experiment that limit the researcher's control. It is even possible that an investigator may not directly participate in the planning and conduct of the "experiment" but may be asked afterward whether a treatment "worked." This kind of situation is clearly the most difficult because important factors may not have been considered in planning or executing the intervention.

EXTERNAL VALIDITY

Field experiments are often conducted with the goal of establishing the external validity of a laboratory finding. The "artificial" environment of the psychology laboratory, which increases the internal validity of research, often decreases the external validity of the findings. Experiments in natural settings may therefore need to be conducted in order to generalize results beyond the laboratory situation.

The external validity of research done in natural settings may be emphasized more if social experimentation is the basis for large-scale social changes. That is, if the results of an experiment are to be used to plan further interventions or to implement similar programs outside the domain in which the experiment was conducted, then it is vital to know to what extent the treatment and results can be generalized. For example, legislators may wish to generalize to a different state certain procedures that have been shown to produce an increase in voter registration in one state. A method to increase employee morale that succeeded in one branch of a company may be considered by company officials for all branches of the company. Will the results of a reading program that is judged to be beneficial at one grade level in one school generalize to other grade levels, other schools, or situations where it is implemented by different personnel? These are, of course, all questions of external validity.

GOALS

Experimentation in natural settings often has different goals from laboratory research. One major difference in goals is that which exists between basic and applied research. **Basic research** is often carried out with the single goal of understanding a phenomenon, of determining how "nature" works. It may be done to gain knowledge merely for knowledge's sake. **Applied research** is also directed toward discovering the reasons for a phenomenon, but it is likely to be done only when knowing the reasons for an event will lead to a change in the status quo. That is, applied research is carried out with the goal of gaining knowledge that will modify or improve the present situation. Experimentation in natural settings, therefore, is more likely to have practical goals.

CONSEQUENCES

During the 1970s the U.S. government experimented with the "new town" concept. Thirteen new towns were created under government sponsorship. Beginning from scratch, designers tried to avoid all the problems of older unplanned urban communities. Towns such as Columbia, Maryland, and Reston, Virginia, are examples. Also in the decade of the 1970s, the government experimented with a program designed to aid prisoners following release from incarceration (see Berk, Boruch, Chambers, Rossi, & Witte, 1987). Individuals released from prison often have little in the way of resources to help them begin a new life, and they frequently have difficulty finding jobs. This economic hardship can contribute to new crime. The program involved random assignment of ex-prisoners to groups that either received financial assistance on leaving prison or did not receive financial assistance. The program targeted as subjects about 2,000 ex-prisoners in Texas and Georgia. In 1988 the National Cancer Institute debated whether to fund a $130 million study to investigate a possible link between breast cancer and fat consumption. The proposed study would require rigorous control over the diets of 10,000 women and monitoring them over 10 years (Sun, 1988).

Clearly, these examples of society's "experiments," as well as those we might imagine being carried out on a smaller scale in natural settings (such as those conducted in schools or businesses), are likely to have consequences of greater immediate impact than laboratory research. Although a few planned communities worked, others did not, and planners and builders went bankrupt (see *Time*, October 16, 1978, p. 84). While the prison release program produced some identifiable positive results, it was also found to be responsible for an increase in crime, apparently due to the ex-prisoners' freedom from having to work (see Berk et al., 1987). The breast-cancer study was voted down when administrators decided that monitoring the 22,000 women needed for a control group could not reasonably be accomplished. A decision was not made at that time as to whether a different study would be undertaken to investigate the cancer link.

The Head Start program for disadvantaged children and the "Sesame Street" television show were social experiments designed to improve the education of literally hundreds of thousands of children across the nation. Experiments in businesses may be carried out with the eventual goal of reducing the number of employees or in other ways affecting the quality of employees' lives. Unfortunately, drawing a meaningful conclusion about the effects of many of these experiments may be impossible without giving more consideration to the design and implementation of these "treatments." This is particularly disturbing, because the consequences of such experiments are often so great in terms of money spent and the number of people whose lives are affected. By contrast, the consequences of a laboratory experiment are often likely to be minimal.

They may directly affect only the lives of a few researchers and of those relatively few subjects recruited to participate.

TRUE EXPERIMENTS AND QUASI-EXPERIMENTS

CHARACTERISTICS OF TRUE EXPERIMENTS

Although many everyday activities (such as altering the ingredients of a recipe) might be called experiments, we would not consider them "true" experiments in the sense in which experimentation has been discussed in this textbook. Analogously, many of the various "social experiments" that are carried out by the government (such as the "new town" concept) and those that are conducted by company officials or educational administrators are also not true experiments. A true experiment is one that leads to an unambigous outcome regarding what caused an event.

True experiments exhibit three important characteristics. First, in a true experiment some type of intervention or treatment is implemented. Using the language of the laboratory researcher, we say that an independent variable is manipulated. Second, true experiments are marked by the high degree of control that an experimenter has over the arrangement of experimental conditions, assignment of subjects, choice of dependent variables, and systematic manipulation of independent variables. The ability to assign subjects randomly to experimental conditions is often seen as the most critical defining characteristic of the true experiment (Judd et al., 1991). Finally, true experiments are characterized by an appropriate comparison. Indeed, the experimenter exerts control over a situation principally in order to establish a proper comparison to evaluate the effectiveness of an independent variable. In the simplest of experimental situations, this comparison is one between two groups that are treated exactly alike except for the variable of interest. Any differences in a dependent variable that arise in such a situation can logically be assigned to the differences between levels of the independent variable.

OBSTACLES TO CONDUCTING TRUE EXPERIMENTS IN NATURAL SETTINGS

Although we have tried to convince you in this and preceding chapters that experimental research is an effective tool for solving problems and answering questions, not everyone agrees with this approach. Those who disagree would hasten to point out the two obstacles that arise when we try to carry out experiments in natural settings. The first problem is obtaining permission to do the research from individuals in positions of authority. Unless they believe that the research will be useful, school board presidents and government and business leaders are unlikely to support research financially or otherwise. We will discuss the problem of the credibility of research later in this chapter when we introduce program evaluation.

The second, and often more pressing, obstacle to doing experiments in natural settings is the problem of access to participants. This problem can prove especially troublesome if participants must agree to be randomly assigned to either a treatment group or a control group before they are allowed to participate in the experiment.

Random assignment to conditions appears unfair at first—after all, random assignment requires that a potentially beneficial treatment be withheld from at least some participants. Suppose that a new approach to the teaching of foreign languages was to be tested at your college or university. Suppose further that, when you went to register for your next semester's classes, you were told that you would be randomly assigned to one of two sections taught at the time you selected—one section involving the old method and one involving the new method. How would you react? Your knowledge of research methods tells you that the two methods must be administered to comparable groups of students and that random assignment is the best way to ensure such comparability. Nonetheless, you might be tempted to feel that random assignment is not fair, especially if you are assigned to the section using the old (old-fashioned?) method. Let's take a closer look at the fairness of random assignment.

If those responsible for selecting the method of foreign language instruction already knew that the new method was more effective than the old method, there would be little justification for testing the method again (unless, of course, the effectiveness of the new method had been demonstrated at schools very different from yours). Under such circumstances we would agree that withholding the new method from students in the control group would be unjust. If we do not know whether the new method is better, however, any approach other than conducting a true experiment will leave us in doubt about the new method's effectiveness. Random assignment to treatments—call it a "lottery" if you prefer—may be the fairest procedure for assigning students to sections. The old method of instruction, after all, was considered effective before the development of the new method. If the new method proves *less* effective, random assignment will have actually "protected" the control participants from receiving an ineffective treatment.

There are ways to offer a potentially effective treatment to all participants while still maintaining comparable groups. Atkinson (1968) randomly assigned students to receive computer-assisted instruction in either English *or* math and then tested both groups in English *and* math. Each group served as a control for the other on the test for which its members had not received instruction. After completing the experiment, both groups could then be given computer-assisted instruction in the subject matter to which they had not been previously exposed.

Establishing a proper control group is possible if there is more demand for a service than an agency can meet. People who are waiting to receive the service can act as what is called a "waiting list" control group. It is essential, however, that people be assigned to the waiting list randomly.

There are also circumstances in which random assignment simply cannot be used. For example, in clinical trials involving tests of new medical treatments, it may be extremely difficult to get patients to agree to be randomly assigned to either the treatment group or the control group. Quasi-experimental designs such as the nonequivalent control group design can be used in these situations. The logic and procedures for these quasi-experimental designs will be described later in this chapter.

THREATS TO INTERNAL VALIDITY CONTROLLED BY TRUE EXPERIMENTS

One way to evaluate an experiment is to determine what kinds of alternative explanations for a phenomenon have been controlled. Prior to doing an experiment, we might look to see what major classes of possible explanations are ruled out by our experimental procedure. Only by eliminating all possible alternative explanations are we able to arrive at a definite conclusion about cause and effect. In previous chapters, we referred to various uncontrolled factors that threaten the internal validity of an experiment as *confounding factors* (they are also called *confounds*). Several types of confounds were identified in earlier chapters (see especially Chapter 6). We will now list eight classes of confounds, using the terminology of Campbell and Stanley (1966; see also Cook & Campbell, 1979). You have already been introduced to some of these **threats to internal validity;** others will be new. After reviewing the major classes of confounds, we will be able to judge the extent to which various experimental procedures control for these kinds of alternative explanations of a treatment effect.

History The occurrence of an event other than the treatment can threaten internal validity if it produces changes in subjects' behavior. A true experiment requires that subjects in the experimental group and in the control group be treated the same (have the same history of experiences) except for the treatment. In the laboratory, this is usually accomplished by balancing or holding conditions constant. For example, the same experimenter might be asked to test subjects in all conditions of an experiment. If different experimenters were to test experimental and control subjects, we would confound the possible effect due to the experimenter and that of the treatment. When doing experiments in natural settings, the researcher may not always be able to exercise these forms of control, so confounding due to history can be a threat to internal validity.

Maturation Subjects in an experiment necessarily change as a function of time. They grow older, become more experienced, and so forth. Change associated with the passage of time per se is called *maturation*. For example, without a proper comparison a researcher might attribute the changes in performance between a pretest and a posttest of a group of schoolchildren to the effect of an intervention when, in reality, the changes were simply due to the normal processes of maturation.

Testing Taking a test generally has an effect on subsequent testing. Consider, for example, the fact that many students often improve from the initial test in a course to the second test. The familiarity with the testing procedure and with the instructor's expectations that they gain during the first test affects their performance on the second test. In the context of a psychology experiment, testing is a threat to internal validity if the effect of a treatment cannot be separated from the effect of testing.

Instrumentation It is possible that changes over time take place not only in the subjects of an experiment but also in the instruments used to measure the subjects' performance. This is most clearly a possibility when human observers are used to assess behavior. As you learned in previous chapters (see especially Chapter 3), observer bias can result from fatigue, expectations, and other characteristics of observers. For example, as a researcher becomes more experienced in making observations, there is likely to be a change in the quality of the observations that she or he makes. Unless controlled for, these changes in instrumentation can threaten internal validity by providing alternative explanations for differences in behavior between one observation period and another. Mechanical instruments also may change with repeated use. A researcher known to the authors once found that a machine used to present material in a learning experiment was not working the same at the end of the experiment as it was at the beginning.

Regression Statistical regression is always a problem when subjects have been selected for an experiment because of "extreme" scores. This source of confounding was discussed in some detail in Chapter 6. As summarized by Cook and Campbell (1979, pp. 52–53), statistical regression

> (1) operates to increase obtained pretest–posttest gain scores among low pretest scores, since this group's pretest scores are more likely to have been depressed by error; (2) operates to decrease obtained change scores among persons with high pretest scores since their pretest scores are likely to have been inflated by error; and (3) does not affect obtained change scores among scorers at the center of the pretest distribution since the group is likely to contain as many units whose pretest scores are inflated by error as units whose pretest scores are deflated by it. Regression is always to the population mean of a group.

Selection When, from the outset of a study, differences exist between the kinds of subjects in one group of an experiment and those in another, there is a confounding due to selection. In the laboratory, this threat to internal validity is generally handled by balancing subject characteristics through random assignment. When one is doing experiments in natural settings, there are often many obstacles to randomization of subjects to treatment and no treatment conditions. These obstacles prevent doing a true experiment and hence present a possible confound due to selection.

Subject Mortality When subjects are lost from an experiment, there is a threat to internal validity. Possible reasons for subject loss were discussed in Chapter 6. The threat to internal validity rests on the assumption that subject loss (*attrition*) changes the nature of a group from that established prior to the introducton of the treatment—for example, by destroying the equivalence of groups that had been established through randomization.

Interactions with Selection Several of the foregoing threats to internal validity can be a source of additional concern to the extent that they interact with characteristics of groups of subjects selected for an experiment. Specifically, there are possible problems due to interactions between (a) selection and history, (b) selection and maturation, and (c) selection and instrumentation. Basically, what this means is that one or more groups of subjects respond differentially to effects associated with history, maturation, or instrumentation. For example, if groups of subjects in an experiment mature at different rates, then differences between groups in the form of changes from pretest to posttest may be due to an interaction of selection and maturation rather than to any treatment. Such might be the case if freshmen in college who served as an experimental group were compared with sophomores who served as a control group. Changes in subjects that occur during the freshman year (as students gain their first acquaintance with the college environment) might be presumed to be greater than those that occur during the sophomore year, and thus they might explain any observed effects.

An interaction of selection and history results when events occurring in time had a different effect on one group of subjects than on another. This is particularly a problem when intact groups are compared. Perhaps due to events that are peculiar to one group's situation, an event may have more of an impact on that group than on another. Consider, for example, research involving a comparison between two classrooms of students at the same school. If the principal of the school were changed during the experiment, it might be expected to have an equal effect on children in both classrooms. However, this would not be the case if children in one classroom had more familiarity with the principal (perhaps because the principal was a previous teacher of these students). Similarly, an interaction of selection and history might be a problem if classrooms at different schools are compared and an event other than the treatment occurs at one school (the principal is changed) and not at the other.

Finally, an interaction of selection and instrumentation might occur should the test instrument be relatively more sensitive to changes in one group's performance than to changes in another's. This occurs, for instance, when ceiling or floor effects are present. Such is the case when a group scores initially so low on an instrument (*floor effect*) that any further drop in scores cannot be reliably measured, or so high (*ceiling effect*) that any more gain cannot be assessed. As you can imagine, a confound would be present if an experimental group showed relatively no change (due to floor or ceiling effects) while a control changed reliably because its mean performance was near neither the low end nor the high end of the measurement scale.

A true experiment controls all of these eight major classes of threats to internal validity. Quasi-experiments can be viewed as compromises between the general aim of gaining valid knowledge regarding the effectiveness of a treatment and the realization that true experiments (and hence control of the major factors threatening internal validity) are not always possible. As Campbell (1969) emphasizes, so-called true experiments should be conducted when possible, but if they are not feasible, quasi-experiments should be conducted. "We must do the best we can with what is available to us" (p. 411).

PROBLEMS THAT EVEN TRUE EXPERIMENTS MAY NOT ELIMINATE

Before considering specific quasi-experimental procedures, we should point out that even true experiments may not control for all possible factors that might cloud the interpretation of an experimental result. Although major threats to internal validity are typically eliminated by the true experiment, there are some additional threats that the investigator must guard against, particularly when working in natural settings. We will use the term *contamination* to describe one general class of threats to internal validity. **Contamination** occurs when there is communication of information about the experiment between groups of subjects. The result of this communication can be resentment on the part of subjects receiving less desirable treatments, rivalry among subjects receiving different treatments, or a general diffusion of treatments across the groups (see Cook & Campbell, 1979).

Consider a situation in which a group of subjects has been randomly assigned to a control group. Further, assume that information is obtained by subjects in this group indicating that "other" subjects are receiving a treatment which appears to be beneficial. What do you think might be the reaction of the control subjects? One possibility is resentment and demoralization. As Cook and Campbell explain, in an industrial setting the person receiving the less desirable treatment may retaliate by lowering productivity. In an educational setting teachers or students might "lose heart" or become angry. This effect of "leaked" information about a treatment may make a treatment look better than it ordinarily would because of the lowered performance of the control group that is demoralized.

Another possible effect of a no treatment group's learning about another group's good fortune is to generate a spirit of competition. That is, a control group might become motivated to reduce the expected difference between itself and the treatment group. As Cook and Campbell point out, this may be likely when intact groups (such as departments, work crews, branch offices, and the like) are assigned to various conditions. Realizing that another group will look better depending on how much it distinguishes itself from the control group, subjects comprising the control group may be motivated to "try harder" so as not to look bad by comparison. Cook and Campbell call this problem compensatory rivalry. Like other contamination effects, it cannot always be assumed to be absent in an experiment.

Yet another possible effect of contamination is diffusion of treatments. According to Cook and Campbell, this occurs when subjects in a no treatment group use information given to others to help them change their own behavior. For example, control subjects may use the information given to subjects in the treatment group to imitate the behavior of the treated subjects. Of course, this reduces the differences between the treated and untreated groups and affects the internal validity of the experiment.

In addition to problems resulting from contamination, true experiments can be weakened by threats to external validity. As you have learned in previous chapters, the extent to which one can generalize across persons, settings, and times depends mainly on how representative one's sample is of the persons, settings, and times to which one wishes to generalize. Representativeness is normally achieved through random sampling. However, because random sampling is used so infrequently, we can rarely say that our sample of subjects, or the situation in which we are making observations, or the times during which we test subjects, are representative samples of all persons, settings, or times. Therefore, the investigator must be aware of possible interactions between the independent variable of an experiment and the type of subject, setting, or time of the experiment. Is a difference between an experimental group and a control group that is found when only volunteers are used, when the setting is an inner-city school, or when the experiment is conducted in the winter also likely to be found when nonvolunteers are tested, when a suburban school is the setting, or when the experiment is performed in the spring of the year?

Cook and Campbell describe several approaches to evaluating threats to external validity, the foremost being determination of the representativeness of the sample. However, they point out that in the last analysis the best test of external validity is replication (see Chapter 6). External validity is an empirical question that is best answered through repetition of the experiment with different types of subjects, in different settings, and at different times. Occasionally these replications can be "built into" an experiment—for example, by selecting more than one group to participate.

Finally, true experiments do not always protect the experimenter from threats due to experimenter expectancy effects or to a "Hawthorne effect." Effects due to experimenter expectancies were discussed in earlier chapters. They occur when the experimenter unintentionally influences the results. Systematic errors in interpretation or mistakes in recording data can be the result of experimenter expectancy effects. Various ways to control experimenter or observer effects were outlined in Chapter 3. The **Hawthorne effect** refers to changes in persons' behavior brought about by the interest that "significant others" show in them. The effect was named after events occurring at the Hawthorne plant of the Western Electric Company in Cicero, Illinois, near Chicago.

Between 1924 and 1932, officials at this plant conducted a series of studies aimed at examining the relationships among productivity, worker satisfaction, and worker motivation (Roethlisberger, 1977). One specific relationship of interest to the researchers was that between illumination level in the plant and productivity in simple, repetitive tasks, such as inspecting small parts and assembling relays and winding coils (Huse & Bowditch, 1977). Results of these early studies were difficult to interpret. According to a researcher involved with the project, the results were "not only inconclusive but also rather curious" (Roethlisberger, 1977, p. 46). Specifically, in one experiment workers were divided into two groups, one working under increasing levels of illumination and the other working under constant illumination. The result was increased productivity in *both* groups, with the rise in output being approximately the same magnitude. "Several further experiments of this character exhibited similar curious outcomes. It looked as if the workers were reacting more to the positive concern of the experimenters about their working conditions than to the actual physical changes in illumination. This response later came to be called the 'Hawthorne effect' " (Roethlisberger, 1977, p. 46). Although there is some controversy surrounding the exact factors responsible for this effect (e.g., Parsons, 1974), a Hawthorne effect generally refers to behavior change resulting from subjects' awareness that someone is interested in them.

As one example of the Hawthorne effect, consider a study wherein prisoners are chosen to participate in research examining the relationship between changes in prison-cell conditions and attitudes toward prison life. If positive changes in prisoners' attitudes are obtained, the results could be due to the actual changes in cell conditions that were made, or they could be due to an increase in morale because prisoners saw the prison administration as expressing concern for them.

Hawthorne effects may be inextricably linked to the action of an independent variable intended to alter the subjects' environment (Sommer, 1968). As Sommer points out, people naturally interpret changes in their environment according to various expectations that they have, according to their needs, and so forth. Just as prisoners may view changes in prison conditions as reflecting concern on the part of the prison staff, so factory workers, schoolchildren, college faculty members, and other groups may interpret changes made in their environment as reflecting interest in them on the part of significant others. Although there is as yet no evidence for widespread Hawthorne effects in field research (see Cook & Campbell, 1979), the psychology investigator must be conscious of the fact that changes in subjects' behavior may be at least partially due to their awareness of the fact that others are interested in them.

QUASI-EXPERIMENTS

A dictionary will tell you that one definition of the prefix *quasi-* is "resembling." A quasi-government, for example, is one resembling, but not actually the same as, a true government. **Quasi-experiments** involve procedures that resemble those that are characteristic of true experiments. Generally speaking, quasi-experiments include some type of intervention or treatment and provide a comparison, but they lack the degree of control found in true experiments. Just as randomization is the hallmark of true experiments, so *lack of randomization* is the hallmark of quasi-experiments. As Campbell and Stanley (1966, p. 34) explain,

> there are many natural social settings in which the research person can introduce something like experimental design into his scheduling of data collection procedures (e.g., the *when* and to *whom* of measurement), even though he lacks the full control over the scheduling of experimental stimuli (the *when* and to *whom* of exposure and the ability to randomize exposures) which makes a true experiment possible. Collectively, such situations can be regarded as quasi-experimental designs.

Quasi-experiments are recommended when true experiments are not feasible. Some knowledge about the effectiveness of a treatment is more desirable than none. The list of possible confounds provided by Campbell and Stanley (1966; Cook & Campbell, 1979), which we reviewed earlier, can be used as a checklist in deciding just how good that knowledge is. Moreover, although a particular experimental procedure may not control for one or more possible types of confounds, the investigator must be prepared to look for additional kinds of evidence that might rule out a confound that is not specifically controlled by an experimental procedure. For example, suppose that a quasi-experiment explicitly controls for only six of the eight major classes of confounds that are eliminated by a true experiment. It may be possible, on the basis of supplementary data or through evidence offered by a logical analysis of the situation, to rule out the remaining two classes of explanations as implausible. In this case a strong argument can be made for the internal validity of the research design, even though a true experiment was not performed. What is important is that the researcher always recognize the specific shortcomings of quasi-experimental procedures and be prepared to address these shortcomings through whatever evidence or logic is available.

With full knowledge of their limitations, then, we present the following information about specific quasi-experimental designs so that you will understand the routes remaining open to an investigator when the path to a true experiment is hopelessly blocked. At the same time, this presentation should help you appreciate the clarity of inference provided by the true experiment. Following a discussion of specific quasi-experimental designs, we look at an alternative to quasi-experimentation—the extension of single-case experimentation to research in natural settings. You may also want to refer to the previous discussion of obstacles to true experiments in natural settings. The difference between the power of the true experiment and that of the quasi-experiment is such that, before facing the problems of interpretation that result from quasi-experimental procedures, the researcher should make every effort possible to approximate the conditions of a true experiment.

SPECIFIC QUASI-EXPERIMENTAL DESIGNS

THE NONEQUIVALENT CONTROL GROUP DESIGN

Perhaps the most serious limitation on experimentation in natural settings is that the experimenter is frequently unable to assign subjects randomly to conditions. This occurs, for instance, when an intact group is singled out for treatment and when administrative decisions or practical considerations prevent randomly assigning subjects. Children in one classroom or school and workers at a particular plant are examples of groups that might be treated in the absence of any random assignment of individuals to conditions. If we assume that behavior is measured both before and after treatment, such an "experiment" can be described as follows:

$$O_1 \; X \; O_2$$

where O_1 refers to the first observation, or pretest, X indicates a treatment, and O_2 refers to the second observation, or posttest.

Campbell and Stanley (1966) call this particular design the "one-group pretest-posttest design." Although it is often used in psychological research, the design has very little internal validity. You should be able to see, for instance, that this design does not control for many factors that can threaten the internal validity of a study. For example, should a difference between pretest and posttest measures be found, how do we know that this difference was not due to some event other than the treatment (*history threat*), that it was not due to the fact that subjects benefited from initial testing (*testing threat*), or that it didn't occur simply because the group of subjects changed over time (*maturation threat*)? This particular design has so little going for it in terms of allowing cause-and-effect inferences that it is sometimes referred to as a "preexperimental design," or one that serves as a "bad experiment" to illustrate possible confounds (see Campbell & Stanley, 1966).

The one-group pretest-posttest design can be modified to create a quasi-experimental design with greatly superior internal validity if two conditions are met: (1) there exists a group "like" the treatment group that can serve as a comparison group and (2) there is an opportunity to obtain pretest and posttest measures from individuals in *both* the treatment and the no treatment groups. Because a comparison group is selected on bases other than random assignment, it cannot be assumed that individuals in the treatment and control groups are equivalent on all important characteristics (a selection threat arises). Therefore it is essential that a pretest be given to both groups to assess their similarity on the dependent measure. Campbell and Stanley (1966) call this quasi-experimental procedure a **nonequivalent control group design.** It can be outlined as follows:

$$\begin{array}{c} O_1 \; X \; O_2 \\ \cdots\cdots\cdots \\ O_1 \quad O_2 \end{array}$$

The dashed line indicates that the treatment and comparison groups were not formed by assigning subjects randomly to conditions. Before considering the strengths and weaknesses of this experimental procedure, let us examine an actual study using this particular quasi-experimental design.

ILLUSTRATION OF THE NONEQUIVALENT CONTROL GROUP DESIGN: THE LANGER AND RODIN STUDY

Langer and Rodin (1976) hypothesized that environmental changes associated with old age contribute, in part, to feelings of loss, inadequacy, and low self-esteem among the elderly. Of particular importance is the change that occurs when elderly persons move into a nursing home. Although they usually care for the elderly quite adequately in physical terms, nursing homes often provide what Langer and Rodin call a "virtually decision-free" environment. The elderly are no longer called on to make even the simplest decisions, such as what time to get up, whom to visit, what movie to watch, and the like. In a nursing home, many or most of these everyday decisions are made for the elderly, leaving them with little personal responsibility and choice.

To test the hypothesis that the lack of opportunity to make personal decisions contributes to the psychological and even the physical debilitation sometimes seen in the elderly, Langer and Rodin carried out a quasi-experiment in a Connecticut nursing home. The independent variable was the type of communication given to two groups of nursing-home residents. One group was given a communication stressing the many decisions that the patients needed to make regarding how their rooms were arranged, visiting, care of plants, movie selection, and so forth. These residents were also given a small plant as a gift (if they decided to accept it) and told to take care of it as they wished. This was the responsibility induced condition. The second group of residents, the comparison group, was also called together for a meeting, but the communication given to this group stressed the staff's responsibility for them. These residents also received a plant as a gift (whether they chose to have one or not) and were told that the nurses would water and care for the plants for them.

Residents of the nursing home had been assigned to a particular floor and room on the basis of availability, and some residents had been there for a long time. As a consequence, randomly assigning residents to the two communication groups was impractical—and probably undesirable from the administration's point of view. Therefore the two communications were given to residents on two different floors of the nursing home. These floors were chosen, in the words of the authors, "because of similarity in the residents' physical and psychological health and prior socioeconomic status, as determined from evaluations made by the home's director, head nurses, and social worker" (Langer & Rodin, p. 193). A different floor was randomly selected for each treatment. In addition, questionnaires containing items that related to "how much control they felt over general events in their lives and how happy and active they felt" (p. 194) were given to residents 1 week before and 3 weeks after the communications. Furthermore, staff members on each floor were asked to rate the residents, before and after the experimental communications, on such traits as alertness, sociability, and activity. The investigators also included a clever posttest measure of social interest by holding a competition that asked participants to guess the number of jelly beans in a large jar. Residents entered the contest if they wished by simply filling out a piece of paper giving their estimate and name.

The Langer and Rodin study nicely illustrates a nonequivalent control group procedure. Moreover, differences between pretest and posttest measures showed that the residents in the responsibility induced group were generally happier, more active, and more alert than residents in the comparison group. Behavioral measures such as frequency of movie attendance also favored the responsibility induced group, and, although ten residents from this group entered the jelly-bean contest, only one resident from the comparison group participated! The investigators point to possible practical implications of these findings. Specifically, they suggest that some of the negative consequences of aging can be reduced or reversed by giving the aged the opportunity to make personal decisions and to feel competent.

SOURCES OF INVALIDITY IN THE NONEQUIVALENT CONTROL GROUP DESIGN

According to Cook and Campbell (1979), the nonequivalent control group design generally controls for all major classes of potential confounds except those due to interactions of (a) selection and maturation, (b) selection and history, (c) selection and instrumentation, and (d) those due to differential statistical regression. We will explore how each of these potential sources of invalidity might pose problems in an effort to interpret the results of the Langer and Rodin study. Then we will explain what evidence or argument the authors offered in defense of their interpretation, which was that the differential communication *caused* the differences in posttest behavior between the two groups of residents. We will also examine how experimenter bias and problems of contamination were controlled, and we will comment briefly on problems of external validity inherent in the nonequivalent control group design.

First, it should be mentioned that Langer and Rodin found that the residents in the two experimental groups did not differ significantly on the pretest measures. Because the residents were not randomly assigned to conditions, it might not have been surprising to find a difference between the two groups before the treatment was introduced. Moreover, it is important to recognize that, even when pretest scores show no difference between groups, as Langer and Rodin reported, one cannot assume that the groups are "equivalent" (Campbell & Stanley, 1966). Why this is so will become apparent in the discussion that follows.

Interaction between Selection and Maturation An interaction between selection and maturation occurs when individuals in one group are growing more experienced, more tired, or more bored at a faster rate than individuals in another group (Cook & Campbell, 1979). Campbell and Stanley (1966) illustrate this problem by describing a nonequivalent control group design using psychotherapy patients as a treatment group and individuals not in therapy as a comparison group. The psychotherapy patients would normally be expected to show some spontaneous remission without the treatment, a change that could be falsely interpreted (given no change in the comparison group) as a treatment effect. Whenever the treatment group consists of individuals who are brighter or more competent than those in the comparison group, differences in rate of maturation may be a confounding factor.

In examining the Langer and Rodin study, we have to ask whether there is any reason to suspect an interaction of selection and maturation. For instance, would residents on the treatment floor be expected to change naturally at a faster rate than patients on the no treatment floor? Several kinds of evidence suggest that this would not be the case. First, the procedure of assigning residents to floors was basically random, and floors were selected randomly for treatment and no treatment. The authors also point out that various measures showed that the residents of the two floors were, on the average, equivalent in socioeconomic status and length of time at the nursing home. Finally, although it is not sufficient evidence in itself, residents on the two floors did not differ on the pretest measures. There is little in the Langer and Rodin study to suggest a confound due to an interaction of selection and maturation.

An interaction of selection and maturation is more likely to be an actual source of invalidity (as are other sources) when the treatment group is self-selected (the members deliberately sought out exposure to the treatment) and when the comparison group is from a different population from the treatment group (Campbell & Stanley, 1966). This occurs when a particular group is singled out for treatment in order to determine whether behavior will improve as a function of the treatment. The example of psychotherapy patients who are compared with normals, which was mentioned earlier, is an example.

An investigator must be aware that, even when pretest scores are the same on the average for the treatment and control groups, it cannot be concluded that the groups are equivalent. This is true for two reasons. First, the pretest is likely to measure respondents on only one measure, or at best on a few measures. The mere fact that individuals do not differ on one measure does not mean that they don't differ on other measures that are relevant to their behavior in this situation. Second, the natural growth rate of two groups from different populations might be different, but the pretest may have been taken at a time when both groups were approximately the same. This problem is illustrated in Figure 11.1. The normal rate of change is greater in Group A than in Group B, but the pretest is likely to show that the groups do not differ. On the other hand, and again because of the differential growth rate, the groups would probably show a difference at the posttest that could be mistaken for a treatment effect. Langer and Rodin selected their groups (but not individuals) randomly from the same population of individuals. Consequently, their design more closely approaches a true experiment than it would if individuals in the two groups came from different populations (Campbell & Stanley, 1966), as would be the case if residents in a nursing home were compared with those attending a sheltered workshop program for the elderly.

Interaction between Selection and History Another type of confound that is not controlled in the nonequivalent control group design is the interaction between selection and history. Cook and Campbell (1979) refer to this problem as *local history effects.* This problem arises when an event other than the treatment affects one group and not the other. Local history, for example, could be a problem in the Langer and Rodin study if an event affecting the residents' happiness and alertness occurred on one floor of the nursing home and not on the other. You can probably imagine a number of possibilities. A change in nursing staff, for instance, might bring about either an increase or a decrease in residents' morale, depending on the nature of the change and the relationship between the behavior of a new nurse and that of an old one. Problems of local history become more problematic the more the locations or settings of the individuals in the treatment and comparison groups differ. Langer and Rodin do not specifically address the problem of local history.

Interaction between Selection and Instrumentation An interaction of selection and instrumentation occurs when changes in a measuring instrument

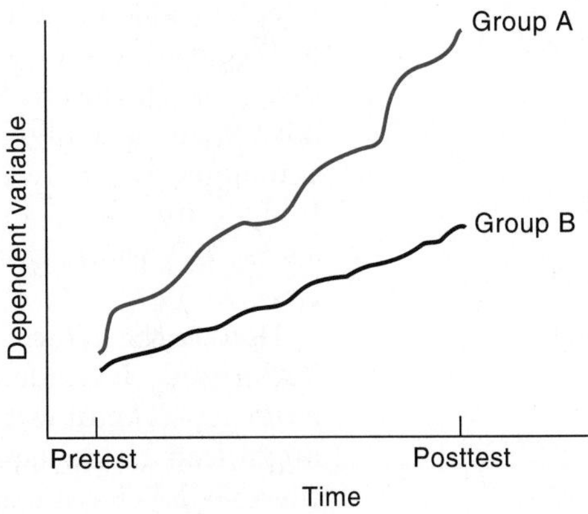

FIGURE 11.1 Possible differential growth rates for two groups (A and B) in the absence of a treatment.

are more likely to be detected in one group than they are in another. Floor or ceiling effects, for instance, could make it difficult to detect behavior change from pretest to posttest. If this is more of a problem in one group than in another, an interaction of selection and instrumentation is present. Cook and Campbell point out that this confound is likely to be more of a problem the greater the nonequivalence of the groups. Because Langer and Rodin's groups did not differ on the pretest, and because performance of the groups did not suggest floor or ceiling effects on the measurement scales that were used, this confound seems implausible in their study.

Differential Statistical Regression Finally, the nonequivalent control group design does not control for differential statistical regression (Cook & Campbell, 1979). This is especially a problem when one group has been singled out for treatment because of its poor performance on some measure. As you are probably aware by now, *whenever* subjects are selected on the basis of extreme scores (the poorest readers, the workers with the lowest productivity, the patients with the most severe problems), regression toward the mean is to be expected. Changes in behavior from pretest to posttest that are due to regression may be mistakenly interpreted as a treatment effect if regression is more likely in the treatment group than in the control group. Because the groups in the Langer and Rodin study came from the same population and there is no evidence that one group's scores were more extreme than another's, a problem of differential statistical regression is not plausible in their study.

Observer Bias and Contamination It is worthwhile to consider how Langer and Rodin handled problems of observer bias and possible effects of contamination and to inquire whether a Hawthorne effect was present. If observers in their study had been aware of the experimental hypothesis, it is possible that they might inadvertently have rated residents as being better after the experimental communication than before. However, all the observers were kept unaware of the experimental hypothesis. Thus, observer bias appears to have been controlled. Langer and Rodin were aware of possible contamination effects. Residents in the control group might have become demoralized if they learned that residents on another floor were given more opportunity to make decisions. In this case, the use of different floors of the nursing home was advantageous; Langer and Rodin indicate that "there was not a great deal of communication between floors" (1976, p. 193). Thus, if one accepts Langer and Rodin's argument, contamination effects do not seem to be present, at least on a scale that would destroy the internal validity of the study.

Hawthorne Effect A Hawthorne effect would be present in the Langer and Rodin study if residents on the treatment floor interpreted the responsibility-inducing communication as a form of special attention. Such an interpretation might lead residents on the treated floor to feel better about themselves. The changes in behavior that Langer and Rodin observed could then be attributed to a change in morale due to a Hawthorne effect as easily as to the opportunity to make decisions and assume personal responsibility that was available to residents in the treatment group. It is difficult to rule out completely a Hawthorne effect in this study. According to the authors, however, "there was no difference in the amount of attention paid to the two groups" (p. 194). In fact, communications to both groups stressed that the staff cared for them and wanted them "to be happy."

Thus, without additional evidence to the contrary, we can conclude that the changes in behavior that Langer and Rodin observed were due to the effect of the independent variable and not to the effect of an extraneous variable that the investigators failed to control.

What should be apparent at this point is that, for an investigator to decide, in the context of a particular experiment, whether an independent variable "worked," it is necessary that he or she be something of a detective. Evidence for and against the interpretation that the treatment actually caused behavior change must be systematically (and sometimes ingeniously) collected and carefully weighed. As Cook and Campbell (1979, pp. 55–56) explain:

> Estimating the internal validity of a relationship is a deductive process in which the investigator has to systematically think through how each of the internal validity threats may have influenced the data. Then, the investigator has to examine the data to test which relevant threats can be ruled out. In all of this process, the researcher has to be his or her own best critic, trenchantly examining all of the threats he or she can imagine. When all of the threats can plausibly be eliminated, it is possible to make confident conclusions about whether a relationship is probably causal. When all of them cannot, perhaps because the appropriate data are not available or because the data indicate that a particular threat may indeed have operated, then the investigator has to conclude that a demonstrated relationship between two variables may or may not be causal.

The Issue of External Validity The investigator must make the same systematic inquiry into the external validity of an experiment. What evidence is there that the particular pattern of results is restricted to a particular group of subjects, setting, or time? For example, although Langer and Rodin suggest that certain changes be made in the way the elderly are cared for, we might question whether the effectiveness of the responsibility-inducing communication would hold for all elderly residents, for all types of nursing homes, and at different times. That the particular nursing home selected by Langer and Rodin was described as "rated by the state of Connecticut as being among the finest care units" (1976, p. 193) suggests that the residents, facilities, and staff there would be different from those found in other homes. For instance, if residents at this particular home were relatively more independent before coming to the home than residents at other homes (perhaps because of differences in socioeconomic status), then the changes experienced upon moving into a home might have had greater impact on them. Consequently, the opportunity to be more independent of staff might be more important to these residents relative to residents in other homes. Similarly, if staff members at this home were more competent than those at other homes, they might be more effective in communicating the experimental communications than would the staff members at other homes.

As we indicated earlier, in the last analysis, the investigator must be ready to replicate an experimental finding under different conditions in order to establish external validity. The deductive process applied to questions of internal validity must also be used to examine a study's external validity. Moreover, an investigator must be ready to live with the fact that one experiment is very unlikely to answer all questions about an experimental hypothesis.

INTERRUPTED TIME-SERIES DESIGNS

In situations where one can observe changes in a dependent variable for some time before and after a treatment is introduced, another quasi-experiment is possible. It is called a **simple interrupted time-series design** (Cook & Campbell, 1979). The essence of this design is the availability of periodic measures before and after a treatment has been introduced. It can be outlined in the following way:

$$O_1 \quad O_2 \quad O_3 \quad O_4 \quad O_5 \quad X \quad O_6 \quad O_7 \quad O_8 \quad O_9 \quad O_{10}$$

Situations such as this may arise when a new product has been introduced, a new social reform instituted, or a special advertising campaign begun. Campbell's (1969) analysis of the effect on traffic fatalities of a crackdown on speeding ordered by the Connecticut governor made use of an interrupted time-series design. Because statistics related to traffic accidents are regularly kept by state agencies, a wealth of archival data was available to yield pretreatment and posttreatment measures. Besides number of fatalities, Campbell looked at number of speeding violations, number of drivers having their licenses suspended, and other measures related to driving behavior. Figure 11.2 shows the percentage of suspensions of licenses for speeding (as a percentage of all license suspensions) before and after the crackdown. There is a clear discontinuity in the time graph that provides evidence for an effect of the treatment. Indeed, the discontinuity in the time series is the major evidence of an effect.

As Campbell points out, only abrupt changes in the time graph can be evaluated because gradual changes are indistinguishable from normal fluctuations over time. Unfortunately, changes often are not nearly so dramatic as those seen in Figure 11.2. In fact, Campbell's analysis of traffic fatalities over the same time period, while revealing evidence of an effect of the crackdown, did not show as abrupt a change as that associated with suspension of drivers' licenses (see Campbell, 1969, Figure 2). A typical outcome of an interrupted time-series design is illustrated by the findings of Ross and White (1987), who examined the effect of newspaper publicity on subsequent crime rates. In June 1984, a metropolitan newspaper instituted a policy of publishing the court

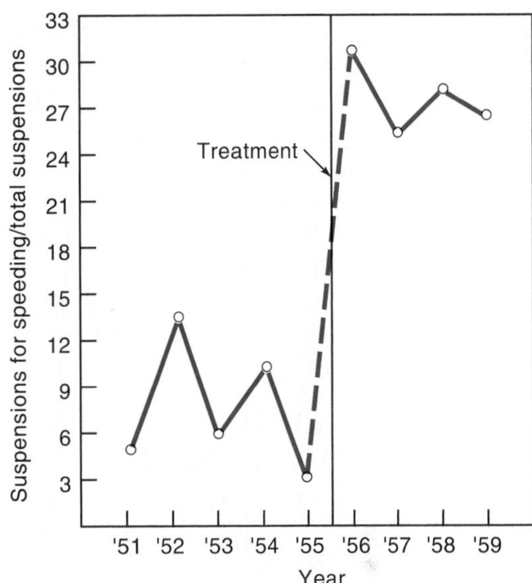

FIGURE 11.2 Suspensions of licenses for speeding, as a percentage of all suspensions (From Campbell, 1969).

results of people convicted of shoplifting, impaired driving, or failure to take a breathalyzer test. The published information identified the individual by name and also furnished details of the incident. For instance, in the case of shoplifting, the item that the individual attempted to shoplift and its value were also noted. Ross and White sought to assess the impact of this publication policy on the frequency of similar offenses. They obtained data from several police and government agencies detailing the incidence of these crimes over a time period beginning several years before the new policy was instituted and continuing for approximately 18 months after the new policy was implemented. The number of shoplifting offenses during this period is shown in Figure 11.3. Visual inspection, confirmed by the results of statistical analyses, revealed an effect of the publication policy on incidence of shoplifting. Interestingly, the policy showed no effect on the incidence of drinking and driving or refusing the breathalyzer test. The investigators suggested that being associated with shoplifting carries a greater social stigma than does driving under the influence of alcohol.

Campbell and Stanley (1966) summarize the problem facing researchers using the simple interrupted time-series design: "The problem of internal validity boils down to the question of plausible competing hypotheses that offer likely alternate explanations of the shift in the time series other than the effect of X" (p. 39). An effect of history is the main threat to internal validity in this type of design (Cook & Campbell, 1979). For instance, considering the results in Figure 11.3, is it possible that some factor other than newspaper publicity was responsible for the reduction in the frequency of shoplifting offenses?

Particularly threatening to the internal validity of the time-series design are

NOTE: Vertical line indicates start of publication policy.

FIGURE 11.3 Shoplifting offenses between January 1980 and December 1985 (From Ross & White, 1987).

influences of a cyclical nature, including seasonal variation (Cook & Campbell, 1979). Thus, when Maki, Hoffman, and Berk (1978) assessed the effect of a water conservation program on water use in a California water district, they had to be sensitive to the possible influence of weather changes, including increased rainfall. Water use also would be expected to drop if population decreased because residents fearful of water shortages left the area when the conservation program was announced. The time-series graph depicting water use revealed a slight dip in water use after the water conservation program was initiated. Only through a detailed and sophisticated analysis, taking into account other facts related to water use, were these researchers able to conclude that the reduction in water use could reasonably be attributed to the conservation program. When analyzing the effect of the Connecticut governor's crackdown on speeding, Campbell (1969) gathered data from neighboring states in order to rule out possible regional trends due to weather or the introduction of automotive safety features in order to strengthen his case for the effect of this particular social-policy change.

Instrumentation must also be considered a threat to internal validity in the simple interrupted time-series design (Cook & Campbell, 1979). When new programs or new social policies are instituted, for example, there are often accompanying changes in the way that records are kept or in the procedures used to collect information. A program intended to reduce crime may lead authorities to modify their definitions of particular crimes or to become more careful when observing and reporting criminal activities. Nevertheless, for an instrumentation threat to be plausible, it must be shown how changes in instrumentation could occur at exactly the time of the intervention (Campbell & Stanley, 1966). Ross and White (1987) showed that they were aware of possible influences due to instrumentation effects. They noted in their Method section that data collected more than 18 months after the newspaper's new policy went into effect were not comparable to prior data because the laws defining a shoplifting offense had been changed. Hence, data were collected only during the 18-month period immediately after the policy change.

Most other threats to internal validity are controlled in the simple interrupted time-series design. Problems of maturation, testing, and regression are pretty much eliminated by the presence of multiple observations both before and after treatment. None of these threats can be ruled out when only a single pretest and posttest measure is available, as in the single-group pretest-posttest design mentioned earlier. For example, an effect of maturation would not normally be expected to show a sharp discontinuity in the time series, although this might be possible in some situations (Campbell & Stanley, 1966). When only one pretest and one posttest observation are available, it is not possible to decide whether performance changes from pretest to posttest reflect a treatment effect or are simply due to maturational processes. The simple time-series design generally permits this decision to be made.

Threats to external validity in the simple interrupted time-series design must be examined carefully. It should be obvious that, if pretreatment observations of behavior are based on multiple tests, then an effect of the treatment on behavior may be restricted to those subjects who have had multiple test experiences. Moreover, because only a single group is generally tested, one that was not randomly selected, it is always possible that the results are limited to subjects with characteristics similar to those who took part in the experiment.

TIME SERIES WITH NONEQUIVALENT CONTROL GROUP

The interrupted time-series design can be enhanced greatly by including a control group. This procedure is identical to that followed in constructing a nonequivalent control group design, which we discussed previously. In this case the researcher must find a group that is comparable to the treatment group and that allows a similar opportunity for multiple observations before and after the time that the treatment is administered to the experimental group. This **time series with nonequivalent control group** design is outlined as follows:

$$\begin{array}{cccccccccccc} O_1 & O_2 & O_3 & O_4 & O_5 & X & O_6 & O_7 & O_8 & O_9 & O_{10} \\ \hdashline O_1 & O_2 & O_3 & O_4 & O_5 & & O_6 & O_7 & O_8 & O_9 & O_{10} \end{array}$$

As before, a dashed line is used to indicate that the control group and the experimental group were not randomly assigned. This interrupted time series with nonequivalent control group permits one to control many threats due to history. As was mentioned earlier, Campbell (1969) used traffic fatality data obtained from neighboring states to provide a comparison with traffic fatality data following the crackdown on speeding in Connecticut. Although traffic fatalities in Connecticut showed a decline immediately following the crackdown, data from comparable states did not exhibit any such decline. This fact tends to rule out changes that might have been due to favorable weather conditions, improved automobile design, or other potentially positive factors.

Archival data, rather than direct observation, frequently provide the basis for time-series designs. For example, the extensive archival data in various fields of sport have furnished social psychologists with an opportunity to test the real-life implications of laboratory-based theories. In particular, Lord and Hohenfeld (1979) used an interrupted time-series design with nonequivalent control group to assess the effects on baseball players' performance of failure to reach a negotiated contract with their club. On the basis of an equity theory, they predicted that players who were playing without a contract would perform more poorly during the year they played out their option because they would feel undercompensated for their services. Their results tended to bear out this prediction, although Duchon and Jago (1981) obtained results suggesting that the external validity of the effect may be limited due to characteristics of the original sample of baseball players. As part of another study in the same vein (see Jackson, Buglione, & Glenwick, 1988), researchers compiled statistics on baseball players who were traded in midseason to a new team. A quasi-experimental analysis revealed that the batting average of these players was higher when playing for the new club than for the old club, confirming a prediction made from a drive theory of social facilitation. The possibility that baseball players, regardless of whether they are traded, increase their batting average over the full-year season was ruled out as an alternative explanation for these findings by demonstrating that averages of a random sample of nontraded players did not show a similar rise.

A particularly good illustration of the interrupted time-series design is provided by McSweeney (1978), who analyzed the frequency of telephone calls asking for directory assistance following initiation of a charge for such calls. Directory assistance calls requesting information about phone numbers listed in standard directories cost the telephone company money, and they pay these expenses by charging more for other services. As McSweeney (1978) pointed out, an intervention that would effectively reduce the frequency of these unnecessary calls would benefit both the telephone company and the consumer.

In 1974, officials at Cincinnati Bell Telephone company initiated charges for local directory assistance calls in excess of three per month. Subscribers were charged 20 cents for each additional call. Because the telephone company keeps extensive archival records, the effect of this intervention could be assessed using a time-series analysis. Furthermore, a simple time series could be expanded by seeking a comparison group. McSweeney chose to use as a control measure the long-distance directory assistance calls that were made from outside the Cincinnati area, for which no charge was made. Although the exact number of "participants" could not be known, it was estimated that the service charge for local directory assistance calls affected more than a million users. From data provided by Cincinnati Bell administrative records, McSweeney created the time-series graph shown in Figure 11.4. The frequency of local calls decreased dramatically after the charge was initiated, while directory assistance calls from outside the area continued to increase gradually.

The time-series analysis revealed a small dip in frequency of local calls before the actual charges were levied. This was apparently in response to the announcement by telephone company officials of the upcoming cost to the user. McSweeney reasonably argued that this change was due to the fact that some

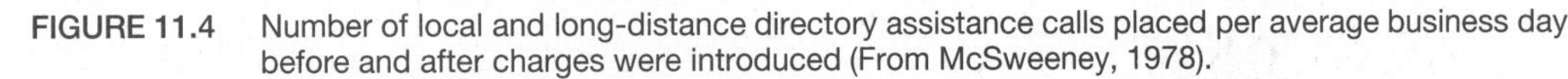

FIGURE 11.4 Number of local and long-distance directory assistance calls placed per average business day before and after charges were introduced (From McSweeney, 1978).

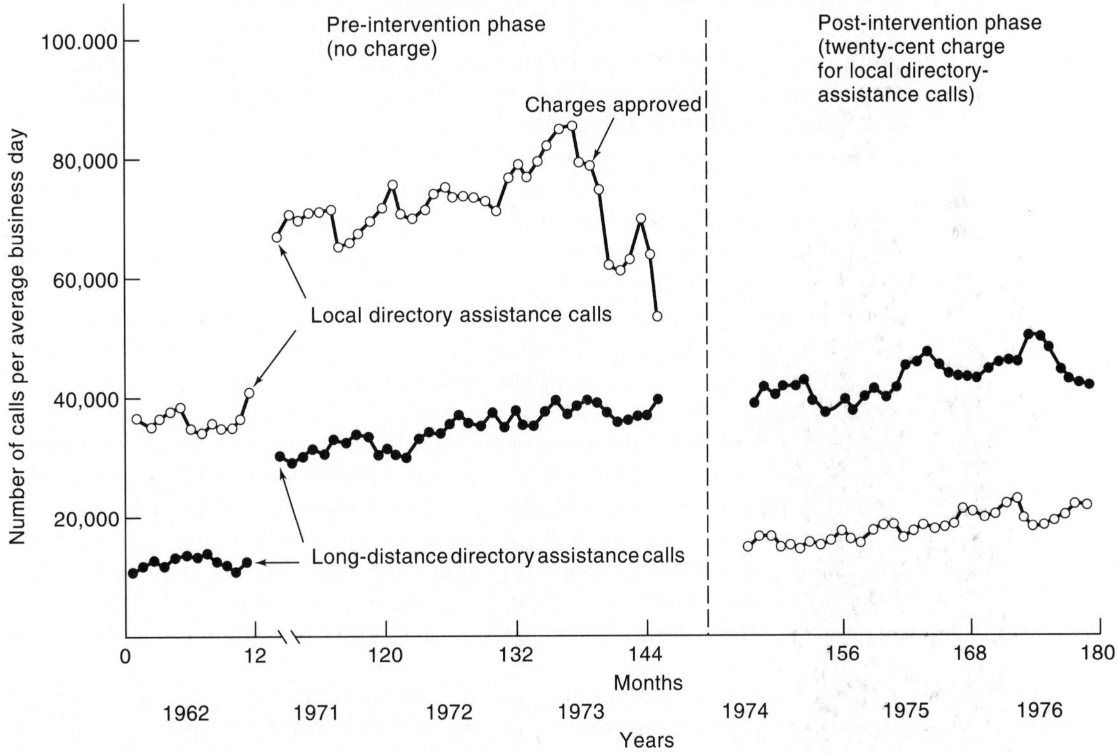

individuals misunderstood the announcement in news reports and thought the charges were already being made. Others may simply have begun to change their calling habits in anticipation of the charges. The clear discontinuity in the time series associated with the treatment group, in conjunction with the absence of any decrease in calls by the comparison group, provides nearly incontrovertible evidence that the effect was due to the intervention made by the telephone company. A subsequent analysis showed that the decrease in local directory assistance calls resulted in an average savings of 65 cents on the telephone bill of each individual residential consumer.

AN EXTENSION OF SINGLE-CASE EXPERIMENTAL DESIGNS TO RESEARCH IN NATURAL SETTINGS

RATIONALE

You may have noticed a similarity between the simple time-series design and the single-case experimental designs discussed in Chapter 10. In both situations, observations made prior to a treatment represent a "baseline" that is compared with observations obtained after the treatment. If there is a clear discontinuity in the behavioral record following the application of an independent variable, it is evidence for the effect of the treatment. Furthermore, for both types of design the major threat to internal validity is history. It is possible that some factor affecting the subjects' behavior, other than the independent variable, is responsible for the observed behavior change. However, the two types of design handle this threat differently.

When a simple time series is used, the investigator must search for historical factors (for example, seasonal variation) that might explain a change in the behavioral record. The addition of a nonequivalent control group greatly enhances the internal validity of the time-series design but does not completely rule out history or other threats, such as instrumentation. Moreover, unless the discontinuity in the time-series record is abrupt and obvious, the investigator must consider the possibility that one of numerous subtle factors produced a change and must rely on sophisticated mathematical models to determine whether an effect is present (see, for example, McCain & McCleary, in Cook & Campbell, 1979). A single-case experimental design controls for effects due to history when changes in the behavioral record correspond systematically to the repeated introduction and withdrawal of an independent variable (as in an ABAB design) or to the staggered introduction of a treatment (as in a multiple-baseline design). Unless observed changes are very small, it may be possible to avoid using complex statistical procedures and to rely instead on visual inspection of the pattern of change associated with the sequential manipulation of a treatment.

Single-case experimental designs offer an alternative to quasi-experimental procedures when one is conducting research in natural settings (for example, Horn & Heerboth, 1982). Although typically used to evaluate changes in a single subject, the single-case experimental design strategy can be used for a group of individuals, such as a classroom singled out for treatment. Examples of single-case experimental designs using groups of subjects are found in Chapter 10 (see, for instance, VanBiervliet et al., 1981). To use an **ABAB design** the investigator must have control over the application and withdrawal of a treatment and an opportunity must be present for periodic observation both during no treatment (baseline) stages and during treatment stages. Clearly this is not always possible in natural settings.

Treatments are often initiated under the assumption that they will "work," and, unfortunately, their effects are often not evaluated. A water conservation program, for example, is not likely to be applied, withdrawn, and then applied again in an attempt to measure its effectiveness on water consumption. However, when control over the application and withdrawal of a treatment is feasible, a single-case experimental design may be used to determine whether a treatment effect exists. The advantage to the researcher is a design whose internal validity is close to, if not the same as, that of a true experiment (see Horn & Heerboth, 1982). The following actual experiment illustrates the possibilities of using this experimental approach in natural settings. This example makes use of a variation of an ABAB design; the multiple-baseline design can also be employed in natural settings (see Horn & Heerboth, 1982).

THE ABAB DESIGN

Schnelle and his associates used a single-case methodology to evaluate the effect of police procedures on reducing crime rate (see, for example, Schnelle et al., 1978). In one study they sought evidence for the effect of a combined police car and helicopter patrol in reducing the frequency of home burglaries in a neighborhood of Nashville, Tennessee. The area was selected because police records showed that it had a chronically high number of burglaries. (Do you see how the *chronic* nature of this extreme measure neutralizes the problem of statistical regression?) The plan was to increase surveillance of the area by adding a helicopter patrol to the usual police-car patrol. When the helicopter was used, the pilots were told to fly low enough to observe suspicious activity. Pilots were in radio contact with the police in the patrol car. The helicopter was flown between 9 A.M. and 5 P.M. (weather permitting), a time that coincides with most home burglaries.

An ABAB procedure was used. Following a baseline observation of frequency of home burglaries in the experimental area, the helicopter was introduced for a period of time, then withdrawn, and then introduced again. The addition of the helicopter was an experimental program by the Nashville police, so the helicopter was again removed following the second treatment stage, providing an additional (and final) baseline period.

Figure 11.5 shows daily frequency of home burglaries during baseline and treatment periods. Visual inspection of the behavioral record clearly shows that the frequency of burglaries decreased when the helicopter was added to the

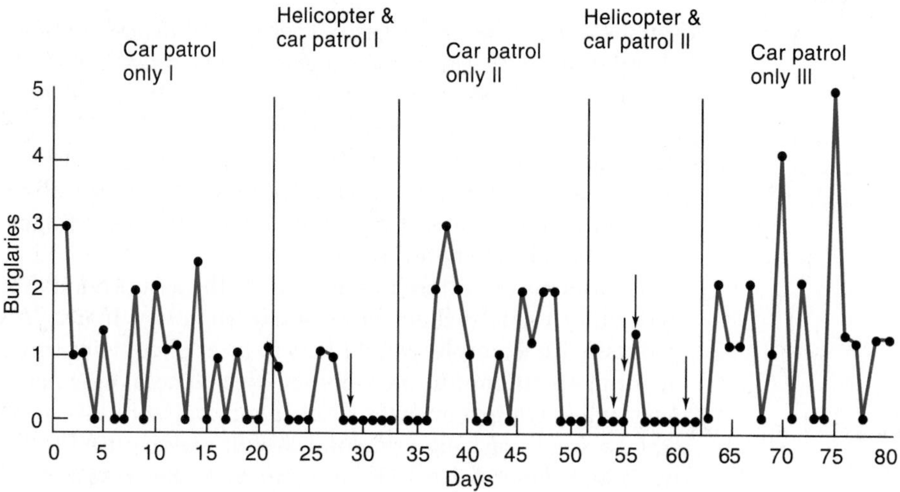

FIGURE 11.5 Daily frequency of home burglaries. Arrows indicate the days the helicopter was prevented from flying (From Schnelle et al., 1978).

police surveillance and increased when no helicopter was present. Interestingly, a check of police records showed no displacement of burglary activity to surrounding neighborhoods. That is, when the frequency of burglaries dropped in the experimental area, there was no corresponding rise in these types of crime in nearby neighborhoods. Note that the dependent variable in this example is frequency based on a *group* of individuals—in this case, residents in an approximately 6-square-mile area. Except for this change in the way behavior is assessed, the design strategy is exactly the same as might be used with a single individual.

PROGRAM EVALUATION

Organizations that produce goods have a ready-made index of success. If a company is set up to make hammers, its success is ultimately determined by its profits from the sale of hammers. At least theoretically, the efficiency and effectiveness of the organization can be easily assessed by examining the company's ledgers. Increasingly, however, organizations of a different sort play a critical role in our society. Because these organizations typically provide services rather than goods, Posavac and Carey (1992) refer to them as *human service organizations.* For example, hospitals, schools, police departments, and government agencies provide a variety of services ranging from emergency room care to fire prevention inspections. Because profit making is not their goal, some other method must be found to distinguish between effective and ineffective agencies. One useful approach to assessing the effectiveness of human service organizations is the discipline of program evaluation.

Posavac and Carey (1992, p. 1) define *program evaluation* as a "collection of methods, skills, and sensitivities necessary to determine whether a human service is needed and likely to be used, whether it is sufficiently intense to meet the unmet need identified, whether the service is offered as planned, and whether the human service actually does help people in need without undesirable side effects." These authors identify the basic goal of program evaluation as *providing feedback regarding human service activities.* Program evaluation represents a hybrid discipline that draws on political science, sociology, economics, education, and psychology. We discuss program evaluation at the end of this chapter on research in natural settings because it represents perhaps the most large-scale application of the principles and methods we have been describing throughout this book.

Program evaluations are designed to provide feedback to the administrators of human service organizations in order to help them decide what services to provide to whom and how to provide them most effectively and efficiently. Specifically, the questions asked by program evaluators are about needs, process, outcome, and efficiency (Posavac & Carey, 1992). An assessment of *needs* seeks to determine the unmet needs of the people for whom an agency might provide a service. If a city government were to consider instituting a program of recreational activities for senior citizens in the community, for example, it would first want to determine whether senior citizens actually need or want such a program and, if they do, what kind of program would be most attractive to them. The methods of survey research are used extensively in studies designed to assess needs. Information obtained in this type of program evaluation is also used to help program planning.

Once a program has been set up, program evaluators may ask about the process that has been established. Programs are not always implemented the way they were planned, and it is essential to know what actually *is* being done when a program is implemented. If the planned activities were not being used by the senior citizens in a recreational program designed specifically for them, it might suggest that the program was inadequately implemented. An evaluation that provides answers to questions about *process,* that is, about how a program is actually being carried out, permits administrators to make adjustments in the delivery of services in order to strengthen the existing program (Posavac & Carey, 1992). Observational methods may be employed in such evaluations.

An evaluation of *outcome* is just that; it asks whether the program has been effective in meeting its stated goals. For example, do senior citizens now have access to more recreational activities, and are they pleased with these activities? Are these particular activities preferred over other activities? The outcome of a community-watch program designed to curb neighborhood crime might be evaluated by assessing whether there were actual decreases in burglaries and assaults following the implementation of the program. Evaluators might also ask about the *efficiency* of the program, that is, about its cost. Choices often have to be made among possible services that a government or other institution is capable of delivering. Information about how successful a program is (outcome evaluation) and information about the program's cost (efficiency evaluation) are necessary if we want to make informed decisions about whether to continue the program, try an alternative program, or cut back on the program's services. These evaluations may use both experimental and quasi-experimental methods for research in natural settings. An evaluator may, for example, use a nonequivalent control group design to assess the effectiveness of a school reform program by comparing students' performance in two different school districts, one with the reform program and one without. It is also possible to use archival data like those described in Chapter 5 to carry out evaluations examining outcome and efficiency. For example, examining police records in order to document the frequency of various crimes was mentioned as one way to assess the effectiveness of a community-watch program.

Earlier in this chapter we described differences between basic and applied research. Program evaluation is perhaps the extreme case of applied research. The purpose of program evaluation is practical, not theoretical. Nevertheless, even in the context of blatantly practical goals, a case can be made for a reciprocal relationship between basic and applied research. Writing in the *International Journal of Psychology*, Salomon (1987) argues that each domain of research serves the other in an ongoing circular way. Specifically, basic research provides us with certain abstractions (for example, scientifically based principles) that express certain regularities in nature. When these principles are examined in the complex and "dirty" world where they supposedly apply, new complexities are recognized and new hypotheses are called for. These new complexities are then tested and evaluated before being tried out again in the real world. Salomon's model looks like this (from Salomon, 1987, p. 444):

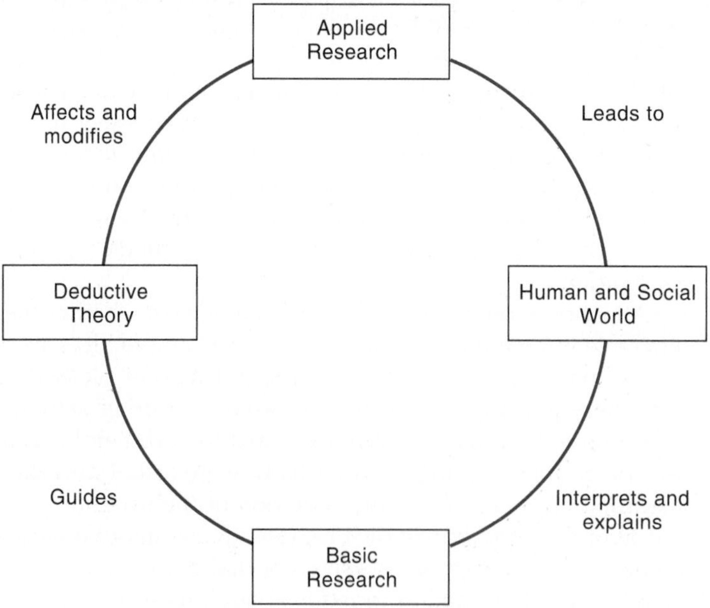

Salomon points to the work of Ellen Langer as a concrete example of this circular relationship. She identified a decline in elderly people's health once they entered nursing homes (see Langer, 1987; Langer & Rodin, 1976, described in this chapter). This led her to develop a theory of mindfulness, which she has tested under controlled experimental conditions and which has implications for more general theories of cognitive development (for example, see Langer & Piper, 1987). The theory provides a guide for her applied work—designing new models of nursing homes. Tests of the practical effects of changes in the care given by nursing homes on the residents' health and well-being will undoubtedly lead to modifications of her theory of mindfulness.

Perhaps the greatest difference between basic research and program evaluation lies in the political and social realities surrounding program evaluation. As was mentioned earlier in this chapter, governments at both local and national levels regularly propose, plan, and execute various types of social reforms. Tax relief programs, work incentive programs, educational reforms, police reforms, and medical care for senior citizens are just a few of the types of social reform programs that a government might initiate. Unfortunately, as Donald Campbell (1969), past president of the American Psychological Association, points out, the outcome of these social reforms often cannot be meaningfully evaluated. Did a change in police techniques lead to greater crime stoppage? Are more elderly people gaining access to public transportation after a reduction in fares? Does a work incentive program take more people off the unemployment rolls? The answers to such questions often cannot be found, says Campbell, because most social reforms are instituted in a political climate that is not ready for hardheaded evaluation. What public official, for instance, wants to be associated with a program that failed? As Campbell suggests, there is "safety under the cloak of ignorance" (pp. 409–410). Furthermore, many social reforms are begun under the assumption that they are certain to be successful. Otherwise why spend all that tax money? For many public administrators it is advantageous to leave that assumption in people's minds rather than face the true facts.

Cambell (p. 409) argues that

> the United States and other modern nations should be ready for an experimental approach to social reform, an approach in which we try out new programs, in which we learn whether or not these programs are effective, and in which we retain, imitate, modify, or discard them on the basis of apparent effectiveness on the multiple imperfect criteria available.

Social scientists must convince administrators to use "true" experiments, if at all possible, or quasi-experiments at the very least, when instituting new social programs. For example, a randomization procedure, perhaps based on public lottery, could be used to decide which group receives a pilot program or gains access to scarce resources. Groups not receiving the program or the available resources would become control groups. The effect of a social "treatment" could then be meaningfully evaluated. At present, decisions regarding who gets what are often influenced by particular interest groups—as the result of intense lobbying, for example—or made on the basis of political favoritism.

According to Campbell, the most significant change needed is for public officials to emphasize the importance of the problem rather than the importance of the solution. Instead of pushing for one certain cure-all (which, in most cases, has little opportunity for success), officials must be ready to execute reform in a manner that permits the clearest evaluation and must be prepared to try different solutions if the first one fails. Public officials must, in other words, be ready to use the experimental method to identify society's problems and to determine effective solutions.

Campbell's (1969) idea that social reforms and experimental methods be routinely brought together has had some impact on social policymakers, but it is still underutilized (see Berk et al., 1987). The reasons are some of the same ones initially identified by Campbell. Nevertheless, without social experimentation, especially that which makes use whenever possible of randomized field experiments, policymakers and the community at large may believe a treatment works when it doesn't or vice versa. Such incorrect decisions lead us to allocate money and resources to ineffective programs.

Not too many years ago, a show called "Scared Straight" was aired on national television. It described a juvenile education program implemented at Rahway State Prison in New Jersey. The program involved taking youthful offenders into a prison to meet with selected convicts from the inmate population. The goal was to inform juveniles about the reality of prison life and, thereby, the program leaders hoped, dissuade them from further illegal activity. Unsubstantiated claims were made for the effectiveness of the program, including some suggesting a success rate as high as 80 to 90 percent (see Locke, Johnson, Kirigin-Ramp, Atwater, & Gerrard, 1986). The Rahway program is just one of several similar programs around the country. But do these programs really work?

Several evaluation studies of the exposure-to-prison programs have produced mixed results, including positive findings, findings of no difference between control and experimental subjects, as well as results suggesting that the program may actually *increase* juvenile crime among some types of delinquents. There is a possibility that less-hardened juvenile offenders may increase their criminal activity after meeting the prisoners. It has been suggested that because these less-hardened offenders have recently begun a life-style wherein they are being recognized and reinforced by their peers for their toughness, this image is also reinforced by the tough image often projected by the prisoners. On the other hand, more frequent juvenile offenders, who have achieved a level of status among their peers for some period of time, may be more threatened by the prospects of prison life because it would mean loss of that status (see Locke et al., 1986).

Attempts to evaluate the effectiveness of this significant social program provide good examples of the difficulties inherent in evaluation research: the difficulty of randomly assigning subjects, of getting administrators to cooperate with experimental procedures, and of dealing with loss of subjects during the evaluation. Nevertheless, program evaluation based on sound experimental methodology offers policymakers at all levels (institution, community, city, state, federal) the information that can help them make rational choices among possible treatments for social problems. Since resources inevitably are in short supply, it is critical that those that are available to help society be put to the best possible use.

Our hope is that your knowledge of research methods will allow *you* to participate knowledgeably and perhaps contribute constructively to the ongoing debate concerning the role of experimentation in society.

SUMMARY

Experimentation in natural settings differs in many ways from experimentation in psychology laboratories. There are likely to be more problems in exerting experimental control in a natural setting, and establishing external validity or generalizing results is more often a key objective. The stated goals of the research and its possible consequences also differ when research is conducted in natural settings. Reasons for doing experiments in natural settings include testing the external validity of laboratory findings and assessing the effects of "treatments" aimed at improving conditions under which people work and live.

Campbell and others have argued that society must be willing to take an experimental approach to social reform—one that will allow the clearest evaluation of the effectiveness of new programs. In many situations (for instance, when available resources are scarce), true experiments involving randomization of individuals to treatment and no treatment conditions are recommended. However, if a true experiment is not feasible, quasi-experimental procedures are the next best approach. Quasi-experiments differ from true experiments in that fewer plausible rival hypotheses for an experimental outcome are controlled. When specific threats to the internal validity of an experiment are not controlled, then the experimenter, by logically examining the situation and by collecting additional evidence, must seek to rule out these threats to internal validity.

A particularly strong quasi-experimental procedure is the nonequivalent control group design. This procedure generally controls for all major threats to internal validity except those associated with interactions of (a) selection and history, (b) selection and maturation, (c) selection and instrumentation, and (d) threats due to differential statistical regression. In addition to the major threats to internal validity, an experimenter must be sensitive to possible contamination resulting from communication between groups of subjects. Problems of observer or experimenter bias, questions of external validity, and Hawthorne effects are potential problems in all experiments, whether conducted in the laboratory or in the field.

When it is possible to observe changes in a dependent measure before and after a treatment is administered, one can carry out a simple interrupted time-series design. The researcher using this design looks for an abrupt change in the time series that coincides with the introduction of treatment. The major threat to internal validity in this design is history—some event other than the treatment may have been responsible for the change in the time series. Instrumentation also can be a problem, especially when the treatment represents a type of social reform that may lead to changes in the way records are kept or data collected. By including a control group that is as similar as possible to the experimental group, one can strengthen the internal validity of a simple time-series design. A time series with nonequivalent control group, for example, controls for many possible history threats.

In this chapter we also discussed how the logic and methodology associated with single-case experimental designs (see Chapter 10) can be applied to experimentation in natural settings. For instance, an ABAB design may be used when a researcher can control the application and withdrawal of a treatment. In such cases the internal validity of the experiment can approach that of a true experiment.

A particularly important goal of research in natural settings is program evaluation. Persons other than psychologists (such as educators, political scientists, and sociologists) are often involved in this process. Types of program evaluation include assessment of needs, process, outcome, and efficiency. Perhaps the most serious constraints on program evaluation are the political and social realities that surround it. The reluctance of public officials to seek an evaluation of social reforms is often an obstacle to be overcome. Nevertheless, social scientists have called on individuals who are knowledgeable about the procedures of program evaluation to make themselves available to those who are responsible for the delivery of social services. By answering this call, we may help change society in a way that will bring the most effective services to those most in need.

KEY CONCEPTS

program evaluation
basic research
applied research
threats to internal validity
contamination
Hawthorne effect
quasi-experiments
nonequivalent control group design
simple interrupted time-series design
time series with nonequivalent control group
ABAB design

REVIEW QUESTIONS

1 What special reasons are there for carrying out experiments in natural settings?
2 Explain how laboratory experiments and those in natural settings differ in control, external validity, goals, and consequences.

3 Distinguish between basic research and applied research.
4 Briefly explain what Donald Campbell meant when he called for an experimental approach to social reform.
5 What are the three distinguishing characteristics of true experiments?
6 What obstacles arise in trying to carry out experiments in natural settings?
7 Comment critically on the "fairness" of random assignment.
8 How can participants be randomly assigned to treatments while still giving all participants access to the experimental treatment?
9 Define by means of an example the eight major threats to internal validity as summarized by Campbell and Stanley (1966).
10 Explain how contamination, threats to external validity, experimenter expectancy effects, and Hawthorne effects threaten the clear interpretation of an experimental result.
11 How are subjects in a control group likely to respond when contamination occurs?
12 What do Cook and Campbell (1979) consider the best test of external validity?
13 Why is the use of a pretest critical in the nonequivalent control group design?
14 Cite one example of a threat to internal validity that is controlled in the nonequivalent control group design and two examples of threats that are not controlled.
15 Explain why we cannot conclude that the treatment and control groups in a nonequivalent control group design are equivalent even when the pretest scores are the same for both groups.
16 What is meant by a "local history effect" in the nonequivalent control group design?
17 How did Langer and Rodin handle problems of observer bias and possible effects of contamination in their study of elderly residents of a nursing home?
18 What is the major evidence for an effect of the treatment in a simple interrupted time-series design?
19 Explain how the addition of a nonequivalent control group to a simple interrupted time-series design reduces the threat to the internal validity of the design.
20 How can single-case experimental designs be used to determine whether an effect is due to a treatment or to the threat to internal validity called *history*?
21 What are the four types of questions typically addressed in program evaluation?
22 In what sense can it be said that basic and applied research have a reciprocal relationship to one another?

CHALLENGE QUESTIONS

1 Because of your extensive background in research design, you have been appointed by a local school board committee to design a definitive study of the effect of a newly developed nutritious breakfast as compared with the current, less nutritious, breakfast on the school performance of young children. The school board is trying to decide whether to establish a "nutritious breakfast program" at the school, and, because of the expense of this proposed program (and because of your persuasive arguments), they have decided to test the effectiveness of the breakfast before implementing the program. For this problem, pretend that you are meeting with the principal of the school to work out the details of the study. You are to respond to each of the following suggestions made by the principal.

A The principal first suggests that students be selected for the treatment during the test phase on the basis of their need. That is, the students who have the lowest nutrition level now will be given the treatment. Explain to the principal why this is not an advisable procedure.

B Having given up his suggestion in Part A, the principal next suggests that the only fair procedure for the test is to give the treatment to all the students to see if there is any improvement in their performance. Explain to the principal what you would have to do under these circumstances to verify the effectiveness of the program, and explain why this could be a "risky" way to test the program.

C Finally, the principal gives up and ask you to outline the design you would propose for the study. Outline the essentials of the design you would propose. In your design be sure to use double-blind procedures and explain to the principal the how and why of these procedures.

2 A psychologist published a book describing the effects of divorce on men, women, and children. She was interested in the effects of divorce that occurred 10 years after the divorce. She found that even 10 years after a divorce half of the women and one-third of the men were still intensely angry. Although half the men and women described themselves as happy, 25 percent of the women and 20 percent of the men remained unable to "get their lives back on track." In only 10 percent of the divorced families did both the former husbands and wives have happy, satisfying lives a decade later. Finally, more than half of the children of divorce entered adulthood as under-achieving and self-deprecating men and women. These findings were based on a 15-year study of sixty divorced couples and their 131 children living in Marin County, California (an affluent suburban area including mostly well-educated people). Explain how the use of a quasi-experimental design would have been helpful in order to specify which of the reported results are due to the effects of divorce.

3 The police force of a large city had to decide between two different approaches to keeping the officers on the force informed about the changes in laws. An enlightened administrator of this force decided to put the two approaches to test in a research study. She decided to use the random groups design and she assigned thirty officers randomly to each of the two programs for a period of 6 months. At the end of this time all the officers who successfully completed the training required under the two approaches were given a final test on their knowledge of the law. The twenty officers who completed Program A showed a reliably higher mean score on this test than did the twenty-eight officers who completed Program B. The administrator wisely chose not to accept these results as decisive evidence of the effectiveness of the two programs. Using only the data reported in this problem, explain why she made this decision. Next, explain how her decision would have been different if twenty officers completed both programs (from the original thirty assigned to each) and there was still a sizable difference favoring Program A. Be sure to mention any limitations on the conclusions she could reach concerning the overall effectiveness of these programs.

4 A small undergraduate college with a new physical fitness center decided to introduce a health enhancement program for faculty and staff. The program is designed to take one semester to complete with three 1-hour sessions per week. Comment critically on each of the following questions regarding the evaluation of this program.

A How might an evaluation of needs have played a role in planning the program?

B What obstacles generally exist in real-world settings, and probably apply in this situation, that prevent the conduct of a true experiment to evaluate the outcome of the program? (Be sure to define the three characteristics of a true experiment.)

C As an alternative to a true experiment, a nonequivalent control group design is proposed in which a group of faculty who did not participate in the program agree

to take the performance tests before the program begins and after the program has ended. Explain why this nonequivalent control group design is superior to a pretest-posttest design in which only the program participants would be tested. State one threat to internal validity that is controlled in the nonequivalent control group design.

ANSWER TO CHALLENGE QUESTION 1

1 A Selecting students on the basis of need may result in problems with regression to the mean, especially if the students are identified on the basis of an unreliable measure of need. If regression were to be a problem, the nutrition program could falsely appear to be effective.

B Administering the program to all students would necessitate projecting what students' performance would have been without the program on the basis of their prior school performance, as is the case in a time-series design. Their prior performance would serve as a baseline, and the risks associated with variable baselines would apply to this situation. The test of the effectiveness of the program would also be potentially challenged by the threats to internal validity that apply to the time-series designs, such as history.

C The most appropriate design for this problem would be a two-group experiment using the random groups design. Both groups should receive comparably packaged breakfast foods that had been previously coded by the manufacturer as containing the newly developed nutritious breakfast or the previously used (and presumably less nutritious) diet. Neither the students nor those responsible for assessing their school performance should know which diet a given student has received. This double-blind procedure avoids potential problems of demand characteristics (students working harder in school because they know they have received the "super" breakfast) and experimenter effects (teachers showing observer bias by varying their assessments of students in light of which treatment the student has received or influencing students' performance differentially by giving more individual attention and instruction to students whom the teachers know are receiving the new diet).

Appendix A

Statistical Methods

Outline

OVERVIEW

This appendix is intended primarily to assist students who have gathered data as part of a research project and who want to analyze their data. The first half of the appendix provides computational procedures for statistics that can be done relatively easily with a calculator. Before presenting the procedures for several statistical tests, we provide a review of some statistical notation with which students will need to be familiar to carry out the tests. Along with the computations for each test, we present a sample data set to illustrate the type of problem for which the statistical test is best suited.

In the second half of the appendix we present sample data sets for different experimental designs for which the analysis of variance is the appropriate inferential statistics test. For these analyses we do not provide computational procedures. Instead, we present the output from a software package that has been used to perform the computations. Our focus is on understanding the output and on interpreting the results of the *F*-tests appropriately. We hope this appendix will help students as they analyze the results of research projects they do in the context of their research methods course.

NOTES ON NOTATION

To learn the computational procedures for specific statistical tests, you need first to learn some general characteristics of statistical notation. A subject's score on a dependent variable is typically called "X." The scores of individual subjects are indicated by subscripts (X_1 X_2 X_3); thus, we refer to the score for the first subject as X_1, that for the second subject as X_2, and so on. If we have two scores for each subject on two different dependent variables, we typically refer to the first score as X and the second score as Y. For example, if we measured the first subject's height as 60 inches and weight as 120 pounds, then $X_1 = 60$ and $Y_1 = 120$.

The number of subjects in each group within a study is indicated using the symbol n. Once again, we use subscripts to differentiate the different groups. If there are thirty subjects in Group 1 and twenty-five subjects in Group 2, we indicate this in symbols as $n_1 = 30$; $n_2 = 25$. The subscripts need not be numbers; if there are ten subjects in the control group and twelve subjects in the experimental group, we could write $n_c = 10$; $n_e = 12$. The total number of subjects across all the groups in the study is indicated by the symbol *N*. If there are three groups in an experiment and if $n_1 = 10$, $n_2 = 15$, and $n_3 = 5$, then $N = 30$.

The summation sign, Σ, indicates that you are to add all the values represented by the symbol(s) that appear to the right of the summation sign. If you had the three scores $X_1 = 4$, $X_2 = 5$, and $X_3 = 6$, the expression ΣX would indicate that you should do the following computation:

$$\Sigma X = X_1 + X_2 + X_3 = 4 + 5 + 6 = 15$$

There are two other common expressions involving the summation sign that appear in many statistical computations, ΣX^2 and $(\Sigma X)^2$. These two expression look very similar, but they require very different computations. The expression ΣX^2 indicates that each individual score should first be squared and then the sum of these squared scores should be determined. The expression $(\Sigma X)^2$ requires the determination of the sum of the individual scores first and then the squaring of this sum. Using our sample of three scores ($X_1 = 4$, $X_2 = 5$, and $X_3 = 6$), the differences between the two calculations can be made clear.

$$\Sigma X^2 = X_1^2 + X_2^2 + X_3^2 = 4^2 + 5^2 + 6^2 = 16 + 25 + 36 = 77$$
$$(\Sigma X)^2 = (X_1 + X_2 + X_3)^2 = (4 + 5 + 6)^2 = (15)^2 = 225$$

DESCRIPTIVE STATISTICS

The scores representing performance of subjects in a particular group can be summarized most completely by constructing a frequency distribution. In a frequency distribution, the possible values of the dependent variable are listed from lowest to highest and the number of subjects obtaining each score is tabulated. While a frequency distribution provides the most complete summary of the results, reporting the frequency distributions for each of the six conditions in an experiment is too cumbersome. Most frequency distributions can be summarized by reporting one measure of central tendency and one measure of dispersion. We will now describe each type of measure in turn.

MEASURES OF CENTRAL TENDENCY: MODE, MEDIAN, AND MEAN

Measures of central tendency indicate the score that identifies the center of the frequency distribution. The *mode* is the crudest measure of central tendency in that it simply indicates the score in the frequency distribution that occurs most often. If two scores in the distribution occur with much higher frequency than do other scores in the distribution, and if these two scores occur at two different locations in the frequency distribution, this two-humped distribution is said to be *bimodal* (to have two modes).

The *median* is defined as the middle score in the frequency distribution. The median is calculated by ranking all the scores from lowest to highest. If there is an odd number of scores, then the middle score is equal to the median. If there is an even number of scores, then the median is the average of the two scores in the middle. For example, if a distribution of scores included the values 4, 7, 2, 1, 9, we would compute the median by first ranking the scores—1, 2, 4, 7, 9—and then selecting the third of the five scores (4) as the median. If a sixth score were included in the distribution (4, 7, 2, 1, 9, 5), we would again rank the scores (1, 2, 4, 5, 7, 9), but this time we would average the third and fourth scores to obtain the median

$$\left(\frac{4 + 5}{2}\right) = 4.5$$

The median is the best measure of central tendency when the distribution includes extreme scores because it is less influenced than is the mean by the extreme scores. For example, the median of the distribution of scores 1, 2, 3, 4, 5 is 3. The median would remain the same even if the distribution were changed to 1, 2, 3, 4, 50.

The *mean* is the most commonly reported measure of central tendency and it is determined by dividing the sum of the scores (ΣX) by the number of scores contributing to that sum (n). The mean of the five scores 4, 7, 2, 1, 9 would be calculated as folows:

$$\text{Mean} = \frac{\Sigma X}{n} = \frac{4 + 7 + 2 + 1 + 9}{5} = 4.6$$

The mean of a population is symbolized as μ (Greek letter mu); the mean of a sample of scores is usually indicated as $\overline{X}$ (read "X bar"), but it is sometimes symbolized as M. The mean should always be reported as a measure of central tendency unless there are extreme scores in the distribution.

The mean of several samples of the same size can be determined by averaging the means of the individual samples. For example, if each of the five groups included ten subjects and the means for these five groups were as follows, $\overline{X}_1 = 4.6$, $\overline{X}_2 = 4.3$, $\overline{X}_3 = 6.2$, $\overline{X}_4 = 4.7$, and $\overline{X}_5 = 5.2$, then the mean across all five groups can be computed using the following equation in which K is the number of groups:

$$\text{Overall mean} = \frac{(\Sigma \overline{X})}{K} = \frac{4.6 + 4.3 + 6.2 + 4.7 + 5.2}{5}$$
$$= \frac{25}{5} = 5.00$$

When the overall mean for a group of samples of different sizes needs to be computed, the simple averaging of the sample means is not appropriate. Simple averaging would give undue weight to the scores for subjects in the smaller groups and would give too little weight to subjects' scores in the larger groups. The overall mean can be computed in a way that gives equal weight to the score for each individual subject. For example, if in Group 1 there are twenty subjects and $\overline{X}_1 = 4.45$, and in Group 2 there are 10 subjects and $\overline{X}_2 = 6.20$, and in Group 3 there are twenty subjects and $\overline{X}_3 = 4.95$, then the overall mean can be computed as follows:

$$\text{Overall mean} = \frac{\Sigma(n)(\overline{X})}{N} = \frac{(20)(4.45) + (10)(6.2) + (20)(4.95)}{50}$$
$$= \frac{89 + 62 + 99}{50}$$
$$= \frac{250}{50} = 5.00$$

MEASURES OF DISPERSION: RANGE AND STANDARD DEVIATION

Whenever you report a measure of central tendency, it should always be accompanied by an appropriate measure of dispersion. Measures of central tendency indicate the center of a frequency distribution, measures of dispersion indicate the breadth or variability of the distribution. The two distributions shown below have the same mean (13), but they clearly differ in how the scores are distributed about that mean. In Distribution A, the scores are tightly packed about the mean, indicating low dispersion. The scores in Distribution B, on the other hand, are more widely distributed about the mean, indicating greater dispersion.

Distribution A	Distribution B
13	9
13	11
13	13
13	15
13	17

The crudest measure of dispersion (the counterpart of the mode) is the range. The *range* is determined by subtracting the lowest score in the distribution from the highest score. In the small distribution made up of the scores 1, 3, 5, 7, the range would be equal to 7–1, or 6.

The most commonly used measure of dispersion (the counterpart of the mean) is the standard deviation. The *standard deviation* tells you approximately how far on the average a score is from the mean. It is equal to the square root of the average squared deviations of the scores in the distribution about the mean. The definitional formula for the standard deviation is

$$\sqrt{\frac{\Sigma(X - \overline{X})^2}{n - 1}}$$

For reasons that need not concern us here the average of the squared deviations about the mean must involve division by n − 1 rather than n so as to provide an unbiased estimate of the population standard deviation based on the sample. The standard deviation of a population is symbolized as σ (Greek letter sigma); the standard deviation of a sample of scores is usually indicated as s, but it sometimes symbolized as SD. The computational formula for the standard deviation is

$$s = \sqrt{\frac{\Sigma X^2 - \frac{(\Sigma X)^2}{n}}{n - 1}}$$

The use of this computational formula can be best illustrated by working through an example for a small distribution of scores: 2, 6, 10, 14, 18.

1 Compute $\Sigma X^2 = 2^2 + 6^2 + 10^2 + 14^2 + 18^2$
$= 4 + 36 + 100 + 196 + 324$
$= 660$

2 Compute $\Sigma X = 2 + 6 + 10 + 14 + 18$
$= 50$

3 Compute $\frac{(\Sigma X)^2}{n} = \frac{(50)^2}{5} = \frac{2,500}{5} = 500$

4 Compute $\Sigma X^2 - \frac{(\Sigma X)^2}{n} = 660 - 500 = 160$

5 Compute $\frac{\Sigma X^2 - \frac{(\Sigma X)^2}{n}}{n - 1} = \frac{160}{4} = 40$

6 Compute $\sqrt{\dfrac{\Sigma X^2 - \dfrac{(\Sigma X)^2}{n}}{n - 1}} = \sqrt{40} = 6.32$

STANDARD ERROR OF THE MEAN

In doing inferential statistics, we use the sample mean as a point estimate of the population mean. That is, we use a single value ($\overline{X}$) to estimate (infer) the population mean (μ). It is often helpful to be able to determine how much error there is in estimating μ on the basis of $\overline{X}$. The Central Limit Theorem in mathematics tells us that if we draw an infinite number of samples of the same size and we compute $\overline{X}$ for each of these samples, the mean of these sample means ($\mu_{\overline{X}}$) will be equal to the population mean (μ), and the standard deviation of the sample means ($\sigma_{\overline{X}}$) will be equal to the population standard deviation (σ) divided by the square root of the sample size ($\sqrt{n}$). The standard deviation of this theoretical sampling distribution of the mean is called the *standard error of the mean*.

Typically, we do not know the standard deviation of the population so we estimate it on the basis of a sample. Thus, the estimate of standard error of the mean ($s_{\overline{X}}$) is computed using the formula $s_{\overline{X}} = s/\sqrt{n}$. Small values of $s_{\overline{X}}$ suggest that we have a good estimate of the population mean, and large values of $s_{\overline{X}}$ suggest that we have only a rough estimate of the population mean. The formula for the standard error of the mean indicates that our ability to estimate the population mean on the basis of a sample is dependent on the size of the sample (large samples lead to better estimates) and on the variability in the population from which the sample was drawn, as estimated by the sample standard deviation (the less variable the scores in a population, the better our estimate of the population mean will be).

If the standard deviation of a sample of twenty-five scores (which can be computed from a set of scores following the procedures described in the previous section) is 5, then the standard error of the mean ($s_{\overline{X}}$) is equal to $s/\sqrt{n}$, which in this case is $5/\sqrt{25} = 5/5 = 1.00$.

CONFIDENCE INTERVALS

Imagine that you are having a physical examination at the campus health clinic. The technician reports that your pulse is 75 beats per minute. You are unlikely to be concerned that your heart is racing if you are also told that the average pulse rate at rest for a person your age is 72 beats per minute. Your knowledge of the variability of pulse rates keeps you from being alarmed. In both physiological and psychological measurement we are often more interested in knowing a range of values that define a "normal" range than we are in specifying a single estimate of a population value. These normal ranges are based on the standard error of the mean and are called *confidence intervals*. In computing a confidence interval we specify a range of values within which we can have a certain degree of confidence that the population mean is included within the interval. As you may suspect, the larger the interval we specify, the greater our confidence that the mean will be included; but larger intervals give us less specific information about the exact value of the population mean. As a compromise, researchers have agreed that the 95 percent confidence interval and the 99 percent confidence interval will be used when an interval estimate of the populaton mean is desired. The confidence interval is centered about our point estimate of the mean ($\overline{X}$), and the boundaries of the 95 percent confidence interval can be calculated using the following formulas:

$$\text{Upper limit of 95 percent confidence interval} = \overline{X} + [t(n - 1)]_{\alpha = .05}[S_{\overline{X}}]$$
$$\text{Lower limit of 95 percent confidence interval} = \overline{X} - [t(n - 1)]_{\alpha = .05}[S_{\overline{X}}]$$

We have already described procedures for computing the sample mean ($\overline{X}$) and the standard error of the mean ($s_{\overline{X}}$). The unfamiliar symbols in the two equations for the limits of the 95 percent confidence interval are $[t(n - 1)]$ and $\alpha = .05$. The level of significance ($\alpha = .05$) may be familiar to you if you have studied the procedures for inferential statistics tests described in Chapter 6. In the case of confidence intervals, $\alpha = (1 - \text{level of confidence})$, expressed as a proportion. So, for the 95 percent confidence interval, $\alpha = 1 - .95 = .05$ and for the 99 percent confidence interval, $\alpha = 1 - .99 = .01$. The t statistic included in the equation is defined by the number of degrees of freedom ($n - 1$), and the t is determined by looking it up in Table A.5.

We are now ready to compute the 95 percent confidence interval for the mean of a sample in which $\overline{X} = 12$, $s = 4$, and $n = 25$.

1 Compute $s_{\overline{X}} = \dfrac{s}{\sqrt{n}} = \dfrac{4}{\sqrt{25}} = \dfrac{4}{5} = .8$

2 Determine degrees of freedom for t: $n - 1 = 25 - 1 = 24$

3 Determine $\alpha = 1 - .95 = .05$

4 Look up in Table A.5 the value for $t(24)_{\alpha = .05} = 2.06$

5 Compute upper limit of 95 percent confidence interval

$$= \overline{X} + [t(n - 1]_{\alpha = .05}[s_{\overline{X}}]$$
$$= 12 + [2.06][.8]$$
$$= 12 + 1.65 = 13.65$$

6 Compute lower limit of 95 percent confidence interval

$$= \overline{X} + [t(n - 1)]_{\alpha = .05}[s_{\overline{X}}]$$
$$= 12 - [2.06][.8]$$
$$= 12 - 1.65 = 10.35$$

7 The 95 percent confidence interval for a sample mean of 12 from a sample size of 25 with a standard deviation of 4 is bounded by 10.35 and 13.65. We can thus be 95 percent confident that the specified interval captures the mean of the population from which the sample was drawn.

CORRELATIONAL ANALYSES

The degree of relationship between two dependent measures for the same sample of subjects is determined by calculating a correlation coefficient. If the two dependent measures both represent at least an interval scale of measurement (see Chapter 3), then the Pearson Product-Moment Correlation Coefficient r is used. If one or both dependent measures represent only an ordinal scale of measurement, however, then the appropriate correlation coefficient is Spearman's Rank-Order Correlation Coefficient r_s. We will illustrate the computational procedures for both correlation coefficients. We will also describe two important correlational analyses using the chi-square test.

PEARSON PRODUCT-MOMENT CORRELATION COEFFICIENT *r*

Each of ten subjects agreed to keep track of how many hours were spent practicing the week before a ping-pong tournament. During the week of the tournament the number of games won by each of these ten subjects was also determined. We will refer to the number of hours of practice as X and to the number of games won as Y. The data for each of the ten subjects on each of these two measures are listed in the following table, and these data were used to carry out the necessary computations for determining r.

Subject	Hours of practice (X)	Games won (Y)
1	40	10
2	20	3
3	10	1
4	15	2
5	18	4
6	35	6
7	27	9
8	16	8
9	4	5
10	33	7

1 Compute $\Sigma X = 40 + 20 + 10 + \ldots + 33 = 218$

2 Compute $\Sigma Y = 10 + 3 + 1 + \ldots + 7 = 55$

3 Compute $\Sigma X^2 = 40^2 + 20^2 + 10^2 + \ldots + 33^2 = 5{,}964$

4 Compute $\Sigma Y^2 = 10^2 + 3^2 + 1^2 + \ldots + 7^2 = 385$

5 Compute $\Sigma XY = (40)(10) + (20)(3) + \ldots (33)(7) = 1{,}404$

6 Compute $\Sigma XY - \dfrac{(\Sigma X)(\Sigma Y)}{n} = 1{,}404 - \dfrac{(218)(55)}{10} = 205$

7 Compute $\Sigma X^2 - \frac{(\Sigma X)^2}{n} = 5{,}964 - \frac{(218)^2}{10} = 1{,}211.60$

8 Compute $\Sigma Y^2 - \frac{(\Sigma Y)^2}{n} = 385 - \frac{(55)^2}{10} = 82.50$

9 Multiply step 7 by step 8 $= (1{,}211.60)(82.50) = 99{,}957$

10 Take the square root of step 9 $= \sqrt{99{,}957} = 316.16$

11 Divide step 6 by step 10 to obtain $r = \frac{205}{316.16} = .65$

The eleven steps we have just outlined have led you successfully through the computational formula for *r*. The computational formula in its complete form is as follows:

$$r = \frac{\Sigma XY - \frac{(\Sigma X)(\Sigma Y)}{n}}{\sqrt{\left(\Sigma X^2 - \frac{(\Sigma X)^2}{n}\right)\left(\Sigma Y^2 - \frac{(\Sigma Y)^2}{n}\right)}}$$

To determine whether your obtained *r* is greater than zero, you can use Table A.2. The degrees of freedom (df) are n − 2, and Table A.2 lists the critical values of *r* for the .05 and .01 levels of significance. If your obtained *r* is *greater* than the tabled value, then the correlation you have obtained is statistically significant. In our example, the degrees of freedom for *r* would be 8 since n is 10. The obtained *r* of .65 is larger than the tabled *r* for a .05 level of significance (.632), so it would be considered statistically significantly larger than zero. Notice, however, if we had used a .01 level of significance, our obtained *r* of .65 would be *less* than the tabled value (.765) and thus judged to be *not* statistically significant. If we concluded that the correlation was statistically significant, then we would also conclude that the more hours a player practices Ping Pong, the more games he or she is likely to win.

SPEARMAN'S RANK-ORDER CORRELATION COEFFICIENT r_s

The director of the admissions office at a very small college selected a random sample of ten students from this year's incoming class to determine whether there was a correlation between the students' high school class ranks and their scores on a national college board test. The scores on the college board test represent an interval scale, with higher scores indicating better performance. The high school ranks, however, represent only an ordinal scale and so Spearman's rank-order correlation must be used.

Student	Class rank	Test score	Test rank	D	D^2
1	2	675	1	1	1
2	4	525	6	−2	4
3	7	500	7.5	−.5	.25
4	9	450	9	0	0
5	6	650	2	4	16
6	1	600	3	−2	4
7	3	550	5	−2	4
8	8	500	7.5	.5	.25
9	10	425	10	0	0
10	5	575	4	1	1

Note: The students' actual high school class ranks would have ranged over ranks larger than 1 to 10. These are their converted class ranks within the sample of 10.

1 Rank the students from highest to lowest on their test scores. For students with the same test score, take the ranks these students would have received and average them. Then, assign the next rank to the next lowest student. For example, students 3 and 8 both have a score of 500. They are in ranks 7 and 8, so both receive a rank of 7.5 $[(7 + 8)/2 = 7.5]$ and the next lowest student (student 4 with a score of 450) receives a rank of 9.

2 Compute D—the difference in the two ranks for each student. See column D in the table.

3 Compute D^2—square each difference score. See column D^2 in the table.

4 Compute $\Sigma D^2 = 1 + 4 + .25 + 0 + 16 + 4 + 4 + .25 + 0 + 1 = 30.5$

5 Multiply ΣD^2 by $6 = (6)(30.5) = 183$

6 Compute $n(n^2 - 1) = 10(10^2 - 1) = 10(100 - 1) = 10(99) = 990$

7 Divide step 5 by step 6: $\frac{183}{990} = .18$

8 Subtract step 7 from 1 to obtain $r_s = 1 - .18 = .82$

Once again, the steps we have just outlined have led you successfully through the computational formula for r_s. The computational formula in its complete form is

$$r_s = 1 - \frac{6(\Sigma D^2)}{n(n^2 - 1)}$$

To determine whether your obtained r_s is greater than zero, you can use Table A.3. The critical information you need in Table A.3 is n (in our example n = 10), and the level of significance you want to use. If the obtained r_s is *greater* than the tabled value, then the correlation you have obtained is statistically significant. In our example, the obtained r_s of .82 is larger than the tabled value for the .05 level of significance (.648), so it would be considered statistically significantly larger than zero. Thus, as you might expect, students' high school class ranks and college board test scores are correlated, although the actual correlation is usually less than .82.

CHI-SQUARE (χ^2) TEST: GOODNESS OF FIT

The chi-square (χ^2) goodness-of-fit test is used to determine whether the obtained frequencies in each of several nominal scale categories correspond to the expected frequencies in each category. The expected frequencies are often based on the laws of chance, but they can also represent expectations based on a formal psychological theory. It is essential that each individual observation be independent and that each observation be classified into one—and only one—category.

The example we will use to illustrate the computation of this test will involve testing the "fairness" of a six-sided die rolled sixty times. You could also consider these data to represent the responses of sixty students to a six-alternative multiple-choice test item on material the students have *not* studied. A fair die and a good test item should lead to equal frequencies across categories. The observed and expected frequencies on which the computations will be based are as follows:

	Outcome categories					
	1	2	3	4	5	6
Observed frequency	7	12	10	12	8	11
Expected frequency	10	10	10	10	10	10
(O – E)	–3	2	0	2	–2	1

1 Compute Observed (O) – Expected (E) frequencies in each category. (See last row of table.)

2 Compute $\chi^2 = \Sigma \frac{(O - E)^2}{E}$

$$= \frac{(-3)^2}{10} + \frac{(2)^2}{10} + \frac{(0)^2}{10} + \frac{(2)^2}{10} + \frac{(-2)^2}{10} + \frac{(1)^2}{10}$$

$$= \frac{9}{10} + \frac{4}{10} + 0 + \frac{4}{10} + \frac{4}{10} + \frac{1}{10}$$

$$= .9 + .4 + 0 + .4 + .4 + .1 = 2.20$$

3 Determine degrees of freedom for χ^2: (number of categories – 1) = 6 – 1 = 5

4 Use Table A.4 to determine critical χ^2 value for 5 degrees of freedom and α = .05

$$\chi^2(5)_{\alpha = .05} = 11.07$$

5 Compare obtained χ^2 with tabled χ^2 value.

a If obtained $\chi^2 <$ tabled χ^2, then the expected frequencies provide a "good fit" for the obtained frequencies.

b If obtained $\chi^2 >$ tabled χ^2, then the expected frequencies do *not* provide a good fit for the obtained frequencies.

6 Our result conforms to step 5a, and so we decide we have a fair die or a good test item.

CHI-SQUARE (χ^2) TEST: CONTINGENCY TABLE

The chi-square (χ^2) contingency test is used to determine whether there is a relationship between two nominal scale variables. This version of the chi-square test is used frequently in the analysis of cross tabulations in survey research. The observations entering into this analysis must be independent, and each observation must be classified into one and only one cell of the contingency table. These assumptions are generally met by making only one observation of each subject, thereby ensuring that the total number of observations entering into the table equals the total number of subjects. In contingency tables having only one degree of freedom (2 × 2 tables), the computations we describe here should not be used if any expected values are less than 10. For chi-square contingency tests with two or more degrees of freedom, it is best if there are no expected frequencies less than 5.

In the following table, the category listed along the rows of the table is the number of hours that subjects reported they habitually slept each night, and the category listed across the columns of the table is the frequency with which these same subjects experienced headaches. The observed frequencies in the body of the table represent the numbers of subjects who experienced the particular combination of sleep and headache frequency.

	Frequency of headaches			
Hours of sleep	Never	Sometimes	Often	Row totals
≥ 8	38 30.98	17 22.74	3 4.28	58
7	37 33.65	21 24.70	5 4.65	63
≤ 6	19 29.37	31 21.56	5 4.06	55
Column totals	94	69	13	176

1 Compute row and column totals of observed frequencies. See table.

2 Compute overall total. Check to be sure both row and column totals sum to the same overall total. See boxed entry in lower right corner of the table.

3 Compute expected frequencies in each cell of the table by multiplying the row total by the column total for that cell and dividing by the overall total. For example, for the cell in the table for subjects getting more than 8 hours of sleep and never reporting headaches, the expected value is equal to

$$\frac{(58)(94)}{176} = \frac{5{,}452}{176} = 30.98$$

The expected values for each cell of the table are entered in the brackets below and to the right of each observed frequency.

4 Compute $\chi^2 = \Sigma \frac{(O - E)^2}{E} =$

$$\frac{(38 - 30.98)^2}{30.98} + \frac{(17 - 22.74)^2}{22.74} + \frac{(3 - 4.28)^2}{4.28} + \frac{(37 - 33.65)^2}{33.65}$$

$$+ \frac{(21 - 24.70)^2}{24.70} + \frac{(5 - 4.65)^2}{4.65} + \frac{(19 - 29.37)^2}{29.37}$$

$$+ \frac{(31 - 21.56)^2}{21.56} + \frac{(5 - 4.06)^2}{4.06}$$

$$= 1.59 + 1.45 + .38 + .33 + .55 + .03 + 3.66 + 4.13 + .22$$

$$= 12.34$$

5 Determine degrees of freedom for χ^2: (number of rows − 1) × (number of columns − 1)

$$= (3 - 1)(3 - 1)$$
$$= (2)(2)$$
$$= 4$$

6 Use Table A.4 to determine critical χ^2 value for 4 degrees of freedom and $\alpha = .05$

$$\chi^2(4)_{\alpha\, =\, .05} = 9.49$$

7 Compare obtained χ^2 with tabled χ^2 value.
   a If obtained χ^2 is greater than the tabled χ^2, then the two variables in the contingency table are significantly related.
   b If obtained χ^2 is less than the tabled χ^2, then the two variables in the contingency table are *not* significantly related.

8 Our result conforms to step 7a, so we conclude that habitual sleep duration and headache frequency are related.

INFERENTIAL STATISTICS FOR TWO-CONDITION EXPERIMENTS

INDEPENDENT SAMPLES *t*-TEST

The independent samples *t*-test is used to determine whether two sample means are sufficiently different so as to be unlikely to have been drawn from the same population. This test is applicable for the analysis of two-group designs involving either the random groups design or the natural groups design (see Chapter 6), although the assumptions underlying the test strictly apply only to the random groups design. If the independent variable has had no effect, then the two samples represent random samples drawn from the same population and they would therefore be expected to provide comparable estimates (within the bounds of sampling error) of the population mean. The independent samples *t*-test is based on the difference between the two sample means, so the expected value of *t* when the independent variable has had no effect is zero. If the independent variable has had an effect, however, the *t* will differ from zero. If the larger mean is subtracted from the smaller mean the *t* will become increasingly smaller than zero as the mean difference increases. If the smaller mean is subtracted from the larger mean, the *t* will become increasingly larger than zero. The difference may be taken in either direction, but you must be careful to note whether it is a positive or negative *t* value. Because sampling error can never be eliminated, the obtained *t* must be compared with a critical value from the appropriate *t*-distribution to determine if it is statistically significant.

The data presented in the following table represent the number of correct responses on a test given after subjects studied the material in one of two groups in a random groups design. Subjects were randomly assigned to either the experimental ($n_e = 4$) or to the control group ($n_c = 6$), and the hypothesis tested in the experiment was that the experimental group would do better on the test.[1] The subject numbers in each group are not in sequence, reflecting their random assignment.

Subject	Experimental group	Subject	Control group
2	20	1	16
5	14	3	15
8	17	4	12
9	21	6	12
		7	14
		10	15

1 Compute $\bar{X}_e = \dfrac{\Sigma X_e}{n_e} = \dfrac{20 + 14 + 17 + 21}{4} = \dfrac{72}{4} = 18$

2 Compute $\bar{X}_c = \dfrac{\Sigma X_c}{n_c} = \dfrac{16 + 15 + 12 + 12 + 14 + 15}{6}$

$$= \frac{84}{6} = 14$$

[1]Some investigators distinguish between directional statistical tests (also called "one-tailed" tests) and nondirectional tests (also called "two-tailed" tests). In a nondirectional test you are testing simply to see if the groups differ from each other; in a directional test you are testing to see if one group has done better (or worse). In this appendix we have tested all hypotheses as if they were nondirectional. Any introductory statistics textbook can be consulted if you need further information concerning the rationale and procedures for one-tailed tests. Table A-5 in this appendix is for nondirectional tests.

3 Compute $\Sigma X_e^2 = 20^2 + 14^2 + 17^2 + 21^2 = 400 + 196 + 289 + 441$
$= 1{,}326$

4 Compute $\Sigma X_c^2 = 16^2 + 15^2 + 12^2 + 12^2 + 14^2 + 15^2 = 256 + 225 + 144 + 144 + 196 + 225 = 1{,}190$

5 Compute $SS_e = \Sigma X_e^2 - \frac{(\Sigma X_e^2)}{n_e} = 1{,}326 - \frac{(72)^2}{4} = 1{,}326 - \frac{5{,}184}{4}$
$= 1{,}326 - 1{,}296 = 30$

6 Compute $SS_c = \Sigma X_c^2 - \frac{(\Sigma X_c)^2}{n_c} = 1{,}190 - \frac{(84)^2}{6} = 1{,}190 - \frac{7{,}056}{6}$
$= 1{,}190 - 1{,}176 = 14$

7 Compute pooled $s^2 = \frac{SS_e + SS_c}{n_e + n_c - 2} = \frac{30 + 14}{4 + 6 - 2} = \frac{44}{8} = 5.50$

8 Compute $s_{\bar{X}_e - \bar{X}_c} = \sqrt{\frac{s^2}{n_e} + \frac{s^2}{n_c}}$

$$= \sqrt{\frac{5.50}{4} + \frac{5.50}{6}} = \sqrt{1.38 + .92} = \sqrt{2.30} = 1.52$$

9 Compute $t = \frac{\bar{X}_e - \bar{X}_c}{s_{\bar{X}_e - \bar{X}_c}} = \frac{18 - 14}{1.52} = \frac{4}{1.52} = 2.63$

10 Determine degrees of freedom for $t = n_e + n_c - 2 = 4 + 6 - 2 = 8$

11 Use Table A.5 to determine critical value for t with 8 degrees of freedom and $\alpha = .5$

$$t\,(8)_{\alpha = .05} = 2.31$$

12 Compare the *absolute value* of your obtained t value with the tabled value.
  a If the absolute value of your obtained t is larger than the tabled value, then the two sampled means likely represent two different populations. That is, the mean difference is statistically significantly larger than zero.
  b If the absolute value of your obtained t is smaller than the tabled value, then the two sample means likely represent the same populaton. That is, the mean difference is *not* statistically significantly larger than zero.

13 Our outcome conforms to step 12a, so we would conclude that the experimental group likely did better.

DIRECT DIFFERENCE *t*-TEST

The direct difference t-test is used to determine the statistical significance of a mean difference in two-condition experiments in which each subject has participated in both conditions. The direct difference t-test is applicable, therefore, to the analysis of complete and incomplete within-subjects design experiments involving two conditions. The procedures for data reduction in these two designs are described in Chapter 9; in this appendix we will assume that these procedures have been completed successfully, and we will present the data for our computational example in its final tabular form.

The following data represent the scores for six subjects, each of whom was tested under the experimental and control conditions in a within-subjects design. The higher the score, the better the subject's performance.

	Condition		
Subject	Experimental	Control	D
1	80	60	20
2	90	75	15
3	65	75	−10
4	95	75	20
5	85	60	25
6	75	55	20

1 Compute a difference score (D) for each subject (see table). Be sure to compute the difference in the same direction for each subject and retain the sign of the difference score.

2 Compute $\Sigma D = 20 + 15 + (-10) + 20 + 25 + 20 = 90$

3 Compute $\bar{D} = \dfrac{\Sigma D}{n} = \dfrac{90}{6} = 15.0$

4 Compute
$$\Sigma D^2 = 20^2 + 15^2 + (-10)^2 + 20^2 + 25^2 + 20^2$$
$$= 400 + 225 + 100 + 400 + 625 + 400$$
$$= 2{,}150$$

5 Compute
$$s_D = \sqrt{\frac{\Sigma D^2 - \dfrac{(\Sigma D)^2}{n}}{n - 1}}$$

$$= \sqrt{\frac{2{,}150 - \dfrac{(90)^2}{6}}{6 - 1}} = \sqrt{\frac{2{,}150 - \dfrac{8{,}100}{6}}{5}} = \sqrt{\frac{2{,}150 - 1{,}350}{5}}$$

$$= \sqrt{\frac{800}{5}} = \sqrt{160} = 12.65$$

6 Compute $s_{\bar{D}} = \frac{s_D}{\sqrt{n}} = \frac{12.65}{\sqrt{6}} = \frac{12.65}{2.45} = 5.16$

7 Compute $t = \frac{\bar{D}}{s_{\bar{D}}} = \frac{15.0}{5.16} = 2.91$

3 Determine degrees of freedom for t: $(n - 1) = 6 - 1 = 5$

9 Use Table A.5 to determine critical value for t with 5 degrees of freedom and $\alpha = .05$

$$t(5)_{\alpha = .05} = 2.57$$

10 Compare the *absolute value* of your obtained t value with the tabled value.
  a If the absolute value of your obtained t is larger than the tabled value, then the mean difference ($\bar{D}$) is statistically significantly larger than zero.
  b If the absolute value of your obtained t is smaller than the tabled value, then the mean difference ($\bar{D}$) is *not* statistically significantly larger than zero.

11 Our result conforms to step 10a, and so we conclude that the experimental group did better.

COMPUTER-ASSISTED ANALYSES

Once an investigator moves beyond a simple correlational design or a two-group experiment, computational procedures become more cumbersome for describing data and for making statistical inferences from data. Fortunately, many researchers now have access to mainframe computers or microcomputers that include appropriate software to carry out the statistical analysis of large data sets. This access to computers has led to a change in the approach taken to introduce students to statistical analysis. Stated simply, the availability of computer-assisted analyses has made knowing step-by-step computational procedures for complex analyses less important. Being able to set up and carry out an analysis using a statistical software package and being able to interpret the "output" have become essential skills that need to be learned by researchers.

Carrying out statistical analyses using computer software requires two types of knowledge. First, the researcher must have a good knowledge of research design and statistics. Second, the researcher must be familiar with the requirements and capabilities of an appropriate statistical software package. Many software packages for statistical analysis are available for use both on mainframe computers and microcomputers. Some of the more popular ones are known by abbreviations like BMDP, SPSS, STATA, and SYSTAT. You may have access to one or more of these programs on the computers in your psychology department or at your campus computer center. Be sure to check with your instructor regarding the availability of these statistical packages on your campus. Should you decide to purchase a statistical software package for your personal computer, be sure to first obtain advice from an experienced researcher who is familiar with the brand of computer you have and with the kinds of statistical analyses you want to perform.

In Chapters 6–9 of this text we introduced various experimental designs and the logic of null hypothesis testing and inferential statistics. This knowledge is essential if you wish to use computer-assisted analysis. A computer is not able to determine what research design you used or the rationale behind the use of that design (although some of the more user-friendly programs provide prompts to guide your thinking). To carry out an analysis, you must provide the computer with information such as: the type of design that was used (e.g., random groups or within subjects); the number of independent variables (e.g., single factor or multifactor); the number of levels of each independent variable; and the number of dependent variables and the level of measurement employed for each. You must also be able to articulate your research hypotheses and to plan appropriate statistical tests of your research hypotheses. For example, you should know what analytical comparisons you plan to do after performing an omnibus *F*-test. A computer will quickly and efficiently perform the computations necessary for obtaining descriptive and inferential statistics. To use the computer effectively as a research tool, however, you must give it specific directions regarding which inferential test you want it to do and which data are to be used in computing the test. Finally, when the computer has carried out the computations, you must be able to interpret correctly the output showing the results of the analysis.

ANALYSIS OF VARIANCE

The most frequently used statistical procedure for analyzing results of psychology experiments is the analysis of variance (ANOVA). An introduction to ANOVA, or the *F*-test, was presented in Chapter 9. In the following sections of this appendix we describe computer-assisted analyses using ANOVA. Our emphasis will be on the interpretation of the output from a statistical software package that was used to compute the ANOVA. We first present the raw data in summary form. Then we provide an illustration of how the results of an ANOVA typically are displayed on a computer screen or on a printed page after the computer has performed the computations. Our examples are based on the SYSTAT program (Systat, Inc., 1800 Sherman Ave., Evanston, IL 60201); however, the output can be expected to be similar to that of other software packages. The steps required to enter the data into the computer in accord with the particular requirements of the software package have been omitted. Procedures for data entry vary from one statistical package to another. Be assured, however, that knowing how to program a computer is *not* required to enter data into a statistical package. Step-by-step instructions are part of the written documentation that accompanies each software package. Through careful reading and a little practice, the procedures for handling data entry can typically be mastered in a relatively short period of time. Once you develop this skill you are freed forever from the chains of laborious statistical calculations!

We turn our attention now to the interpretation of the output for the ANOVA for four research designs: single-factor analysis for independent-groups designs; single-factor analysis for within-subjects designs; two-factor analysis for independent-groups designs; and two-factor analysis for mixed designs.

SINGLE-FACTOR ANALYSIS OF VARIANCE FOR INDEPENDENT GROUPS DESIGNS

The single-factor analysis of variance for independent groups designs is used to analyze the results of random groups and natural groups designs involving one independent variable with two or more levels. (The assumptions underlying the test strictly apply only to the random-groups design.) The logic of this statistical test is described in detail in Chapter 9. We will first describe the procedures for computer-assisted analysis of an omnibus *F*-test. We will then describe the procedures for developing the coefficients for analytical comparisons and for testing the statistical significance of the comparison. We will consider only the case when all groups in the experiment are the same size.

The data in the following table represent the number of words correctly identified (out of a possible twenty) on a vocabulary test. Five subjects were randomly assigned to each of four groups (defined by the method of study that subjects were instructed to use to learn the words in preparation for the vocabulary test). The control method involved no specific instructions, but in the three experimental methods subjects were instructed either to study a synonym of the to-be-learned word (synonym method), or a dictionary definition of the to-be-learned word (dictionary method), or a literary passage in which the to-be-learned word was used in context (passage method). The independent variable being manipulated is instruction, and it can be symbolized by the letter A. The levels of this independent variable can be differentiated by using the symbols a_1, a_2, a_3, and a_4 for the four respective groups. The number of subjects within each group is referred to as n; in this case, n = 5. The total number of subjects in the experiment is symbolized as *N*; in this case, *N* = 20. Finally, the number of groups is referred to as *a*; in this case, *a* = 4.

				Instruction (A)			
Subject	Control (a_1)	Subject	Synonym (a_2)	Subject	Definition (a_3)	Subject	Passage (a_4)
1	12	6	15	11	16	16	14
2	10	7	14	12	16	17	14
3	9	8	13	13	13	18	15
4	11	9	12	14	12	19	12
5	8	10	12	15	15	20	12
Mean	10.0		13.2		14.4		13.4
Standard deviation	1.6		1.3		1.8		1.3

The first step in the analysis of any experiment is to set up a data matrix like the one above. The number of correct responses is listed for each subject in each of the four groups with each subject identified with a unique subject number. Below the data matrix the mean and standard deviation are provided for each group. The mean and standard deviation can be computed with such a small data set using the procedures described earlier in this appendix. For most experiments, however, there will be more subjects in each group and the mean and standard deviation can be obtained using the same statistical program that is used to compute the omnibus *F*-test. As we discussed in Chapter 9, it is essential to have the means along with the outcome of the *F*-test to interpret the results of an experiment.

Screen A.1 represents the output of the SYSTAT statistical program after it has computed the omnibus *F*-test for the data in this experiment. The first line on the screen indicates that the program encountered four levels during processing that were identified as groups 1–4. The next line indicates that the dependent variable was called "words" and that the total number of

SCREEN A.1

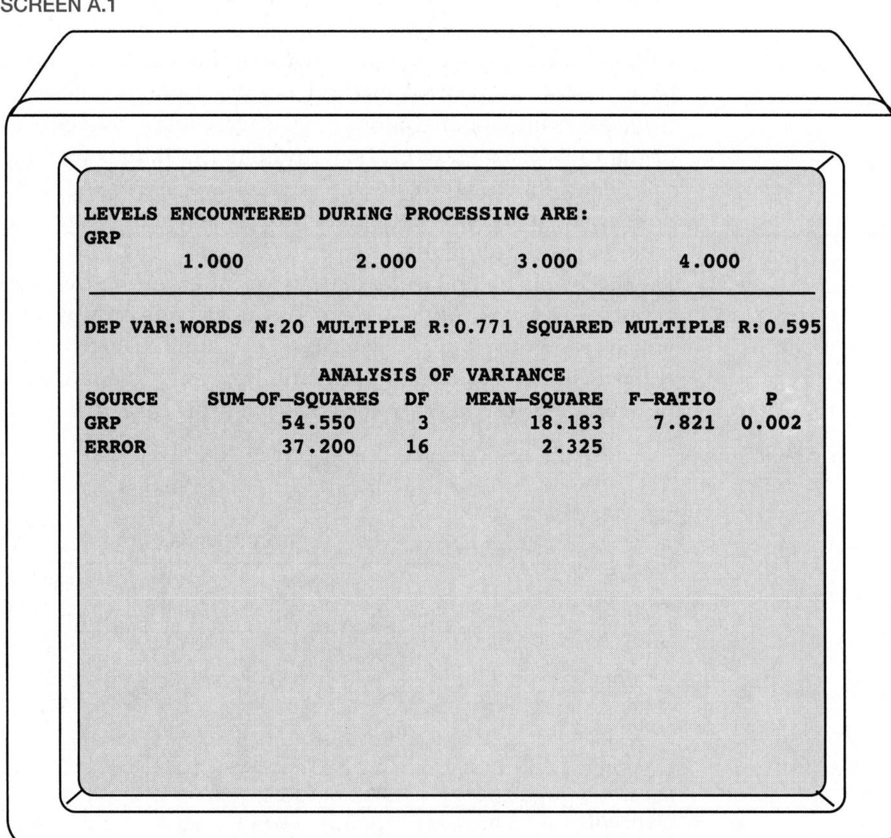

subjects (N) was 20. On that same line the multiple R (.771) and the squared multiple R (.595) appear. These values pertain to the use of the correlational technique called regression analysis, which is related to the analysis of variance. But, these values are not critical in interpreting the statistical significance of an *F*-test. To interpret an *F*-test, the most critical information is the analysis of variance summary table that fills the remainder of the screen.

The first column of the table, labeled "Source," includes the two major sources of variation in the analysis of a single-factor analysis of variance: Variation due to the independent variable (GRP for group) and Error variation reflecting variation within the groups. The second column presents the Sum-of-Squares for each of the two sources of variation. These values reflect the amount of variation produced in the experiment by each source of variation. The statistical program computes these values based on the data matrix, and it is these computations that would be cumbersome to compute with a calculator. The third column indicates the degrees of freedom (DF) for each source of variation. The DF for Group is equal to the number of groups minus 1 (in this case, $4 - 1 = 3$). The DF for Error is equal to the number of subjects in each group minus 1 times the number of groups. There were 5 subjects in each of the four groups so the DF for Error is: $(5 - 1)\,4 = 16$.

The fourth column presents the Mean-Square for each source of variation. The mean square reflects somewhat of an average amount of variation for each source in the sense that it adjusts for the number of entries contributing to each source of variation. There is a potential bias in estimating a variance; so, instead of using the number of entries themselves, the sums of squares are adjusted using the degrees of freedom. Therefore, the Mean-Squares are obtained in the summary table by dividing the Sum-of-Squares by the corresponding DF. The *F*-ratio is computed by forming a ratio of the Mean-Square for Groups over the Mean-Square Error. In this experiment the *F*-ratio was 7.821, the value that is shown in the second column from the right of the summary table. The final piece of information that is provided by a computer-based statistical analysis of variance is the probability of the *F*-ratio assuming the null hypothesis is true. The probability for the *F*-ratio in this experiment of .002 appears in the far right column of the summary table. Since this probability is less than the conventional level of significance (.05), we can conclude that this *F*-ratio is statistically significant.

At this point we know that the omnibus *F*-test was statistically significant. So, we know that there was an overall effect of the independent variable of type of instruction in the experiment. This tells us that something happened in the experiment, but it does not specify what has happened. Analytical comparisons can be computed to specify the source of the overall effect of the independent variable. Typically, a small set of comparisons would be required to locate the sources of systematic variation in a single-factor experiment (see Chapter 9). We will illustrate the procedure for doing analytical comparisons by describing the computer-based analysis of only one comparison. We will use as our example the analytical comparison of the control group with the average of the three experimental groups to see if this is one source of systematic variation contributing to the overall effect of the instructional variable.

STEPS IN DEVELOPING COEFFICIENTS FOR ANALYTICAL COMPARISON

1 State hypothesis in words: Compare control method with average of three experimental methods.

2 State null hypothesis for comparison: $\mu_{a_1} = \dfrac{\mu_{a_2} + \mu_{a_3} + \mu_{a_4}}{3}$

3 Set null hypothesis statement equal to zero:

$$\mu_{a_1} - \left[\frac{\mu_{a_2} + \mu_{a_3} + \mu_{a_4}}{3}\right] = 0$$

4 Expand expression by taking minus sign inside brackets and isolating terms over common denominator:

$$\mu_{a_1} - \frac{\mu_{a_2}}{3} - \frac{\mu_{a_3}}{3} - \frac{\mu_{a_4}}{3} = 0$$

5 Eliminate fractions by multiplying expression by common denominator:

$$3\mu_{a_1} - \mu_{a_2} - \mu_{a_3} - \mu_{a_4} = 0$$

6 The coefficients for each group are the multipliers for each mean in this equation.

$$C_1 = +3$$
$$C_2 = -1$$
$$C_3 = -1$$
$$C_4 = -1$$

7 Computation check: The coefficients for an analytical comparison must sum to zero.

8 If a group is not included in a comparison, its coefficient is 0.

F-TEST FOR ANALYTICAL COMPARISON

Once you have determined the coefficients for the analytical comparison you want to do, using the procedures described in the preceding section, you are ready to run the program to compute the *F*-test for your comparison. The output for the analysis of the comparison of the control group to the average of the three experimental groups appears in Screen A.2. The critical information among that appearing in the upper-left corner of the screen is the

```
>output*
>hypothesis
>effect = grp
>contrast
>3 -1 -1 -1
>test

TEST FOR EFFECT CALLED:    GRP

TEST OF HYPOTHESIS

      SOURCE            SS        DF      MS          F        P
  HYPOTHESIS          50.417       1    50.417     21.685   0.000
       ERROR          37.200      16     2.325
```

SCREEN A.2

coefficients that were entered for the comparison. The format of the summary table is very similar to that for the single-factor analysis we described earlier. In fact, the Source of variation labeled "Error" is exactly the same as for the omnibus *F*-test for this experiment. In general, the error term for analytical comparisons is the same as the error term for the omnibus test.

The source of variation being tested in this analysis is labeled "Hypothesis." It reflects the potential systematic variation due to the analytical comparison being tested. Since analytical comparisons reflect the contrast between two sets of means, they always have only one degree of freedom. In this case, the contrast is between the mean for the control group and the mean of the three means in the experimental group. The *F*-ratio for testing the effect of the analytical comparison (called hypothesis in the summary table) is the ratio of the Mean-Square (MS) for Hypothesis over the MS Error. The resulting *F* shown in the summary table is 21.685. The probability of this *F* (with 1 and 16 degrees of freedom) under the null hypothesis is less than one in a thousand. This probability is less than the conventional level of significance (.05), and so we conclude that this analytical comparison is statistically significant.

The mean for the control group was 10.0, and the mean across the three experimental groups was 13.7. These means along with the statistically significant *F*-ratio lead to the conclusion that the three experimental groups recalled more vocabulary words than did the control group. This conclusion based on the test of an analytical comparison is much more specific than the conclusion based on the omnibus test that something happened in the experiment.

SINGLE-FACTOR ANALYSIS OF VARIANCE FOR WITHIN-SUBJECTS DESIGNS

The results of experiments which involve within-subjects designs (see Chapter 7) that include one independent variable manipulated at two or more levels are analyzed using a single-factor analysis of variance. The within-subjects designs involve the repeated testing of subjects, and so the analyses of the within-subjects designs are also called repeated-measures analyses. The underlying logic and the interpretation of the *F*-test are the same for the within-subjects designs and for the independent-groups designs. There are a few characteristics, however, that are sufficiently different to warrant a brief description of the analyses of the within-subjects designs.

One distinctive characteristic is the procedure used to prepare the data matrix for the within-subjects designs. These procedures were illustrated in Chapter 9 using an example of a time-perception experiment involving the complete within-subjects design. The independent variable was interval length, and there were four levels: 12, 24, 36, and 48 seconds. The means of the median time estimates for each of five subjects for the four intervals were 12.6, 22.0, 38.0, and 39.4 seconds.

The data from the time-perception experiment outlined in Chapter 9 were analyzed with a single-factor analysis of variance for the within-subjects designs using the SYSTAT statistical software package. The purpose of the analysis was to determine if the subjects' estimates of the intervals changed with increasing interval length. The output of this analysis is shown on Screen A.3.

As was the case for the single-factor analysis of the independent-groups designs, the results of the analysis of the within-subjects designs are summarized in an analysis of variance summary table. The output begins, however, by indicating that the number of cases (i.e., subjects) in the analysis was five. The output next displays the means for the four levels of the interval length variable. The program labels these levels with the generic indicators A(1), A(2), A(3), and A(4). It is important that these labels are correctly identified with the actual levels of the independent variable—in this case, A(1) is 12 seconds, A(2) is 24 seconds, and so on.

The summary table begins with a clear label indicating that this is a within-subjects analysis. This label is important because the body of the summary table looks just like the one for the analysis of independent-groups designs experi-

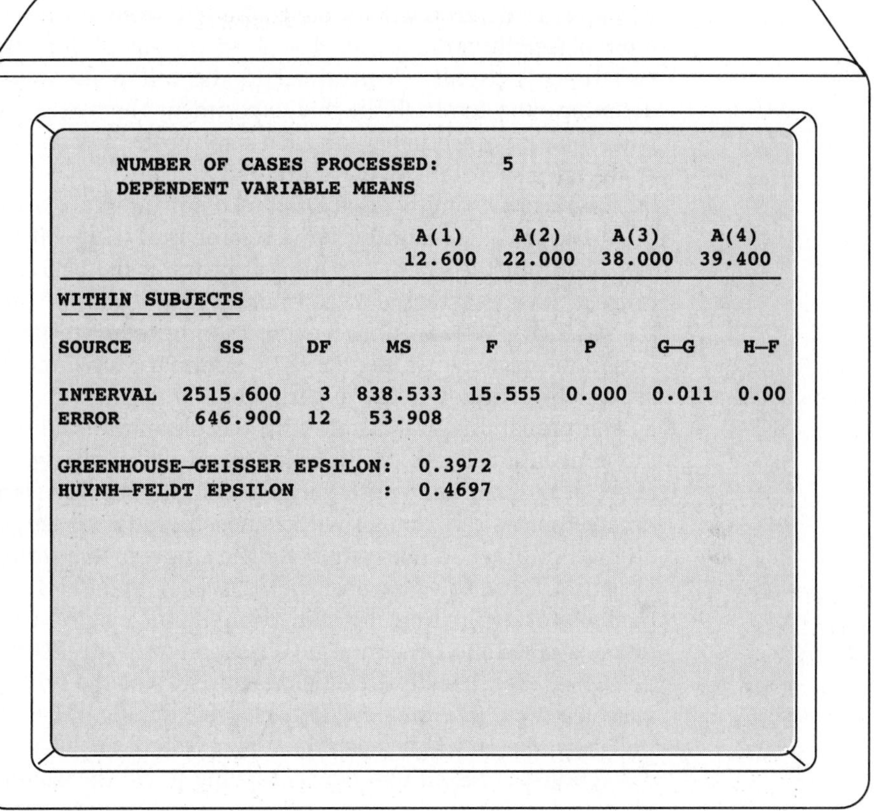
NUMBER OF CASES PROCESSED: 5
DEPENDENT VARIABLE MEANS

A(1)	A(2)	A(3)	A(4)
12.600	22.000	38.000	39.400

WITHIN SUBJECTS

SOURCE	SS	DF	MS	F	P	G–G	H–F
INTERVAL	2515.600	3	838.533	15.555	0.000	0.011	0.00
ERROR	646.900	12	53.908				

GREENHOUSE–GEISSER EPSILON: 0.3972
HUYNH–FELDT EPSILON : 0.4697

SCREEN A.3

ments. The *F*-ratio is still made up of a numerator reflecting potential systematic variation and a denominator reflecting only error variation. As we described in Chapter 9, however, the error variation in the within-subjects designs is different from the error variation in the independent-groups designs. In the within-subjects designs, error variation reflects the residual variation (see Chapter 9) after the variation due to the independent variable and the variation due to subjects have been subtracted from the total variation in the analysis. This is a good illustration of why statistical programs should not be used "blind." That is, the person doing the analysis must understand the nature of the analysis before trying to interpret the computer output. The computer does well the computing it is programmed to do. It is you, however, who has to interpret the output of these computations.

The summary table for the single-factor within-subjects design includes the familiar columns of Source, Sum of Squares, Degrees of Freedom, Mean Square, *F*, and Probability (see the single-factor independent-groups design in this appendix if these terms are not familiar). The DF for the Interval source of variation is determined by subtracting 1 from the number of levels of the interval length variable (i.e., 4 − 1 = 3). The DF for the error term (residual variation) is usually determined in the following way. The first step is to determine the total DF. In this experiment there was a total of five subjects with four time estimates for each subject for a total of twenty scores to be analyzed. The Total DF, therefore, is 19 (20 − 1). The DF for error is obtained by subtracting from the total DF the DF for Interval (3) and the DF for Subjects (5 − 1 = 4). The resulting DF for error is 12 (19 − 3 − 4). Neither Subjects Variation nor the Total Variation appears in the SYSTAT summary table because neither is essential to computing the *F*-ratio for Interval. To understand the summary table well, however, it is important to know that the sources of variation presented in the SYSTAT summary table may not represent all the sources of variation in the experiment.

The probability associated with the obtained *F*-ratio of 15.555 is less than the conventional level of significance of .05 so we would conclude that the effect of the interval length variable was statistically significant. The subjects' time estimates did change with increasing interval length. There are two additional columns in this output for the single-factor within-subjects analysis of variance. These columns are labeled "G–G" and "H–F." They reflect two corrections for evaluating the statistical significance of a within-subjects *F*-ratio that are called the Greenhouse-Geisser and Huynh-Feldt corrections (see Keppel, 1991). Because of certain characteristics of the within-subjects analysis of variance there is a greater likelihood of making a Type I error (rejecting the null hypothesis when it is true). The Greenhouse-Geisser and Huynh-Feldt corrections represent two ways of trying to compensate for the increased likelihood of a Type I error. As you can see, the corrections have led to larger probabilities in the last two columns than the one in column P. In this case, however, all three probabilities are less than the conventional level of significance of .05 so they lead to the same conclusion—the *F*-ratio is statistically significant.

Appropriate use of corrections for the Type I error rates in the analysis of within-subjects designs is a topic typically covered in graduate-level statistics classes. Their appearance on this SYSTAT summary table illustrates an important point about the use of statistical software packages. The statistical packages are designed to serve users with varying degrees of sophistication regarding methodological and statistical issues. It is likely that less sophisticated users will encounter information in the computer output that is unfamiliar. When this occurs, it is important to seek assistance and advice from someone who is an expert in the use of the statistical software package. When it comes to the analysis of data, it is definitely the case that what you don't know can hurt you.

The statistically significant *F*-test for the overall effect of interval length is an omnibus *F*-test. As was the case in the analysis of independent-groups designs experiments, analytical comparisons can be used to identify the source of the effect of an independent variable more specifically. In the within-subjects designs the Residual Mean Square can be used as the error term for analytical comparisons (see Keppel, 1991, for more specific guidelines regarding appropriate error terms for analytical comparisons).

One common type of analytical comparison that is used for within-subjects designs is called trend analysis. Trend analysis is used to determine whether the effect of an independent variable can best be described as linear or nonlinear. Trend analysis was used in the analysis of our time-perception experiment, and the trend analysis showed that the changes in subjects' time estimates with increasing interval lengths were best described as linear. The important point is that trend analysis represents a type of analytical comparison. As such, trend analysis allows a much more specific conclusion to be drawn than is possible based only on an omnibus *F*-test.

TWO-FACTOR ANALYSIS OF VARIANCE FOR INDEPENDENT GROUPS DESIGNS

The two-factor analysis of variance for independent groups designs is used for the analysis of experiments in which each of two independent variables has been manipulated at at least two levels. The logic of complex designs with two independent variables and the conceptual basis for the analysis of these experiments are described in Chapter 8. We will focus in this appendix on the computer-assisted analysis of a complex design which involves an *F*-test for the main effect of A, the main effect of B, and the interaction effect, A $\times$ B. Our example will involve a significant A $\times$ B interaction, and so we will also illustrate the computations for a simple main effect. The two-factor analysis for independent groups is applicable to experiments in which both independent variables are manipulated using a random groups design, in which both independent variables represent the natural groups design, and in which one independent variable represents the natural groups design and the other represents the random groups design. In the last section of this appendix we will describe the computations for a mixed design in which one independent variable represents an independent groups design and the second independent variable represents a within-subjects design.

The data in the following table represent the number of correct responses on a simple motor learning task as a function of two independent variables. The first independent variable was the hand the subject used to perform the task, and the two levels of this variable were the dominant and the nondominant hand. The second independent variable was the delay (in seconds) between successive trials on the task, and it was manipulated at three levels (0, 30, and 60 seconds). The hand variable will be referred to as A, with the dominant hand being a_1, and the nondominant hand being a_2. The delay variable will be referred to as B with the 0-second delay as b_1, the 30-second delay as b_2, and the 60-second delay as b_3. Five subjects were randomly assigned to each of the six groups resulting from the factorial combination of the two independent variables.

Hand Dominance (Variable A) × Delay Interval (Variable B)

Dominant/0 sec		Dominant/30 sec		Dominant/60 sec	
Subject	a_1b_1	Subject	a_1b_2	Subject	a_1b_3
1	18	6	17	11	18
2	17	7	19	12	20
3	19	8	22	13	21
4	21	9	20	14	22
5	20	10	17	15	19
Nondominant/0 sec		**Nondominant/30 sec**		**Nondominant/60 sec**	
Subject	a_2b_1	Subject	a_2b_2	Subject	a_2b_3
16	9	21	15	26	16
17	11	22	17	27	19
18	10	23	16	28	18
19	11	24	17	29	20
20	12	25	14	30	18

The first step in carrying out a computer-assisted analysis of a two-factor analysis of variance is to enter the data matrix like the one in the preceding table into the computer. Typically the data for the three levels of the B variable (in this case, delay) are entered successively for each level of the A variable (in this case, hand dominance). That is, the Dominant/0 second group would be entered first, followed by the Dominant/30 second group, and ending with the Nondominant/60 second group. For this data matrix, therefore, the number of correct responses would be entered in the order of the subject numbers from 1 to 30. Once the data are entered into the computer, the next step is to examine the output for the descriptive statistics for a two-factor experiment.

Two screens are required to contain the output from SYSTAT. These screens show the descriptive statistics for a two-factor analysis of variance using the data for the experiment involving hand dominance and delay. The first set of results, displayed on Screen A.4, are the results for level 1 of hand and level 1 of delay. Once again, it is essential that the actual levels of the independent variables be identified. For this experiment, the first set of results corresponds to the group using their dominant hand with a 0-second delay. The corresponding groups for the results in the middle and at the bottom of Screen A.4 are dominant hand/30-second delay and dominant hand/60-second delay, respectively.

Screen A.4 displays the descriptive statistics for the dominant-hand groups across the three delay groups. Screen A.5 displays the descriptive statistics for the nondominant-hand groups across the three delay groups. Because the type of information provided for each of these six groups is the same, we will describe in detail only the data displayed for the first group on Screen A.4. The two columns headed Hand and Delay indicate the respective levels of these two independent variables in each group. The column headed Response is the most critical column. Entries in this column represent values on the dependent

```
THE FOLLOWING RESULTS ARE FOR:
          HAND     =          1.000
         DELAY     =          1.000
TOTAL OBSERVATIONS:       5
                 RESPONSE            HAND          DELAY
   N OF CASES              5            5              5
      MINIMUM         17.000        1.000          1.000
      MAXIMUM         21.000        1.000          1.000
      MEAN            19.000        1.000          1.000
      STANDARD DEV     1.581        0.000          0.000

THE FOLLOWING RESULTS ARE FOR:
          HAND     =          1.000
         DELAY     =          2.000
TOTAL OBSERVATIONS:       5
                 RESPONSE            HAND          DELAY
      N OF CASES           5            5              5
      MINIMUM         17.000        1.000          2.000
      MAXIMUM         22.000        1.000          2.000
      MEAN            19.000        1.000          2.000
      STANDARD DEV     2.121        0.000          0.000

THE FOLLOWING RESULTS ARE FOR:
          HAND     =          1.000
         DELAY     =          3.000
TOTAL OBSERVATIONS:       5
                 RESPONSE            HAND          DELAY
      N OF CASES           5            5              5
      MINIMUM         18.000        1.000          3.000
      MAXIMUM         22.000        1.000          3.000
      MEAN            20.000        1.000          3.000
      STANDARD DEV     1.581        0.000          0.000
```

SCREEN A.4

variable, in this case, number of correct responses (abbreviated as Response). The number of cases (5) is shown first, indicating that five subjects provided scores on the dependent variable in this group. The minimum and maximum scores in the group are shown in the next two rows; the minimum number correct in this group was 17 and the maximum was 21. The difference between these two indicates the range of scores in this group (see measures of dispersion earlier in this appendix). The minimum and maximum values can also be useful in identifying basement and ceiling effects (see Chapter 8) when the absolute minimum and maximum possible values in the experiment are known.

The most important descriptive statistic is the next one listed for the first group, the mean (19). It is the means for the six groups that are used to describe what happened in the experiment. These means should be summarized in a table or a figure (see Chapter 8 and Appendix C) before examining the analysis of variance summary table. It is also a good idea to use the raw data to check the computations of these means to be sure of their accuracy and to be sure

```
THE FOLLOWING RESULTS ARE FOR:
              HAND      =          2.000
             DELAY      =          1.000
TOTAL OBSERVATIONS:           5
                    RESPONSE              HAND            DELAY
    N OF CASES                    5                5                5
     MINIMUM                  9.000            2.000            1.000
     MAXIMUM                 12.000            2.000            1.000
     MEAN                    10.600            2.000            1.000
     STANDARD DEV             1.140            0.000            0.000

THE FOLLOWING RESULTS ARE FOR:
              HAND      =          2.000
             DELAY      =          2.000
TOTAL OBSERVATIONS:           5
                    RESPONSE              HAND            DELAY
     N OF CASES                   5                5                5
     MINIMUM                 14.000            2.000            2.000
     MAXIMUM                 17.000            2.000            2.000
     MEAN                    15.800            2.000            2.000
     STANDARD DEV             1.304            0.000            0.000

THE FOLLOWING RESULTS ARE FOR:
              HAND      =          2.000
             DELAY      =          3.000
TOTAL OBSERVATIONS:           5
                    RESPONSE              HAND            DELAY
     N OF CASES                   5                5                5
     MINIMUM                 16.000            2.000            3.000
     MAXIMUM                 20.000            2.000            3.000
     MEAN                    18.200            2.000            3.000
     STANDARD DEV             1.483            0.000            0.000
```

SCREEN A.5

that the data have been entered into the computer properly. The table of means and the analysis-of-variance summary table are the essential tools needed to interpret the results of a factorial experiment.

The last descriptive statistic displayed for the first group is the standard deviation. The standard deviation provides helpful information about the variation in each group. Looking across the six groups displayed on the two screens, we can see that the largest standard deviation was in the dominant hand/30-second delay group (2.121) and the smallest standard deviation was in the nondominant hand/0-second delay group (1.14). The small difference between these two values indicates that there was little difference in the amount of variation across the six groups in the experiment. The fact that the largest standard deviation in any group was just over two correct responses indicates that there was not much variation within any of the six groups. We are now ready to examine the analysis-of-variance summary table for our two-factor experiment to see if there were any statistically significant sources of variation.

Screen A.6 displays the output from the SYSTAT program for a two-factor

TABLE OF MEANS

HAND	DELAY 0	30	60
DOMINANT	19.0	19.0	20.0
NONDOMINANT	10.6	15.8	18.2

LEVELS ENCOUNTERED DURING PROCESSING ARE:

HAND	1.000	2.000	
DELAY	1.000	2.000	3.000

DEP VAR:RESPONSE N:30 MULTIPLE R:0.915 SQUARED MULTIPLE R:0.838

ANALYSIS OF VARIANCE

SOURCE	SUM-OF-SQUARES	DF	MEAN-SQUARE	F-RATIO	P
HAND	149.633	1	149.633	61.075	0.000
DELAY	93.800	2	46.900	19.143	0.000
HAND * DELAY	60.467	2	30.233	12.340	0.000
ERROR	58.800	24	2.450		

SCREEN A.6

analysis of variance for independent groups. At the top of the screen we have added a table of means for the experiment being analyzed. This table is based on the two screens of descriptive statistics with which we were just working, but it is not part of the output from SYSTAT. The actual output begins with the heading "LEVELS ENCOUNTERED DURING PROCESSING ARE:" near the middle of the screen. We included the table of means to make it easier to understand the interpretation of the summary table. The means indicate that there was little change in the number of correct responses as a function of delay for the dominant-hand groups. For the nondominant-hand groups, however, there was an apparent change across the three levels of delay. With this pattern of results in mind, we can turn to the analysis-of-variance summary table.

The output from SYSTAT near the middle of Screen A.6 begins by displaying that there were two levels of the independent variable of hand and three levels of the independent variable of delay encountered in the processing of the analysis. The presence of more than one independent variable marks this as a multifactor design, and the levels of the independent variables indicate that it is a 2 × 3 design. The next line of the output begins by indicating that the name of the dependent variable is Response (shorthand for number of correct responses). On that same line the total N of thirty is shown; the total N results from there being five subjects in each of the six groups of the experiment. The multiple R and the squared multiple R are indicated at the end of the same line. As we said in our description of the analysis of the single-factor analysis of variance for independent groups, the multiple R's are related to regression analysis which is not directly related to the interpretation of the analysis-of-variance summary table.

The analysis-of-variance summary table for a two-factor design is shown in the lower third of the screen. In a single-factor experiment there is only one independent variable that can be a potential source of systematic variation in an experiment. In a two-factor design, there are three sources of potential systematic variation: the main effect of each independent variable and the interaction of the two independent variables (see Chapter 8). These three sources of potential systematic variation are reflected in the summary table as the first three entries in the source column. The main effect of hand appears first, then the main effect of delay, and finally, the interaction of the two independent variables. The interaction of the two appears on the screen as HAND*DELAY; more typically interactions are written as Hand X Delay. Much more critical than the form of the notation for interactions is that interactions represent an important new dimension made possible by multifactor experiments. Interactions allow us to determine whether the effect of one independent variable differs depending on the level of a second independent variable. The final source of variation is a familiar one. The error variation that is used in the computation of the *F*'s for the two main effects and for the interaction is the variation within groups in the experiment.

The degrees of freedom for each independent variable are determined in the same way as in a single-factor experiment, namely, the number of levels of the variable minus 1. Since there were two levels of the hand variable and three levels of the delay variable, the corresponding DF for these variables are 1 and 2, respectively (as is indicated in the DF column of the summary table). The degrees of freedom for the interaction of the two variables are obtained by multiplying the DF for the two variables. The DF shown in the summary table for HAND*DELAY is 2 (1 × 2). The DF for the within-groups error is determined in the usual way by computing the DF within each group (number of subjects minus 1; in this case, 5 − 1 = 4) and multiplying by the number of groups. Thus, the DF for error in the summary table is 24 (4 × 6).

The three *F*-ratios in a two-factor design have the same form as when the experiment involves only the independent-groups designs. The Mean Square Error is used as the denominator for all three *F*-tests. The Mean Square for each main effect and for the interaction are used as the numerators for three independent *F*-ratios. The three *F*-ratios appear in the summary table in the *F*-

RATIO column. It is best to evaluate the *F*-ratio for the interaction first (see Chapter 9). The obtained probability of less than one in a thousand for the *F* of 12.34 for the interaction is less than the conventional level of significance of .05. So, we can conclude that the interaction was statistically significant. A statistically significant interaction indicates that the effect of the delay variable was different as a function of which hand was used. The pattern in the table of means at the top of the screen indicates the nature of the interaction. The delay variable had less of an effect on the groups using their dominant hand than on those using their nondominant hand. In the next section we will describe simple main effects, a type of analysis that can be used to specify the nature of an interaction even better.

After examining the interaction effect, the two main effects should be examined. The *F*-ratio for the main effect of hand was 61.075, with a probability of less than one in a thousand. Because the probability is less than the conventional level of significance of .05, the main effect of hand was statistically significant. The means for this main effect can be obtained by averaging across the columns of the table at the top of the screen, thereby computing a mean for the dominant hand of 19.3 and for the nondominant hand of 14.9. These means along with the statistically significant *F*-test indicate that those working with their dominant hand made more correct responses than those working with their nondominant hand. The *F*-ratio for the main effect of delay was 19.143, with a probability of less than one in a thousand. As was true for the main effect of hand, this probability is less than the conventional level of significance of .05, and thus the main effect of delay was statistically significant. The means for the main effect of delay are obtained by averaging across the rows of the table of means at the top of the screen. These three means for the main effect of delay are 14.8, 17.4, and 19.1 for the 0, 30, and 60 second delays, respectively. These means and the accompanying statistically significant *F*-test for the main effect of delay indicate that the number of correct responses increased with increasing delay. Analytical comparisons could be used to specify the nature of the changes as a function of delay more precisely.

ILLUSTRATION OF SIMPLE MAIN EFFECT

Simple main effects are used in the analysis of two-factor designs to identify more specifically the nature of statistically significant interactions (see Chapters 8 and 9). A simple main effect involves the overall effect of one independent variable at one level of a second independent variable. Statistical software packages vary as to whether they include the computation of simple main effects. We will illustrate the computation using calculations that can be done with a calculator. For these computations we will use the data for the three delay groups who used their nondominant hand. These data are in the bottom half of the data matrix near the beginning of the section on the analysis of the two-factor design for independent groups. This simple main effect would be referred to as the effect of delay at the nondominant hand (or more generally, the effect of variable B at A2). We will first present the computations and then briefly describe the interpretation of simple main effects.

Computing the simple main effect of B at a_2 (B/a_2).

1 Compute $SS_{B/a_2} = \dfrac{(\Sigma X_{a_2b_1})^2 + (\Sigma X_{a_2b_2})^2 + (\Sigma X_{a_2b_3})^2}{n} - \dfrac{(\Sigma X_{a_2b_1} + \Sigma X_{a_2b_2} + \Sigma X_{a_2b_3})^2}{(b)(n)}$

$$= \frac{(53)^2 + (79)^2 + (91)^2}{5} - \frac{(53 + 79 + 91)^2}{(3)(5)}$$

$$= \frac{2{,}809 + 6{,}241 + 8{,}281}{5} - \frac{(223)^2}{15}$$

$$= \frac{17{,}331}{5} - \frac{49{,}729}{15}$$

$$= 3{,}466.20 - 3{,}315.27 = 150.93$$

2 Compute $df_{B/a_2} = b - 1 = 3 - 1 = 2$

3 Compute $MS_{B/a_2} = \dfrac{SS_{B/a_2}}{df_{B/a_2}} = \dfrac{150.93}{2} = 75.47$

4 Compute $F\ (df_{B/a_2}, df_{WG}) = \dfrac{MS_{B/a_2}}{MS_{WG}} = \dfrac{75.47}{2.45} = 30.80$

The final computation of the *F*-ratio involved the use of the Mean Square Error (within groups) from the SYSTAT output for the two-factor design shown on Screen A.6. The computations of all the other values needed to compute a simple main effect are shown in the four steps we have outlined. As with any *F*-test, it is necessary to determine the probability of the *F* under the null hypothesis. The obtained $F\ (2, 24) = 30.8$ is associated with a probability of less than one in a thousand which is less than the conventional level of significance of .05. Thus, the simple main effect of delay at the level of nondominant hand was statistically significant. Although we will not illustrate the computations here, we did compute the simple main effect of delay for those subjects using their dominant hand. The resulting $F\ (2, 24)$ was .68. An *F*-ratio less than 1 cannot be statistically significant so this nonsignificant simple main effect indicates that there was no effect of delay when subjects used their dominant hand.

Together, the two simple main effects help us to specify the source of the statistically significant interaction of delay and hand dominance. As described in Chapter 9, the source of an interaction can be specified even more exactly by using simple comparisons to follow up statistically significant simple main effects.

TWO-FACTOR ANALYSIS OF VARIANCE FOR A MIXED DESIGN

The two-factor analysis of variance for a mixed design is appropriate when one independent variable represents either the random groups or natural groups design and the second independent variable represents the within-subjects design. The first independent variable is called the *between-subjects factor* and is symbolized as A. The second independent variable is called the *within-subjects factor* and is symbolized as B. The two-factor analysis for a mixed design is somewhat of a hybrid of the single-factor analysis for independent groups and the single-factor analysis for the within-subjects designs.

The data presented in the following table represent the mean frequency judgments subjects gave to four brief segments of popular songs. The subjects listened to a tape including several songs; half the subjects did not expect the frequency judgment test (incidental group), and half did expect the test (intentional group). In addition, all subjects judged songs that had been presented either one, two, or three times. Thus, the experiment was a 2 × 3 design in which instructions were manipulated in a random groups design with five subjects assigned to each of two groups and in which the presented frequency variable was manipulated in a complete within-subjects design. The following data matrix shows the mean frequency judgments at three levels of presentation frequency for each subject in each group.

		Presentation Frequency (B)		
	Subject	1(b_1)	2(b_2)	3(b_3)
	1	1.2	2.2	3.0
	2	.8	2.0	3.2
	3	1.2	1.8	2.8
Incidental	4	1.5	2.0	2.5
group (a_1)	5	1.2	2.5	3.2
	6	1.2	1.5	2.0
	7	1.0	2.0	2.5
	8	1.0	1.2	3.2
Intentional	9	1.2	2.2	2.8
group (a_2)	10	1.0	2.2	3.5

The thirty scores in the data matrix were entered into the SYSTAT program for a two-factor analysis of variance for a mixed design. The output from the program is presented in Screen A.7. The output begins by indicating that there were ten cases (i.e., ten subjects) in the analysis. The next portion of the output presents the means for the three levels of the presentation (frequency) variable. These means describe the main effect of the presentation variable, and

```
NUMBER OF CASES PROCESSED:       10
DEPENDENT VARIABLE MEANS

                    PRESENT(1)  PRESENT(2)  PRESENT(3)
                         1.130       1.960       2.870
_______________________________________________________

BETWEEN SUBJECTS
----------------

SOURCE         SS     DF     MS       F       P

GROUP        0.225     1   0.225   1.718   0.226
ERROR        1.049     8   0.131

WITHIN SUBJECTS
---------------

SOURCE         SS     DF     MS       F       P      G-G    H-F

PRESENT     15.149     2   7.574  58.640  0.000  0.000  0.00
PRESENT
*GROUP       0.045     2   0.022   0.173  0.843  0.810  0.84
ERROR        2.067    16   0.129

GREENHOUSE-GEISSER EPSILON:  0.8539
HUYNH-FELDT EPSILON       :  1.0000
```

SCREEN A.7

they are presented because this main effect was the only statistically significant effect in the analysis. Means for the main effect of group and for the interaction could be obtained by running the descriptive statistics program on SYSTAT or by computing the means directly from the data matrix. It is important to examine the means for both statistically significant and nonsignificant effects.

The summary table in Screen A.7 is divided into two parts. The Between Subjects section includes the *F*-test for the main effect of groups. The form of this part of the table is like that of a single-factor analysis for the independent-groups design. The Error listed in this section is the within-groups variation. The *F*-ratio for the effect of group was not statistically significant since the obtained probability of .226 was greater than the conventional level of statistical significance of .05.

The second part of the summary table in Screen A.7 is headed Within Subjects. It includes the main effect of the within-subjects variable of presentation frequency and the interaction of presentation frequency and group. In general, any effect including a within-subjects variable (main effect or interaction) must be tested with the residual error term used in the within-subjects design. The

F-ratio for the interaction is less than 1 and so was not statistically significant. The main effect of presentation frequency, however, did result in a statistically significant F. As was true in the analysis of the single-factor within-subjects design, the SYSTAT output for the analysis of the mixed design provides corrected probability values for effects that include a within-subjects factor. The Greenhouse-Geisser and the Huynh-Feldt corrections attempt to adjust for the higher probability of a Type I error in the within-subjects design (see Keppel, 1991, for more details about these corrections).

The two-factor analysis for a mixed design follows the logic for any complex design (see Chapter 9). That is, the interaction is examined first, and if the interaction is statistically significant, then simple main effects and simple comparisons are used to identify the source of the interaction. The main effects are then examined, and analytical comparisons can be used to analyze further statistically significant main effects of independent variables with more than two levels. Care must be taken, however, when analyzing a mixed design to use the appropriate error term for analyses beyond those listed in the summary table (i.e., simple main effects, simple comparisons, and analytical comparisons). It is fitting that we end this appendix by encouraging you to seek expert advice when facing this or any other challenge in the analysis of your research findings.

STATISTICAL TABLES

TABLE A.1 TABLE OF RANDOM NUMBERS*

Col. / Line	(1)	(2)	(3)	(4)	(5)	(6)	(7)	(8)	(9)	(10)	(11)	(12)	(13)	(14)
1	10480	15011	01536	02011	81647	91646	69179	14194	62590	36207	20969	99570	91291	90700
2	22368	46573	25595	85393	30995	89198	27982	53402	93965	34095	52666	19174	39615	99505
3	24130	48360	22527	97265	76393	64809	15179	24830	49340	32081	30680	19655	63348	58629
4	42167	93093	06243	61680	07856	16376	39440	53537	71341	57004	00849	74917	97758	16379
5	37570	39975	81837	16656	06121	91782	60468	81305	49684	60672	14110	06927	01263	54613
6	77921	06907	11008	42751	27756	53498	18602	70659	90655	15053	21916	81825	44394	42880
7	99562	72905	56420	69994	98872	31016	71194	18738	44013	48840	63213	21069	10634	12952
8	96301	91977	65463	07972	18876	20922	94595	56869	69014	60045	18425	84903	42508	32307
9	89579	14342	63661	10281	17453	18103	57740	84378	25331	12566	58678	44947	05585	56941
10	85475	36857	53342	53988	53060	59533	38867	62300	08158	17983	16439	11458	18593	64952
11	28918	69578	88231	33276	70997	79936	56865	05859	90106	31595	01547	85590	91610	78188
12	63553	40961	48235	03427	49626	69445	18663	72695	52180	20847	12234	90511	33703	90322
13	09429	93969	52636	92737	88974	33488	36320	17617	30015	08272	84115	27156	30613	74952
14	10365	61129	87529	85689	48237	52267	67689	93394	01511	26358	85104	20285	29975	89868
15	07119	97336	71048	08178	77233	13916	47564	81506	97735	85977	29372	74461	28551	90707

(continued)

TABLE A.1 TABLE OF RANDOM NUMBERS* *(continued)*

Line \ Col.	(1)	(2)	(3)	(4)	(5)	(6)	(7)	(8)	(9)	(10)	(11)	(12)	(13)	(14)
16	51085	12765	51821	51259	77452	16308	60756	92144	49442	53900	70960	63990	75601	40719
17	02368	21382	52404	60268	89368	19885	55322	44819	01188	65255	64835	44919	05944	55157
18	01011	54092	33362	94904	31273	04146	18594	29852	71585	85030	51132	01915	92747	64951
19	52162	53916	46369	58586	23216	14513	83149	98736	23495	64350	94738	17752	35156	35749
20	07056	97628	33787	09998	42698	06691	76988	13602	51851	46104	88916	19509	25625	58104
21	48663	91245	85828	14346	09172	30168	90229	04734	59193	22178	30421	61666	99904	32812
22	54164	58492	22421	74103	47070	25306	76468	26384	58151	06646	21524	15227	96909	44592
23	32639	32363	05597	24200	13363	38005	94342	28728	35806	06912	17012	64161	18296	22851
24	29334	27001	87637	87308	58731	00256	45834	15398	46557	41135	10367	07684	36188	18510
25	02488	33062	28834	07351	19731	92420	60952	61280	50001	67658	32586	86679	50720	94953
26	81525	72295	04839	96423	24878	82651	66566	14778	76797	14780	13300	87074	79666	95725
27	29676	20591	68086	26432	46901	20849	89768	81536	86645	12659	92259	57102	80428	25280
28	00742	57392	39064	66432	84673	40027	32832	61362	98947	96067	64760	64584	96096	98253
29	05366	04213	25669	26422	44407	44048	37937	63904	45766	66134	75470	66520	34693	90449
30	91921	26418	64117	94305	26766	25940	39972	22209	71500	64568	91402	42416	07844	69618
31	00582	04711	87917	77341	42206	35126	74087	99547	81817	42607	43808	76655	62028	76630
32	00725	69884	62797	56170	86324	88072	76222	36086	84637	93161	76038	65855	77919	88006
33	69011	65795	95876	55293	18988	27354	26575	08625	40801	59920	29841	80150	12777	48501
34	25976	57948	29888	88604	67917	48708	18912	82271	65424	69774	33611	54262	85963	03547
35	09763	83473	73577	12908	30883	18317	28290	35797	05998	41688	34952	37888	38917	88050
36	91567	42595	27958	30134	04024	86385	29880	99730	55536	84855	29080	09250	79656	73211
37	17955	56349	90999	49127	20044	59931	06115	20542	18059	02008	73708	83517	36103	42791
38	46503	18584	18845	49618	02304	51038	20655	58727	28168	15475	56942	53389	20562	87338
39	92157	89634	94824	78171	84610	82834	09922	25417	44137	48413	25555	21246	35509	20468
40	14577	62765	35605	81263	39667	47358	56873	56307	61607	49518	89696	20103	77490	18062
41	98427	07523	33362	64270	01638	92477	66969	98420	04880	45585	46565	04102	46880	45709
42	34914	63976	88720	82765	34476	17032	87589	40836	32427	70002	70663	88863	77775	69348
43	70060	28277	39475	46473	23219	53416	94970	25832	69975	94884	19661	72828	00102	66794
44	53976	54914	06990	67245	68350	82948	11398	42878	80287	88267	47363	46634	06541	97809
45	76072	29515	40980	07391	58745	25774	22987	80059	39911	96189	41151	14222	60697	59583
46	90725	52210	83974	29992	65831	38857	50490	83765	55657	14361	31720	57375	56228	41546
47	64364	67412	33339	31926	14883	24413	59744	92351	97473	89286	35931	04110	23726	51900
48	08962	00358	31662	25388	61642	34072	81249	35648	56891	69352	48373	45578	78547	81788
49	95012	68379	93526	70765	10592	04542	76463	54328	02349	17247	28865	14777	62730	92277
50	15664	10493	20492	38391	91132	21999	59516	81652	27195	48223	46751	22923	32261	85653

* *Source: Table of 105,000 Random Decimal Digits,* Statement no. 4914, File no. 261-A-1, Interstate Commerce Commission, Washington, D.C. May 1949.

TABLE A.2 VALUES OF r AT THE .05 AND .01 LEVELS OF SIGNIFICANCE*

df	.05	.01	df	.05	.01	df	.05	.01
1	.997	1.000	16	.468	.590	35	.325	.418
2	.950	.990	17	.456	.575	40	.304	.393
3	.878	.959	18	.444	.561	45	.288	.372
4	.811	.917	19	.433	.549	50	.273	.354
5	.754	.874	20	.423	.537	60	.250	.325
6	.707	.834	21	.413	.526	70	.232	.302
7	.666	.798	22	.404	.515	80	.217	.283
8	.632	.765	23	.396	.505	90	.205	.267
9	.602	.735	24	.388	.496	100	.195	.254
10	.576	.708	25	.381	.487			
11	.553	.684	26	.374	.478			
12	.532	.661	27	.367	.470			
13	.514	.641	28	.361	.463			
14	.497	.623	29	.355	.456			
15	.482	.606	30	.349	.449			

* Adapted from Table VII of Fisher and Yates, *Statistical Tables for Biological, Agricultural, and Medical Research,* 6th ed., 1974. Published by Oliver and Boyd, Limited, Publishers, Edinburgh, by permission of the authors and publishers. Published by Longman Group Ltd., London.

TABLE A.3 VALUES OF RANK-ORDER CORRELATION COEFFICIENT (r_s) AT THE .05 AND .01 LEVELS OF SIGNIFICANCE*

N	.05	.01
5	1.000	—
6	.886	1.000
7	.786	.929
8	.715	.881
9	.700	.834
10	.649	.794
12	.588	.735
14	.539	.680
16	.503	.636
18	.474	.600
20	.447	.570
22	.426	.544
24	.407	.521
26	.391	.501
28	.376	.484
30	.363	.467

* Adapted from Table 1 (p. 385) of McCall, R. B. (1980). *Fundamental Statistics for Psychology,* 3d ed., Harcourt, Brace, Jovanovich. Reproduced by permission of publisher.

TABLE A.4 CRITICAL VALUES OF THE CHI SQUARE (χ^2) DISTRIBUTION*

Instructions for use: To find the critical value of χ^2, locate the row in the left-hand column of the table corresponding to the number of degrees of freedom (df) associated with χ^2, and select the value of χ^2 listed for the desired level of significance (α).

df	α = .05	α = .01	df	α = .05	α = .01
1	3.84	6.63	16	26.30	32.00
2	5.99	9.21	17	27.59	33.41
3	7.81	11.34	18	28.87	34.81
4	9.49	13.28	19	30.14	36.19
5	11.07	15.09	20	31.41	37.57
6	12.59	16.81	21	32.67	38.93
7	14.07	18.48	22	33.92	40.29
8	15.51	20.09	23	35.17	41.64
9	16.92	21.67	24	36.42	42.98
10	18.31	23.21	25	37.65	44.31
11	19.68	24.72	26	38.89	45.64
12	21.03	26.22	27	40.11	46.96
13	22.36	27.69	28	41.34	48.28
14	23.68	29.14	29	42.56	49.59
15	25.00	30.58	30	43.77	50.89

* This table is abridged from Table 8 in *Biometrika tables for statisticians,* vol. 1 (3d ed.), New York: Cambridge University Press, 1970, edited by E. S. Pearson and H. O. Hartley, by permission of the *Biometrika* Trustees.

TABLE A.5 SELECTED VALUES FROM THE *t* DISTRIBUTION*

Instructions for use: To find a value of *t*, locate the row in the left-hand column of the table corresponding to the number of degrees of freedom (df) associated with the standard error of the mean, and select the value of *t* listed for your choice of α. The value given in the column labeled α = .05 is used in the calculation of the 95 percent confidence interval, and the value given in the column labeled α = .01 is used to calculate the 99 percent confidence interval.

df	α = .05	α = .01	df	α = .05	α = .01
1	12.71	63.66	18	2.10	2.88
2	4.30	9.92	19	2.09	2.86
3	3.18	5.84	20	2.09	2.84
4	2.78	4.60	21	2.08	2.83
5	2.57	4.03	22	2.07	2.82
6	2.45	3.71	23	2.07	2.81
7	2.36	3.50	24	2.06	2.80
8	2.31	3.36	25	2.06	2.79
9	2.26	3.25	26	2.06	2.78
10	2.23	3.17	27	2.05	2.77
11	2.20	3.11	28	2.05	2.76
12	2.18	3.06	29	2.04	2.76
13	2.16	3.01	30	2.04	2.75
14	2.14	2.98	40	2.02	2.70
15	2.13	2.95	60	2.00	2.66
16	2.12	2.92	120	1.98	2.62
17	2.11	2.90	Infinity	1.96	2.58

* This table is adapted from Table 12 in *Biometrika tables for statisticians,* vol. 1 (3d ed.), New York: Cambridge University Press, 1970, edited by E. S. Pearson and H. O. Hartley, by permission of the *Biometrika* Trustees.

TABLE A.6 CRITICAL VALUES OF THE *F*-DISTRIBUTION*

Instructions for use: To find the critical value of *F*, locate the cell in the table formed by the intersection of the row containing the degrees of freedom associated with the denominator of the *F*-ratio and the column containing the degrees of freedom associated with the numerator of the *F*-ratio. The numbers listed in boldface type are the critical values of *F* at $\alpha = .05$; the numbers listed in Roman type are the critical values of *F* at $\alpha = .01$. As an example, suppose we have adopted the 5 percent level of significance and wish to evaluate the significance of an *F* with $df_{num} = 2$ and $df_{denom} = 12$. From the table we find that the critical value of $F(2, 12) = 3.89$ at $\alpha = .05$. If the obtained value of *F* equals or exceeds this critical value, we will reject the null hypothesis; if the obtained value of *F* is smaller than this critical value, we will not reject the null hypothesis.

Degrees of freedom for denominator	Degrees of freedom for numerator																	
	1	2	3	4	5	6	7	8	9	10	12	15	20	24	30	40	60	Infinity
1	**161**	**200**	**216**	**225**	**230**	**234**	**237**	**239**	**241**	**242**	**244**	**246**	**248**	**249**	**250**	**251**	**252**	**254**
	4052	4999	5403	5625	5764	5859	5928	5981	6022	6056	6106	6157	6209	6235	6261	6287	6313	6366
2	**18.5**	**19.0**	**19.2**	**19.2**	**19.3**	**19.3**	**19.4**	**19.4**	**19.4**	**19.4**	**19.4**	**19.4**	**19.4**	**19.4**	**19.5**	**19.5**	**19.5**	**19.5**
	98.5	99.0	99.2	99.2	99.3	99.3	99.4	99.4	99.4	99.4	99.4	99.4	99.4	99.5	99.5	99.5	99.5	99.5
3	**10.1**	**9.55**	**9.28**	**9.12**	**9.01**	**8.94**	**8.89**	**8.85**	**8.81**	**8.79**	**8.74**	**8.70**	**8.66**	**8.64**	**8.62**	**8.59**	**8.57**	**8.53**
	34.1	30.8	29.5	28.7	28.2	27.9	27.7	27.5	27.4	27.2	27.0	26.9	26.7	26.6	26.5	26.4	26.3	26.1
4	**7.71**	**6.94**	**6.59**	**6.39**	**6.26**	**6.16**	**6.09**	**6.04**	**6.00**	**5.96**	**5.91**	**5.86**	**5.80**	**5.77**	**5.75**	**5.72**	**5.69**	**5.63**
	21.2	18.0	16.7	16.0	15.5	15.2	15.0	14.8	14.7	14.6	14.4	14.2	14.0	13.9	13.8	13.8	13.6	13.5
5	**6.61**	**5.79**	**5.41**	**5.19**	**5.05**	**4.95**	**4.88**	**4.82**	**4.77**	**4.74**	**4.68**	**4.62**	**4.56**	**4.53**	**4.50**	**4.46**	**4.43**	**4.26**
	16.3	13.3	12.1	11.4	11.0	10.7	10.5	10.3	10.2	10.0	9.89	9.72	9.55	9.47	9.38	9.29	9.20	9.02
6	**5.99**	**5.14**	**4.76**	**4.53**	**4.39**	**4.28**	**4.21**	**4.15**	**4.10**	**4.06**	**4.00**	**3.94**	**3.87**	**3.84**	**3.81**	**3.77**	**3.74**	**3.67**
	13.8	10.9	9.78	9.15	8.75	8.47	8.26	8.10	7.98	7.87	7.72	7.56	7.40	7.31	7.23	7.14	7.06	6.88
7	**5.59**	**4.74**	**4.35**	**4.12**	**3.97**	**3.87**	**3.79**	**3.73**	**3.68**	**3.64**	**3.57**	**3.51**	**3.44**	**3.41**	**3.38**	**3.34**	**3.30**	**3.23**
	12.2	9.55	8.45	7.85	7.46	7.19	6.99	6.84	6.72	6.62	6.47	6.31	6.16	6.07	5.99	5.91	5.82	5.65
8	**5.32**	**4.46**	**4.07**	**3.84**	**3.69**	**3.58**	**3.50**	**3.44**	**3.39**	**3.35**	**3.28**	**3.22**	**3.15**	**3.12**	**3.08**	**3.04**	**3.01**	**2.93**
	11.3	8.65	7.59	7.01	6.63	6.37	6.18	6.03	5.91	5.81	5.67	5.52	5.36	5.28	5.20	5.12	5.03	4.86
9	**5.12**	**4.26**	**3.86**	**3.63**	**3.48**	**3.37**	**3.29**	**3.23**	**3.18**	**3.14**	**3.07**	**3.01**	**2.94**	**2.90**	**2.86**	**2.83**	**2.79**	**2.71**
	10.6	8.02	6.99	6.42	6.06	5.80	5.61	5.47	5.35	5.26	5.11	4.96	4.81	4.73	4.65	4.57	4.48	4.31
10	**4.96**	**4.10**	**3.71**	**3.48**	**3.33**	**3.22**	**3.14**	**3.07**	**3.02**	**2.98**	**2.91**	**2.85**	**2.77**	**2.74**	**2.70**	**2.66**	**2.62**	**2.54**
	10.0	7.56	6.55	5.99	5.64	5.39	5.20	5.06	4.94	4.85	4.71	4.56	4.41	4.33	4.25	4.17	4.08	3.91
11	**4.84**	**3.98**	**3.59**	**3.36**	**3.20**	**3.09**	**3.01**	**2.95**	**2.90**	**2.85**	**2.79**	**2.72**	**2.65**	**2.61**	**2.57**	**2.53**	**2.49**	**2.40**
	9.65	7.21	6.22	5.67	5.32	5.07	4.89	4.74	4.63	4.54	4.40	4.25	4.10	4.02	3.94	3.86	3.78	3.60
12	**4.75**	**3.89**	**3.49**	**3.26**	**3.11**	**3.00**	**2.91**	**2.85**	**2.80**	**2.75**	**2.69**	**2.62**	**2.54**	**2.51**	**2.47**	**2.43**	**2.38**	**2.30**
	9.33	6.93	5.95	5.41	5.06	4.82	4.64	4.50	4.39	4.30	4.16	4.01	3.86	3.78	3.70	3.62	3.54	3.36
13	**4.67**	**3.81**	**3.41**	**3.18**	**3.03**	**2.92**	**2.83**	**2.77**	**2.71**	**2.67**	**2.60**	**2.53**	**2.46**	**2.42**	**2.38**	**2.34**	**2.30**	**2.21**
	9.07	6.70	5.74	5.21	4.86	4.62	4.44	4.30	4.19	4.10	3.96	3.82	3.66	3.59	3.51	3.43	3.34	3.17
14	**4.60**	**3.74**	**3.34**	**3.11**	**2.96**	**2.85**	**2.76**	**2.70**	**2.65**	**2.60**	**2.53**	**2.46**	**2.39**	**2.35**	**2.31**	**2.27**	**2.22**	**2.13**
	8.86	6.51	5.56	5.04	4.69	4.46	4.28	4.14	4.03	3.94	3.80	3.66	3.51	3.43	3.35	3.27	3.18	3.00
15	**4.54**	**3.68**	**3.29**	**3.06**	**2.90**	**2.79**	**2.71**	**2.64**	**2.59**	**2.54**	**2.48**	**2.40**	**2.33**	**2.29**	**2.25**	**2.20**	**2.16**	**2.07**
	8.68	6.36	5.42	4.89	4.56	4.32	4.14	4.00	3.89	3.80	3.67	3.52	3.37	3.29	3.21	3.13	3.05	2.87
16	**4.49**	**3.63**	**3.24**	**3.01**	**2.85**	**2.74**	**2.66**	**2.59**	**2.54**	**2.49**	**2.42**	**2.35**	**2.28**	**2.24**	**2.19**	**2.15**	**2.11**	**2.01**
	8.53	6.23	5.29	4.77	4.44	4.20	4.03	3.89	3.78	3.69	3.55	3.41	3.26	3.18	3.10	3.02	2.93	2.75
17	**4.45**	**3.59**	**3.20**	**2.96**	**2.81**	**2.70**	**2.61**	**2.55**	**2.49**	**2.45**	**2.38**	**2.31**	**2.23**	**2.19**	**2.15**	**2.10**	**2.06**	**1.96**
	8.40	6.11	5.18	4.67	4.34	4.10	3.93	3.79	3.68	3.59	3.46	3.31	3.16	3.08	3.00	2.92	2.83	2.65
18	**4.41**	**3.55**	**3.16**	**2.93**	**2.77**	**2.66**	**2.58**	**2.51**	**2.46**	**2.41**	**2.34**	**2.27**	**2.19**	**2.15**	**2.11**	**2.06**	**2.02**	**1.92**
	8.29	6.01	5.09	4.58	4.25	4.01	3.84	3.71	3.60	3.51	3.37	3.23	3.08	3.00	2.92	2.84	2.75	2.57
19	**4.38**	**3.52**	**3.13**	**2.90**	**2.74**	**2.63**	**2.54**	**2.48**	**2.42**	**2.38**	**2.31**	**2.23**	**2.16**	**2.11**	**2.07**	**2.03**	**1.98**	**1.88**
	8.18	5.93	5.01	4.50	4.17	3.94	3.77	3.63	3.52	3.43	3.30	3.15	3.00	2.92	2.84	2.76	2.67	2.49
20	**4.35**	**3.49**	**3.10**	**2.87**	**2.71**	**2.60**	**2.51**	**2.45**	**2.39**	**2.35**	**2.28**	**2.20**	**2.12**	**2.08**	**2.04**	**1.99**	**1.95**	**1.84**
	8.10	5.85	4.94	4.43	4.10	3.87	3.70	3.56	3.46	3.37	3.23	3.09	2.94	2.86	2.78	2.69	2.61	2.42
22	**4.30**	**3.44**	**3.05**	**2.82**	**2.66**	**2.55**	**2.46**	**2.40**	**2.34**	**2.30**	**2.23**	**2.15**	**2.07**	**2.03**	**1.98**	**1.94**	**1.89**	**1.78**
	7.95	5.72	4.82	4.31	3.99	3.76	3.59	3.45	3.35	3.26	3.12	2.98	2.83	2.75	2.67	2.58	2.50	2.31
24	**4.26**	**3.40**	**3.01**	**2.78**	**2.62**	**2.51**	**2.42**	**2.36**	**2.30**	**2.25**	**2.18**	**2.11**	**2.03**	**1.98**	**1.94**	**1.89**	**1.84**	**1.73**
	7.82	5.61	4.72	4.22	3.90	3.67	3.50	3.36	3.26	3.17	3.03	2.89	2.74	2.66	2.58	2.49	2.40	2.21

(continued)

TABLE A.6 CRITICAL VALUES OF THE *F*-DISTRIBUTION* (*continued*)

Degrees of freedom for denominator	Degrees of freedom for numerator																	
	1	2	3	4	5	6	7	8	9	10	12	15	20	24	30	40	60	Infinity
26	**4.23**	**3.37**	**2.98**	**2.74**	**2.59**	**2.47**	**2.39**	**2.32**	**2.27**	**2.22**	**2.15**	**2.07**	**1.99**	**1.95**	**1.90**	**1.85**	**1.80**	**1.69**
	7.72	5.53	4.64	4.14	3.82	3.59	3.42	3.29	3.18	3.09	2.96	2.81	2.66	2.58	2.50	2.42	2.33	2.13
28	**4.20**	**3.34**	**2.95**	**2.71**	**2.56**	**2.45**	**2.36**	**2.29**	**2.24**	**2.19**	**2.12**	**2.04**	**1.96**	**1.91**	**1.87**	**1.82**	**1.77**	**1.65**
	7.64	5.45	4.57	4.07	3.75	3.53	3.36	3.23	3.12	3.03	2.90	2.75	2.60	2.52	2.44	2.35	2.26	2.06
30	**4.17**	**3.32**	**2.92**	**2.69**	**2.53**	**2.42**	**2.33**	**2.27**	**2.21**	**2.16**	**2.09**	**2.01**	**1.93**	**1.89**	**1.84**	**1.79**	**1.74**	**1.62**
	7.56	5.39	4.51	4.02	3.70	3.47	3.30	3.17	3.07	2.98	2.84	2.70	2.55	2.47	2.39	2.30	2.21	2.01
40	**4.08**	**3.23**	**2.84**	**2.61**	**2.45**	**2.34**	**2.25**	**2.18**	**2.12**	**2.08**	**2.00**	**1.92**	**1.84**	**1.79**	**1.74**	**1.69**	**1.64**	**1.51**
	7.31	5.18	4.31	3.83	3.51	3.29	3.12	2.99	2.89	2.80	2.66	2.52	2.37	2.29	2.20	2.11	2.02	1.80
60	**4.00**	**3.15**	**2.76**	**2.53**	**2.37**	**2.25**	**2.17**	**2.10**	**2.04**	**1.99**	**1.92**	**1.84**	**1.75**	**1.70**	**1.65**	**1.59**	**1.53**	**1.39**
	7.08	4.98	4.13	3.65	3.34	3.12	2.95	2.82	2.72	2.63	2.50	2.35	2.20	2.12	2.03	1.94	1.84	1.60
120	**3.92**	**3.07**	**2.68**	**2.45**	**2.29**	**2.17**	**2.09**	**2.02**	**1.96**	**1.91**	**1.83**	**1.75**	**1.66**	**1.61**	**1.55**	**1.50**	**1.43**	**1.25**
	6.85	4.79	3.95	3.48	3.17	2.96	2.79	2.66	2.56	2.47	2.34	2.19	2.03	1.95	1.86	1.76	1.66	1.38
INFINITY	**3.84**	**3.00**	**2.60**	**2.37**	**2.21**	**2.10**	**2.01**	**1.94**	**1.88**	**1.83**	**1.75**	**1.67**	**1.57**	**1.52**	**1.46**	**1.39**	**1.32**	**1.00**
	6.63	4.61	3.78	3.32	3.02	2.80	2.64	2.51	2.41	2.32	2.18	2.04	1.88	1.79	1.70	1.59	1.47	1.00

* This table is abridged from Table 18 in *Biometrika tables for statisticians,* vol. 1 (3d ed.), New York: Cambridge University Press, 1970, edited by E. S. Pearson and H. O. Hartley, by permission of the *Biometrika* Trustees.

Appendix B

Questionnaire Construction

Outline

INTRODUCTION

In Chapter 4 we discussed procedures for administering a survey without describing in detail the nature of the most common survey research instrument, the questionnaire. Even if the sample used was perfectly representative, the response rate was 100 percent, and the research design was elegantly planned and perfectly executed, the results of a survey will be useless if the questionnaire was poorly constructed. Although there is no substitute for experience when it comes to preparing a good questionnaire, there are a few general principles of sound questionnaire construction with which you should be familiar before you do your first survey. In this appendix we describe six basic steps in preparing a questionnaire and then offer some more specific guidelines for writing and administering individual questions. This material will be most useful should you decide to make use of a questionnaire as part of a research project you are doing.

STEPS IN PREPARING A QUESTIONNAIRE

Six basic steps in preparing a questionnaire are listed in Table B.1. The warning "Watch out for that first step!" is appropriate here. The first step in questionnaire construction, deciding what information is to be sought, should actually be the first step in planning the survey as a whole. This decision, of course, determines the nature of the questions to be included in the questionnaire. It is important to project the likely results of the survey if the proposed questionnaire is used and then to decide whether these "findings" will answer the questions the study is intended to address. Surveys are frequently done under

TABLE B.1 SIX BASIC STEPS IN PREPARING A QUESTIONNAIRE

1 Decide what information should be sought.
2 Decide what type of questionnaire should be used.
3 Write a first draft of the questionnaire.
4 Reexamine and revise the questionnaire.
5 Pretest the questionnaire.
6 Edit the questionnaire and specifiy the procedures for its use.

considerable time pressure, and inexperienced researchers are especially prone to impatience. Just remember that a poorly conceived questionnaire takes just as much time and effort to administer and analyze as does a well-conceived questionnaire. The difference is that a well-constructed questionnaire leads to interpretable results. The best that can be said for a poorly designed one is that it is a good way to learn how important careful deliberation is in the planning stages.

Once the information to be sought from respondents has been clearly specified, the next step is to decide on the type of questionnaire to be used. For example, will it be self-administered, or will trained interviewers be using it? This decision is determined primarily by the survey method that has been selected. For instance, if a telephone survey is to be done, trained interviewers will be needed. In designing the questionnaire, one should also consider using items that have been prepared by other researchers. There is no reason to develop your own instrument to assess racial prejudice if a reliable and valid one is already available. Besides, if you use items from a questionnaire that has already been used, you can compare your results directly with those of earlier studies.

If you decide that no available instrument suits your needs, you will have to take the third step and write a first draft of your own questionnaire. Guidelines concerning the format and ordering of questions, as well as suggestions for wording questions effectively, will be presented in later sections of this appendix.

The fourth step in questionnaire construction, reexamining and rewriting, is an essential one. Questions that appear objective and unambiguous to you may strike others as slanted and ambiguous. It is most helpful to have your questionnaire reviewed by experts, both those who have knowledge of survey research methods and those with expertise in the area on which your study is focused. For example, if you are doing a survey of students' attitudes toward the campus food service, it would be advisable to have your questionnaire reviewed by the campus food service director. When you are dealing with a controversial topic, it is especially important to have representatives of both sides of the issue screen your questions for possible bias. Sometimes no one particular wording can be agreed on by all. In such cases, the *split-ballot technique* is helpful. In this technique, different wordings of the same questions are used for equivalent samples of respondents. The effect of the wording can be directly examined by comparing responses made in these two (or more) samples. For example, Schuman and Bobo (1988) used the split-ballot technique to embed randomized experiments within their survey design. Their overall objective was to examine the opposition of whites to the rights of blacks to open housing. They used the split-ballot technique to assign subgroups within their samples randomly to different versions of questions. Comparing the responses of these subgroups led to the identification of factors that affect attitudes toward open housing, factors such as people's general resistance to government coercion.

By far the most critical step in the development of a sound questionnaire is step 5, the pretest. A pretest involves actually administering the questionnaire to a small sample of respondents under conditions as much as possible like those to be used in the final administration of the survey. Pretest respondents must also be typical of those to be included in the final sample; it makes little sense to pretest a survey of nursing home residents by administering the questionnaire to college students. There is one way, however, in which a pretest does differ from the final administration of the survey. Respondents should be interviewed at length regarding their reactions to individual questions and to the questionnaire as a whole. This provides information about potentially ambiguous or offensive items.

The pretest should also serve as a "dress rehearsal" for interviewers, who should be closely supervised during this stage to ensure that they understand and adhere to the proper procedures for administering the questionnaire. If major changes have to be made as a result of problems arising during the pretest, a second pretest may be needed to determine whether these changes solved the problems originally encountered. After pretesting is completed, the final step is to edit the questionnaire and specify the procedures to be followed in its final administration.

In the next two sections, we return to two issues pertinent to the third step in preparing a questionnaire—writing a first draft. We will consider two sets of guidelines: one for writing questions and one for the general format of a questionnaire.

GUIDELINES FOR THE EFFECTIVE WORDING OF QUESTIONS

Lawyers have long known that how a question is phrased has great impact on how that question is answered. Survey researchers need to be equally conscious of this principle. This point is illustrated in a survey Loftus (1979a) conducted for the manufacturer of a leading headache remedy. She found that people reported having more headaches when they were asked "Do you get headaches frequently and, if so, how often?" than when they were asked "Do you get headaches occasionally and, if so, how often?" Unfortunately, the extent of the influence of the wording of questions in a given survey can almost never be determined precisely. The problem is clearer than the solution. Schuman and Scott (1987) argue that investigators should realize the limitations on assessing, in an absolute sense, people's opinions or attitudes based on any one set of questions. They encourage researchers to emphasize subjects' reponses to the same set of questions over time. At a minimum, the exact wording of critical questions should always be reported along with the data describing respondents' answers. The problem of the potential influence of the wording of questions is yet another illustration of why a multimethod approach is so essential in investigating behavior.

There are certain guidelines to follow to minimize problems arising from the phrasing of survey questions. These guidelines can be applied to *free-response* (open-ended) questions and to *closed* (multiple-choice) questions. Free-response questions, like the essay questions on a classroom test, merely specify the area to be addressed in a response. For example, the question "What are your views on the legalizing of abortion?" is a free-response question. By contrast, closed questions provide specific response alternatives. "Is police protection very good, fairly good, neither good nor bad, not very good, or not good at all?" is a closed question about the quality of police protection in a community.

The advantages of free-response questions are that they can be written more quickly and that they offer the respondent greater flexibility. However, these advantages are often more than offset by the difficulties that arise in recording and scoring responses to free-response questions. For example, extensive coding is frequently necessary before rambling responses to free-response questions can be summarized succinctly. Closed questions, on the other hand, are more difficult to write, but they can be answered more easily and quickly and fewer scoring problems arise. It is also much easier to summarize responses to closed questions because the answers are readily comparable across respondents. A major disadvantage of closed questions is that they reduce expressiveness and spontaneity. Further, the possibility exists that the respondent will have to choose a less than preferred response because no presented alternative really captures his or her views. Hence, the responses obtained may not accurately reflect the respondent's opinion.

Newcomb, Koenig, Flacks, and Warwick (1967) used both free-response and closed questions in a survey of students' attitudes. Their survey was done in two stages. In the first stage, student respondents were asked a series of free-response questions about how their lives had changed as a result of attending college. The trained interviewers used probes extensively and effectively in this stage. A self-administered questionnaire was then developed for the second stage of the survey. During this second stage, a different sample of students rated how much they had changed in each of a number of areas. The researchers wrote closed questions for the second stage of the survey using specific areas of change that had been indicated in the answers to the original set of free-response questions. This survey illustrates the complementary strengths of free-response and closed questions. The findings of the survey showed that one area in which change did occur was in the students' political views. What is more, these changes were shown to persist well after the students had left college.

Closed questions frequently include a scale which is used to measure the degree or amount of response to the question. A typical scale would include the categories "strongly agree," "agree," "neutral," "disagree," and "strongly disagree." Alternatively, degree of response can be measured by asking respondents to rank several alternatives from "most preferred" to "least preferred." The scale using strength of agreement is an illustration of category scaling. The scale ranking preferences is an illustration of rank-order scaling. Rank-order scaling has the advantage that it forces the respondent to make discriminations among alternatives. Rank-order scaling is thus more sensitive in measuring differences that respondents *can* detect.

The disadvantage of rank-order scaling is that it is not informative about the absolute judgment of any one alternative. For example, respondents could rank the beauty of fifteen photographs even if they judged all the photographs to be ugly; they could reliably identify the least ugly (most beautiful) of the group even if they judged them all to be ugly. If they were asked to use category scaling to rate the beauty of the photographs, it would be possible to measure the absolute level of rated beauty of each photograph. It would also be possible to interpret the relative distances between the ratings for different photographs, something that is not possible with rank-order scaling. (The winner and runner-up in a race can be decided in a photo finish or "by a mile," and the winner will still be first and the runner-up second.) The ability to obtain absolute judgments and to interpret distances between ratings are the primary advantages of category scaling. The major disadvantage is that respondents may fail to make discriminations that they are capable of making. They may, for example, give the same rating of beauty to all the photographs. In general, rank-order scaling is preferred if the researcher is interested in relative preferences; category scaling is preferred if the researcher is interested in the absolute level of the respondents' reactions.

Several characteristics of good questionnaire items are listed in Table B.2. For instance, regardless of the type of question used, the vocabulary should be simple, direct, and familiar to all respondents. Questions should be as clear and specific as possible. Double-barreled questions should be avoided. An example of a double-barreled question is: "Have you suffered from headaches and nausea recently?" A person may respond "no" if both symptoms have not occurred at exactly the same time or may respond "yes" if either symptom has

TABLE B.2 GOOD QUESTIONNAIRE ITEMS SHOULD:

1 Include vocabulary that is simple, direct, and familiar to all respondents.
2 Be clear and specific.
3 *Not* involve leading, loaded, or double-barreled questions.
4 Be as short as possible (twenty or fewer words).
5 Include all conditional information prior to the key idea.
6 Be edited for readability.

occurred. The solution to the problem of double-barreled questions is a simple one—rewrite them as separate questions. Survey questions should be as short as possible without sacrificing the clarity of the questions' meaning. Twenty or fewer words should suffice for most survey questions. Each question should be carefully edited for readability and should be phrased in such a way that all conditional information precedes the key idea. For example, it would be better to ask, "If you were forced to leave your present job, what type of work would you seek?" than to ask, "What type of work would you seek if you were forced to leave your present job?"

Leading or loaded questions should also be avoided in a questionnaire. *Leading questions* take the form "Most people favor the use of nuclear energy. What do you think?" To avoid bias, it is better to mention all possible perspectives or to mention none. A survey question about attitudes toward nuclear energy could read either "Some people favor the use of nuclear energy, some people oppose the use of nuclear energy, and some people have no opinion one way or the other. What do you think?" or "What do you think about the use of nuclear energy?" *Loaded questions* are questions that contain emotion-laden words. For example, terms such as *radical* and *racist* should be avoided. To guard against loaded questions, it is best to have your questionnaire reviewed by individuals representing a range of social and political perspectives.

GUIDELINES FOR THE GENERAL FORMAT OF A QUESTIONNAIRE

Two aspects of the general format should be considered in constructing the final copy of a questionnaire: the design or layout of the questionnaire and the ordering of questions.

DESIGN

An effort should be made to make the design of the questionnaire attractive, but the emphasis should be on making it as easy as possible to use.

A section of a questionnaire designed for personal or phone interviews is shown in Table B.3. This questionnaire was used by trained interviewers in a survey done by the Institute for Social Research at the University of Michigan. The aim of the survey was to examine the quality of American life (Campbell, Converse, & Rogers, 1975). Several characteristics of this questionnaire are noteworthy. Each question is identified with a letter indicating the section of the questionnaire and a number specifying the individual question. This is done to facilitate later scoring and analysis of responses. The arrangement of the questions on each page is compact, but the structure is designed to make it easy to read the questions and to record responses. Whenever possible, questions with the same response format appear together. When closed questions are asked, a note is included to remind the interviewer to give the respondent a card listing the response alternatives so that the respondent can concentrate on the question and not on remembering the alternatives. At the

TABLE B.3 SAMPLE QUESTIONNAIRE FORMAT FOR PERSONAL OR PHONE INTERVIEW

Section A: City and Neighborhood

A1 In this study we are interested in measuring the quality of life of people in this country—that is, the things people like and dislike about their homes, cities, neighborhoods, jobs, and so on. The first question is: How long have you lived in (INSERT NAME OF COMMUNITY, OR OF COUNTY IF RURAL)? ____________. (IF LESS THAN TWO YEARS, GET NUMBER OF MONTHS.)

_______YEARS _______MONTHS, OR SINCE ____________

A2 And how long have you lived here in this (house/apartment)? (IF *LESS* THAN TWO YEARS. GET NUMBER OF MONTHS.)

_______YEARS _______MONTHS, OR SINCE ____________

A3 I'd like to ask how satisfied you are with some of the main public services you are supposed to receive. (HAND R CARD 1, YELLOW) Please tell me how you feel about each thing I mention, using one of the answers on this card. First, how about the way streets and roads are kept up around here. Would you say this service is *very good, fairly good, neither good nor bad, not very good, or not good at all?*

1. VERY GOOD	2. FAIRLY GOOD	3. NEITHER GOOD NOR BAD	4. NOT VERY GOOD	5. NOT GOOD AT ALL

A4 How do you feel about the quality of the *public* schools that the children from around here go to—would you say it is *very good, fairly good, neither good nor bad, not very good, or not good at all?* [DK is don't know.]

1. VERY GOOD	2. FAIRLY GOOD	3. NEITHER GOOD NOR BAD	4. NOT VERY GOOD	5. NOT GOOD AT ALL	8. DK

IF R LIVES IN A CITY, TOWN, OR VILLAGE, ASK A5 AND A6: IF RURAL, TURN TO A7

A5 How good is garbage collection in this neighborhood? Is it *very good, fairly good, neither good nor bad, not very good, or not good at all?* [DK is don't know.]

1. VERY GOOD	2. FAIRLY GOOD	3. NEITHER GOOD NOR BAD	4. NOT VERY GOOD	5. NOT GOOD AT ALL	8. DK

A6 What about the parks and playgrounds for children in this neighborhood? Are they *very good, fairly good, neither good nor bad, not very good, or not good at all?* [DK is don't know.]

1. VERY GOOD	2. FAIRLY GOOD	3. NEITHER GOOD NOR BAD	4. NOT VERY GOOD	5. NOT GOOD AT ALL	8. DK

ASK EVERYBODY:

A7 How about police protection around here. Is it *very good, fairly good, neither good nor bad, not very good, or not good at all?* [DK is don't know.]

1. VERY GOOD	2. FAIRLY GOOD	3. NEITHER GOOD NOR BAD	4. NOT VERY GOOD	5. NOT GOOD AT ALL	8. DK

beginning of the first question, the respondent is given a brief rationale for the study as a whole, but this preamble is kept short so as to require as little of the respondent's time as possible.

The format of a questionnaire that is meant to be self-administered must be somewhat different. The first section of a self-administered questionnaire distributed to passengers on Amtrak trains is shown in Table B.4. The items are arranged in a clear and uncluttered manner, and the order of the questions is clearly indicated by the large boldface numbers. Each item is short and direct, and the instructions for each question are simple. The small numbers next to each blank are used to computer-code the responses. The numbers in parentheses indicate column numbers in a computer file, and the other numbers are the ones to be entered if the respondent checks that blank. Such prior coding saves time when the data are to be analyzed and helps reduce the number of errors in data entry. In designing a self-administered questionnaire, one should spare no effort to make it visually appealing; visual appeal increases the response rate. It is most important that the questions be self-explanatory and that respondents be able to complete the questionnaire quickly and correctly.

ORDERING OF QUESTIONS

A crucial issue in deciding the order of the questions in a survey is which question or questions to ask first. The first few questions set the tone for the rest of the questionnaire and determine how willingly and conscientiously respondents will work on subsequent questions. For example, it is best to begin self-administered questionnaires with the most interesting set of questions in order to capture the respondent's attention. Demographic data should be obtained at the end of a self-administered questionnaire. In surveys involving personal or telephone interviews, on the other hand, demographic questions are frequently asked at the beginning because they are easy for the respondent to answer and thus bolster the respondent's confidence. They also allow time for the interviewer to establish rapport before asking questions about more sensitive matters.

The order in which particular questions are asked can have dramatic effects, as illustrated in a study by Schuman, Presser, and Ludwig (1981). They found differential responding depending on the order of two questions concerning abortion, one general and one specific. The general question was "Do you think it should be possible for a pregnant woman to obtain a legal abortion if she is married and does not want any more children?" The more specific question was "Do you think it should be possible for a pregnant woman to obtain a legal abortion if there is a strong chance of a serious defect in the baby?" When the general question was asked first, 60.7 percent of respondents said "yes," but when the general question followed the specific question, only 48.1 percent of respondents said "yes." The corresponding values for the specific question were 84 percent and 83 percent agreement in the first and second positions, respectively. The generally accepted method for dealing with this problem is

TABLE B.4 SAMPLE FORMAT FOR SELF-ADMINISTERED QUESTIONNAIRE

Illinois Department of Transportation
Survey of Amtrak Passengers

Dear Amtrak Passenger:

The Illinois Department of Transportation is conducting a study of rail passenger service on the Chicago–St. Louis corridor to determine what improvements should be made to upgrade service on this route. This survey is designed to identify the preferences and travel needs of passengers on Amtrak trains. Your cooperation in filling out this questionnaire will be greatly appreciated.

A Department representative will collect the survey when you have finished. If you leave your seat before the representative returns, kindly leave the questionnaire on your seat. If you have filled out this survey previously, please take a few minutes to answer questions 1 through 7 and 21 through 26.

Have an enjoyable trip and thank you for your cooperation.

1 Please check the station where you boarded this train and the station where you will get off.

Station	Boarded	Will Get Off
Chicago	______01 (1–6)	______01 (7–8)
Joliet	______02	______02
Pontiac	______03	______03
Bloomington	______04	______04
Lincoln	______05	______05
Springfield	______06	______06
Carlinville	______07	______07
Alton	______08	______08
St. Louis	______09	______09
Points in Missouri	______10	______10
Points in Arkansas	______11	______11
Points in Texas	______12	______12

2 Please indicate how you reached the station to board this train and how you will reach your next destination after you get off this train. (Check as many as apply.)

	To Station Where You Got On	From Station Where You Will Get off
Automobile	______01 (9–11)	______01 (12–14)
Taxi	______02	______02
City Bus	______03	______03
Airline	______04	______04
Commuter Train	______05	______05
Amtrak Train	______06	______06
Amtrak Shuttle	______07	______07
Intercity Bus	______08	______08
Walker	______09	______09
Other	______10	______10

3 Is your car parked at or near an Amtrak Station during this trip?
Yes ______15.1 No ______15.2

4 What is the zip code of the place you left to get to this train? (If zip code is unknown, the city and a nearby major street intersection will be sufficient.)
Zip Code ______
16 17 18 19 20
OR: City ______
Street
Intersection ______
______

5 What is the zip code (or city and nearby street intersection) of the place where you will be going upon leaving this train?
Zip Code ______
21 22 23 24 25
OR: City ______
Street
Intersection ______
______

6 Which one of the following best describes the main purpose of this trip? (Mark only one)
26-1______ Business or work
2 ______Vacation or recreation
3 ______Travel to or from school
4 ______Personal business
5 ______Shopping
6 ______Visit family or friends
7 ______Entertainment/Spectator sport
8 ______Other (Please specify) ______

7 How long before the departure time of this train did you leave for the station?
27-1 ______ 10–15 minutes
2 ______ 16–30 minutes
3 ______ 31–45 minutes
4 ______ 46–60 minutes
5 ______ more than 1 hour

to use *funnel questions,* which means proceeding from the most general to the most specific when ordering the questions pertaining to a given topic.[1]

Problems resulting from the order of questions can also arise when several questions on the same topic are asked, all at the same level of specificity. For example, we might ask a series of questions regarding a person's views about several minority groups. Our interest might be in how the person's responses differ for the different minority groups. But responses could also be affected by the sequence in which the various questions were asked within each of the minority groups. A person's reaction to one question, for example, might influence how the next question is interpreted. Effects due to the order in which such questions are asked can be handled in one of two ways. The first technique is to use exactly the same order for all samples to be compared, thus holding the effect of order constant. This technique does not allow us to determine what the effects of order were. Alternatively, many different orders of the questions might be used within each of the samples to be compared, thus neutralizing the effect of order. This problem of dealing with order effects is discussed much more fully in Chapter 7.

The final aspect of the ordering of survey questions that we will consider is the use of *filter questions*—general questions asked of respondents to find out whether they need to be asked more specific questions. For example, the question "Do you own a car?" might precede a series of questions about the costs of maintaining a car. In this instance, the respondent would answer the specific questions only if her or his response to the general question was "yes." If that answer was "no," the interviewer would not ask the specific questions (in a self-administered questionnaire, the respondent would be instructed to skip that section). When the filter questions involve objective information ("Are you over 65?"), their use is relatively straightforward. Caution must be exercised, however, in using behavioral or attitudinal questions as filter questions. Smith (1981) first asked respondents whether they approved of hitting another person in "any situations you can imagine." Logically, a negative response to this most general question should imply a negative response to any more specific questions. Nonetheless, over 80 percent of the people who responded "no" to the general question then reported that they approved of hitting another person in specific situations, such as in self-defense. Although findings such as this suggest that filter questions should be used cautiously, the need to demand as little of the respondent's time as possible makes filter questions an essential tool in the design of effective questionnaires.

[1]Oppenheim (1966) describes in detail the question-wording plan developed by Gallup called the Quintamensional Plan of Question Design. The first step is to ask the respondent whether he or she has thought about the issue at all. This is followed by open-ended questions about general feelings and closed questions about specific aspects of the issue. The fourth step involves asking for the respondent's reasons for the views he or she holds. Finally, the interviewer inquires how strongly the respondent's views are held.

Appendix C

Scientific Research Reports

Outline

INTRODUCTION

Scientific research is a public activity. A clever hypothesis, an elegant research design, meticulous data collection procedures, reliable results, and an insightful theoretical interpretation of the findings are all useless to the scientific community unless they are made public. As one writer suggests most emphatically, "Until its results have gone through the painful process of publication, preferably in a refereed journal of high standards, scientific research is just play. Publication is an indispensable part of science" (Bartholemew, 1982, p. 233). A "refereed" journal is one in which submitted manuscripts are reviewed by other researchers who are experts in the field addressed in the paper under review. These so-called peer reviewers decide whether the research is methodologically sound and whether it makes a substantive contribution to the field of psychology. These reviews are then submitted to a senior researcher who serves as editor of the journal. It is the editor's job to decide which papers warrant publication.

As we have already noted, the most common vehicle for making a research study available to the scientific community is the professional journal. *Memory & Cognition, Child Development, Journal of Personality and Social Psychology,* and *Journal of Clinical and Consulting Psychology* are but a few of the journals that publish research studies of interest to investigators in a variety of fields in psychology. Editors of these journals decide which manuscripts will be published. Their decisions are based on (a) the quality of the research and (b) the effectiveness of its presentation in the written manuscript. Thus both content and style are important. Editors seek the best research, clearly described. Journal editors set rigorous standards; only about one of every four manuscripts submitted to the leading psychology journals is accepted for publication (American Psychological Association, 1992b).

Editorial review and the publication process itself are time-consuming. More than a year can elapse between when a paper is submitted and when it finally appears in the journal. To provide a more timely means of reporting research findings, professional societies such as the American Psychological Association, the American Psychological Society, the Psychonomic Society, and the Society for Research in Child Development sponsor conferences at which researchers give brief oral presentations describing their recent work. Such conferences also provide an opportunity for discussion and debate among investigators interested in the same research questions.

In order to do research, whether it will eventually be reported at a conference or published in a journal, investigators must often obtain financial support in the form of a grant from a government or private agency. These grants are typically awarded on the basis of a competitive review of research proposals. Because these proposals are written before the research is actually done, they require a slightly different style and format from a journal article.

What do journal articles, oral presentations, and research proposals have to do with you? If you attend graduate school in psychology, you will probably have to describe your research using all three types of scientific communication. Even if you do not pursue a professional career in psychology, the principles of good written and oral presentations are applicable to a wide variety of employment situations. For example, a memo to your department manager describing the outcome of a recent sale may have much the same content and format as a short journal article. Of more immediate concern, however, your course in research methods may require you to write or deliver a research report. This appendix will help you do it well. First we will review some guidelines for effective writing. Then we will discuss the preparation of research reports, both written and oral, as well as the writing of research proposals.

Throughout this appendix we have drawn heavily on the *Publication Manual* (3d ed., 1983) of the American Psychologicial Association.[1] Editors and authors use this manual to ensure a consistent style across the many different journals in psychology. The manual answers questions ranging from appropriate content for each section of the article to rules for typing the final manuscript. If graduate study in psychology is in your future, we recommend that you add the *Publication Manual* to your personal library. (Order from the American Psychological Association, 750 First Street, N.E., Washington, DC 20002-4242.)

GUIDELINES FOR EFFECTIVE WRITING

Learning to write well is like learning to swim, drive a car, or play the piano. Improvement is unlikely to result solely from reading about how the activity is to be done. A person learns to write well by writing and by getting critical feedback from writing "coaches" (teachers, friends, editors). Lee Cronbach (1992, p. 391), the author of several of the most widely cited articles in the *Psychological Bulletin*, writes: "My advice must be like the legendary recipe for jugged hare, which begins, 'First catch your hare.' First, have a message worth delivering. Beyond that, it is care in writing that counts. . . . Rework any sentence that lacks flow or cadence, any sentence in which first-glance reading misplaces the emphasis, and any sentence in which comprehension comes less than instantly to that most knowledgeable of readers, the writer of the sentence. At best, technical writing can aspire to literary virtues—a change of pace from abstract thesis to memorable example, from brisk to easeful, from matter-of-fact to poetic." These are the goals. To reach them, it is helpful to take a brief look at the basic and familiar rules of effective writing.

Professional writer Jack Ridl provides the first maxim for effective writing: "Write, not assuming that you will be understood, but trying to avoid being misunderstood." Good writing, like good driving, is best done defensively. Assume that whatever *can* be misunderstood will be! The first way to avoid being misunderstood is to *know your audience.* If you assume your readers know more than they actually do, you will leave them confused. If you underestimate your readers, you risk boring them with unnecessary details. Either risk seriously increases the likelihood that what you have written will not be read. But if you must err, it is better to underestimate your readers. For example, when you prepare a research report you might reasonably assume that your intended audience is your instructor. Writing for your instructor might lead you to leave a lot out of your paper because, after all, you assume your instructor knows all that anyway. It would probably be better to consider your fellow students your audience. This might result in your including more detail than necessary, but it will be easier for your instructor to help you learn to "edit out" the nonessential material than to "edit in" essential material that you have omitted. Whatever audience you choose, make the selection *before* you begin to write, and keep that audience in mind every step of the way.

A second task that you must complete before you begin to write is to *identify your purpose.* The principal purposes of a journal article are to describe and to convince. You want first to describe what you have done and what you have found, and second to convince the reader that your interpretation of these results is a sound one. A research proposal, on the other hand, is principally written to persuade someone that the proposed research is worth doing. Because they are typically brief, oral presentations can be expected to do little more than get the listener interested enough to read more about the topic. Knowing the purpose for which you are writing should help you choose what information to present and decide how that information should be presented.

Although the specific purposes of research reports and proposals vary, all reports and proposals fall within the general category of expository writing. Webster's dictionary defines *exposition* as "discourse designed to convey information or explain what is difficult to understand." The foundation of good expository writing is clarity of thought and expression. The *Publication Manual* (1983) clearly outlines the road to clarity: "Clear communication, which is the prime objective of scientific reporting, may be achieved by presenting ideas in an orderly manner and by expressing oneself smoothly and precisely" (p. 31).

One avenue to clarity is adherence to grammatical rules, the mechanics of good writing. For example, the words *affect* and *effect* are not interchangeable. As a verb, *affect* means "to influence," and as a noun it means "emotion" or "feeling." As a verb, *effect* means "to cause to come into being," and as a noun it means "outcome" or "result." Another problem that often arises involves words of Latin and Greek origin with unusual plural forms. Words such as *data, phenomena,* and *criteria* are plural. They require a plural verb form and plural adjective modifiers: "These data show that . . . ." The *Publication Manual* (pp. 34–35) also contains sage advice regarding diction: the choice of the right word at the right time.

> Make certain that every word means exactly what you intend it to mean. Sooner or later most authors discover a discrepancy between their accepted meaning of a term and its dictionary definition. In informal style, for example, *feel* broadly substitutes for *think* or *believe,* but such latitude is not acceptable in scientific style.
>
> Likewise, avoid colloquial expressions (e.g., *write up* for *report*), which diffuse meaning. Approximations of quantity (e.g., *quite a large part, practically all,* or *very few*) are interpreted differently by different readers or in different contexts. They weaken statements, especially those describing empirical observations.

The mere avoidance of flagrant violations of grammatical rules does not guarantee effective writing. Grammatical rules do not address questions of organization and style. As you will see in the next section, a generally agreed-upon structure has evolved for research reports, and this structure dictates the basic organization of research papers. Although certain stylistic conventions are often suggested, they are less consistently adhered to than are structural conventions. For instance, at one time scientific writing was assumed to require the use of the third person passive: "It has been shown that behavior is affected by the drug." Such constructions were intended to connote increased objectivity, but all too often they resulted only in deadly dull prose. The sentence construction to use is the one that is the most direct and concise: "The drug affected behavior." Increasingly, the use of third person constructions ("The authors believe. . .") are being replaced by the use of the first person ("We believe. . ."; see Polyson & Levinson, 1982).

The American Psychological Association has issued a policy statement (*Publication Manual*, p. 43) regarding one aspect of the style of research papers.

> APA as a publisher accepts journal authors' word choices unless those choices are inaccurate, unclear, or ungrammatical. Because APA as an organization is committed

> both to science and to the fair treatment of individuals and groups, however, authors of journal articles are required to avoid writing in a manner that reinforces questionable attitudes and assumptions about people.

Although APA is concerned with the general problem of the fair treatment of all individuals and groups, it gives one aspect of language use special attention. APA has developed guidelines for the use of nonsexist language "to help authors recognize and change instances in which word choices may be inaccurate, misleading, or discriminatory" (p. 43). These guidelines are presented in Table C.1. Most psychology journals now require all published manuscripts to conform to these guidelines, so it would be wise (and considerate) to get into the habit of using nonsexist language. There is already evidence that the new requirements have had an influence on the language used in APA journals. Gannon et al. (1992) examined the language used in 4,952 articles published in 1970, 1975, 1980, 1985, and 1990 in four different areas of psychology (developmental, clinical, physiological, and social) in APA journals. They found a significant decrease over these years in the percentage of articles in which sexist language was used. Gannon et al. (1992, p. 392) found that by 1990, the journals they examined "had approached the total elimination of sexist language." (See also Chapter 5.)

As we noted at the outset, our review of the essentials of effective writing is neither exhaustive nor thorough enough to make you a good writer. Developing your writing skill requires several trips through the cycle of writing, reading, and rewriting, preferably with critical feedback from others in the reading stage. The *Publication Manual* again provides a clear statement of the goal: "By developing ideas clearly and logically you invite readers to read,

TABLE C.1 GUIDELINES FOR NONSEXIST LANGUAGE

Sexism in journal writing may be classified into two categories: problems of *designation* and problems of *evaluation.*

Problems of designation

When you refer to a person or persons, choose words that are accurate, clear, and free from bias. Long-established cultural practice can exert a powerful, insidious influence on even the most conscientious author. For example, the use of *man* as a generic noun can be ambiguous and may convey an implicit message that women are of secondary importance. You can choose nouns, pronouns, and adjectives to eliminate, or at least to minimize, the possibility of ambiguity in sex identity or sex role. Problems of designation are divided into two subcategories: *ambiguity of referent,* where it is unclear whether the author means one or both sexes, and *stereotyping,* where the writing conveys unsupported or biased connotations about sex roles and identity.

Problems of evaluation

Scientific writing, as an extension of science, should be free of implied or irrelevant evaluation of the sexes. Difficulties may derive from the habitual use of clichés, or familiar expressions, such as "man and wife." The use of "man and wife" implies differences in the freedom and activities of each and may inappropriately prompt the reader to evaluate the roles. "Husband and wife" are parallel; "man and wife" are not. Problems of evaluation, like problems of designation, are classified in terms of ambiguity of referent and stereotyping.

Avoiding sexist language

The task of changing language may seem awkward at first. Nevertheless, careful attention to meaning and practice in rephrasing will overcome any initial difficulty (Bass, 1979). The result of such effort, and the purpose of the guidelines in this table, is accurate, unbiased communication.

encourage them to continue, and make their task agreeable by leading them smoothly from thought to thought" (p. 31). With this goal in mind, we now turn our attention to the "nuts and bolts" of a research report by considering the structure of a typical journal article.

STRUCTURE OF A RESEARCH REPORT

The structure of a research report serves two major purposes. First, it offers an organizational framework within which the author can provide a clear description of the research and a convincing interpretation of the findings. In this sense, the structure is like that provided by the various acts of a Shakespearean play. Both the playwright and the audience share certain expectations about what should occur in each act as the play unfolds. For example "the stage is set" in the first act, and the climax can be expected in the third act. Similarly, in a research report both author and reader share expectations about the content of each section of the report. The structure is not intended to shackle the playwright or the author. It simply provides a vehicle to make it easier for the audience to focus on the particular point being made in the play or the research report.

A research report is like a play, but it is also like a telephone directory. The structure of a telephone directory is intended to facilitate access to specific information. The structure of a research report also serves this "ready reference" function. If you wanted to know how an experiment was done, you would look in the Method section; if you were seeking specific information about some particular research finding, you would look in the Results section.

Even though research reports can be used like telephone directories, they should not read like telephone directories. As the *Publication Manual* puts it, "Although scientific writing differs in form from literary writing, it need not and should not lack style or be dull" (p. 22). When writing a research report you should keep the analogy of the play in mind; when mining the research literature to set up your next experiment, you may find the telephone directory analogy more helpful.

A research report consists of the following sections:

Title Page
Abstract
Body of Report {
Introduction
Method
Results
Discussion
}
References
Footnotes
Appendices

The four sections from the introduction to the discussion make up the body of the report (the four acts of the "play"). The title page and the abstract are like the playbill you see before the play itself begins, and the remaining sections are the counterpart of the credits. In this appendix we will provide descriptions of the content and format of each of these sections, but these descriptions will not suffice for teaching you how to write a report. The best preparation for that is to read journal articles in some area of psychology that interests you. Even so, you will perfect your skill at writing research reports only by actually writing them.

TITLE PAGE

The first page of a research report is the title page. It includes the title of the research report, the name(s) of the author(s), and the institutional affiliation(s) of the author(s). An illustration of a correctly typed title page and succeeding pages of a research report is presented in the sample paper at the end of this appendix. The title page indicates what the research is about, who did the research, and where the research was done. The title is perhaps the most critical aspect of your paper because it is the part that is most likely to be read! The title should clearly indicate what the central topic of your paper is. In the words of the *Publication Manual* (pp. 22–23):

> A title should summarize the main idea of the paper simply and, if possible, with style. It should be a concise statement of the main topic and should identify the actual variables or theoretical issues under investigation and the relation between them.
>
> Titles are commonly indexed and compiled in numerous reference works. Therefore, avoid words that serve no useful purpose; they increase length and can mislead indexers. For example, the words *method* and *results* do not normally appear in a title, nor should such redundancies as "A Study of" or "An Experimental Investigation of" begin a title.

A common format for the title of students' research reports is "[The Dependent Variable(s)] as a Function of [the Independent Variable(s)]." For example, "Anagram Solution Time as a Function of Problem Difficulty" and "Accuracy of Mirror Tracing as a Function of Gender and Background Luminance" would be good titles. The title must not only be informative, but it should also be brief; the recommended maximum length is fifteen words. At all costs avoid uninformative or ambiguous titles such as "Operant Conditioning Results," "Laboratory Report #1," or "Personality Differences in Subjects." Be sure your title describes as specifically as possible the content of your research.

ABSTRACT

The second page of the report, the abstract, appears under that single word, which is typed as a centered heading (see sample paper). The abstract is a one-paragraph summary of the content and purpose of the research report. The abstract should be 100 to 175 words long (about ten to fifteen double-spaced typewritten lines), and it should highlight the critical points made in each of the four sections of the body of the report (introduction, method, results, discussion). The abstract should also specify the population from which subjects were drawn, the nature of the test instruments or research apparatus employed, and the data-gathering procedures—all in sufficient detail to reflect their importance in the research study. Next to the title, the abstract is the part of the paper that is most likely to be read. And, like the title, it will help determine whether readers will go on to the rest of the paper. Because so much information must be presented in a single paragraph, you may find the abstract difficult to write. The best approach is to write it last! If you write the abstract after you have written the rest of the report, you will be able to *abstract*, or paraphrase, your own words more easily. The *Publication Manual* (pp. 23–24) summarizes these points well.

> An abstract is a brief, comprehensive summary of the contents of the article; it allows readers to survey the contents of an article quickly and, like the title, is used by abstracting and information services to index and retrieve articles.
>
> A well-prepared abstract can be the single most important paragraph in the article. . . . Do not include in an abstract information that does not appear in the body of the paper. . . . Make each sentence maximally informative, especially the lead sentence. Be as brief as possible. . . . An abstract that is accurate, succinct, quickly comprehensible, and informative will increase the audience and the future retrievability of your article.

INTRODUCTION

Objectives The title of your report appears at the top of the third page as a centered heading, and then the first paragraph of the introduction section begins immediately. This is the only section of the report that does *not* begin with a centered section heading (see sample paper). The introduction serves three purposes. The order in which these objectives are met in any given report may vary, but the order in which we will describe them here is the most common one.

First, the introduction should provide a general statement of the problem being addressed. This places the paper in perspective. The second objective is to summarize briefly the relevant background literature that led you to the present research problem and approach. Finally, the introduction includes an outline of the present study and a logical development of the predictions or hypotheses (if any) guiding the research. All three of these objectives share a common purpose: to give the reader a firm sense of what you are doing and why you are doing it.

The *Publication Manual* suggests four questions to keep in mind while writing the introduction: "What is the point of the study? How do the hypothesis and the experimental design relate to the problem? What are the theoretical implications of the study, and how does the study relate to previous work in the area? and What are the theoretical propositions tested, and how were they derived?'' (p. 24).

The purpose of summarizing related research studies is *not* to provide an exhaustive literature review. Instead, care should be taken to select the most pertinent studies to develop the rationale of your experiment. In summarizing these selected studies, you should emphasize whatever details of the earlier work will best help the reader understand what *you* have done and why. You must acknowledge the contributions of other researchers to your understanding of the problem. Of course, if you quote directly from another person's work, you must use quotation marks.

More commonly, however, reference is made to the work of other researchers in one of two ways. Either you refer to the authors of the article you are citing by their last names, with the year in which the paper was published appearing in parentheses immediately after the names, or you make a general reference to their work and follow it with *both* the names and the year of publication in parentheses. For example, if you were citing a study by David G. Myers and Jane R. Dickie that was published in 1989, you would write either ''Myers and Dickie (1989) have found. . . '' or ''Recent research (Myers & Dickie, 1989) has shown that. . . '' Complete bibliographical information on Myers and Dickie's paper, including the journal title, volume number, and specific pages, would appear in the references section. Footnotes are *not* used to cite references in a research report in psychology.

You should include in your paper only those references that you have actually read. If you read a paper by Barney (1990) in which the research of Ludwig (1988) is described, you should not cite the Ludwig paper unless you have actually read that paper. Instead, you should use some form such as ''Ludwig (1988), as reported by Barney (1990), found that. . . '' You should use this approach for two reasons. The first and most obvious one is that you should accurately report what you have read. If this appeal to scholarly integrity does not suffice, you should recognize the risk you are taking. If Barney (1990) has misreported the work of Ludwig (1988) and you repeat this misrepresentation, you are equally subject to criticism. You won't subsequently be able to say, ''Barney (1990) made me do it.'' The general rule is simple: *Cite only what you have read.* (See also Chapter 2.)

Searching the Psychological Literature In the long run, the best way to develop ideas for research and to become familiar with the relevant literature is to read the journals in your area of interest regularly. Reading journal articles requires an approach different from reading newspaper articles or textbooks. In the spirit of ''well begun is half done,'' we present ten commandments for reading journal articles in Table C.2. The comments below the commandments provide a brief interpretation of each one. Following these dictums will help you to read more critically and successfully.

At the time you are taking your research methods course, you may not have

TABLE C.2 TEN COMMANDMENTS FOR READING RESEARCH ARTICLES CRITICALLY

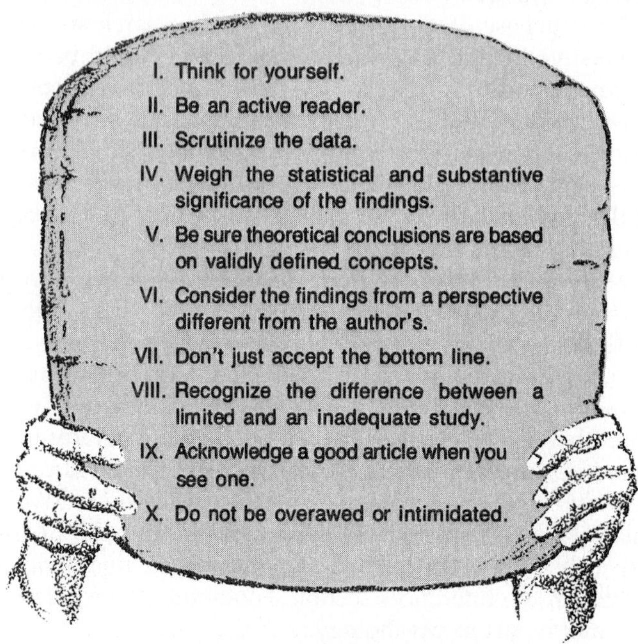

Comments on the commandments

(1) Read the paper with the goal of gaining your own understanding of the research. The best source for an independent view of what was done and what was found is the method and results sections, respectively.

(2) Read the paper actively from start to finish. Whenever possible, outline, paraphrase, or write down questions about the details of the study.

(3) Examine the data very carefully, especially those in tables and figures. Are the findings internally consistent; do they support the author's expectations?

(4) Examine not only whether a given effect is statistically significant but also what its magnitude is. Are the conclusions based on strong or marginal results?

(5) Often conclusions found in the discussion are stated in terms of theoretical concepts and make no mention of their defining operations. This is appropriate but only when the operations validly define the concepts.

(6) An independent view of the findings is one that is free of bias. Viewing the findings from a different perspective involves purposely adopting a bias different from the author's.

(7) Any "bottom-line" conclusion is the result of several transformations of the original data. Be sure you get to the bottom of these transformations before accepting the bottom line.

(8) A study that confounds the age of the subjects in each of two treatment groups is inadequate. One that tests only fifth graders in both groups is of limited generality, but it is interpretable.

(9) A good study asks and answers a good question. If the method is sound and the conclusions are supported by the results, then the study passes the critical test for good research.

(10) Remember the tremendous assets you have in reading research articles. The article contains technical language, including statistics, and the author is likely an authority about the research itself, but you have the advantage of objectivity and a fresh perspective.

Adapted from Table 1 in Anisfeld (1987). Used by permission of the author and publisher.

had a chance to read the research literature widely or to have settled on a principal area of interest in psychology. So when you are faced with the task of writing a research report, you may need help in searching the psychological literature. For example, you may have an idea for an experiment and you may wonder whether this experiment has already been done. Or you may have read an article describing an experiment on which you would like to base your experiment, and you may be interested in finding other studies related to this topic. Fortunately, resources are available to help you answer such questions without plodding through every issue of every psychology journal in the campus library.

Perhaps the most useful reference tool for psychology students is *Psychological Abstracts,* in which the abstracts from over 1,000 national and international periodicals are published monthly. These abstracts are organized under sixteen general categories, such as "Experimental Psychology (Human)" and "Physical and Psychological Disorders." Under each category, abstracts are arranged alphabetically by the first author's name, and the abstracts are numbered consecutively in one or two volumes each year. In 1987 over 36,000 abstracts appeared in *Psychological Abstracts* (that's over 3,000 abstracts in each monthly issue). Obviously, browsing aimlessly through issues of the *Abstracts* would be only slightly less time-consuming than browsing through the journals themselves.

The most efficient way to search through *Psychological Abstracts* is to use one of the two indices that have been published with each volume since 1984. An author index is an alphabetical listing of the authors of the articles in that volume along with the number of the abstract of each author's article. If you were interested in doing research in perception, you could use an undergraduate textbook to identify well-known researchers in this area and then use the author index to locate the abstracts of their most recent work. The second type of index, the subject index, is a bit more cumbersome to use, but it is obviously essential if you have not identified specific researchers whose work you want to locate. The subject index is psychology's version of the Yellow Pages. However, your fingers may have to do a lot of walking before you finally find what you are looking for. To make matters worse, the language of psychology is an ever-changing one, so the topics listed in the subject index vary somewhat from year to year. Nonetheless, careful and industrious use of the subject index can be an excellent route to invaluable references. If you want to use the subject index to locate abstracts of articles related to your research in perception, you must focus your topic. Perhaps terms such as "motion perception" or "apparent movement" would lead you to the references you want.

Once you have identified a few recent articles (within the last three to five years), your best bet for continuing to search the literature would be to use the references sections of these key articles. If an article keeps appearing in the references section of other articles, you can be fairly sure that it is an important paper. There is even a reference index called the *Social Science Citation Index* that records the reference history of an article. That is, once an article has been published, the citation index searches the references sections of all future articles in that area and notes whenever the original article is cited. You can use the index to determine how many times a given article has been cited or to identify the specific articles in which the given article is cited. In a sense, *Psychological Abstracts* allows you to search backward from the present, and the *Social Science Citation Index* allows you to search forward from the past. Like *Psychological Abstracts,* the *Citation Index* permits you to trace the work of a specific author. Detailed instructions regarding the use of the *Citation Index* are best left to a reference librarian.

We will conclude this section on searching the psychological literature with a brief look at the most popular approach to doing a literature search: computerized literature search. A useful overview of online information retrieval is provided by Lewis (1986). Our discussion of this topic will be limited to the description of a computer-assisted search done by one of our undergraduate students, Janet Swim. Janet was interested in conducting a survey to determine the incidence of rapes and other sexual assaults on dates. She had come across a few references to this topic in her general reading in the area of women's studies, and now she wanted to make a more systematic search of the psychological literature. A reference librarian helped Janet make a search of the computer-based counterparts of both *Psychological Abstracts* and the *Social Science Citation Index.*

Janet used a keyword technique to search *Psychological Abstracts,* and she had a chapter on rape by Klemmack and Klemmack (1976) to serve as the basis of her search of the *Citation Index.* A keyword search is possible because of the computer's ability to access large amounts of information quickly. The computer is able to scan the titles and abstracts of articles in its memory and to identify all those that contain particular keywords. The most effective approach to this type of search is to have intersecting keywords *both of which* need to be present before the computer will "tag" an article. For example, Janet used the keyword RAPE and the letter string DAT to guide her search. She chose the letter string DAT in order to catch such variants as DATE, DATES, and DATING. This intersection led to the identification of seventy-five references, seventy-three of which were written in English. Janet also obtained eleven additional references that had cited the Klemmack and Klemmack (1976) paper when she had the computer search the *Social Science Citation Index.*

The major advantage of the computer-assisted search is speed; Janet completed both searches in less than half an hour. There are also a few disadvantages. One is that many of the references the computer locates do not prove useful. For example, Janet obtained one reference on rape among mallard ducks on specific chronological dates. Keywords can also prove tricky. The string DAT identified all studies using the word DATA, so a number of Janet's references provided data about rape—but not solely in the context of dating. One final potential disadvantage of doing a computer search is that there is sometimes a fee associated with using this service. Nonetheless, when used properly, a computer-assisted literature search is a useful tool. Parr (1979) concludes that

"Online information retrieval adds a new dimension to bibliographic inquiry while at the same time reinforcing use of traditional bibliographic sources" (p. 62).

METHOD

The second major section of the body of a research report is the method section. The method section is usually identified by a centered heading ("Method") with a double space separating it from the preceding and following text (see sample paper). The method section follows right after the introduction. The introduction has provided a broad outline of the research you have done; the method fills in the nitty-gritty details. The *Publication Manual* presents a straightforward description of the goals of the method section: "The method section describes in detail how the study was conducted. Such a description enables the reader to evaluate the appropriateness of your methods and the reliability and the validity of your results. It also permits experienced investigators to replicate the study if they so desire" (p. 25). Writing a good method section can be difficult. It sounds easy because all you have to do is describe exactly what you have done. But if you want to get a sense of how challenging this can be, just try to write a clear and interesting paragraph describing how to tie your shoelaces.

The key to writing a good method section is organization. Fortunately, the structure of this section is so consistent that a few basic subsections provide the pattern of organization you need for most research reports. Before describing the content of these subsections, however, we must address the question that students writing their first research report ask most frequently: "How much detail should I include?" The quality of your paper will be adversely affected if you include either too much or too little detail. The rule stated in the *Publication Manual* seems simple enough: "Include in these subsections only the information essential to comprehend and replicate the study" (p. 26). As we have said before, the best way to learn how to follow this rule is to read the method sections of journal articles and to write your own research reports. Be sure to get feedback from your instructor concerning appropriate level of detail.

The four most common subsections of the method section are subjects (participants), design, materials (apparatus), and procedure. Each of these subsections is introduced by an underlined subheading that usually begins at the left margin (see sample paper). The *Publication Manual* (p. 26) aptly summarizes the content of the subjects subsection.

> The subsection on subjects answers three questions: Who participated in the study? How many participants were there? How were they selected? Give the total number of participants and the number assigned to each experimental condition. If any participants did not complete the experiment, give the number of participants and the reasons they did not continue. When humans are the participants, report the procedures for selecting and assigning subjects and the agreements and payments made. Give major demographic characteristics such as general geographic location,

type of institutional affiliation, sex, and age. When animals are the participants, report the genus, species, and strain number or other specific identification, such as the name of the supplier. Give the number of animals and the animal's sex, age, weight, and physiological condition. In addition, specify all essential details of their treatment and handling so that the investigation can be successfully replicated.

The design subsection contains such information as the operational definitions of independent and dependent variables, along with the specific design used for each independent variable. The procedures used to form groups of subjects (such as random assignment or matching) should be described. Counterbalancing or randomization techniques for arranging the levels of within-subjects variables could also be included in this subsection. Often the information in this subsection and that in the subjects subsection are presented together in a combined subsection called *Design and Subjects*. Another common practice is to include the material that would be presented in the design subsection in the procedure subsection. Where the design information appears in the method section is optional; that it appear *somewhere* in the method section is required.

The apparatus subsection is also optional. If the only equipment you used is paper, pencils, and a stopwatch, it is better to include this information in the procedure subsection than in a separate apparatus section. On the other hand, if the apparatus or materials played a central role in the study, a separate subsection is useful. In an operant-conditioning experiment, it would be essential to describe the conditioning chamber in which the animal was trained. If complex or custom-made equipment has been used, a diagram or drawing is helpful for both the reader and the writer of an apparatus subsection. In general, the label *Apparatus* is used when mechanical equipment is described. The label *Materials* is used when less mechanical instruments, such as a paper-and-pencil personality test, have been constructed or used. If you use equipment or materials developed by another investigator, you should cite the work of that investigator, but you should also include the general characteristics of the materials in your own report.

The procedure subsection is the most critical component of the method section. It is here that you describe what happened from the beginning to the end of the sessions in which you tested your participants. As the previous sentence implies, the organization of the procedure subsection is usually chronological. You should begin writing this subsection by outlining the important steps in testing participants in each group of your study. Next you can either describe the procedure for each group in turn or describe the procedures common to all groups and then point out the distinguishing features of each group. Whichever organization you choose (you may not learn which works best until you have tried to write both), it is best to begin writing only after you have prepared a checklist of the important features of your procedure. The instructions given to subjects should be presented in paraphrase form unless they define an experimental manipulation, in which case they should be reported verbatim. The *Publication Manual* recommends that the method section, and especially the procedure subsection, "should tell the reader *what* you did and *how* you did it" (p. 26).

RESULTS

The centered heading "Results" introduces this third major section of the body of a research report (see sample paper). Like the third act of a dramatic play, the results section contains the climax of the research report—the actual findings of the study. For many students, though, the excitement of describing the climax is blunted by anxiety. The source of their anxiety is the necessity of reporting statistical information in the results section. The best way to alleviate this anxiety, of course, is to develop the same command of statistical concepts that you have of other concepts. While you are acquiring this mastery of statistics, however, you need a way to deal effectively with the problem of presenting statistical information. The solution to this problem is to adopt a simple organizational structure to guide your writing of the results section.

You should use your results section to answer the questions you raised in your introduction. In a sense, the results section is like the evidence presented during the testimony of witnesses in a criminal trial. The introduction serves as the counterpart of the attorney's opening statement, and the discussion (to be described in the next section of this appendix) parallels the attorney's closing statement to the jury. The guiding principle in the results section is to "stick to the facts, just the facts."

Reporting Statistics The *Publication Manual* provides a clear statement of the objectives of a results section: "The Results section summarizes the data collected and the statistical treatment of them. First, briefly state the main results or findings. Then report the data in sufficient detail to justify the conclusions" (p. 27). As we mentioned, there is a structure for the paragraphs of the results section that will help you meet these objectives. This structure is outlined in Table C.3, and an illustration of a paragraph from the results section of a published article appears after the table. The paragraph should begin by stating the purpose of the analysis. The reason(s) for doing an analysis should be stated succinctly; often, no more than a phrase is necessary. You might introduce an inferential test by saying, "An analysis of variance was done to determine the main effect of the drug variable" or "In order to determine the overall effect of the drug variable . . . ." There are two reasons for making the rationale for each analysis explicit. It helps your reader follow the logic of your analysis plan. And it ensures that you will never try to report an analysis whose purpose you do not understand.

The second step is to identify the descriptive statistic that will be used to summarize the results for a given dependent variable. For example, you might use the mean number of correct responses, the median reaction time, or the

TABLE C.3 STRUCTURE OF A TYPICAL PARAGRAPH IN THE RESULTS SECTION

1. State the purpose of the analysis.
2. Identify the descriptive statistic to be used to summarize results.
3. Present a summary of this descriptive statistic across conditions in the text itself, in a table, or in a figure.
4. If a table or figure is used, point out the major findings on which the reader should focus.
5. Present the reasons for, and the results of, inferential statistics tests.
6. State the conclusion that follows from each test, but do not discuss implications. These belong in the discussion section.

Sample paragraph

To examine retention as a function of instructions given at the time of study, the number of words recalled by each subject in each instruction condition was determined. Words were scored as correct only if they matched a word that had appeared on the target list. Thus, synonyms were not counted as correct; misspelled words were accepted if the spelling was sufficiently similar to a target item that it could be reasonably concluded that the intended word had actually appeared on the list. Mean numbers of words recalled were 15.6, 15.2, and 10.1 in the bizarre imagery condition, the standard imagery condition, and the control condition, respectively. Overall, mean recall differed significantly among the conditions, $F(2, 72) = 64.84$, $MS_e = 0.44$, $p < .05$. Two analytical comparisons were performed to determine the source of this effect. These tests revealed that the two groups given imagery instructions when averaged together differed significantly from the control condition, $F(1, 72) = 44.62$, $p < .05$; however, the two imagery conditions did not differ significantly from each other, $F(1, 72) = 1.66$, $p > .05$. In conclusion, retention by subjects instructed to use imagery was higher than that by subjects given no specific study instructions, but retention did not differ for the two types of imagery instructions.

cumulative number of bar presses per minute to summarize the results in each condition of your study. Next, a summary of this descriptive statistic across conditions should be provided. Whenever possible, measures of central tendency should be accompanied by corresponding measures of variability. If there are only two or three conditions in your experiment, this summary can be presented in the text itself. For instance, you could summarize the results of a two-group study by saying, "The mean number of correct responses for the experimental group was 10.5 ($s = 2.1$), whereas that for the control group was 5.2 ($s = 1.8$)."

More commonly, however, you will have more data to summarize and you will need to present your findings in either a table or a figure (graph). We will describe the procedures for constructing tables and figures later in this section. For now, it will be sufficient if you simply look at the examples of tables and figures in the sample paper at the end of the appendix.

We should not expect a table or figure to be self-sufficient. Instead, it should be used more like a map that you are given as you enter a large and unfamiliar museum. For most of us, the map is not sufficient to guarantee a satisfying visit to the exhibits without some commentary from a tour guide. Similarly, your reader needs some help to gain as much information as possible from a table or figure. You are in the best position to offer this assistance because you are the person most familiar with your results. You should direct your reader's attention to the highlights of the data in the table or figure, focusing especially on those aspects of the results that are consistent (or discrepant) with the hypotheses you proposed in the introduction. Usually the same data are not reported in both a table and a figure. Tables provide a more precise description of the results, but figures make it easier to see trends or patterns in the data. Whichever you choose, be sure to highlight in the text itself the critical results that the table or figure reveals.

The fourth step in writing a paragraph of the results section is to present the results of inferential statistical tests. Three pieces of information should always be reported with any inferential statistics test: the name of the test (usually indicated by a symbol such as t, r, χ^2, or F); the degrees of freedom for the test; and the value of the test statistic that you obtained. Until quite recently, the convention had been to report the probability level along with each test relative to the chosen level of significance, such as $p < .05$ or $p < .01$. An example of the conventional format would be, "The mean in the experimental group (5.20) was significantly higher than the mean in the control group (3.00), $t(24) = 2.75$, $p < .05$." More recently, editors have suggested that the significance level for all inferential tests be specified early in the results section and that each reported test be accompanied by the estimate of error variation for that test. For instance, you might see "The overall effect of the drug variable was statistically significant, $F(3, 64) = 7.15$, $MS_{error} = 2.4$." When you write the results section, you should assume that your reader has a basic knowledge of inferential statistics. Therefore, you do not need to refer to concepts such as the null hypothesis or mention whether your outcome falls in or out of the critical region. All that is required is that you use the term "statistically significant" correctly. It is helpful to report measures of effect size along with the results of the inferential statistics tests (see Chapter 9).

The final step in writing a good paragraph in the results section is to state a brief conclusion that follows from each test you report. This is accomplished by referring to the descriptive statistics on which the inferential test is based. For example, if the mean number correct in the experimental group is 10, that in the control group is 5, and this difference is statistically significant, an appropriate concluding statement would be "The control group did worse than the experimental group." In this simple example the conclusion may seem obvious, but appropriate concluding statements are essential in more complex analyses. It is discouraging when a student strings together a series of inferential statistical tests with appropriate commentary on the statistical significance of each test—and then never reports the descriptive statistics or any conclusion. It is almost useless for your readers to know that an independent variable has had a statistically significant effect if you have failed to describe the nature of that effect. *Descriptive* statistics are essential in providing such a description.

As we mentioned earlier, each paragraph of the results section follows the structure outlined in Table C.3. The idea is not to overload your reader with statistics. The challenge is to select those findings that are most critical, being sure to report all the data pertinent to the questions raised in your introduction. Before concluding our discussion of the results section, we will briefly describe the basic procedures for constructing tables and figures, two key tools in reporting results effectively.

Presenting Data in Tables Tables are an effective and efficient means of presenting large amounts of data in concise form. The table should supplement and not duplicate information in the text of the paper, but it should be well integrated into the text. The tables in your paper should be numbered consecutively (arabic numerals are used to number tables) so that they can be referred to easily in the text by their numbers. Each table should also have a brief explanatory title, and the columns and rows of the table should be labeled clearly. The data entries in the table should all be reported to the same degree of precision (that is, all values should have the same number of decimal places), and the values should be consistently aligned with the corresponding row and column headings. An appropriately constructed table appears in the sample manuscript at the end of this appendix.

When manuscripts are submitted for publication, each table is typed on a separate page and the tables appear at the end of the paper after the references and footnotes sections. This is done principally for the convenience of the typesetter, who will be positioning the tables in the printed journal article. When this format is used, the position of the table in the paper is indicated by typing "Insert Table 1 here" as a centered heading either immediately before or immediately after the paragraph in which the first reference to the table appears. You separate this heading from the preceding and the following paragraphs by double-spacing before and after typing the heading (see sample paper). Some instructors prefer to have their students type the table in the text itself at the point where reference to the table is made. A table number and title are required even when the table is placed directly in the text.

Presenting Data in Figures Figures, like tables, are a concise way to present large amounts of information. Of course, the format of a figure differs from that of a table. A figure has two principal axes: the horizontal axis, or X-axis, and the vertical axis, or Y-axis. Typically, the levels of the independent variable are plotted on the X-axis and those of the dependent variable are plotted on the Y-axis. When there are two or more independent variables, the levels of the second and succeeding independent variables serve as labels for the curves within the figure or are indicated in a figure legend. Two illustrations of the format for figures are presented in Figures C.1 and C.2. In Figure C.1 the values of the dependent variable are plotted on the Y-axis, the levels of one independent variable (serial position) are indicated on the X-axis, the levels of the

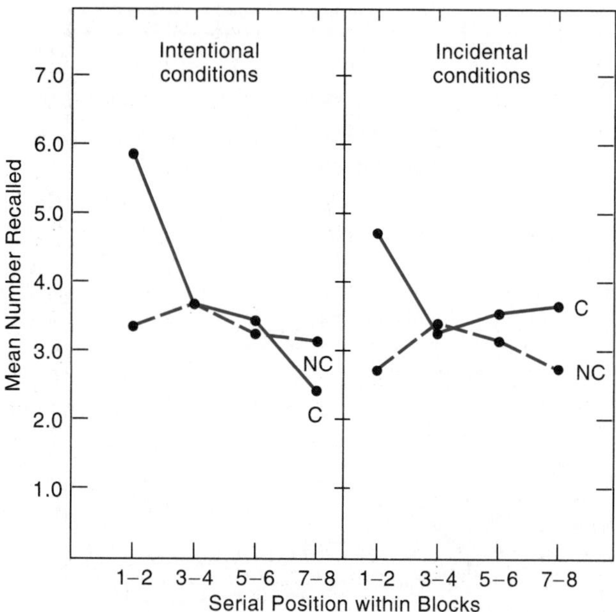

FIGURE C.1 Mean number of words recalled (of a possible ten) as a function of serial position within blocks and instructional condition (C = Cued; NC = Noncued).

second independent variable (C versus NC) label the curves, and the levels of the third independent variable (instructions) serve as the headings for each of the two panels of the figure. There are also three independent variables represented in Figure C.2: one on the X-axis and two differentiated by symbols that can be interpreted by using the legend at the top of the figure. For example, the reversal groups are represented by circles and the control groups are represented by squares. Here again, the Y-axis indicates values of the dependent variable.

The two sample figures illustrate that there are alternative ways to construct useful graphic presentations. All figures must include certain features, however. The X- and Y-axes must be clearly labeled, with each label printed parallel to the corresponding axis. Selected points (called *grid points*) on each axis must be identified with labeled grid marks, and the grid labels are always printed horizontally. Each figure is accompanied by a figure caption that corresponds to the title of a table.

Figures are numbered consecutively in the paper with arabic numerals, and they are referred to by number. The numbering of figures is done separately from the numbering of tables. It is common in psychology to enclose figures in a boxed outline, as has been done in Figures C.1 and C.2. The grid points of the X-axis are repeated on the top and those of the Y-axis are repeated on the right for ease of reading the figure, but these additional grid points are usually

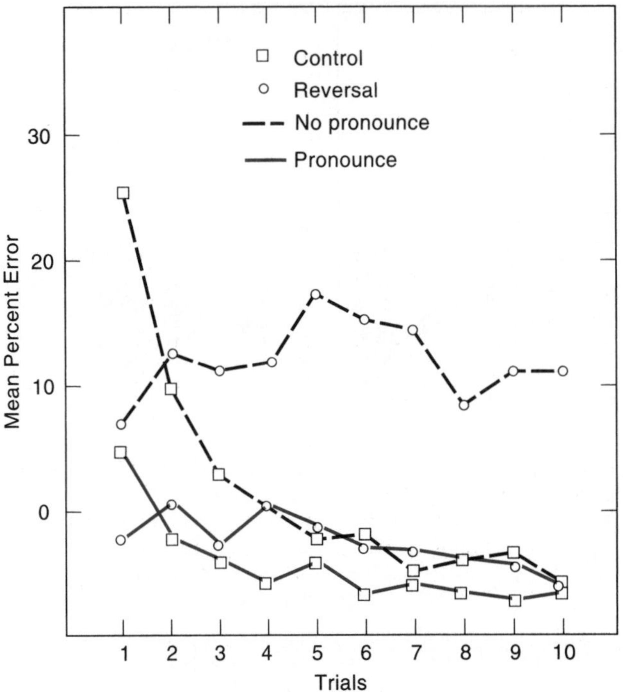

FIGURE C.2 Mean percent error across trials for TCC transfer as a function of type of transfer task and pronunciation instructions.

not labeled. Finally, the grid scale for the X- and Y-axes should be chosen such that the plotted curves are legible and span the entire illustration. Although the word *caption* actually means "at the head," the captions of Figure C.1 and Figure C.2 appear at the bottom of the corresponding figures because this is a common format that instructors use for students' research reports. When a manuscript is submitted for publication, each figure appears on a separate page but the figure captions do not appear on the figures themselves. They are presented on a separate page under the centered heading "Figure Captions." This page follows the tables at the end of the manuscript but precedes the figures, which are presented in order.

Two general types of figures are commonly used in psychology: bar graphs and line graphs. A bar graph is often used when the independent variable plotted on the X-axis is a nominal-scale variable (see Chapter 3). For example, if you were plotting the mean GPA (dependent variable) of students enrolled in different academic majors (independent variable), you could use a bar graph. An illustration of a bar graph is presented in Figure C.3. By far the most common type of figure is the line graph. Figures C.1 and C.2 represent this

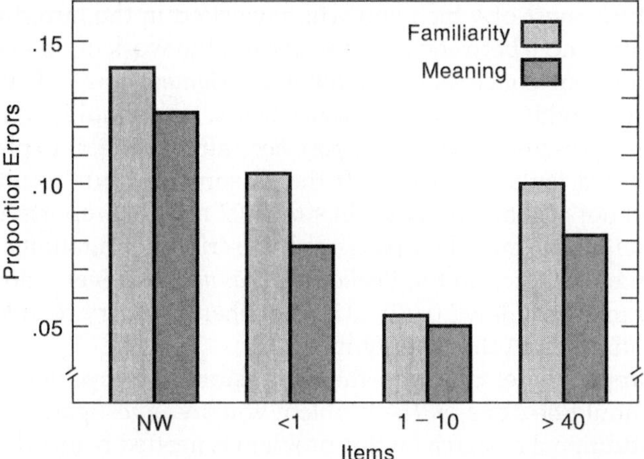

FIGURE C.3 Proportion recognition errors made by two groups of college students after rating verbal items for either familiarity or meaning. The items were nonwords (NW) and words appearing less than one time, one through ten times, and more than forty times per million in the Thorndike-Lorge count.

type of figure, and we have already discussed the procedures for constructing it.

DISCUSSION

The fourth section of the body of your report, the discussion, opens with a centered head (see sample paper). After presenting the evidence in the results section, you are ready for your "closing statement to the jury." In the words of the *Publication Manual* (p. 27):

> After presenting the results, you are in a position to evaluate and interpret their implications, especially with respect to your original hypothesis. In the Discussion section, you are free to examine, interpret, and qualify the results, as well as to draw inferences from them.

The discussion should begin with a succinct statement of the essential findings, and you should give particular attention to how your findings support or refute your original hypotheses. You do not repeat the descriptive statistics in this summary, nor do you necessarily refer to the statistical significance of the findings. The discussion is written in a tone and style consistent with the introduction. Be careful, however, to keep the statements you make in the discussion consistent with the data reported in the results. For instance, you should not report that one group did better than another if the comparison between these groups was not statistically significant—at least not without some qualification of what you mean by "better."

The second step in the discussion is to tie your findings in with the relevant literature, most of which you will have cited in the introduction. "Similarities and differences between your results and the work of others should clarify and confirm your conclusions" (*Publication Manual*, p. 27). If your results are not consistent with your original hypotheses, you should suggest an explanation for these discrepancies. Such *post hoc* (after-the-fact) explanations should be considered tentative at best. If the reasons for your results are unclear, you should not hesitate to say so. In students' research reports, it is often necessary and helpful to include a paragraph describing limitations or problems in the research. As noted in the *Publication Manual*, however, "do not dwell compulsively on every flaw" (p. 28). On the other hand, try to anticipate criticisms of your study that others might make.

If appropriate, conclude the discussion by proposing additional research that should be done on the problem you are investigating. Avoid clichés such as "Additional research on this problem is needed before definitive conclusions can be reached." Instead, be specific about what research should be done and *why* it needs to be done. That is, be sure to explain what the new research should reveal that we do not already know. Do not just say, "It would be interesting to do this experiment with younger subjects." Explain how you would expect the results to differ with younger subjects and what you would conclude if the results of the proposed experiment were to turn out as expected. Remember, the watchword in proposing new research is to *be specific*. Your emphasis should definitely be on quality, not quantity.

Some students (as well as some professional researchers) find it hard to separate their description of their findings from their interpretation of the results. A potential solution for such students is to write a combined results and discussion section. If you choose this option, however, you must still meet the objectives of both sections. The objectives for the discussion are clearly summarized in the *Publication Manual* (p. 28):

> In general, be guided by these questions: What have I contributed here? How has my study helped to resolve the original problem? What conclusions and theoretical implications can I draw from my study? The responses to these questions are the core of your contribution, and readers have a right to clear, unambiguous, and direct answers.

REFERENCES

We have already described the procedure for citing references within the body of a research report by using the name(s) of the author(s) and the date of publication. The references section, which appears with a centered heading on a separate page after the discussion (see sample paper), includes the complete citation for each reference. "Just as data in the paper support interpretations and conclusions, so reference citations document statements made about the literature" (*Publication Manual*, p. 28).

There are three types of references that will cover almost all those needed for students' research reports: journal articles, books, and chapters in edited books. The format for each of these reference types is illustrated in Table C.4. As this table shows, the second and succeeding lines of each reference are slightly indented. The journal article reference includes the authors, the year of publication, the title of the article, the name of the journal, the volume number, and the page numbers. The book citation includes the authors, the copyright date, the title, the city in which the book was published, and the publisher. The reference for a chapter in an edited volume includes the author of the chapter, the date, the chapter title, the editors of the book, the title of the book, the page numbers of the chapter, the city of publication, and the publisher. You can save your readers much aggravation if you follow the reference formats closely and proofread your reference list *carefully*. The references are listed in alphabetical order by the last name of the first author of each article. If there are two articles by the same author(s), they are arranged in ascending order by year of publication.

FOOTNOTES

Because they are not used for citing references, footnotes are rare in journal articles and even more rare in students' research reports. Should you find that you do need to use footnotes, number them consecutively in the text. They appear on a separate page following the references section under the centered heading "Footnotes."

APPENDICES

Appendices are slightly less common than footnotes, and they, too, appear at the end of the paper following the references (or footnotes, if there are any). Appendices are a bit more common in students' research reports than in published articles. Instructors may require you to submit an appendix including

TABLE C.4 ILLUSTRATION OF FORMAT OF REFERENCE CITATIONS

Journal article
Loftus, E. F., & Burns, T. E. (1982). Mental shock can produce retrograde amnesia. Memory & Cognition, 10, 318–323.
Book
Posavac, E. J., & Carey, R. G. (1992). Program evaluation (4th ed.). Englewood Cliffs, NJ: Prentice-Hall.
Chapter in an edited book
Weiss, J. M. (1977). Psychological and behavioral influences on gastrointestinal lesions in animal models. In J. D. Maser & M. E. P. Seligman (Eds.), Psychopathology: Experimental models (pp. 232–269). San Francisco: W. H. Freeman.

your raw data, the worksheets for a statistical analysis, or the computer printout of the analyses. The appendix can also be used to provide a verbatim copy of the instructions to subjects or a list of the specific materials used in an experiment. Each appendix is identified by letter (A, B, C, and so on), and any reference to the appendix in the body of the text is made using this letter. For instance, you might write, "The complete instructions can be found in Appendix A."

ORAL PRESENTATIONS

Research psychologists regularly attend professional conventions at which they present brief oral descriptions of their research. Similarly, students in a research-methods class may be required to give oral presentations of their research either in class or at a research symposium involving students from a number of different classes or at undergraduate research conferences (Palladino, Carsrud, Hulicka, & Benjamin, 1982). All of these settings share one characteristic—the time allowed for the presentation is usually no more than 10 to 15 minutes. In this length of time it is impossible to provide the detailed description that is included in a journal article. In general, as noted in the *Publication Manual*, "Material delivered verbally should differ from written material in its level of detail, organization, and presentation" (p. 192). Schlosberg (1965) summarizes the task one faces in giving an oral presentation and offers a word of sage advice: "Your primary purpose is to communicate clearly to an audience [under less-than-ideal conditions]. The important thing is to concentrate your efforts on getting across only one or two main points" (p. 606). In getting the main points across, the person giving the oral presentation must remember that a listener, unlike a reader, has no opportunity to review what has been said before.

One consequence of the constraints we have just described is that a brief oral presentation may require more preparation than that required for writing a research report. In giving your presentation, you will draw on the same questions that you use to organize the body of a written research report: Why was the research done? What was done? What was found? What are the implications of the findings? You probably recognize these as the guiding questions for organizing the introduction, method, results, and discussion sections. All four questions are relevant to an oral presentation, but the time constraints (and the attention span of your listeners) require that you choose *one* of these questions as your focus. For example, if you were describing a completed research project, you would probably focus on the question, What was found? But if the research had been done principally to develop a new technique to study a problem, you would probably focus on the question, What was done? Choose one focus and stick to it.

A colleague of ours in the biology department has developed five principles that he distributes to his cell physiology students to help them prepare the oral

TABLE C.5 PRINCIPLES TO FOLLOW FOR AN EFFECTIVE ORAL PRESENTATION

1. Avoid the temptation to tell everything you know in 10 minutes.
2. Cultivate a good platform presence.
3. Accompany your talk with useful visual aids.
4. Leave at least 2 minutes of your allotted time for questions.
5. Practice your talk before a critical audience before you give it.

presentation required in his class. These five principles are listed in Table C.5. Like all good maxims these five sound simple enough, but they are all too frequently ignored even by experienced researchers. The temptation described in the first prinicple can best be avoided by following the advice we gave earlier about limiting your presentation to one or two main points. The brief time available for an oral presentation is barely sufficient to allow you to present the evidence supporting these main points. There simply will not be time to discuss any side issues.

The second principle, cultivation of a good platform presence, can best be achieved by developing public speaking skills. Most people need a written copy of their presentation in front of them while they are presenting, but your presentation will be more effective if you can *appear* not to be reading. Many people speak too quickly in front of an audience, particularly if they are reading; it is best to use simple, direct sentences presented at a moderate rate. Most important, speak loudly and clearly.

The third principle, the use of effective visual aids, can help your listeners follow your presentation. To be effective, slides or material written on a blackboard must be distinct enough to be seen clearly at a distance (see Figure C.4). If you are not an audiovisual whiz, consider developing your skills in this area. In the meantime, use printed handouts for visual aids. Be sure that whatever visual aids you use are as close to self-explanatory as you can make them.

You need to keep in mind the fourth principle, leaving time for questions, because most professional conferences and classroom presentations will require that you reserve time for questions. Though it is somewhat intimidating, this opportunity for questions gives your listeners a chance to become actively involved in your presentation.

The final principle is perhaps the most important one. The presence of an audience is more critical than the practice you can get by simply rehearsing the talk over and over by yourself. Such private rehearsal is a good way to prepare for your "dress rehearsal," but it is no substitute for practicing before others.

The five principles listed in Table C.5 provide a good coaching manual for oral presentations. The best way to develop this skill, however, is to deliver as many oral presentations as possible under "game conditions." Practice may not make perfect, but it is the best route we know to improvement.

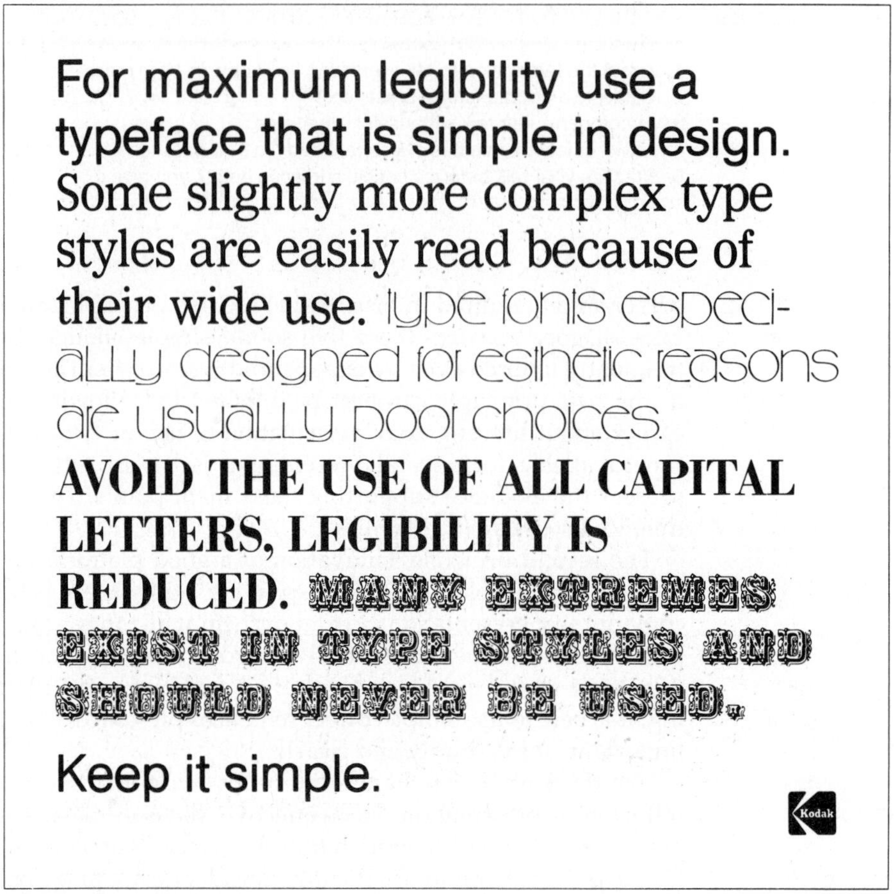

For maximum legibility use a typeface that is simple in design. Some slightly more complex type styles are easily read because of their wide use. Type fonts especially designed for esthetic reasons are usually poor choices.

AVOID THE USE OF ALL CAPITAL LETTERS, LEGIBILITY IS REDUCED. MANY EXTREMES EXIST IN TYPE STYLES AND SHOULD NEVER BE USED.

Keep it simple.

Kodak

M3-193 Lettering Styles

FIGURE C.4 A visual aid that speaks for itself.

RESEARCH PROPOSALS

In the last section of this appendix, we discuss writing again—but this time the writing of research proposals. As we mentioned at the beginning of the appendix, researchers must often seek financial support for their research by submitting grant proposals to private or government agencies. Students in research-methods classes are also sometimes required to submit proposals describing research they might do. Even if a written proposal is not required, only a foolhardy researcher would tackle a research project without careful *prior* consideration of related literature, possible practical problems, workable statistical analyses of the data, and eventual interpretation of the expected results. Without a carefully constructed plan for the research, the unprepared investigator is likely to produce an unworkable, unanalyzable, or uninterpretable piece of research.

The purpose of a research proposal is to ensure a workable experimental design that, when implemented, will result in an interpretable empirical finding of significant scientific merit. No research proposal, no matter how carefully prepared, can guarantee important results. Researchers learn early in their careers about Murphy's Law. In essence, Murphy's Law states that "anything that can go wrong will go wrong." Nonetheless, it is worthwhile to develop a research proposal, if only to avoid the research problems that *are* avoidable.

A written research proposal follows the general format of a journal article, but the headings of the various sections are slightly different. The proposal should include the following main sections:

Introduction
Method
Expected results and statistical treatment
References
Appendix

An abstract is not included in a research proposal. The introduction of a research proposal should include a more extensive review of the relevant literature than is required for a journal article. The statement of the research problem and the logical development of hypotheses in a research proposal are the same as required in a journal article. Similarly, the method section in the proposal should be as close as possible to the one that will accompany the finished research. Thus our remarks about the format and content of the method section of a research report apply equally to the writing of a proposal.

The section of the proposal entitled Expected results and statistical treatment should include a brief discussion of the anticipated results of the research. In most cases the exact nature of the results will not be known. Nevertheless, you will always have some idea (in the form of a hypothesis or prediction) of the outcome of the research. The expected-results section should outline what results might be expected and highlight those that are most important to the project. This section may include tables or figures of the results as you expect (hope) that they will come out. A statistical analysis plan for the proposed results should be in this section. Reasonable alternatives to the expected results should also be mentioned, as well as possible problems of interpretation that will arise if the results deviate from the research hypothesis.

The references section should be exactly like that same section as it would be submitted with the final report. An appendix should complete the research proposal and should include a list of *all* materials that will be used in doing the experiment. In most cases this will mean that a copy of the instructions to subjects will be included, as well as the type of apparatus used, a list of stimulus materials or a description of the stimuli, and so on. To repeat, *all materials* should be listed. For example, if you are doing a study involving subjects' memory for lists of words, the following must be included in the appendix: actual lists with randomizations made, type of apparatus used for presentation, instructions to subjects for all conditions, and randomizations of conditions.

A SAMPLE RESEARCH REPORT

The first two or three words of the title are typed above each page number in order to identify the manuscript. Note that the title page is the first numbered page.

The title of the article, the author's name, and the institutional affiliation of the author are each typed on separate lines. Use uppercase and lowercase letters, with double spacing between lines; center these lines slightly above the middle of the page. A good title will identify for the reader the topic and the major variables under investigation.

A *running head* is an abbreviated title. It should be a meaningful phrase and appear, centered, in all-uppercase letters, near the bottom margin of the title page. The running head appears in the manuscript only here; however, it appears at the top of every other page in a journal article.

Memory for Frequency

1

Memory for Frequency of Hearing Popular Songs

Nancy A. Norton

Loyola University of Chicago

Running head: MEMORY FOR SONGS

The abstract is found on page 2 of the manuscript. The word *Abstract* appears centered on a line double-spaced above the first line of the abstract. The abstract is typed as a single paragraph, but without indenting the first line.

The abstract should be a concise summary of the problem, methodology, major findings, and conclusion of the study. It should not exceed approximately 150 words.

Double-space between *all* lines in a manuscript, including between lines in footnotes, tables, and figure captions. Page margins should be about 1 to $1\frac{1}{2}$ inches on all sides of each page.

Memory for Frequency

2

Abstract

Memory for frequency of occurrence of popular songs was investigated. College students (N = 26) listened to a lengthy series of 10-s excerpts from popular songs, judged the number of times each song was heard, and tried to identify the titles and artists of the songs. Each excerpt was presented 0, 1, 2, 3, or 4 times. All students were informed that their memory for the names of various popular songs would be tested, and that some songs would be repeated, but only half the students were also informed that a frequency test would be given. Mean frequency estimates corresponded closely to actual frequencies and did not differ as a function of instructions regarding a frequency judgment test. However, accuracy of frequency judgments was significantly correlated with degree of knowledge of the popular songs, suggesting that memory for frequency of songs may not be a strictly automatic process.

The title of the article (without the author's name or affiliation) is typed in lowercase and uppercase letters and centered above the first line of the introduction to the study. Note that the word *Introduction* does not appear in the manuscript.

An ampersand (&) is used for "and" when referring to a study with more than one author when that reference is enclosed within parentheses.

The word *and* is used to join names of multiple authors when a reference is not enclosed within parentheses. First names or initials of authors are typically not used when identifying a reference.

Memory for Frequency

3

Memory for Frequency of Hearing Popular Songs

Memory for the number of times that an event has been experienced is often remarkably good. This is true whether the event to be remembered has been experienced in a particular situation, for example, as part of a laboratory experiment, or whether the event is one that an individual has experienced in many different situations as part of a lifetime of experiences (see Zechmeister & Nyberg, 1982, for a brief review of frequency judgment studies). This sensitivity to event frequency is assumed to play a role in many kinds of cognitive decisions. For example, frequency information is relevant when discriminating between old and new events as part of a recognition memory task (Underwood, 1971) or when assessing our degree of certainty about the truth or validity of statements (Hasher, Goldstein, & Toppino, 1977).

Hasher and Zacks (1979) have suggested that frequency information is encoded automatically. Automatic processes, in their view, are those that are completed without effort, are not affected by intention to learn, are not improved with practice, and are developmentally quite stable. Automatic encoding may, in fact, be something that humans are genetically "prepared" to do.

Hasher and Chromiak (1977) have provided empirical support for this theory of automatic encoding of frequency information. In one experiment, these investigators presented a list of 48 words to students in the second, fourth, and sixth grades, and to

A useful analogy for writing an introduction is a funnel. A good introduction often begins with rather broad or general statements about the topic under consideration. Then, the author narrows somewhat the focus by referring to relevant examples of previous research on this topic. Finally, the author identifies the specific goals (hypotheses) of the present research.

college students. The critical words were presented zero to four times. Half the students at each grade level were warned that a frequency judgment test would be forthcoming; the other half were not told that memory for frequency would be tested. Results revealed that students at all levels judged frequency relatively accurately, that this ability did not differ across grade levels, and that students forewarned about a frequency test did not do better than those not forewarned. In a second experiment, Hasher and Chromiak investigated whether memory for frequency improved with practice. It did not.

Studies investigating memory for event frequency have generally examined retention of verbal stimuli, such as words or parts of words (e.g., letters, bigrams), or pictorial stimuli. Nevertheless, automatic encoding of frequency information is assumed to extend potentially to all stimuli, whether meaningful or not (Hasher & Chromiak, 1977). In the present experiment, the generality of automatic encoding of frequency was tested by examining memory for frequency of hearing popular songs. College students listened to a lengthy series of brief excerpts from popular songs that were presented zero to four times. After listening to the presentation series all students were asked to judge the number of times that different songs had been heard. Half of the students were informed that a frequency test would be administered; half were not informed. If frequency of hearing popular songs is encoded automatically then students' estimates

After reading the introduction, does the reader know exactly why you are doing this study and what you expect to find?

The word *Method* is centered prior to the first line of the second major part of the body of the manuscript. Do not begin a new page when starting the Method, Results, or Discussion sections.

It is advisable to use headings, such as Subjects, Materials, and Procedure, to sequence the writing of the Method section. Although there is no "right" order of appearance of headings, a Subjects heading most often appears first in a research manuscript. Sometimes a Design heading is used, particularly when the design is complex; moreover, headings can be combined, for example, Subjects and Design.

of situational frequency should correspond closely to actual frequency of occurrence and should not differ between students told that a frequency test would be given and those not told.

Method

Subjects

Twenty-six students from a college psychology class participated in the study. These students were randomly assigned to either the informed or uninformed groups. Thus, each group consisted of 13 students.

Materials

An audio cassette tape was prepared containing 52, 10-s segments of popular songs. All of the song segments were taken from rock songs that had been in the "top 20" at some point in the past 3 years. The same song segment was never repeated in successive positions on the tape; there were always 4 to 10 intervening presentations between the repetitions of any one song. Segments contained no lyrics and were taken from the beginning of the song. Each segment was separated from the next by silent intervals of 5 to 7 s.

The 16 critical songs were presented either 1, 2, 3, or 4 times on the tape. The tape was divided into two halves. In each half different critical songs were represented twice at each of the four levels of frequency. Therefore, there were four songs presented at each of the frequency levels. To increase the apparent range of frequencies on the tape, one song was recorded

Numbers 10 or greater appear as numerals (e.g., 13), unless they begin a sentence, in which case they are expressed in words (e.g., Twenty-six. . .).

Words are used to express numbers less than 10 (e.g., five), unless they precede a unit of measure (3 years), occur in a series (4, 6, 8, 10, and 12), or represent specific numerical forms, such as dates, time, sums of money, points on a scale, and so forth (e.g., January 1; 7-point scale; $N = 9$).

six times and presented through both halves of the tape. In addition, to avoid possible primacy or recency effects, one filler song segment was presented twice and two different segments were each played once at the beginning of the tape (primacy), and two songs were each played once at the end of the tape (recency).

The test tape was prepared in similar fashion. The 16 critical song segments, each of 10-s duration, were randomly ordered and recorded. In addition, four additional song segments that had not been on the presentation tape were included on the test. Thus, 20 song segments were on the test tape, four at each of five frequency levels: 0, 1, 2, 3, or 4. Each segment was separated by a 5-s silent interval to allow subjects time to record their frequency judgment for each song.

Test booklets were prepared for all students. The first page of these booklets contained instructions that were to be read prior to listening to the tape. The second page of the booklet was a questionnaire that was not to be inspected until the presentation tape had ended. The items on the questionnaire asked (a) how many hours per day the student spent listening to music, (b) which type of music the student preferred, and (c) whether the student had ever played a musical instrument. Additional items on the questionnaire asked students to use a 7-point rating scale to indicate (a) how much they liked rock music, (b) how knowledgeable they felt they were about

Avoid including trivial details in the Method section (e.g., A Number 2 pencil was used.)

When writing the Procedure subsection of the Method section, try to tell a story from beginning to end of what happened.

contemporary music, and (c) how good they felt their memory was for music heard previously. The last page in the booklet was the answer sheet for the frequency judgment test. Space was provided for frequency judgments for each of the 20 songs. Space was also provided for identification of each song title and of the artist or group.

Procedure

All students were assembled in a classroom and a tape player was positioned at the front of the room so that each student could hear the song segments. The previously prepared booklets were distributed to the students in a random order. Students were then told to read the instructions on the first page of the booklet, but to keep the booklet closed until after the tape had been played. Booklets for students in the informed group contained general memory instructions indicating that the experiment involved a test of "your memory for the names of various popular songs." Students in the informed group were also asked to attend to the frequency of each song segment so that they could later make accurate frequency judgments. Students in the uninformed group received similar instructions but they were not told that their memory for the frequency of occurrence of song segments would be tested. The instructions also informed students in both groups about the general nature of what would be played on the tape, and the fact that some songs would be repeated.

Units of measure are abbreviated without trailing periods (e.g., seconds = s; minutes = min).

After reading the Method section, can the reader carry out your study exactly as you did it?

The Results section begins immediately following the Method section. The word *Results* is centered above the first line of the Results section.

The Results section should begin with a description of the major dependent variables, the summary statistics used (e.g., means and standard deviations), and the results obtained across conditions of the study.

After the presentation tape was played, students were asked to fill out the brief questionnaire on the second page of the booklet. This took approximately 2 min. This questionnaire was used primarily as a filler activity to introduce a delay between hearing the tape and the frequency judgment test. The test tape, containing the 20 song segments, was then played and students were asked to estimate how many times each song was heard on the previous tape. Students were told to guess if they were not sure.

Finally, the test tape was played again, and students were asked to try to identify the title and the name of the artist for each song segment. The tape was stopped after each segment and approximately 30 s were allowed for the two identifications.

Results

Before carrying out the analysis of the frequency judgment test, the characteristics of the students tested in the experiment were examined using their responses to the questionnaire. The mean responses of the students in the informed and uninformed groups to four critical items on the questionnaire are summarized in Table 1. Although there were slight differences across groups, the mean responses indicated that the two groups of students were comparable in terms of the number of hours each day they spent listening to music, their liking of rock music, and their self-assessed memory ability for previously heard music.

Tables or figures appear on separate pages toward the end of the manuscript. When a table or figure is included in the Results section, lines are used to separate a phrase telling the printer where to insert the relevant table or figure in the final printed version of the article. In the text do not refer to a table or figure by position (e.g., See Figure 1 below.) because the actual position will be determined when the article is typeset. Always refer to tables or figures by their number.

When writing the Results section, you may assume that your reader has a basic knowledge of statistical procedures and thus you may omit reference to such concepts as the null hypothesis or whether an outcome falls within the critical region for your test.

Insert Table 1 about here

Two dependent variables were considered in assessing the accuracy of students' frequency judgment performance. First, as a measure of what could be called absolute accuracy, the number of times each student correctly judged the actual frequency of presentation was recorded. The mean number of these "hits" was 9.46 (SD = 3.04) for students in the informed group, and 9.00 (SD = 2.89) for students in the uninformed group. The difference between these means was not statistically significant, $t(24) = .40$, $p > .05$.

An alternative method for measuring the accuracy of frequency judgment performance is to assess the ability to discriminate among items of different presentation frequencies. This relative measure of frequency judgment accuracy was used as a second dependent variable in this study. The mean estimated frequency as a function of actual frequency was determined on the basis of the four frequency judgments made at each of five levels of frequency. Thus, for each student the mean estimated frequency for the four zero-presented songs, the four once-presented songs, and so forth, was calculated. The means of these means for each frequency level and for both informed and uninformed students are shown in Figure 1. As can be seen in the figure, frequency estimates in both groups increased as actual

Note that a figure is a graph or other pictorial representation of results; a table is used to summarize numbers or verbal expressions (e.g., descriptions of scale labels).

An analysis of variance for a complex design is indicated by using numerals to represent the independent variables and the number of levels associated with each variable. Numerals are separated by an x, which is read "by." For example, a 2 × 5 ("two by five") analysis of variance indicates that the statistical test involved two independent variables; one variable had 2 levels and the other variable had 5 levels. Degrees of freedom associated with results of an analysis of variance (*F*-test) are presented in parentheses with the obtained *F* values.

Be careful to use signs for inequality correctly when referring to the probability of a statistical outcome.

Memory for Frequency

10

frequency of occurrence increased. Moreover, an inspection of the data in Figure 1 reveals that there were only slight differences in mean frequency judgments as a function of being informed or not being informed about an upcoming frequency judgment test.

Insert Figure 1 about here

A 2 x 5 analysis of variance including the two independent variables of instructions and frequency level was carried out on the data summarized in Figure 1. Although there was some suggestion of an interaction in the nonparallel lines in the figure, there was no statistically significant interaction between instructions and frequency level, $F(4, 96) = 1.82$, $p > .05$. There was also no significant difference in the mean judgments for students in the informed group (2.20) as compared to those in the uninformed group (2.34), $F(1, 24) < 1$. However, actual frequency was a statistically significant variable, $F(4, 96) = 129.40$, $p < .01$. The mean estimates for frequencies 0, 1, 2, 3, and 4, were 0.39, 1.38, 2.52, 3.31, and 3.76, respectively. Therefore, there was evidence that accurate relative frequency judgments for excerpts from popular songs can be made. But there was no evidence that students differed in their memory for frequency of hearing songs as a function of the instructions given to them regarding a frequency judgment test.

All statistical terms are abbreviated and should be underlined to indicate italics printing (e.g., t, M, SD).

Footnotes should be used sparingly in a manuscript. A footnote is indicated with the proper numerical superscript at the end of a line, and the footnote itself is typed on a separate page following the References section.

After reading the Results section, does your reader know all the important findings in your study?

The word *Discussion* is centered on a line immediately following the Results section and before the first line of the Discussion section.

The number of titles and artists correctly identified by each student was also determined. Among all 26 students the range of song titles (of 20 possible) identified correctly was 0 to 18, ($M = 8.81$). The range of correct identification of artists was the same ($M = 8.27$). The numbers of titles and artists correctly identified were highly correlated, $r(24) = .90$. Because of this close relationship, the number of titles correctly identified was chosen to indicate the degree of knowledge that a student had about the songs heard. The correlation was determined between students' knowledge of the songs and the accuracy of their frequency judgments as reflected by the number of "hits" on the frequency judgment test.[1] The obtained correlation was $r(24) = .70$, which is reliably larger than zero, $t(24) = 4.79$, $p < .01$. The significant correlation suggests that frequency judgment accuracy varies with a person's knowledge of the to-be-judged stimuli.

Discussion

The present experiment investigated people's abilities to judge the frequency with which they heard a number of popular songs. Prior to listening to the songs, college students were either informed or not informed about the later frequency judgment task. In agreement with results of other published studies in this area (e.g., Hasher & Chromiak, 1977), no significant difference in frequency judgment performance was observed as function of instructions to remember frequency.

The Discussion section should begin with a brief review of the rationale and procedure of the study, and then provide a succinct statement of the essential findings, emphasizing those findings that relate to the hypotheses or goals of the study that were stated in the Introduction.

The year of publication appears in parentheses after the authors' surnames even when that particular reference has appeared previously in the text.

A good Discussion section will mention possible alternative explanations for the results of the study.

Moreover, in both the informed and uninformed conditions of the experiment, frequency estimates increased as frequency of actual occurrence increased. These findings support the notion that frequency information for musical stimuli, like that for verbal or pictorial stimuli, is encoded "automatically."

The finding, however, that accuracy of frequency judgments correlated with students' knowledge of the musical stimuli, poses a challenge for the strictly automatic encoding process proposed by Hasher and Zacks (1979) There are apparently individual differences in frequency judgment performance that are linked to knowledge of the stimuli to be judged. One possibility is that memory for frequency is likely to be encoded more easily when stimuli are meaningful than when they are not meaningful. Although Hasher and Chromiak (1977) have indicated that meaningfulness is not a critical factor in determining automatic encoding of frequency information, the present results suggest otherwise.

Although meaningful elaboration of the stimuli to be judged may influence memory for frequency, this suggestion must be made tentatively. The relationship between knowledge (defined by number of song titles identified) and memory for frequency (defined by number of "hits") is only correlational. There are several other possible factors that may be responsible for this relationship. For example, students who know more song titles are likely to be more familiar with music in general than are

The conclusion of a good Discussion often contains information that can direct future research; vacuous statements such as, "More research needs to be done" should be avoided.

students who do not know many titles. The correlation between knowledge of the songs and accuracy of frequency judgments may be attributable to this general expertise in music rather than to meaningful elaboration. An "expert" might be able to make finer discriminations among stimuli than can a nonexpert. This alternative explanation could be tested by administering a frequency judgment test for musical stimuli to groups of people selected on the basis of their musical expertise. If general musical expertise is a critical factor, then frequency judgment accuracy should be greater for groups with greater expertise. Of course, in testing this possible explanation it would be essential to demonstrate that frequency judgment accuracy for nonmusical stimuli does not vary with changes in musical expertise.

Because all students were advised that their memory for song titles would be tested, it is possible that students who knew many titles were less frustrated or less anxious than those who knew only a few titles. Such affective differences could account for the original correlation if it were argued that frequency judgment accuracy decreased with increasing anxiety or frustration. An account based on differences in frequency judgment performance as a function of mild emotional changes would also provide evidence against automatic encoding (see Hasher & Zacks, 1979).

After reading the Discussion section, does your reader know what your findings mean?

In summary, the present results confirm that accurate frequency judgments can be made for musical stimuli, thereby extending the generality of frequency encoding beyond verbal and pictorial stimuli. The absence of a difference in frequency judgment accuracy for informed and uninformed groups supports the notion that frequency information is encoded automatically. The automatic encoding of frequency appears inconsistent, however, with the obtained correlation between knowledge of the musical stimuli and frequency judgment accuracy. The basis of this correlation and the extent of the challenge it poses to the automatic encoding theory are unclear at this time.

The References section begins on a new page, with the word *References* centered on a line that is two lines below the page number.

The authors' names are typed flush with the margin with the second and subsequent lines indented three spaces; initials, but not first names of authors, are provided. Names of two authors, and the last two names in a series, are separated by an ampersand (&). The year of publication of a book or article appears in parentheses, followed by a period, immediately after the authors' names and before a title.

Only the first letter of the first word of titles of articles and books is capitalized, whereas the first letters of all major words in the name of a journal are capitalized.

Page numbers of a specific article or chapter are shown in parentheses following the title of the book in which the material appears.

The volume number of a journal, as well as the name of a journal or book, are underlined.

Memory for Frequency

15

References

Hasher, L., & Chromiak, W. (1977). The processing of frequency information: An automatic mechanism? Journal of Verbal Learning and Verbal Behavior, 16, 173-184.

Hasher, L., Goldstein, D., & Toppino, T. (1977). Frequency and the conference of referential validity. Journal of Verbal Learning and Verbal Behavior, 16, 107-112.

Hasher, L., & Zacks, R. T. (1979). Automatic and effortful processes in memory. Journal of Experimental Psychology: General, 108, 356-388.

Underwood, B. J. (1971). Recognition memory. In H. H. Kendler & J. T. Spence (Eds.), Essays in neobehaviorism (pp. 313-335). New York: Appleton-Century-Crofts.

Zechmeister, E. B., & Nyberg, S. E. (1982). Human memory: An introduction to research and theory. Monterey, CA: Brooks/Cole.

Author notes are used to acknowledge technical, financial, editorial, or other forms of assistance with the study, and to identify the address of the author or authors from whom additional information about the study, as well as reprints (copies), may be obtained.

Memory for Frequency

16

Author Notes

The data reported in this study are "real" and are based on an experiment performed as a classroom demonstration in an undergraduate course taught by E. B. Zechmeister. The author was asked, along with other members of the class, to be a subject in this experiment. Then, in order to pass the course the author was required to prepare a written manuscript, using strict American Psychological Association (APA) editorial style, which reported the results of this experiment. Subsequently, the instructor had the nerve to ask whether he might use the manuscript (after some "editing") in his book!

Both the author and the instructor wish to acknowledge the help of Jim Fidler in preparing the audio tapes used in this experiment.

Requests for reprints should be addressed to Nancy A. Norton, Psychology Department, Loyola University of Chicago, 6525 N. Sheridan Road, Chicago, IL 60626.

Footnotes, if they are present, are indicated in the text by typing numerals slightly above the last letter of the last word in a sentence or phrase that is noted (. . .end.[1]). The notes themselves are numbered consecutively and are typed on a separate page under the heading Footnote(s). The footnote page follows immediately after the page titled Author Notes.

Footnote

[1]Typically a single correlation should not be computed across two or more groups of subjects who have been treated differently. Instead, the correlation of interest should be computed within each group of subjects and an average correlation across groups would then be used to describe the overall correlation. In the present study there were no significant differences between groups in either knowledge of the songs or accuracy of frequency judgments. Therefore, for the sake of simplicity, only one correlation was computed.

Tables and figures appear on separate pages at the end of the manuscript following the References, Author Notes, and Footnotes. Tables are numbered consecutively (using arabic numerals) in the order in which the tables appear in the manuscript.

Table titles are typed flush with the margin in uppercase and lowercase letters. The title is also underlined.

A note that clarifies or explains the table as a whole is put below the table with the word *Note,* underlined, followed by a period, typed flush to the left margin, introducing the note. If a specific footnote is needed to explain a particular item in the table, then a superscript letter is used following the item in the table (45[a]) and also before the first letter of the note which appears on the line after any general notes ([a]This number. . .).

Memory for Frequency

18

Table 1

Mean Responses of Students in Informed and Uninformed Groups to Questionnaire Items

Item	Condition	
	Informed	Uninformed
Hours listening to music	2.44	2.29
Liking of rock music	4.92	5.71
Knowledge of contemporary music	4.54	4.85
Memory for music previously heard	5.38	5.15

Note. Means for "hours listening" item are based on students' judgments of number of hours; means for remaining items are based on students' responses using a 7-point scale, with 7 being the high end of the scale.

Figure captions are numbered consecutively (using arabic numerals) on one page in the order in which they appear in the text.

Figure Caption

Figure 1. Estimated frequency of occurrence as a function of actual frequency of occurrence.

The actual figures are presented, each on a separate page, following the list of figure captions. When graphs are figures, they should be drawn carefully on white paper of good quality. Be sure to label correctly and clearly the axes and curves of any line graph.

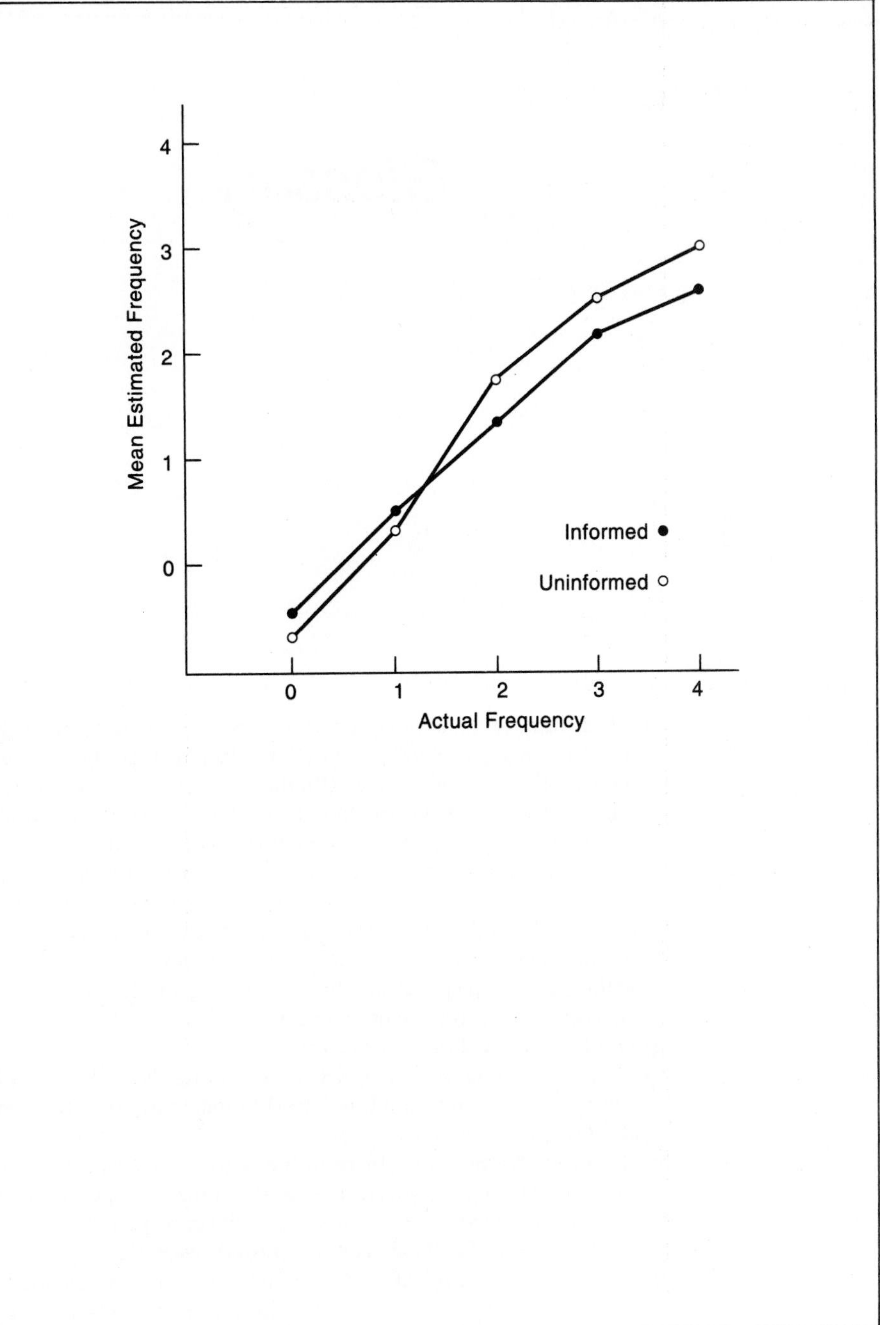

Glossary

ABAB design (reversal design) A single-case experimental design in which an initial baseline stage (A) is followed by a treatment stage (B), a return to baseline (A), and then another treatment stage (B); the researcher observes whether behavior changes on introduction of the treatment, reverses when the treatment is withdrawn, and improves again when the treatment is reintroduced.

ABBA counterbalancing A technique for balancing stage-of-practice effects in the complete within-subjects design that involves presenting the conditions in one sequence followed by the opposite of the same sequence.

accidental sample A type of nonprobability sample that results when availability and willingness to respond are the overriding factors used in selecting respondents; generally low in representativeness.

alpha (α) See **level of significance.**

analytical comparisons A statistical technique that can be applied (usually after obtaining a significant omnibus *F*-test) to locate the specific source of systematic variation in an experiment.

anticipation effects A problem in the within-subjects design, especially when ABBA counterbalancing is used, whenever the subject's expectations about which condition should occur next influence how the subject responds.

applied research See **basic versus applied research.**

archival data A source of evidence that is based upon records or documents relating the activities of individuals, institutions, governments, and other groups; used as an alternative to or in conjunction with other research methods.

baseline stage The first stage of a single-case experiment in which a record is made of the individual's behavior prior to any intervention.

basement effect See **ceiling effect.**

basic versus applied research Whereas basic research mainly seeks knowledge about nature simply for the sake of understanding it better, applied research seeks knowledge that will modify or improve the present situation; however, basic and applied research are considered to have a reciprocal relationship, for example, when basic research is used to identify abstract principles that can be applied in real-world settings, and when applied research is used to reveal possible limitations or extensions of these principles.

behaviorism An approach to the study of psychology that emphasizes observable behavior as the only legitimate source of scientific evidence and that defines psychology's goal as the prediction and control of behavior.

behavior modification The application of learning-conditioning principles in order to change behavior; first used synonymously with behavior therapy.

behavior therapy The application of learning-conditioning principles to clinical populations; first used synonymously with behavior modification.

biased sample A sample in which the distribution of characteristics is systematically different from that of the parent population.

block randomization The most common technique for carrying out random assignment in the random groups design; each block includes a random order of the conditions and there are as many blocks as there are subjects in each condition of the experiment.

case study An intensive description and analysis of a single individual.

causal inference The identification of the cause or causes of a phenomenon, by establishing covariation of cause and effect, a time-order relationship with cause preceding effect, and the elimination of plausible alternative causes.

ceiling (basement) effect A measurement problem whereby the researcher cannot measure the effects of an independent variable or a possible interaction because performance has reached a maximum (minimum) in any condition of the experiment.

checklist An instrument used to record the presence or absence of something in the situation under observation.

clinical significance A measure of the strength of a treatment as indicated by the extent to which it has improved the life of a client in a real-world setting; usually assessed using either subjective evaluation or social comparison.

cluster sampling A type of probability sample in which the sampling unit is an aggregate or cluster of elements for which an appropriate sampling frame is available.

coding The initial step in data reduction, especially with narrative records, in which units of behavior or particular events are identified and classified according to specific criteria.

complete within-subjects design A type of within-subjects design in which practice effects are balanced by administering the conditions several times to each subject such that results for each subject are interpretable.

complex design An experiment in which two or more independent variables are studied simultaneously.

confederate Someone in the service of a researcher who is instructed to behave in a certain way in order to help produce an experimental treatment.

confounding What results when the independent variable of interest systematically covaries with a second, unintended independent variable.

construct validity When referring to a psychological test, construct validity asks the question: Is this test measuring the theoretical construct that the test is intended to measure?

contamination What results when there is communication of information about the experiment between groups of subjects.

content analysis Any of a variety of techniques for making inferences by objectively identifying specific characteristics of messages, usually written communications but may be any form of message; used extensively in the analysis of archival data.

control A key component of the scientific method whereby the effect of various factors possibly responsible for a phenomenon are isolated; three basic types of control are manipulation, holding conditions constant, and balancing.

correlation A correlation exists when two different measures of the same people, events, or things vary together; the presence of a correlation makes it possible to predict values on one variable by knowing the values on the second variable.

correlation coefficient A statistic that indicates how well two measures vary together; absolute size ranges from 0.0 (no correlation) to 1.00 (perfect correlation); direction of covariation is indicated by the sign of the coefficient, a plus (+) indicating that both measures covary in the same direction and a minus (−) indicating that the variables vary in opposite directions.

correlational research Research which has the goal of identifying predictive relationships among naturally occurring variables.

cross-sectional design A survey research design in which one or more samples of the population are selected and information is collected from the samples at one time.

data reduction The process in the analysis of behavioral data whereby results are meaningfully organized and statements summarizing important findings are prepared.

debriefing A process following a research session through which participants are informed about the rationale for the research in which they participated, about the need for any deception, and about their specific contribution to the research. Important goals of debriefing are to clear up any misconceptions and to leave participants with a positive feeling toward psychological research.

deception Intentionally withholding information about significant aspects of a research project from a participant or presenting misinformation about the research to participants.

demand characteristics The cues and other information used by participants to guide their behavior in a psychological study, often leading participants to do what they believe the observer (experimenter) expects them to do.

dependent variable Measure of behavior used by the researcher to assess the effect (if any) of the independent variables.

differential transfer Potential problem in within-subjects designs when performance in one condition differs depending on which of two other conditions precedes it.

double-blind experiment Both the subject and the observer are kept unaware (blind) of what treatment is being administered.

ecological psychology Has as its goal the comprehensive description of individuals in everyday contexts.

effect size An index of the strength of the relationship between the independent variable and dependent variable that is independent of sample size.

element Each member of the population of interest.

empirical approach An approach to acquiring knowledge that emphasizes direct observation and experimentation as a way of answering questions.

ethogram A complete catalog of all the behavior patterns of an organism, including information as to frequency, duration, and context of occurrence.

ethology The study of the behavior of organisms in relation to their natural environment; generally considered a branch of biology.

event sampling A procedure whereby the observer records each event that meets a predetermined definition; more efficient method than time sampling when event of interest occurs infrequently.

experimenter effects The experimenters' expectations that may lead them to treat subjects differently in different groups or to record data in a biased manner.

external validity The extent to which the results of a research study can be generalized to different populations, settings, and conditions.

***F*-test** A statistical test based on the ratio of variation between groups and variation within groups; under the null hypothesis both sources of variation represent error variation only and the expected value of F is 1.00.

field experiment A procedure in which one or more independent variables is manipulated by an observer in a natural setting to determine the effect on behavior.

field notes Verbal records of a trained observer that provide a running description of participants, events, settings, and behaviors.

Hawthorne effect Changes in a person's behavior brought about by the interest shown in that person by significant others.

hypothesis A tentative explanation for a phenomenon.

idiographic approach The intensive study of an individual, with an emphasis on both individual uniqueness and lawfulness.

incomplete within-subjects design A type of within-subjects design in which each condition is administered to each subject only once and the order of administering the conditions is varied across subjects such that practice effects are neutralized by combining the results for all subjects.

independent groups design Each separate group in the experiment represents a different condition as defined by the level of the independent variable.

independent variable A factor for which the researcher either selects or manipulates at least two levels in order to determine its effect on behavior.

inferential statistics A means to test whether the differences in a dependent variable that are associated with various conditions of an experiment are reliable, that is, larger than would be expected on the basis of error variation alone.

informed consent Explicitly expressed willingness to participate in a research project based on clear understanding of the nature of the research, of the consequences of not participating, and of all factors that might be expected to influence willingness to participate.

interaction What occurs when the effect of one independent variable differs depending on the level of a second independent variable.

internal validity The degree to which differences in performance can be attributed unambiguously to an effect of an independent variable, as opposed to an effect of some other (uncontrolled) variable; an internally valid study is free of confounds.

interobserver reliability The degree to which two independent observers are in agreement.

interrupted time-series design See **simple interrupted time-series design** and **time series with nonequivalent control group.**

interviewer bias What occurs when the interviewer tries to adjust the wording of a question to "fit" the respondent or records only selected portions of the respondent's answers.

irreversible task A problem that arises in the incomplete within-subjects design when a specific task cannot be administered more than once to the same subjects; necessitates special balancing procedures to ensure that practice effects, task, and independent variable are appropriately controlled.

level of significance (alpha α) When the probability of an outcome under the null hypothesis is less than this value, then the outcome is statistically significant.

longitudinal design A survey research design in which the same sample of respondents is interviewed more than once.

main effect The overall effect of an independent variable in a complex design.

margin of error In survey research, an estimate of the difference between a result obtained from a sample (e.g., the sample mean) and the corresponding true population value (e.g., population mean).

matched groups design A type of independent groups design in which the researcher forms comparable groups by matching subjects on a pretest task and then randomly assigning the members of these matched sets of subjects to the conditions of the experiment.

measurement scale One of four levels of physical and psychological measurement: nominal (categorizing), ordinal (ranking), interval (specifying distance between stimuli), and ratio (having an absolute zero point).

mechanical subject loss What occurs when a subject fails to complete the experiment because of equipment failure or because of experimenter error.

meta-analysis The analysis of results of several (often, very many) independent experiments investigating the same research area; the measure used in a meta-analysis is typically effect size.

minimal risk A research participant is said to experience minimal risk when probability and magnitude of harm or discomfort anticipated in the research are not greater than that ordinarily encountered in daily life or during the performance of routine tests.

mixed design When different designs (independent groups, within-subjects) are used for the different independent variables in a complex design the overall experiment is described as a mixed design.

multimethod approach An approach to hypothesis testing that seeks evidence by collecting data using several different measures of behavior; a recognition of the fact that any single measure of behavior can result from some artifact of the measuring process.

multiple-baseline design (across subjects, across behaviors, across situations) A single-case experimental design in which the effect of a treatment is demonstrated by showing that behaviors in more than one baseline change as a consequence of the introduction of a treatment; multiple baselines are established for different individuals, for different behaviors in the same individual, or for the same individual in different situations.

natural groups design A type of independent groups design in which the conditions represent the selected levels of a naturally occurring independent variable, for example, the subject variable age.

***N* = 1 designs** See **single-case experiment.**

narrative record A record intended to provide a more or less faithful reproduction of behavior as it originally occurred.

naturalistic observation An observation of behavior in a more or less natural setting without any attempt by the observer to intervene.

nomothetic approach An approach to research that seeks to establish broad generalizations or laws that apply to large groups (populations) of individuals; the average or typical performance of a group is emphasized.

nonequivalent control group design A quasi-experimental procedure in which a comparison is made between control and treatment groups that have been established on some basis other than through random assignment of subjects to groups.

nonprobability sampling A sampling procedure in which there is no way to estimate the probability of each element's being included in the sample; two common types are accidental sampling and purposive sampling.

nuisance factors Potential independent variables that are not directly of interest to the researcher but serve as possible sources of confounding.

null hypothesis The assumption used as the first step in statistical inference whereby the independent variable is said to have had no effect.

observer bias Systematic errors in observation often resulting from the observer's expectancies regarding the outcome of a study (i.e., expectancy effects).

omnibus *F*-test An initial overall analysis of the experiment for which the null hypothesis is that all the group means are equal.

operant In the experimental analysis of behavior, operants are behavioral responses emitted by an organism, such as the "voluntary" responses of walking and talking.

operational definition A procedure whereby a concept is defined solely in terms of the operations used to produce and measure it.

participant observation An observation of behavior by someone who also has an active and significant role in the situation or context in which behavior is recorded.

percentile score The percentage of people in a normative sample who scored below a given raw score.

physical traces A source of evidence that is based on the remnants, fragments, and products of past behavior; used as an alternative to or in conjunction with other research methods.

placebo control Procedure by which a substance that resembles a drug or other active substance but that is actually an inert, or inactive, substance is given to subjects.

plagiarism The presentation of another's ideas or work without clearly identifying the source.

population The set of all the cases of interest.

power The power of a statistical test is the probability that a false null hypothesis will be rejected; power is related to the level of significance selected, the size of the treatment effect, and the sample size.

privacy The right of individuals to decide how information about them is to be communicated to others.

probability sampling A sampling procedure in which the probability that each element of the population will be included in the sample can be specified.

program evaluation Research that seeks to determine whether a change proposed by an institution, government agency, or other unit of society is needed and likely to have an effect as planned or, when implemented, to actually have an effect.

purposive sample A type of nonprobability sample in which the elements to be included in the sample are selected by the investigator on the basis of special characteristics of the respondents.

quasi-experiments Procedures that resemble those characteristics of true experiments, for example, that some type of intervention or treatment is used and a comparison is provided, but are lacking in the degree of control that is found in true experiments.

random assignment The most common technique for forming groups as part of an independent groups design; the goal is to establish equivalent groups by balancing subject characteristics.

random groups design The most common type of independent groups design in which individuals are randomly selected or randomly assigned to each group such that groups are considered comparable at the start of the experiment.

random sampling See **simple random sampling.**

reactivity The influence that an observer has on the behavior under observation; behavior influenced by an observer may not be representative of behavior when an observer is not present.

regression to the mean Because some component of a test score is due to error (as opposed to true score), extreme scores on one test are likely to be closer to the mean on a second test, thus posing a threat to the validity of an experiment in which extreme groups are selected; the amount of this regression will be greater for less reliable tests.

relevant independent variable An independent variable that has been shown to influence behavior, either directly, by producing a main effect, or indirectly, by resulting in an interaction in combination with a second independent variable.

reliability A measurement is reliable when it is consistent.

replication Repeating the exact procedures used in an experiment to determine whether the same results are obtained.

representativeness A sample is representative to the extent that it has the same distribution of characteristics as the population from which it was selected; our ability to generalize from sample to population is critically dependent on representativeness.

residual variation When conducting an *F*-test for a within-subjects design, residual variation is the estimate of error variation which serves as the denominator of the *F*-ratio.

respondent In the experimental analysis of behavior, a respondent is a behavioral response elicited naturally from the environment, such as the withdrawal of one's hand after touching a hot stove.

risk/benefit ratio A subjective evaluation of the risk to a research participant relative to the benefit both to the individual and to society of the results of the proposed research.

sample Something less than all the cases of interest; in survey research, a subset of the population actually drawn from the sampling frame.

sampling frame A specific listing of all the members of the population of interest; an operational definition of the population.

scientific method An approach to knowledge that emphasizes empirical rather than intuitive processes, testable hypotheses, systematic and controlled observation of operationally defined phenomena, data collection using accurate and precise instrumentation, valid and reliable measures, and objective reporting of results; scientists tend to be critical and, most importantly, skeptical.

selective deposit The bias that results from the way physical traces are laid down and the way archival sources are produced, edited, or altered, as they are established; when present, the bias severely limits generality of research findings.

selective subject loss What occurs when subjects are lost differentially across the conditions of the experiment as the result of some characteristic of each subject that is related to the outcome of the study.

selective survival The bias that results from the way physical traces and archives survive over time; when present, the bias severely limits the external validity of research findings.

sensitivity The sensitivity of an experiment refers to the likelihood that the effect of an independent variable will be detected when that variable does, indeed, have an effect; sensitivity is increased to the extent that error variation is reduced (e.g., by holding variables constant rather than balancing them).

simple comparison A special type of analytical comparison that is used to determine the specific source of variation within a simple main effect in a complex design.

simple interrupted time-series design A quasi-experimental procedure in which changes in a dependent variable are observed for some period of time both before and after a treatment is introduced.

simple main effect The effect of one independent variable at one level of a second independent variable in a complex design.

simple random sampling and random selection A type of probability sampling in which each possible sample of a specified size in the population has an equal chance of being selected.

single-case experiment A procedure that focuses on behavior change in one individual ($N = 1$) by systematically contrasting conditions within that individual while continuously monitoring behavior.

situation sampling The random or systematic selection of situations in which observations are to be made with the goal of representativeness across circumstances, locations, and conditions.

social comparison A measure of clinical significance of a treatment in which the researcher compares the behavior of a client after treatment with the behavior of a "normal" group of subjects.

social desirability The pressures on survey respondents to answer as they think they should respond in accordance with what is most socially acceptable, and not in accordance with what they actually believe.

spurious relationship What exists when evidence falsely indicates that two or more variables are associated.

stage-of-practice effects The changes subjects undergo across repeated testing in within-subjects designs; subjects may get better if a skill is being developed or worse because of factors such as fatigue or boredom.

standard score Expresses the distance of a given test taker's raw score from the mean of the normative population in standard deviation units.

statistically significant When the probability of an obtained difference in an experiment is smaller than would be expected if error variation alone were assumed to be responsible for the difference, the difference is statistically significant.

stratified random sampling A type of probability sampling in which the population is divided into subpopulations called *strata* and random samples are drawn from each of these strata.

structured observation A variety of observational methods using intervention in which the degree of control is often less than in field experiments; frequently used by clinical and developmental psychologists when making behavioral assessments.

subject variables The characteristics subjects bring with them to the laboratory, such as their gender; subject variables are often studied as independent variables in the natural groups design.

subjective evaluation A measure of clinical significance of a treatment in which the judgments of people who have contact with the client are used to assess whether the behavior of the client is perceptibly different after treatment from what it was before treatment.

successive independent samples design A survey research design in which a series of cross-sectional surveys is done and the same questions are asked of each succeeding sample of respondents.

test-retest reliability A measure of the consistency of test scores obtained by administering the test to the same sample of individuals on two separate occasions.

theory A logically organized set of propositions which serves to define events, describe relationships among events, and explain the occurrence of these events; scientific theories guide research and organize empirical knowledge.

threats to internal validity Possible causes of a phenomenon which must be controlled so that a clear cause-effect inference can be made.

time sampling The selection of observation intervals either systematically or randomly with the goal of obtaining a representative sample of behavior.

time series with nonequivalent control group (See also **simple interrupted time-series design.**) A quasi-experimental procedure that improves on the validity of a simple time-series design by including a nonequivalent control group; both treatment and comparison groups are observed for a period of time both before and after the treatment.

token economy A procedure in behavior modification in which behavior is reinforced with tokens which can then be used to "purchase" desired reinforcers.

unobtrusive (nonreactive) measures Measures of behavior that eliminate the problem of reactivity, because observations are made in such a way that the presence of the observer is not detected by those being observed.

validity The "truthfulness" of a measure; a valid measure is one that measures what it claims to measure.

within-subjects design A design in which the independent variable is implemented by administering all the levels of the independent variable to each subject.

References

Abramson, L. Y., & Seligman, M. E. P. (1977). Modeling psychopathology in the laboratory: History and rationale. In J. D. Maser & M. E. P. Seligman (Eds.), *Psychopathology: Experimental models* (pp. 1–26). San Francisco: Freeman.

Adair, J. G., Dushenko, T. W., & Lindsay, R. C. L. (1985). Ethical regulations and their impact on research practice. *American Psychologist, 40,* 59–72.

Addison, W. E. (1986). Agonistic behavior in preschool children: A comparison of same-sex versus opposite-sex interactions. *Bulletin of the Psychonomic Society, 24,* 44–46.

Adjang, O. M. J. (1986). Exploring the social environment: A developmental study of teasing in chimpanzees. *Ethology, 73,* 136–160.

Adler, A. (1973). *Practice and theory of individual psychology,* trans. P. Radin. Totowa, NJ: Littlefield, Adams.

Adler, T. (1991, December). Outright fraud rare, but not poor science. *APA Monitor,* 11.

Allison, M. G., & Ayllon, T. (1980). Behavioral coaching in the development of skills in football, gymnastics, and tennis. *Journal of Applied Behavior Analysis, 13,* 297–314.

Allport, G. W. (1946). Letters from Jenny. *Journal of Abnormal and Social Psychology, 41,* nos. 3 and 4.

Allport, G. W. (1961). *Pattern in growth and personality.* New York: Holt, Rinehart and Winston.

Allport, G. W. (1965). *Letters from Jenny.* New York: Harcourt, Brace & World.

Altmann, J. (1974). Observational study of behavior: Sampling methods. *Behavior, 48,* 1–41.

American Psychiatric Association. (1987). *Diagnostic and statistical manual of mental disorders* (3rd ed. rev.). Washington, DC: Author.

American Psychological Association. (1983). *Publication Manual* (3d ed.). Washington, DC: Author.

American Psychological Association. (1991). Five-year report of the policy and planning board, 1990; Five years of turbulence, change, and growth within APA. *American Psychologist, 46,* 678–688.

American Psychological Association. (1992a). Ethical principles of psychologists and code of conduct. *American Psychologist, 47,* 1597–1611.

American Psychological Association. (1992b). Summary report of journal operations, 1991. *American Psychologist, 47,* 968.

Anastasi, A. (1988). *Psychological testing* (6th ed.). New York: Macmillan.

Anderson, C. R. (1976). Coping behaviors as intervening mechanisms in the inverted-U stress-performance relationship. *Journal of Applied Psychology, 61,* 30–34.

Anderson, J. R. (1990). *The adaptive character of thought.* Hillsdale, NJ: Erlbaum.

Anderson, J. R., & Milson, J. R. (1989). Human memory: An adaptive perspective. *Psychological Review, 96,* 703–719.

Anderson, K. J., & Revelle, W. (1982). Impulsivity, caffeine, and proofreading: A test of the Easterbrook hypothesis. *Journal of Experimental Psychology: Human Perception and Performance 8,* 614–624.

Anisfeld, M. (1987). A course to develop competence in critical reading of empirical research in psychology. *Teaching of Psychology, 14,* 224–227.

Asch, S. E. (1951). Effects of group pressure upon the modification and distortion of judgments. In H. Guetzkow (Ed.), *Groups, leadership, and men* (pp. 177–190). Pittsburgh: Carnegie.

Asch, S. E. (1955). Opinions and social pressure. *Scientific American, 193,* 31–35.

Atkinson, R. C. (1968). Computerized instruction and the learning process. *American Psychologist, 23,* 225–239.

Atkinson, R. C. & Shiffrin, R. M. (1968). Human memory: A proposed system and its control processes. In K. W. Spence & J. T. Spence (Eds.), *The psychology of learning and motivation,* vol. 2 (pp. 89–195). New York: Academic Press.

Babbie, E. (1992). *The practice of social research* (6th ed.). Belmont, CA: Wadsworth.

Bailey, J. (1987). The editor's page. *Journal of Applied Behavior Analysis, 20,* 305–307.

Barash, D. P. (1977). Human ethology: Exchanging cheetahs for Chevrolets? *Environment and Behavior 9,* 487–490.

Barker, R. G., Wright, H. F., Schoggen, M. F., & Barker, L. S. (1978). Day in the life of Mary Ennis. In R. G. Barker et al. (Eds.), *Habitats, environments, and human behavior* (pp. 51–98). San Francisco: Jossey-Bass.

Baron, J. N., & Reiss, P. C. (1985). Same time, next year: Aggregate analyses of the mass media and violent behavior. *American Sociological Review, 50,* 347–363.

Bartholomew, G. A. (1982). Scientific innovation and creativity: A zoologist's point of view. *American Zoologist, 22,* 227–335.

Bartlett, F. C. (1932). *Remembering: A study in experimental and social psychology.* Cambridge: Cambridge University Press.

Bass, B. M. (1979). Confessions of a former male chauvinist. *American Psychologist, 34,* 194–195.

Berk, R. A., Boruch, R. F., Chambers, D. L., Rossi, P. H., & Witte, A. D. (1987). Social policy experimentation: A position paper. In D. S. Cordray & M. W. Lipsey (Eds.), *Evaluation Studies Review Annual,* vol. 11 (pp. 630–672). Newbury Park, Calif.: Sage.

Bickman, L. (1976). Observational methods. In C. Selltiz, L. S. Wrightsman, & S. W. Cook (Eds.), *Research methods in social relations* (pp. 251–290). New York: Holt, Rinehart and Winston.

Blanck, P. D., Bellack, A. S., Rosnow, R. L., Rotheram-Borus, M. J., & Schooler, N. R.

(1992). Scientific rewards and conflicts of ethical choices in human subjects research. *American Psychologist, 47,* 959–965.

Bloom, B. L., Asher, S. J., & White, S. W. (1978). Marital disruption as a stressor: A review and analysis. *Psychological Bulletin, 85,* 867–894.

Bolgar, H. (1965). The case study method. In B. B. Wolman (Ed.), *Handbook of clinical psychology* (pp. 28–39). New York: McGraw-Hill.

Bond, C. F., Jr., & Titus, L. J. (1983). Social facilitation: A meta-analysis of 241 studies. *Psychological Bulletin, 94,* 265–292.

Booth, W. (1988). Chimps and research: Endangered? *Science, 241,* 777–778.

Bootzin, R. R., Acocella, J. R., & Alloy, L. B. (1993). *Abnormal psychology: Current perspectives* (6th ed.). New York: McGraw-Hill.

Boring, E. G. (1950). *A history of experimental psychology.* New York: Appleton-Century-Crofts.

Boring, E. G. (1954). The nature and history of experimental control. *American Journal of Psychology, 67,* 573–589.

Bornstein, M. T., Bellack, A. S., & Hersen, M. (1977). Social-skills training for unassertive children: A multiple-baseline analysis. *Journal of Applied Behavior Analysis, 10,* 183–195.

Brainerd, C. J. (1978). *Piaget's theory of intelligence.* Englewood Cliffs, NJ: Prentice-Hall.

Brandt, R. M. (1972). *Studying behavior in natural settings.* New York: Holt, Rinehart and Winston; University Press of America, 1981.

Bridgwater, C. A., Bornstein, P. H., & Walkenbach, J. (1981). Ethical issues and the assignment of publication credit. *American Psychologist, 36,* 524–525.

Broach, D. (1992, June). Non-cognitive predictions of performance in radar-based air traffic control training. Paper presented at the Fourth Annual Convention of the American Psychological Society, San Diego, CA.

Brown, R., & Kulik, J. (1977). Flashbulb memories. *Cognition, 5,* 73–99.

Browne, M. A., & Mahoney, M. J. (1984). Sport psychology. *Annual Review of Psychology, 35,* 605–625.

Brush, S. G. (1991). Women in science and engineering. *American Scientist, 79,* 404–419.

Burns, M. S., Haywood, H. C., & Delclos, V. R. (1987). Young children's problem-solving strategies: An observational study. *Journal of Applied Developmental Psychology, 8,* 113–121.

Campbell, A. (1981). *The sense of well-being in America.* New York: McGraw-Hill.

Campbell, A., Converse, P. E., & Rodgers, W. L. (1975). *The quality of American life; July–August, 1971.* Ann Arbor: ISR Social Science Archive.

Campbell, D. T. (1969). Reforms as experiments. *American Psychologist, 24,* 409–429.

Campbell, D. T., & Stanley, J. C. (1966). *Experimental and quasi-experimental designs for research.* Chicago: Rand McNally.

Chambers, J. H., & Ascione, F. R. (1987). The effects of prosocial and aggressive video-games on children's donating and helping. *Journal of Genetic Psychology, 148,* 499–505.

Cherlin, A. J., Furstenberg, F. F., Jr., Chase-Lansdale, P. L., Kiernan, K. E., Robins, P. K., Morrison, D. R., & Teitler, J. O. (1991). Longitudinal studies of effects of divorce on children in Great Britain and the United States. *Science, 252,* 1386–1389.

Chow, S. L. (1988). Significance test or effect size? *Psychological Bulletin, 103,* 105–110.

Cohen, D. (1979). *J. B. Watson: The founder of behaviorism.* London: Routledge & Kegan Paul.

Cohen, J. (1988). *Statistical power analysis for the behavioral sciences* (2nd ed.). Hillsdale, NJ: Erlbaum.

Cohen, J. (1992). A power primer. *Psychological Bulletin, 112,* 155–159.

Cohen, N. J., McCloskey, M., & Wible, C. G. (1990). Flashbulb memories and underlying cognitive mechanisms: Reply to Pillemer. *Journal of Experimental Psychology: General, 119,* 97–100.

Cohen, S., Evans, G. W., Krantz, D. S., & Stokols, D. (1980). Physiological, motivational, and cognitive effects of aircraft noise on children: Moving from the laboratory to the field. *American Psychologist, 35,* 231–243.

Cook, T. D. & Campbell, D. T. (1979). *Quasi-experimentation: Design and analysis issues for field settings.* Chicago: Rand McNally.

Cordaro, L., & Ison, J. R. (1963). Psychology of the scientist: X. Observer bias in classical conditioning of the planarian. *Psychological Reports, 13,* 787–789.

Coren, S., & Porac, C. (1977). Fifty centuries of right-handedness: The historical record. *Science, 198,* 631–632.

Coughlin, E. K. (1988). Scholar who submitted bogus article to journals may be disciplined. *The Chronicle of Higher Education, 35,* 1, A7.

Courneya, K. S., & Carron, A. V. (1992). The home advantage in sport competitions: A literature review. *Journal of Sport & Exercise Psychology, 14,* 13–27.

Cronbach, L. J. (1992). Four *Psychological Bulletin* articles in perspective. *Psychological Bulletin, 12,* 389–392.

Crusco, A. H., & Wetzel, C. G. (1984). The Midas touch: The effects of interpersonal touch on restaurant tipping. *Personality and Social Psychology Bulletin, 10,* 512–517.

Curtiss, S. R. (1977). *Genie: A psycholinguistic study of a modern-day "wild child."* New York: Academic Press.

Dawes, R. M. (1988). *Rational choice in an uncertain world.* San Diego, CA: Harcourt, Brace, Jovanovich.

Dawes, R. M. (1991, June). *Problems with a psychology of college sophomores.* Paper presented at the Third Annual Convention of the American Psychological Society, Washington, DC.

Dawes, R. M. (1992, June). *Why believe that for which there is no good evidence?* Paper presented at the Fourth Annual Convention of the American Psychological Society, San Diego, CA.

Dickie, J. R. (1987). Interrelationships within the mother-father-infant triad. In P. W. Berman & F. A. Pedersen (Eds.), *Men's transitions to parenthood: Longitudinal studies of early family experience* (pp. 113–143). Hillsdale, NJ: Erlbaum.

Diener, E., & Crandall, R. (1978). *Ethics in social and behavioral research.* Chicago: The University of Chicago Press.

Dittmar, M. L., Berch, D. B., & Warm, J. S. (1982). Sustained visual attention in deaf and hearing adults. *Bulletin of the Psychonomic Society 19,* 339–342.

Divorce of the year. *Newsweek,* March 12, 1973, pp. 48–49.

Duchon, D., & Jago, A. G. (1981). Equity and the performance of major league baseball players: An extension of Lord and Hohenfeld. *Journal of Applied Psychology, 66,* 728–732.

Eibl-Eibesfeldt, I. (1975). *Ethology: The biology of behavior.* New York: Holt, Rinehart and Winston.

Erber, R. (1991). Affective and semantic priming: Effects of mood on category accessibility and inference. *Journal of Experimental Social Psychology, 27,* 480–498.

Evans, R., & Donnerstein, E. (1974). Some implications for psychological research of early versus late term participation by college subjects. *Journal of Research in Personality, 8,* 102–109.

Fenney, D. M. (1987). Human rights and animal welfare. *American Psychologist, 42*, 593–599.

Festinger, L., Riecken, H., & Schachter, S. (1956). *When prophecy fails.* Minneapolis: University of Minnesota Press.

Fischer, K., Schoeneman, T. J., & Rubanowitz, D. E. (1987). Attributions in the advice columns: II. The dimensionality of actors' and observers' explanations for interpersonal problems. *Personality and Social Psychology Bulletin, 13*, 458–466.

Fossey, D. (1981). Imperiled giants of the forest. *National Geographic, 159*, 501–523.

Fossey, D. (1983). *Gorillas in the mist.* Boston: Houghton-Mifflin.

Fowler, R. D. (1992). Report of the chief executive officer: A year of building for the future. *American Psychologist, 47*, 876–883.

Frame, C. L. & Strauss, C. C. (1987). Parental informed consent and sample bias in grade-school children. *Journal of Social and Clinical Psychology, 5*, 227–236.

Frank, M. G., & Gilovich, T. (1988). The dark side of self- and social perception: Black uniforms and aggression in professional sports. *Journal of Personality and Social Psychology, 54*, 74–85.

Friedman, M. P., & Wilson, R. W. (1975). Application of unobtrusive measures to the study of textbook usage by college students. *Journal of Applied Psychology, 60*, 659–662.

Gallup, G., Jr. (1988). The Gallup poll: Public opinion 1987. Wilmington, DE: Scholarly Resources, Inc.

Gallup, G. H. (1976). Human needs and satisfaction: A global survey. *Public Opinion Quarterly, 40*, 459–467.

Gannon, L., Luchetta, T., Rhodes, K., Pardie, L., & Segrist, D. (1992). Sex bias in psychological research. *American Psychologist, 47*, 389–396.

Gazzaniga, M. S. (1972). One brain—Two minds? *American Scientist, 60*, 311–317.

Geller, E. S., Russ, N. W., & Altomari, M. G. (1986). Naturalistic observations of beer drinking among college students. *Journal of Applied Behavior Analysis, 19*, 391–396.

Goldstein, R. S., Minkin, B. L., Minkin, N., & Baer, D. M. (1978). Finders, keepers?: An analysis and validation of a free-found-ad policy. *Journal of Applied Behavior Analysis, 11*, 465–473.

Goleman, D. (1981, January). The new competency tests: Matching the right people to the right jobs. *Psychology Today*, pp. 35–46.

Goodall, J. (1987). A plea for the chimpanzees. *American Scientist, 75*, 574–577.

Grammer, K., Schiefenhovel, W., Schleidt, M., Lorenz, B., & Eibl-Eibesfeldt, I. (1988). Patterns on the face: The eyebrow flash in crosscultural comparison. *Ethology, 77*, 279–299.

Gray, J. N., & Melton, G. B. (1985). The law and ethics of psychosocial research on AIDS. *Nebraska Law Review, 64*, 637–688.

Greenberg, R. P., Bornstein, R. F., Greenberg, M. D., & Fisher, S. (1992). A meta-analysis of antidepressant outcome under "blinder" conditions. *Journal of Consulting and Clinical Psychology, 60*, 664–669.

Grice, G. R., & Hunter, J. J. (1964). Stimulus intensity effects depend upon the type of experimental design. *Psychological Review, 71*, 247–256.

Griffin, J. H. (1960). *Black like me.* New York: New American Library.

Grisso, T., Baldwin, E., Blanck, P. D., Rotheram-Borus, M. J., Schooler, N. R., & Thompson, T. (1991). Standards in research: APA's mechanisms for monitoring the challenges. *American Psychologist, 46*, 758–766.

Guerin, B. (1986). Mere presence effects in humans: A review. *Journal of Experimental Social Psychology, 22*, 38–77.

Haas, R. G., Katz, I., Rizzo, N., Bailey, J., & Eisenstadt, D. (1991). Cross-racial appraisal as related to attitude ambivalence and cognitive complexity. *Personality and Social Psychology Bulletin, 17,* 83–92.

Haber, L. R., & Haber, R. N. (1982). Does silent reading involve articulation? Evidence from tongue twisters. *American Journal of Psychology, 95,* 409–419.

Halpern, A. R., & Bower, G. H. (1982). Musical expertise and melodic structure in memory for musical notation. *American Journal of Psychology, 95,* 31–50.

Harlow, H. F., & Harlow, M. K. (1966). Learning to love. *American Scientist, 54,* 244–272.

Hartup, W. W. (1974). Aggression in childhood: Development perspectives. *American Psychologist, 29,* 336–341.

Hays, R. (1980). Honesty requiring a self-initiated response. *Psychological Reports, 46,* 87–90.

Heath, L., & Davidson, L. (1988). Dealing with the threat of rape: Reactance or learned helplessness? *Journal of Applied Social Psychology, 18,* 1334–1351.

Henderson, B. B., & Dias, L. (1987). An exploratory study of infant problem solving in natural environments. *Ethology and Sociobiology, 8,* 205–213.

Henrick, C. (1990). Replications, strict replications, and conceptual replications: Are they important? In J. W. Neuliep (Ed.), *Handbook of replication research in the behavioral and social sciences.* [Special Issue] *Journal of Social Behavior and Personality,* vol. 5 (pp. 41–49).

Hersen, M., & Barlow, D. H. (1976). *Single-case experimental designs: Strategies for studying behavior change.* New York: Pergamon Press.

Hinrichs, J. V. & Novick, L. R. (1982). Memory for numbers: Nominal vs. magnitude information. *Memory & Cognition, 10,* 479–486.

Hirschberg, N., & Itkin, S. (1978). Graduate student success in psychology. *American Psychologist, 33,* 1083–1093.

Hite, S. (1987). *Women and love: A cultural revolution in progress.* New York: Knopf.

Holden, C. (1987). Animal regulations: So far, so good. *Science, 238,* 880–882.

Holsti, O. R. (1969). *Content analysis for the social sciences.* Reading, MA.: Addison-Wesley.

Hops, J., Biglan, A., Sherman, L., Arthur, J., Friedman, L., & Osteen, V. (1987). Home observations of family interactions of depressed women. *Journal of Consulting and Clinical Psychology, 55,* 341–346.

Horn, W. F., & Heerboth, J. (1982). Single-case experimental designs and program evaluation. *Evaluation Review, 6,* 403–424.

Horton, S. V. (1987). Reduction of disruptive mealtime behavior by facial screening. *Behavior Modification, 11,* 53–64.

Hughes, H. M., & Haynes, S. N. (1978). Structured laboratory observation in the behavioral assessment of parent-child interactions: A methodological critique. *Behavior Therapy, 9,* 428–447.

Huse, E. F., & Bowditch, J. L. (1977). *Behavior in organizations: A systems approach to managing* (2nd ed.). Reading, MA: Addison-Wesley.

Intons-Peterson, M. J. (1983). Imagery paradigms: How vulnerable are they to experimenters' expectations? *Journal of Experimental Psychology: Human Perception and Performance, 9,* 394–412.

Jackson, J. M., Buglione, S. A., & Glenwick, D. S. (1988). Major league baseball performance as a function of being traded: A drive theory analysis. *Personality and Social Psychology Bulletin, 14,* 46–56.

Jenni, D. A., & Jenni, M. A. (1976). Carrying behavior in humans: Analysis of sex differences. *Science, 194,* 859–860.

Jenni, M. A. (1976). Sex differences in carrying behavior. *Perceptual and Motor Skills, 43,* 323–330.

Jessor, R., Chase, J. A., & Donovan, J. E. (1980). Psychosocial correlates of marijuana use and problem drinking in a national sample of adolescents. *American Journal of Public Health, 70,* 604–613.

Johnson, D. (1990). Animal rights and human lives: Time for scientists to right the balance. *Psychological Science, 1,* 213–214.

Johnson, J. E., Petzel, T. P., Hartney, L. M., & Morgan, R. A. (1983). Recall and importance ratings of completed and uncompleted tasks as a function of depression. *Cognitive Therapy and Research, 7,* 51–56.

Judd, C. M., Smith, E. R., & Kidder, L. H. (1991). *Research methods in social relations* (6th ed.). Fort Worth, TX: Holt, Rinehart and Winston.

Kagan, J., Reznick, J. S., & Snidman, N. (1988). Biological bases of childhood shyness. *Science, 240,* 167–171.

Kahneman, D., & Tversky, A. (1973). On the psychology of prediction. *Psychological Review, 80,* 237–251.

Kazdin, A. E. (1977). Assessing the clinical or applied significance of behavior change through social validation. *Behavior Modification, 1,* 427–452.

Kazdin, A. E. (1978a). *History of behavior modification: Experimental foundations of contemporary research.* Baltimore: University Park Press.

Kazdin, A. E. (1978b). Methodological and interpretive problems of single-case experimental designs. *Journal of Consulting and Clinical Psychology, 46,* 629–642.

Kazdin, A. E. (1980a). *Behavior modification in applied settings* (rev. ed.). Homewood, IL: Dorsey Press.

Kazdin, A. E. (1980b). *Research design in clinical psychology.* New York: Harper & Row.

Kazdin, A. E. (1982a). Single-case experimental designs. In P. C. Kendall & J. N. Butcher (Eds.), *Handbook of research methods in clinical psychology* (pp. 416–490). New York: Wiley.

Kazdin, A. E. (1982b). The token economy: A decade later. *Journal of Applied Behavior Analysis, 15,* 431–446.

Kazdin, A. E., & Bootzin, R. R. (1972). The token economy: An evaluation review. *Journal of Applied Behavior Analysis, 5,* 343–372.

Kazdin, A. E., & Erickson, L. M. (1975). Developing responsiveness to instructions in severely and profoundly retarded residents. *Journal of Behavior Therapy and Experimental Psychiatry, 6,* 17–21.

Keith, T. Z., Reimers, T. M., Fehrmann, P. G., Pottebaum, S. M., & Aubrey, L. W. (1986). Parental involvement, homework, and TV time: Direct and indirect effects on high school achievement. *Journal of Educational Psychology, 78,* 373–380.

Keller, F. S. (1937). *The definition of psychology.* New York: Appleton-Century-Crofts.

Kelly, J. A. (1986). Psychological research and the rights of animals: Disagreement with Miller. *American Psychologist, 41,* 839–841.

Kelman, H. C. (1967). Human use of human subjects: The problem of deception in social psychological experiments. *Psychological Bulletin, 67,* 1–11.

Kelman, H. C. (1972). The rights of the subject in social research: An analysis in terms of relative power and legitimacy. *American Psychologist, 27,* 989–1016.

Kenny, D. A. (1979). *Correlation and causality.* New York: Wiley.

Keppel, G. (1991). *Design and analysis: A researcher's handbook* (3rd ed.). Englewood Cliffs, NJ: Prentice-Hall.

Kimble, G. A. (1989). Psychology from the standpoint of a generalist. *American Psychologist, 44,* 491–499.

Kirkham, G. L. (1975). Doc cop. *Human Behavior, 4,* 16–23.

Kirmeyer, S. L., & Biggers, K. (1968). Environmental demand and demand engendering behavior: An observational analysis of the Type A pattern. *Journal of Personality and Social Psychology, 54,* 997–1005.

Kirsch, I. (1978). Teaching clients to be their own therapists: A case-study illustration. *Psychotherapy: Theory, Research and Practice, 15,* 302–305.

Klemmack, S. H., & Klemmack, D. L. (1976). The social definition of rape. In M. J. Walker & S. L. Brodsky (Eds.), *Sexual assault.* Lexington, MA: Lexington Books.

Krantz, D. S. (1979). A naturalistic study of social influences on meal size among moderately obese and nonobese subjects. *Psychosomatic Medicine, 41,* 19–26.

Kratochwill, T. R., & Brody, G. H. (1978). Single subject designs: A perspective on the controversy over employing statistical inference and implications for research and training in behavior modification. *Behavior Modification, 2,* 291–307.

Kratochwill, T. R., & Levin, J. R. (Eds.). (1992). *Single-case research design and analysis.* Hillsdale, NJ: Erlbaum.

LaFrance, M., & Mayo, C. (1976). Racial differences in gaze behavior during conversations: Two systematic observational studies. *Journal of Personality and Social Psychology, 33,* 547–552.

Lakatos, I. (1978). *The methodology of scientific research.* London: Cambridge University Press.

Landers, S. (1987a, September). CARE urges protection for animals and labs. . . . *APA Monitor,* 28–29.

Landers, S. (1987b, December). Lab checks: Rigid or reciprocal? *APA Monitor,* 6–7.

Landers, S. (1988, September). Adolescent study presents dilemma. *APA Monitor,* 6.

Langer, E. J. (1989). *Mindfulness.* Reading, MA: Addison-Wesley.

Langer, E. J., & Piper, A. I. (1987). The prevention of mindlessness. *Journal of Personality and Social Psychology, 53,* 280–287.

Langer, E. J., & Rodin, J. (1976). The effects of choice and enhanced personal responsibility for the aged: A field experiment in an institutional setting. *Journal of Personality and Social Psychology, 34,* 191–198.

Latané, B., & Darley, J. M. (1970). *The unresponsive bystander: Why doesn't he help?* New York: Appleton-Century-Crofts.

Latané, B., Williams, K., & Harkin, S. (1979). Many hands make light the work: The causes and consequences of social loafing. *Journal of Personality and Social Psychology, 37,* 822–832.

Lau, R. R., & Russell, D. (1980). Attributions in the sports pages. *Journal of Personality and Social Psychology, 39,* 29–38.

Levine, R. V. (1990). The pace of life. *American Scientist, 78,* 450–459.

Levine, R. V., West, L. J., & Reis, H. T. (1980). Perceptions of time and punctuality in the United States and Brazil. *Journal of Personality and Social Psychology, 38,* 541–550.

Lewis, L. K. (1986). Bibliographic computerized searching in psychology. *Teaching of Psychology, 13,* 38–40.

Linton, M. (1978). Real world memory after six years: An *in vivo* study of very long term memory. In M. M. Gruneberg, P. E. Morris, & R. N. Sykes (Eds.), *Practical aspects of memory* (pp. 69–76). New York: Academic Press.

Locke, T. P., Johnson, G. M., Kirigin-Ramp, K., Atwater, J. D., & Gerrard, M. (1986). An evaluation of a juvenile education program in a state penitentiary. *Evaluation Review, 10,* 281–298.

Loftus, E. F. (1979a). *Eyewitness testimony.* Cambridge, MA: Harvard University Press.

Loftus, E. F., (1979b). The malleability of human memory. *American Scientist, 67,* 312–320.

Loftus, E. F., & Burns, T. E. (1982). Mental shock can produce retrograde amnesia. *Memory & Cognition, 10,* 318–323.

Lord, R. G., & Hohenfeld, J. A. (1979). Longitudinal field assessment of equity effects on the performance of major league baseball players. *Journal of Applied Psychology, 64,* 19–26.

Lovaas, O. I., Newsom, C., & Hickman, C. (1987). Self-stimulatory behavior and perceptual reinforcement. *Journal of Applied Behavior Analysis, 20,* 45–68.

Lubin, B., Zuckerman, M., Breytspraak, L. M., Bull, N. C., Gumbhir, A. K., & Rinck, C. M. (1988). Affects, demographic variables, and health. *Journal of Clinical Psychology, 44,* 131–141.

Luria, A. R. (1968). *The mind of a mnemonist.* New York: Basic Books.

McCain, L. J., & McCleary, R. (1979). The statistical analysis of the simple interrupted time-series quasi-experiment. In T. D. Cook & D. T. Campbell (Eds.), *Quasi-Experimentation: Design & analysis issues for field settings* (pp. 233–293). Chicago: Rand McNally.

McCloskey, M., Wible, C. G., & Cohen, N. J. (1988). Is there a special flashbulb-memory mechanism? *Journal of Experimental Psychology: General, 117,* 171–181.

McGaugh, J. L. (1990, September). Happy birthday APA. *APS Observer,* 2.

McGrew, W. C. (1972). *An ethological study of children's behavior.* New York: Academic Press.

McKinney, J. D., Mason, J., Perkerson, K., & Clifford, M. (1975). Relationship between classroom behavior and academic achievement. *Journal of Educational Psychology, 67,* 198–203.

McSweeney, A. J. (1978). Effects of response cost on the behavior of a million persons: Charging for directory assistance in Cincinnati. *Journal of Applied Behavior Analysis, 11,* 47–51.

Maki, J. E., Hoffman, D. M., & Berk, R. A. (1978). A time series analysis of the impact of a water conservation campaign. *Evaluation Quarterly, 2,* 107–118.

Marx, M. H. (1963). The general nature of theory construction. In M. H. Marx (Ed.), *Theories in contemporary psychology* (pp. 4–46). New York: Macmillan.

Maser, J. D., & Seligman, M. E. P. (Eds.). (1977). *Psychopathology: Experimental models.* San Francisco: Freeman.

Meehl, P. E. (1954). *Clinical versus statistical prediction: A theoretical analysis and review of the literature.* Minneapolis: University of Minnesota Press.

Meehl, P. E. (1978). Theoretical risks and tabular asterisks: Sir Karl, Sir Ronald, and the slow progress of soft psychology. *Journal of Consulting and Clinical Psychology, 46,* 806–834.

Meehl, P. E. (1990a). Appraising and amending theories: The strategy of Lakatosian defense and two principles that warrant it. *Psychological Inquiry, 1,* 108–141.

Meehl, P. E. (1990b). Why summaries of research on psychological theories are often uninterpretable. *Psychological Reports, 66,* 195–244 (Monograph Supplement 1–V66).

Meehl, P. E. (1992, June). *Philosophy of science: Help or hindrance?* Paper presented at the Fourth Annual Convention of the American Psychological Society, San Diego, CA.

Melton, G. B., & Gray, J. N. (1988). Ethical dilemmas in AIDS research: Individual privacy and public health. *American Psychologist 43,* 60–64.

Melton, G. B., Levine, R. J., Koocher, G. P., Rosenthal, R., & Thompson, W. C. (1988). Community consultation in socially sensitive research. *American Psychologist, 43,* 573–581.

Merritt, C. B., & Fowler, R. G. (1948). The pecuniary honesty of the public at large. *Journal of Abnormal and Social Psychology, 43,* 90–93.

Milgram, S. (1977). Subject reaction: The neglected factor in the ethics of experimentation. Hastings Center Report, October.

Milgram, S., Liberty, H. J., Toledo, R., & Wackenhut, J. (1986). Response to intrusion into waiting lines. *Journal of Personality and Social Psychology, 51,* 683–689.

Miller, J. D. (1986, May). Some new measures of scientific illiteracy. Paper presented at the meeting of the American Association for the Advancement of Science, Philadelphia.

Miller, N. E. (1985). The value of behavioral research on animals. *American Psychologist, 40,* 423–440.

Miller, T. Q., Heath, L., Molcan, J. R., & Dugoni, B. L. (1991). Imitative violence in the real world: A reanalysis of homicide rates following championship prize fights. *Aggressive Behavior, 17,* 121–134.

Mook, D. G. (1983). In defense of external invalidity. *American Psychologist, 38,* 379–387.

Mooney, L. A., & Brabant, S. (1987). Deviance, deference, and demeanor: Birthday cards as ceremonial tokens. *Deviant Behavior, 8,* 377–388.

Moore, B. R. & Stuttard, S. (1979). Dr. Guthrie and *Felis domesticus* or: Tripping over the cat. *Science, 205,* 1031–1033.

Myers, D. G. (1990). *Social Psychology* (3rd ed.). New York: McGraw-Hill.

Neisser, U. (1981). John Dean's memory: A case study. *Cognition, 9,* 1–22.

Newcomb, T. M., Koenig, K. E., Flacks, R., & Warwick, D. P. (1967). *Persistence and change: Bennington College and its students after twenty-five years.* New York: Wiley.

New town blues: HUD abandons a disaster. *Time,* October 16, 1978, p. 84.

Novak, M. A. (1991, July). 'Psychologists care deeply' about animals. *APA Monitor,* 4.

O'Leary, K. D., & Borkovec, T. D. (1978). Conceptual, methodological, and ethical problems of placebo groups in psychotherapy research. *American Psychologist, 33,* 821–830.

Oppenheim, A. N. (1966). *Questionnaire design and attitude measurement.* New York: Basic Books.

Orne, M. T. (1962). On the social psychology of the psychological experiment: With particular reference to demand characteristics and their implications. *American Psychologist, 17,* 776–783.

Osgood, C. E., & Walker, E. G. (1959). Motivation and language behavor: A content analysis of suicide notes. *Journal of Abnormal and Social Psychology, 59,* 58–67.

Palladino, J. J., Carsrud, A. L., Hulicka, I. M., & Benjamin, L. T., Jr. (1982). Undergraduate research in psychology: Assessment and directions. *Teaching of Psychology, 9,* 71–74.

Parr, V. H. (1979). Online information retrieval and the undergraduate. *Teaching of Psychology, 6,* 61–62.

Parry, H. J., & Crossley, H. M. (1950). Validity of responses to survey questions. *Public Opinion Quarterly, 14,* 61–80.

Parsons, H. M. (1974). What happened at Hawthorne? *Science, 183,* 922–932.

Parsonson, B. S., & Baer, D. M. (1992). The visual analysis of data, and current research into the stimuli controlling it. In T. R. Kratochwill & J. R. Levin (Eds.), *Single-case research design and analysis* (pp. 15–40). Hillsdale, NJ: Erlbaum.

Patton, J. E., Routh, D. K., & Stinard, T. A. (1986). Where do children study? Behavioral observations. *Bulletin of the Psychonomic Society, 24,* 439–440.

Peplau, L. A., & Gordon, S. L. (1985). Women and men in love: Gender differences in close heterosexual relationships. In R. K. Unger & B. S. Wallston (Eds.), *Women, gender, and social psychology* (pp. 257–291). Hillsdale, NJ: Erlbaum.

Phillips, D. P. (1977). Motor vehicle fatalities increase just after publicized suicide stories. *Science, 196*, 1464–1465.

Phillips, D. P. (1978). Airplane accident fatalities increase just after newspaper stories about murder and suicide. *Science, 201*, 748–750.

Phillips, D. P. (1983). The impact of mass media violence on U. S. homicides. *American Sociological Review, 48*, 560–568.

Phillips, D. P., & Bollen, K. A. (1985). Same time, last year: Selective data dredging for negative findings. *American Sociological Review, 50*, 364–371.

Piaget, J. (1965). *The child's conception of number.* New York: Norton.

Pillemer, D. B. (1990). Clarifying the flashbulb memory concept: Comment on McCloskey, Wible, & Cohen (1988). *Journal of Experimental Psychology: General, 119*, 92–96.

Pishkin, V., & Shurley, J. T. (1983). Electrophysiological parameters in anxiety and failure: Evaluation of doxepin and hydroxyzine. *Bulletin of the Psychonomic Society, 21*, 21–23.

Pitman, R. K., Kolb, B., Orr, S. P., deJong, J., Yadati, S., & Singh, M. M. (1987). On the utility of ethological data in psychiatric research: The example of facial behavior in schizophrenia. *Ethology and Sociobiology, 8*, 111S–116S.

Polyson, J., & Levinson, M. (1982). Writing styles: A survey of psychology journal editors. *American Psychologist, 37*, 335–338.

Popper, K. R. (1959). *The logic of scientific discovery.* New York: Basic Books.

Popper, K. R. (1976). *Unended quest.* Glasgow: Fontana/Collins.

Posavac, E. J., & Carey, R. G. (1992). *Program evaluation.* (4th ed). Englewood Cliffs, NJ: Prentice-Hall.

Posner, M. I. (1973). *Cognition: An introduction.* Glenview, IL: Scott, Foresman.

Poulton, E. C. (1973). Unwanted range effects from using within-subject experimental designs. *Psychological Bulletin, 80*, 113–121.

Poulton, E. C. (1975). Range effects in experiments on people. *American Journal of Psychology, 88*, 3–32.

Poulton, E. C. (1982). Influential companions. Effects of one strategy on another in the within-subjects designs of cognitive psychology. *Psychological Bulletin, 91*, 673–690.

Poulton, E. C., & Freeman, P. R. (1966). Unwanted asymmetrical transfer effects with balanced experimental designs. *Psychological Bulletin, 66*, 1–8.

Reynolds, G. S. (1968). *A primer of operant conditioning.* Glenview, IL: Scott, Foresman.

Richardson, D. R., Pegalis, L., & Britton, B. (1992). A technique for enhancing the value of research participation. *Contemporary Social Psychology, 16*, 11–13.

Riley, D. A. (1962). Memory for form. In L. Postman (Ed.), *Psychology in the making* (pp. 402–465). New York: Knopf.

Rimm, D. C., & Masters, J. C. (1979). *Behavior therapy: Techniques and empirical findings* (2nd ed.). New York: Academic Press.

Rodman, J. L., & Burger, J. M. (1985). The influence of depression on the attribution of responsibility for an accident. *Cognitive Therapy and Research, 9*, 651–657.

Roethlisberger, F. J. (1977). *The elusive phenomena: An autobiographical account of my work in the field of organized behavior at the Harvard Business School.* Cambridge, MA: Division of Research, Graduate School of Business Administration (distributed by Harvard University Press).

Rollin, B. E. (1985). The moral status of research animals in psychology. *American Psychologist, 40*, 920–926.

Rosenfeld, A. (1981). Animal rights vs. human health. *Science, 81*, 18, 22.

Rosenhan, D. L. (1973). On being sane in insane places. *Science, 179*, 250–258.

Rosenthal, R. (1963). On the social psychology of the psychological experiment: The experimenter's hypothesis as unintended determinant of experimental results. *American Scientist, 51*, 268–283.

Rosenthal, R. (1966). *Experimenter effects in behavioral research.* New York: Appleton-Century-Crofts.

Rosenthal, R. (1976). *Experimenter effects in behavioral research.* (Enlarged ed.). New York: Irvington.

Rosenthal, R. (1990). Reflections in behavioral research. In J. W. Neuliep (Ed.), *Handbook of replication research in the behavioral and social sciences.* [Special Issue] *Journal of Social Behavior and Personality*, vol. 5 (pp. 1–30).

Ross, A. S., & White, S. (1987). Shoplifting, impaired driving, and refusing the breathalyzer: On seeing one's name in a public place. *Evaluation Review, 11*, 254–260.

Rotter, J. B. (1966). Generalized expectancies for internal versus external control of reinforcement. *Psychological Monographs, 80* (1, Whole No. 609), 1–28.

Sackheim, H. A., Gur, R. C., & Saucy, M. C. (1978). Emotions are expressed more intensely on the left side of the face. *Science, 202*, 434–436.

Salomon, G. (1987). Basic and applied research in psychology: Reciprocity between two worlds. *International Journal of Psychology, 22*, 441–446.

Schaller, G. B. (1963). *The mountain gorilla.* Chicago: University of Chicago Press.

Schlosberg, H. (1965). Hints on presenting a paper at an APA convention. *American Psychologist, 20*, 606–607.

Schnelle, J. F., Kirchner, R. E., Macrae, J. W., McNees, M. P., Eck, R. H., Snodgrass, S., Casey, J. D., & Uselton, P. H., Jr. (1978). Police evaluation research: An experimental and cost-benefit analysis of a helicopter patrol in a high-crime area. *Journal of Applied Behavior Analysis, 11*, 11–21.

Schoeneman, T. J., & Rubanowitz, D. E. (1985). Attributions in the advice columns: Actors and observers, causes and reasons. *Personality and Social Psychology Bulletin, 11*, 315–325.

Schulz, R., & Bazerman, M. (1980). Ceremonial occasions and mortality: A second look. *American Psychologist, 35*, 253–261.

Schuman, H., & Bobo, L. (1988). Survey-based experiments on white racial attitudes toward residential integration. *American Journal of Sociology, 94*, 273–299.

Schuman, H., Presser, S., & Ludwig, J. (1981). Context effects on survey responses to questions about abortion. *Public Opinion Quarterly, 45*, 216–233.

Schuman, H., & Scott, J. (1987). Problems in the use of survey questions to measure public opinion, *Science, 236*, 957–959.

Scoville, W. B., & Milner, B. (1957). Loss of recent memory after bilateral hippocampal lesions. *Journal of Neurology, Neurosurgery, and Psychiatry, 20*, 11–19.

Seligman, M. E. P. (1988, August). Why is there so much depression today? The waxing of the individual and the waning of the commons. The G. Stanley Hall Lecture presented at the American Psychological Association, Atlanta.

Shapiro, K. J. (1991, July). Use morality as basis for animal treatment. *APA Monitor*, 5.

Sharma, S., & Moskowitz, H. (1972). Effect of marijuana on the visual autokinetic phenomenon. *Perceptual and Motor Skills, 35*, 891–894.

Simon, H. A. (1992). What is an "explanation" of behavior? *Psychological Science, 3*, 150–161.

Singer, B., & Benassi, V. A. (1981). Occult beliefs. *American Scientist, 69*, 49–55.

Singer, M. (1982). Comparing memory for natural and laboratory reading. *Journal of Experimental Psychology: General, 111*, 331–347.

Skinner, B. F. (1937). Two types of conditioned reflex: A replay to Konorski and Miller. *Journal of General Psychology, 16*, 272–279.

Skinner, B. F. (1958). Teaching machines. *Science, 128*, 969–977.

Skinner, B. F. (1966). Operant behavior. In W. K. Honig (Ed.), *Operant behavior: Areas of research and application* (pp. 12–32). New York: Appleton-Century-Crofts.

Smith, P. K., & Lewis, K. (1985). Rough-and-tumble play, fighting, and chasing in nursery school children. *Ethology and Sociobiology, 6*, 175–181.

Smith, R. J. (1977). Electroshock experiment at Albany violates ethics guidelines. *Science, 198*, 383–386.

Smith, T. W. (1981). Qualifications to generalized absolutes: "Approval of hitting" questions on the GSS. *Public Opinion Quarterly, 45*, 224–230.

Sommer, R. (1968). Hawthorne dogma. *Psychological Bulletin, 70*, 592–595.

Spitz, R. A. (1965). *The first year of life.* New York: International Universities Press.

Squire, L. R., Knowlton, B., & Musen, G. (1993). The structure and organization of memory. *Annual Review of Psychology, 44*, 453–495.

Sternberg, R. J. (1986). A triangular theory of love. *Psychological Review, 93*, 119–135.

Strauss, A., & Corbin, J. (1990). *Basics of qualitative research.* Newbury Park, CA: Sage.

Sun, M. (1981). Laetrile brush fire is out, scientists hope. *Science, 212*, 758–759.

Sun, M. (1988). Debate rages over breast cancer study. *Science, 239*, 17–18.

Tedeschi, J. T., Lindskold, S., & Rosenfeld, P. (1985). *Introduction to social psychology.* St. Paul, MN: West.

Thomas, L. (1992). *The fragile species.* New York: Charles Scribner's Sons.

Thompson, T. L. (1982). Gaze toward and avoidance of the handicapped: A field experiment. *Journal of Nonverbal Behavior, 6*, 188–196.

Till, R. E. (1985). Verbatim and inferential memory in young and elderly adults. *Journal of Gerontology, 40*, 316–323.

Tversky, A. (1974). Judgment under uncertainty: Heuristics and biases. *Science, 185*, 1124–1131.

Tversky, A., & Kahneman, D. (1971). Belief in the law of small numbers. *Psychological Bulletin, 76*, 105–110.

Ulrich, R. E. (1991). Animal rights, animal wrongs and the question of balance. *Psychological Science, 2*, 197–201.

Ulrich, R. E. (1992). Animal research: A reflective analysis. *Psychological Science, 3*, 384–386.

Underwood, B. J. (1957). *Psychological research.* New York: Appleton-Century-Crofts.

Underwood, B. J. (1975). Individual differences as a crucible in theory construction. *American Psychologist, 30*, 128–134.

Underwood, B. J., & Shaughnessy, J. J. (1975). *Experimentation in psychology.* New York: Wiley: Robert E. Krieger, 1983.

VanBiervliet, A., Spangler, P. F., & Marshall, A. M. (1981). An ecobehavioral examination of a simple strategy for increasing mealtime language in residential facilities. *Journal of Applied Behavior Analysis, 14*, 295–305.

Van Nuys, D. (1975). On the phrasing of hypnotic suggestions: A brief case report. *Psychotherapy: Theory, Research and Practice, 12*, 302–304.

Wallace, W. P., & Underwood, B. J. (1964). Implicit responses and the role of intralist similarity in verbal learning by normal and retarded subjects. *Journal of Educational Psychology, 55*, 362–370.

Wallraff, H. G., & Sinsch, U. (1988). The role of "outward-journey information" in homing experiments with pigeons: New data on ontogeny of navigation and general survey. *Ethology, 77, 10–27.*

Ward, W. D., & Jenkins, H. M. (1965). The display of information and the judgment of contingency. *Canadian Journal of Psychology, 19,* 231–241.

Warwick, D. P., & Lininger, C. A. (1975). *The sample survey: Theory and practice.* New York: McGraw-Hill.

Watson, J. B. (1913). Psychology as the behaviorist views it. *Psychological Review, 20,* 158–177.

Watson, J. B. [1914] (1967). *Behavior: An introduction to comparative psychology.* New York: Holt, Rinehart and Winston.

Webb, E. J., Campbell, D. T., Schwartz, R. D., Sechrest, L., & Grove, J. B. (1981). *Nonreactive measures in the social sciences* (2nd ed.). Boston: Houghton-Mifflin.

Weigel, R. H., Loomis, J. W., & Soja, M. J. (1980). Race relations on prime time television. *Journal of Personality and Social Psychology, 39,* 884–893.

Weiss, J. M. (1977). Psychological and behavioral influences on gastrointestinal lesions in animal models. In J. D. Maser & M. E. P. Seligman (Eds.), *Psychopathology: Experimental models* (pp. 232–269). San Francisco: Freeman.

Willems, E. P. (1969). Planning a rationale for naturalistic research. In E. P. Willems & H. L. Raush (Eds.), *Naturalistic viewpoints in psychological research* (pp. 44–71). New York: Holt, Rinehart and Winston.

Willems, E. P., & Raush, H. L. (Eds.). (1969). *Naturalistic viewpoints in psychological research.* New York: Holt, Rinehart and Winston.

Williams, K. D., Harkins, S., & Latané, B. (1981). Identifiability as a deterrent to social loafing: Two cheering experiments. *Journal of Personality and Social Psychology, 40,* 303–311.

Willingham, W. W. (1974). Predicting success in graduate education. *Science, 183,* 273–278.

Wilson, G. T. (1978). On the much discussed nature of the term "behavior therapy." *Behavior Therapy, 9,* 89–98.

Wortman, C. B., & Loftus, E. F. (1981). *Psychology.* New York: Knopf.

Yeaton, W. H., & Sechrest, L. (1981). Critical dimensions in the choice and maintenance of successful treatments: Strength, integrity, and effectiveness. *Journal of Consulting and Clinical Psychology, 49,* 156–167.

Yeaton, W. H., & Sechrest, L. (1986). Use and misuse of no-difference findings in eliminating threats to validity. *Evaluation Review, 10,* 836–852.

Zechmeister, E. B., & Johnson, J. E. (1992). *Critical thinking: A functional approach.* Pacific Grove, CA: Brooks/Cole.

Zechmeister, E. B., & Nyberg, S. E. (1982). *Human memory: An introduction to research and theory.* Pacific Grove, CA: Brooks/Cole.

Name Index

Subject Index